WORD
BIBLICAL
COMMENTARY

To Joe,
An esteemed colleague,
in friendship!
Cordially,
Wick

General Editors
David A. Hubbard
Glenn W. Barker †

Old Testament Editor
John D. W. Watts

New Testament Editor
Ralph P. Martin

WORD

BIBLICAL

COMMENTARY

VOLUME 41

Galatians

RICHARD N. LONGENECKER

WORD BOOKS, PUBLISHER • DALLAS, TEXAS

Word Biblical Commentary
GALATIANS
Copyright © 1990 by Word, Incorporated

Library of Congress Cataloging-in-Publication Data
Main entry under title:

Word biblical commentary.

   Includes bibliographies.
   1. Bible—Commentaries—Collected works.
BS491.2.W67 220.7'7 81-71768
ISBN 0-8499-0240-1 (vol.41) AACR2

Printed in the United States of America

The author's own translation of the text appears in italic type under the heading "Translation," as well as in brief Scripture quotations in the body of the commentary, except where otherwise indicated.

01239 AGF 987654321

To my doctoral students
of the past dozen years,
who have taught me much!

Contents

Editorial Preface

The launching of the *Word Biblical Commentary* brings to fulfillment an enterprise of several years' planning. The publishers and the members of the editorial board met in 1977 to explore the possibility of a new commentary on the books of the Bible that would incorporate several distinctive features. Prospective readers of these volumes are entitled to know what such features were intended to be; whether the aims of the commentary have been fully achieved time alone will tell.

First, we have tried to cast a wide net to include as contributors a number of scholars from around the world who not only share our aims, but are in the main engaged in the ministry of teaching in university, college, and seminary. They represent a rich diversity of denominational allegiance. The broad stance of our contributors can rightly be called evangelical, and this term is to be understood in its positive, historic sense of a commitment to Scripture as divine revelation, and to the truth and power of the Christian gospel.

Then, the commentaries in our series are all commissioned and written for the purpose of inclusion in the *Word Biblical Commentary*. Unlike several of our distinguished counterparts in the field of commentary writing, there are no translated works, originally written in a non-English language. Also, our commentators were asked to prepare their own rendering of the original biblical text and to use those languages as the basis of their own comments and exegesis. What may be claimed as distinctive with this series is that it is based on the biblical languages, yet it seeks to make the technical and scholarly approach to a theological understanding of Scripture understandable by—and useful to—the fledgling student, the working minister, and colleagues in the guild of professional scholars and teachers as well.

Finally, a word must be said about the format of the series. The layout, in clearly defined sections, has been consciously devised to assist readers at different levels. Those wishing to learn about the textual witnesses on which the translation is offered are invited to consult the section headed *Notes*. If the readers' concern is with the state of modern scholarship on any given portion of Scripture, they should turn to the sections of *Bibliography* and *Form/Structure/Setting*. For a clear exposition of the passage's meaning and its relevance to the ongoing biblical revelation, the *Comment* and concluding *Explanation* are designed expressly to meet that need. There is therefore something for everyone who may pick up and use these volumes.

If these aims come anywhere near realization, the intention of the editors will have been met, and the labor of our team of contributors rewarded.

General Editors: *David A. Hubbard*
                            Glenn W. Barker †
   Old Testament: *John D. W. Watts*
  New Testament: *Ralph P. Martin*

Author's Preface

Why another Galatians commentary? The question is pertinent, particularly with such commentaries as those by Lightfoot (1865), Burton (1921), Mussner (1974), Betz (1979), and Bruce (1982) already existing. Ultimately, the answer to why another scholarly commentary can only be given in terms of (1) new approaches or new data of relevance to the subject, and (2) the interests and expertise of the commentator. That there are both new approaches to and new data for the study of Galatians is a thesis I hope to demonstrate throughout the *Introduction* and *Commentary* proper. As for my interests and expertise, the first can be itemized briefly below. The second, of course, must be left to the judgment of others.

My interests in NT study are most concisely stated as follows. First, I am always concerned with the history of interpretation—that is, with how a subject has been treated in the past, so as to profit from either advances or false starts in the discussion and to give direction to my own research through the isolation of crucial issues. Second, I want to know as much as possible about the circumstances behind the writing and the purposes for which its author wrote. Third, I approach the material in question asking about its literary structures—in the case of letters, epistolary and rhetorical structures—and their relations to the conventions of the day. Then, of course, I am concerned with the meaning of words in a text, both as to how particular expressions were used in the day and as to how a given author shaped those expressions for his own purposes. Following hard on the heels of philology is my concern with what may be called phenomenological historiography—that is, the identification and tracing of similar themes and parallel ways of looking at things in roughly cognate bodies of literature with the hope of spawning fresh interpretive insights. A sixth interest is in the development of thought in the apostolic period and beyond, while a seventh has to do with the relevance of the NT for Christian faith and life today.

Paul's letter to the Galatians has been a favorite of mine. In large measure, repeated study of Galatians has generated my own scholarly interests in the NT generally. Furthermore, the letter has been of late the object of a great deal of research and specialized study. So I have worked on this commentary with great relish. Where I believe my work on Galatians is most distinctive is in (1) its stress on Hellenistic epistolary conventions, (2) its eclectic treatment of Greco-Roman rhetorical features, (3) its highlighting of Jewish themes and exegetical procedures, and (4) its Antiochian style of interpretation. I would also like to believe that at many other points—e.g., on addressees, date, opponents, and a host of specific exegetical issues—I have made a contribution as well. Most of all, however, as one who views the NT in terms of salvation history and not just with a history-of-religions perspective, it is my desire that through what follows the reader will experience something of the same impact on his or her life as I have experienced from a close study of Paul's letter to the Galatians. Only then will the question of why one wants to write another Galatian commentary be truly answered.

In the course of research and writing I have had help from a number of former doctoral candidates who have worked under my supervision at Toronto, and to them I express my heartfelt thanks. Dr. Terry Donaldson and Dr. Steve Mason prepared a great deal of material on Pauline chronology, rabbinic parallels, parallels in Josephus, and ethical treatises in the ancient world. Dr. Walter Hansen's dissertation on "The Abraham Story in Galatians, in Light of Epistolary and Rhetorical Analyses" (published 1989) and Dr. Murray Barron's dissertation on "The Relational Function of the Spirit in Galatians" (unpublished), while incorporating some of my interests and ideas, were foundational in many ways for my writing of this commentary. Dr. Tom Sappington and my son, Dr. Bruce Longenecker, helped greatly with regard to bibliography. In addition, my wife Fran and Allan Martens (Th. D. cand.) aided in a number of ways, including proofreading. To all these faithful helpers I express my heartfelt thanks. Also, of course, I owe much to the vast host of scholars who have written on Galatians before me. I trust that in the way I handle their materials my debt will be evident. All I can pray is that my attempt to carry on their work will to some extent be a fulfillment of their endeavors, and so be to the greater benefit of the Church at large.

October 1990   RICHARD N. LONGENECKER
Wycliffe College

Abbreviations

A. General Abbreviations

ad	comment on	masc.	masculine
Akkad.	Akkadian	mg.	margin
א	Codex Sinaiticus	MS(S)	manuscript(s)
Ap. Lit.	Apocalyptic Literature	MT	Masoretic text (of the Old
Apoc.	Apocrypha		Testament)
Aq.	Aquila's Greek Transla-	n.	note
	tion of the OT	n.d.	no date
Arab.	Arabic	Nestle	Nestle (ed.), *Novum*
Aram.	Aramaic		*Testamentum Graece*[26],
c.	*circa*, about		rev. by K. and B. Aland
cent.	century	no.	number
cf.	*confer*, compare	n.s.	new series
chap(s).	chapter(s)	NT	New Testament
cod., codd.	codex, codices	obs.	obsolete
contra	in contrast to	o.s.	old series
DSS	Dead Sea Scrolls	OT	Old Testament
ed.	edited by, editor(s)	p., pp.	page, pages
e.g.	*exempli gratia*, for ex-	pace	with due respect to, but
	ample		differing from
et al.	*et alii*, and others	//, par(s).	parallel(s)
ET	English translation	par.	paragraph
EV	English Versions of the	passim	elsewhere
	Bible	pl.	plural
f., ff.	following (verse or verses,	Pseudep.	Pseudepigrapha
	pages, etc.)	Q	Quelle ("Sayings" source
fem.	feminine		for the Gospels)
frag.	fragments	q.v.	*quod vide*, which see
FS	Festschrift, volume	rev.	revised, reviser, revision
	written in honor of	Rom.	Roman
ft.	foot, feet	RVmg	Revised Version margin
gen.	genitive	Sam.	Samaritan recension
Gr.	Greek	*sc.*	*scilicet*, that is to say
hap. leg.	*hapax legomenon*, sole	Sem.	Semitic
	occurrence	sing.	singular
Heb.	Hebrew	Souter	A. Souter, ed., *Novum*
Hitt.	Hittite		*Testamentum Graece*,
ibid.	*ibidem*, in the same place		2nd ed. (1947)
id.	*idem*, the same	Sumer.	Sumerian
i.e.	*id est*, that is	s.v.	*sub verbo*, under the word
impf.	imperfect	Symm.	Symmachus
infra	below	Tg.	Targum
in loc.	*in loco*, in the place cited	Theod.	Theodotion
Jos.	Josephus	Tisch.	C. Tischendorf, ed.,
loc. cit.	the place cited		*Novum Testamentum*
LXX	Septuagint		*Graece*, 8th ed., 1869–
m.	Mishna		72

TR	Textus Receptus	*v.l.*	*varia lectio*, alternative reading
tr.	translator, translated by		
UBSGT	The United Bible Societies Greek Text	vol.	volume
		WH	B. F. Westcott & F. J. A. Hort, ed., *The New Testament in the Original Greek* (1881)
Ugar.	Ugaritic		
UP	University Press		
u.s.	*ut supra*, as above		
v, vv	verse, verses	x	times (2x = two times, etc.)
viz.	*videlicet*, namely		

Note: The textual notes and numbers used to indicate individual manuscripts are those found in the apparatus criticus of *Novum Testamentum Graece*, ed. E. Nestle and K. Aland et al. (Stuttgart: Deutsche Bibelgesellschaft, 1979[26]). This edition of the Greek New Testament is the basis for the *Translation* sections.

B. Abbreviations for Translations and Paraphrases

AmT	Smith and Goodspeed, *The Complete Bible, An American Translation*		*Vulgate in the Light of the Hebrew and Greek Original*
ASV	American Standard Version, American Revised Version (1901)	Moffatt	J. Moffatt, *A New Translation of the Bible* (NT 1913)
AV	Authorized Version = KJV	NAB	The New American Bible
Berkeley	G. Verkuyl, ed., *The Holy Bible: The Berkeley Version in Modern English* (NT 1945, OT 1959)	NEB	The New English Bible
		NIV	The New International Version (1978)
		NJB	New Jerusalem Bible (1985)
		Phillips	J. B. Phillips, *The New Testament in Modern English*
GNB	Good News Bible = Today's English Version	RSV	Revised Standard Version (NT 1946, OT 1952, Apoc. 1957)
JB	Jerusalem Bible		
JPS	Jewish Publication Society, *The Holy Scriptures*	RV	Revised Version, 1881–85
		Wey	R. F. Weymouth, *The New Testament in Modern Speech*
KJV	King James Version (1611) = AV	Wms	C. B. Williams, *The New Testament: A Translation in the Language of the People*
Knox	R. A. Knox, *The Holy Bible: A Translation from the Latin*		

C. Abbreviations of Commonly Used Periodicals, Reference Works, and Serials

AAS	*Acta apostolicae sedis*	*ADAJ*	*Annual of the Department of Antiquities of Jordan*
AARSR	American Academy of Religion Studies in Religion	*AER*	*American Ecclesiastical Review*
AASOR	Annual of the American Schools of Oriental Research	*AfO*	*Archiv für Orientforschung*
AB	Anchor Bible	AGJU	Arbeiten zur Geschichte des antiken Judentums und des Urchristentums
ABR	*Australian Biblical Review*		
AbrN	*Abr-Nahrain*	AGSU	Arbeiten zur Geschichte des Spätjudentums und Urchristentums
ACNT	Augsburg Commentary on the New Testament		
AcOr	*Acta orientalia*	*AH*	F. Rosenthal, *An Aramaic Handbook*
ACW	Ancient Christian Writers		

AHR	*American Historical Review*	ARM	Archives royales de Mari
AHW	W. von Soden, *Akkadisches Handwörterbuch*	*ArOr*	*Archiv orientální*
AION	*Annali dell'istituto orientali di Napoli*	ARSHLL	Acta Reg. Societatis Humaniorum Litterarum Lundensis
AJA	*American Journal of Archaeology*	*ARW*	*Archiv für Religionswissenschaft*
AJAS	*American Journal of Arabic Studies*	ASNU	Acta seminarii neotestamentici upsaliensis
AJBA	*Australian Journal of Biblical Archaeology*	ASS	Acta sanctae sedis
		AsSeign	*Assemblées du Seigneur*
AJBI	*Annual of the Japanese Biblical Institute*	ASSR	*Archives des sciences sociales des religions*
AJP	*American Journal of Philology*	*ASTI*	*Annual of the Swedish Theological Institute*
AJSL	*American Journal of Semitic Languages and Literature*	ATAbh	Alttestamentliche Abhandlungen
AJT	*American Journal of Theology*	ATANT	Abhandlungen zur Theologie des Alten und Neuen Testaments
ALBO	Analecta lovaniensia biblica et orientalia		
ALGHJ	Arbeiten zur Literatur und Geschichte des hellenistischen Judentums	ATD	Das Alte Testament Deutsch
		ATDan	Acta Theologica Danica
ALUOS	Annual of Leeds University Oriental Society	*ATJ*	*African Theological Journal*
		ATR	*Anglican Theological Review*
AnBib	Analecta Biblica	*AUSS*	*Andrews University Seminary Studies*
AnBoll	Analecta Bollandiana		
ANEP	J. B. Pritchard (ed.), *Ancient Near East in Pictures*	*BA*	*Biblical Archaeologist*
ANESTP	J. B. Pritchard (ed.), *Ancient Near East Supplementary Texts and Pictures*	BAC	Biblioteca de autores cristianos
		BAG	W. Bauer, *A Greek-English Lexicon of the New Testament and Other Early Christian Literature*, ET, ed. W. F. Arndt and F. W. Gingrich (1957)
ANET	J. B. Pritchard (ed.), *Ancient Near Eastern Texts*		
ANF	The Ante-Nicene Fathers		
Ang	*Anglicum*		
AnOr	Analecta orientalia		
ANQ	*Andover Newton Quarterly*	BAH	Bibliothèque archéologique et historique
ANRW	*Aufstieg und Niedergang der römischen Welt*, ed. H. Temporini and W. Haase, Berlin	*BangTF*	*Bangalore Theological Forum*
		BAR	*Biblical Archaeology Review*
ANT	Arbeiten zur Neutestamentlichen Textforschung	*BASOR*	*Bulletin of the American Schools of Oriental Research*
		BASP	*Bulletin of the American Society of Papyrologists*
Anton	*Antonianum*		
AOAT	Alter Orient und Altes Testament	BBB	Bonner biblische Beiträge
		BCSR	*Bulletin of the Council on the Study of Religion*
AOS	American Oriental Series		
AP	J. Marouzeau (ed.), *L'année philologique*	BDB	F. Brown, S. R. Driver, and C. A. Briggs, *Hebrew and English Lexicon of the Old Testament* (Oxford: Clarendon, 1907)
APOT	R. H. Charles (ed.), *Apocrypha and Pseudepigrapha of the Old Testament*		
ARG	*Archiv für Reformationsgeschichte*	BDF	F. Blass, A. Debrunner, and R. W. Funk, *A Greek Grammar*

	of the New Testament (University of Chicago/University of Cambridge, 1961)	BLS	Bible and Literature Series
		BNTC	Black's New Testament Commentaries
BDR	F. Blass, A. Debrunner, and F. Rehkopf, *Grammatik des neutestamentlichen Griechisch*	*BO*	*Bibliotheca orientalis*
		BR	*Biblical Research*
		BRev	*Bible Review*
BeO	*Bibbia e oriente*	BS	Biblische Studien
BET	Beiträge zur biblischen Exegese und Theologie	*BSac*	*Biblica Sacra*
BETL	Bibliotheca ephemeridum theologicarum lovaniensium	*BSO(A)S*	*Bulletin of the School of Oriental (and African) Studies*
		BSR	Bibliothèque de sciences religieuses
BEvT	Beiträge zur evangelischen Theologie	*BT*	*The Bible Translator*
		BTB	*Biblical Theology Bulletin*
BFCT	Beiträge zur Förderung christlicher Theologie	BU	Biblische Untersuchungen
		BulCPE	*Bulletin du Centre Protestant d'Études* (Geneva)
BGBE	Beiträge zur Geschichte der biblischen Exegese	*BVC*	*Bible et vie chrétienne*
BGU	Berliner griechische Urkunden	*BW*	*Biblical World*
BHH	*Biblisch-Historisches Handwörterbuch*	BWANT	Beiträge zur Wissenschaft vom Alten und Neuen Testament
BHK	R. Kittel, *Biblia hebraica*	*BZ*	*Biblische Zeitschrift*
BHS	*Biblia hebraica stuttgartensia*	BZAW	Beihefte zur ZAW
BHT	Beiträge zur historischen Theologie	BZET	Beihefte zur Evangelische Theologie
Bib	*Biblica*	BZNW	Beihefte zur ZNW
BibB	Biblische Beiträge	BZRGG	Beihefte zur ZRGG
BibLeb	*Bibel und Leben*		
BibNot	*Biblische Notizen*	*CAD*	*The Assyrian Dictionary of the Oriental Institute of the University of Chicago*
BibOr	Biblica et orientalia		
BibS(F)	Biblische Studien (Freiburg, 1895-)		
		CAH	*Cambridge Ancient History*
BibS(N)	Biblische Studien (Neukirchen, 1951-)	CAT	Commentaire de l'Ancien Testament
BiTod	*The Bible Today*	*CB*	*Cultura biblica*
BIES	*Bulletin of the Israel Exploration Society* (= *Yediot*)	*CBG*	*Collationes Brugenses el Gandavenses*
BIFAO	*Bulletin de l'institut français d'archéologie orientale*	*CBQ*	*Catholic Biblical Quarterly*
		CBQMS	CBQ Monograph Series
BILL	Bibliothèque des cahiers de l'Institut de Linguistique de Louvain	*CBVE*	*Comenius Blätter für Volkserziehung*
		CCath	Corpus Catholicorum
BJRL	*Bulletin of the John Rylands University Library of Manchester*	CChr	Corpus Christianorum
		CG	Cairenensis Gnosticus (Nag Hammadi Codex)
BJS	Brown Judaic Studies		
BK	*Bibel und Kirche*	CGTC	Cambridge Greek Testament Commentary
BKAT	Biblischer Kommentar: Altes Testament	CGTSC	Cambridge Greek Testament for Schools and Colleges
BL	*Book List*		
BLE	*Bulletin de littérature ecclésiastique*	*CH*	*Church History*
		CHR	*Catholic Historical Review*
BLit	*Bibel und Liturgie*	*CIG*	*Corpus inscriptionum*

	graecarum	*DT*	*Deutsche Theologie*
CII	*Corpus inscriptionum iudaicarum*	*DTC*	*Dictionnaire de théologie catholique*
CIL	*Corpus inscriptionum latinarum*	*DTT*	*Dansk teologisk tidsskrift*
CIS	*Corpus inscriptionum semiticarum*	*DunRev*	*Dunwoodie Review*
CJT	*Canadian Journal of Theology*	EBib	Etudes bibliques
ClerRev	*Clergy Review*	*EBT*	*Encyclopedia of Biblical Theology*
CLit	*Christianity and Literature*	*EcR*	*Ecclesiastical Review*
CM	*Cahiers marials*	*ED*	*Euntes Docete (Rome)*
CNT	Commentaire du Nouveau Testament	*EE*	*Estudios Eclesiásticos*
ComLit	*Communautes et liturgies*	*EglT*	*Église et théologie*
ConB	Coniectanea biblica	EHAT	Exegetisches Handbuch zum Alten Testament
Concil	*Concilium*	EKKNT	Evangelisch-katholischer Kommentar zum Neuen Testament
ConNT	*Coniectanea neotestamentica*		
CQ	*Church Quarterly*	*EKL*	*Evangelisches Kirchenlexikon*
CQR	*Church Quarterly Review*		
CRAIBL	*Comptes rendus de l'Académie des inscriptions et belles-lettres*	*Emman*	*Emmanuel*
CrQ	*Crozier Quarterly*	*EncJud*	*Encyclopedia judaica (1971)*
CSCO	Corpus scriptorum christianorum orientalium	*EnchBib*	*Enchiridion biblicum*
		EpR	*Epworth Review*
CSEL	Corpus scriptorum ecclesiasticorum latinorum	*ER*	*Ecumenical Review*
		ErJb	*Eranos Jahrbuch*
CTA	A. Herdner, *Corpus des tablettes en cunéiformes alphabétiques*	*EstBib*	*Estudios biblicos*
		ETL	*Ephemerides theologicae lovanienses*
CTJ	*Calvin Theological Journal*	*ETR*	*Etudes théologiques et religieuses*
CTQ	*Concordia Theological Quarterly*	ETS	Erfurter Theologische Studien
CurTM	*Currents in Theology and Mission*	EvK	Evangelische Kommentar
CV	*Communio viatorum*	*EvQ*	*Evangelical Quarterly*
		EvT	*Evangelische Theologie*
DACL	*Dictionnaire d'archéologie chrétienne et de liturgie*	*EW*	*Exegetisches Wörterbuch zum Neuen Testament (EWNT)*, ed. H. Balz and G. Schneider, 3 vols. (Stuttgart: Kohlhammer, 1980–83)
DBSup	*Dictionnaire de la Bible, Supplément*		
Diak	*Diakonia*		
DISO	C. -F. Jean and J. Hoftijzer, *Dictionnaire des inscriptions semitiques de l'ouest*	*Exp*	*Expositor*
		ExpTim	*The Expository Times*
DJD	Discoveries in the Judean Desert	FB	Forschung zur Bibel
		FBBS	Facet Books, Biblical Series
DL	*Doctrine and Life*	FC	Fathers of the Church
DOTT	D. W. Thomas (ed.), *Documents from Old Testament Times*	*FM*	*Faith and Mission*
		FRLANT	Forschungen zur Religion und Literatur des Alten und Neuen Testaments
DR	*Downside Review*		
DS	Denzinger-Schönmetzer, *Enchiridion symbolorum*	FTS	Frankfurter Theologische Studien

GAG	W. von Soden, *Grundriss der akkadischen Grammatik*	IB	*Interpreter's Bible*
GCS	Griechischen christlichen Schriftsteller	IBD	*Illustrated Bible Dictionary*, ed. J. D. Douglas and N. Hillyer
GKB	Gesenius-Kautzsch-Bergsträsser, *Hebräische Grammatik*	IBS	*Irish Biblical Studies*
		ICC	International Critical Commentary
GKC	*Gesenius' Hebrew Grammar*, ed. E. Kautzsch, tr. A. E. Cowley	IDB	G. A. Buttrick (ed.), *Interpreter's Dictionary of the Bible*
GNT	Grundrisse zum Neuen Testament	IDBSup	Supplementary volume to *IDB*
GOTR	*Greek Orthodox Theological Review*	IEJ	*Israel Exploration Journal*
		IER	*Irish Ecclesiastical Record*
GRBS	*Greek, Roman, and Byzantine Studies*	ILS	H. Dessau (ed.), *Inscriptiones Latinae Selectae* (Berlin, 1892)
Greg	*Gregorianum*		
GThT	*Geformelet Theologisch Tijdschrift*	Int	*Interpretation*
		ISBE	*International Standard Bible Encyclopedia*, ed. G. W. Bromiley
GTJ	*Grace Theological Journal*		
GuL	*Geist und Leben*		
		ITQ	*Irish Theological Quarterly*
HALAT	W. Baumgartner et al., *Hebräisches und aramäisches Lexikon zum Alten Testament*	ITS	*Indian Theological Studies*
		JA	*Journal asiatique*
HAT	Handbuch zum Alten Testament	JAAR	*Journal of the American Academy of Religion*
HB	*Homiletica en Biblica*	JAC	Jahrbuch für Antike und Christentum
HDR	Harvard Dissertations in Religion		
HeyJ	*Heythrop Journal*	JAMA	*Journal of the American Medical Association*
HibJ	*Hibbert Journal*	JANESCU	*Journal of the Ancient Near Eastern Society of Columbia University*
HKAT	Handkommentar zum Alten Testament		
HKNT	Handkommentar zum Neuen Testament	JAOS	*Journal of the American Oriental Society*
HL	*Das heilige Land*	JAS	*Journal of Asian Studies*
HNT	Handbuch zum Neuen Testament	JBC	R. E. Brown et al., eds., *The Jerome Biblical Commentary*
HNTC	Harper's NT Commentaries	JBL	*Journal of Biblical Literature*
HR	*History of Religions*	JBR	*Journal of Bible and Religion*
HSM	Harvard Semitic Monographs	JCS	*Journal of Cuneiform Studies*
		JDS	Judean Desert Studies
HTKNT	Herders theologischer Kommentar zum Neuen Testament	JEA	*Journal of Egyptian Archaeology*
		JEH	*Journal of Ecclesiastical History*
HTR	*Harvard Theological Review*	JES	*Journal of Ecumenical Studies*
HTS	Harvard Theological Studies	JETS	*Journal of Evangelical Theological Society*
HUCA	*Hebrew Union College Annual*	JHS	*Journal of Hellenic Studies*
HUTH	Hermeneutische Untersuchungen zur Theologie	JIBS	*Journal of Indian and Buddhist Studies*
		JIPh	*Journal of Indian Philosophy*

JJS	*Journal of Jewish Studies*	LCC	Library of Christian Classics
JMES	*Journal of Middle Eastern Studies*	LCL	Loeb Classical Library
		LD	Lectio divina
JMS	*Journal of Mithraic Studies*	*Leš*	*Lešonénu*
JNES	*Journal of Near Eastern Studies*	*LingBib*	*Linguistica Biblica*
JPOS	*Journal of the Palestine Oriental Society*	*LLAVT*	E. Vogt, *Lexicon linguae aramaicae Veteris Testamenti*
JQR	*Jewish Quarterly Review*	*LouvStud*	*Louvain Studies*
JQRMS	Jewish Quarterly Review Monograph Series	*LPGL*	G. W. H. Lampe, *Partistic Greek Lexicon*
JR	*Journal of Religion*	*LQ*	*Lutheran Quarterly*
JRAS	*Journal of the Royal Asiatic Society*	*LR*	*Lutherische Rundschau*
		LSJ	Liddell-Scott-Jones, *Greek-English Lexicon*
JRE	*Journal of Religious Ethics*	*LTK*	*Lexikon für Theologie und Kirche*
JRelS	*Journal of Religious Studies*		
JRH	*Journal of Religious History*	*LTSB*	*Lutheran Theological Seminary Bulletin*
JRomH	*Journal of Roman History*		
JRT	*Journal of Religious Thought*	LUÅ	Lunds universitets årsskrift
JSJ	*Journal for the Study of Judaism*	*LumVie*	*Lumière et Vie*
		LVit	*Lumen Vitae*
JSNT	*Journal for the Study of the New Testament*	LW	Lutheran World
JSNTSup	JSNT Supplement Series	*MC*	*Modern Churchman*
JSOT	*Journal for the Study of the Old Testament*	*McCQ*	*McCormick Quarterly*
		MDOG	Mitteilungen der deutschen Orient-Gesellschaft
JSOTSup	JSOT Supplement Series		
JSS	*Journal of Semitic Studies*	*MelT*	*Melita Theologica*
JSSR	*Journal for the Scientific Study of Religion*	MeyerK	H. A. W. Meyer, *Kritisch-exegetischer Kommentar über das Neue Testament*
JTC	*Journal for Theology and the Church*	MM	J. H. Moulton and G. Milligan, *The Vocabulary of the Greek Testament* (1930)
JTS	*Journal of Theological Studies*		
JTSA	*Journal of Theology for South Africa*	MNTC	Moffatt NT Commentary
		MPAIBL	*Mémoires présentés à l'Académie des inscriptions et belles-lettres*
Jud	*Judaica*		
		MQR	*Michigan Quarterly Review*
KAI	H. Donner and W. Röllig, *Kannaanäische und aramäische Inschriften*	*MS*	*Milltown Studies*
		MScRel	Mélanges de science religieuse
KAT	E. Sellin, ed., *Kommentar zum Alten Testament*	MTS	Marburger theologische Studien
KB	L. Koehler and W. Baumgartner, *Lexicon in Veteris Testamenti libros*	*MTZ*	*Münchener theologische Zeitschrift*
		MUSJ	*Mélanges de l'université Saint-Joseph*
KD	*Kerygma und Dogma*		
KEK	Kritisch-exegetischer Kommentar über das Neue Testament	MVAG	Mitteilungen der vorder-asiatisch-ägyptischen Gesellschaft
KlT	Kleine Texte		
KTR	*King's Theological Review* (London)	*NAG*	*Nachrichten von der Akademie der Wissenschaften in Göttingen*

NB	New Blackfriars
NCB	New Century Bible (new ed.)
NCCHS	R. C. Fuller et al., eds., New Catholic Commentary on Holy Scripture
NCE	M. R. P. McGuire et al., ed., New Catholic Encyclopedia
NCIB	New Clarendon Bible
NedTTs	Nederlands theologisch tijdschrift
Neot	Neotestamentica
NESTR	Near East School of Theology Reveiw
NewDocs	New Documents Illustrating Early Christianity, A Review of Greek Inscriptions, etc., ed. G. H. R. Horsley, North Ryde, NSW, Australia
NFT	New Frontiers in Theology
NGS	New Gospel Studies
NHS	Nag Hammadi Studies
NICNT	New International Commentary on the New Testament
NiewTT	Niew theologisch tijdschrift
NIGTC	New International Greek Testament Commentary
NJDT	Neue Jahrbücher für deutsche Theologie
NKZ	Neue kirchliche Zeitschrift
NorTT	Norsk Teologisk Tijdsskrift
NovT	Novum Testamentum
NovTSup	Supplement to NovT
NPNF	Nicene and Post-Nicene Fathers
NRT	La nouvelle revue théologique
NTA	New Testament Abstracts
NTAbh	Neutestamentliche Abhandlungen
NTD	Das Neue Testament Deutsch
NTF	Neutestamentliche Forschungen
NTL	New Testament Library
NTS	New Testament Studies
NTSR	The New Testament for Spiritual Reading
NTTS	New Testament Tools and Studies
Numen	Numen: International Review for the History of Religions
NZM	Neue Zeitschrift für Missionswissenschaft
OBO	Orbis biblicus et orientalis
ÖBS	Österreichische biblische Studien
OCD	Oxford Classical Dictionary
OGI	W. Dittenberger, ed., Orientis graeci inscriptiones selectae (Leipzig: Hirzel, 1903–5)
OIP	Oriental Institute Publications
OLP	Orientalia lovaniensia periodica
OLZ	Orientalische Literaturzeitung
Or	Orientalia (Rome)
OrAnt	Oriens antiquus
OrChr	Oriens christianus
OrSyr	L'orient syrien
ÖTKNT	Ökumenischer Taschenbuch-Kommentar zum NT
OTM	Oxford Theological Monographs
OTS	Oudtestamentische Studiën
PAAJR	Proceedings of the American Academy of Jewish Research
PAmh	Amherst Papyri
PC	Proclamation Commentaries
PCB	M. Black and H. H. Rowley, eds., Peake's Commentary on the Bible
PEFQS	Palestine Exploration Fund, Quarterly Statement
PEnteux	Enteuxeis Papyri (Cairo)
PEQ	Palestine Exploration Quarterly
PFay	Fayûm Papyri
PG	Parologia graeca, ed. J. P. Migne
PGiess	Giessen Papyri
PGM	K. Preisendanz, ed., Papyri graecae magicae
PGrenf	An Alexandrian Erotic Fragment and Other Greek Papyri, ed. B. P. Grenfell
PhEW	Philosophy East and West
PhRev	Philosophical Review
PJ	Palästina-Jahrbuch
PL	Patrologia Latina, ed. J. P. Migne
PLond	Greek Papyri in the British Museum (London)
PMich	Michigan Papyri
PNTC	Pelican New Testament commentaries

PO	Patrologia orientalis	RGG	*Religion in Geschichte und*
POxy	Oxyrhynchus Papyri		*Gegenwart*
ProcIBA	*Proceedings of the Irish Biblical*	RHE	*Revue d'histoire ecclésiastique*
	Association	RHPR	*Revue d'histoire et de*
PRS	*Perspectives in Religious*		*philosophie religieuses*
	Studies	RHR	*Revue de l'histoire des religions*
PRU	*Le Palais royal d'Ugarit*	RivB	*Rivista biblica*
PSTJ	*Perkins (School of Theology)*	RM	*Rheinisches Museum für*
	Journal		*Philologie*
PTebt	Tebtunis Papyri	RNT	Regensburger Neues
PTMS	Pittsburgh Theological		Testament
	Monograph Series	RR	*Review of Religion*
PTR	*Princeton Theological Review*	RSLR	*Rivista di Storiae Letteratura*
PVTG	Pseudepigrapha Veteris		*Religiosa* (Turin)
	Testamenti graece	RSO	*Rivista degli studi orientali*
PW	Pauly-Wissowa, *Real-*	RSPT	*Revue des sciences philoso-*
	Encyklopädie der klassischen		*phiques et théologiques*
	Altertumswissenschaft	RSR	*Recherches de science religieuse*
PWSup	Supplement to PW	RTL	*Revue théologique de Louvain*
		RTP	*Revue de théologie et de*
QDAP	*Quarterly of the Department of*		*philosophie*
	Antiquities in Palestine	RTR	*Reformed Theological Review*
		RUV	*La Revue de l'Université Laval*
RA	*Revue d'assyriologie et*	RUO	*Revue de l'université Ottawa*
	d'archéologie orientale		
RAC	*Reallexikon für Antike und*	SacPag	*Sacra Pagina*
	Christentum	SAH	*Sitzungsberichte der*
RArch	*Revue archéologique*		*Heidelberger Akademie der*
RB	*Revue biblique*		*Wissenschaften (phil.-hist.*
RBén	Revue Bénédictine		*Klasse)*
RCB	*Revista de cultura biblica*	Sal	*Salmanticensis*
RE	*Realencyklopädie für*	SANT	Studien zum Alten und
	protestantische Theologie und		Neuen Testament
	Kirche	SAQ	Sammlung ausgewählter
REA	*Revue des Études*		kirchen- und
	Augustiniennes		dogmengeschichtlicher
RechBib	Recherches bibliques		Quellenschriften
REg	*Revue d'égyptologie*	SAWB	*Sitzungsberichte der (königlich*
REJ	*Revue des études juives*		*preussischen) Akademie der*
RelArts	Religion and the Arts		*Wissenschaften zu Berlin*
RelS	*Religious Studies*		*(phil.-hist. Klasse)*
RelSoc	*Religion and Society*	SB	Sources bibliques
RelSRev	*Religious Studies Review*	SBB	Stuttgarter biblische
RES	*Répertoire d'épigraphie*		beiträge
	sémitique	SBFLA	*Studii biblici franciscani liber*
RestQ	*Restoration Quarterly*		*annuus*
RevExp	*Review and Expositor*	SbGU	*Sammelbuch griechischen*
RevistB	*Revista Biblica*		*Urkunden*, ed. F. Preisigke
RevQ	*Revue de Qumrân*	SBJ	*La sainte bible de Jérusalem*
RevRel	*Review for Religious*	SBLASP	Society of Biblical Literature
RevScRel	*Revue des sciences religieuses*		Abstracts and Seminar
RevSém	*Revue sémitique*		Papers
RevThom	*Revue thomiste*	SBLDS	SBL Dissertation Series

SBLMasS	SBL Masoretic Studies
SBLMS	SBL Monograph Series
SBLSBS	SBL Sources for Biblical Study
SBLSCS	SBL Septuagint and Cognate Studies
SBLTT	SBL Texts and Translations
SBM	Stuttgarter biblische Monographien
SBS	Stuttgarter Bibelstudien
SBT	Studies in Biblical Theology
SC	Source Chrétiennes
ScEccl	Sciences ecclésiastique
ScEs	Science et esprit
SCR	Studies in Comparative Religion
Scr	Scripture
ScrB	Scripture Bulletin
SD	Studies and Documents
SE	Studia Evangelica 1, 2, 3, 4, 5, 6 (= TU 73 [1959], 87 [1964], 88 [1964], 102 [1968], 103 [1968], 112 [1973])
SEÅ	Svensk exegetisk årsbok
Sef	Sefarad
SeinSend	Sein Sendung
Sem	Semitica
SémiotBib	Sémiotique et Bible
SHAW	Sitzungsberichte heidelbergen Akademie der Wissenschaften
SHT	Studies in Historical Theology
SHVL	Skrifter Utgivna Av Kungl. Humanistika Vetenskapßamfundet i Lund
SJLA	Studies in Judaism in Late Antiquity
SJT	Scottish Journal of Theology
SMSR	Studi e materiali di storia delle religioni
SNT	Studien zum Neuen Testament
SNTSMS	Society for New Testament Studies Monograph Series
SNTU	Studien zum Neuen Testament und seiner Umwelt
SO	Symbolae osloenses
SOTSMS	Society for Old Testament Study Monograph Series
SPap	Studia papyrologica
SPAW	Sitzungsberichte der preussischen Akademie der Wissenschaften
SPB	Studia postbiblica
SR	Studies in Religion/Sciences Religieuses
SSS	Semitic Study Series
ST	Studia theologica
STÅ	Svensk teologisk årsskrift
StBibT	Studia biblica et theologica
STDJ	Studies on the Texts of the Desert of Judah
STK	Svensk teologisk kvartalskrift
Str-B	H. Strack and P. Billerbeck, Kommentar zum Neuen Testament, 4 vols. (1926–28)
StudBib	Studia biblica
StudNeot	Studia neotestamentica
SUNT	Studien zur Umwelt des Neuen Testaments
SVTP	Studia in Veteris Testamenti pseudepigrapha
SWJT	Southwestern Journal of Theology
SymBU	Symbolae biblicae upsalienses
TantY	Tantur Yearbook
TAPA	Transactions of the American Philological Association
TB	Theologische Beiträge
TBC	Torch Bible Commentaries
TBl	Theologische Blätter
TBü	Theologische Bücherei
TC	Theological Collection (SPCK)
TD	Theology Digest
TDNT	G. Kittel and G. Friedrich, eds., Theological Dictionary of the New Testament, 10 vols., ET (1964–76)
TextsS	Texts and Studies
TF	Theologische Forschung
TGl	Theologie und Glaube
Th	Theology
ThA	Theologische Arbeiten
ThBer	Theologische Berichte
THKNT	Theologischer Handkommentar zum Neuen Testament
ThViat	Theologia Viatorum
TJ	Trinity Journal
TJT	Toronto Journal of Theology

TLZ	*Theologische Literaturzeitung*		Konkordanz zum griechischen
TNTC	Tyndale New Testament		*Neuen Testament*
	Commentaries	VoxEv	*Vox Evangelica* (London)
TP	*Theologie und Philosophie*	VS	Verbum salutis
	(ThPh)	VSpir	*Vie spirituelle*
TPQ	*Theologisch-Praktische*	VT	*Vetus Testamentum*
	Quartalschrift	VTSup	Vetus Testamentum,
TQ	*Theologische Quartalschrift*		Supplements
TRev	*Theologische Revue*		
TRu	*Theologische Rundschau*	WA	M. Luther, *Kritische Gesamt-*
TS	*Theological Studies*		*ausgabe* (= "Weimar" edition)
TSAJ	Texte und Studien zum	WBC	Word Biblical Commentary
	Antiken Judentum	WC	Westminister Commentary
TSFB	*Theological Students Fellowship*	WD	*Wort und Dienst*
	Bulletin	WDB	*Westminster Dictionary of the*
TSK	*Theologische Studien und*		*Bible*
	Kritiken	WF	Wege der Forschung
TT	*Teologisk Tidsskrift*	WHAB	*Westminster Historical Atlas of*
TTKi	*Tidsskrift for Teologi og Kirke*		*the Bible*
TToday	*Theology Today*	WMANT	Wissenschaftliche
TTS	Trier theologische Studien		Monographien zum Alten
TTZ	*Trierer theologische Zeitschrift*		und Neuen Testament
TU	Texte und Untersuchungen	WO	*Die Welt des Orients*
TWAT	G. J. Botterweck and H.	WTJ	*Westminster Theological*
	Ringgren, eds., *Theologisches*		*Journal*
	Wörterbuch zum Alten	WUNT	Wissenschaftliche
	Testament		Untersuchungen zum
TWNT	G. Kittel and G. Friedrich,		Neuen Testament
	eds., *Theologisches Wörterbuch*	WW	*Word and World*
	zum Neuen Testament	WZKM	*Wiener Zeitschrift für die*
TynB	*Tyndale Bulletin*		*Kunde des Morgenlandes*
TZ	*Theologische Zeitschrift*	WZKSO	*Wiener Zeitschrift für die*
			Kunde Süd- und Ostasiens
UCL	Universitas Catholica		
	Lovaniensis	ZA	*Zeitschrift für Assyriologie*
UF	*Ugaritische Forschungen*	ZAW	*Zeitschrift für die*
UFHM	University of Florida		*alttestamentliche Wissenschaft*
	Humanities Monograph	ZDMG	*Zeitschrift der deutschen*
UNT	Untersuchungen zum		*morgenländischen Gesellschaft*
	Neuen Testament	ZDPV	*Zeitschrift des deutschen*
US	*Una Sancta*		*Palästina-Vereins*
USQR	*Union Seminary Quarterly*	ZEE	*Zeitschrift für evangelische*
	Review		*Ethik*
UT	C. H. Gordon, *Ugaritic*	ZHT	*Zeitschrift für historiche*
	Textbook		*Theologie*
UUÅ	Uppsala universitetsårsskrift	ZKG	*Zeitschrift für Kirchengeschichte*
		ZKNT	Zahn's *Kommentar zum NT*
VC	*Vigiliae christianae*	ZKT	*Zeitschrift für katholische*
VCaro	*Verbum caro*		*Theologie*
VD	*Verbum domini*	ZMR	*Zeitschrift für Missionskunde*
VetC	*Vetera Christianorum*		*und Religionswissenschaft*
VF	*Verkündigung und Forschung*	ZNW	*Zeitschrift für die*
VKHNT	K. Aland, ed., *Vollständige*		*neutestamentliche Wissenschaft*

| ZRGG | Zeitschrift für Religions- und Geistesgeschichte | ZTK | Zeitschrift für Theologie und Kirche |
| ZST | Zeitschrift für systematische Theologie | ZWT | Zeitschrift für wissenschaftliche Theologie |

D. Abbreviations for Books of the Bible, the Apocrypha, and the Pseudepigrapha

OLD TESTAMENT

Gen	2 Chr	Dan
Exod	Ezra	Hos
Lev	Neh	Joel
Num	Esth	Amos
Deut	Job	Obad
Josh	Ps(Pss)	Jonah
Judg	Prov	Mic
Ruth	Eccl	Nah
1 Sam	Cant	Hab
2 Sam	Isa	Zeph
1 Kgs	Jer	Hag
2 Kgs	Lam	Zech
1 Chr	Ezek	Mal

NEW TESTAMENT

Matt	1 Tim
Mark	2 Tim
Luke	Titus
John	Philem
Acts	Heb
Rom	Jas
1 Cor	1 Peter
2 Cor	2 Peter
Gal	1 John
Eph	2 John
Phil	3 John
Col	Jude
1 Thess	Rev
2 Thess	

APOCRYPHA

1 Esd	1 Esdras	Ep Jer	Epistle of Jeremy
2 Esd	2 Esdras	S Th Ch	Song of the Three Children (or Young Men)
4 Ezra	4 Ezra		
Tob	Tobit	Sus	Susanna
Jdt	Judith	Bel	Bel and the Dragon
Add Esth	Additions to Esther	Pr Man	Prayer of Manasseh
Wis	Wisdom of Solomon	1 Macc	1 Maccabees
Sir	Ecclesiasticus (Wisdom of Jesus the son of Sirach)	2 Macc	2 Maccabees
		3 Macc	3 Maccabees
Bar	Baruch	4 Macc	4 Maccabees

E. Abbreviations of the Names of Pseudepigraphical and Early patristic Books

Adam and Eve	Life of Adam and Eve	Sib. Or.	Sibylline Oracles
Apoc. Abr.	Apocalypse of Abraham (1st to 2nd cent. A.D.)	T. 12 Patr.	Testaments of the Twelve Patriarchs
2–3 Apoc. Bar.	Syriac, Greek Apocalypse of Baruch	T. Abr.	Testament of Abraham
		T. Judah	Testament of Judah
Apoc. Mos.	Apocalypse of Moses	T. Levi	Testament of Levi, etc.
As. Mos.	(see T. Mos.)		
1–2–3 Enoch	Ethiopic, Slavonic, Hebrew Enoch	Apoc. Pet.	Apocalypse of Peter
		Ep. Pet.	Epistle of Peter to James
Ep. Arist.	Epistle of Aristeas		(Kerygmata Petrou)
Jub.	Jubilees	Gos. Eb.	Gospel of the Ebionites
Mart. Isa.	Martyrdom of Isaiah	Gos. Eg.	Gospel of the Egyptians
Odes Sol.	Odes of Solomon	Gos. Heb.	Gospel of the Hebrews
Pss. Sol.	Psalms of Solomon	Gos. Naass.	Gospel of the Naassenes

Gos. Pet.	Gospel of Peter	Rom.	Ignatius, *Letter to the Romans*
Gos. Thom.	Gospel of Thomas		
Prot. Jas.	Protevangelium of James	Smyrn.	Ignatius, *Letter to the Smyrnaeans*
Barn.	Barnabas		
1–2 Clem.	1–2 Clement	Trall.	Ignatius, *Letter to the Trallians*
Did.	Didache		
Diogn.	Diognetus	Mart. Pol.	Martyrdom of Polycarp
Herm. Man.	Hermas, Mandates	Pol. Phil.	Polycarp to the Philippians
Sim.	Similitudes	Iren.	
Vis.	Visions	Adv. Haer.	Irenaeus, Against All Heresies
Ign. Eph.	Ignatius, *Letter to the Ephesians*	Tert.	
Magn.	Ignatius, *Letter to the Magnesians*	De Praesc. Haer.	Tertullian, On the Proscribing of Heretics
Phil.	Ignatius, *Letter to the Philadelphians*	Ps.-Clem. Hom.	Pseudo-Clementine Homilies
Pol.	Ignatius, *Letter to the Polycarp*	Ps.-Clem. Recog.	Pseudo-Clementine Recognitions

F. Abbreviations of Names of Dead Sea Scrolls and Related Texts

CD	Cairo (Genizah text of the) Damascus (Document)	1QS	Serek hayyahad (Rule of the Community, Manual of Discipline)
Hev	Naḥal Ḥever texts	1QSa	Appendix A (Rule of the Congregation) to 1QS
Mas	Masada texts		
Mird	Khirbet Mird texts	1QSb	Appendix B (Blessings) to 1QS
Mur	Wadi Murabba'at texts		
P	Pesher (commentary)	3Q15	Copper Scroll from Qumran Cave 3
Q	Qumran		
1Q, 2Q, 3Q, etc.	Numbered caves of Qumran, yielding written material; followed by abbreviation of biblical or apocryphal book	4QFlor	Florilegium (or Eschatological Midrashim) from Qumran Cave 4
		4QMess ar	Aramaic "Messianic" text from Qumran Cave 4
		4QPrNab	Prayer of Nabonidus from Qumran Cave 4
QL	Qumran literature	4QShirShab	Angelic Liturgy from Qumran Cave 4
1QapGen	Genesis Apocryphon of Qumran Cave 1	4QTestim	Testimonia text from Qumran Cave 4
1QH	Hôdāyôt (Thanksgiving Hymns) from Qumran Cave 1	4QTLevi	Testament of Levi from Qumran Cave 4
1QIsaᵃ,ᵇ	First or second copy of Isaiah from Qumran Cave 1	4QPhyl	Phylacteries from Qumran Cave 4
1QpHab	Pesher on Habakkuk from Qumran Cave 1	11QMelch	Melchizedek text from Qumran Cave 11
1QpMic	Pesher on Micah from Qumran Cave 1	11QtgJob	Targum of Job from Qumran Cave 11
1QM	Milḥāmāh (War Scroll)	11QTemple	Temple Scroll from Qumran Cave 11

G. Abbreviations of Targumic Material

Tg. Onq.	Targum Onqelos	Tg. Ps.-J.	Targum Pseudo-Jonathan
Tg. Neb.	Targum of the Prophets	Tg. Yer. I	Targum Yerušalmi I*
Tg. Ket.	Targum of the Writings	Tg. Yer. II	Targum Yerušalmi II*
Frg. Tg.	Fragmentary Targum	Yem. Tg.	Yemenite Targum
Sam. Tg.	Samaritan Targum	Tg. Esth. I, II	First or Second Targum of
Tg. Isa.	Targum of Isaiah		Esther
Pal. Tgs.	Palestinian Targums		
Tg. Neof.	Targum Neofiti I	*optional title	

H. Abbreviations of Other Rabbinic Works

'Abot R. Nat.	'Abot de Rabbi Nathan	Pesiq. Rab Kah.	Pesiqta de Rab Kahana
'Ag. Ber	'Aggadat Berešit	Pirqe R. El.	Pirqe Rabbi Eliezer
Bab.	Babylonian	Rab.	Rabbah (following
Bar.	Baraita		abbreviation for biblical
Der. Er. Rab.	Derek Ereṣ Rabba		book: Gen. Rab. [with
Der. Er. Zuṭ.	Derek Ereṣ Zuṭa		periods] = Genesis
Gem.	Gemara		Rabbah)
Kalla	Kalla	ṣem.	ṣemaḥot
Mek.	Mekilta	Sipra	Sipra
Midr.	Midraš; cited with usual	Sipre	Sipre
	abbreviation for biblical	Sop.	Soperim
	book; but Midr. Qoh. =	S. 'Olam Rab.	Seder ' Olam Rabbah
	Midraš Qohelet	Talm.	Talmud
Pal.	Palestinian	Yal.	Yalquṭ
Pesiq. R.	Pesiqta Rabbati		

I. Abbreviations of Orders and Tractates in Mishnaic and Related Literature

'Abot	'Abot	Ketub.	Ketubot
'Arak.	'Arakin	Kil.	Kil'ayim
'Abod. Zar.	'Aboda Zara	Ma'aś.	Ma'śerot
B. Bat.	Baba Batra	Mak.	Makkot
Bek.	Bekorot	Makš.	Makširin (= Mašqin)
Ber.	Berakot	Meg.	Megilla
Beṣa	Beṣa (= Yom Tob)	Me'il.	Me'ila
Bik.	Bikkurim	Menaḥ.	Menaḥot
B. Meṣ.	Baba Meṣi' a	Mid.	Middot
B. Qam.	Baba Qamma	Miqw.	Miqwa'ot
Dem.	Demai	Mo'ed	Mo'ed
'Ed.	'Eduyyot	Mo'ed Qat.	Mo'ed Qaṭan
'Erub.	'Erubin	Ma'aś. Š.	Ma'aśer Šeni
Giṭ.	Giṭṭin	Našim	Našim
Ḥag.	Ḥagiga	Nazir	Nazir
Ḥal.	Ḥalla	Ned.	Nedarim
Hor.	Horayot	Neg.	Nega 'im
Ḥul.	Ḥullin	Nez.	Neziqin
Kelim	Kelim	Nid.	Niddah
Ker.	Keritot	Ohol.	Oholot

'Or.	'Orla	Sukk.	Sukka
Para	Para	Ta'an.	Ta'anit
Pe 'a	Pe 'a	Tamid	Tamid
Pesaḥ.	Pesaḥim	Tem.	Temura
Qinnim	Qinnim	Ter.	Terumot
Qidd.	Qiddušin	Ṭohar.	Ṭoharot
Qod.	Qodašin	T. Yom	Tebul Yom
Roš. Haš.	Roš Haššana	'Uq.	'Uqṣin
Sanh.	Sanhedrin	Yad.	Yadayim
Šabb.	Šabbat	Yebam.	Yebamot
Šeb.	Šebi 'it	Yoma	Yoma (= Kippurim)
Šebu.	Šebu 'ot	Zabim	Zabim
Šeqal.	Šeqalim	Zebaḥ	Zebaḥim
Soṭa	Soṭa	Zer.	Zera'im

J. Abbreviations of Nag Hammadi Tractates

Acts Pet. 12 Apost.	Acts of Peter and the Twelve Apostles	Marsanes	Marsanes
		Melch.	Melchizedek
Allogenes	Allogenes	Norea	Thought of Norea
Ap. Jas.	Apocryphon of James	On Bap. A	On Baptism A
Ap. John	Apocryphon of John	On Bap. B	On Baptism B
Apoc. Adam	Apocalypse of Adam	On Bap. C	On Baptism C
1 Apoc. Jas.	First Apocalypse of James	On Euch. A	On the Eucharist A
2 Apoc. Jas.	Second Apocalypse of James	On Euch. B	On the Eucharist B
Apoc. Paul	Apocalypse of Paul	Orig. World	On the Origin of the World
Apoc. Pet.	Apocalypse of Peter	Paraph. Shem	Paraphrase of Shem
Asclepius	Asclepius 21–29	Pr. Paul	Prayer of the Apostle Paul
Auth. Teach.	Authoritative Teaching	Pr. Thanks	Prayer of Thanksgiving
Dial. Sav.	Dialogue of the Savior	Prot. Jas.	Protevangelium of James
Disc. 8–9	Discourse on the Eighth and Ninth	Sent. Sextus	Sentences of Sextus
		Soph. Jes. Chr.	Sophia of Jesus Christ
Ep. Pet. Phil.	Letter of Peter to Philip	Steles Seth	Three Steles of Seth
Eugnostos	Eugnostos the Blessed	Teach. Silv.	Teachings of Silvanus
Exeg. Soul	Exegesis on the Soul	Testim. Truth	Testimony of Truth
Gos. Eg.	Gospel of the Egyptians	Thom. Cont.	Book of Thomas the Contender
Gos. Phil.	Gospel of Philip		
Gos. Thom.	Gospel of Thomas	Thund.	Thunder, Perfect Mind
Gos. Truth	Gospel of Truth	Treat. Res.	Treatise on Resurrection
Great Pow.	Concept of our Great Power	Treat. Seth	Second Treatise of the Great Seth
Hyp. Arch.	Hypostasis of the Archons	Tri. Trac.	Triparite Tractate
Hypsiph.	Hypsiphrone	Trim. Prot.	Trimorphic Protennoia
Interp. Know.	Interpretation of Knowledge	Val. Exp.	A Valentinian Exposition
		Zost.	Zostrianos

Commentary Bibliography

Allan, J. A. *The Epistle of Paul the Apostle to the Galatians.* TBC. London: SCM, 1951. **Ambrosiaster.** *Commentarium in Epistulam Beati Pauli ad Galatas* (*PL* 17:357–94). **Amiot, F. S.** *Paul: Epître aux Galates.* Paris: Beauchesne et ses Fils, 1946. **Augustine.** *Commentarium in Epistulam ad Galatas* (*PL* 35:2105–48). **Barclay, W.** *The Letters to the Galatians and Ephesians.* Daily Study Bible. Rev. ed. Edinburgh: St. Andrew Press, 1976. **Betz, H. D.** *Galatians: A Commentary on Paul's Letter to the Churches in Galatia.* Hermeneia. Philadelphia: Fortress, 1979. **Beyer, W.** *Der Brief an die Galater.* Rev. P. Althaus. NTD. Göttingen: Vandenhoeck & Ruprecht, 1962. **Bligh, J.** *Galatians: A Discussion of St. Paul's Epistle.* London: St. Paul, 1969. **Blunt, A. W. F.** *The Epistle of Paul to the Galatians.* Clarendon Bible. Oxford: Clarendon, 1925. **Boice, J. M.** "Galatians." In *The Expositor's Bible Commentary*, Vol. 10, ed. F. E. Gaebelein. Grand Rapids: Zondervan, 1976. 407–508. **Bonnard, P.** *L'Epître de Saint Paul aux Galates.* 2nd ed. CNT. Neuchâtel and Paris: Delachaux & Niestle, 1972. **Bousset, W.** "Der Brief an die Galater." In *Die Schriften des Neuen Testaments.* 2nd ed. Göttingen: Vandenhoeck & Ruprecht, 1908. 2:28–72. **Bring, R.** *Commentary on Galatians.* Tr. E. Wahlstrom. Philadelphia: Muhlenberg, 1961. **Bruce, F. F.** *The Epistle to the Galatians.* NIGTC. Grand Rapids: Eerdmans, 1982. **Burton, E. deW.** *A Critical and Exegetical Commentary on the Epistle to the Galatians.* ICC. Edinburgh: T. & T. Clark, 1921. **Calvin, J.** *The Epistles of Paul the Apostle to the Galatians, Ephesians, Philippians, and Colossians.* Tr. T. H. L. Parker, in *Calvin's New Testament Commentaries*, ed. D. W. Torrance and T. F. Torrance, Vol. 11. Grand Rapids: Eerdmans, 1965. 3–119. **Chrysostom, J.** *Commentary on the Epistle to the Galatians and Homilies on the Epistle to the Ephesians.* Oxford: Parker, 1840 (*PG* 61:611–82). **Cole, R. A.** *The Epistle of Paul to the Galatians.* TNTC. Grand Rapids: Eerdmans, 1965. **Cousar, C. B.** *Galatians.* Interpretation. Atlanta: John Knox, 1982. **DeWolf, L. H.** *Galatians: A Letter for Today.* Grand Rapids: Eerdmans, 1971. **Duncan, G. S.** *The Epistle of Paul to the Galatians.* MNTC. London: Hodder & Stoughton, 1934. **Eadie, J.** *A Commentary on the Greek Text of the Epistle of Paul to the Galatians.* Edinburgh: T. & T. Clark, 1869. **Ellicott, C. J.** *A Critical and Grammatical Commentary on St. Paul's Epistle to the Galatians.* Andover: Draper, 1860. **Emmet, C. W.** *St. Paul's Epistle to the Galatians.* The Reader's Commentary. New York: Funk & Wagnalls, 1912. **Erasmus, D.** *Collected Works of Erasmus.* Vol. 42: *Paraphrases on Romans and Galatians.* Ed. R. D. Sider. Toronto: University of Toronto Press, 1984. **Findlay, G. G.** *The Epistle to the Galatians.* 3rd ed. Expositor's Bible. London: Hodder & Stoughton, 1891. **Fitzmyer, J. A.** "The Letter to the Galatians." In *The Jerome Biblical Commentary.* Englewood Cliffs, NJ: Prentice-Hall, 1968. 2:236–46. **Fung, R. Y. K.** *The Epistle to the Galatians.* NICNT. Grand Rapids: Eerdmans, 1988. **Guthrie, D.** *Galatians.* NCB. London: Marshall, Morgan & Scott, 1973. **Hendriksen, W.** *The Epistle to the Galatians.* New Testament Commentary. Grand Rapids: Baker, 1969. **Hilgenfeld, A.** *Der Galaterbrief übersetzt, in seinen geschichtlichen Beziehungen untersucht und erklärt.* Leipzig: Breitkopf & Härtel, 1852. **Jerome.** *Commentarium in Epistulam ad Galatas* (*PL* 26:307–438). **Knox, J.** "Galatians, Letter to the." In *IDB* (1962) 2:338–43. **Lagrange, M.-J.** *Saint Paul, Epître aux Galates.* 2nd ed. Paris: Gabalda, 1925. **Lietzmann, H.** *An die Galater.* 4th ed. HNT 10. Tübingen: Mohr-Siebeck, 1971. **Lightfoot, J. B.** *Saint Paul's Epistle to the Galatians.* 10th ed. 1890; repr: London: Macmillan, 1986. **Lipsius, R. A.** *Briefe an die Galater, Römer, Philipper.* 2nd ed. Freiburg: Mohr-Siebeck, 1892. **Loisy, A.** *L'Epître aux Galates.* Paris: Nourry, 1916. **Luther, M.** *Luthers Werke*, Vol. 2 (1519 and 1523 editions); Vols. 40[1] and 40[2a] (1538 edition). Weimar: Bohlaus, 1884, 1911, 1914. ————. *Luther's Works*, Vols. 26 and 27. Ed. J. Pelikan. St. Louis: Concordia, 1963–64. ————. *A Commentary on St. Paul's Epistle to the Galatians.* Tr. P. S. Watson, based on the Middleton edition of the English version of 1575. London: James Clarke, 1953. **Lyonnet, S.** *Les Epîtres de Saint Paul aux Galates, aux Romains.* Paris: Cerf, 1953. **Machen, J. G.** *Machen's Notes on Galatians*, ed. J. H. Skilton. Nutley, NJ: Presbyterian &

Reformed, 1977. **McDonald, H. D.** *Freedom in Faith: A Commentary on Paul's Epistle to the Galatians.* Old Tappan, NJ: Revell, 1973. **Mussner, F.** *Der Galaterbrief.* HTKNT 9. Freiburg, Basel, and Vienna: Herder, 1974. **Neil, W.** *The Letter of Paul to the Galatians.* Cambridge Bible Commentary. Cambridge: Cambridge University Press, 1967. **Neill, S.** *Paul to the Galatians.* New York: Association Press, 1958. **Oepke, A.** *Der Brief des Paulus an die Galater.* 3rd ed., ed. J. Rohde. THKNT. Berlin: Evangelische Verlagsanstalt, 1973. **Origen.** *Ex Libris Origenis in Epistulam Galatas* (*PG* 14:1293–98). **Osiek, C.** *Galatians.* New Testament Message. Wilmington, DE: Michael Glazier, 1980. **Pelagius.** *Expositions of the Thirteen Epistles of St. Paul.* Ed. A. Souter. Cambridge: Cambridge University Press, 1922. **Ramsay, W. M.** *A Historical Commentary on St. Paul's Epistle to the Galatians.* 2nd ed. London: Hodder & Stoughton, 1900. **Ridderbos, H. N.** *The Epistle of Paul to the Churches of Galatia.* Tr. H. Zylstra. NICNT. Grand Rapids: Eerdmans, 1953. **Schlier, H.** *Der Brief an der Galater.* KEK 7, 10th ed. Göttingen: Vandenhoeck & Ruprecht, 1949. **Sieffert, F.** *Der Brief an die Galater.* KEK 7, 9th ed. Göttingen: Vandenhoeck & Ruprecht, 1899. **Stamm, R. T.,** and **Blackwelder, O. F.** "The Epistle to the Galatians." In *IB,* Vol. 10. New York: Abingdon, 1953. **Stott, J. R. W.** *The Message of Galatians.* Downers Grove, IL: Inter-Varsity, 1968. **Tertullian.** *Adversus Marcionem.* Ed., tr., and intro. E. Evans. Oxford: Clarendon, 1972 (*PL* 2:239–524), esp. Book 5. **Theodore of Mopsuestia.** *Commentaries on the Minor Epistles of St. Paul.* 2 vols., ed. H. B. Swete. Cambridge: Cambridge University Press, 1880–82 (*PG* 66:911–22). **Theodoret of Cyrrhus.** *Commentarii in omnes Pauli Epistulas.* Oxford: Parker, 1852 (*PG* 82:505–58). **Victorinus.** *Marii Victorini Afri commentarii in epistulas Pauli.* Ed. A. Locher. Leipzig: Teubner, 1972. **Watkins, C. H.** *St. Paul's Fight for Galatia.* London: James Clarke, 1914. **Williams, A. L.** *The Epistle of Paul the Apostle to the Galatians.* Cambridge Greek Testament. Cambridge: Cambridge University Press, 1911. **Zahn, T.** *Der Brief des Paulus an die Galater.* 3rd ed. Kommentar zum Neuen Testament. Leipzig: Deichert, 1922.

General Bibliography

Askwith, E. H. *The Epistle to the Galatians: An Essay on Its Destination and Date.* New York: Macmillan, 1899. **Aurray, P.** "S. Jerome et S. Augustin—La controverse au sujet de l'incident d'Antioche." *RSR* 29 (1939) 594–610. **Aus, R. D.** "Three Pillars and Three Patriarchs: A Proposal Concerning Gal 2:9." *ZNW* 70 (1979) 252–61. **Bacon, B. W.** "Peter's Triumph at Antioch." *JR* 9 (1929) 204–23. **Bahr, G. J.** "Paul and Letter Writing in the First Century." *CBQ* 28 (1966) 465–77. ⸻. "The Subscriptions in the Pauline Letters." *JBL* 87 (1968) 27–41. **Bammel, E.** "Gottes ΔΙΑΘΗΚΗ (Gal. III.15–17) und das jüdische Rechtsdenken." *NTS* 6 (1960) 313–19. ⸻. "Νόμος Χριστοῦ." In *Studia Evangelica* III, ed. F. L. Cross. TU 88. Berlin: Akademie, 1964. 12–28. ⸻. "Galater 1, 23." *ZNW* 59 (1968) 108–12. ⸻. "πτωχός." *TDNT* 6:888–915. **Bandstra, A. J.** *The Law and the Elements of the World: An Exegetical Study in Aspects of Paul's Teaching.* Kampen: Kok, 1964. **Barclay, J. M. G.** "Mirror-Reading a Polemical Letter: Galatians as a Test Case." *JSNT* 31 (1987) 73–93. ⸻. *Obeying the Truth: A Study of Paul's Ethics in Galatians.* Edinburgh: T. & T. Clark, 1988. **Barclay, W.** *Flesh and Spirit: An Examination of Galatians 5:19–23.* London: SCM, 1962; Grand Rapids: Baker, 1976. **Barrett, C. K.** *The Holy Spirit and the Gospel Tradition.* London: SPCK, 1947. ⸻. "Paul and the 'Pillar' Apostles." In *Studia Paulina.* FS J. de Zwaan, ed. J. N. Sevenster and W. C. van Unnik. Haarlem: Bohn, 1953. 1–19. ⸻. "Titus." In *Neotestamentica et Semitica.* FS M. Black, ed. E. E. Ellis and M. Wilcox. Edinburgh: T. & T. Clark. 1969. 1–14. ⸻. *The Signs of an Apostle.* London: Epworth, 1970. ⸻.

"The Allegory of Abraham, Sarah, and Hagar in the Argument of Galatians." In *Rechtfertigung*. FS E. Käsemann, ed. J. Friedrich, W. Pohlmann, and P. Stuhlmacher. Tübingen: Mohr-Siebeck, 1976. 1–16. ————. "*Shaliaḥ* and Apostle." In *Donum Gentilicium*. FS D. Daube, ed. C. K. Barrett, E. Bammel, and W. D. Davies. London: Oxford University Press, 1978. 88–102. ————. *Freedom and Obligation: A Study of the Epistle to the Galatians*. London: SPCK, 1985. **Barth, M.** "The Kerygma of Galatians." *Int* 21 (1967) 131–46. ————. "The Faith of the Messiah." *HeyJ* 10 (1969) 363–70. **Bauckham, R. J.** "Barnabas in Galatians." *JSNT* 2 (1979) 61–70. **Bauer, W.** *Orthodoxy and Heresy in Earliest Christianity*. Tr. and ed. R. A. Kraft and G. Krodel. Philadelphia: Fortress, 1971. 61–76. **Bauernfeind, O.** "Die Begegnung zwischen Paulus und Kephas, Gal 1:18–20." *ZNW* 47 (1956) 268–76. ————. "τρέχω, δρόμος, πρόδρομος." *TDNT* 8:226–35. **Baur, F. C.** "Die Christuspartei in der korinthischen Gemeinde: Der Gegensatz des petrinischen und paulinischen Christentums in der ältesten Kirche." *Tübinger Zeitschrift für Theologie* (1831) 61–206. ————. *Paul: His Life and Works*. 2 vols., tr. E. Zeller from *Paulus, der Apostel Jesu Christi* (Stuttgart: Becher & Muller, 1845). London: Williams & Norgate, 1875, 1:245–57. **Beare, F. W.** "The Sequence of Events in Acts 9–15 and the Career of Peter." *JBL* 62 (1943) 293–306. **Behm, J.** "ἀνάθημα, ἀνάθεμα, κατάθεμα." *TDNT* 1:354–55. ————. "καρδία." *TDNT* 3:605–13. **Beker, J. C.** *Paul the Apostle: The Triumph of God in Life and Thought*. Philadelphia: Fortress, 1980. **Belleville, L. L.** "'Under Law': Structural Analysis and the Pauline Concept of Law in Galatians 3.21–4.11." *JSNT* 26 (1986) 53–78. **Berger, K.** "Apostelbrief und apostolische Rede: Zum Formular frühchristlicher Briefe." *ZNW* 65 (1974) 190–231. ————. "Almosen für Israel: Zum historischen Kontext der paulinischen Kollekte." *NTS* 23 (1977) 180–204. **Bertram, G.** "νήπιος." *TDNT* 4:912–23. **Best, E.** *One Body in Christ: A Study in the Relationship of the Church to Christ in the Epistles of the Apostle Paul*. London: SPCK, 1955. **Betz, H. D.** "Geist, Freiheit und Gesetz: Die Botschaft des Paulus an die Gemeinden in Galatien." *ZTK* 71 (1974) 78–93 (ET "Spirit, Freedom, and Law: Paul's Message to the Galatian Churches," *SEÅ* 39 [1974] 145–60). ————. "The Literary Composition and Function of Paul's Letter to the Galatians." *NTS* 21 (1975) 353–79. ————. "In Defense of the Spirit: Paul's Letter to the Galatians as a Document of Early Christian Apologetics." In *Aspects of Religious Propaganda in Judaism and Early Christianity*, ed. E. Schüssler Fiorenza. Notre Dame, IN: University of Notre Dame Press, 1976. 99–114. **Betz, O.** "στίγμα." *TDNT* 7:657–64. **Bjerkelund, C.** *Parakalô: Form, Funktion und Sinn der Parakalô-Sätze in den paulinischen Briefen*. Bibliotheca Theologica Norwegica 1. Oslo: Universitetsforlaget, 1967. **Blackman, E. C.** *Marcion and His Influence*. London: SPCK, 1948. **Bläser, P. P.** *Das Gesetz bei Paulus*. Münster: Aschendorff, 1941. **Bonsirven, J.** "Exégèse allegorique chez les rabbins tannaites." *RSR* 23 (1933) 522–24. ————. *Exégèse rabbinique et exégèse paulinienne*. Paris: Beauchesne, 1939. **Bornkamm, G.** "The Revelation of Christ to Paul on the Damascus Road and Paul's Doctrine of Justification and Reconciliation: A Study in Galatians I." Tr. J. M. Owen, in *Reconciliation and Hope*. FS L. L. Morris, ed. R. Banks. Exeter: Paternoster, 1974. 90–103. **Bradley, D. G.** "The TOPOS as a Form in the Pauline Paraenesis." *JBL* 72 (1953) 238–46. **Bring, R.** *Christus und das Gesetz: Die Bedeutung des Gesetzes des Alten Testaments nach Paulus und seine Glauben an Christus*. Leiden: Brill, 1969. **Brinsmead, B. H.** *Galatians as Dialogical Response to Opponents*. SBLDS 65. Chico, CA: Scholars, 1982. **Brown, R. E.**, and **Meier, J. P.** *Antioch and Rome: New Testament Cradles of Catholic Christianity*. New York: Paulist, 1982. **Bruce, F. F.** "Galatian Problems. 2: North or South Galatians?" *BJRL* 52 (1970) 243–66. ————. "Further Thoughts on Paul's Biography: Galatians 1:11–2:14." In *Jesus und Paulus*. FS W. G. Kümmel, ed. E. E. Ellis and E. Grässer. Tübingen: Mohr-Siebeck, 1975. 21–29. ————. *Paul: Apostle of the Heart Set Free*. Grand Rapids: Eerdmans, 1977. ————. "The Curse of the Law." In *Paul and Paulinism*. FS C. K. Barrett, ed. M. D. Hooker and S. G. Wilson. London: SPCK, 1982. 27–36. **Büchsel, F.** "ἀλληγορέω." *TDNT* 1:260–63. **Buck, C. H.** "The Date of Galatians." *JBL* 70 (1951) 113–22. **Buck, C. H.,** and **Taylor, G.** *Saint Paul: A Study in the Development of His Thought*. New York: Scribner's Sons, 1969. 82–102. **Bultmann, R.** *Der Stil der paulinischen Predigt und die kynisch-stoische Diatribe*. FRLANT 13. Göttingen: Vandenhoeck & Ruprecht, 1910. **Buri, F.** *Clemens Alexandrinus und* *der paulinische Freiheitsbegriff.* Zürich: Niehmans, 1939. **Burkitt, F. C.** *Christian Beginnings.* London: University of London, 1924. **Burton, E. deW.** *Spirit, Soul, and Flesh.* Chicago: University of Chicago Press, 1918. **Byrne, B.** *"Son of God"—"Seed of Abraham": A Study of the Idea of the Sonship of God of All Christians in Paul against the Jewish Background.* AnBib 83. Rome: Biblical Institute Press, 1979. **Caird, G. B.** "Chronology of the NT." *IDB.* New York: Abingdon, 1962. 1:599–607. ————. *The Language and Imagery of the Bible.* London: Duckworth, 1980. **Calder, W. M.** "Adoption and Inheritance in Galatia." *JTS* 31 (1930) 372–74. **Callan, T.** "Pauline Midrash: The Exegetical Background of Gal 3:19b." *JBL* 99 (1980) 549–67. **Campbell, T. H.** "Paul's 'Missionary Journeys' as Reflected in His Letters." *JBL* 74 (1955) 80–87. **Carrington, P.** "Peter in Antioch." *ATR* 15 (1933) 1–15. ————. *The Early Christian Church.* 2 vols. Cambridge: Cambridge University Press, 1957. **Chase, F. H.** *Chrysostom: A Study in the History of Biblical Interpretation.* Cambridge: Deighton, Bell, 1887. **Chilton, B. D.** "Galatians 6:15: A Call to Freedom before God." *ExpTim* 89 (1977–78) 311–13. **Clark, K. W.** "The Meaning of ἐνεργέω and καταργέω in the New Testament." *JBL* 54 (1935) 93–101. **Clarke, W. K. L.** "St. Paul's 'Large Letters.'" *ExpTim* 24 (1913) 285. **Clemens, J. S.** "St. Paul's Handwriting." *ExpTim* 24 (1913) 380. **Corbett, E. P. J.** *Classical Rhetoric for the Modern Student.* New York: Oxford, 1965, 1971. **Corbett, E. P. J.,** ed. *Rhetorical Analyses of Literary Works.* New York: Oxford, 1969. **Cosgrove, C. H.** "Arguing like a Mere Human Being: Galatians 3:15–18 in Rhetorical Perspective." *NTS* 34 (1988) 536–49. **Cranfield, C. E. B.** "St. Paul and the Law." *SJT* 17 (1964) 43–68. **Crownfield, F. C.** "The Singular Problem of the Dual Galatians." *JBL* 63 (1945) 491–500. **Cullmann, O.** *Peter: Disciple, Apostle, Martyr.* Tr. F. V. Filson. London: SCM, 1953. ————. *The Christology of the New Testament.* Tr. S. C. Guthrie and C. A. M. Hall. Philadelphia: Westminster, 1962. **Cuming, G. J.** "Service-endings in the Epistles." *NTS* 22 (1975) 110–13. **Dahl, N. A.** "Der Name Israel: Zur Auslegung von Gal 6, 16." *Judaica* 6 (1950) 161–70. ————. "The Atonement—An Adequate Reward for the Akedah? (Ro 8:32)." In *Neotestamentica et Semitica.* FS M. Black, ed. E. E. Ellis and M. Wilcox. Edinburgh: T. & T. Clark, 1969. 15–29. ————. "Paul's Letter to the Galatians: Epistolary Genre, Content, and Structure." Unpublished SBL Paul Seminar paper, 1974. ————. *Studies in Paul: Theology for the Early Christian Mission.* Minneapolis: Augsburg, 1977. **Danby, H.,** tr. *The Mishnah.* London: Oxford University Press, 1933. **Daniélou, J.** *Origen.* Tr. W. Mitchell. London & New York: Sheed & Ward, 1955. **Daube, D.** "Rabbinic Methods of Interpretation and Hellenistic Rhetoric." *HUCA* 22 (1949) 239–64. ————. "Alexandrian Methods of Interpretation and the Rabbis." In *Festschrift Hans Lewald.* Basel: Helbing & Lichtenbahn, 1953. 27–44. ————. *The New Testament and Rabbinic Judaism.* London: Athlone, 1956. **Davies, W. D.** *Paul and Rabbinic Judaism: Some Rabbinic Elements in Pauline Theology.* 4th ed. Philadelphia: Fortress, 1980. ————. "A Note on Josephus, *Antiquities* 15.136." *HTR* 47 (1954) 135–40. ————. "Paul and the Dead Sea Scrolls: Flesh and Spirit." In *The Scrolls and the New Testament,* ed. K. Stendahl. New York: Harper, 1957. 157–82. ————. "Paul and the People of Israel." *NTS* 24 (1977) 4–39. ————. "Paul and the Law: Reflections on Pitfalls in Interpretation." In *Paul and Paulinism.* FS C. K. Barrett, ed. M. D. Hooker and S. G. Wilson. London: SPCK, 1982. 4–16. **Deidun, T. J.** *New Covenant Morality in Paul.* AnBib 89. Rome: Biblical Institute, 1981. **Deissmann, A.** *Die neutestamentliche Formel "In Christo Jesu."* Marburg: Elwert, 1892. ————. *Bible Studies.* Tr. A. Grieve. Edinburgh: T. & T. Clark, 1901. ————. *Light from the Ancient East: The New Testament Illustrated by Recently Discovered Texts of the Graeco-Roman World.* Tr. L. R. M. Strachan. London: Hodder & Stoughton, 1909. **Delacey, D. R.** "Paul in Jerusalem." *NTS* 20 (1983) 82–86. **Delling, G.** "καιρός." *TDNT* 3:455–62. ————. "πληρόω, πλήρωμα." *TDNT* 6:286–306. ————. "στοιχέω, συστοιχέω, στοιχεῖον." *TDNT* 7:666–87. **Derrett, J. D. M.** *Law in the New Testament.* London: Darton, Longman & Todd, 1970. **DeVries, C. E.** "Paul's 'Cutting' Remarks about a Race: Galatians 5:1–12." In *Current Issues in Biblical and Patristic Interpretation.* FS M. C. Tenney, ed. G. F. Hawthorne. Grand Rapids: Eerdmans, 1975. 115–20. **Dibelius, M.** *A Fresh Approach to the New Testament and Early Christian Literature.* London: Nicholson & Watson, 1936. ————. *From Tradition to Gospel.* Tr. B. L. Woolf. New York:

Scribners, 1965. ————. *A Commentary on the Epistle of James.* Rev. H. Greeven, tr. M. A. Williams. Hermeneia. Philadelphia: Fortress, 1976. **Dinkler, E.** "Der Brief an die Galater." *VF* 1–3 (1953–55) 182–83. **Dion, P. E.** "The Aramaic 'Family Letter' and Related Epistolary Forms in Other Oriental Languages and in Hellenistic Greek." *Semeia* 22 (1981) 59–76. **Dix, G.** *Jew and Greek: A Study in the Primitive Church.* London: Dacre, 1953. **Dixon, P.** *Rhetoric.* London: Methuen, 1971. **Dodd, C. H.** *The Mind of Paul: A Psychological Approach.* Manchester: John Rylands Library, 1934 (= *BJRL* 17 [1933] 91–106; idem, *New Testament Studies* [Manchester: Manchester UP, 1953] 67–82). ————. *The Mind of Paul: Change and Development.* Manchester: John Rylands Library, 1934 (= *BJRL* 18 [1934] 69–110; idem, *New Testament Studies* [Manchester: Manchester UP, 1953] 83–128). ————. *Gospel and Law.* Cambridge: Cambridge University Press; New York: Columbia University Press, 1951. ————. *According to the Scriptures: The Sub-structure of New Testament Theology.* London: Nisbet, 1952. ————. "ΕΝΝΟΜΟΣ ΧΡΙΣΤΟΥ." In *Studia Paulina.* FS J. de Zwaan, ed. W. C. van Unnik and J. N. Sevenster. Haarlem: Bohn, 1953. 96–110 (repr. idem, *More New Testament Studies* [Manchester: Manchester University Press, 1968] 134–48). **Donaldson, T. L.** "The 'Curse of the Law' and the Inclusion of the Gentiles: Galatians 3.13–14." *NTS* 32 (1986) 94–112. ————. "Zealot and Convert: The Origin of Paul's Christ-Torah Antithesis." *CBQ* 51 (1989) 655–82. **Doty, W. G.** "The Classification of Epistolary Literature." *CBQ* 31 (1969) 185–89. ————. *Letters in Primitive Christianity.* Philadelphia: Fortress, 1973. **Downey, G.** *A History of Antioch in Syria from Seleucus to the Arab Conquest.* Princeton: Princeton University Press, 1961. ————. *Antioch in the Age of Theodosius the Great.* Norman, OK: University of Oklahoma Press, 1961. ————. *Ancient Antioch.* Princeton: Princeton University Press, 1963. **Drane, J. W.** *Paul, Libertine or Legalist? A Study in the Theology of the Major Pauline Epistles.* London: SPCK, 1975. **Dunn, J. D. G.** *Baptism in the Holy Spirit.* SBT 2:15. London: SCM, 1970. ————. *Unity and Diversity in the New Testament: An Inquiry into the Character of Earliest Christianity.* London: SCM; Philadelphia: Westminster, 1977. ————. *Christology in the Making.* London: SCM, 1980. ————. "The Incident at Antioch (Gal 2.11–18)." *JSNT* 18 (1983) 7–11. ————. "The New Perspective on Paul." *BJRL* 65 (1983) 95–122. ————. "Works of the Law and the Curse of the Law (Galatians 3.10–14)." *NTS* 31 (1985) 523–42. **Dupont, J.** "Pierre et Paul à Antioche et à Jérusalem." *RSR* 45 (1957) 42–60, 225–39. ————. "La Revelation du Fils de Dieu en faveur de Pierre (Mt 16, 17) et de Paul (Ga 1, 16)." *RSR* 52 (1964) 411–20. ————. "The Conversion of Paul and Its Influence on His Understanding of Salvation by Faith." In *Apostolic History and the Gospel.* FS F. F. Bruce, ed. W. W. Gasque and R. P. Martin. Exeter: Paternoster, 1970. 176–94. **Easton, B. S.** "New Testament Ethical Lists." *JBL* 51 (1932) 1–12. **Eckert, J.** *Die urchristliche Verkündigung im Streit zwischen Paulus und seinen Gegnern nach dem Galaterbrief.* Münchener Universitäts-Schriften, Katholisch-theologische Fakultät. Regensburg: Pustet, 1971. **Eger, O.** "Rechtswörter und Rechtsbilder in den paulinischen Briefen." *ZNW* 18 (1917) 105–8. **Elliott, J. K.** "The Use of ἕτερος in the New Testament." *ZNW* 60 (1969) 140–41. **Ellis, E. E.** *Paul's Use of the Old Testament.* Edinburgh: Oliver & Boyd; Grand Rapids: Eerdmans, 1957. ————. "Paul and His Opponents: Trends in the Research." In *Christianity, Judaism, and Other Greco-Roman Cults.* FS M. Smith, ed. J. Neusner. 4 vols. Leiden: Brill, 1975. 1:264–98. **Emmet, C. W.** "The Case for the Tradition." In *The Beginnings of Christianity, Part I: The Acts of the Apostles.* 5 vols. Ed. F. J. Foakes Jackson and K. Lake. London: Macmillan, 1922. 2:265–97. **Exler, F.** *The Form of the Ancient Greek Letter: A Study in Greek Epistolography.* Washington, D.C.: Catholic University of America, 1923. **Faw, C. E.** "The Anomaly of Galatians." *BR* 4 (1960) 25–38. **Féret, H. M.** *Pierre et Paul à Antioche et à Jérusalem: Le 'conflict' des deux apostres.* Paris: Cerf, 1955. **Filson, F. V.** *Three Crucial Decades.* London: Epworth, 1963. **Fitzmyer, J. A.** "St. Paul and the Law." *The Jurist* 27 (1967) 18–36. ————. "Some Notes on Aramaic Epistolography." *JBL* 93 (1974) 201–25. **Foerster, W.** "Die δοκοῦντες" in Gal. 2." *ZNW* 36 (1937) 286–92. ————. "Abfassungszeit und Ziel des Galaterbriefes." In *Apophoreta.* FS E. Haenchen, ed. W. Eltester and F. H. Kettler. Berlin: Töpelmann, 1964. 135–41. ————. "κληρονόμος." *TDNT* 3:767–85. **Fridrichsen, A.** *The Apostle and His Message.* Uppsala: Almquist & Wiksells, 1947. **Friedrich, G.** "Lohmeyers These über 'Das paulinische Briefpräskript' kritisch beleuchtet." *ZNW* 46 (1955) 272–74. **Fuller, D. P.** *Gospel and Law: Contrast or Continuum?* Grand Rapids: Eerdmans, 1980. **Fuller, R. H.** *A Critical Introduction to the New Testament.* London: Duckworth, 1966. 23–26. **Funk, R. W.** "The Enigma of the Famine Visit." *JBL* 75 (1956) 130–36. ————. *Language, Hermeneutic, and Word of God: The Problem of Language in the New Testament and Contemporary Theology.* New York: Harper & Row, 1966. 250–74. ————. "The Apostolic Parousia: Form and Significance." In *Christian History and Interpretation.* FS J. Knox, ed. W. R. Farmer, C. F. D. Moule, and R. R. Niebuhr. Cambridge: Cambridge University Press, 1967. 249–68. **Furnish, V. P.** *Theology and Ethics in Paul.* Nashville & New York: Abingdon, 1968. **Gaechter, P.** "Petrus in Antiochia (Gal 2:11–14)." *ZKT* 72 (1950) 177–212. **Gamble, H.** *The Textual History of the Letter to the Romans.* Grand Rapids: Eerdmans, 1977. 57–83. **Gardiner, E. N.** *Greek Athletic Sports and Festivals.* Oxford: Clarendon, 1955. **Gaston, L.** "Paul and the Torah." In *Antisemitism and the Foundations of Christianity,* ed. A. T. Davies. New York: Paulist, 1979. 48–71. ————. *Paul and the Torah.* Vancouver: University of British Columbia Press, 1987. **Geyser, A. S.** "The Earliest Name of the Earliest Church." In *De Fructu Oris Sui.* FS A. van Selms, ed. I. H. Eybers, et al. Leiden: Brill, 1971. 58–66. **Goldin, J.** "Not by Means of an Angel and Not by Means of a Messenger." In *Religions in Antiquity.* FS E. R. Goodenough, ed. J. Neusner. Leiden: Brill, 1968. 412–24. **Goppelt, L.** "τύπος κτλ." *TDNT* 8:246–59. **Gordon, T. D.** "A Note on ΠΑΙΔΑΓΩΓΟΣ in Galatians 3.24–25." *NTS* 35 (1989) 150–54. **Grafe, E.** *Die paulinische Lehre vom Gesetz.* Leipzig: Mohr, 1893. **Grant, R. M.** "Hellenistic Elements in Galatians." *ATR* 34 (1952) 223–26. ————. *The Letter and the Spirit.* London: SPCK, 1957. ————. "Jewish Christianity at Antioch in the Second Century." In *Judeo-Christianisme.* FS J. Daniélou. *RSR* 60 (1972) 97–108. **Gunther, J. J.** *St. Paul's Opponents and Their Background: A Study of Apocalyptic and Jewish Sectarian Teachings.* NovTSup 35. Leiden: Brill, 1973. **Gutbrod, W.** "νόμος." *TDNT* 4:1022–85. **Hall, D. R.** "St. Paul and Famine Relief: A Study in Galatians 2¹⁰." *ExpTim* 82 (1971) 309–11. **Hansen, G. W.** *Abraham in Galatians: Epistolary and Rhetorical Contexts.* JSNTSup 29. Sheffield: Sheffield Academic Press, 1989. **Hanson, A. T.** *Studies in Paul's Technique and Theology.* London: SPCK, 1974. ————. *The Paradox of the Cross in the Thought of St. Paul.* JSNTSup 17. Sheffield: JSOT Press, 1987. **Hanson, R. P. C.** *Allegory and Event: A Study of the Sources and Significance of Origen's Interpretation of Scripture.* London: SCM; Richmond, VA: John Knox, 1959. **Harrison, E. F.** *Introduction to the New Testament.* Grand Rapids: Eerdmans, 1964. 257–64. **Harvey, A. E.** "The Opposition to Paul." In *Studia Evangelica* IV, ed. F. L. Cross. TU 102. Berlin: Akademie, 1968. 319–32. **Haussleiter, J.** *Der Glaube Jesu und der christliche Glaube.* Leipzig: Dörffling & Franke, 1891. ————. "Was versteht Paulus unter christlichen Glauben?" In *Theologische Abhandlungen.* FS H. Cremer. Gütersloh: Bertelsmann, 1895. 159–81. **Hawkins, J. G.** "The Opponents of Paul in Galatia." Ph.D. diss., Yale, 1971. **Hay, D. M.** "Paul's Indifference to Authority." *JBL* 88 (1969) 36–44. ————. "What Is Proof? Historical Verification in Philo, Josephus, and Quintilian." *SBLASP* 17:2 (1979) 87–100. **Hays, R. B.** *The Faith of Jesus Christ: An Investigation of the Narrative Substructure of Galatians 3:1–4:11.* SBLDS 56. Chico, CA: Scholars, 1983. **Hebert, A. G.** "'Faithfulness' and 'Faith.'" *Th* 58 (1955) 373–79. **Hemer, C. J.** "Acts and Galatians Reconsidered." *Themelios* 2 (1977) 81–88. **Hengel, M.** "Christologie und neutestamentliche Chronologie." In *Neues Testament und Geschichte: Historisches Geschehen und Deutung im Neuen Testament.* FS O. Cullmann, ed. H. Baltensweiler and B. Reicke. Zürich: Theologischer Verlag, 1972. 43–67 (ET "Christology and New Testament Chronology," in idem, *Between Jesus and Paul: Studies in the Earliest History of Christianity* [Philadelphia: Fortress, 1983] 30–47). ————. *Judaism and Hellenism: Studies in Their Encounter in Palestine during the Early Hellenistic Period.* 2 vols. Tr. J. Bowden. Philadelphia: Fortress, 1974. ————. *Crucifixion in the Ancient World and the Folly of the Message of the Cross.* Tr. J. Bowden. London: SCM, 1977. ————. *Acts and the History of Earliest Christianity.* Tr. J. Bowden. London: SCM, 1979. **Hester, J. D.** *Paul's Concept of Inheritance: A Contribution to the Understanding of Heilsgeschichte.* Edinburgh and London: Oliver & Boyd, 1968. **Hill, D.** "Salvation Proclaimed: IV. Galatians 3:10–14: Freedom and Acceptance." *ExpTim* 93 (1982)

196–200. **Hirsch, E.** "Zwei Fragen zu Gal 6." *ZNW* 29 (1930) 192–97. **Hoffmann-Aleith, E.** *Das Paulusverständnis in der alten Kirche.* Berlin: Töpelmann, 1937. ————. "Das Paulusverständnis des Johannes Chrysostomus." *ZNW* 38 (1939) 181–88. **Holmberg, B.** *Paul and Power: The Structure of Authority in the Primitive Church as Reflected in the Pauline Epistles.* ConB 11. Lund: Gleerup, 1978. **Hooker, M. D.** "ΠΙΣΤΙΣ ΧΡΙΣΤΟΥ." *NTS* 35 (1989) 321–42. **Hort, F. J. A.** *Judaistic Christianity.* London: Macmillan, 1894. **Howard, G.** "Notes and Observations on the 'Faith of Christ.'" *HTR* 60 (1967) 459–65. ————. "The 'Faith of Christ.'" *ExpTim* 85 (1974) 212–15. ————. "Was James an Apostle? A Reflection on a New Proposal for Gal. i.19." *NovT* 19 (1977) 63–64. ————. *Paul: Crisis in Galatia: A Study in Early Christian Theology.* SNTSMS 35. Cambridge: Cambridge University Press, 1979. **Hübner, H.** *Law in Paul's Thought.* Studies of the New Testament and Its World. Tr. J. C. G. Greig. Edinburgh: T. & T. Clark, 1984. **Hunter, A. M.** *Paul and His Predecessors.* 2nd ed. London: SCM, 1961. **Hurd, J. C.** *The Origin of 1 Corinthians.* New York: Seabury, 1965. ————. "Pauline Chronology and Pauline Theology." In *Christian History and Interpretation.* FS J. Knox, ed. W. R. Farmer, C. F. D. Moule, and R. R. Niebuhr. Cambridge: Cambridge University Press, 1967. 225–48. ————. "The Sequence of Paul's Letters." *CJT* 14 (1968) 189–200. **Hurtado, L. W.** "The Jerusalem Collection and the Book of Galatians." *JSNT* 5 (1979) 46–62. **Jeremias, J.** "Paul and James." *ExpTim* 66 (1955) 368–71. ————. "Chiasmus in den Paulusbriefen." *ZNW* 49 (1958) 145–56. ————. "The Key to Pauline Theology." *ExpTim* 76 (1965) 27–30. ————. *The Central Message of the New Testament.* London: SCM; New York: Scribner's, 1965. ————. *Abba: Studien zur neutestamentlichen Theologie und Zeitgeschichte.* Göttingen: Vandenhoeck & Ruprecht, 1966 (ET of "Adam," in idem, *The Prayers of Jesus.* SBT 2:6. London: SCM, 1967. 11–66). ————. "Paulus als Hillelit." In *Neotestamentica et Semitica.* FS M. Black, ed. E. E. Ellis and M. Wilcox. Edinburgh: T. & T. Clark, 1969. 88–94. **Jewett, R.** "The Form and Function of the Homiletic Benediction." *ATR* 51 (1969) 13–34. ————. "The Agitators and the Galatian Congregation." *NTS* 17 (1971) 198–212. ————. *A Chronology of Paul's Life.* Philadelphia: Fortress, 1979. **Johnson, S. E.** "Asia Minor and Early Christianity." In *Christianity, Judaism, and Other Greco-Roman Cults.* FS M. Smith, ed. J. Neusner. 4 vols. Leiden: Brill, 1975. 2:77–145. **Jones, A. H. M.** *The Cities of the Eastern Roman Provinces.* Oxford: Clarendon, 1937. **Kamlah, E.** *Die Form der katalogischen Paränese im Neuen Testament.* WUNT 7. Tübingen: Mohr-Siebeck, 1964. **Käsemann, E.** *New Testament Questions of Today.* Tr. W. J. Montague. London: SCM, 1969. ————. "The Pauline Theology of the Cross." *Int* 24 (1970) 151–77. **Keck, L.** "The Poor among the Saints in the New Testament." *ZNW* 56 (1965) 100–29. ————. "The Poor among the Saints in Jewish Christianity and Qumran." *ZNW* 57 (1966) 54–78. **Kennedy, G. A.** *The Art of Persuasion in Greece.* Princeton: Princeton University Press, 1963. ————. *The Art of Rhetoric in the Roman World: 300 B.C.—A.D. 300.* Princeton: Princeton University Press, 1972. ————. *New Testament Interpretation through Rhetorical Criticism.* Chapel Hill, NC: University of North Carolina Press, 1984. **Kennedy, H. A. A.** *The Theology of the Epistles.* London: Duckworth, 1919. **Kepple, R. J.** "An Analysis of Antiochene Exegesis of Galatians 4:24–26." *WTJ* 39 (1977) 239–49. **Kessler, M.** "A Methodological Setting for Rhetorical Criticism." *Semitics* 4 (1974) 22–36. ————. "An Introduction to Rhetorical Criticism of the Bible: Prolegomena." *Semitics* 7 (1980) 1–27. **Kilpatrick, G. D.** "Gal 2, 14 ὀρθοποδοῦσιν." In *Neutestamentliche Studien.* FS R. Bultmann. BZNW 21. Berlin: Töpelmann, 1957. 269–74. ————. "Galatians 1:18 ΙΣΤΟΡΗΣΑΙ ΚΗΦΑΝ." In *New Testament Essays.* FS T. W. Manson, ed. A. J. B. Higgins. Manchester: University of Manchester Press, 1959. 144–49. **Kim, C. H.** *The Form and Structure of the Familiar Greek Letter of Recommendation.* SBLDS 4. Missoula, MT: Scholars, 1972. ————. "The Papyrus Invitation." *JBL* 94 (1975) 391–402. **Kim, S.** *The Origin of Paul's Gospel.* WUNT 2:4. Tübingen: Mohr-Siebeck; Grand Rapids: Eerdmans, 1984. **Kittel, G.** "πίστις Ἰησοῦ Χριστοῦ bei Paulus." *TSK* 79 (1906) 419–36. ————. "ἀββᾶ." *TDNT* 1:5–6. ————. "ἀκοτύω." *TDNT* 1:216–21. **Klausner, J.** *From Jesus to Paul.* Tr. W. F. Stinespring. New York: Macmillan, 1943. **Knox, J.** *Chapters in a Life of Paul.* Nashville: Abingdon, 1950. **Knox, W. L.** *St. Paul and the Church of Jerusalem.* Cambridge: Cambridge University Press, 1925. **Koester, H.** "GNOMAI

DI APHOROI: The Origin and Nature of Diversification in the History of Early Christianity." *HTR* 58 (1965) 279–318. **Koskenniemi, H.** *Studien zur Idee und Phraseologie des griechischen Briefes bis 400 n. Chr.* Helsinki: Suomalaien Tiedeakatemie, 1956. **Kraeling, C. H.** "The Jewish Community at Antioch." *JBL* 51 (1932) 130–60. **Kramer, W.** *Christ, Lord, Son of God.* Tr. B. Hardy. SBT 50. London: SCM, 1966. **Kreller, H.** *Erbrechtliche Untersuchungen auf Grund der gräco-ägyptischen Papyruskunden.* Aalen: Scientia, 1919, 1970. **Kümmel, W.** *Introduction to the New Testament.* Tr. A. J. Mattill, Jr. London: SCM, 1965. ———. "'Individualgeschichte' und 'Weltgeschichte' in Galater 2, 15–21." In *Christ and Spirit in the New Testament.* FS C. F. D. Moule, ed. B. Lindars and S. S. Smalley. Cambridge: Cambridge University Press, 1973. 157–73. **Ladd, G. E.** "Paul and the Law." In *Soli Deo Gloria.* FS W. C. Robinson. Grand Rapids: Eerdmans, 1968. 50–67. **Lake, K.** *The Earlier Epistles of St. Paul: Their Motive and Origin.* London: Rivingtons, 1911. ———. "The Apostolic Council of Jerusalem." In *The Beginnings of Christianity, Part I: The Acts of the Apostles.* 5 vols. Ed. F. J. Foakes Jackson and K. Lake. London: Macmillan, 1922. 5:195–212. **Lambrecht, J.** "The Line of Thought in Gal. 2.14b–21." *NTS* 24 (1978) 484–95. **Lampe, G. W. H.** "The Reasonableness of Typology." In *Essays in Typology,* ed. G. W. H. Lampe and K. J. Woollcombe. London: SCM, 1957. 9–38. **Lauterbach, J. Z.** "Ancient Jewish Allegorists." *JQR* 1 (1911) 291–333, 503–31. **Lawson, J.** *The Biblical Theology of Saint Irenaeus.* London: Epworth, 1948. **Lieberman, S.** *Hellenism in Jewish Palestine: Studies in the Literary Transmission, Beliefs, and Manners of Palestine in the I Century BCE —IV Century CE.* New York: Jewish Theological Seminary of America, 1962. **Liebeschuetz, J. H. W. G.** *Antioch: City and Imperial Administration in the Later Roman Empire.* Oxford: Clarendon, 1972. **Lietzmann, H.** *A History of the Early Church.* Tr. B. Woolf. New York: Meridian Books, 1961. **Ljungman, H.** *Das Gesetz erfüllen: Matth. 5, 17ff. und 3, 15 untersucht.* LUÅ 50:6. Lund: Gleerup, 1954. ———. *Pistis: A Study of Its Presuppositions and Its Meaning in Pauline Use.* Lund: Gleerup, 1964. **Lohmeyer, E.** "Probleme paulinischer Theologie: I. Briefliche Grussüberschriften." *ZNW* 26 (1927) 158–73. **Lohse, E.** "Ursprung und Prägung des christlichen Apostolats." *TZ* 9 (1953) 259–75. **Longenecker, R. N.** *Paul, Apostle of Liberty.* New York: Harper & Row, 1964; Grand Rapids: Baker, 1976. ———. *The Christology of Early Jewish Christianity.* SBT 2:17. London: SCM, 1970; Grand Rapids: Baker, 1981. ———. "Ancient Amanuenses and the Pauline Epistles." In *New Dimensions in New Testament Study,* ed. R. N. Longenecker and M. C. Tenney. Grand Rapids: Zondervan, 1974. 281–97. ———. *Biblical Exegesis in the Apostolic Period.* Grand Rapids: Eerdmans, 1975. 19–50, 104–32. ———. "The 'Faith of Abraham' Theme in Paul, James, and Hebrews: A Study in the Circumstantial Nature of New Testament Teaching." *JETS* 20 (1977) 203–12. ———. "The Acts of the Apostles." In *The Expositor's Bible Commentary.* Vol. 9, ed. F. E. Gaebelein. Grand Rapids: Zondervan, 1981. 207–573. ———. "The Pedagogical Nature of the Law in Galatians 3:19–4:7." *JETS* 25 (1982) 53–61. ———. "On the Form, Function, and Authority of the New Testament Letters." In *Scripture and Truth,* ed. D. A. Carson and J. D. Woodbridge. Grand Rapids: Zondervan, 1983. 101–14. ———. *New Testament Social Ethics for Today.* Grand Rapids: Eerdmans, 1984. ———. "The Nature of Paul's Early Eschatology." *NTS* 31 (1985) 85–95. ———. "Antioch of Syria." In *Major Cities of the Biblical World,* ed. R. K. Harrison. Nashville: Nelson, 1985. 8–21. **Luedemann, G.** *Paul, Apostle to the Gentiles: Studies in Chronology.* Tr. F. S. Jones. Philadelphia: Fortress, 1984. **Lührmann, D.** "Gal 2:9 und die katholischen Briefe: Bemerkungen zum Kanon und zur *regula fidei.*" *ZNW* 72 (1981) 65–87. **Lull, D. J.** *The Spirit in Galatia: Paul's Interpretation of PNEUMA as Divine Power.* SBLDS 49. Chico, CA: Scholars, 1980. ———. "'The Law Was Our Pedagogue': A Study in Galatians 3:19–25." *JBL* 105 (1986) 481–98. **Lütgert, W.** *Gesetz und Geist: Eine Untersuchung zur Vorgeschichte des Galaterbriefes.* Gütersloh: Bertelsmann, 1919. **Luther, M.** "The Freedom of a Christian," *Luther's Works. American ed.* Vol. 31, tr. W. A. Lambert, rev. H. J. Grimm. Philadelphia: Muhlenburg, 1957, 327–77. **Lyall, F.** "Roman Law in the Writings of Paul—Adoption." *JBL* 88 (1969) 458–66. **Macgregor, W. M.** *Christian Freedom.* London: Hodder & Stoughton, 1914. **Magie, D.** *Roman Rule in Asia Minor.* Princeton: Princeton University Press, 1950. **Malherbe, A. J.** *Social Aspects of Early*

Christianity. 2nd ed. Philadelphia: Fortress, 1983. ————. *Moral Exhortation: A Greco-Roman Sourcebook.* Library of Early Christianity 4. Philadelphia: Westminster, 1986. ————. *Ancient Epistolary Theorists.* SBLSBS 19. Atlanta: Scholars, 1988. **Martyn, J. L.** "A Law-Observant Mission to Gentiles: The Background of Galatians." *MQR* 22 (1983) 221–36. **Maurer, C.** "μετατίθημι." *TDNT* 8:161–62. **McCullough, W. S.** *A Short History of Syriac Christianity.* Toronto: University of Toronto Press, 1982. **McNamara, M.** "'to de (Hagar) Sina oros estin en te Arabia'* (Gal. 4:25a): Paul and Petra." *MS* 2 (1978) 24–41. **Meecham, H. G.** *Light from Ancient Letters: Private Correspondence in the Non-Literary Papyri of Oxyrhynchus of the First Four Centuries and Its Bearing on New Testament Language and Thought.* London: Allen & Unwin, 1923. **Meeks, W. A.,** and **Wilken, R. L.** *Jews and Christians in Antioch in the First Four Centuries of the Common Era.* SBLSBS 13. Missoula, MT: Scholars, 1978. **Menoud, P. H.** "Revelation and Tradition: The Influence of Paul's Conversion on His Theology." *Int* 7 (1953) 131–41. **Merk, O.** "Der Beginn der Paränese im Galaterbrief." *ZNW* 60 (1969) 83–104. **Metzger, B. M.** "Antioch-on-the-Orontes." *BA* 11 (1948) 69–88. **Michaelis, W.** "Judaistische Heidenchristen." *ZNW* 30 (1931) 83–89. **Michel, O.** *Paulus und seine Bibel.* Gütersloh: Bertelsmann, 1929. ————. "οἰκοδομέω." *TDNT* 5:136–44. ————. "οἰκονόμος." *TDNT* 5:149–51. **Milligan, G.** *The New Testament Documents: Their Origin and Early History.* London: Macmillan, 1913. **Milne, H. J. M.** *Greek Shorthand Manuals: Syllabary and Commentary.* London: Oxford University Press, 1934. **Moffatt, J.** *An Introduction to the Literature of the New Testament.* 3rd ed. Edinburgh: T. & T. Clark, 1918. 83–107. **Molland, E.** *The Conception of the Gospel in Alexandrian Theology.* Oslo: Dybwad, 1938. **Momigliano, A.** *The Development of Greek Biography.* Cambridge, MA: Harvard University Press, 1971. **Moreau, J.** *Die Welt der Kelten.* Stuttgart: Cotta, 1958. **Moule, C. F. D.** *An Idiom-Book of New Testament Greek.* 2nd ed. Cambridge: Cambridge University Press, 1959. ————. *Worship in the New Testament.* Ecumenical Studies in Worship 9. London: Lutterworth, 1961. ————. "Obligation in the Ethic of Paul." In *Christian History and Interpretation.* FS J. Knox, ed. W. R. Farmer, C. F. D. Moule, and R. R. Niebuhr. Cambridge: Cambridge University Press, 1967. 389–406. ————. "Fulfilment-Words in the New Testament: Use and Abuse." *NTS* 14 (1968) 293–320. **Mulka, A. L.** "Fides quae per caritatem operatur." *CBQ* 28 (1966) 174–88. **Mullins, T. Y.** "Petition as a Literary Form." *NovT* 5 (1962) 46–54. ————. "Disclosure as a Literary Form in the New Testament." *NovT* 7 (1964) 44–50. ————. "Greeting as a New Testament Form." *JBL* 87 (1968) 418–26. ————. "Formulas in New Testament Epistles." *JBL* 91 (1972) 380–90. ————. "Visit Talk in the New Testament Letters." *CBQ* 35 (1973) 350–58. ————. "Benediction as a New Testament Form." *AUSS* 15 (1977) 59–64. **Munck, J.** "Paul, the Apostles, and the Twelve." *ST* 3 (1951) 96–110. ————. *Paul and the Salvation of Mankind.* Tr. F. Clarke. Richmond, VA: John Knox, 1959. ————. "Jewish Christianity in Post-Apostolic Times." *NTS* 6 (1960) 103–16. **Mussner, F.** "Hagar, Sinai, Jerusalem." *TQ* 135 (1955) 56–60. ————. *Theologie der Freiheit nach Paulus.* Freiburg: Herder, 1976. **Nauck, W.** "Das οὖν-paräneticum." *ZNW* 49 (1958) 134–35. **Nijenhuis, J.** "The Greeting in My Own Hand." *BT* 19 (1981) 225–58. **O'Brien, P. T.** *Introductory Thanksgivings in the Letters of Paul.* NovTSup 49. Leiden: Brill, 1977. **Oepke, A.** "βάπτω, βαπτίζω." *TDNT* 1:529–45. ————. "ἐν." *TDNT* 2:537–43. ————. "ἐνδύω." *TDNT* 2:319–20. **O'Neill, J. C.** *The Recovery of Paul's Letter to the Galatians.* London: SPCK, 1972. **Orchard, B.** "The Ellipsis between Galatians 2, 3 and 2, 4." *Bib* 54 (1973) 469–81. **Pack, R. A.** *The Greek and Latin Literary Texts from Greco-Roman Egypt.* 2nd ed. Ann Arbor: University of Michigan Press, 1965. **Pagels, E. H.** *The Gnostic Paul: Gnostic Exegesis of the Pauline Letters.* Philadelphia: Fortress, 1975. **Parker, T. H. L.,** tr. *Calvin's New Testament Commentaries,* Vol. 11. London: SCM; Grand Rapids: Eerdmans, 1971. **Peake, A. S.** *Paul and the Jewish Christians.* Manchester: Manchester University Press, 1929. **Pfitzner, V. C.** *Paul and the Agon Motif: Traditional Athletic Imagery in the Pauline Literature.* NovTSup 16. Leiden: Brill, 1967. **Pieper, K.** "Antiochien am Orontes in apostolischen Zeitalter." *TGl* 22 (1930) 710–28. **Räisänen, H.** *Paul and the Law.* WUNT 29. Tübingen: Mohr-Siebeck, 1983. ————. "Galatians 2.16 and Paul's Break with Judaism." *NTS* 31 (1985) 543–53. **Ramsay, W. M.** *The Church in the Roman Empire before A.D. 170.*

London: Hodder & Stoughton, 1893. ————. *The Cities and Bishoprics of Phrygia.* Oxford: Clarendon, 1895. ————. *St. Paul the Traveller and the Roman Citizen.* 14th ed. London: Hodder & Stoughton, 1920. ————. *The Teaching of Paul in Terms of the Present Day.* London: Hodder & Stoughton, 1913. 372–92. **Reicke, B.** "The Law and This World According to Paul: Some Thoughts Concerning Gal 4:1–11." *JBL* 70 (1951) 259–76. ————. "Der geschichtliche Hintergrund des Apostelkonzils und der Antiochia-Episode." In *Studia Paulina.* FS J. de Zwaan, ed. J. N. Sevenster and W. C. van Unnik. Haarlem: Bohn, 1953. 172–87. **Rengstorf, K. H.** "ἀπόστολος." *TDNT* 1:407–45. ————. "ζυγός." *TDNT* 2:896–901. **Reumann, J.** "'Stewards of God': Pre-Christian Religious Application of οἰκονόμος in Greek." *JBL* 77 (1958) 339–49. **Richardson, P.** *Israel in the Apostolic Church.* SNTSMS 10. Cambridge: Cambridge University Press, 1969. 74–102. ————. *Paul's Ethic of Freedom.* Philadelphia: Westminster, 1979. ————. "Pauline Inconsistency: 1 Cor 9:19–23 and Gal 2:11–14." *NTS* 26 (1980) 347–61. **Roberts, C. H.** "A Note on Galatians 2:14." *JTS* 40 (1939) 55–56. ————. *Greek Literary Hands, 350 B.C.–A.D. 400.* Oxford: Clarendon, 1956. **Robinson, D. W. B.** "The Circumcision of Titus, and Paul's 'Liberty.'" *ABR* 12 (1964) 24–42. ————. "Distinction between Jewish and Gentile Believers in Galatians." *ABR* 13 (1965) 29–44. ————. "'Faith of Jesus Christ'—A New Testament Debate." *RTR* 29 (1970) 71–81. **Robinson, J. A. T.** *Redating the New Testament.* London: SCM, 1976. 55–57. **Roller, O.** *Das Formular der paulinischen Briefe: Ein Beitrag zur Lehre vom antiken Briefe.* Stuttgart: Kohlhammer, 1933. **Ropes, J. H.** *The Singular Problem of the Epistle to the Galatians.* Cambridge, MA: Harvard University Press, 1929. **Rossell, W. H.** "New Testament Adoption—Graeco-Roman or Semitic?" *JBL* 71 (1952) 233–34. **Round, D.** *The Date of St. Paul's Epistle to the Galatians.* Cambridge: Cambridge University Press, 1906. **Sampley, J. P.** "'Before God, I Do Not Lie' (Gal. I.20): Paul's Self-Defence in the Light of Roman Legal Praxis." *NTS* 23 (1977) 477–82. **Sanday, W.** "The Early Visits of St. Paul to Jerusalem." *The Expositor,* 5th series, 3 (1896) 253–63. **Sanders, E. P.** *Paul and Palestinian Judaism: A Comparison of Patterns of Religion.* Philadelphia: Fortress, 1977. ————. "On the Question of Fulfilling the Law in Paul and Rabbinic Judaism." In *Donum Gentilicum.* FS D. Daube, ed. E. Bammel, C. K. Barrett, and W. D. Davies. Oxford: Clarendon, 1978. 103–26. ————. *Paul, the Law, and the Jewish People.* Philadelphia: Fortress, 1983. **Sanders, J. T.** "The Transition from Opening Epistolary Thanksgiving to Body in the Letters of the Pauline Corpus." *JBL* 81 (1962) 348–62. **Schelkle, K. H.** *Paulus Lehrer der Väter.* Düsseldorf: Patmos, 1956. **Schmithals, W.** "Die Heretiker in Galatien." *ZNW* 47 (1956) 25–67 (rev. ET "The Heretics in Galatia," in *Paul and the Gnostics,* 13–64). ————. *Paul and James.* Tr. D. M. Barton. SBT 46. London: SCM, 1965. ————. *The Office of Apostle in the Early Church.* Tr. J. E. Steely. Nashville: Abingdon, 1969. ————. *Paul and the Gnostics.* Tr. J. E. Steely. Nashville: Abingdon, 1972. **Schnider, F.,** and **Stenger, W.** *Studien zum neutestamentlichen Brieffformular.* NTTS 11. Leiden: Brill, 1987. **Schoenberg, M. W.** "HUIOTHESIA: The Word and the Institution." *Scripture* 15 (1963) 115–23. **Schoeps, H. J.** *Paul: The Theology of the Apostle in the Light of Jewish Religious History.* Tr. H. Knight. Philadelphia: Westminster, 1961. **Schrage, W.** *Die konkreten Einzelgebote in der paulinischen Paränese.* Gütersloh: Mohn, 1961. ————. *Ethik des Neuen Testaments.* Göttingen: Vandenhoeck & Ruprecht, 1982 (ET *The Ethics of the New Testament.* Tr. D. E. Green. Philadelphia: Fortress, 1988). **Schrenk, G.** "Was bedeutet 'Israel Gottes'?" *Judaica* 5 (1949) 81–94. ————. "Der Segenwunsch nach der Kampfepistel." *Judaica* 6 (1950) 170–90. **Schubert, P.** "Form and Function of the Pauline Letters." *JR* 19 (1939) 365–77. ————. *Form and Function of the Pauline Thanksgivings.* BZNW 20. Berlin: Töpelmann, 1939. **Schürmann, H.** "'Das Gesetz des Christus' (Gal 6, 2): Jesu Verhalten und Wort als letztgültige sittliche Norm nach Paulus." In *Neues Testament und Kirche.* FS R. Schnackenburg, ed. J. Gnilka. Freiburg: Herder, 1974. 282–300. **Schütz, J. H.** *Paul and the Anatomy of Apostolic Authority.* SNTSMS 26. Cambridge: Cambridge University Press, 1975. **Schweizer, E.** "Zum religionsgeschichtlichen Hintergrund der 'Sendungsformel' Gal 4,4f., Rm 8,3f., Joh 3,16f., 1 Joh 4,9." *ZNW* 57 (1966) 199–210. ————. "πνεῦμα, πνευματικός." *TDNT* 6:332–451. ————. "υἱός κτλ." *TDNT* 8:334–92. ————. "υἱοθεσία." *TDNT* 8:399. ————. "Paul's Christology and Gnosticism." In *Paul and Paulinism.* FS C. K. Barrett, ed. M. D. Hooker and S. G. Wilson. London: SPCK, 1982, 115–23. ————. "Slaves of the Elements and Worshipers of Angels: Gal 4:3, 9 and Col 2:8, 18, 20." *JBL* 107 (1988) 455–68. **Scott, C. A. A.** *Christianity According to St. Paul.* Cambridge: Cambridge University Press, 1961. **Seeseman, H.** "Das Paulusverständnis des Clemens Alexandrinus." *TSK* 107 (1936) 312–46. **Selby, D. J.** *Toward the Understanding of St. Paul.* Englewood Cliffs, NJ: Prentice-Hall, 1962. **Sherk, R. K.** *Roman Documents from the Greek East: Senatus Consulta and Epistulae to the Age of Augustus.* Baltimore: Johns Hopkins, 1969. **Snodgrass, K.** "Spheres of Influence: A Possible Solution to the Problem of Paul and the Law." *JSNT* 32 (1988) 93–113. **Souter, A.** *A Study of Ambrosiaster.* Cambridge: Cambridge University Press, 1905. ————. *The Character and History of Pelagius' Commentary on the Epistles of St. Paul.* London: Oxford University Press, 1916. ————. *The Earliest Latin Commentaries on the Epistles of St. Paul.* Oxford: Clarendon, 1927. **Stähelin, F.** *Geschichte der kleinasiatischen Galater.* 2nd ed. 2 vols. Leipzig: Teubner, 1907. **Stählin, G.** "προκοπή, προκόπτω." *TDNT* 6:703–19. **Stein, R. H.** "The Relationship of Galatians 2:1–10 and Acts 15:1–35: Two Neglected Arguments." *JETS* 17 (1974) 239–42. **Stendahl, K.** *Paul among Jews and Gentiles, and Other Essays.* Philadelphia: Fortress, 1976. **Stowers, S. K.** *Letter Writing in Greco-Roman Antiquity.* Library of Early Christianity 5. Philadelphia: Westminster, 1986. **Stuhlmacher, P.** "Zur paulinischen Christologie." *ZTK* 74 (1977) 449–63 (ET "On Pauline Christology," in idem, *Reconciliation, Law, and Righteousness* [Philadelphia: Fortress, 1986] 169–81). **Suggs, M. J.** "The Christian Two Way Tradition: Its Antiquity, Form, and Function." In *Studies in the New Testament and Early Christian Literature.* FS A. P. Wikgren, ed. D. E. Aune. NovTSup 33. Leiden: Brill, 1972, 60–74. **Sykutris, J.** "Epistolographie." In *PW,* Supplement 5, 218–19. **Talbert, C. H.** "Again: Paul's Visits to Jerusalem." *NovT* 9 (1967) 26–40. **Taubenschlag, R.** *The Law of Greco-Roman Egypt in the Light of the Papyri, 332 B.C.—640 A.D.* 2nd ed. Warsaw: Pánstwowe Wydawnictwo Naukowe, 1955, 109–207. **Taylor, G. M.** "The Function of ΠΙΣΤΙΣ ΧΡΙΣΤΟΥ in Galatians." *JBL* 85 (1966) 58–76. **Thomas, J.** "Formgesetze des Begriffskatalogs im Neuen Testament." *TZ* 24 (1968) 15–28. **Torrance, T. F.** "One Aspect of the Biblical Conception of Faith," *ExpTim* 68 (1957) 111–14. **Trudinger, L. P.** "ΕΤΕΡΟΝ ΔΕ ΤΩΝ ΑΠΟΣΤΟΛΩΝ ΟΥΚ ΕΙΔΟΝ ΕΙ ΜΗ ΙΑΚΩΒΟΝ: A Note on Galatians i.19." *NovT* 17 (1975) 200–202. **Turner, C. H.** "Greek Patristic Commentaries on the Pauline Epistles." In *Hastings Dictionary of the Bible,* rev. F. C. Grant and H. H. Rowley. New York: Scribner, 1963, 484–531. **Turner, E. G.** *Greek Manuscripts of the Ancient World.* Princeton: Princeton University Press, 1971. **Tyson, J. B.** "Paul's Opponents in Galatia." *NovT* 10 (1968) 241–54. ————. "'Works of Law' in Galatians." *JBL* 92 (1973) 423–31. **Vielhauer, P.** "Gesetzesdienst und Stoicheiadienst im Galaterbrief." In *Rechtfertigung.* FS E. Käsemann, ed. J. Friedrich, W. Pohlmann, and P. Stuhlmacher. Tübingen: Mohr-Siebeck, 1976. 543–55. **Vögtle, A.** *Die Tugend- und Lasterkataloge im Neuen Testament.* NTAbh 16. Münster: Aschendorff, 1936. **Wallace-Hadrill, D. S.** *Christian Antioch: A Study of Early Christian Thought in the East.* Cambridge: Cambridge University Press, 1982. **Walton, F. R.** "The Messenger of God in Hecataeus of Abdera." *HTR* 48 (1955) 255–57. **Weder, H.** *Das Kreuz Jesu bei Paulus: Ein Versuch über den Geschichtsbezug des christlichen Glaubens nachzudenken.* FRLANT 125. Göttingen: Vandenhoeck & Ruprecht, 1981. **Wendland, P.** *Die urchristlichen Literaturformen.* HNT 1:3. Tübingen: Mohr, 1912. 339–45. **Werner, J.** *Der Paulinismus des Irenaeus.* Leipzig: Hinrichs, 1889. **Westerholm, S.** "Letter and Spirit: The Foundation of Pauline Ethics." *NTS* 30 (1984) 229–48. ————. "On Fulfilling the Whole Law (Gal. 5:14)." *SEÅ* 51–52 (1986–87) 229–37. ————. *Israel's Law and the Church's Faith: Paul and His Recent Interpreters.* Grand Rapids: Eerdmans, 1988. **White, J. L.** "Introductory Formulae in the Body of the Pauline Letter." *JBL* 90 (1971) 91–97. ————. *The Form and Function of the Body of the Greek Letter: A Study of the Letter-Body in the Non-Literary Papyri and in Paul the Apostle.* SBLDS 5. Missoula, MT: Scholars, 1972. ————. *The Form and Structure of the Official Petition: A Study in Greek Epistolography.* SBLDS 5. Missoula, MT: Scholars, 1972. ————. "Epistolary Formulas and Cliches in the Greek Papyrus Letters." *SBLASP* 14 (1978) 289–319. ————. "The Greek Documentary Letter Tradition: Third Century B.C.E. to Third Century C.E." *Semeia* 22 (1981)

89–106. ————. *Light from Ancient Letters.* Philadelphia: Fortress, 1986. ————. "Ancient Greek Letters." In *Greco-Roman Literature and the New Testament,* ed. D. E. Aune. SBLSBS 21. Atlanta: Scholars, 1988. 85–106. **White, J. L.,** and **Kensinger, K.** "Categories of Greek Papyrus Letters." *SBLASP* 10 (1976) 79–91. **Wibbing, S.** *Die Tugend- und Lasterkataloge im Neuen Testament und ihre Traditionsgeschichte unter besonderer Berücksichtigung der Qumran Texte.* Berlin: Töpelmann, 1959. **Wickert, U.** *Studien zu den Pauluskommentaren Theodors von Mopsuestia.* Berlin: Töpelmann, 1962. **Wikenhauser, A.** *Pauline Mysticism: Christ in the Mystical Teaching of St. Paul.* Tr. J. Cunningham. New York: Herder & Herder, 1960. **Wilckens, U.** "στῦλος." *TDNT* 7:732–36. **Wilcox, M.** "'Upon the Tree'—Deut 21:22–23 in the New Testament." *JBL* 96 (1977) 85–99. ————. "The Promise of the 'Seed' in the New Testament and the Targumim." *JSNT* 5 (1979) 2–20. **Wiles, M. F.** *The Divine Apostle: The Interpretation of St. Paul's Epistles in the Early Church.* Cambridge: Cambridge University Press, 1967. **Williams, S. K.** "The Hearing of Faith: ΑΚΟΗ ΠΙΣΤΕΩΣ in Galatians 3." *NTS* 35 (1989) 82–93. **Wilson, R. McL.** "Gnostics in Galatia?" In *Studia Evangelica IV,* ed. F. L. Cross. TU 102. Berlin: Akademie, 1968. 358–67. **Winnett, F. V.,** and **Reed, W. L.** *Ancient Records from North Arabia.* Toronto: University of Toronto Press, 1970. **Winter, J. G.** "Another Instance of ὀρθοποδεῖν." *HTR* 34 (1941) 161–62. **Woollcombe, K. J.** "Biblical Origins and Patristic Development of Typology." In *Essays in Typology,* ed. G. W. H. Lampe and K. J. Woollcombe. London: SCM, 1957. 39–75. **Yaron, R.** *Gifts in Contemplation of Death in Jewish and Roman Law.* Oxford: Clarendon, 1960. **Young, N. H.** "*Paidagōgos:* The Social Setting of a Pauline Metaphor." *NovT* 29 (1987) 150–76. **Ziemann, F.** *De Epistularum Graecarum Formulis.* Berlin: Hass, 1912. 362–65. **Ziesler, J. A.** *The Meaning of Righteousness in Paul: A Linguistic and Theological Inquiry.* SNTSMS 20. Cambridge: Cambridge University Press, 1972.

Introduction

All of our NT manuscripts arrange the Pauline letters roughly according to length, from the longest to the shortest: Romans, 1 and 2 Corinthians, Galatians, Ephesians, Philippians, Colossians, 1 and 2 Thessalonians, 1 and 2 Timothy, Titus, and Philemon. Where Hebrews was thought to be by Paul, it was included either after his letters to various churches and before those to individuals (i. e., after 2 Thessalonians and before 1 Timothy, as in Codex A; cf. Athanasius' *Festal Letter* 39 of A.D. 367) or after Romans and before 1 Corinthians, evidently because of its length (as in P[46]). The sixty-three tractates of the Jewish Mishnah are arranged in their six divisions (*Sĕdārîm*) according to descending order of size, and this seems to have been the original criterion for the arrangement of Paul's letters as well.

The Muratorian Canon, however, gives two different arrangements for the Pauline letters. The first lists only the major missionary letters: "first of all to the Corinthians . . . then to the Galatians . . . and then to the Romans." The second, which follows immediately on the heels of the first, reads: "The blessed apostle Paul himself, following the rule of his predecessor John [*sic*], writes by name only to seven churches in the following order: to the Corinthians the first, to the Ephesians the second, to the Philippians the third, to the Colossians the fourth, to the Galatians the fifth, to the Thessalonians the sixth, to the Romans the seventh." The Muratorian Canon then goes on to say that "he wrote to the Corinthians and to the Thessalonians once more for their reproof" and "to Philemon one, and to Titus one, and to Timothy two, out of goodwill and love." But these two listings seem to be primarily thematic in nature, and so cannot set aside the normal order of the MSS. Furthermore, the Muratorian Canon may date later than A.D. 200, as usually supposed. Likewise, the catalogue of OT and NT writings inserted between Philemon and Hebrews in Codex D (Codex Claromontanus)—where the Pauline letters are listed as Romans, 1 and 2 Corinthians, Galatians, Ephesians, 1 and 2 Timothy, Titus, Colossians, and Philemon, with Philippians and 1 and 2 Thessalonians missing—does not over-rule the order of the letters in the Codex itself. At least it does not bring into question the traditional order of the four major missionary letters of Paul. (On Marcion's arrangement, see below.)

Yet whatever its place in the lists of antiquity, the letter to the Galatians takes programmatic primacy for (1) an understanding of Paul's teaching, (2) the establishing of a Pauline chronology, (3) the tracing out of the course of early apostolic history, and (4) the determination of many NT critical and canonical issues. It may even have been the first written of Paul's extant letters. Possibly as well, excluding the confessional portions incorporated throughout the NT, it antedates everything else written in the NT. It is necessary, therefore, to understand Galatians aright if we are to understand Paul and the rest of the NT aright.

THE IMPACT OF GALATIANS ON CHRISTIAN THOUGHT AND ACTION

Bibliography

Patristic Materials

Tertullian. *Adversus Marcionem.* Ed., tr., and intro. E. Evans. Oxford: Clarendon, 1972 (*PL* 2:239–524). ————. *Adversus Valentinianos* (*PL* 2:523–96). *Evangelium Thomae.* Ed. and tr. A. Guillaumont, H. C. Puech, G. Quispel, W. Till, Y.' Abd al Masih. Leiden: Brill, 1959. *Evangelium Veritatis.* Ed. and tr. M. Malinine, H. C. Puech, G. Quispel, W. Till. Zürich: Rascher, 1961. **The Nag Hammadi Library.** *The Nag Hammadi Library in English.* Ed. J. M. Robinson. Leiden: Brill; San Francisco: Harper & Row, 1977. **Irenaeus.** *Adversus Haereses.* Ed. W. W. Harvey. Cambridge: Cambridge University Press, 1857 (*PG* 7:1263–1322). **Hippolytus.** *Refutationis Omnium Haeresium.* In *Opera* 3, ed. P. Wendland. Leipzig: Hinrichs, 1916. **Clement of Alexandria.** *Stromata* I–VI. In GCS, Vol. 2, ed. O. Stählin. 1905–36. Berlin: Akademie, 1960. ————. In LCL, tr. G. W. Butterworth. London: Heinemann, 1919. **Origen.** *Commentariorum in Epistulam S. Pauli ad Romanos* (*PG* 14:833–1292). ————. *Ex Libris Origenis in Epistulam Galatas* (*PG* 14:1293–98). ————. *Le commentaire d' Origene sur Rom III.5–V. 7* (Greek text). Ed. J. Scherer. Cairo: Institut français d'archaologie orientale, 1957. ————. *Contra Celsum.* Tr., intro., and notes H. Chadwick. Cambridge: Cambridge University Press, 1953. ————. *On First Principles.* Tr., intro., and notes G. W. Butterworth. New York: Harper & Row, 1966. ————. "Fragments on Romans." Ed. H. Rambsbotham, *JTS* 13 (1912) 210–24, 357–68, and 14 (1913) 10–22. ————. *The Writings of Origen.* Tr. F. Crombie, *Ante-Nicene Christian Library,* 10, 23. Edinburgh: T. & T. Clark, 1869. ————. *Selections from the Commentaries and Homilies of Origen.* Tr. R. B. Tollinton. London: SPCK, 1929. **Chrysostom, John.** *Commentary on the Epistle to the Galatians and Homilies on the Epistle to the Ephesians.* Oxford: Parker, 1840 (*PG* 61:611–82). ————. *Chrysostom and His Message: A Selection from the Sermons of St. John Chrysostom of Antioch and Constantinople.* Ed. S. Neill. London: Lutterworth, 1962. ————. *The Homilies of S. John Chrysostom on the First Epistle of S. Paul the Apostle to the Corinthians.* Part II. Oxford: Parker, 1839. **Theodore of Mopsuestia.** *Commentaries on the Minor Epistles of St Paul.* 2 vols., ed. H. B. Swete. Cambridge: Cambridge University Press, 1880–82 (*PG* 66:911–22). **Theodoret of Cyrrhus.** *Commentarii in omnes Pauli Epistulas.* Oxford: Parker, 1852 (*PG* 82:505–58). **Greek Commentaries.** *Pauluskommentare aus der griechischen Kirche aus Katenenhandschriften gesammelt und herausgegeben.* Ed. K. Staab. Münster: Aschendorffe, 1933. **Victorinus.** *Marii Victorini Afri commentarii in epistulas Pauli.* Ed. A. Locher. Leipzig: Teubner, 1972. **Ambrosiaster.** *Commentarium in Epistulam Beati Pauli ad Galatas* (*PL* 17:357–94). **Jerome.** *Commentarium in Epistulam ad Galatas* (*PL* 26:307–438). **Augustine.** *Commentarium in Epistulam ad Galatas* (*PL* 35:2105–48). **Pelagius.** *Expositions of the Thirteen Epistles of St. Paul.* Ed. A. Souter. Cambridge: Cambridge University Press, 1922.

Reformation Writings

Erasmus, D. *Collected Works of Erasmus,* Vol. 42: *Paraphrases on Romans and Galatians.* Ed. R. D. Sider. Toronto: University of Toronto, 1984. **Luther, M.** *Luthers Werke,* Vol. 2 (1519 and 1523 editions of Galatians); Vols. 40[1] and 40[2a] (1538 edition). Weimar: Bohlaus, 1884, 1911, 1914. ————. *Luther's Works,* Vols. 26 and 27. Ed. J. Pelikan. St. Louis: Concordia, 1963–64. **Calvin, John.** *The Epistles of Paul the Apostle to the Galatians, Ephesians, Philippians, and Colossians.* Tr. T. H. L. Parker (*Calvin's Commentaries,* ed. D. W. Torrance and T. F. Torrance, Vol. 11). Grand Rapids: Eerdmans, 1965. 3–119.

Contemporary Authors

Blackman, E. C. *Marcion and His Influence.* **Buri, F.** *Clemens Alexandrinus.* **Chase, F. H.** *Chrysostom.* **Daniélou, J.** *Origen.* **Grant, R. M.** *The Letter and the Spirit.* **Hanson, R. P. C.** *Allegory and Event.* **Hoffmann-Aleith, E.** *Das Paulusverständnis in der alten Kirche.* ————. "Das Paulusverständnis des Johannes Chrysostomus." *ZNW* 38 (1939) 181–88. **Lawson, J.** *The Biblical Theology of Saint Irenaeus.* **Lightfoot, J. B.** "The Patristic Commentaries on This Epistle." In *Galatians* (1890), 227–36. **Molland, E.** *The Conception of the Gospel in Alexandrian Theology.* **Pagels, E. H.** *The Gnostic Paul.* **Parker, T. H. L.** *Calvin's New Testament Commentaries.* **Schelkle, K. H.** *Paulus Lehrer der Väter.* **Seeseman, H.** "Das Paulus erständnis des Clemens Alexandrinus." *TSK* 107 (1936) 312–46. **Souter, A.** *A Study of Ambrosiaster.* ————. *The Character and History of Pelagius' Commentary on the Epistles of St. Paul.* ————. *The Earliest Latin Commentaries on the Epistles of St. Paul.* **Turner, C. H.** "Greek Patristic Commentaries on the Pauline Epistles." In *Hastings' Dictionary of the Bible,* rev. F. C. Grant and H. H. Rowley. New York: Scribner, 1963. 484–531. **Watson, P. S.** "Editor's Preface." In M. Luther, *A Commentary on St. Paul's Epistle to the Galatians,* tr. based on the Middleton edition of the English version of 1575. London: James Clarke, 1953. 1–15. **Werner, J.** *Der Paulinismus des Irenaeus.* **Wickert, U.** *Studien zu den Pauluskommentaren Theodors von Mopsuestia.* **Wiles, M. F.** *The Divine Apostle.*

Historically, Galatians has been foundational for many forms of Christian doctrine, proclamation, and practice. And it remains true today to say that how one understands the issues and teaching of Galatians determines in large measure what kind of theology is espoused, what kind of message is proclaimed, and what kind of lifestyle is practiced.

1. Marcion

Marcion of Sinope (a village of the region of Pontus in northeastern Asia Minor along the southern shore of the Black Sea), sometime around A.D. 140, compiled a truncated canon of the NT that contained only ten letters of Paul and the Gospel according to Luke—all with omissions and alterations to suit his understanding of Christianity. Marcion read Paul's letters in the following order: Galatians, 1 and 2 Corinthians, Romans, 1 and 2 Thessalonians, Laodiceans (Ephesians?), Colossians, Philippians, and Philemon (cf. Tertullian, *Adv. Marc.* 5.2–21, who is our earliest witness for Marcion's order; see also Epiphanius, *Haer.* 42.9). So at the head of his *Apostolikon* ("Apostolic Writings") stood Galatians, which served as the interpretive key to the Christian religion vis-à-vis Judaism.

As Marcion understood it, Galatians was directed against Judaism and everything Jewish. It declares the abolition of the Jewish law and repudiates the Creator God of the Jewish Scriptures, who, according to Marcion, is an entirely other deity than the God whom Paul proclaimed. Thus as Marcion read Galatians, he saw 1:6–9, for example, as setting up a sharp contrast between Paul's preaching and the tenets of Judaism, with the angel from heaven of 1:8 who preached another gospel being a messenger of this Jewish Creator God whom Paul opposed. He interpreted the Hagar-Sarah allegory of 4:21–31 as representing two distinctly different "revelations" (not just "testaments"), the former being the Jewish religion that Paul directs his converts to cast out. And he insisted that Paul's words of 6:14, that through the cross of Christ "the world has been crucified to me and I to the world," have reference to the renunciation of the Jewish God and the Jewish law (cf. Tertullian, *Adv. Marc.* 5.2–4). Nor did the Jerusalem apostles fare any better, for they were "too close kindred with Judaism" (ibid. 5.3.1). As Marcion viewed matters, the Jerusalem apostles and Paul proclaimed two entirely different gospels, which is why Paul says in 2:11–14 that he censured Peter at Antioch for not walking uprightly according to the truth of the Christian gospel (ibid. 5.3.6–7).

2. Tertullian

Tertullian of Carthage (the ancient city-state port on the north coast of Africa, nine miles northeast of modern Tunis) published in A.D. 208 the third edition of his *Adversus Marcionem* (the first edition probably appeared in A.D. 198, with the third being the only extant edition of the work), which sets out in Book 5, sections 2–4, Tertullian's understanding of Galatians in opposition to that of Marcion. Tertullian agreed with Marcion on the importance of Galatians vis-à-vis Judaism: "We too claim that the primary epistle against Judaism is that addressed to the Galatians" (ibid. 5.2.1). But he went on to insist that Marcion was terribly wrong to renounce the Creator God and to set aside the Jewish Scriptures, for both the abolition of the law and the establishment of the gospel derive from the Creator's own ordinance and are rooted in the prophecies of the Jewish Scriptures. So Tertullian argued that it is the same God as preached in the gospel who had been known in the law, though "the rule of conduct" is not the same.

Specifically, Tertullian insisted that Galatians must be understood to teach that the Christian renunciation of the law stems from the Creator's own will and came about through the work of the Creator's Christ. As for the Jerusalem apostles, he saw them as basically one with Paul in soteriology and Christology, though he says that their faith in those early days was "unripe and still in doubt regarding the observance of the law," just as Paul's practice was inconsistent at times (e.g., in circumcising Timothy, Acts 16:3), though only "for circumstances' sake." As for the "false brothers" of 2:4–5, they were Jewish Christians who perverted the gospel by their retention of the old rule of conduct. Tertullian held, however, that their endeavors came to an end when Peter, James, and John officially recognized the legitimacy of the Pauline mission by giving to Paul and Barnabas (presumably at the Jerusalem Council) "the right hand of fellowship."

So Tertullian, on the basis of his reading of Galatians, taught that the law was meant by God for the early instruction of his people, but that with the fulfillment of his redemptive purposes in the coming of Christ, God abolished the law that he himself had appointed ("Better he than someone else!")—though God also confirms the law (i. e., the moral law) in society to the extent that he must (ibid. 5.2.1–4). Tertullian's views on God as having both abolished and confirmed the law, however, must be read with care. For only here does he speak in an unqualified manner of God's having abolished the law. Usually he distinguishes between (1) the ceremonial aspect of the law that was abolished, and (2) the moral aspect that was confirmed and heightened by Christ (cf. *De Pudicitia* 6.3–5; *De Monogamia* 7.1; *De Oratione* 1.1). As for Marcion's deletions in Galatians (deleting 1:18–24; 2:6-9a; 3:6–9; and parts of 3:10–12, 14a, 15–25; 4:27–30, with extensive alterations in 4:21–26), Tertullian exclaimed: "Let Marcion's eraser be ashamed of itself" (*Adv. Marc.* 5.4.2). And as for Marcion's treatment of Paul generally, Tertullian's argument throughout Book 5 of *Adversus Marcionem* is presented in confirmation of the thesis set out at the beginning of the work: "the most barbarous and melancholy thing about Pontus [dismal as the region is of itself] is that Marcion was born there" (ibid. 1.1.4).

3. The Gnostics

Gnostics within the early Church also looked to Paul, often revering him as the gnostic initiate and teacher *par excellence.* Gnosticism appeared in many forms and among many groups in the second and third centuries—the Sethians, Ophites or Naassenes, Simonians, Basilidians, Marcosians, Marcellians, Carpocrations, and Cerinthians being some of the better known. Probably most significant and closest to catholic Christianity were the Valentinians, who claimed succession to the apostle Paul through Theudas, a disciple of Paul, who instructed Valentinus. Valentinus himself seems to have been a man of considerable brilliance, with great eloquence and a considerable following, who about A.D. 140 was a candidate for the office of bishop at Rome (cf. Tertullian, *Adv. Valentinianos* 4). His gnostic inclinations may have been known at the time and been part of the reason for his failing to gain that post, or he may have espoused such views only later. At any rate, sometime during the middle-to-late second century, Valentinus and his disciples Ptolemy, Heracleon, and Theodotus developed a system of gnostic-Christian speculation that we know about from extant fragments of their writings, from refutations of their position by Irenaeus, Hippolytus, Tertullian, Clement of Alexandria, and Origen, and from those Nag Hammadi texts that are generally considered to be Valentinian, particularly the *Gospel of Truth.*

The Valentinians accepted Romans, 1 and 2 Corinthians, Galatians, Ephesians, Philippians, Colossians, and Hebrews as having been written by Paul—perhaps also 1 and 2 Thessalonians and Philemon, but certainly not 1 and 2 Timothy or Titus (which denounce heresies that sound too much like Gnosticism). While there is no evidence that they looked on Galatians as being more important than the other letters of Paul, they thought very highly of Galatians for a number of reasons. Chiefly, they took Paul's denials in chaps. 1–2 that his apostleship and gospel came by means of human agency and his insistence that they came rather by revelation (1:1, 11–12; cf. 2:2) as support for their distinction between tradition and revelation. Furthermore, they understood Paul's treatment of the relations between Jews and Gentiles in chaps. 3–4 as a parable having to do with relations between the called and the elect—that is between "psychics" and "pneumatics." Like Marcion, the Valentinians contrasted the God of the Jews, who is the God of the psychics, with the God of the Christians, that is of the pneumatics, and lumped the Jerusalem apostles and their preaching with the former, since they were still under the influence of Jewish opinions. They differed from Marcion, however, in that while he jettisoned the religion of Israel and the proclamation of the Jerusalem apostles, they accepted all this as valid on a psychic level, but sought to go beyond what had been received from tradition so as to glory in what was true on a pneumatic level as received by direct revelation and the private teachings of Paul. Thus, for example, the Hagar-Sarah allegory of 4:21–31 presents two "sonships": the first, a psychic sonship, which is in reality no better than slavery, and the second, the pneumatic sonship, which is free from the traditions of the past and lives by promise and revelation. Both sonships, the Valentinians said, are valid, but the second is far better! So when the Valentinians read Gal 5 with its stress on freedom from the law and the supremacy of the Spirit, they understood Paul to be teaching their position of what it means to be a pneumatic and not a psychic Christian. And when in Gal 6 Paul speaks of his converts as pneumatics ("spirituals," πνευματικοί) and not as merely psychics (vv 1–5), and then concludes by calling them "the Israel of God" (v 16), they found their theology to be explicitly confirmed (cf. E. H. Pagels, *The Gnostic Paul*, 101–14).

Opponents of Gnosticism within the Church included Irenaeus (*Adv. Haer.*), Hippolytus (*Refutationis Omnium Haeresium*), Tertullian (*Adv. Valentinianos*), Clement of Alexandria (esp. *Stromateis* 7; *Excerpta et Theodoto*), and Origen (cf. his many anti-Valentinian comments in treating the Pauline letters). Much of the argument of the church fathers was to the effect that Christianity as proclaimed among the Gentiles is really in continuity with all that God did redemptively in the past, and that it truly carries on the apostles' message. So in opposition to the Gnostics' claim of being in apostolic succession because they were carrying on Paul's private and oral teachings, the church fathers laid stress on the apostolic centers of the Gentile world, where presumably the apostolic witness would be most alive, arguing that in these centers there is no remembrance of anything having been proclaimed by the apostles other than what can be found in their writings as contained in the NT. Irenaeus and Tertullian even went so far as to claim that Gal. 2:5 should be read, "We *did* give in to them for a time, so that the truth of the gospel might remain with you," thereby omitting the negative οὐδέ contained in our better manuscripts (Irenaeus, *Adv. Haer.* 3.13.3; Tertullian, *Adv. Marc.* 5.3). On this basis they asserted that Paul did, in fact, submit to the authority of the Jerusalem apostles, and so they sought to refute the gnostic distinction between Paul and the Jerusalem apostles.

4. The Alexandrian Fathers

We do not have any Greek commentaries on Galatians from either of the two great Christian teachers of Alexandria at the end of the second century and the beginning of the third: Clement and Origen. Jerome in commenting on Gal 5:13 tells us that Origen produced fifteen books and seven homilies on Galatians, but only fragments of two or three of these have been preserved in Latin dress (see Pamphilus' *Apology* and Jerome's *Commentarium in Epistulam ad Galatas*). There are, however, numerous references and allusions to Galatians in these two church fathers' other extant writings, and from these it is possible to piece together something of their understanding of the letter.

Clement of Alexandria was an adult convert to Christianity and after a long spiritual pilgrimage settled in Alexandria as a pupil of Pantaenus, whom he succeeded as head of the Catechetical School during A.D. 190–202. He left Alexandria in A.D. 202 when severe persecution of Christians broke out under Septimius Severus, and died in Asia Minor about A.D. 214. While Clement's extant works are fewer and more theological in nature than those of his successor, there can be no doubt as to how he viewed Paul's teaching in Galatians. Most succinct is the following quotation from "The Rich Man's Salvation":

Now the works of the law are good—who will deny it? For "the commandment is holy" [Rom 7:12], but only to the extent of being a kind of training, accompanied by fear and preparatory instruction, leading on to the supreme law-giving and grace of Jesus [cf. Gal 3:24]. On the other hand, "Christ is the fulfilment [i.e., the πλήρωμα, not τέλος] of the law unto righteousness to every one who believes" [Rom 10:4], and those who perfectly observe the Father's will he makes not slaves, in the manner of a slave, but sons and brothers and joint-heirs [cf. Gal 3:26–4:7] (Clement, *Quis Dives Salvetur?* 9.2; see *Stromateis* 4.130.3

for the other occasion where Clement uses πλήρωμα in commenting on Rom 10:4).

Here Clement reveals something of his understanding of Paul's teaching in Galatians: as to the nature of the law, it is "good" and "holy"; as to the purpose of the law, it was to be "a kind of training, accompanied by fear and preparatory instruction"; as to the focus of the law, it is to be found in its "leading on to the supreme law-giving and grace of Jesus"; as to Christ's work in relation to the law, "Christ is the fulfilment of the law"; as to the Christian's status before God, it is one of being righteous apart from the law (no longer slaves under the law but "sons and brothers and joint-heirs"); and as to the Christian's responsibility to God, it is to believe and perfectly observe the Father's will.

Origen (A.D. 185–254), the pious and precocious son of the Greek grammarian and Christian martyr Leonides, who became head of the Catechetical School at Alexandria at the age of eighteen in A.D. 203, published during his lifetime a prodigious number of critical, exegetical, theological, apologetic, and practical writings. There is extant among all these materials, however, no commentary on Galatians. Yet we are not left to wonder how Origen understood Galatians or what impact it made on him, for there are numerous hints and several direct statements on these matters in the many Greek fragments we have of his commentaries on Matthew, John, and Romans, in the few Latin portions of his Galatians commentary preserved by Pamphilus and Jerome, and in the two hundred or so extant homilies we have from Origen on various biblical passages. In addition, in *De Principiis* Origen spells out quite explicitly his principles of biblical interpretation.

In *Contra Celsum*, which was written near the end of his life, Origen uses Gal 5:17 in support of his sharp distinction between the flesh and the spirit, with primacy, of course, being given to the spirit: "It is impossible for a man, who is a compound being, in which 'the flesh lusts against the spirit and the spirit against the flesh,' to keep the feast [i. e., the Lord's Day, Preparation, Passover, Pentecost, or any other] with his whole nature; for either he keeps the feast with his spirit and afflicts the body, which through the lust of the flesh is unfit to keep it along with the spirit, or else he keeps it with the body, and the spirit is unable to share in it" (8.23; cf. 4.52 where Origen applauds Numenius the Pythagorean who said: "The soul [ψυχή] is the work of God, while the nature of the body is different. And in this respect there is no difference between the body of a bat, or of a worm, or of a frog, and that of a man; for the matter [ὕλη] is the same, and their corruptible part is alike"). Earlier in *De Principiis* Origen made this same distinction using Gal 5:17 in support as well (1.3.4; 3.2.3; 3.4.1–5). So it seems safe to say, though without his Galatians commentary, that Galatians with its flesh-spirit dichotomy was foundational for Origen's thought.

Likewise, the Hagar-Sarah allegory of 4:21–31 seems to have been foundational for Origen's exegetical method, for in *Contra Celsum* it is that passage which he uses to justify his allegorical or spiritual exegesis:

Scripture frequently makes use of the histories of real events in order to present to view more important truths, which are but obscurely intimated; and of this kind are the narratives relating to the "wells" and to the "marriages" and to the various acts of "sexual intercourse" recorded of righteous persons, for which, however, it will be more reasonable to offer an explanation in the exegetical writings referring to those very passages. But that wells were constructed by righteous men in the land of the Philistines, as related in the book of Genesis, is manifest from the wonderful wells which are shown at Ascalon, and which are deserving of mention on account of their structure, so foreign and peculiar compared to that of other wells. Moreover, that both young men and female servants are to be understood metaphorically, is not our doctrine merely, but one which we have received from the beginning from wise men, among whom a certain one [Paul] said, when exhorting his hearers to investigate the figurative meaning: "Tell me, you that read the law, do you not hear the law? For it is written that Abraham had two sons: the one by a bond maid, the other by a free woman. But he who was of the bond woman was born after the flesh; he of the free woman was by promise. Which things are an allegory, for these are the two covenants: the one from Mount Sinai, which genders to bondage, which is Agar." And a little after, "But Jerusalem which is above is free, which is the mother of us all." And any one who will take up the Epistle to the Galatians may learn how the passages relating to the "marriage" and the "intercourse with the maid-servants" have been allegorized—the Scripture desiring us to imitate not the literal acts of those who did these things, but, as the apostles of Jesus are accustomed to call them, the spiritual (4.44).

And in that same work, Gal 2:15 is used to buttress his view of Paul vis-à-vis the Jerusalem apostles that he was "mightier than they" (ibid. 7.21) and Gal 2:12 to support his understanding of the nature of the Jerusalem apostles' actions that they had "not yet learned from Jesus to ascend from the law that is regulated according to the letter to that which is interpreted according to the spirit" (ibid. 2.1).

In his Romans commentary, Origen deals extensively with Paul's teaching on the law—a subject of great importance, of course, for Galatians as well. He notes that not every reference to law in Paul's writings has the Mosaic law in view, and so insists that distinctions must be made in Paul's usage if we are to understand his meaning (*Comm. ad Rom.* on Rom 3:19 [*PG* 14:958]). He lists six ways in which the word "law" is used and illustrates them from Paul's letters: (1) the Mosaic law according to the letter (Gal 3:10, 19, 24; 5:4); (2) the Mosaic law according to its spiritual sense (Rom 7:12,14); (3) natural law (Rom 2:14); (4) Mosaic history (Gal 4:2); (5) the prophetic books (1 Cor 14:21); and (6) the teachings of Christ (1 Cor 9:21)—though this latter sense is suggested only somewhat tentatively ("Fragments on Romans," *JTS* 13 [1912] 216–18 [on Rom 2:21–25] and 14 [1913] 13 [on Rom 7:7]). With regard to distinguishing between the Mosaic law and natural law, Origen posits that the presence or absence of the article with νόμος is of help, though he never claims this to be an invariable rule (*Comm. ad Rom.* on Rom 3:21 [*PG* 14:959]).

More particularly, when commenting on Paul's teaching regarding the Christian's relation to the law, Origen—in concert with Tertullian, Irenaeus, and the Alexandrians generally—separates the law into two parts: (1) the ceremonial laws of Leviticus, which interpreted according to the flesh have come to an end with Christ, and (2) the moral requirements of the law, which have been retained and amplified by Christ (ibid. on Rom 8:3 and 11:6; cf. Tertullian, *De Pudicitia* 6.3–

5; *De Monogamia* 7.1; *De Oratione* 1.1; Irenaeus, *Adv. Haer.* 4.16.4; *Apostolic Constitutions* 6.20). And when relating law and gospel, while not without an understanding of the gospel as the fulfillment of the law, "his main emphasis," as Maurice Wiles points out, "was placed on the more static and less dynamic conception of the already present but hidden spiritual meaning of the law" (*The Divine Apostle*, 65). For example, commenting on Rom 6:14 Origen interprets "you are not under law but under grace" as a contrast between the letter of the law and the spirit of the law, without any attention being given to historical developments either within or between the testaments (*Comm. ad Rom.* on Rom 6:1 [*PG* 14:1035]). It is, in fact, this separation of law into its ceremonial and moral parts and this type of static understanding of relations between the testaments that characterizes Origen's thinking. And it is no exaggeration to say that these same features have been ingrained in most succeeding treatments of Galatians, with only a few exceptions.

5. The Antiochian Fathers

At Antioch of Syria, however, another brand of Christian interpretation arose: one that owed much to Origen for its critical spirit and grammatical precision, but stood in opposition to many of the Alexandrian exegetical tenets. John Chrysostom (A.D. 345–407), who became famous in his native Antioch as a great Christian leader and outstanding preacher ("John the Golden Mouth") and who then served as Archbishop of Constantinople during A.D. 398–407, is one of the most important, particularly with regard to Galatians. For while his treatment of all the other NT writings is in the form of homilies on various passages, sometime during the last decade of his life he wrote a commentary on Galatians that moves from verse to verse in extended fashion. Chrysostom's Galatian commentary cannot have been written earlier than A.D. 395, for, commenting on Gal 1:16, he refers his readers to his earlier discussion on the change of Paul's name from Saul to Paul, and that discussion is in *Hom. de Mut. Nom.* 3, which can be dated A.D. 395. Some argue that the Galatians commentary must have been written before A.D. 398, the date when Chrysostom became Archbishop at Constantinople, because its character is suited to oral delivery, which would characterize better his Antioch residence. (Chrysostom also wrote an OT commentary on the first six chapters of Isaiah.)

Theodore of Mopsuestia (died A.D. 429), a contemporary and colleague of Chrysostom, is also important. He was born in Tarsus, but lived in Antioch and became bishop of the ecclesiastical see of Mopsuestia. He wrote commentaries on all of Paul's letters, of which only fragments remain in Greek, though there are Latin translations for those on Galatians through Philemon. Likewise of importance is Theodoret (A.D. 393–460), a native of Antioch and disciple of Theodore, who later became Bishop of Cyrrhus in Syria. Because of their terseness of expression, good sense, and absence of faults, his commentaries on Paul have often been credited as being superior to all other patristic expositions of Scripture. But, as J. B. Lightfoot observed, "they have little claim to originality, and he who has read Chrysostom and Theodore of Mopsuestia will find scarcely anything in Theodoret which he has not seen before" ("Patristic Commentaries," 230).

With regard to the major introductory questions of the day—that is, regarding the identity of the opponents, the nature of their teaching, and the situation Paul faced at Galatia—Chrysostom says quite clearly:

Some of the Jews who believed, being held down by the prepossessions of Judaism, and at the same time intoxicated by vain-glory, and desirous of obtaining for themselves the dignity of teachers, came to the Galatians, and taught them that the observance of circumcision, sabbaths, and new-moons, was necessary, and that Paul in abolishing these things was not to be borne. For, said they, Peter and James and John, the chiefs of the Apostles and the companions of Christ, forbade them not. Now in fact they did not forbid these things, but this was not by way of delivering positive doctrine, but in condescension to the weakness of the Jewish believers, which condescension Paul had no need of when preaching to the Gentiles; but when he was in Judea, he employed it himself also [cf. Acts 21:20–26]. But these deceivers, by withholding the causes both of Paul's condescension and that of his brethren, misled the simpler ones, saying that he was not to be tolerated, for he appeared but yesterday, while Peter and his colleagues were from the first— that he was a disciple of the Apostles, but they of Christ; that he was single, but they many, and pillars of the Church. They accused him too of acting a part, saying: "this very man who forbids circumcision observes the rite elsewhere, and preaches one way to you and another way to others" (*Commentary* on Gal 1:1–3).

In so stating, Chrysostom was only drawing together the lines of early patristic understanding, in opposition to Marcion and the Gnostics. Likewise, in his constant correlation of Gal 2:1–10 and the Jerusalem Council (cf. ibid. on Gal 1:17; 2:1–12; and 2:17) and his parallels between Galatians and 2 Corinthians (e.g., ibid. on 1:10, correlating 2 Cor 11:23 with Galatians), Chrysostom appears to be only repeating a settled opinion among all interpreters of his day: that Galatians was written toward the close of Paul's missionary travels in the eastern part of the Roman empire, somewhere around A.D. 56–57.

But while Chrysostom and his Antiochian colleagues agreed with the Alexandrian Fathers on the introductory issues of pertinence to Galatians, exegetically and theologically they differed widely. For while the Alexandrians (and Tertullian), in opposition to Marcion, did everything they could to assure that Paul's opposition to the law was kept to a minimum—and so tended to view the relations between the testaments in somewhat static fashion—the Antiochian church fathers emphasized historical development and redemptive fulfillment, and so understood Paul's teaching differently regarding such matters as gospel and law and the Christian's relation to the law. Likewise, the Antiochian church fathers stood diametrically opposed to allegorical exegesis and denied the legitimacy of dividing the law into two unequal parts—the ceremonial law, which came to an end with Christ and the moral law, which was reaffirmed by Christ. And while they acknowledged that Paul used the word "law" differently in his writings to refer at times to natural law or to the whole OT, as well as to the Mosaic law, they tended not to appeal to these distinctions in explicating difficult passages, but preferred to interpret such passages along the lines of only one sense per passage for the word "law." So, for example, whereas Origen held that Paul's use of "law" changed frequently and without notice in Rom 7, Chrysostom insisted that Rom 7 must be understood in terms of the Mosaic law throughout, with ideas about natural law and/or a paradisal command to be ruled out altogether (see esp. *Hom. in Rom.* 12.6 on Rom 7:12; though in treating Rom 2:14–

15 Chrysostom distinguished among written law, natural law, and law as revealed in action).

Themes of development and fulfillment come to the fore at many places in the Antiochian church fathers' treatment of Galatians. For example, though he refused to separate gospel and law as opposing forces, Chrysostom was not prepared to see the law as an ethical guide for Christians. Thus on Paul's statement, "Now that faith has come, we are no longer under the supervision of the law; for you are all sons of God through faith in Christ Jesus" (Gal 3:25–26), Chrysostom writes:

> The Law, then, as it was our tutor, and we were kept shut up under it, is not the adversary but the fellow-worker of grace. But if when grace is come it continues to hold us down, it becomes an adversary; for if it confines those who ought to go forward to grace, then it is the destruction of our salvation. If a candle which gave light by night kept us, when it became day, from the sun, it would not only not benefit, it would injure us. And so does the Law, if it stands between us and greater benefits. Those then are the greatest traducers of the Law who still keep it, just as the tutor makes a youth ridiculous by retaining him with himself when time calls for his departure (*Commentary* on Gal 3:25–26).

And though he failed to apply the verse either to the anti-Semitism prevalent in his day or to male chauvinism, in a remarkable sermon delivered at Constantinople toward the end of his life Chrysostom interpreted Gal 3:28 as having relevance for the question of slavery. Thus while agreeing with Christians of his day that slavery is "the penalty of sin and the punishment of disobedience," Chrysostom went on to assert:

> But when Christ came he annulled even this, for in Christ Jesus "there is no slave nor free." Therefore, it is not necessary to have a slave; but if it should be necessary, then only one or at most a second. . . . Buy them and after you have taught them some skill by which they may maintain themselves, set them free (*Homily* 40 on 1 Corinthians 10).

In so speaking, Chrysostom was knowingly breaking away from a common Christian view that since slavery arose because of sin it could only be eradicated in the eschaton when God deals finally with sin. Based on a more dynamic understanding of redemption, Chrysostom argued for an application of the gospel to the question of slavery in the present—not just reserving such matters for the future (cf. my *New Testament Social Ethics for Today*, 60–65).

It is fair to say, then, that the Antiochian church fathers, while not denying continuity to the redemptive activities of God throughout history, had a livelier sense of historical development and redemptive fulfillment than did their Alexandrian counterparts. And because of their more dynamic approach to Scripture, they treated questions concerning gospel and law, relations between the testaments, and the Christian's attitude toward the law differently from the Alexandrians.

6. Other Latin and Greek Commentators

Many others wrote commentaries on Galatians in the post-Nicene period. The important critical and exegetical issues, however, were taken to have been largely settled in the second and third centuries, with the result that most of these later works simply built on what had gone before. Four great Latin commentaries deserve mention: one by Ambrosiaster (Hilary), which was written sometime during A.D. 366–84; one by Jerome about A.D. 387; one by Augustine about A.D. 394; and one by Pelagius sometime before A.D. 410. The commentary of Marius Victorinus is earlier, written about A.D. 360, but it is not in the same class as these four among Latin commentaries.

Jerome refers to a number of commentaries he consulted in writing his own commentary, but singles out Origen's as having been especially important and the one he followed most closely. Jerome's work on Galatians is characterized by extensive learning, acute criticism, and some fanciful and even perverse interpretations, coupled with lively and vigorous exposition (so Lightfoot, "Patristic Commentaries," 232). In the main, however, it comes off as a reconstituted Alexandrian treatment of the letter. The commentary ascribed to Ambrosiaster (so called because it was wrongly credited to Ambrose and has been commonly printed with his writings) is one of the best of the Latin commentaries. But it too is heavily dependent on Alexandrian tenets. Augustine's commentary claims no knowledge of the writings of others on Galatians, and the work evidences that to be the case. While important for its spiritual insights and great thoughts at numerous places, as a critical commentary it falls far short. And Pelagius' commentaries on Paul's letters, though perceptive and vital in the portions we have, were purged of what were considered to be their heretical features, so we are unable to judge either their sources or their distinctive contributions.

All other commentaries on Galatians in the Middle Ages are derivative writings. Those in Greek by John of Damascus (c. A.D. 750), Ecumenius (10th cent.), and Theophylactus (late 11th cent.) are largely dependent on Chrysostom and Theodore of Mopsuestia, as is also the anonymous *Catena* (date uncertain) published by Cramer in 1842. Those by the many Latin writers of this period are equally unoriginal, being derived from Ambrosiaster (Hilary), Jerome, Augustine, and Pelagius—and through Jerome, in particular, rooted in an Alexandrian approach to the interpretation of Galatians.

7. *The Protestant Reformers*

During the Protestant Reformation, Galatians took on heightened importance. In 1517 Erasmus published his *Paraphrase on Romans*, which was followed in 1518 or 1519 by his *Paraphrase on Galatians*. These paraphrases seem to have been done as a kind of relief from his work as a critical editor and as preparations for full-scale commentaries, though Erasmus never got around to writing commentaries. The paraphrases on Romans and Galatians were immediately popular on the continent and later in Britain. "For the interpretation of Romans and Galatians," as J. B. Payne, A. Rabil, Jr., and W. S. Smith, Jr., observe, "Erasmus' favourite interpreters were clearly Origen and Jerome, respectively" (*Collected Works of Erasmus*, 42:xviii). Erasmus' Alexandrian proclivities are clearly evident in his frequent insistence that Paul rejected not the whole law but only its ceremonial parts—thereby viewing the ceremonial law as coming to an end in Christ and the moral law as reaffirmed by Christ—and in his arguments for the spiritual law of Christ as taking the place of the ceremonial law of Moses. In opposition to the ceremonialism of his day, Erasmus read Galatians more in terms of the contrast between personal and formal expressions of religion than in terms of eschatological redemption.

Martin Luther (1483–1546) lectured repeatedly on Galatians at the university of Wittenburg, where he was professor of biblical exegesis. In 1519 he published a commentary on Galatians that was largely dependent on Jerome and Erasmus. Then in 1523 he produced an abbreviated and revised form of that 1519 work, which in its omissions and revisions began to depart from both Jerome and Erasmus (see *Luthers Werke*, 2:436–758; *Luther's Works*, 27:151–410). During the fall of 1531, Luther gave another series of lectures on Galatians. That series was taken down in full by three of his students and published in 1535. It was then republished with revisions in 1538 as his definitive exposition of Galatians (*Werke*, 40^1 and 40^{2a}; *Works*, 26 and 27a). In this later commentary Luther frequently opposes Jerome on matters of exegesis and interpretation, occasionally taking issue with Erasmus as well. In effect, though seemingly without being aware of it himself, Luther's 1538 commentary stands firmly in an Antiochian tradition of interpretation.

Luther loved Galatians, finding in it a source of strength for his own life and an armory of weapons for his reforming work. He called it "my own epistle, to which I have plighted my troth; my Katie von Bora" (*Werke*, 40^1:2; Katie von Bora, of course, was Luther's wife). When just two years before his death the complete Latin edition of his works was being prepared, Luther commented: "If they took my advice, they would print only the books containing doctrine, like Galatians" (*Werke*, 40^1:2)

In his 1538 commentary on Galatians, Luther stresses the doctrine of justification by faith, fighting against opponents on two fronts. He opposed, of course, scholastic theology and the Papists in their equation of gospel and law. But he also argued against the radical reformers of his day (the Enthusiasts or *Schwärmer*, as he called them) in their separation of the letter and the spirit and of flesh and spirit. The former he saw as modern equivalents to the Judaizers and against them argued for the contrast between gospel and law—though, it must be noted, without denying continuity in God's redemptive activity throughout history or negating the ultimate unity of purpose in both. The latter, however, he saw as contemporary dualists and allegorists, and insisted that they failed to understand Paul's use of flesh and spirit aright.

In 1527, when commenting on Christ's words "This is my body," Luther—against the Enthusiasts and with an allusion to Gal 5:20—had said:

> Everything is and is called spirit and spiritual that proceeds from the Holy Spirit, no matter how corporeal, external and visible it may be. And everything is flesh and carnal that proceeds without the Spirit from the natural powers of the flesh, no matter how inward and invisible it may be. Thus St. Paul in Romans 7 calls the carnal mind "flesh," and in Galatians 5 he reckons among the works of the flesh "heresy, hatred, envy," etc., which are entirely inward and invisible (*Werke*, 23:203).

And this emphasis continues in his Galatians commentary of 1538.

On matters having to do with the identity of the opponents at Galatia, the nature of their teaching, and the situation Paul faced, Luther was quite traditional, accepting positions arrived at by the church fathers and those who preceded him. All that he did that was new in these areas was to identify the Papists as the Judaizers of his day and to spell out Paul's teaching on justification vis-à-vis their position. Likewise, Luther was traditional in equating Gal 2:1–10 with the Jerusalem Council of Acts 15, and so viewing Galatians as having been written late in Paul's career. Exegetically, however, Luther broke with his Latin tradition by arguing for the contrast between gospel and law, on the one hand, and for the union of flesh and spirit and letter and spirit, on the other. In so doing, he was in line with an Antiochian tradition of exegesis and interpretation, in contradistinction to the Alexandrian church fathers and the Latin commentators.

John Calvin (1509–64) is often thought of as a man of only one book, *The Institutes of the Christian Religion,* which he completed in 1536 at the age of twenty-seven. But Calvin was also a pastor and a statesman, who delivered sermons and wrote letters—and who, in carrrying out his pastoral duties in Geneva, became a prolific writer of commentaries. In addition to commentaries on the OT, he wrote commentaries on all the books of the NT except 2 and 3 John and Revelation. His commentary on Galatians was published in 1548 when he was thirty-nine.

With regard to critical issues Calvin, like Luther, was thoroughly traditional. For example, Calvin held that the claim of the Judaizers to represent the apostles at Jerusalem was false, for they, in contradistinction to the Jerusalem apostles, both (1) undercut Paul's authority as an apostle, and (2) taught that observance of the Jewish ceremonies was still necessary—so attacking not just Paul but also the truth of the gospel (see Calvin's introductory "The Theme of the Epistle to the Galatians," in *The Epistles of Paul,* 3–7). Also, following his predecessors, Calvin believed that the Galatian Christians to whom Paul wrote were located somewhere in the northern regions of the Roman province of Galatia (cf. the opening statement of Calvin's Galatian commentary: "It is well known in what parts of Asia the Galatians lived and what were the boundaries of their country" [ibid., 3]), and so presumably evangelized during the latter part of Paul's missionary activity. Yet, interestingly, Calvin identifies the Jerusalem visit of Gal 2:1–10 with the famine visit of Acts 11:27–30, and not with Acts 15:1–30 as might be expected. For on Gal 2:1, Calvin says: "This [visit] can hardly be regarded definitely as the journey mentioned by Luke in Acts 15:2. The course of the history leads us to the contrary conclusion" (ibid., 24). He then goes on to argue for the identification of this visit with the famine visit.

Exegetically, Calvin deplored allegorizing the text in search of deeper, more spiritual meanings. Rather, he argued for the "literal sense"—that is, the plain and single meaning of the words as understood in their historical context. On Paul's use of ἀλληγορούμενα in Gal 4:24, which was being used to validate allegorical exegesis, Calvin writes:

Origen, and many others along with him, have seized this occasion of twisting Scripture this way and that, away from the genuine sense. For they inferred that the literal sense is too meagre and poor and that beneath the bark of the letter there lie deeper mysteries which cannot be extracted but by hammering out allegories. And this they did without difficulty, for the world always has and always will prefer speculations which seem ingenious to solid doctrine. With such approbation the licence increased more and more, so that he who played this game of allegorizing Scripture not only was suffered to pass unpunished but even obtained the highest applause. For many centuries no man was thought clever who lacked the cunning and daring to transfigure with subtlety the sacred Word of God. This was undoubtedly a trick of Satan to impair the authority of Scripture and remove any true advantage out of the reading of it. God avenged this profanation with a just judgment when He suffered the pure meaning to be buried under false glosses.

Scripture, they say, is fertile and thus bears multiple meanings. I acknowledge that Scripture is the most rich and inexhaustible fount of all wisdom. But I deny that its fertility consists in the various meanings which anyone may fasten to it at his pleasure. Let us know, then, that the true meaning of Scripture is the natural and simple one, and let us embrace and hold it resolutely. Let us not merely neglect as doubtful, but boldly set aside as deadly corruptions, those pretended expositions which lead us away from the literal sense (ibid., 84–85).

Likewise, in contradistinction to the medieval habit of modernizing history, Calvin refused to contemporize the text for the sake of relevance. He was convinced that a faithful exposition of the apostolic message in its first-century dress was what was necessary and most significant for the issues confronting Christians in the sixteenth century. And while, as in the *Institutes*, he viewed man as consisting of two parts, a soul and a body, and spoke of the soul as "the nobler part of him" (1.15.1–8), in his Galatians commentary Calvin stands in opposition to an Alexandrian separation of flesh and spirit and to the radical reformers' separation of letter and spirit (see his statements in the Galatians commentary on Gal 5:17, with references to his earlier comments on Romans 8).

Yet while Calvin was in many ways Antiochian in his historical and exegetical sensibilities, he was basically Alexandrian in his theological orientation, in his understanding of the relation of the testaments, and in his treatment of the interaction between gospel and law in the Christian life. Frequently, in fact, having dealt historically and exegetically with a text, and having come to a dilemma in the interpretation, he solved the issue on a theological basis—not, at all times, inappropriately, but often much too quickly. And while exegetically he tried to keep separate the first and the sixteenth centuries, in applying the message of a passage the "then" and the "now" often became so intertwined as to become one and the same.

"The sixteenth century was, above all things," as T. H. L. Parker reminds us, "the age of the Bible" (*Calvin's New Testament Commentaries*, vii). Not only Erasmus, Luther, and Calvin, but also Melanchthon, Zwingli, Beza, Musculus, Pellican, Brenz, Bugenhagen, Bullinger, Bucer, Mercerus, and a host of others call for attention. Much more research needs to be done on each of these commentators before they can be treated in any such summary fashion as we have done for those above. Nonetheless, Erasmus, Luther, and Calvin set the tone for much of what followed in commentary writing in the succeeding centuries, with distinctly new approaches not being proposed until the modern critical period.

8. The Modern Critical Period

The modern critical period of Pauline studies began with Ferdinand Christian Baur, who in 1831 first proposed his Hegelian understanding of the course of early Christian history ("Die Christuspartei in der korinthischen Gemeinde: Der Gegensatz des petrinischen und paulinischen Christentums in der ältesten Kirche,"

Tübinger Zeitschrift für Theologie [1831] 61–206; see also his *Paul: His Life and Works*, 2 vols, tr. E. Zeller [London: Williams & Norgate, 1875] 1:105–45, 250–57). Baur saw Galatians as a polemic by Paul against legalistic Jewish Christians from Jerusalem who were unimpeded by the Jerusalem apostles—or, as Baur's position was developed by his disciples, against the full authority of the Jerusalem church, including that of Peter and James. This understanding of early Christianity in general and of Galatians in particular was directly opposed by J. B. Lightfoot, whose 1865 commentary on the letter set the standard for all commentary writing from his day to the present (*Saint Paul's Epistle to the Galatians*, 1st ed. [London: Macmillan, 1865]).

In the 1890s William M. Ramsay challenged the traditional understanding of the provenance of Galatians, proposing instead what has become known as the South Galatian hypothesis (*The Church in the Roman Empire before A.D. 170* [London: Hodder & Stoughton, 1893]; *The Cities and Bishoprics of Phrygia* [Oxford: Clarendon, 1895]; *St. Paul the Traveller and the Roman Citizen* [London: Hodder & Stoughton, 1896]; *A Historical Commentary on St. Paul's Epistle to the Galatians* [London: Hodder & Stoughton, 1899]). In 1919 Wilhelm Lütgert (*Gesetz und Geist: Eine Untersuchung zur Vorgeschichte des Galaterbriefs* [Gütersloh: Bertelsmann]), followed in 1929 by James Hardy Ropes (*The Singular Problem of the Epistle to the Galatians* [Cambridge, MA: Harvard University Press]), in opposition to the unitary nature of Paul's Galatian opponents, argued a "Two Front Theory" that postulated both judaizing legalists and pneumatic radicals as being addressed, though in different sections of the letter. In 1921 Ernest deWitt Burton set the model for what a true exegetical commentary on Galatians should be (*A Critical and Exegetical Commentary on the Epistle to the Galatians* [ICC; Edinburgh: T. & T. Clark]). In 1948 W. D. Davies set the pattern for the interpretation of Paul in terms of his background in Pharisaic Judaism, with those studies having profound implications for the understanding of Paul's use of Jewish exegetical procedures and theological themes in Galatians (*Paul and Rabbinic Judaism* [London: SPCK]). In 1950 John Knox argued for the disengagement of Paul's letters from the portrayals of Paul in Acts, with interpreters being called on to understand Galatians in its historical circumstances, date, and teachings apart from Acts (*Chapters in a Life of Paul* [Nashville: Abingdon]). In 1956 Walter Schmithals proposed a gnostic setting for the situation at Galatia ("Die Heretiker in Galatien," *ZNW* 47 [1956] 25–67, which, as revised in 1965, now appears as "The Heretics in Galatia," in *Paul and the Gnostics*, tr. J. E. Steely [Nashville: Abingdon, 1972] 13–64). In 1971 Robert Jewett proposed a Zealot background ("The Agitators and the Galatian Congregation," *NTS* 17 [1971] 198–212).

During the 1960s and 1970s a great deal of study on the epistolary structures of first-century letters was undertaken, much of which has direct bearing on the structure of Galatians. In 1975 and 1979 Hans Dieter Betz stressed the rhetorical forms of the Greco-Roman world, particularly the "apologetic letter" genre of forensic rhetoric, as providing the basic interpretive key to Galatians ("The Literary Composition and Function of Paul's Letter to the Galatians," *NTS* 21 [1975] 353–79; idem, *Galatians: A Commentary on Paul's Letter to the Churches in Galatia* [Hermeneia; Philadelphia: Fortress, 1979]). And throughout the past quarter-century, Galatians has become prominent in various liberation theologies—whether of a Latin American or South American variety (e.g., G. Gutierrez, *A Theology of Liberation* [Maryknoll, NY: Orbis Books, 1973] 158–61), or black liberation (e.g., J. H. Cone,

Black Theology and Black Power [Maryknoll, NY: Orbis Books, 1979] 39, 60, 125), or women's liberation (e. g., R. Scroggs, "Paul and the Eschatological Woman," *JAAR* 40 [1972] 283–303).

Much of what follows will deal directly with the issues raised and the approaches taken as cited above for the modern critical period. I must, therefore, leave the discussion of each of these matters to those fuller treatments (see particularly the discussions of "Authorship," "Addressees," "Date," "Opponents and Situation," and "Epistolary and Rhetorical Structures"). All I have attempted to do here by means of a selective reading of the history of interpretation is (1) to make the point that Paul's letter to the Galatians has been and continues to be foundational for many forms of Christian thought, proclamation, and practice, (2) to highlight certain distinctive ways in which Galatians has been treated in the past so as to alert the reader to crucial issues that must be dealt with in interpretation, and (3) to whet the reader's appetite for a fresh study of the letter itself. Paul's Galatians is, in fact, like a lion turned loose in the arena of Christians. It challenges, intimidates, encourages, and focuses our attention on what is really essential as little else can. How we deal with the issues it raises and the teachings it presents will in large measure determine how we think as Christians and how we live as Christ's own.

Authorship

Bibliography

Bahr, G. J. "Paul and Letter Writing in the First Century." *CBQ* 28 (1966) 465–77. ———. "The Subscriptions in the Pauline Letters." *JBL* 87 (1968) 27–41. **Baur, F. C.** *Paul: His Life and Works*, 1:245–57. **Burton, E. deW.** *Galatians*, lxv–lxxi. **Deissmann, A.** *Light from the Ancient East*. **Doty, W. G.** *Letters in Primitive Christianity*. **Funk, R. W.** *Language, Hermeneutic, and Word of God*, 250–74. ———. "The Apostolic Parousia: Form and Significance." In *Christian History and Interpretation*. FS J. Knox, ed. W. R. Farmer, C. F. D. Moule, and R. R. Niebuhr. Cambridge: Cambridge University Press, 1967. 249–68. **Koskenniemi, H.** *Studien zur Idee und Phraseologie des griechischen Briefes bis 400 n. Chr.* **Longenecker, R. N.** "Ancient Amanuenses and the Pauline Epistles." In *New Dimensions in New Testament Study*, ed. R. N. Longenecker and M. C. Tenney. Grand Rapids: Zondervan, 1974. 281–97. ———. "On the Form, Function, and Authority of the New Testament Letters." In *Scripture and Truth*, ed. D. A. Carson and J. D. Woodbridge. Grand Rapids: Zondervan, 1983. 101–14. **Milligan, G.** *Documents*, 21–30, 241–47. **Milne, H. J. M.** *Greek Shorthand Manuals*. **O'Neill, J. C.** *Recovery*. **Pack, R. A.** *Greek and Latin Literary Texts*. **Roberts, C. H.** *Greek Literary Hands, 350 B.C.—A.D 400*. Oxford: Clarendon, 1956. **Roller, O.** *Das Formular*. **Schubert, P.** "Form and Function of the Pauline Letters." *JR* 19 (1939) 365–77. **Sherk, R. K.** *Roman Documents from the Greek East*. **Turner, E. G.** *Greek Manuscripts*. **Wendland, P.** *Die urchristlichen Literaturformen*, 339–45. **White, J. L.** *The Form and Function of the Body of the Greek Letter*.

1. Author

The most uncontroverted matter in the study of Galatians is that the letter was written by Paul, the Christian apostle whose ministry is portrayed in the Acts of the Apostles. The letter begins by naming him as its author (1:1). Furthermore, the nature of its theological argument, its distinctive use of Scripture in support of that argument, the character of its impassioned appeals, and the style of writing all point to Paul as its author. If Galatians is not by Paul, no NT letter is by him, for none has any better claim.

Marcion, the Gnostics, the Alexandrian church fathers, the Antiochian church fathers, the Protestant Reformers, and almost all scholars since have accepted Paul's authorship without question, with many seeing Galatians as the programmatic basis for all Pauline thought and the touchstone for all Christian theology. There is, in fact, no recorded opposition to Paul's authorship of Galatians until the nineteenth century. Even the Tübingen scholar F. C. Baur accepted Galatians as by Paul and built his case for early Christianity on "the four great Epistles of the Apostle which take precedence of the rest in every respect, namely, the Epistle to the Galatians, the two Epistles to the Corinthians, and the Epistle to the Romans" (the so-called *Hauptbriefe*), for, insisted Baur, "there has never been the slightest suspicion of unauthenticity cast on these four epistles, and they bear so incontestably the character of Pauline originality, that there is no conceivable ground for the assertion of critical doubts in their case" (*Paul: His Life and Works*, 1:246). And the vast majority of scholars today agree.

Not everyone, of course, has concurred. In the nineteenth century Bruno Bauer outdid F. C. Baur in the application of "Tendency Criticism" and even denied that the *Hauptbriefe* were written in the first century (*Kritik der paulinischen Briefe* [Berlin: Hempel, 1852]). He argued that since Galatians is so full of obscurities, contradictions, improbabilities, and non sequiturs, it could hardly have been written by Paul. Others of his day followed him, among whom were A. D. Loman, A. Pierson, S. A. Naber, Rudolf Steck, Daniel Volter, W. C. van Manen, C. H. Weisse, and Jacob Cramer (for diverse discussions of those denying authenticity, see E. deW. Burton, *Galatians*, lxix–lxxi; J. C. O'Neill, *Recovery*, 3–10). The twentieth century has also witnessed similar denials (e.g., L. G. Rylands, *A Critical Analysis of the Four Chief Pauline Epistles* [London: Watts, 1929]; F. R. McGuire, "Did Paul Write Galatians?" *HibJ* 66 [1967–68] 52–57). But such denials are widely considered today to be aberrations in the history of NT study, and rightly so.

J. C. O'Neill has lately revived both Bruno Bauer's criticisms and C. H. Weisse's interpolation theory, and so proposes that Galatians should be seen as a strictly anti-Judaic writing to which a number of glosses have been added (*Recovery*). Starting from the thesis that Paul was "a coherent, argumentative, pertinent Writer" who wrote with method, order, and clarity (ibid., 1–2), O'Neill identifies over thirty passages in Galatians that appear to him to be disparate from Paul's central anti-Judaic argument and assigns them to a later editor. The paraenetic section of 5:13–6:10, for example, which is the longest of the supposed interpolations, O'Neill believes "has nothing in particular to do with the urgent problem Paul was trying to meet in his original letter" (ibid., 67)—in fact, it shows quite clearly in its opposition to antinomianism that it has no vital connection with the concerns of the letter. As O'Neill sees it, "The present text of Galatians contains such obscurity, inconsequence, and contradiction that some solution must be found. If the choice lies between supposing that Paul was confused and contradictory and supposing that his text has been commented upon and enlarged, I have no hesitation in choosing the second" (ibid., 86). So O'Neill sets forth what he calls "an Old Approach": that Galatians consists of an original anti-Judaic writing by Paul to which has been added over thirty glosses at the time the letter was edited for publication, and that these later interpolations can be recognized by their disparate character.

The disparities that O'Neill sees in Galatians have, of course, been the building blocks for W. Lütgert and J. H. Ropes in their "Two-Front Theory" and for Walter Schmithals in his Jewish-Christian gnostic approach. Neither of these positions, however, is widely accepted today. Yet it must be said that Lütgert, Ropes, and Schmithals, each in his own way, have dealt with the data of Galatians in a much more responsible fashion than does O'Neill. For O'Neill simply dismisses the data on which their views are based, and then dismisses their positions because they are founded on passages he rejects. Later in our discussion of the opponents at Galatia, as well as at various places in the commentary proper, we will deal with the views of Lütgert, Ropes, and Schmithals. Suffice it here to say with Kümmel regarding O'Neill's position, "The older, frequently represented hypotheses of interpolation or compilation of Gal are nowadays scarcely discussed, and this is no doubt correct" (*Introduction to the New Testament*, rev. ed., tr. H. C. Kee [Nashville: Abingdon, 1975] 304).

2. Amanuensis

What, however, most commentators have not taken into account when dealing with the authorship of Galatians is the probable presence of an amanuensis in the composition of the letter—for that matter, of most, if not all, of the NT letters. The extant nonliterary Greek papyri, the bulk of which (some 40,000 to 60,000) were found during the 1890s in the Fayûm of Egypt, indicate quite clearly that an amanuensis or secretary was frequently, if not commonly, used in the writing of letters in the years before, during, and after the first Christian century. And there are reasons to believe that the writers of the NT followed this custom as well. Literary men of the day may have preferred, as did Quintilian (c. A.D. 35–95), not to use an amanuensis for their personal correspondence. Or they may have agreed with Cicero (106–43 B.C.) that dictation to a secretary was an expedient necessitated only by illness or the press of duties. But the papyrus materials show that the common practice for more ordinary men was to use an amanuensis to write out their letters, after which the sender himself would often, though not always, add in his own handwriting a word of farewell, his personal greetings, and the date (cf. my "Ancient Amanuenses," 281–97; idem, "On the Form," 101–14).

Writing skills among amanuenses undoubtedly varied. A third-century A.D. Latin payment schedule reads: "To a scribe for best writing, 100 lines, 25 denarii; for second-quality writing, 100 lines, 20 denarii; to a notary for writing a petition or legal document, 100 lines, 10 denarii" (*Edictum Diocletiani de pretiis rerum venalium*, col. vii, 39–41). The Greek biographer Plutarch (c. A.D. 46–120) credited Cicero (106–43 B.C.) with the invention of a system of Latin shorthand, relating how Cicero placed scribes in various locations in the senate chamber to record the speeches and taught them in advance "signs having the force of many letters in little and short marks" (*Parallel Lives* 23, on Cato the Younger)—though it may have been Tiro, the freedman of Cicero, who was actually the originator, for inventions of slaves were often credited to their masters. The reference by Seneca (4 B.C.–A.D. 65) to slaves having invented among their other notable accomplishments "signs for words, with which a speech is taken down, however rapid, and the hand follows the speed of the tongue" (*Ad Lucilium Epistulae Morales* 90.25) lends credence to Tiro, or someone like him, as the originator, and suggests that at least by A.D. 63–64, when Seneca's letters to Lucilius were written, a system of Latin shorthand was widely in use.

The earliest comparable evidence for a system of Greek shorthand is contained in POxy 724, dated March 1, A.D. 155 ("the fifth of Phamenouth in the eighteenth year of the emperor Titus Ailios Hadrian Antonius Augustus Eusebius"), wherein a former official of Oxyrhynchus by the name of Panechotes binds his slave Chaerammon to a stenographer named Apollonius for a term of two years in order to learn shorthand from him. Though Panechotes' letter is a second-century writing, the developed system of shorthand that it assumes (which Chaerammon was to take two years to learn) presupposes an earlier workable system of Greek shorthand, dating, at least, from the first Christian century, and probably earlier.

The extent of freedom that amanuenses had in drafting letters is impossible to determine from the evidence presently at hand. Undoubtedly it varied from case to case. Amanuenses may have written their clients' messages word for word or even syllable by syllable; they may have been given the sense of a message and left to work out the wording themselves; or they may have been asked to write on a particular subject in a sender's name without being given explicit directions as to how to develop the topic, especially if the sender felt his amanuensis already knew his mind on the matter. Scholarly opinion on this is sharply divided. Otto Roller, for example, believed that ancient amanuenses had a great deal of freedom and that dictation of a word for word variety was rare (*Das Formular*, 333), whereas F. R. M. Hitchcock drew exactly the opposite conclusion ("The Use of *graphein*," *JTS* 31 [1930] 273–74). But whatever method or methods may have been used in the writing of any particular letter, the sender usually added a personal subscription in his own hand, thereby attesting to all that was written. At times he even included in that subscription a resume of what had been said in the body of the letter, thereby acknowledging further the contents and highlighting some of its details.

Though we possess no autograph of any of the NT letters, it may be assumed that their authors followed current letter-writing conventions and so used amanuenses as well—though in these cases, the secretaries were probably more personal companions than trained scribes. In 2 Thess 3:17 Paul says that it was his practice to add a personal subscription to his letters in his own handwriting, thereby attesting to what was written and assuring his converts of the letter's authenticity. Such a statement is in line with the epistolary practice of the day and alerts us to the likely presence of other such subscriptions among his other letters, though it gives no guidance as to how to mark them off. Likewise, the words of 1 Cor 16:21 and Col 4:18 ("I, Paul, write this greeting in my own hand") suggest that the subscriptions were distinguishable in handwriting from the material that preceded— necessitating, of course, the involvement of an amanuensis in what preceded. The "I, Tertius, who wrote this letter in the Lord" of Rom 16:22 cannot be understood in any way other than that an amanuensis was involved to some extent in Paul's letter to Christians at Rome (or, as some suggest, to believers at Ephesus). And Gal 6:11, while allowing some uncertainty as to the precise extent of the reference, recalls certain features in the subscriptions of Greco-Roman letters when it declares "See what large letters I use as I write to you with my own hand!"

Philem 19 may also be the beginning of such a personal subscription: "I, Paul, am writing this with my own hand." Of the non-Pauline materials in the NT, 1 Peter and the Gospel of John are most plausibly seen as having been written by amanuenses. As George Milligan observed, "In the case of the First Epistle of St

Peter, indeed, this seems to be distinctly stated, for the words διὰ Σιλουανοῦ, 'by Silvanus,' in c. v.12, are best understood as implying that Silvanus was not only the bearer, but the actual scribe of the Epistle. And in the same way an interesting tradition, which finds pictorial representation in many mediaeval manuscripts of the Fourth Gospel, says that St. John dictated his Gospel to a disciple of his named Prochorus" (*Documents*, 22–23; cf. 160–61 and Plate V).

Just how closely Paul supervised his companions in their writing down of his letters is impossible from the data to say. As we have seen, the responsibilities of an amanuensis could vary, ranging all the way from taking dictation verbatim to "fleshing out" a general line of thought. Paul's own practice probably varied with the circumstances encountered and the companions available. Assuming, as Otto Roller proposed, that amanuenses were often identified in the salutations of letters (particularly if they were known to the addressees), more might be left to the discretion of Silas and Timothy (cf. 1 Thess 1:1, 2 Thess 1:1) or to Timothy alone (cf. 2 Cor 1:1; Col 1:1; Phil 1:1; Philem 1) than to Sosthenes (cf. 1 Cor 1:1) or Tertius (cf. Rom 16:22)—and perhaps much more to Luke, who is referred to as being the only one with Paul during his final imprisonment (cf. 2 Tim 4:11). Furthermore, if in one case Paul closely scrutinized and revised a letter, at another time he may have only read it over and allowed it to go out practically unaltered.

Later we will speak more extensively about the epistolary features of Galatians. Suffice it here to say that when we think of the authorship of Paul's letters we should probably also think of various companions of Paul acting as his secretaries and writing out the major portions of his letters at his direction. Perhaps Paul's secretary for the writing of Galatians was one of the "brothers" referred to in the salutation (1:2), and perhaps that secretary had more input into the composition than merely writing it down. On such matters we can only conjecture. What can be said with confidence, however, is (1) that Gal 6:11 implies a distinction between the handwriting of the subscription and that of the body of the letter, with the involvement of an amanuensis the most likely inference to be drawn, and (2) that the impassioned nature of Galatians suggests that Paul's secretary, whoever he was, did little in this letter either to moderate the apostle's expressions (e.g., 5:12) or to buffer his emotions.

Addressees

Bibliography

Betz, H. D. *Galatians*, 1–5. **Bruce, F. F.** "Galatian Problems. 2. North or South Galatians?" *BJRL* 52 (1970) 243–66. ———. *Galatians*, 3–18. **Burton, E. deW.** *Galatians*, xvii–xliv. **Fitzmyer, J. A.** "The Letter to the Galatians." In *JBC*, 2:236–46. **Hemer, C. J.** "Acts and Galatians Reconsidered." *Themelios* 2 (1977) 81–88. **Jones, A. H. M.** *The Cities of the Eastern Roman Provinces.* **Lake, K.** *The Earlier Epistles*, 253–65, 309–16. **Lightfoot, J. B.** *Galatians* (1890) 1–35. **Magie, D.** *Roman Rule in Asia Minor.* **Moffatt, J.** *Introduction*, 83–107. **Moreau, J.** *Die Welt der Kelten.* Stuttgart: Cotta, 1958. **Ramsay, W. M.** *The Church in the Roman Empire.* ———. *The Cities and Bishoprics.* ———. *St. Paul the Traveller.* ———. *Galatians.* **Robinson, J. A. T.** *Redating*, 55–57. **Stähelin, F.** *Geschichte der kleinasiatischen Galater.* **Stein, R. H.** "The Relationship of Galatians 2:1–10 and Acts 15:1–35: Two Neglected Arguments." *JETS* 17 (1974) 239–42.

Paul's letter to the Galatians is so called because it is addressed to "the churches in Galatia" (1:2), with those addressees later characterized as "foolish Galatians" (3:1). But who were the Galatians? Where did they come from? Were they Galatians ethnically, or were they called Galatians because they lived in the Roman province of Galatia? Where exactly in the province did they live? When in Paul's missionary endeavors were they evangelized, and what contacts did Paul have with them afterwards?

1. Celts, Gauls, Galatians

Greek writers commonly used Γαλάται (Galatians) and Κέλται or Κελτοί (Celts) interchangeably, as did Latin authors with *Celtae* (Celts), *Galli* (Gauls), and *Galatae* (Galatians). Originating in the Danube River basin of central Europe, the Celts migrated into Switzerland, southern Germany, and northern Italy, then into France and Britain, and finally southeastward into the Balkan peninsula and Asia Minor. In Britain they were most commonly known as Celts; in France as Gauls and their territory there as Gallia; in Asia Minor as Galatians and their region as Galatia or Gallograecia ("the land of the Greek-speaking Gauls").

The southeast migration of the Gauls and their settlement in Asia Minor took place in several stages. In 281 B.C., searching for new homelands, they ravaged Thrace, Macedonia, and Thessaly, but in 279 B.C. were stopped at Delphi from going further into the heartland of Greece. In 278–277 B.C. some 20,000 Gauls crossed the Hellespont into Asia Minor at the invitation of Nicomedes, king of Bithynia, who wanted to use them as mercenaries against his enemies. Settling around Ancyra, they menaced neighboring populations and came close to overrunning all of Asia Minor. About 232 B.C., after a series of battles, they were finally defeated by Attalus I, king of Pergamum, and confined to a region in northern Asia Minor bounded by Bithynia and Paphlagonia to the north, by Pontus to the east, by Phrygia to the west, and by Cappadocia and Lycaonia to the south—a region traversed by the rivers Halys and Sangarius. In 190 B.C. the Seleucid king Antiochus III was defeated by Rome at Magnesia, and in 189 B.C. Galatia shared the same fate as the rest of Asia Minor and came under Roman authority.

Governed by Rome, Galatia was at first classed a dependent kingdom. But though they had stood with Antiochus III against Rome, the Galatians came to appreciate the wisdom of being on good terms with Rome. So in 64 B.C., because of its friendship, Pompey rewarded Galatia by designating it a client kingdom. About 40 B.C., at the death of Deiotaros, king of Galatia, Mark Antony conferred the kingdom of Galatia, together with the eastern part of Paphlagonia, on Kastor, the son-in-law of Deiotaros, and gave to Amyntas, the able secretary of the late Deiotaros, a new kingdom made up of portions of Pisidia and Phrygia. But Kastor died in 36 B.C., and at his death eastern Paphlagonia was given to his brother, while Galatia was turned over to Amyntas, who also retained his Phrygio-Pisidian inheritance. In the same year Amyntas received as well a part of Pamphylia. Later, in order to bring together the separate territories of Galatia and Phrygio-Pisidia, Amyntas was given Lycaonia—or, at least, a large part of it. And after the battle of Actium, Augustus also gave him Cilicia Tracheia as a reward for his aid.

When in 25 B.C. Amyntas was killed in battle with the Homonades from northern Taurus, his kingdom was reorganized as a Roman province (*Provincia Galatia*) and governed by a praetorian legate (*legatus pro praetore*). It was also decreased somewhat in size, with the part of Pamphylia that Amyntas had controlled given back to Pamphylia and Cilicia Tracheia given to Archelaus. In 5 B.C., however, a large part of Paphlagonia to the north was added to Galatia, and three or four years later the province was extended farther to the northeast by the addition of some areas that had formerly belonged to Pontus—with this northeastern section of the province now being called, it seems, Pontus Galaticus, as distinguished from Pontus Polemonianus. Sometime shortly before or during the reign of Claudius (A.D. 41–54) the territory of the Homonades in northern Taurus became a part of Galatia as well.

In Paul's day the Roman province of Galatia stretched right through the heart of Asia Minor, from Pontus on the Black Sea to Pamphylia on the Mediterranean (cf. Pliny [A.D. 23–79], *Historia Naturalis* 5.147: "Galatia touches on Cabalia in Pamphylia"). The churches addressed by Paul, therefore, might theoretically have been located anywhere within these boundaries. The question is: Were these churches situated in the old ethnic region of the original Galatian tribal lands in northern Asia Minor, where Ancyra, Pessinus, and Tavium were the chief cities, or were they located somewhere else in the province, perhaps in "Phrygia Galatica" where Antioch and Iconium were prominent cities and "Lycaonia Galatica" where Lystra and Derbe were villages? (Reference to "Phyrgia Galatica" and "Lycaonia Galatica" is by way of analogy with "Pontus Galatica," which is known to have been an official Roman designation.) The former view is what is called the North Galatian hypothesis. It takes Acts 16:6 and 18:23 as allusions to Paul's ministry there. The latter is the South Galatian hypothesis. It sees Acts 13:14–14:23 as an account of the establishment of the Galatian churches and Acts 16:6 and 18:23 as referring to Paul's further visits in the same area.

In addition to Gal 1:2; 3:1 and Acts 16:6; 18:23, references to Galatia or the Galatian churches appear in the NT at 1 Cor 16:1; 2 Tim 4:10; and 1 Peter 1:1. 1 Cor 16:1 undoubtedly has in mind the same churches as addressed in Galatians, with their location dependent on what is decided regarding the addressees of Paul's Galatian letter. 2 Tim 4:10 is not readily identifiable, and its significance is complicated by the variant reading Γαλλίαν for Γαλατίαν. 1 Peter 1:1 seems to denote the province in general, since it is associated with the other Anatolian provinces of Pontus, Cappadocia, Asia, and Bithynia.

2. North and South Galatian Hypotheses

It is hardly surprising that patristic, medieval, and Reformation commentators assumed that Galatians was written to Christians of Gaulish or Celtic descent whose churches were located in northern Asia Minor. About A.D. 74 Vespasian detached almost all of Pisidia from Galatia, and about A.D. 137 Lycaonia Galatica was removed from Galatia and joined to Cilicia and Isaurica to form an enlarged province of Cilicia. Then about A.D. 297 southern Galatia was united with various adjoining regions to become the new province of Pisidia, with Antioch its capital and Iconium its second city. So with the province of Galatia reduced to its original ethnological dimensions, early commentators generally assumed that Paul's addressees were located there. Only Asterius (d. A.D. 340), Bishop of Amaseia in Pontus, seems to have thought differently, for he identified "the Galatic region and Phrygia" of Acts 18:23 as "Lycaonia and the cities of Phrygia" (*Homilia VIII in SS. Petrum et Paulum* [*PG* 40:293D]). But there is no evidence that this identification was made by anyone else—though Ramsay saw in Asterius's statement a persisting, yet admittedly scantily attested, South Galatian tradition ("The 'Galatia' of St. Paul and the 'Galatic Territory' of Acts," in *Studia Biblica et Ecclesiastica* IV [Oxford: Clarendon, 1896] 16ff.). In fact, until the nineteenth century the North Galatian hypothesis held the field almost unchallenged. Besides Asterius, the only exceptions seem to have been (1) John Calvin, who assumed a North Galatian view but understood Galatians to have been written before the Jerusalem Council and equated Gal 2:1–10 with the famine visit of Acts 11:30 (on such a combination of views, Bruce muses: "One wonders when he supposed the evangelization of North Galatia to have taken place" [*Galatians*, 7]), and (2) J. J. Schmidt, who in 1748 advocated what might be called a Pan-Galatian hypothesis. Calvin, however, never meant his statements as a challenge to the traditional view of his day; and a Pan-Galatian hypothesis, though accepted by such nineteenth-century scholars as J. P. Mynster, R. Cornely, E. Jacquier, and (for a time) T. Zahn, never really got off the ground.

J. B. Lightfoot in 1865 summed up the classical North Galatian hypothesis in definitive fashion, arguing that "Galatia" in both Paul's letter and Luke's Acts should be understood in an ethnic and not a political sense, and that therefore Paul wrote to the churches of Ancyra, Pessinus, Tavium, and (perhaps) Juliopolis, the first three being cities of North Galatia (Juliopolis was in Bithynia), on his third missionary journey (as depicted in Acts) sometime around A.D. 57–58 from Macedonia or Achaia, after having written 1 and 2 Corinthians but before writing to Christians at Rome (cf. *Galatians*, 18–56). Lightfoot built his case as follows:

1. That since both Paul and Luke commonly use popular, geographical, and ethnic language when referring to people and regions, and not official, provincial, or political designations, we should understand "Galatia" in Gal 1:2; 3:1 and Acts 16:6; 18:23 as referring not to the Roman province of that name but to the land of the Gauls and the people of that name;
2. That Paul's account of a second visit to Jerusalem in Gal 2:1–10 most likely is to be correlated with Luke's portrayal of the Jerusalem Council in Acts 15;
3. That Acts 16:6 and 18:23 speak of two visits of Paul to Galatia, with the language of these verses suggesting that the Galatia in question is beyond Lycaonia and not to be equated with the cities of southern Galatia;
4. That Paul's allusion to two visits in Gal 4:13 (cf. τὸ πρότερον) fits nicely the situation suggested by Acts 16:6 and 18:23;
5. That it would be strange for Paul, in trying to regain their allegiance, to address Christians of Phrygia and Lycaonia as Galatians, when, in fact, they were not Galatians ethnically but only so politically under Roman rule;
6. That various ancient authors have referred to the Gauls as a fickle and super-stitious people (esp. Caesar, *De Bello Gallico* 2.1; 4.5; 6.16; Cicero, *De Divinatione* 1.5; 2.36–37), which is how Paul characterizes his addressees as well; and
7. That the style and subject matter of Paul's letter to the Galatians is very compatible with letters known to have been written on Paul's third missionary journey, particularly with the tone of 2 Corinthians (which it follows) and the content of Romans (which it precedes).

But while Lightfoot is to be credited with giving definitive expression to the classical form of the North Galatian hypothesis, there are contemporary forms of the position that must be taken into account as well. Chief among these is that of

Introduction

James Moffatt, who in 1911 set out the position in a way most commonly held today (*Introduction*, 83–107).

While agreeing with Lightfoot's overall conclusions and his major supporting arguments, Moffatt discounted as irrelevant Lightfoot's stress on (1) the fickleness of the Gauls, and (2) affinities between Galatians and the other *Hauptbriefe*. Likewise, in part because of his refusal to base any argument on relative order among the *Hauptbriefe*, Moffatt disagreed with Lightfoot on matters of provenance and date (i.e., from Macedonia or Achaia, about A.D. 57–58), preferring rather to argue from the "so quickly" (οὕτως ταχέως) of Gal 1:6 that the letter was probably written from Ephesus soon after Paul left Galatia a second time (Acts 18:23)—so somewhere around A.D. 53, a few years before the composition of the other *Hauptbriefe*. Furthermore, still influenced by Paul's οὕτως ταχέως, Moffatt suggested that the letter's recipients were probably located in the western part of Galatia and not around its capital Ancyra and the cities Pessinus and Tavium, as Lightfoot thought. On this latter point, however, most North Galatianists today prefer to remain uncommitted.

As Moffatt saw it, the major objections to a South Galatian view are:

1. That "it arbitrarily makes the burning question of circumcision for Gentile Christians emerge in an acute shape some time before the period of Acts 15—a view for which there is no evidence in Acts and against which the probabilities of the general situation tell heavily" (ibid., 92);
2. That "it involves the incredible idea that Paul circumcised Timotheus (Acts 16:3) after he had written Gal 5:2" (ibid., 92);
3. That "if Luke had viewed Derbe, Lystra, and the rest of Paul's earlier mission field as belonging to Γαλατία proper, it is inexplicable why the name should not occur in Acts 13–14" (ibid., 93);
4. That "Derbe and Lystra belonged to Lykaonia (Acts 14:6, 11), not to Phrygia, so that the South Galatian view, that Acts 16:6 is recapitulatory, breaks down at the outset" (ibid., 93);
5. That "if the opening of the South Galatian mission is so fully described in Acts 13–14, why is there no mention of the illness which Paul specially mentions in Gal 4:13?" (ibid., 99);
6. That "the Galatians received Paul ὡς ἄγγελον θεοῦ, ὡς Χριστὸν Ἰησοῦν (Gal 4:14), in spite of his illness—a very different thing from hailing him in full health as the pagan Hermes (Acts 14:12)" (ibid., 99);
7. That "there is not a hint in the epistle of any persecution or suffering endured by him in his evangelisation of Galatia, whereas his South Galatian mission was stormy in the extreme (Acts 13–14, 2 Tim 3:11)" (ibid., 99); and,
8. That "if Paul had evangelised S. Galatia prior to the Council, it is not easy to understand why he did not say so in Gal 1:21" (ibid., 99; which objection, of course, assumes a "classical" South Galatian view of provenance and date).

More significantly, Moffatt's main reasons for accepting a North Galatian view are as follows:

1. That the comparative πρότερον, "former," of Gal 4:13 indicates that "Paul had visited the Galatian churches twice," and this fact corresponds nicely with Acts 16:6 and 18:23 (ibid., 84);

2. That the expressions τὴν Φρυγίαν καὶ Γαλατικὴν χώραν, "the country of Phrygia and Galatia," of Acts 16:6 and τὴν Γαλατικὴν χώραν καὶ Φρυγίαν, "the country of Galatia and Phrygia," of Acts 18:23 must be understood as popular and geographical terms that denote "not one district but two," and so cannot be equivalent to Phrygia-Galatia (ibid., 93); and

3. That because the purposes of the visits are the same, "the identity of Gal 2:1–10 with Acts 15 must be maintained" (ibid.,100).

In opposition to a North Galatian view, W. M. Ramsay, in a number of books and articles published in the 1890s (e.g., *The Church in the Roman Empire*; *The Cities and Bishoprics*; *St Paul the Traveller*; *Galatians*), set out a South Galatian view. Earlier, J. J. Schmidt in 1748 and J. P. Mynster in 1825, arguing a "Pan-Galatian" position, held that the churches of South Galatia as presented in Acts 13–14 are included among those addressed by Paul in his letter (cf. W. G. Kümmel, *Introduction to the New Testament*, tr. A. J. Mattill, Jr. [London: SCM, 1965] 192). But their view failed to do justice to the evident homogeneity among the churches addressed and raised more difficulties than it solved. The first scholar, in fact, to propose a distinctly South Galatian position was Georges Perrot in 1867 (*De Galatia provincia Romana* [Paris: 1867] 43–44), whose views were adopted by Ernest Renan in 1869 (*Saint Paul*, Bk. III: *The History of the Origins of Christianity* [London: Mathieson, 1869] 24–26, 63–64, 169–73). It was, however, W. M. Ramsay who did the original historical research on the question and who presented the South Galatian hypothesis in its definitive form.

Ramsay's treatment of the Galatian question began by focusing on "the history and character of the people, and the geography of the country" (*Galatians*, 6). It is impossible here to summarize his data or to marshall all his arguments. Most important for our purposes are the following three conclusions:

1. That "so early as the second century B.C. the Phrygian origin of the larger half of the Galatian population [in northern Asia Minor] was forgotten by ordinary people of the surrounding countries; and the whole state was thought of as Galatia and its people Galatians" (ibid., 84);

2. That when Galatia was expanded and became a province in 25 B.C., this became true as well for people in the south, for "the status of each non-Roman person in the Empire was that of a 'provincial'; and he was designated as a member of the Roman Empire, not by his nation, but by his Province" (ibid., 119); and

3. That since foreigners, enemies, and slaves were related ideas in Roman theory, any courteous orator or writer would certainly not address Antiocheans as Phrygians or Lystrans as Lycaonians—particularly, though not only, if there were Roman citizens among them—but "would designate them either as *Galatae*, i.e., members of the Roman empire as being members of the Province Galatia, or as *Coloni*, citizens of Roman *Coloniae*, which would have been an even more honorific term" (ibid., 120).

Then turning to Galatians and its relation to Acts, Ramsay argued:

1. That Paul's visit to Jerusalem of Gal 2:1–10 is not to be correlated with the Jerusalem Council of Acts 15, for their purposes are quite different and their

descriptions too disparate, but should be identified with the famine visit of Acts 11:30 (ibid., 293–301);

2. That "Paul writes as a Roman and a citizen of the Empire," and so in all his letters "never uses wide geographical names except those of Roman provinces" (ibid., 314; also 147–64 and 314–21; idem, *St. Paul the Traveller*, passim); and,

3. That Luke, who generally follows popular, geographical, and colloquial usage, would never as a Greek of the educated class use "Galatia" to denominate the Roman province, but would speak of geographical regions or ethnic groupings within a province (as he does in Acts 13–14 of "Pisidia," "Phrygia" and "Lycaonia") or would use some such buffer expression as "the Galatic Eparchy"—as he does in Acts 16:6 and 18:23 when he writes τὴν Γαλατικὴν χώραν (ibid., 315–16).

Thus Ramsay argued that when Paul speaks of the Galatians (Gal 1:2; 3:1) he means the four churches in the south of the province of Galatia and that when Luke refers to "the Galatic territory" (Acts 16:6; 18:23) he means quite specifically provincial Galatia as opposed to ethnic Galatia.

On the related issues of when and where the Galatian letter was written, Ramsay assumed in his earlier writings a date of A.D. 50 and a provenance somewhere on Paul's second missionary journey—that is, shortly after the visit of Acts 16:6, with "the former" (τὸ πρότερον) visit referred to in Gal 4:13 being that depicted in Acts 13–14. This, of course, raised the question as to why Paul in Galatians did not mention a third visit to Jerusalem (i.e., the Jerusalem Council visit of Acts 15), and Ramsay found that question somewhat difficult. Usually he answered that it was because reference to a third visit was beside the point of Paul's argument. He also suggested that this Jerusalem visit found no place in Paul's letter simply because it occurred after the Galatian churches were founded and Paul's point in Gal 1–2 is that the Jerusalem apostles gave him no directions when he *first* brought the gospel to Galatia. Later, however, feeling the thrust of this objection, Ramsay revised his views as to date and provenance to argue that Galatians was written just prior to the Jerusalem Council of Acts 15 and probably from Antioch in Syria (see his *The Teaching of Paul*, 372–92; also the preface added to the 14th edition of *St. Paul the Traveller and Roman Citizen* [London: Hodder & Stoughton, 1920], which is not included in the American reprint of 1962 taken from the 3rd edition of 1897)—so making Galatians the earliest of Paul's extant letters.

In effect, then, the South Galatian hypothesis (as is true also for the North Galatian hypothesis) appears in two forms: what might be called the classical form of the earlier Ramsay—that is, to churches of South Galatia, written about A.D. 50 on Paul's second missionary journey—and the contemporary form of the later Ramsay—that is, to churches of South Galatia, written prior to the Jerusalem Council, about A.D. 49, from Syrian Antioch. E. deW. Burton was one of the most able supporters of the first. After exegetical surveys of the data he argued:

1. That "the evidence of the Pauline epistles is, therefore, decidedly more favourable to a uniformly Roman use of geographical terms by the apostle and the view that by Galatia he means both in 1 Cor 16:1 and Gal 1:2, the Roman province, than to a mixed usage such as is found, for example in Acts" (*Galatians*, xxvii);

lxviii   INTRODUCTION

2. That it does not seem possible to suggest any other name for the churches of southern Galatia that would have been inclusive enough for Paul's purpose, for "if the churches addressed were those of Derbe, Lystra, Iconium, and Antioch, which he founded on his first missionary journey, he could not well address their members by any single term except Galatians" (ibid., xxix); and

3. That the Greek of Acts 16:6 and 18:23 must be read as referring not to two localities but to one, that is to "the Phrygic-Galatic territory," for "the joining of the words Φρυγίαν and Γαλατικήν by καί, with the article before the first one only, implies that the region designated by χώρα is one, Phrygian and Galatian" (ibid., xxxii).

F. F. Bruce has been the most prolific supporter of the contemporary form of the South Galatian hypothesis (see *The Acts of the Apostles: The Greek Text with Introduction and Commentary* [Grand Rapids: Eerdmans, 1951]; *The Book of Acts: The English Text with Introduction, Exposition, and Notes* [NICNT; Grand Rapids: Eerdmans, 1954]; *BJRL* 52 [1970] 243–66; *Paul: Apostle of the Heart Set Free*; *Galatians*).

3. Some Observations on the Question of Destination

Modern discussions of the North and South Galatian hypotheses are often not concerned with the historical merits of the case, nor even as seriously interested in the exegetical issues as they once were. Rather, the discussions today are usually carried on in terms of internal chronological considerations alone—principally in terms of where Gal 2:1–10 fits in the life of Paul and vis-à-vis his visits to Jerusalem as given in Acts. Many, in fact, simply call the historical and exegetical considerations "mostly speculative" (e.g., H. D. Betz, *Galatians*, 5). But the issue of destination is too important for such a cavalier attitude. We will deal later with Gal 2:1–10 and the question of establishing a relative chronology. Here, however, since we believe that historical and exegetical matters regarding the addressees must be treated first, we want to make some observations with regard to destination. Following that, we will suggest some biographical indices of importance for identifying the letter's recipients.

Certain caveats, however, are in order before proceeding further. First of all it need be recognized that though the question has important historical, exegetical, and interpretive ramifications, the deriving of either doctrinal insight or spiritual benefit from Paul's letter to the Galatians is not dependent on a final solution as to provenance. Furthermore, it must be insisted that it is impossible to correlate positions taken on this matter with the theological stances of the various interpreters, whether liberal or conservative. Lightfoot as a North Galatianist and Ramsay and Burton as South Galatianists, for example, never intended such a correlation, and neither have their more able supporters. Likewise, it must be said that there is no necessary correlation between an acceptance of a South Galatian position and a high estimate of the historical reliability of Acts, or between a North Galatian view and a more skeptical view of Acts. Ramsay and Burton, both South Galatianists, varied in their opinions of Acts. R. H. Fuller, who adopts a southern Galatian destination for Paul's letter, has a low view of the historical accuracy of Acts (*Introduction*, 23–26), whereas J. G. Machen, H. N. Ridderbos, E. F. Harrison, and R. H. Stein have accepted a North Galatian hypothesis coupled with great respect for Acts (see J. G. Machen, *Machen's Notes*, 86–94; H. N. Ridderbos, *The Epistle of Paul to the Churches of Galatia*; E. F. Harrison, *Introduction*, 257–64; R. H. Stein, *JETS* 17 [1974] 239–42).

What, then, can be said regarding the Galatian question? The issues are notoriously complex, and every interpreter weighs the data somewhat differently. For my part, I find some of the arguments both pro and con ambiguous, inconclusive, or faulty. For example:

1. That northern Galatia was more inaccessible to Paul than southern Galatia—which disregards the Roman road system and would be a problem only if Paul were a tourist and not an evangelist;
2. That people of northern Galatia were culturally more impoverished and religiously less open to Paul's message than those of southern Galatia— which disregards the mixing of populations, cultures, and religions in both areas and assumes a knowledge of what constitutes a proper prolegomenon for the Christian gospel;
3. That Jews would have been present in the churches of the south, but were not living in the north—which is patently false;
4. That Paul's missionary strategy was to concentrate on the main cities of the empire, and so he would have gone to cities of the south rather than to those of the north—which ignores the insignificance of Lystra and Derbe in the south compared to Ancrya and Pessinus in the north and forces on Paul a policy that even Acts suggests was not always the case;
5. That affinities between Galatians and the other Pauline *Hauptbriefe* require all of them to have been written in the same period of missionary activity— which is denied by many North Galatianists today and can be explained in other ways;
6. That the Gauls of northern Galatia were fickle and superstitious, qualities that conform to Paul's characterization of his addressees—which is a selective reading of history, relegating such rather common human characteristics to only one people;
7. That the delegation of Acts 20:4 had representatives from southern Galatia (Gaius and Timothy), but none from northern Galatia—which is interesting, but inconclusive;
8. That Luke's interest in Acts is primarily, if not exclusively, in Paul's mission in the south of the Galatian province—which, again, is interesting but not conclusive;
9. That the omission in Acts of Paul's sickness mentioned in Gal 4:13 and the omission in Galatians of any reference to being stoned at Lystra as reported in Acts 14:19 speak against equating the people of the south with the recipients of the letter; and,
10. That Paul's statement of Gal 4:14 that the Galatians at first received him as an "angel of God" carries some remembrance of the Lystran reception of Barnabas and Paul as Zeus and Hermes (Acts 14:11–13), or that his closing words in Gal 6:17, "I bear in my body the marks of the Lord Jesus," has some reference to his being stoned at Lystra (Acts 14:19).

Ultimately, determination as to the Galatian addressees boils down to three sets of issues: historical issues, exegetical issues, and chronological issues. The latter of these will be dealt with in the section to follow. The first two, however, must be commented on here. It is, however, quite impossible in the space available to reproduce the data or to represent adequately the argumentation involved, and so we must refer the reader to those who have done so, as cited above.

For my part, I consider W. M. Ramsay's research on the historical issues convincing in the main: that from 25 B.C. to at least A.D. 74, the Roman province of Galatia included the cities of Paul's first missionary journey (Acts 13:14–14:23); that non-Romans in the Galatian province would have been known and addressed by Romans by their provincial designation and not by their race; and that "Paul writes as a Roman and a citizen of the Empire," and so addresses his Galatian converts by their official, provincial name, whereas Luke generally follows popular, geographical, and colloquial usage (see esp. Ramsay's *St. Paul the Traveller*, passim, and *Galatians*, 1–234). On the exegetical issues, I find Burton's treatment of the data most responsible, and repeat his conclusions here for emphasis:

1. That "the evidence of the Pauline epistles is, therefore, decidedly more favourable to a uniformly Roman use of geographical terms by the apostle and the view that by Galatia he means both in 1 Cor 16:1 and Gal 1:2, the Roman province, than to a mixed usage such as is found, for example, in Acts";
2. That it does not seem possible to suggest any other name for the churches of southern Galatia that would have been inclusive enough for Paul's purpose, for "if the churches addressed were those of Derbe, Lystra, Iconium, and Antioch, which he founded on his first missionary journey, he could not well address their members by any single term except Galatians"; and,
3. That the Greek of Acts 16:6 and 18:23 must be read as referring not to two localities but to one, that is "the Phrygic-Galatic territory," for "the joining of the words Φρυγίαν and Γαλατικήν by καί, with the article before the first one only, implies that the region designated χώρα is one, Phrygian and Galatian" (*Galatians*, xxv–xliv).

So on the basis of historical and exegetical considerations, I conclude in favor of a South Galatian understanding of the letter's addressees.

4. Biographical Indices of Importance

In addition to such matters, there are a number of biographical and theological indices in the Galatian letter that, while they cannot establish a case on their own, serve to substantiate a South Galatian position arrived at for more basic reasons. Later in discussing a relative chronology for Paul's correspondence and the date of the Galatian letter I will suggest some theological indices. Here, however, I want to mention four biographical indices that have some bearing on the question.

Our first biographical index has to do with Timothy. This may seem strange, for Timothy does not appear in the letter at all. Nevertheless, he has a bearing on the discussion by the very fact that he is not mentioned. Like the incident in the Sherlock Holmes story of the dog that did not bark in the night, this silence is a curious fact that may speak louder than many other pieces of evidence in the case.

According to Acts, Timothy was a more or less constant companion of Paul from Lystra at the start of Paul's second missionary journey (Acts 16:1–4) through to Paul's final trip to Jerusalem (Acts 20:4). Even if we disregard Acts and confine ourselves to the evidence from Paul's letters alone, a similar picture emerges: Timothy was actively involved in Paul's missionary activities (cf. 1 Thess 1:1; 3:1, 6; 2 Thess 1:1; 1 Cor 4:17; 16:10; 2 Cor 1:1, 19; Rom 16:21) and present with Paul during his imprisonment(s) (cf. Phil 1:1; 2:19; Col 1:1; Philem 1). In fact, with the exception of Ephesians and Titus, Timothy is mentioned in every Pauline letter but Galatians.

Now if the recipients of the Galatian letter were residents of northern Galatia, it must be assumed that Timothy was as involved in their evangelization as he was in the founding of churches in the provinces of Asia, Macedonia, and Achaia. Yet Paul does not mention him in Galatians. And that failure to mention Timothy (also, of course, Silas, though without as strong circumstantial support), along with his repeated references to Barnabas, argues strongly against a North Galatian hypothesis. Not only so, but it also speaks against the classical form of the South Galatian hypothesis (which places the writing of Galatians after Acts 16:6), for it is virtually unthinkable that Paul would have addressed a letter to Christians in an area that included Lystra without sending news or making any mention of their native son. Thus the absence of Timothy in Galatians is strong circumstantial evidence in favor of the view that Paul wrote before Timothy joined the missionary party and that the addressees of the letter lived in the southern portion of the province—necessitating that (to anticipate a later discussion) the letter was sent before Paul made his return trip to the region as recounted in Acts 16:1–5.

A second biographical index concerns Barnabas, who is mentioned three times in Galatians (2:1, 9, 13). The fact that Barnabas is the main Pauline associate referred to in the letter may be taken as presumptive evidence that he was known to the addressees—that is, to those evangelized by Paul and Barnabas on the mission to southern Galatia of Acts 13–14. Admittedly, (1) these references to Barnabas occur in the course of Paul's account of events at Jerusalem and Syrian Antioch, without any direct reference made to Barnabas' being in Galatia, and (2) Barnabas is referred to in 1 Cor 9:6 without any necessary suggestion that he had ever been at Corinth. It is, however, not just the fact of Paul's mention of Barnabas in Galatians that is significant, but the manner of his reference to him, particularly in 2:13.

North Galatianists, of course, often correlate Gal 2:11–14 with the rift between Paul and Barnabas reported in Acts 15:36–41, and so understand the former as Paul's version of what led to the breakup of the missionary team after the Jerusalem Council. But it is extremely difficult to believe that shortly after the Jerusalem Council Barnabas would have so given in to these "men from James" as to undercut the decision of the council itself. On the other hand, it is quite possible that sometime before the council Barnabas vacillated in his actions at Syrian Antioch and inadvertently became involved in a damaging compromise—or, as Paul viewed it, in "hypocrisy." Though standing with Paul on the legitimacy of a direct mission to Gentiles during their work in southern Galatia, he may have become uncertain when he returned to Syrian Antioch regarding law observance for Jewish Christians and table fellowship of Jews with Gentiles. So when Paul writes that "even Barnabas" (καὶ Βαρναβᾶς) was led astray, that would have been very meaningful to those who knew him well in southern Galatia and understandable before the Jerusalem Council. But to those of northern Galatia, Paul's "even Barnabas" comment would have seemed strange and Barnabas' defection after the council difficult to imagine.

Titus is mentioned in Gal 2:1–5 as having accompanied Paul and Barnabas on their second visit to Jerusalem, and as there having become something of a test case.

On a North Galatian view, this took place at the Jerusalem Council and Titus was one of the "some other believers" (τινὰς ἄλλους ἐξ αὐτῶν) of Acts 15:2. There is much in this account that must be reserved for our discussion in the commentary proper, particularly the textual issue in v 5 as to whether Paul and Barnabas did or did not give in to the demand of the stricter Jewish Christians. If they did give in to such a request, of course, even though not by compulsion, it becomes difficult to square Paul's words with the portrayal of Acts 15. But whether they did or did not, it is hard to believe that pressure for the circumcision of a single individual would have been mounted in the midst of a meeting called to deal with the whole issue of Jewish-Gentile relations. One would have thought that the principles involved would have been treated first and a decision reached before demands for the circumcision of a particular person were made—and, further, that with such a decision as reported in Acts 15:19–29, such a demand on Titus would never have been made. On the other hand, it is understandable that a conservative party of Jewish Christians might have decided at the time of the famine visit (Acts 11:30) to make Titus a test case. Thus the reference to Titus in Galatians provides us with a third biographical index of pertinence to the question of the letter's destination, and suggests—though, assuredly, does not demand—a South Galatian understanding.

A fourth biographical index that can be cited has to do with Peter, and particularly Paul's depiction of him in the Antioch episode of Gal 2:11–14. We know next to nothing of Peter's travels and activities apart from Acts, and even in Acts the picture is too hazy and imprecise to be of much use as a chronological index in resolving the Galatian question. What we can be certain of, however, is that Peter was an active participant in the Jerusalem Council. And while it is often claimed that his action in the Antioch affair is understandable when Gal 2:11–14 is seen as occurring after the council, it is much more understandable as having taken place before the council and as having been part of the controversy that precipitated it.

Other resolutions of the North-South Galatian quandary, of course, are possible, for the historical, exegetical, and biographical factors have been evaluated differently by various scholars. But not every possibility is a probability. And we believe that the balance of probability favors a South Galatian hypothesis.

Such a position, of course, leaves certain exegetical issues yet unresolved. For example, what is the significance of τὸ πρότερον in Gal 4:13? Is this temporal adverb used as a true comparative (i.e., the former of two visits) or is it to be understood simply in the sense of the first of a series (i.e., "previously")? And if a comparative, does it have in mind the visit of Acts 16:6 (with the latter being that of Acts 18:23), or the visit of Acts 13:14–14:23 (with the latter being that of Acts 16:6), or the eastward journey from Antioch to Derbe of Acts 13:14–14:21a (with the latter being the westward return summarized in Acts 13:21b–23)? Furthermore, such a position needs to be integrated with matters having to do with chronology. Thus we must deal with the question of date in the following section, as well as with related exegetical issues in their appropriate places in the commentary proper.

DATE

Bibliography

Beare, F. W. "The Sequence of Events in Acts 9–15 and the Career of Peter." *JBL* 62 (1943) 295–306. **Betz, H. D.** "Geist, Freiheit und Gesetz: Die Botschaft des Paulus an die Gemeinden in Galatien." *ZTK* 71 (1974) 78–93. ————. "In Defense of the Spirit: Paul's Letter to the Galatians as a Document of Early Christian Apologetics." In *Aspects of Religious Propaganda in Judaism and Early Christianity*, ed. E. Schüssler Fiorenza. Notre Dame, IN: University of Notre Dame Press, 1976. 99–114. ————. *Galatians*, 9–12. **Bruce, F. F.** *Galatians*, 43–56. **Buck, C. H.** "The Date of Galatians." *JBL* 70 (1951) 113–22. **Buck, C. H.**, and **Taylor, G.** *Saint Paul*, 82–102. **Burton, E. deW.** *Galatians*, xliv–liii. **Caird, G. B.** "Chronology of the NT." *IDB*, 1:599–607. **Campbell, T. H.** "Paul's 'Missionary Journeys' as Reflected in His Letters." *JBL* 74 (1955) 80–87. **Drane, J. W.** *Paul, Libertine or Legalist?* 140–43. **Duncan, G. S.** *Galatians*, xxi–xxxii. **Funk, R. W.** "The Enigma of the Famine Visit." *JBL* 75 (1956) 130–36. **Hurd, J. C.** *The Origin of 1 Corinthians*. 12–42. ————. "Pauline Chronology and Pauline Theology." In *Christian History and Interpretation*. FS J. Knox, ed. W. R. Farmer, C. F. D. Moule, and R. R. Niebuhr. Cambridge: Cambridge University Press, 1967. 225–48. **Jewett, R.** *Chronology*. **Knox, J.** *Chapters*. **Lake, K.** *The Earlier Epistles*. 265–304. **Lightfoot, J. B.** *Galatians* (1890), 36–56. **Luedemann, G.** *Paul*, 44–80, 90–92. **Machen, J. G.** *Machen's Notes*, 86–94. **Ramsay, W. M.** *The Teaching of Paul*, 372–92. **Robinson, J. A. T.** *Redating*, 55–57. **Round, D.** *The Date*. **Sanday, W.** "The Early Visits of St. Paul to Jerusalem." *Exp*, 5th series, 3 (1896) 253–63. **Stein, R. H.** "The Relationship of Galatians 2:1–10 and Acts 15:1–35: Two Neglected Arguments." *JETS* 17 (1974) 239–42. **Talbert, C. H.** "Again: Paul's Visits to Jerusalem." *NovT* 9 (1967) 26–40.

It is impossible to discuss the date of Galatians without taking into account the question of the letter's destination (as we have attempted to do above). Yet destination does not necessarily determine date. Most North Galatianists posit that the letter was written on Paul's third missionary journey (if the framework of Acts is accepted), sometime between A.D. 53 and 58—though Betz suggests between A.D. 50 and 55 (*Galatians*, 9–12). Most South Galatianists view it as having been written either during the early part of Paul's second missionary journey sometime around A.D. 49–50, or after Paul's first missionary journey but before the Jerusalem Council in A.D. 49—though Burton thought A.D. 53–54 to be most likely (*Galatians*, xliv–liii), and Robinson suggests about A.D. 56 (*Redating*, 55–57, citing E. H. Askwith, *The Epistle to the Galatians* [1899]). Without a doubt, the date of Galatians is one of the most knotty problems in Pauline studies. It is not, however, an incidental problem or one that can be ignored. Because the letter deals with such important matters as the salvation of Gentiles apart from the Jewish law and relationships between Paul and the Jerusalem church, one's view as to date has wide-ranging implications for one's understanding of Paul's theology and the reconstruction of the history of early Christianity.

1. Paul's Jerusalem Visits in Galatians and Acts

Any attempt to establish a chronology for Paul and to date Galatians must begin with Paul's own statements in Gal 1–2. This is not merely because priority must be given to primary sources (Paul's own letters) over secondary sources (Luke's Acts), but because Paul writes under oath (Gal 1:20) and any slip or dissimulation would have played into the hands of his opponents. Historiographically speaking, Paul's statements in Gal 1–2 are the most important in the entire NT.

In Galatians Paul speaks of two visits, and only two, which he made as a Christian to Jerusalem: a visit three years after his conversion, in 1:18–20; and a visit "fourteen years later," in 2:1–10 (Paul speaks of a third visit, the collection visit, in Rom 15:25–33, 1 Cor 16:1–4, and 2 Cor 1:16). Five visits to Jerusalem, however, are given in Acts, which may conveniently be labeled (1) the conversion visit, 9:26–30;

(2) the famine visit, 11:27–30; (3) the Jerusalem Council, 15:1–30; (4) the hasty visit, 18:22 (while the name "Jerusalem" does not appear in 18:22, Jerusalem is certainly implied by the absolute use of "the church" [τὴν ἐκκλησίαν] and the expressions "went up" [ἀναβάς] and "went down" [κατέβη]; and (5) the collection visit, 21:15–17. Six Jerusalem visits may be seen in Acts if εἰς Ἰερουσαλήμ of 12:25 is accepted; but though εἰς is better attested externally, scholars usually conclude on the basis of internal factors that ἐξ Ἰερουσαλήμ was the original reading (see my "The Acts of the Apostles," in *The Expositor's Bible Commentary*, 9:417). Most find little difficulty in identifying Gal 1:18–20 with Acts 9:26–30. The problem has to do with Gal 2:1–10 vis-à-vis the visits of Acts.

A number of positions on this question have been taken. C. H. Talbert lists seven (*NovT* 9 [1967] 26 n. 3), to which can be added the view of D. R. Delacey that Gal 2:1–10 is the conversion visit of Acts 9:26–30 and that Luke did not know of the visit of Gal 1:18–20 (*NTS* 20 [1983] 82–86). The following five options, however, are the most viable and important:

1. That Gal 2:1–10 is the Jerusalem Council visit of Acts 15:1–30, with the famine visit of Acts 11:27–30 left unrelated to the question or seen as unimportant for Paul's polemic in Galatians. This is the traditional view that held the field virtually unchallenged until the early twentieth century. Only John Calvin, it seems, demurred in identifying Gal 2:1–10 with Acts 11:27–30, though without defense (see his *Commentary on Galatians*, tr. T. H. L. Parker [Grand Rapids: Eerdmans, 1965] 24, commenting on Gal 2:1).
2. That Gal 2:1–10 is the famine visit of Acts 11:27–30, with the Jerusalem Council visit of Acts 15:1–30 taking place after Galatians was written. This view became an option when the revised form of the South Galatian hypothesis was proposed. Among those who have argued it are D. Round, *The Date*; K. Lake, *The Earlier Epistles*, 297ff. (though later he abandoned the position in favor of Acts 11:27–30 and 15:1–30 as doublets); C. W. Emmet, *Galatians*, xivff.; idem, "The Case for the Tradition," 2:265–97; W. M. Ramsay, *The Teaching of Paul*, 372–92; idem, *St. Paul the Traveller*, 14th ed., xxi, xxxi; A. W. F. Blunt, *The Acts of the Apostles* (Oxford: Clarendon, 1922) 182ff.; idem, *Galatians*, 21–25; F. C. Burkitt, *Christian Beginnings*, 116ff.; G. S. Duncan, *Galatians*, xxiiff.; F. Amiot, *S. Paul: Epître aux Galates*, 32; W. L. Knox, *The Acts of the Apostles* (Cambridge: Cambridge University Press, 1948) 40ff.; R. Heard, *Introduction to the New Testamant* (New York: Harper & Row, 1950) 183; H. F. D. Sparks, *The Formation of the New Testament* (London: SCM, 1952) 60–61; D. Guthrie, *New Testamant Introduction: The Pauline Epistles* (London: Tyndale, 1961) 79–87; idem, *Galatians*, 27–37; J. W. Drane, *Paul, Libertine or Legalist?* esp. 140–43; F. F. Bruce, *Galatians*, 43–56.
3. That Gal 2:1–10 is the Jerusalem Council visit of Acts 15:1–30, which Luke has turned into two visits by misunderstanding the parallel nature of two reports he received about the council and so fabricating the visit of Acts 11:27–30. Among the many who have argued this view are K. Lake, "The Apostolic Council of Jerusalem," 5:201; E. Haenchen, "The Book of Acts as Source Material for the History of Early Christianity," in *Studies in Luke–Acts*, ed. L. E. Keck and J. L. Martyn (Nashville: Abingdon, 1966), 271; idem, *The Acts of the Apostles*, tr. R. McL. Wilson (Philadelphia: Westminster, 1971), 400–404, 438–39.

4. That Gal 2:1–10 is the Jerusalem Council visit of Acts 15:1–30, with Acts 11:27–30 being a misplaced report of the collection visit which was originally connected with the material of Acts 21:15–17 but which Luke has chosen to place earlier in order to support his schematic portrayal of the expansion of the church. Among proponents of this view are F. W. Beare, *JBL* 62 (1943) 298; R. W. Funk, *JBL* 75 (1956) 130–36.

5. That Gal 2:1–10 is the Jerusalem Council visit of Acts 15:1–30, with Acts 11:27–30 being an invention of Luke (for reasons given in either positions three or four above) and with the Jerusalem Council visit to be identified with the hasty visit of Acts 18:22. Major advocates of this position are J. Knox, *Chapters*; J. C. Hurd, "Pauline Chronology," 225–48; idem, *CJT* 14 (1968) 189–200; C. Buck and G. Taylor, *Saint Paul,* 7–9, passim; R. Jewett, *Chronology,* 63–104; G. Luedemann, *Paul,* 13ff., 71ff., 149ff.

The first two of these positions mount no attack against Acts. They seek, rather, to correlate the visits given in Galatians with those of the Acts narrative. The third and fourth positions view Acts as having less credibility, and explain Acts 11:27–30 as either an inadvertent doublet of Acts 15:1–30 or a conscious insertion into Acts 11 of some material that was originally associated with Acts 21:15–17. The fifth dispenses with the framework of Acts altogether. It argues on the basis of Gal 1–2 and data from his other letters that Paul's biography can be reconstructed in terms of only three visits to Jerusalem: (1) the conversion visit of Gal 1:18–20 (cf. Acts 9:26–30); (2) the Jerusalem Council visit of Gal 2:1–10 (cf. Acts 15:1–30, which is to be identified with the hasty visit of Acts 18:22 and probably to be located at that time historically); and (3) the collection visit of Rom 15:25–33; 1 Cor 16:1–4; and 2 Cor 1:16 (which is represented in Acts 11:27–30 and 21:15–17 in quite garbled fashion).

2. An Evaluation of the Three-Visit Hypothesis

Because of the nature of current chronological discussions, it is necessary to deal first with John Knox's three-visit hypothesis before taking up directly the question of whether or not Gal 2:1–10 is Paul's version of the Jerusalem Council. Arguments in favor of the historical reliability of Acts, or even specific demonstrations of agreement between Paul and Luke on the course of Paul's missionary outreach (where an itinerary can be inferred from Paul's own letters), do not go far in dealing with Knox's reconstruction, since proponents of the three-visit hypothesis have largely disengaged Acts from considerations of Pauline chronology. It is necessary, therefore, to take the Knox hypothesis on its own terms when evaluating it. And when dealt with on its own terms—apart from any argument that depends on the validity of Acts—four problems, at least, arise that serve to highlight certain inconsistencies within the position and that suggest a failure to account for the data better than does Acts.

One major difficulty with the Knox hypothesis is the fact that Barnabas is not mentioned at all in Paul's letters in connection with the founding of any of the churches in Macedonia and Achaia. Rather, 2 Cor 1:19 states that Silas and Timothy were Paul's co-workers in founding the Corinthian church. Furthermore, Barnabas does not figure in any significant way in any of the continuing correspondence with these churches (1 Cor 9:6 is no real exception, and certainly 2 Cor 8:22 and Col 4:10 cannot be so claimed). Yet on Knox's reconstruction, all of these churches were founded prior to the Jerusalem Council. And Gal 2:1–10 makes it clear that Paul and Barnabas were confederates in a Gentile ministry before the convening of that council.

It is, of course, theoretically possible to argue that Paul for one reason or another just inadvertently failed to mention Barnabas in connection with their joint ministries to Macedonia and Achaia—or perhaps that Paul and Barnabas were independent missionaries to the Gentiles who just before the council decided to go up together to Jerusalem to discuss common problems with the Jerusalem leaders. A more straightforward interpretation of Gal 2:1–10, however, is that Paul and Barnabas were partners in mission at least up until the time of the council. And this being so, the absence of Barnabas from Paul's letters that have to do with Macedonia and Achaia is difficult to square with Knox's hypothesis. Unless it is asserted that a Paul-Barnabas missionary team has no basis in reality at all, the Acts account, in which the split between Paul and Barnabas occurs after the Jerusalem Council of Acts 15, gives a far more satisfactory explanation for the presence of Barnabas in Gal 2:1, 9, 13 and his absence from Paul's other letters.

A second problem with Knox's hypothesis arises from Paul's narration in Gal 1:21–24, for there he says quite explicitly that he spent his time between his two visits to Jerusalem in the regions of Syria and Cilicia. Now if, as Knox proposes, the Jerusalem Council visit occurred late in Paul's ministry and is to be identified with the so-called hasty visit of Acts 18:22, Paul's statements in Gal 1:21–24 do not appear to leave room for such missionary activity in Macedonia and Achaia as the Corinthian correspondence and Rom 15 require. They may allow by a slight extension travel and ministry in the neighboring province of Galatia (as North Galatianists and some South Galatianists posit). But they can hardly be read to include an extensive ministry as far away as Macedonia and Achaia. This is, of course, exactly what John Knox does (*Chapters*, 58–60), repeating Johannes Weiss's claim: "Gal 1:21 cannot be taken to mean that for the fourteen years, he worked *only* in Syria and Cilicia. The statement merely indicates the point from which his work at that time began, but does not in any way describe this work as a whole" (*The History of Primitive Christianity* [New York: Wilson-Erickson, 1937] 1:204; so also C. H. Buck and G. Taylor, *Saint Paul*, 251). Yet to include missions to Macedonia and Achaia within Gal 1:21–24 seems to make a mockery of language and to discredit entirely Paul's endeavor to be truthful (cf. 1:20). The framework of events in Acts accommodates the data of Gal 1:21–24 in a much simpler and more straightforward manner.

A further internal problem with the three-visit hypothesis has to do with the timing of the Jerusalem Council vis-à-vis the Gentile mission. For in Knox's reconstruction, this crucial conference, at which the status of Gentile Christians was resolved, took place only after a fourteen-year period during which Paul had established churches of a Gentile character throughout the eastern part of the Roman empire. But if the issue was as serious as all the reports indicate, it is difficult to understand why it was not dealt with by the leaders of the first-century church before the problem had spread as far as Macedonia and Achaia. This is, of course, an argument based on "what is likely to have happened," and so—with history being what it is—only of limited value. Yet it must be said that the Acts account of these relationships, wherein the Jerusalem Council takes place soon after the Gentile mission expanded beyond Syrian Antioch, appears more likely.

A fourth difficulty with Knox's hypothesis has to do with the conclusion to the collection project. For as Paul prepared to leave for Jerusalem to deliver the collection to the Christians there, he expressed anxiety as to whether the collection would actually be accepted by the Jerusalem church (Rom 15:25–32). And his fears appear to have been well-founded, for from Luke's reticence to speak of the collection in his description of Paul's final visit to Jerusalem (cf. my "The Acts of the Apostles," in *The Expositor's Bible Commentary*, 9:519) and from the fact of Paul's arrest and imprisonment in Jerusalem, it would seem that the collection was not well received by the Jerusalem church. Yet one important feature in Knox's reconstruction is that the collection was an obligation laid on Paul by the Jewish Christians at the Jerusalem Council, which he then made haste to fulfill. If, however, this was the case—that is, if the collection was something that the Jerusalem church had demanded from Paul and was expecting as part of an agreement—it is difficult to account for Paul's fears and the subsequent failure of the project. It would appear, rather, that the impetus and rationale for the collection came from Paul himself. But if the collection was not an obligation laid on Paul at the Jerusalem Council, then one of the main arguments that Knox and others have used for placing the council so late in Paul's career is seriously weakened. Admittedly, this is no argument for the validity of Acts, for Luke makes no reference (except at 24:17 in reporting Paul's defense before Felix) to such a collection. But it weighs heavily against Knox's reconstruction of events.

Thus even when taken on its own terms, it must be concluded that the Knox reconstruction gives a much less satisfactory account of a series of details found in Paul's own letters than does the traditional framework of Acts. Taken together with T. H. Campbell's earlier demonstration that, where they can be checked, Paul and Luke are in essential agreement as to the pattern of Paul's itinerary (*JBL* 74 [1955] 80–87), these considerations stand in opposition to the three-visit reconstruction of Knox, Hurd, Jewett, Luedemann, and others. It is, therefore, not simple naiveté that causes us to prefer Luke's framework in Acts to Knox's reconstruction, and so we feel free to raise directly the question of the relation of Gal 2:1–10 to Acts 15:1–30.

3. On Identifying Gal 2:1–10 with Acts 15:1–30

The strongest and most obvious argument in favor of identifying Gal 2:1–10 with Acts 15:1–30 is the marked similarity between the two passages. Both speak of a meeting held at Jerusalem to deal with the question of Gentile Christians having to observe the Jewish law. In both, the discussion is prompted by Jewish Christian legalists. In both, the main participants are Paul and Barnabas, on the one hand, and Peter and James, on the other. And in both, the decision reached is in favor of a law-free mission to Gentiles. It cannot be denied that on first impression these two passages seem to refer to the same event—and so they have been understood by almost everyone until the twentieth century.

This general impression of similarity, however, is diminished when the passages are subjected to closer scrutiny, for there are a number of differences and omissions that suggest that the similarities may be more superficial than substantial. Prominent among the differences are matters having to do with (1) the role of Paul at the meeting, (2) the motivation for the trip to Jerusalem, and (3) the nature of the meeting itself. As for the first matter, it can be asked: Was Paul a major participant and at the center of the discussion, as in Gal 2:2, or was he overshadowed by Barnabas, Peter, and James, as in Acts 15? As for the second: Was the trip to Jerusalem made in response to a revelation (κατὰ ἀποκάλυψιν), as in Gal 2:2, or because of a sending by the Antioch church, as in Acts 15:1–3? And third: Was the meeting private (κατ᾽ ἰδίαν) with a few leaders, as in Gal 2:2, or a public conference, as in Acts 15:6, 12?

These differences are immediately apparent on any close study of the two passages. Yet they may be attributable simply to the differing purposes and perspectives of Paul and Luke in their respective writings. And if these were the only problems in equating the passages, matters could be left at that. There are, however, two omissions in Galatians that weigh more heavily against an identification of Gal 2:1–10 with Acts 15:1–30. Also, there is an observation of some importance that arises from the schism reported in Gal 2:11–14 that has some bearing on the question.

To speak of omissions in Galatians, of course, presupposes a certain attitude toward Acts, for one cannot make comparisons without also leveling value judgments on the materials being compared. And though we cannot here enter into a full discussion of Acts as a historical source (for an introductory treatment, see my "The Acts of the Apostles," in *The Expositor's Bible Commentary*, 9:208–31), some remarks need be made apropos the question.

Suffice it here to say that, on the one hand, we believe the current widespread skepticism toward the historical reliability of Acts to be ill-founded, resting as it does on an inadequate consideration of ancient historiography and a false dichotomization of history and theology. On the other hand, it is necessary to use Acts critically, for, as 2 Cor 11:23–27 illustrates, Luke's account by no means contains a complete record of Paul's ministry. Even where Paul and Luke treat the same event, as is generally thought to be the case with respect to Gal 1:18–20 and Acts 9:26–30, the differences between the accounts is a clear indication that the two authors wrote from different perspectives, shaping their presentations in strikingly different ways. Indeed, in comparison with Paul's letters, Acts is a secondary source, which is a fact that must constantly be kept in mind when judging between them. Yet it is not at all inappropriate to take seriously Luke's account of Paul's itinerary in attempting to unravel the problems posed by Gal 1–2.

Assuming, then, the basic reliability of Acts in its presentation of Paul's itinerary, the identification of Gal 2:1–10 with Acts 15:1–30 forces one to say that Paul in Galatians has omitted reference to the famine visit of Acts 11:27–30 for reasons of his own. But it is difficult to imagine how Paul, who affirms his truthfulness so vehemently in Gal 1:20, could have failed to mention that visit in the recitation of his contacts with the Jerusalem leaders in Gal 1–2. In the context of his emphasis on the minimal nature of his contacts with the Jerusalem leaders (Gal 1:16–17, 18–19; 2:1) and their confirmation of his ministry on those few occasions when they did meet (Gal 1:23–24; 2:6–9), such an omission is hard to justify since it tends to discredit his argument. Would not his opponents have been quick to seize on such an omission? Would they not have said that, after all, there was a second visit of Paul to Jerusalem, which Paul has failed to mention—perhaps because it showed that he was no independent apostle, as he claimed, but a mere disciple whose authority stemmed from the apostles at Jerusalem?

Those who posit a late date for Galatians and yet hold to the reliability of Acts are forced to say that, for one reason or another, Paul saw no polemical importance in the famine visit, and so omitted it in his narration of events. J. G. Machen, for example, argued that there is a transition between Gal 1:18–24 with its assertion of a full accounting and Gal 2:1–10 where "an entirely different argument" is made (*Machen's Notes*, 91–92). So Machen insisted:

> Rightly regarded, therefore, Paul's argument does not demand that the famine visit should be mentioned, supposing it took place prior to the visit recorded in Gal 2:1–10, unless it involved the important event of a real conference between the original apostles and Paul regarding the content of Paul's gospel and an expression of opinion by the original apostles about that gospel and about Paul's right to preach it. . . . Paul was not obliged to mention it in his argument, and his omission of mention of it before Gal 2:1 does not prove either that the visit narrated in Gal 2:1–10 is to be identified with it or that the Book of Acts is in error in representing it as having occurred (ibid., 93–94).

To some, such an explanation may be convincing. If, however, Gal 1:11–2:10 is taken to be a connected biographical argument (as will be argued later in discussing the letter's structure and in the commentary proper) and Acts 11:27–30 is accepted as authentic, certainly the omission in Galatians of any reference to the famine visit is a factor that must weigh heavily against the identification of Gal 2:1–10 with Acts 15:1–30.

A second omission in Galatians that stands in the way of taking Gal 2:1–10 as Paul's account of the Jerusalem Council (assuming, again, the basic reliability of Acts) is Paul's silence as to the major decision of the council, which decision would have served as the coup de grâce to the conflict at Galatia. Now it is not difficult to believe that Paul may have been somewhat reluctant, for various reasons, to refer to the four prohibitions tacked on to the decision of the council (Acts 15:20, 29), even if they had to do not with the salvation of Gentiles but with their table fellowship with Jewish Christians (cf. my *Paul, Apostle of Liberty*, 232–35, 239–43). But it is difficult to see why in the midst of the Galatian conflict he chose to be silent about the decision reached at Jerusalem—or how, in fact, he could have avoided any mention of it—if he were writing after the Jerusalem Council. Paul certainly did not draw his punches or refrain from using arguments advantageous for his position elsewhere in his Galatian letter. It seems, therefore, inconceivable that he would not have brought in the decision of the Jerusalem Council in his debate with the Judaizers—indeed, that he would not have driven its major point home in his argument—had he known about the council's decision when writing Galatians.

Perhaps it could be argued that Paul's Galatian converts had not yet heard of the decision reached at Jerusalem, and so he did not bring it into his argument when writing them. Yet surely Paul would have realized, were this the case, that by not taking the opportunity afforded him of being the first to inform them of the decision—when, in fact, he would have been in a position to present it as an overwhelming victory for the Gentile mission—he was paving the way for serious difficulties later in allowing the Judaizers an opportunity to take the initiative and to misrepresent the intentions of the council. And after allowing the Judaizers the privilege of first telling the Galatians about the four prohibitions included with the council's decision, it would have been very difficult for Paul to have made the bare assertion that "those who seemed to be important . . . added nothing to my message" (Gal 2:6) without playing right into the hands of his opponents.

Nor can it be argued that since the letter from the council was addressed "to the Gentile believers in Antioch, Syria, and Cilicia" (Acts 15:23), its decision and prohibitions had no relevance to Gentile Christians in Galatia, nor that Paul only first heard about the council's action from James on his last visit to Jerusalem (Acts 21:25) and so was unaware of it when writing to the Galatians. With respect to the first of these suggestions, it is apparent from Acts 16:4 and 21:25 that the action taken was intended to have a more general applicability—to the whole Gentile mission, of which the church at Syrian Antioch was the mother church. And as for the second of these arguments, not only is Acts 21:25 open to other interpretations (cf. my "The Acts of the Apostles," in *The Expositor's Bible Commentary*, 9:520), but it seems apparent from the discussions of 1 Cor 8–10 and Rom 14 that the Jerusalem prohibitions were being discussed in these churches even before Paul's final visit to Jerusalem and that Paul was already defending the keeping of such prohibitions in his churches, even if his defense was on his own terms. Thus the absence in Galatians of any mention of the major decision of the council remains a significant problem for those who want to see Gal 2:1–10 as Paul's account of the Jerusalem Council.

Furthermore, assuming that Paul's clash with Peter of Gal 2:11–14 took place after the Jerusalem Council, Paul's account of that clash undercuts his whole argument and turns to the advantage of his judaizing opponents. Indeed, it would reveal Paul's recognition of a chasm that still existed between himself and the Jerusalem apostles, which had only superficially been bridged over at the Jerusalem Council. The inclusion of this Antioch episode in Paul's argument at a time *before* the council is understandable. But to use it in support of his polemic *after* the decision of the council, and without reference to that decision, casts considerable doubt on Paul's logical powers. One might, of course, attempt to rescue Paul's logic by reversing the order of events in Gal 2, so that Gal 2:11–14 refers to a time before the Jerusalem Council and Gal 2:1–10 is Paul's version of that council (for a defense of this position together with a list of its adherents, see J. Dupont, *RSR* 45 [1957] 42–60, 225–39). That, however, is a rather drastic expedient for which there is no manuscript support and which flies in the face of any normal reading.

Despite, therefore, certain superficial similarities between Gal 2:1–10 and Acts 15:1–30, closer inspection reveals a number of serious problems with identifying the Jerusalem visits of which these two passages speak. The seriousness of these problems, in fact, suggests that we must attempt to find a place for the events of Gal 2:1–10 elsewhere in the historical sequence of events.

4. On Identifying Gal 2:1–10 with Acts 11:27–30

Though Gal 2:1–10 and Acts 11:27–30 may not at first glance display many similarities, it is by no means impossible that they present the same Jerusalem visit from two different perspectives. Since Barnabas had been sent to Antioch by the Jerusalem church because of the Gentile outreach there, it is not unreasonable to expect that he would have taken advantage of a return trip to Jerusalem, whatever its immediate purpose, to discuss such an outreach with the Jerusalem leaders. Moreover, such a visit would have been a much more likely setting for the private sort of meeting described in Gal 2. Furthermore, the injunction of the Jerusalem apostles to "*continue to remember* [μνημονεύωμεν] the poor" reported in Gal 2:10 may well have in mind and be building on the delivery of the famine relief from Antioch Christians.

Three bits of autobiographical information relative to Paul's career as a missionary tend to favor the identification of Gal 2:1–10 with the famine visit. The first is the brief statement of Gal 1:21, "Later I went to Syria and Cilicia." Indeed, as noted above, there have been frequent attempts to read these words as not excluding a more extensive missionary outreach on the part of Paul during this time—either in the neighboring province of Galatia, as traditional North Galatianists and some South Galatianists believe, or throughout Asia Minor and the Balkan peninsula, as John Knox and others hold. Yet certainly the more natural reading of the text is that Paul spent his time between the two Jerusalem visits of Gal 1:18–20 and 2:1–10 *only* in Syria and Cilicia—that is, in missionary activity that centered first in Tarsus and then in Antioch. And if this be the case, then his missionary endeavors in the province of Galatia did not take place until after his second visit described in Gal 2:1–10.

A second bit of important autobiographical information is to be found in Gal 2:2, 7–9, where Paul tells us that when he went up to Jerusalem on his second visit he considered himself to be a missionary to the Gentiles, and that during that visit he was recognized as such by the leaders of the Jerusalem church. Now it may be argued that this would hardly have been the case at the time of the famine visit, when Paul's missionary travels had not yet begun, for how could Paul have thought of himself as an apostle to the Gentiles and been so recognized if none of his missionary journeys had yet taken place (so W. Sanday, *Exp*, 5th series, 3 [1896] 253–63; R. H. Stein, *JETS* 17 [1974] 239–42)? But this is an artificial argument, which arises only on the basis of a perception of Paul that depends too heavily on Acts. As far as Paul himself was concerned, his call to preach the gospel to the Gentiles was coincident with his conversion, as he tells us plainly in Gal 1:15–16. And while the events portrayed in Acts on his various missionary journeys were certainly confirmatory of such a call—perhaps may even have served to explicate the nature of that call more fully—Paul himself rooted that call in his conversion experience and seems at the time of writing Galatians to have looked on his activities at Tarsus (which Luke omits) and Antioch (which Luke only summarizes) as confirmations of his call. So if we really take Galatians to be the primary evidence here, we must conclude that Paul's conversion (1:15–16) and his early activities at Tarsus and Antioch (1:21–24) were entirely sufficient, from his perspective, to account for his claims in Gal 2:2, 7–9. In fact, it is possible to interpret vv 7–9 as the agreement that opened the way for him to engage in a wider Gentile mission.

The third bit of data has to do with the Antioch episode of Gal 2:11–14, to which we have referred earlier. Acts locates Paul at Antioch both after the famine visit (Acts 12:25–13:3; 14:26–28) and after the Jerusalem Council (Acts 15:30–35), so theoretically the events of 2:11–14 could have taken place at either time. Yet it is difficult to imagine why Peter and Barnabas (καὶ Βαρναβᾶς, "even Barnabas") would have caved in under the pressure of Jewish Christians from Jerusalem if the decision and decrees of the Jerusalem Council had then been in existence. The situation at Syrian Antioch, it seems, could only have arisen where there were no clear guidelines to govern table fellowship between Jewish and Gentile Christians. While one could posit various reasons for Peter's action, only in the confusion of the pre-council period would such a pioneer in the Gentile mission as Barnabas have pulled back from full fellowship with Gentiles under Jewish Christian pressure.

In addition to these bits of autobiographical data that look in the direction of identifying Gal 2:1–10 with Acts 11:27–30, reference should also be made to the nature of the judaizing activity as represented in Galatians. It is often assumed that a late date for Galatians allows time for a judaizing opposition to arise in the Pauline mission and for tensions to be reported back to the Jerusalem church. Galatians, however, does not view the judaizing opposition as indigenous to Paul's mission, but as stemming entirely from Jerusalem (whether with or without the backing of the Jerusalem leaders, which is what must be investigated later). In connection with his second visit to Jerusalem, Paul alludes to "some false brothers" who called for Titus' circumcision (2:4–5); in relating the Antioch episode, he speaks of "certain men . . . from James" who caused the trouble (2:12); and, of course, in the Galatian situation the agitators have ties with Jerusalem. We must deal later with the identity and message of Paul's opponents. Suffice it here to note that Galatians represents their activity as having arisen first in Jerusalem and then as moving out to Antioch and Galatia, and not vice versa. So it need be stressed that the information that Galatians itself provides as to the activities of Paul's opponents does not require a late date for the events of either 2:1–10 or 2:11–14. Nor does it require such a date for the writing of the Galatian letter itself.

There are, in fact, some rather striking similarities between the conflict reported in Gal 2:11–14 and the occasion for the convening of the Jerusalem Council as given in Acts 15:1–2. In both, the agitators come from Jerusalem and stir up controversy at Antioch. In both, questions as to the necessity of the Jewish law for Gentile Christians are raised. If the events of Gal 2:11–14 occurred after the Jerusalem Council—which has suggested to some a permanent rift between Paul and his two former colleagues, Peter and Barnabas—it is difficult to see why Paul would have wanted to mention the incident at all, particularly in light of his opponents' accusations. But if the events took place before the issues were dealt with at Jerusalem and Paul was writing in the midst of the ensuing controversy, the inclusion of the incident is understandable. It seems best, therefore, to conclude that Paul wrote Galatians on the eve of the Jerusalem Council, before the issues arising from the Antioch episode had been resolved.

The identification of Paul's visit to Jerusalem of Gal 2:1–10 with the famine visit of Acts 11:27–30 is not, however, without its problems. The most serious concerns the time spans of Gal 1:18 ("after three years") and 2:1 ("after fourteen years"). Two dates are usually taken as benchmarks in establishing a NT chronology: (1) Paul's ministry at Corinth, which began shortly after the edict of Claudius against Jews of Rome in the ninth year of Claudius' reign as emperor (Acts 18:2; i.e., January 25, A.D. 49, to January 24, A.D. 50) and which continued during Gallio's brief time as proconsul of Achaia (Acts 18:12; i.e., July 1, A.D. 51, to probably July 1, A.D. 52), and (2) Jesus' crucifixion, which, it is generally agreed, took place either in A.D. 30 or 33. Working from these two rather fixed points, scholars have dated the famine visit at about A.D. 46 or 47 and the Jerusalem Council at A.D. 49 (though, of course, later on a three-visit hypothesis). In whatever way, therefore, we correlate the visits of Galatians with those of Acts, the time spans given in Gal 1:18 and 2:1 must be taken into account.

On first reading, of course, it appears that Paul is saying that between his conversion and his visit to Jerusalem of Gal 2:1–10 was a period of seventeen years (i.e., three years plus fourteen years). And that span of time fits nicely an identification of Gal 2:1–10 with the Jerusalem Council—assuming Jesus' crucifixion in A.D. 30 and Paul's conversion two or three years later (or, assuming Jesus' crucifixion in A.D. 33, Paul's conversion in A.D. 35–37, and the Jerusalem Council occurring at the time of the so-called hasty visit of Acts 18:22 in the early or middle 50s). But the time spans of Gal 1:18 and 2:1 have greater difficulty fitting into the widely accepted NT chronological framework when Gal 2:1–10 is identified with the famine visit of Acts 11:27–30.

In order to accommodate the three-year and fourteen-year time spans of Gal 1:18 and 2:1 within the limits imposed by the dates for Jesus' crucifixion and Paul's initial Corinthian ministry, and still hold to the identification of Gal 2:1–10 with Acts 11:27–30, at least two of the following three assumptions must be made:

1. That the three years and fourteen years are concurrent, not consecutive—that is, that both are to be measured from Paul's conversion, and not that the fourteen years of Gal 2:1 are to be counted from Paul's first visit;
2. That Paul in Gal 1:18 and 2:1 is using a method of computation wherein parts of years are counted as full years; and
3. That Jesus' crucifixion took place in A.D. 30, with Paul's conversion two or three years afterwards.

Admittedly, such assumptions may not appear immediately evident to everyone. But they are not at all impossible. The thesis of an early date for the writing of Galatians is supported by such historical, exegetical, and critical evidence as we have cited above. And though the time spans of Gal 1:18 and 2:1 may not at first glance easily fit into such an understanding, they do not, given certain possible assumptions, discredit that thesis. Furthermore, the thesis of an early date for Galatians can be supported by reference to certain theological indices of importance, to which we must now turn.

5. Theological Indices of Importance

It was F. C. Baur who first attempted to assign dates to the NT writings on the basis of their ideological tendencies and doctrinal content (see his "Die Christuspartei in der korinthischen Gemeinde," *Tübinger Zeitschrift für Theologie* [1831] 61–206; also his *Paul: His Life and Works*). And though he strongly opposed Baur in most of his "Tendency Criticism," J. B. Lightfoot also in his 1865 commentary laid heavy emphasis on matters of style and content in dating Galatians vis-à-vis 1 and 2 Corinthians and Romans—arguing that in tone, feeling, and expression, Galatians is closest to 2 Corinthians (which Lightfoot assumed to be a single letter), but that in argumentation and doctrine it stands in relation to Romans "as the rough model to the finished statue," and so must be seen as having been written shortly after 2 Corinthians but before Romans (*Galatians*, 42–50). Lightfoot's comparisons of Galatians with 2 Corinthians, however, hardly demonstrate that the two letters were written at approximately the same time. The most they show is that the same author wrote both. Likewise, the claim that Galatians and Romans treat the same topics in similar fashion, only with greater development in Romans, can be challenged.

lxxxiv   INTRODUCTION

At any rate, once 2 Cor 10–13 (from whence Lightfoot drew his comparisons of tone and feeling, as well as many parallels of expression) came to be viewed as a separate letter ("the Severe Letter") written prior to 2 Cor 1–9 ("the Conciliatory Letter"), Lightfoot's observations in this regard tended to be forgotten.

In 1951 C. H. Buck tried to revive Lightfoot's position by focusing on the Pauline antitheses of faith-works and flesh-spirit in 2 Corinthians (3:17; 4:10–5:5), Galatians (4:1–7; 5:13–25), and Romans (8:2–25), arguing that—even apart from the data of 2 Cor 10–13—it is evident that 2 Cor 1–9, Galatians, and Romans share the same underlying approach to these matters, and so these three letters must be seen as having been written at about the same time and in that order (*JBL* 70 [1951] 113–22; cf. C. H. Buck and G. Taylor, *Saint Paul*, 82–102). But while Buck has had his supporters (e.g., C. E. Faw, *BR* 4 [1960] 25–38; J. C. O'Neill, *The Theology of Acts in Its Historical Setting* [London: SPCK, 1961] 96–97), most consider dating Galatians on the basis of such considerations not very compelling, since the data can be interpreted in too subjective a fashion (so, e.g., Betz, *Galatians*, 11; Bruce, *Galatians*, 48–51).

The attempt to establish a date for Galatians solely by reference to theological indices within the letter is a dubious one. Historical, exegetical, and critical considerations (such as we have treated above) must be dealt with first if we are to have any hope of grounding the discussion on a solid, evidential basis. If we move the debate away from these considerations and carry it on exclusively in terms of the theology of Galatians vis-à-vis the theology of Paul's other letters, we run the risk of a completely subjective criticism. Yet it must also be said that having dealt first with historical, exegetical, and critical issues concerning the addressees and date, it is necessary to ask as well how the theology of the letter correlates with what has been concluded as to provenance on other grounds. The evidence drawn from various theological indices, therefore, may not be foundational for the case, but it certainly ought to be supportive, at least in the main, if there is to be any confidence in conclusions drawn from historical, exegetical, and critical inquiries.

Much has been done in this area, particularly of late, but not everything is equally important. Nor does all the evidence point in the same direction. There are, however, certain theological indices in Galatians that lend credence to the idea of an early date in Paul's missionary career for the writing of the letter, and to these we must refer.

John Drane in 1975 proposed three important indices in support of an early date for Galatians (see his *Paul, Libertine or Legalist?* Appendix B: "The Date of Galatians," 140–43; actually Drane adds a fourth index, "Paul's stated surprise at the unexpected way in which the Galatians had deserted his message [Galatians 1:6]," but this is not of the same nature or quality as his first three). The first of Drane's indices has to do with the role of revelation in Gal 1:11ff. vis-à-vis that of tradition in 1 Cor 15:1ff. On this Drane comments:

> It is inconceivable that Paul moved from an emphasis on the tradition of the church duly handed on in 1 Corinthians to the opposite emphasis on an individualistic revelatory experience in Galatians. Nor, after his experience with the Gnosticizing tendencies met in Corinth, is it likely that Paul would subsequently have made such an unguarded statement as that in Galatians 1:11ff. But it is easy to think that the Galatians statement was earlier than the Corinthians

passage, written at a time when Paul was unaware of the possibly Gnostic understanding of his words, and that in the meantime such an understanding had come into the Corinthian church, to which his statements in 1 Corinthians 15 were in part the reply (ibid.,142).

A second theological index to which Drane points concerns differences in Paul's teaching on the Mosaic law in Galatians and in Romans, for in Galatians there is a very negative attitude expressed in comparison to the more positive statements of Romans. On this Drane says:

> Now it is easy to understand how Paul could have had a very pessimistic view of the Law at a relatively early stage in his ministry, before he had experienced some of the immorality into which "free" Christians could fall. But it is almost impossible to think either that he initially held a positive attitude to it, which later changed, or that (as would be required if Galatians is dated close to 1 and 2 Corinthians and Romans) he could have held the two together at one and the same time (ibid.,142–43).

The third matter Drane cites has to do with the moral freedom proclaimed in Gal 5:13–6:10 as compared to the moral principles laid out in both 1 Corinthians and Romans, where quotations from Jesus' teaching are used as guidelines for Christian morality. And on this third theological index, Drane comments:

> In Galatians Paul adopts the idealistic view that, if all believers are under the control of the Holy Spirit, they will naturally do what is right both individually and socially. In 1 Corinthians and Romans, and to a lesser extent 2 Corinthians, he adopts a more realistic position, and introduces elementary moral rules to form guidelines for behaviour in specific situations, a process which again is more easily explicable in terms of an early date for Galatians than the other way around (ibid.,143).

One may object to Drane's characterization of Galatians as an "extreme" representation of Paul's thought and to his rather constricted thesis-antithesis-synthesis procrustean grid into which he casts the data of Paul's letters. Yet without acceding to his sharp either-or categories, it must be acknowledged that the direction of development which Drane points out in these three theological indices is from Galatians to the Corinthian letters and Romans, and not vice versa.

Hans Dieter Betz in 1976 argued on the basis of the manner of Paul's references to the Spirit in Galatians for a relatively early date for the letter (see his "In Defense of the Spirit," 99–114; cf. his earlier "Geist, Freiheit und Gesetz," *ZTK* 71 [1974] 78–93). And in his 1979 Galatians commentary he summarizes his position as follows:

> On the whole, an early date is more commendable than a late date. Paul's theological position is different from the later letter to the Romans. As a matter of fact, it closely resembles the "enthusiastic" or even "gnostic" position. Paul does not find it necessary to protect himself against misunderstandings, but emphasizes the "Spirit" without any qualification. The letter seems to belong to

the beginning of his difficulties with his opponents, rather than to an advanced stage (*Galatians*, 12).

Of course, having previously asserted that "it is more probable that the Galatian churches were located in central Anatolia" (ibid., 5), Betz cannot speak of a date earlier than A.D. 50. So he concludes: "The most likely date would fall into the beginning of the middle period of his mission in Asia Minor, the first period being that of the founding of the Galatian churches. The years between 50–55 as the date of writing may be accepted as a reasonable guess" (ibid., 12). Nonetheless, Betz's observation about the enthusiastic and unguarded nature of Paul's references to the Spirit in Galatians, despite his North Galatian proclivities and assumed gnostic parallels, is highly significant. For, indeed, though the Spirit never becomes a topic on its own in the letter, the Spirit is central in Paul's Galatian defense of the gospel, underlying and tying together all that Paul writes by way of theological argument (esp. in 3:2–14) and personal appeal (esp. in 5:13–26). And while admittedly Paul's enthusiastic and unguarded manner of referring to the Spirit in Galatians is not decisive of itself for the question of dating, it tends to support an earlier rather than a later date as the time of writing.

Another theological index that points in the direction of an early date for Galatians is what might be called the functional Christology of the letter vis-à-vis the more developed Christology of the Corinthian correspondence and Romans. The salutation of Galatians sets the tone in this regard by identifying Jesus Christ as the one whom God "raised . . . from the dead" (1:1) and "who gave himself for our sins to rescue us from the present evil age" (1:4). Furthermore, Richard B. Hays has recently argued persuasively that in Gal 3:1–4:11 "the framework of Paul's thought is constituted neither by a system of doctrines nor by his personal religious experience but by a 'sacred story,' a narrative structure," which, "while not all-determinative, is *integral* to Paul's reasoning" (*The Faith of Jesus Christ*, quoting from 5–6 [italics his]). Though Hays himself draws no conclusions from this for the question of date, his demonstration of Jesus-narrative elements in 3:1–4:11 (citing materials in 3:1, 13–14, 22, 26–28; 4:3–6) that are more functional in nature—and so presumably earlier—than those in Paul's other letters suggests an early date for the letter's composition.

One might also cite the elemental nature of Paul's ecclesiology in Galatians. An early use of this theological index is to be found in G. S. Duncan's 1934 Moffatt commentary:

As at least *pointers* in the direction of an early date we may cite the character of his references to the Church and the fact that, though he comes so near to it in thought, he never uses the expression "the body of Christ." Similarly, he does not use the term "the mystery" with regard to the Gospel, even though all that is implied by that phrase in Col. i. 25ff. is already present to his mind. The simple expression found in iii.29, v. 24, "those who belong to Christ" (lit. "who are of Christ") has a parallel in the name "Christ's men" (*Christianoi*) which about this time came to be applied to the believers at Antioch (Acts xi.26) (*Galatians*, xxxi).

Duncan's observations, of course, have to do principally with relations between Galatians and the Prison Epistles, which is not a matter at issue here. There is, however, one further ecclesiological indicator of some significance for the question at hand—the way Paul speaks of the church in the various salutations of his letters.

Assuming for a moment the priority of Galatians, it is instructive to note that the salutations of Paul's earlier letters generally seem to develop from a more mundane understanding of the church (i.e., local congregations in particular areas or cities) to a more elevated understanding (i.e., the Church universal):

> *Gal 1:2*—"to the churches in Galatia" (ταῖς ἐκκλησίαις τῆς Γαλατίας)—though, of course, Paul speaks in 1:13 of having persecuted "the church of God" (τὴν ἐκκλησίαν τοῦ θεοῦ), but in another context;
> *1 Thess 1:1; 2 Thess 1:1*—"to the church of the Thessolonians in God the/our Father and the Lord Jesus Christ" (τῇ ἐκκλησίᾳ Θεσσαλονικέων ἐν θεῷ πατρὶ [ἡμῶν] καὶ κυρίῳ Ἰησοῦ Χριστῷ);
> *1 Cor 1:2; 2 Cor 1:1*—"to the church of God at Corinth" (τῇ ἐκκλησίᾳ τοῦ θεοῦ τῇ οὔσῃ ἐν Κορίνθῳ).

The salutations of Romans and the Prison Epistles, however, are of another type, for they speak of Christians as "loved by God," "holy ones," and "faithful brothers," but leave the word ἐκκλησία, "church," and/or the discussion of the church for later, more developed treatments:

> *Rom 1:7*—"to all at Rome who are loved by God and called holy ones" (πᾶσιν τοῖς οὖσιν ἐν Ῥώμῃ ἀγαπητοῖς θεοῦ, κλητοῖς ἁγίοις);
> *Col 1:2*—"to the holy and faithful brothers in Christ at Colosse" (τοῖς ἐν Κολοσσαῖς ἁγίοις καὶ πιστοῖς ἀδελφοῖς ἐν Χριστῷ);
> *Eph 1:1*—"to the holy ones [at Ephesus], the faithful in Christ Jesus" (τοῖς ἁγίοις τοῖς οὖσιν [ἐν Ἐφέσῳ] καὶ πιστοῖς ἐν Χριστῷ Ἰησοῦ);
> *Phil 1:1*—"to all the holy ones in Christ Jesus at Philippi, together with the overseers and deacons" (πᾶσιν τοῖς ἁγίοις ἐν Χριστῷ Ἰησοῦ τοῖς οὖσιν ἐν Φιλίπποις σὺν ἐπισκόποις καὶ διακόνοις).

A further index to be cited is Paul's use of σύν-compound words, which seems to be in line with his developing ecclesiology and to suggest an early date for Galatians. They appear frequently with reference to fellow Christians in Romans, Colossians, Ephesians, Philippians, and Philemon—once even in 1 Thessalonians and once in 1 Corinthians: συνεργός ("fellow worker") in 1 Thess 3:2; Rom 16:3, 9, 21; Phil 2:25; 4:3; Philem 1, 24; συγκληρονόμος ("fellow heir") in Rom 8:17; Eph 3:6; συγκοινωνός ("partner") in 1 Cor 9:23; Phil 1:7; συμμιμητής ("fellow imitator") in Phil 3:17; συναιχμάλωτος ("fellow prisoner") in Rom 16:7; Col 4:10; Philem 23; σύνδουλος ("fellow servant") in Col 1:7; 4:7; συστρατιώτης ("fellow soldier") in Phil 2:25; Philem 2; σύσσωμος ("belonging to the same body") in Eph 3:6. The σύν-compounds of Galatians, however, are of another type, being devoid of any reference to fellow Christians: συνηλικιώτης ("contemporary" of others in Judaism) in 1:14; συστοιχέω ("in line with" or "corresponds to" the present city of Jerusalem) in 4:25; and συσταυρόω ("be crucified together with" Christ) in 2:20 (also Rom 6:6).

One major theological objection to dating Galatians early, of course, has to do with its relative lack of eschatological teaching, particularly in comparison with that of 1 and 2 Thessalonians and 1 and 2 Corinthians. It is fairly common today to explain the development of NT thought along the lines of an early fixation on the future and progressive shifts brought about by the Parousia's delay (so E. Käsemann, *New Testament Questions of Today*, 236–37). On such a view, it was eschatology that dominated Paul's outlook in his early days, while such matters as soteriology, Christology, ecclesiology, and ethics came to assume importance in his teaching only later (for a brief history of this eschatological understanding of Paul from J. Weiss to E. P. Sanders, see my "The Nature of Paul's Early Eschatology," *NTS* 31 [1985] 85–86). I have argued, however, that the Thessalonian letters show that Paul's basic Christian conviction and the starting point for all his Christian theology was not apocalyptic eschatology but functional Christology—that is, that his commitment was not first of all to a program or some timetable of events, but to a person, Jesus the Messiah, with the result that what Jesus did and said were the controlling factors for even his eschatology (ibid., 87–95). Thus, without denying the importance of either eschatology or development in Pauline thought, I see no reason to invoke an eschatological criterion in establishing a relative chronology for Galatians vis-à-vis the Thessalonian and Corinthian correspondence.

In light, therefore, of the cumulative evidence as to date drawn from historical, exegetical, and critical considerations, and supported by certain theological indices of importance, we conclude in agreement with F. C. Burkitt (and others) that "the most natural interpretation of the biographical statements in Galatians i and ii is that they were written before the 'Council' at Jerusalem" (*Christian Beginnings*, 116). And while there remain difficulties in holding to an early date for the writing of Galatians, Philip Carrington was probably right to assert that "the arguments which perplexed the older theologians and still go on in the schools were due in no small degree to the fact that they accepted the later date of Galatians, which was traditional in their time" (*The Early Christian Church*, 1:91).

OPPONENTS AND SITUATION

Bibliography

Barclay, J. M. G. "Mirror-Reading a Polemical Letter: Galatians as a Test Case." *JSNT* 31 (1987) 73–93. **Baur, F. C.** "Die Christuspartei in der korinthischen Gemeinde," *Tübinger Zeitschrift für Theologie* [1831] 61–206. ————. *Paul: His Life and Works*, 1:105–45, 250–57. **Betz, H. D.** *Galatians*, 5–9. **Brinsmead, B. H.** *Dialogical Response.* **Bruce, F. F.** *Galatians*, 19–32. **Burton, E. deW.** *Galatians*, liii–lxv. **Crownfield, F. C.** "The Singular Problem of the Dual Galatians." *JBL* 63 (1945) 491–500. **Duncan, G. S.** *Galatians*, xxvi–xxxiv. **Ellis, E. E.** "Paul and His Opponents: Trends in the Research." In *Christianity, Judaism, and Other Greco-Roman Cults.* FS M. Smith, ed. J. Neusner. Leiden: Brill. 1975, 264–98. **Gunther, J. J.** *St. Paul's Opponents.* Harvey, A. E. "The Opposition to Paul." In *Studia Evangelica IV*, ed. F. L. Cross. TU 102. Berlin: Akademie, 1968. 319–32. **Hawkins, J. G.** "The Opponents of Paul in Galatia." Ph.D. diss., Yale, 1971. **Hort, F. J. A.** "The Church of Antioch." In *Judaistic Christianity*, 61–83. **Howard, G.** *Paul: Crisis in Galatia*, 1–19. **Jewett, R.** "The Agitators and the Galatian Congregation." *NTS* 17 (1971) 198–212. **Knox, W. L.** *St. Paul and the Church of Jerusalem.* **Lake, K.** *The Earlier Epistles*, 304–8. **Lightfoot, J. B.** "St. Paul and the Three." In *Galatians* (1890), 292–374. **Longenecker, R. N.** "Christianity in Jerusalem." In *Paul, Apostle of Liberty*, 271–88. **Lull, D. J.** *The Spirit in Galatia*, 29–52. **Lütgert, W.** *Gesetz und Geist.* **Munck, J.** *Paul and the Salvation of Mankind*, 87–134. ————. "Jewish Christianity in Post-Apostolic Times." *NTS* 6 (1960) 103–16. **Mussner, F.** *Galaterbrief*, 11–29. **Ropes, J. H.**

Singular Problem. **Schlier, H.** *Galater.* **Schmithals, W.** *Paul and the Gnostics.* ————. *Paul and James.* **Schoeps, H. J.** *Paul,* 63–87. **Schütz, J. H.** *Paul and the Anatomy of Apostolic Authority,* 124–28. **Tyson, J. B.** "Paul's Opponents in Galatia." *NovT* 10 (1968) 241–54. **Wilson, R. McL.** "Gnostics in Galatia?" In *Studia Evangelica* IV, ed. F. L. Cross. TU 102 Berlin: Akademie, 1968. 358–67. **Zahn, T.** *Galater,* 1–9.

The identity of Paul's opponents, the nature of their opposition, and the substance of their teaching are alluded to throughout Galatians, but are never spelled out precisely as entities on their own. It is, therefore, only from some type of "mirror reading" of the letter itself that we are able to speak of the opponents and their message, and so to reconstruct the situation to which Paul speaks. Mirror reading, however, is always difficult and dangerous. Its difficulty lies in the fact that it is not always possible to distinguish among (1) exposition, (2) polemic (i.e., an aggressive explication), and (3) apology (i.e., a defensive response), and mirror reading works only where there is reasonable assurance that we are dealing with either polemic or apology. Its danger, of course, is that it is all too easy to see our own image or concerns in the reflection and so to project our own favorite theses into the evidence. Nevertheless, despite its difficulties, dangers, and frequent abuse, mirror reading is the only method here available to us. Other materials, indeed, must be used to check our hypotheses and to supplement whatever profile may be drawn from Galatians itself, but we possess no other writing from antiquity that speaks so directly to the situation as does Paul's own letter.

Having affirmed the necessity of mirror reading in the study of Galatians, however, a caveat is in order. B. H. Brinsmead's monograph is to date the most thorough-going treatment of Galatians in terms of mirror reading. Yet one must take care not to interpret everything in Galatians as a response to the opponents' position. Certainly Galatians is dialogical, but its dialogue is with the Galatian Christians and not directly with the opponents. As H. D. Betz observes: "Paul never addresses his opponents directly, but he addresses the issues which they had introduced" (*Galatians,* 5; cf. 267 n. 143). So it is necessary to begin with the issues that Paul addresses and to try to distinguish (1) how the opponents understood them, (2) how the Galatian Christians understood them, and (3) how Paul understood them. Simply to reverse Paul's affirmations is at times helpful in gaining a handle on what the opponents taught and why they taught as they did. At other times, it may reflect more how the Galatian Christians understood matters. Often, however, such a procedure gives us only how Paul in the heat of controversy characterized (even caricatured) their teaching and activity, which may not have been how they themselves saw them.

1. The Identity of the Opponents

So much has been written on the identity of Paul's opponents at Galatia and there is such a welter of opposing opinions and conflicting theories that exegesis can easily become swamped. As we noted earlier, the common, almost uncontested view during the patristic and Reformation periods was that Paul's opponents were Jewish Christian Judaizers. But that identification has been both challenged and considerably refined during the past 150 years or so. In what follows, we desire to sketch out the main lines of the modern debate and propose a working hypothesis.

F. C. Baur, with whom the modern period of Pauline studies began, proposed in 1831 that primitive Christianity must be seen as composed of two rival factions:

XCINTRODUCTION

a Petrine group, which included a so-called Christ party, and a Pauline group, with which the Apollos party was associated ("Die Christuspartei in der korinthischen Gemeinde," *Tübinger Zeitschrift für Theologie* [1831] 61–206). The former faction he saw constituting the overwhelming majority in the Jerusalem church, founding the Christian community at Rome, furnishing the opposition to Paul at Corinth and Galatia, and later being known as the Ebionites. The Jerusalem apostles were part of this group; though being unable to oppose his arguments in support of a Gentile mission, they had somewhat reluctantly acknowledged Paul's independence. They were, however, never fully reconciled to Paul's type of Gentile outreach, and so they did not oppose the more legalistic members of the Jerusalem church in their opposition to Paul, but remained passive in the ensuing conflict. Thus, as Baur set out his views more fully in 1845, Paul's opponents were these zealous Jewish Christians from Jerusalem, who, unopposed by the Jerusalem apostles, infiltrated his churches in order to complete the work of conversion by imposing on the Gentiles the requirements of the Jewish law (*Paul: His Life and Works*, 1:105–45, 250–57).

Baur's position, however, was adjusted by his disciples Albert Schwegler and Eduard Zeller (Baur's son-in-law) to read that behind Paul's opponents stood the full authority of the Jerusalem church, including that of Peter and James (F. K. A. Schwegler, *Das nachapostolische Zeitalter in den Hauptmomenten seiner Entwicklung*, 2 vols. [Tübingen, 1846]; E. Zeller, *Apostelgeschichte nach ihrem Inhalt und Ursprung kritisch and untersucht* [Stuttgart, 1854], which is based on a series of articles written between 1848 and 1851 for the *Theologische Jahrbücher*). And it was in this form that the Tübingen view of the situation at Galatia became disseminated (cf., e.g., A. Hilgenfeld, *Der Galaterbrief*).

In 1865, J. B. Lightfoot, in direct opposition to Tübingen, argued that, though their ministries differed, Paul's relationship with the apostles at Jerusalem was one of mutual recognition and acceptance (see esp. his "St. Paul and the Three," 292–374). So while those who brought a deviant gospel to Galatia were from the mother church at Jerusalem—and may, in fact, even have been personal disciples of Jesus himself—they were not supported by the Jerusalem apostles in their judaizing activities, and therefore must be seen as having taken a line of their own. On the "certain men [who] came from James" of Gal 2:12, for example, Lightfoot writes:

> Did they bear any commission from him? If so, did it relate to independent matters, or to this very question of eating with the Gentiles? It seems most natural to interpret this notice by the parallel case of the Pharisaic brethren, who had before troubled this same Antiochene Church, "going forth" from the Apostles and insisting on circumcision and the observance of the law, though they "gave them no orders" (Acts XV.24)" (ibid., 371).

If the Jerusalem apostles were slow in checking the Judaizers' activities it was probably because they had hopes of conciliating them. And if James was more reticent than Peter to approve Paul's missionary outreach to Gentiles, that at worst must be seen only as a case of his understanding "in this, as in his recognition of Jesus as the Christ, moving more slowly than the Twelve" (ibid., 372).

A variation of Lightfoot's position is that of F. J. A. Hort, his Cambridge colleague, who held that the opposition to Paul at both Antioch and Galatia probably did, in fact, stem from James, but mistakenly so (see his *Judaistic Christi-*

anity). Being pastorally concerned about Jewish-Gentile relations in the Christian communities founded outside of Palestine, James may very well have sent a delegation from Jerusalem to check on affairs. But the emissaries from James mistook his interests and turned his practical concerns into justification for their claim that Gentile Christians must be circumcised and take on a Jewish lifestyle. In effect, they shifted an original practical concern of the Jerusalem church over into the area of a theological principle—a "present policy" of caution into a "permanent principle" of necessity (ibid., pp. 80–81)—and so denied the legitimacy of a direct ministry to Gentiles and the validity of the conversion of Gentiles to Christ apart from any commitment to Judaism. Hort insisted that all of their theological judaizing, however, was a mistaken reading of James' real concern, and so unsupported by the Jerusalem apostles.

A decided shift in the understanding of the problem at Galatia came with the "Two Front Theory" of Wilhelm Lütgert in 1919 and James Hardy Ropes in 1929. Lütgert argued that Galatians was directed against not one but two types of opponents—a judaizing group, which exaggerated the Jewish features in Paul's message, and a pneumatic group of spiritual radicals (*freien Geister*), which exaggerated Paul's teaching on freedom—and that these two groups were fighting with each other (*Gesetz und Geist*). To view matters in this light, Lütgert insisted, explains the contradictions between (1) Paul being charged with being both too independent of the Jerusalem apostles (by the Judaizers) and too dependent on them and on the Jewish moral tradition (by the Pneumatics), and (2) Paul having to assert his own equality with the Jerusalem apostles and argue for the futility of the Jewish law in 1:1–5:12 (against the Judaizers), and then having to check certain ethical excesses by appealing to a summation of the Jewish law and to "the law of Christ" in 5:13–6:10 (against the Pneumatics). Ropes built on Lütgert's thesis, but developed it by claiming that neither group appears from the way in which Paul deals with them to be Jewish (*Singular Problem*). The Pneumatics certainly were not. Nor were the Judaizers, who most likely were simply Gentiles enamored with the Hebraic elements of their Christian faith.

In 1945 Frederic C. Crownfield rejected the Lütgert-Ropes position, because he could see no evidence for such a twofold opposition (*JBL* 63 [1945] 491–500). Instead, Crownfield proposed that the opponents were syncretistic in their stance, probably with a background in a Jewish mystery cult that sought union with God in various ritualistic ways, including that of circumcision. So when they became Christians, Crownfield speculated, they must have brought with them "the combination of some Jewish rites with laxity in morals" (ibid., 493). To such opponents, therefore, Paul had to stress (1) his own independence from the Jerusalem apostles, (2) the mutual exclusiveness of gospel and law, and (3) the moral imperative of Christian liberty.

In 1954 Johannes Munck leveled a broadside against the Tübingen understanding of the course of apostolic history (*Paul and the Salvation of Mankind*). As Munck saw it, the difference between the Jerusalem apostles and Paul was not one of message (i.e., the sufficiency of the work of Christ, the futility of the law, and the inclusion of Gentiles) but had to do with *Heilsgeschichte*—that is, with whether Gentiles were to be reached only after Israel's full conversion, as the Jerusalem apostles expected, or, as Paul believed, a representative number of Gentiles must first be won to Christ before the Parousia and its accompanying full salvation for Jews would take place (ibid., 87–134). So Munck argued that Paul's opponents at Galatia could not have been Jewish Judaizers, since there were no such persons before A.D. 70 (see also his "Jewish Christianity in Post-Apostolic Times," *NTS* 6 [1960] 103–16), but must have been Gentiles who misunderstood Paul's teaching about Jerusalem and were unduly affected by their reading of the OT. Munck focused for support of his thesis on the present substantival participle οἱ περιτεμνόμενοι of Gal 6:13, arguing that it should be read as a permissive middle and not as a passive (or as a "causative middle," which would be equivalent to a passive):

> As the present participle in the middle voice of περιτέμνω never means "those who belong to the circumcision," but everywhere else "those who receive circumcision," that must also be the case in Gal 6:13. That is made specially clear by the connexion between the two sentences. The thought here is not of the Jews or Judaizers in general, but specifically of the Judaizers among the Galatians. Paul's opponents, who are agitating for Judaism among the Gentile Christian Galatians, are therefore themselves Gentile Christians. Their circumcision is still in the present, so that all this Judaizing movement is of recent date (*Paul and the Salvation of Mankind,* 89).

Strangely, while laying great emphasis on 6:13, Munck gave little attention to the reference to persecution in 6:12 ("the only reason they do this is to avoid being persecuted for the cross of Christ"), and so did not attempt to explain how this very important feature in Paul's profile of his opponents could have been true for Gentile Christians who had no connection with Jerusalem. A. E. Harvey, however, sought to fill in this lacuna in Munck's thesis by proposing that the pressure on these Gentile Judaizers came from local Jews in their endeavors to recover former proselytes who had become Christians ("The Opposition to Paul").

Walter Schmithals, in a 1956 article which he later revised for inclusion in his 1965 *Paulus und die Gnostiker,* advanced the thesis that Paul's opponents were Jewish-Christian Gnostics, who, though they practiced circumcision, prided themselves in not being dependent on the Jerusalem apostles and opposed Paul because he was ("Die Heretiker in Galatien," *ZNW* 47 [1956] 25–67; which, as revised in 1965, was translated as "The Heretics in Galatia," in *Paul and the Gnostics,* 13–64). As Schmithals sees it, Paul was "only meagerly informed" about the situation at Galatia. Therefore, his discussion of faith and the law in chaps. 3–4 contains only "current *topoi*" such as were usually brought in when dealing with Jews about salvation, but which have nothing necessarily to do with the Galatian situation. So setting aside the relevance of Gal 3–4, Schmithals finds no basis for the Lütgert-Ropes two-front theory—nor, more importantly, any reason to postulate a judaizing problem among Paul's converts. As Schmithals sees it, it is the paraenetic section of Galatians that best reflects Paul's information about the situation and that alone takes us into the real issues at stake. He insists, therefore, that at the heart of matters was the question of apostolic independence, for in the eyes of the Gnostics the "purity of the gospel and the non-mediated character of the apostolate are inseparable" (ibid., 19). Thus it was that Paul's opponents at Galatia, taking a stance diametrically opposed to that of the Jerusalem apostles, claimed that in being dependent on the Jerusalem apostles Paul was perverting the purity of the Christian gospel.

In 1971 Robert Jewett proposed an explanation of Paul's opponents at Galatia in terms of the Zealot movement that was rising in Palestine, particularly during the procuratorship of Ventidius Cumanus (A.D. 48–52; *NTS* 17 [1971] 198–212). During the period from the late forties until the outbreak of the Jewish war in A.D. 66, the Zealots sought to purge Israel of all Gentile elements in the hope that God would then bring in the Messianic Age. Absolute separation from the heathen world was what they wanted, and so their activities were directed against all who had Gentile sympathies and all who associated with Gentile sympathizers. As Jewett puts it:

> Jewish Christians in Judea were stimulated by Zealot pressure into a nomistic campaign among their fellow Christians in the late forties and early fifties. Their goal was to avert the suspicion that they were in communion with lawless Gentiles. It appears that the Judean Christians convinced themselves that circumcision of Gentile Christians would thwart Zealot reprisals (ibid., 205).

Thus it was about this time, Jewett believes, that agitators first appeared at Antioch (Gal 2:11–14), and then later at Galatia.

As Jewett sees it, the Judaizers' strategy was not to oppose Paul but to offer a supplement to the Pauline message and so bring the Galatian Christians to perfection. "The promise of perfection," Jewett observes, "would have a powerful appeal to the Hellenistic Christians of Galatia, for such was the aim of the mystery religions as well as of classical philosophy" (ibid., 207). Circumcision and the observance of the cultic calendar, in fact, would be most congenial to Paul's Galatian converts—though, so as not to weaken their case, the Judaizers made no mention of being obligated to keep all the Mosaic law. At the same time, the Galatian Christians with their pagan backgrounds were as susceptible to libertinism as to Judaism. So since they believed that the Spirit gave them immediate immortality, they had little interest in ethical distinctions and were just as much in danger of ethical excesses as apostasy.

Taking up Jewett's suggestion that it was the opponents' strategy not to oppose Paul directly but to offer a completion of his gospel, George Howard in 1979 has gone further to argue that probably the opponents actually thought of themselves as in no way opposing Paul, either directly or indirectly, but considered him to be teaching circumcision and treated him as an ally (*Paul: Crisis in Galatia*, 1–19). Howard concisely states his position as follows:

> The view presented here is that rather than assuming that the opponents held the opposite position from the one they ascribed to Paul, they held in fact the same position they ascribed to him and considered him as their ally. If this is true it is most likely that the agitators were Jewish Christian judaizers from Jerusalem who preached circumcision and who said that Paul did the same because he like them was dependent on the Jerusalem apostles for his gospel (ibid., 9).

As Howard views them, therefore, Paul's Galatian opponents believed that they were only carrying on a ministry to Gentiles as they thought Paul would have done had he been able to remain longer in Galatia, and that it was Paul alone who saw their activities as opposed to the gospel. Thus Howard makes two assertions with regard to the identity of Paul's opponents: "First it is clear that there is no need to

postulate an opposition of syncretists, radical spiritualists, gnostics, or any combination of them. The opponents were Jewish Christian judaizers connected with
Jerusalem. Secondly, the opposition which appears in the letter is from the
viewpoint of Paul" (ibid., 11). In explication, Howard writes:

> While Paul was hostile to the judaizers, there is no indication that they were
> hostile to him. Paul's hostility to them was caused by his earlier clashes with
> other judaizers who had sought to undermine his work. Paul had hoped that
> such clashes were over since the Jerusalem meeting with the "pillar" apostles
> and his reprimand of Peter; hence his disappointment at the turn of events is
> understandable. But there is no reason to believe that the current judaizers
> were privy to these earlier clashes or to the agreements made at Jerusalem
> (ibid., 11).

The range of opinions as to the identity of Paul's opponents at Galatia seems at
first glance rather staggering. Each of the above-mentioned views has a history,
each has modern defenders, and each has been nuanced in various ways (for
further treatments, cf. E. E. Ellis, "Paul and His Opponents"; J. G. Hawkins, "The
Opponents of Paul in Galatia"). It may be, as some believe, that we must admit
scholarship's inability to make an identification, and so remain somewhat agnostic
on the matter (so H. Schlier, *Galater*, 19–24). Yet most are convinced that with
suitable caution it is possible to delineate at least a general profile of those who were
troubling the Galatian churches.

Negatively, there is rather widespread agreement on a few crucial points. First,
almost all scholars today agree that the "Two-Front Theory" of Lütgert and Ropes
is impossible to maintain, simply because Paul speaks to his Galatian converts as a
more-or-less homogeneous group. Likewise, most find Schmithal's identification
of the opponents as Gnostics to be difficult, since it must begin by resorting to the
assumption that Paul was poorly informed about the situation and then goes on to
deny the relevance of what most interpreters consider to be the central portion of
the letter (i.e., chaps. 3–4). Furthermore, it has difficulty in showing how or why the
Gnostics argued for circumcision when they themselves had no judaizing tendencies
(cf. R. McL. Wilson, "Gnostics in Galatia?"). A third negative conclusion accepted
by most is that Munck's argument for the Gentile nature of the judaizing opposition
to Paul is strained, being unsupported by his treatment of 6:13 and hindered by his
neglect of 6:12. A fourth generally accepted point is that the opponents were hardly
indigenous to the situation, for Paul repeatedly refers to them as distinguishable
from the Galatian Christians (cf. 1:7–9; 3:1; 4:17; 5:7, 12; 6:12–13). Indeed, Paul
seems not to have known them, either personally or by name. He refers to them
generally as "some people" (τινές) and "anybody" (τις) in his opening statement
of the problem (1:7–9); he asks during the course of his treatment such questions as
"Who has bewitched you?" (3:1) and "Who cut in on you and kept you from obeying
the truth?" (5:7); and he warns, "The one who is throwing you into confusion will
pay the penalty, whoever he may be" (5:10), with the singulars of 1:9 and 5:10 best
seen as generic singulars. Finally, it is generally agreed that, though they may have
come from the Jerusalem congregation and been in personal contact with the
apostles there, the opponents in their judaizing activity were probably taking a line
of their own, and so were unsupported by the Jerusalem apostles.

The closest thing we get to a clear description of Paul's opponents in Galatians is in the opening statement of 1:6–9 and the postscript of 6:11–18. In the first of these passages we learn that the agitators were perverting the gospel and throwing believers into confusion, with the ironic allusion to "an angel from heaven" suggesting that they came with high qualifications and/or were appealing to a higher authority than Paul. In the postscript we are told that they were promoting circumcision for Gentile Christians and that Paul views their motivation as being a desire to avoid persecution. It is, therefore, these two passages that must hold center stage in any attempt to characterize the opponents.

Various inferences, however, can also be drawn from other data in the letter, though with diminished clarity. For instance, from the way in which Paul defends his apostleship in 1:1 and 1:11–2:10, it may legitimately be inferred that his standing as an apostle was in some way a focus of the opponents' attack, and that it was being unfavorably compared to that of the "pillar" apostles at Jerusalem. Likewise, from the way in which Paul deals with (1) the futility of the Mosaic law as a means of salvation in 2:15–3:18 and (2) its purpose as a pedagogue in 3:19–4:7, it seems reasonable to assume that the opponents stressed the importance of observing the law not only for being fully accepted by God but also as a proper Christian lifestyle. Such features—coupled with Paul's specific counterarguments having to do with Abraham (3:6–9), righteousness vis-à-vis the law (3:10–14), the covenant and its promise (3:15–18), the purpose of the law (3:19–4:7), and the supremacy of "Jerusalem that is above" over "the present city of Jerusalem" (4:21–31)—strongly suggest that the opponents had a Jewish background and a Jerusalem orientation. On the other hand, their preaching of a "gospel" message (1:6–7, which, of course, Paul calls "another gospel") and their desire to avoid persecution "for the cross of Christ" (6:12) point conclusively to their being Christians.

We conclude, therefore, that Paul's opponents were Jewish Christians—or, more accurately, Christian Jews—who came from the Jerusalem church to Paul's churches in Galatia with a message stressing the need for Gentiles to be circumcised and to keep the rudiments of the cultic calendar, both for full acceptance by God and as a proper Christian lifestyle. Undoubtedly they presented their message as being theologically based and claimed to be only interested in Gentiles being fully integrated into the chosen people of Israel, and so full recipients of the blessings of the Abrahamic covenant. Probably, as well, they claimed not to be opposing Paul but to be completing his message, and so bringing the Galatian Christians to perfection. Perhaps they also claimed to be representing James' pastoral concerns regarding Jewish-Gentile relations in the Christian communities outside of Palestine. Paul, however, accuses them of being primarily motivated by a desire to avoid persecution, and so to boast about Gentiles being circumcised (6:12–13).

In fact, Paul's evaluation of their motives in 6:12–13—"they want to put up a good show in the flesh" in order "to avoid being persecuted for the cross of Christ" and so "that they may boast about your flesh"—is probably the key to understanding the Judaizers. For, as Jewett points out, in the rising tide of Jewish nationalism in Palestine, with the antagonism of the Zealots being directed against all who had Gentile sympathies and all who associated with Gentile sympathizers:

If they could succeed in circumcising the Gentile Christians, this might effectively thwart any Zealot purification campaign against the Judean church! . . .

The nomistic Christians in Judea would have ample reason to boast if they could induce the Gentile churches to enter the ranks of the circumcised, for such an achievement would release them from a mortal threat levelled against all who dared to associate themselves with the ungodly and the uncircumcised. It was this hope of public recognition for their loyalty to the Torah which lay behind Paul's bitter words: "they wish to put up a good show in the flesh" (vi 12) (*NTS* 17 [1971] 206).

2. The Message of the Opponents

Having identified Paul's Galatian opponents as Jewish Christians from Jerusalem who were motivated by concern for the welfare of Palestinian Christians amidst the rising pressures of Jewish nationalism and so carried on a judaizing campaign among Paul's converts in the Diaspora in order to thwart any Zealot purification campaign against the church back home, the question arises: Is it possible to go further and delineate the contours of their teaching in Galatia? The problem, of course, is that such an endeavor requires an even more extensive use of "mirror reading," and we cannot always be sure in Paul's letter where exposition alone is to the fore and where polemic or apology is dominant. Nevertheless, since exposition, polemic, and apology so often seem to merge, some inferences can be drawn. While an outline or order of presentation must remain obscure, some features of the Judaizers' message can legitimately be highlighted.

For openers, it seems safe to say that the opponents made it a major feature of their presentation to discredit Paul's apostolic credentials. For from the way in which he so vigorously and extensively defends both the independence and the equality of his apostleship vis-à-vis that of the Jerusalem apostles in Gal 1–2—even to the point of recounting his opposition to Peter, the "men from James," and "even Barnabas" at Antioch (2:11–14)—it can be concluded that the opponents were arguing that Paul was, in fact, dependent on and subordinate to the leadership of the mother church at Jerusalem (from whence, of course, they came and were accredited representatives). F. F. Bruce aptly draws together what can be inferred from a mirror reading of Paul's defense on this matter, and so speculates that the Judaizers must have argued as follows:

"The Jerusalem leaders are the only persons with authority to say what the true gospel is, and this authority they received direct from Christ. Paul has no comparable authority: any commission he exercises was derived by him from the Jerusalem leaders, and if he differs from them on the content or implications of the gospel, he is acting and teaching quite arbitrarily. In fact," they may have added, "Paul went up to Jerusalem shortly after his conversion and spent some time with the apostles there. They instructed him in the first principles of the gospel and, seeing that he was a man of uncommon intellect, magnanimously wiped out from their minds his record as a persecutor and authorized him to preach to others the gospel which he had learned from them. But when he left Jerusalem for Syria and Cilicia he began to adapt the gospel to make it palatable to Gentiles. The Jerusalem leaders practised circumcision and observed the law and the customs, but Paul struck out on a line of his own, omitting circumcision and other ancient observances from the message he preached, and thus he betrayed his ancestral heritage. This law-free gospel has no authority but his own;

he certainly did not receive it from the apostles, who disapproved of his course of action. Their disapproval was publicly shown on one occasion at Antioch, when there was a direct confrontation between Peter and him on the necessity of maintaining the Jewish food-laws" (*Galatians*, 26).

A further feature of the Judaizers' message must have been on being rightly related to Abraham and the Abrahamic covenant, and so on being legitimately Abraham's sons and experiencing fully the blessings of God's covenant with Abraham (and, by extension, the people of Israel). Paul's exposition of the faith of Abraham in 3:6–9 ("he believed God, and it was credited to him as righteousness"; "all nations will be blessed in you"), his polemic on the nature of the covenant and the focus of its promise in 3:15–18 (established with Abraham apart from the law, with its promises being focused particularly on Abraham's Seed, "who is Christ"), his application of that polemic to the situation at hand in 3:29 ("if you belong to Christ, then you are Abraham's seed, and heirs according to the promise"), his allegorical treatment of Hagar and Sarah and their sons in 4:21–31, and his use of the expression "the Israel of God" for his Galatian converts in 6:16—all these, to judge by their prominence in Paul's argument, strongly suggest that Abraham and the Abrahamic covenant loomed large in the Judaizers' teaching.

Throughout his treatment of these matters Paul seems to be interacting with a typically Jewish attitude, as expressed most clearly in the Talmud, that truth comes in two guises, the first in an elemental form and the second in a developed form (cf. D. Daube, "Public Retort and Private Explanation," *The New Testament and Rabbinic Judaism* [London: Athlone, 1965] 141–50)—and that he is countering in particular the Judaizers' application of this Jewish motif to the effect that Paul's message was an elemental form of the gospel proclamation while theirs is the developed. The Judaizers' argument could very well have run along the following lines: (1) while Paul directed the Galatians to Gen 15:6, they must realize that the developed form of God's covenant with Abraham appears in Gen 17:4–14, with its requirement of circumcision emphatically stated in vv 10–14; (2) while Paul spoke only of Abraham, the full development of Israel's religious legislation came with Moses; (3) while Paul spoke of the promises of the gospel, the promises were in actuality made to Abraham and to his "seed," which means the nation; and (4) while Paul assured his converts that by accepting the gospel they became sons of Abraham, the question must be raised as to which son they represent, for Abraham had two sons—the first being Ishmael, with Isaac born later.

To this line of argument, as we have seen, Paul responds by asserting that Christ and Christ's own are Abraham's true "seed" (3:16, 29). Furthermore, he insists that the covenant with Abraham was confirmed by God four hundred and thirty years before the giving of the Mosaic law, and so having been confirmed, it can neither be annulled nor added to by later developments (3:15–18). And in regard to the claim that his message represents an Ishmaelian form of truth, he responds in rather circumstantial and ad hominem fashion (note the two uses of μέν, "indeed," in vv 23–24) that he can allegorize as well: it is Hagar, who has contacts with Mt. Sinai (from whence came the law that the Judaizers so extol), who should be associated with the present Jerusalem, which explains the bondage of Jerusalem and her emissaries; it is, however, Sarah, Isaac, and spiritual Jerusalem who are involved in the promises of God, and we are children of promise in association with them (4:22–28).

Included as well in the Judaizers' presentation seem to be charges that Paul, as a matter of fact, actually did preach and practice circumcision, but that he withheld this more developed rite only so as to gain his converts' initial favorable response. Thus, in effect, he was more interested in winning their approval than God's approval (cf. 1:10), since he really did believe in circumcision and made it a part of his ministry elsewhere (cf. 5:11). So as they saw it, there was need for accredited emissaries from Jerusalem to bring Paul's truncated ministry at Galatia to completion (cf. 1:6–7). Perhaps the Judaizers charged Paul with advocating circumcision because of their garbled version of the Titus episode at Jerusalem (2:1–5)—or, if Galatians be dated later than we've proposed, because of Paul's circumcision of Timothy (cf. Acts 16:1–3), whose status in Jewish eyes stemmed from his Jewish mother. Perhaps the charge arose from their knowledge that Paul approved of Jewish believers in Jesus expressing their faith in the traditional forms of Judaism (cf. his later words on this matter in 1 Cor 7:17–20). Or perhaps they simply knew that Paul himself continued to live a basically Jewish lifestyle (cf. 1 Cor 9:19–23; see also my "The Problem Practices of Acts," in *Paul, Apostle of Liberty*, 245–63). What, however, they evidently failed to appreciate is that Paul made a distinction between Jewish Christians and Gentile Christians—though, obviously, not at all in the same way as they did. So while he saw it as perfectly legitimate for Jewish Christians to express their faith in Jesus through the traditional Jewish practices, he strenuously opposed the imposition of these practices on Gentile Christians either for full acceptance by God or as a normative way of life.

On a practical basis, the opponents at Galatia must also have included in their message an emphasis on the Jewish law as the divinely appointed way to check libertinism within the church. Paul's emphases on (1) the pedagogical function of the law coming to an end with Christ, in 3:19–4:7, and (2) living by the direction of the Spirit (as opposed to life directed by law) as the antidote to libertinism, in 5:13–26, suggest that not only did the opponents argue circumcision as a prerequisite for being fully accepted by God but also that they asserted that life lived under the Torah—which meant for them a Jewish lifestyle—was the only way to bring the excesses of the flesh into line. The repeated mention of "the flesh" (σάρξ, or "the sinful nature") in 5:13–21 implies quite clearly that the Galatian churches were having ethical problems or at least were acutely conscious of ethical failures. For such problems the Judaizers offered a rather straightforward and seemingly God-honoring solution: accept a Jewish nomistic lifestyle and you will have clear guidance as to what is right and wrong, and so be able to live a life that pleases God. Just as Paul's message, they probably added, being only elemental in nature, was not able to relate you properly to Abraham and the Abrahamic covenant for full salvation, so it failed to relate you to the divine Torah and a Jewish lifestyle for proper Christian living. Thus you need to accept circumcision to be fully accepted by God into the Abrahamic covenant, and you need to take on a Jewish lifestyle in order to live in a manner that checks the excesses of your sinful, Gentile natures and enables you to please God in your lives. Their message was, therefore, in effect, one of both legalism for full salvation and nomism for Christian living (cf. my *Paul, Apostle of Liberty*, 78–83, on the use of "legalism" and "nomism").

3. The Situation in the Churches

The situation at Galatia was serious, not just, of course, because of the presence of Judaizers, but because the Judaizers had persuaded Gentile Christians to turn away from "the truth of the gospel" (2:5, 14) to "a different gospel—which is not at all the same gospel" (1:6–7). Their arguments were persuasive (cf. 3:1; 5:7–8), and those who claimed the name of Christ were beginning to carry out their directives (cf. 4:9–11). As yet, however, Paul's converts seem not to have submitted to the rite of circumcision, and so Paul exhorts them to stand firm in their Christian freedom (5:1)—even, in fact, expressing confidence that they will (5:10).

In addition to this judaizing threat brought in from the outside, there was in the Galatian churches the threat of libertinism, which appears to have been present from the very beginning. In the midst of his treatment of libertinism in 5:13–6:10, Paul tells his converts: "I warn you, *as I did before,* that those who live like this will not inherit the kingdom of God" (5:21). So while it is clear that in dealing with the judaizing problem Paul is countering a theology brought in by others, in treating the threat of libertinism it is equally clear that he is opposing a view that was indigenous.

Are we then to think of two parties in the churches of Galatia that were diametrically opposed to each other—a legalistic group and a libertine group— something like the warring parties in the Corinthian congregation (cf. 1 Cor 1:10– 12)? By the way in which Paul seems to be addressing rather homogeneously all his Galatian converts in both his anti-judaizing polemic and his anti-libertine argument, probably not. In countering the judaizing threat, he seems to characterize all the Galatian Christians as "foolish Galatians" (3:1); in speaking to the libertine problem, he likewise seems to assume that he is speaking to all the believers, as the equation of ὑμεῖς οἱ πνευματικοί, "you who are spiritual," with ἀδελφοί, "brothers," suggests (6:1). Furthermore, as Robert Jewett points out:

> In the anti-libertinistic section (v. 13–vi. 10) there are answers to questions raised by the nomistic influx. In v. 14 Paul shows that Christian love replaces the law while in v. 23 he assures the Galatians that the law will not condemn the fruits which flow from the Spirit. In vi. 2 he states that behaviour based on love would "fulfil the law of Christ." This shows that the ethic arrayed against libertinism was phrased as a replacement of the law and was directed to the congregation as a whole just as the earlier portions of the letter were (*NTS* 17 [1971] 210).

So with Jewett we conclude:

> Paul viewed the congregation as a more or less homogeneous unit capable of being swayed in this direction and that. . . . The Hellenistic assumptions of this congregation were as susceptible to the propaganda of the agitators as to the lures of libertinism (ibid., 209).

On the much more difficult question of exactly how much of the Mosaic law the Galatian Christians expected to assume—or how much the Judaizers taught them it was necessary to assume—it is impossible to say. Paul, of course, argues that "every man who lets himself be circumcised . . . is obligated to obey the whole law" (5:3) and accuses his opponents of not fully obeying the law themselves (6:13). From these statements it has been variously argued that (1) "these false teachers can hardly have been Judaizers" else Paul would not have been able to point out their deficiencies of teaching and practice (W. Schmithals, *Paul and the Gnostics*, 33–34; cf. F. C. Crownfield, "The Singular Problem," *JBL* 63 [1945] 500: "This would be impossible for real Judaizers, but quite natural for the syncretists"), (2) the opponents were from non-Pharisaic Jewish backgrounds and so did not themselves hold to a rigid understanding of the law (e.g., J. G. Hawkins, "The Opponents of Paul in Galatia," 344–46), (3) the opponents agreed theoretically with Paul and so taught the Galatians, but were insincere in their own practice (e.g., J. B. Lightfoot, *Galatians*, 222), or (4) the opponents taught complete obedience to the law, but from Paul's perspective they were not keeping it as scrupulously as their teaching demanded (e. g., G. Howard, *Paul: Crisis in Galatia*, 15). Mirror reading Paul's words at this point, however, seems to fail us, for though 5:3 and 6:13 clearly express his criticisms, they tell us nothing necessarily about how his opponents themselves or their intended converts viewed matters. I tend to agree with Jewett that probably the Judaizers asked for the Galatians' observance of only the most obvious requirements, and so did not impose on them the whole law, which would have been unnecessary for their purpose and would only weaken their case. But that opinion is drawn from conclusions reached as to the Judaizers' primary purpose and does not arise as an inference from Paul's words in 5:3 and 6:13, though it is not in conflict with such statements.

EPISTOLARY AND RHETORICAL STRUCTURES

Bibliography

Aune, D. "Review of Hans Dieter Betz, *Galatians*," *RSR* 7 (1981) 323–28. **Betz, H. D.** "The Literary Composition and Function of Paul's Letter to the Galatians," *NTS* 21 (1975) 353–79. ———. *Galatians*, 14–33. **Bjerkelund, C.** *Parakalô*. **Bligh, J.** *Galatians*. **Brinsmead, B. H.** *Dialogical Response*. **Caird, G. B.** *The Language and Imagery of the Bible*. **Corbett, E. P. J.** *Classical Rhetoric for the Modern Student*. **Corbett, E. P. J.**, ed. *Rhetorical Analyses of Literary Works*. **Dahl, N. A.** "Paul's Letter to the Galatians: Epistolary Genre, Content, and Structure." Unpublished Society of Biblical Literature Paul Seminar paper, 1974. **Daube, D.** "Rabbinic Methods of Interpretation and Hellenistic Rhetoric." *HUCA* 22 (1949) 239–64. **Deissmann, A.** *Light from the Ancient East*, 224–46. **Dixon, P.** *Rhetoric*. **Doty, W. G.** "The Classification of Epistolary Literature." *CBQ* 31 (1969) 185–89. ———. *Letters in Primitive Christianity*. **Exler, F.** *The Form of the Ancient Greek Letter*. **Funk, R. W.** *Language, Hermeneutic, and Word of God*, 250–74. ———. "The Apostolic Parousia: Form and Significance." In *Christian History and Interpretation*. FS J. Knox, ed. W. R. Farmer, C. F. D. Moule, and R. R. Niebuhr. Cambridge: Cambridge University Press, 1967. 249–68. **Grant, R. M.** "Hellenistic Elements in Galatians." *ATR* 34 (1952) 223–26. **Hansen, G. W.** *Abraham in Galatians*. **Hay, D. M.** "What Is Proof? Historical Verification in Philo, Josephus, and Quintilian." *SBLASP* 17:2 (1979) 87–100. **Jeremias, J.** "Chiasmus in den Paulusbriefen." *ZNW* 49 (1958) 145–56. **Kennedy, G. A.** *The Art of Persuasion in Greece*. ———. *The Art of Rhetoric in the Roman World: 300 B.C.–A.D. 300*. ———. *New Testament Interpretation through Rhetorical Criticism*, esp. 144–52. **Kessler, M.** "A Methodological Setting for Rhetorical Criticism." *Semitics* 4 (1974) 22–36. ———. "An Introduction to Rhetorical Criticism of the Bible: Prolegomena." *Semitics* 7 (1980) 1–27. **Kim, C. H.** *The Form and Structure of the Familiar Greek Letter of Recommendation*. ———. "The Papyrus Invitation." *JBL* 94 (1975) 391–402. **Koskenniemi, H.** *Studien zur Idee und Phraseologie des griechischen Briefes bis 400 n. Chr*. **Longenecker, R. N.** "On the Form." **Malherbe, A. J.** *Social Aspects.* ———. *Moral Exhortation.* **Meecham, H. G.** *Light from Ancient Letters.* **Meeks, W. A.** "Review of H. D. Betz, *Galatians." JBL* 100 (1981) 304–7. **Milligan, G.** *Documents*, 83–107, 255–61. **Mullins, T. Y.** "Petition as a Literary Form." *NovT* 5 (1962) 46–54. ———. "Disclosure as a Literary Form in the New Testament." *NovT* 7 (1964) 44–50. ———. "Formulas in New Testament Epistles." *JBL* 91 (1972) 380–90. ———. "Visit Talk in the New Testament Letters." *CBQ* 35 (1973) 350–58. **Roller, O.** *Das Formular.* **Sanders, J. T.** "The Transition from Opening Epistolary Thanksgiving to Body in the Letters of the Pauline Corpus." *JBL* 81 (1962) 348–62. **Schubert, P.** *Pauline Thanksgivings.* **Stowers, S. K.** *Letter Writing.* **Sykutris, J.** "Epistolographie." In PW, Supplement 5, 218–19. **Wendland, P.** *Die urchristlichen Literaturformen.* **White, J. L.** "Introductory Formulae in the Body of the Pauline Letter." *JBL* 90 (1971) 91–97. ———. *The Form and Function of the Body of the Greek Letter.* ———. *The Form and Structure of the Official Petition.* ———. "Epistolary Formulas and Cliches in the Greek Papyrus Letters." *SBLASP* 14 (1978) 289–319. ———. "The Greek Documentary Letter Tradition, Third Century B.C.E. to Third Century C.E." *Semeia* 22 (1981) 89–106. **White, J. L.** and **Kensinger, K.** "Categories of Greek Papyrus Letters." *SBLASP* 10 (1976) 79–91.

Since form and content are inseparable in the study of any writing, it is necessary to give attention not only to what is said but also to how it is said—that is, to the forms used to convey meaning and to the function served by each particular form. Therefore, prior to considering the specific content of Galatians (i.e., prior to exegesis proper), it is essential that we analyze the epistolary and rhetorical structures of the letter (for a more extensive analysis, see G. W. Hansen, *Abraham in Galatians*, Part 1, 21–93), with those analyses then being taken into account at each stage in the interpretation.

1. The Literary Genre

As is well known, Adolf Deissmann was so impressed by the correspondence in form between Paul's letters and the "true" or "real letters" (*wirkliche Briefe*) of the nonliterary papyri—that is, letters that arose from a specific situation and were intended only for the eyes of the person or persons to whom they were addressed, and not for the public at large or with the studied art of the "literary epistles" of the day—that he concluded: "I have no hesitation in maintaining the thesis that all the letters of Paul are real, non-literary letters. Paul was not a writer of epistles but of letters; he was not a literary man" (*Light from the Ancient East*, 232; cf. 224–46). What Deissmann was trying to correct by such a statement were views then current of Paul as a systematic theologian, or as a rather decadent classicist, or as mechanically inspired by God (cf. W. G. Doty, *CBQ* 31 [1969] 185–89). What, on the other hand, he was attempting to highlight were the genuine, unaffected religious impulses that can be seen in Paul's letters and the definite, unrepeatable situations to which they spoke. With regard to Galatians, Deissmann characterized it as "the offspring of passion, a fiery utterance of chastisement and defense, not at all a treatise 'De lege et evangelio'; the reflection rather of genius flashing like summer lightning" (*Light from the Ancient East*, 237).

Deissmann's emphasis on Paul's letters as real letters written to specific people in response to particular situations has been accepted by most as valid and helpful (e.g., P. Wendland, *Die urchristlichen Literaturformen*, 344; J. Sykutris, "Epistolographie," 218–19; O. Roller, *Das Formular*, 32). Yet laudatory and important as it is, subsequent study has brought to light at least four ways in which Deissmann's thesis needs to be nuanced more carefully. In the first place, it is widely recognized today that Deissmann's classification of Paul's letters as "private" letters as opposed to "public" letters is somewhat misleading, for Paul's letters are not merely private, personal communications—at least not "private" and "personal" in the usual sense of those terms. They were written to Christian believers for instruction in their common life together by one who was self-consciously an apostle, and so an official representative of early Christianity. As George Milligan long ago pointed out:

> The letters of St. Paul may not be epistles, if by that we are to understand literary compositions written without any thought of a particular body of readers. At the same time, in view of the tone of authority adopted by their author, and the general principles with which they deal, they are equally far removed from the unstudied expression of personal feeling, which we associate with the idea of a true letter. And if we are to describe them as letters at all, it is well to define the term still further by the addition of some such distinguishing epithet as "missionary" or "pastoral." It is not merely St. Paul the man, but St. Paul the spiritual teacher and guide who speaks in them throughout (*Documents*, 95).

Or as Donald J. Selby says: "These letters are not, strictly speaking, private letters. As their character clearly shows, they were written to be read before the congregation to which they were addressed. The second person plural, the allusions to various persons, and the greetings and salutations make them group communications" (*Toward the Understanding of St. Paul*, 239). Galatians in particular, while comparable in many ways to the private letters of the nonliterary papyri, indicates by its stress on apostleship (e.g., 1:1, 11–12; 2:8; 6:17), its address to "the churches of Galatia" (1:2; cf. 3:1), its tone of authority, and its style of teaching that it is more than merely a private letter, but must be understood as a missionary or pastoral letter written to a community (or communities) of Christians.

A second correction that needs to be made in Deissmann's thesis has to do with his contention that Paul's letters lack form or structure, except for a few stereotyped conventions and customary formulae in the salutations, thanksgivings, and closings. This was a deduction Deissmann drew from his premise that Paul's letters are nonliterary, personal communications as opposed to literary, artistic productions. But the conclusion is a non sequitur, for recent study has demonstrated the existence of many conventional forms and structural features both in the common, private letters of the Hellenistic period and in the Pauline corpus (cf. esp. J. L. White, *The Form and Function of the Body of the Greek Letter*; idem, *The Form and Structure of the Official Petition*; C. H. Kim, *The Form and Structure of the Familiar Greek Letter of Recommendation*). There is, of course, a wide range of literary styles in the extant, real letters of Paul's day. Yet there are certain epistolary conventions that can be observed in those letters as well as in Paul's letters—conventions to be found not only in the salutations, thanksgivings, and closings, but also in the bodies of the letters (contra B. H. Brinsmead, *Dialogical Response*, 78 n. 2, who sides with Deissmann and J. Weiss in claiming that "the Pauline letters at least will continue to be conceived as salutation, thanksgiving, and closing, with virtually anything in any order thrown in between"). So while it is proper to speak of Galatians as a passionate, real letter, that should not be taken to mean that we may ignore the various epistolary conventions and formulae that appear throughout its body. An awareness of such literary forms, in fact, enables us to move beyond Deissmann's view that Galatians in its central sections is rather chaotic and unstructured—and so to interpret Paul's message more adequately.

A third way in which Deissmann's thesis needs to be modified has to do with his distinction between a letter and an epistle, which distinction must be stated more carefully in view of the wide variety of types of letters found among the nonliterary papyri (cf. my treatments of "Letters in Antiquity," "Pastoral Letters," and "Tractate Letters," in "On the Form," 101–6). Demetrius in his handbook *On Style* listed twenty-one types of real letters, with Proclus expanding the list to forty-one—for example, letters of friendship, recommendation, request, information, instruction, consolation, praise, thanksgiving, accusation, apology, introduction, interrogation, invitation, and rebuke, with some letters evidencing a mixture of types (cf. W. G. Doty, *Letters in Primitive Christianity*, 10; also T. Y. Mullins, *NovT* 5 [1962] 46–54; C. H. Kim, *JBL* 94 [1975] 391–402; J. L. White and K. Kensinger, *SBLASP* 10 [1976] 79–91). Of course, none of Paul's letters corresponds exactly to the types described in the handbooks or as exemplified in the papyri. Nevertheless, an examination of the purpose, mood, style, and structure of each of Paul's letters provides a basis for classifying it roughly according to one or the other of the then-existing types of Hellenistic letters. One example would be Philemon as a letter of recommendation; others are Philippians as a letter of thanksgiving and 1 Corinthians as a letter of response and instruction. Likewise, to anticipate our discussion in what follows, Galatians should probably be seen as a letter of rebuke and request.

Finally, it needs be said that Deissmann's rather simple classification of Paul's letters as real letters needs to be amended further to take into account Paul's use of other literary traditions as well, such as his use of then-current rhetorical forms and modes of persuasion, chiastic structures, midrashic exegetical procedures, early Christian hymns and/or confessional formulae, and fixed paraenetic material. So though Deissmann was right to insist on the real, private Hellenistic letter as "the primary literary *Gattung* to which Paul's letters belong" (so J. L. White, *The Form and Function of the Body of the Greek Letter*, xii), that must not be taken to exclude Paul's eclectic use of other literary traditions as well, as drawn from his Hellenistic, Jewish, and Christian backgrounds.

Hans Dieter Betz dismisses the real, private letter as an appropriate literary genre for understanding the structure of Galatians, arguing instead for what he calls the "apologetic letter" genre (*NTS* 21 [1975] 354; idem, *Galatians*, 14; so also B. H. Brinsmead, *Dialogical Response*, 42, passim). Betz sees in Plato's *Epistle* 7 the precedent for such a genre, and cites Isocrates' *Antidosis*, Demosthenes' *De Corona*, Cicero's *Brutus*, and Libanius's *Oratio* 1 in support. He admits, however, that "the subsequent history of the genre is difficult to trace since most of the pertinent literature did not survive" (*Galatians*, 15). Nevertheless, he quotes with approval Arnaldo Momigliano's remark that "one vaguely feels the Platonic precedent in Epicurus, Seneca, and perhaps St. Paul"—and goes on to assert, "the cautious 'perhaps' is no longer necessary" (ibid.). Betz also sees Galatians as an example of the "magical letter" (*Himmelsbrief*), though not so much to describe the epistolary genre of Galatians as to provide a basis for his suggestion that Paul expected his letter to bring immediate curses (cf. 1:8–9) or blessings (cf. 6:16) on his converts, depending on their response. So he cites a number of examples of magical letters from K. Preisendanz *Papyri Graecai Magicae* (new ed. A. Henrichs, 2 vols. [Stuttgart: Teubner, 1973–74]. But as W. A. Meeks rhetorically asks, "Will anyone who has actually read the *Zauberpapyri* to which Betz refers, and then reads Galatians, really imagine that he is reading the same kind of literature?" (*JBL* 100 [1981] 306).

The basis for Betz's confidence in Galatians as typical of the apologetic letter genre of antiquity, however, starts to crumble when one looks more closely at the Greek and Roman autobiographical essays with which he compares Galatians, for there is a fundamental difference between them and Galatians: these so-called letters of apology are in reality not real letters at all. As R. G. Bury in his introduction to Plato's *Letter* 7 observes:

> [It is] probable that not only is this letter an "open" letter addressed rather to the general public than to the parties named in the superscription, but that the superscription itself is merely a literary device. The letter was never meant to be sent to Sicily at all . . . so that what Plato is doing in this letter is to indulge in a literary fiction which enables him to publish in epistolary form what is at once a history, an apology, and a manifesto (*Plato*, LCL [London: Heinemann, 1966] 9:474).

Likewise, Isocrates' *Antidosis* is not a letter but, as its author himself calls it, "a discourse which would be, as it were, a true image of my thought and of my whole life" (*Antidosis* 7), and so a defense calculated to dissipate prejudice against him. Isocrates' defense clearly echoes Socrates' defense as presented by Plato in the *Apology* (so A. Momigliano, *Development of Greek Biography*, 59). Yet the *Antidosis* is more discursive than strictly a legal defense to be presented before a court, for, as Isocrates points out, "some things in my discourse are appropriate to be spoken in a courtroom; others are out of place amid such controversies, being frank discussions about philosophy" (*Antidosis* 10).

Demosthenes' *De Corona* is also hardly to be compared to a real letter, being a speech delivered in August, 330 B.C., before a jury of more than five hundred citizens of Athens (cf. C. A. Vance's comments in *Demosthenes*, LCL [London: Heinemann, 1963] 2:14–15). As well, Cicero's *Brutus* is no letter but a lengthy defense of his position by means of a review of Roman procedures of oratory (cf. *Cicero*, LCL [London: Heinemann, 1962] 5:5), while Libanius's autobiography, his *Oratio 1*, is an imitation of Isocrates' *Antidosis* (so A. Momigliano, *Development of Greek Biography*, 60)—with neither comparable either in form or in content to Paul's Galatians. In fact, none of these claimed precedents for Galatians really illuminates the epistolary structure of Galatians, for none is a real letter. Thus we must agree with Wayne Meeks' criticism of Betz and his proposed "apologetic letter" genre: "Betz does not inspire confidence in his thesis . . . by referring almost exclusively to rhetorical and epistolary *theory* rather than to specific examples of real apologies and real letters from antiquity. He does not offer us a single instance of the apologetic letter with which we can compare Galatians. We are therefore asked to interpret Galatians as an example of a genre for which no other example can apparently be cited" (*JBL* 100 [1981] 306).

The classification of Galatians as an apologetic letter has more to do with the style of the letter's argument than with its epistolary structure. Indeed, autobiography, apology, and defense are important factors for any rhetorical analysis of Galatians. But rhetorical analyses must not be confused with or replace attempts to describe the letter's structure. Betz, of course, believes that the epistolary framework of Galatians can be easily removed "as a kind of external bracket for the body of the letter" (*Galatians*, 15), so that what is left is rhetoric or an "apologetic speech"—which Betz, followed by Brinsmead, then analyzes in terms of the rules for forensic speech as found in the classical rhetorical handbooks. Certainly, rhetorical analyses of Galatians are often of great value, and must be discussed at greater length later. Here I would only point out that neither Betz nor Brinsmead has given sufficient attention to an epistolary analysis of Galatians, and so they have too quickly concluded that "the epistolary nature of Galatians has little consequence for the structure of its contents" (quoting Brinsmead, *Dialogical Response*, 37, who even asserts that "papyri give us no help in understanding the overall structure of Paul's letters" [ibid., 39]). In contradistinction, I agree with J. L. White and others that "the common letter tradition, though certainly not the only tradition on which Paul depends, is the primary literary *Gattung* to which Paul's letters belong" (*The Form and Function of the Body of the Greek Letter*, xii). And it is on this basis that I intend to begin the discussion of the structure of Galatians.

2. Epistolary Analysis

Greek letters began with an opening formula ("A to B," or at times "To B from A," with the greeting χαίρειν, lit. "rejoice"; collogically "hail" or "greetings") and ended with a closing formula (e.g., ἐρρῶσθαι σε εὔχομαι, "I pray you good health," ἐρρῶσθαι σε βούλομαι, "I wish you good health," or simply ἔρρωσο, "good health, farewell"). Between the opening and the closing, a number of rather conventional formulae commonly appeared. Analyses of the nonliterary papyri have produced a substantial list of such formulae, of which the following for our purposes are most significant (for texts and ET, see J. L. White, *The Form and Function of the Body of the Greek Letter*):

Thanksgiving: γινώσκειν σε θέλω, πάτερ, ὅτι εὐχαριστῶ πολλὰ Ἰσιδώρῳ τῷ ἐπιτρόπῳ ἐπεὶ συνέστακέ μοι, "I wish you to know, father, that I am greatly thankful to Isidorus the guardian, since he has advised me" (BGU 816);

Prayer: πρὸ μὲν πάντων εὔχομέ σαι ὑγειένειν καὶ προκόπτειν, ἅμα δὲ καὶ τὸ προσκύνημά σου ποιοῦμε ἡμερησίως παρὰ τοῖς πατρώες θεοῖς, "before all things I pray for your health and success; at the time I also make daily obeisance for you before our ancestral gods" (PMich 209:3–6);

Expression of Joy: λιὰν ἐχάρην ἀκούσασα ὅτι, "I rejoiced exceedingly when I heard that" (PGiess 21:3);

Astonishment-Rebuke: θαυμάζω πῶς, "I am surprised how" (POxy 113:20);

Expression of Grief or Distress: ἀκούσας ὅτι νωθρεύῃ ἀγωνιοῦμεν, "I am anxious because I heard you were ill" (BGU 449:4);

Reminder of Past Instruction: ὡς ἠρώτηκά σε, "as I have asked you" (PMich 202:3);

Disclosure: γινώσκειν σε θέλω ὅτι, "I want you to know that" (PGiess 11:4), or γνώριζε οὖν, "know therefore" (PMich 28:16), or ἀλλὰ οἶδα ὅτι, "but I know that" (POxy 1219:11);

Request: παρακαλῶ σαι, μῆτηρ, διαλάγητί μοι, "I beg you, mother, be reconciled to me" (BGU 846:10), or ἐρωτηθεὶς οὖν, ἄδελφε, τάχιόν μοι γράφιν, "I therefore ask you, brother, to write me at once" (PMich 209:9–10), or δέομαι οὖν σου, βασιλεῦ, εἴ σοι δοκεῖ, "I entreat you therefore, king, if it pleases you" (PEnteux 82:6);

Use of the Verb for Hearing or Learning: ἀκούσας δὲ τὰ κατὰ τὸν Πτολεμαῖον ἐλυπήθην σφόδρα, "I was deeply grieved to hear about the case of Ptolemaeus"

(PTebt 760:20); ἐλοιπήθην ἐπιγνοῦσα παρά, "I was grieved to learn from" (POxy 930:4);

περί *with the Genitive*: καὶ περὶ τῶν χωρίων, "and about the fields" (POxy 1220:23);

Notification of a Coming Visit: θεῶν οὖν βουλομένων, πρὸς τὴν ἑορτὴν ... πειράσομαι πρὸς ὑμᾶς γενέσθαι, "If the gods will, therefore, I will try to come to you ... for the feast" (POxy 1666:11);

Reference to Writing: ἔγραψας ἡμῖν ὅτι, "you wrote us that" (PMich 36:1);

Verbs of Saying and Informing: ἐρῖ σοι δὲ Ἀπολινάρις πῶς, "Apolinarius will tell you how" (POxy 932:3); καὶ δηλωσόν μοι πόσαι ἐξέβησαν ἵνα εἰδῶ, "and inform me how many came out so that I may know" (PFay 122:14);

Expression of Reassurance: τοῦτο μὴ νομίσης ὅτι, "do not think that" (PMich 206:11);

Responsibility Statement: μὴ ἀμελήσης ἐν τῇ αὔριον ἀπαντῆσαι πρὸς ἡμᾶς, do not neglect to come and meet us tomorrow" (PAmh 143:2);

The Use of the Vocative to Indicate Transition: φανερόν σοι ποιῶ, ἄδελφε, "I make known to you, brother" (PMich 206:4–5).

Two matters with regard to the frequency and function of these formulae in ancient letters need here to be highlighted. In the first place, as T. Y. Mullins points out, "*The use of one form tends to precipitate the use of others with it*" (*JBL* 91 [1972] 387 [italics his]); and second, "They almost always punctuate a break in the writer's thought" (ibid.). Thus, as Mullins goes on to elaborate:

> The opening is a sort of warm-up for the main issue and provides a convenient clustering place for matters less important than the main issue (but not necessarily introductory to it). The closing constitutes the final communication and is a natural clustering place for matters of minor importance which the writer wants to add before breaking off. But in a letter of any considerable length there will be places where a writer will pause and break the flow of his thought for a moment. He may mark such places with epistolary forms whose relevance to the main subject matter will vary according to the way the writer thinks and expresses himself (ibid.).

So in studying a Greek letter (Galatians included), we need to be alert to the clustering of various epistolary formulae at certain strategic points *and* the use of such clusters to signal significant breaks or turning points in the letter.

A scanning of Paul's letters reveals that they are usually constructed according to the following pattern, which is in line with the structure of Hellenistic letters generally:

1. *Opening* (sender, addressee or addressees, greeting);
2. *Thanksgiving* or *Blessing* (often with an intercession);
3. *Body* (formal opening, connective and transitional formulae, eschatological climax, and sometimes a travelogue);
4. *Paraenesis* (with vocatives prevalent);
5. *Closing* (greetings, doxology, benediction, with a reference to the writing process sometimes included).

Furthermore, a scanning of his letters indicates that Paul used rather freely many of the epistolary formulae of his day. Yet though he used the conventions and formulae of Hellenistic letter writing, he seems not confined to them. For example, the thanksgiving sections which follow most of his salutations (except in Galatians) are generally in line with Greek epistolary style, but also appear to reflect Christian liturgical practice. Nor does Paul use the current epistolary conventions and formulae in any slavish manner. These were matters that were "in the air" and widely practiced, and Paul's use of them should therefore probably be seen as more unconscious adaptations of standard conventions than studied attempts to write in an acceptable fashion. As Robert Funk aptly says in closing his review of the formal features of Paul's letters:

> It should be emphasized that these elements are subject of variation in both context and order, and that some items are optional, although the omission of any one calls for explanation. It is put this way around on the view that Paul is not rigidly following an established pattern, but is creating his own letter form—in relation, of course, to the letter as a literary convention. If he has molded this particular pattern out of the circumstances of his apostolic ministry and on the basis of his theological understanding, he seems to follow it without conscious regard to its structure. It is just the way he writes letters. It is only in this sense that we can legitimately speak of "form" (*Language, Hermeneutic, and Word of God*, 270; see also W. G. Doty, *Letters in Primitive Christianity*, 27–43).

A close analysis of Galatians produces the following list of phrases that by comparison with those of the nonliterary papyri should probably be judged to be based on rather conventional epistolary formulae:

1:1–2 (*salutation*): Παῦλος... ταῖς ἐκκλησίαις τῆς Γαλατίας, "Paul... to the churches of Galatia"
1:3 (*greeting*): χάρις ὑμῖν καὶ εἰρήνη, "grace and peace to you"
1:6 (*rebuke formula*): θαυμάζω ὅτι, "I am astonished that"
1:9 (*reminder of past teaching*): ὡς προειρήκαμεν, καὶ ἄρτι πάλιν λέγω, "as we have said before, so now I say again"
1:11 (*disclosure formula*): γνωρίζω δὲ ὑμῖν, "I want you to know"
1:13 (*disclosure formula*): ἠκούσατε γάρ, "for you have heard"
3:1 (*vocative-rebuke*): ὦ ἀνόητοι Γαλάται, "you foolish Galatians"
3:2 (*verb of hearing*): τοῦτο μόνον θέλω μαθεῖν ἀφ᾽ ὑμῶν, "only this I want to learn from you"
3:7 (*disclosure formula*): γινώσκετε ἄρα ὅτι, "you know then"
3:15 (*vocative-verb of saying*): ἀδελφοί, ... λέγω, "brothers, ... let me take an example"
3:17 (*verb of saying*): τοῦτο δὲ λέγω, "so this I say"
4:1 (*verb of saying*): λέγω δέ, "what I am saying is this"
4:11 (*expression of distress*): φοβοῦμαι ὑμᾶς, "I fear for you"
4:12 (*request formula*): ἀδελφοί, δέομαι ὑμῶν, "I plead with you, brothers"
4:13 (*disclosure formula*): οἴδατε δὲ ὅτι, "you know that"
4:15 (*disclosure formula*): μαρτυρῶ γὰρ ὑμῖν ὅτι, "I testify on your behalf that"
4:19 (*vocative*): τέκνία μου, "my little children"
4:20 (*apostolic parousia*): ἤθελον δὲ παρεῖναι πρὸς ὑμᾶς, "how I wish I could be with you"

4:21   (*verb of saying*): λέγετέ μοι, "tell me"
4:28   (*vocative*): ὑμεῖς δέ, ἀδελφοί, "so you, brothers"
4:31   (*vocative*): διό, ἀδελφοί, "therefore, brothers"
5:2   (*motive for writing formula*): ἴδε ἐγὼ Παῦλος λέγω ὑμῖν ὅτι, "mark my words! I, Paul, tell you that"
5:3   (*disclosure-attestation*): μαρτύρομαι δὲ πάλιν, "again I testify"
5:10   (*confidence formula*): ἐγὼ πέποιθα εἰς ὑμᾶς ἐν κυρίῳ ὅτι, "I am confident in the Lord regarding you that"
5:11   (*vocative*): ἐγὼ δέ, ἀδελφοί, "brothers, if I"
5:13   (*vocative*): ὑμεῖς γὰρ . . . ἀδελφοί, "you, brothers"
5:16   (*verb of saying*): λέγω δέ, "so I say"
6:1   (*vocative*): ἀδελφοί, "brothers"
6:11   (*autographic subscription*): ἴδετε πηλίκοις ὑμῖν γράμμασιν ἔγραψα, "see what large letters I use as I write to you"
6:16   (*benediction*): εἰρήνη ἐπ᾽ αὐτοὺς καὶ ἔλεος, "peace and mercy upon them"
6:18   (*grace wish, vocative*): ἡ χάρις . . . ἀδελφοί, "the grace . . . brothers"

In surveying this list, it is particularly important to note that these formulaic phrases do not appear evenly distributed throughout the letter but are grouped in clusters. Indeed, as Mullins observed with regard to frequency, "one form tends to precipitate the use of others with it" (*JBL* 91 [1972] 387). Equally important, however, is Mullins' point with regard to function: that the clusters of such formulae tend to signal breaks or turning points in the development of a writer's argument (ibid.).

Disregarding for a moment the "verb of saying" formulae (3:15, 17; 4:1, 21; 5:16), which seem to be used mainly to knit portions of the letter's body together, it should be observed that the clusters of formulaic phrases appear in only certain sections:

1:1–3   salutation (sender to addressees) and a greeting;
1:6–13   astonishment-rebuke formula; disclosure statements;
3:1–7   vocative; rebuking questions; disclosure statement;
4:11–20   expression of distress; request formula; disclosure statements; travelogue and a visit wish;
4:28–5:13 vocatives; summary appeal; disclosure-attestation statement; expression of confidence; vocatives;
6:11–18   autographic subscription; benediction; grace wish; vocative.

The opening salutation (1:1–5) and the closing subscription (6:11–18) are clearly identifiable sections. On this everyone agrees. Furthermore, Galatians has no thanksgiving section. So the remainder of the material between the opening salutation and the closing subscription is made up of the body of the letter and the paraenesis. And in this material, as based on the identifiable clusters of formulaic phrases, it is possible to argue that Paul's Galatian letter develops in the following way: (1) a rebuke section (θαυμάζω) that begins at 1:6; (2) a theological section that begins at 3:1; (3) a request section (ἀδελφοί, δέομαι ὑμῶν) that begins at 4:12; and (4) a paraenesis section that begins somewhere between 4:28 (ὑμεῖς δέ, ἀδελφοί) and 5:13 (ὑμεῖς γὰρ . . . ἀδελφοί), with request blending into and becoming explicitly exhortation.

We must deal more fully with all of these matters later in the commentary proper. Suffice it here to say that on the basis of Paul's use of rather standard epistolary formulae, Galatians can be seen to be made up of six identifiable sections: salutation (1:1–5), rebuke (1:6ff.), theological arguments (3:1ff.), request (4:12ff.), paraenesis (beginning somewhere between 4:28 and 5:13), and subscription (6:11–18). The difficulty of identifying precisely where the paraenesis begins suggests that the request and paraenesis sections work together as one unit, with exhortation being an aspect of Paul's overall appeal. Likewise, the way Paul sets up his arguments in 3:1–4:11 by the Antioch episode of 2:11–14 and the material of 2:15–21 indicates that he saw 3:1–4:11 as part of what he began at 1:6. So we may go further to suggest that the basic epistolary structure of Galatians should be seen as follows:

1:1–5   *Salutation;*

1:6–4:11   *Rebuke Section,* with the inclusion of autobiographical details and theological arguments;

4:12–6:10 *Request Section,* with the inclusion of personal, scriptural, and ethical appeals;

6:11–18   *Subscription.*

It is, in fact, this structure that will serve as the basis for our outline of the letter and that will inform our exegesis in the commentary proper.

3. Diachronic Rhetorical Analysis

It is necessary, however, to understand Galatians not only in terms of its epistolary structure. Attention must also be given to its argumentative structures—that is, to the way in which within the letter's epistolary structure Paul has developed his argument by means of then-current rhetorical forms and modes of persuasion. Two ways of analyzing a writing as to its rhetorical structures are possible. The first lays emphasis on the rhetorical forms in their historical context and seeks to trace out lines of genetic relations with other writings of the time. The second examines the argument on its own, classifying its stages of development in terms of general, more universal modes of persuasion. The first method is the historical, comparative method, which has of late been called "diachronic rhetorical criticism"; the second is strictly a compositional method, which has been given the name "synchronic rhetorical criticism" (cf. M. Kessler, *Semitics* 4 [1974] 22–36; see also idem, *Semitics* 7 [1980] 1–27). It is with the first that we are here concerned. The second will be treated in what immediately follows.

Hans Dieter Betz's work on Galatians is to date the most serious and significant attempt to interpret the letter on the basis of a diachronic rhetorical analysis (*NTS* 21 [1975] 353–79; idem, *Galatians,* 14–25). As Betz sees it, Galatians is an "apologetic letter" that conforms closely to the requirements of forensic rhetoric (i.e., rhetoric addressed to a jury or judge, which seeks to defend or accuse someone with regard to certain past actions) as set out in the handbooks on rhetoric by Aristotle (*Rhetoric*), Cicero (*De Inventione* and *De Optimo Genere Oratorum*), Quintilian (*Institutio Oratoria*), and others (esp. the anonymous *Rhetorica ad*

Herennium of about 85 B.C., which was formerly attributed to Cicero), and as exemplified in Plato's *Epistle* 7, Isocrates's *Antidosis,* Demosthenes's *De Corona,* Cicero's *Brutus,* and Libanius's *Oratio* 1.

The basic elements of forensic rhetoric as developed by the classical rhetoricians are as follows:

1. *Exordium* (introduction), which sets out the character of the speaker and defines the central issues being addressed;
2. *Narratio* (narration), which is a statement of the facts that relate to the issues of the case;
3. *Propositio* (proposition), which states the points of agreement and disagreement and the central issues to be proved;
4. *Probatio* (confirmation), which develops the central arguments;
5. *Refutatio* (refutation), which is a rebuttal of the opponents' arguments;
6. *Peroratio* (conclusion), which summarizes the case and evokes a sympathetic response.

Betz argues that Galatians, when compared with this classical model, should be seen as Paul's letter of apology to his converts in Asia Minor—wherein they are the jury, he is the defendant, and the intruders are his accusers. Set within an epistolary framework that "separates so easily that it appears as a kind of external bracket for the body of the letter" (*Galatians,* 15), its argument proceeds as follows:

I.	Epistolary Prescript	1:1–5
II.	*Exordium*	1:6–11
III.	*Narratio*	1:12–2:14
IV.	*Propositio*	2:15–21
V.	*Probatio*	3:1–4:31
VI.	*Exhortatio*	5:1–6:10
VII.	Epistolary Postscript, with a *Peroratio* included (vv 12–17)	6:11–18.

Now there is no doubt that Betz's treatment of Galatians must be considered a landmark in NT scholarship. It is a bold, new conception of the form and function of the letter that is supported by magisterial control of the ancient literary parallels and by precise exegesis of the text itself. Compared to many descriptions of Galatians as a passionate but confused writing, Betz's stress on Paul's care in the construction of the argument is to be welcomed—even though, as we must argue, Betz can be faulted for viewing that care in too scholastic and rigid a manner. As Wayne Meeks rightly says in praise of Betz's work, particularly on Gal 1–2: "With great deftness Betz leads us step by step through the first two chapters, showing how the apparently ambiguous and even disjointed allusions to the events in Jerusalem and in Antioch serve not only a very precisely conceived defensive strategy, but also a profound theological *peripeteia*" (*JBL* 100 [1981] 305). At many places, in fact, Betz has demonstrated through diachronic rhetorical analysis how one part of Paul's letter relates to other parts, thereby revealing something of the underlying rhetorical structure of Paul's argument. From now on, any interpretation of Galatians that treats one section as independent from the rest must be considered suspect because of Betz's rhetorical analysis.

Yet there are certain major criticisms that must be raised against Betz's work, despite its great strengths. And it is in these areas that a diachronic rhetorical analysis such as Betz proposes must be carefully qualified.

In the first place, it needs to be pointed out that Betz's attempt to interpret *all* of Galatians in terms of forensic rhetoric breaks down on a number of counts. His thesis works best for the first two chapters, where Paul begins by accusing his opponents of perverting the gospel (1:7) and by defending himself against their accusations (1:10). Indeed, Paul's vehement denials throughout these chapters (1:1, 11–12, 16–17, 19–20, 22; 2:5, 6, 17, 21) and his accompanying autobiographical narrative in support of his statements (1:13–2:21) make the imagery of a judicial proceeding an appropriate analogy and feasible backdrop for this section of the argument (cf. J. P. Sampley, *NTS* 23 [1977] 477–82). Yet Betz's thesis has tougher sledding when it moves into chaps. 3–4 and 5–6. As for chaps. 3–4, Betz himself concedes, "Admittedly, an analysis of these chapters in terms of rhetoric is extremely difficult" (*Galatians*, 129). The "apparent confusion" of these chapters he explains on the basis of Quintilian's advice "to diversify by a thousand figures." But that appears to be a somewhat thin and rather desperate justification for keeping Galatians within the bounds of classical forensic rhetoric (cf. D. E. Aune, "Review of H. D. Betz, *Galatians*," *RSR* 7 [1981] 325, who notes that Gal 3–4 "does not easily fit the role assigned it in the rhetorical analysis proposed by Betz"). Actually, besides Paul's use of *interrogatio* in 3:1–5 and *exemplum* in 3:6–7, Betz is not able to find any other significant feature in these chapters that relates directly to the category of forensic rhetoric. So he breaks up the material of these chapters into separate proofs and discusses each in isolation from its context. Likewise with regard to chaps. 5–6, Betz says, "It is rather puzzling to see that parenesis plays only a marginal role in the ancient rhetorical handbooks, if not in rhetoric itself" (*Galatians*, 254). And he laments the fact that even Quintilian has no special treatment of it.

What Betz has done, in effect, has been to push a good thesis too hard and too far. He has tried to force all of Galatians into the mold of forensic rhetoric, whereas Paul's biblical exegesis in chaps. 3–4 reflects more Jewish rhetorical conventions and his exhortations in chaps. 5–6 are more congenial to a deliberative form of Greco-Roman rhetoric than a forensic form (for definitions of forensic, deliberative, and demonstrative rhetoric, see P. Dixon, *Rhetoric*, 22–23; for claims that "Galatians is probably best viewed as deliberative rhetoric," see G. A. Kennedy, *New Testament Interpretation through Rhetorical Criticism*, 145–47, and F. F. Church, "Rhetorical Structure and Design in Paul's Letter to Philemon," *HTR* 71 [1978] 17–33). Furthermore, in his concentration on forensic rhetoric as providing the basic structure and the argumentative forms for Galatians, Betz has failed to appreciate the dramatic shift in mood that occurs at 4:12 and to ignore such epistolary evidence as we have cited above as would signal the start of a major new section there. And even where the analogy of a judicial proceeding best fits the data of Galatians (i.e., chaps. 1–2), Betz has been too rigid in application. For at times in those chapters Paul is the accuser and the prosecutor as well as the defendant, and his converts are in the dock as deserters as well as being the jury.

A second major criticism that can be raised against Betz's treatment of Galatians is that he uses the parallels drawn from classical forensic rhetoric in a strictly genealogical manner, without giving due consideration to their presence in other types of ancient literature and so without acknowledging their appearance in Paul's letter as being more analogical than strictly genealogical in nature. Indeed, Betz has shown that certain features of Greco-Roman judicial rhetoric can be paralleled in Galatians—for example, as per Betz's analysis, the expression of astonishment in 1:6 (cf. Cicero, *De Inventione* 1.17.25); the discussion of adversaries in 1:7 (cf. *Rhetorica ad Herennium* 1.5.8); the statement of *causa* in 1:6–7 (cf. *Rhetorica ad Herennium* 1.4.7); the transition of 1:10–11 (cf. Quintilian, *Institutio Oratoria* 4.1.76–79); the subdivisions of the *narratio* throughout 1:12–2:14 (cf. Quintilian, *Institutio Oratoria* 4.2.47–51); the support of denials throughout 1:12–2:14 (cf. Quintilian, *Institutio Oratoria* 4.2.1–11); the assigning of reasons or motives for major events in 1:16 and 2:2 (cf. Quintilian, *Institutio Oratoria* 4.2.52); the characterization of persons in 2:4, 6, 11–14 (cf. Quintilian, *Institutio Oratoria* 4.2.52); the statement of the proposition to be elaborated and defended in 2:19–20 (cf. Quintilian, *Institutio Oratoria* 4.4.1); the interrogation of witnesses in 3:1–5 and 4:8–11 (cf. Aristotle, *Rhetoric* 1.15.15); the use of examples in 3:6, 15 and 4:22 (cf. Quintilian, *Institutio Oratoria* 5.11.6 and 32–35); the diversity of arguments in 3:1–4:31 (cf. Quintilian, *Institutio Oratoria* 5.14.3); the recapitulation in 6:11–18 (cf. Quintilian, *Institutio Oratoria* 6.1.1–2); and the appeal to the emotions in 6:12–17 (cf. Cicero, *De Inventione* 1.55.106). Some of these features, however, are also paralleled by certain epistolary conventions of the day—for example, the expression of astonishment (1:6), subdivisions of the narrative (1:12–2:14), recapitulation (6:11–18), and appeal to the emotions (6:12–17). Furthermore, a number of these features are common to the rhetoric of the OT, which Paul knew well—for example, the characterization of his opponents in 1:7 as οἱ ταράσσοντες ("the troublers," see also 5:10 and 6:17) may very well be an allusion to Achar "the troubler of Israel" (cf. 1 Chr 2:7); the use of curses in 1:8–9 was an essential part of the covenant form; the appeal to revelation in 1:12, 16; 2:2 as the basis for a prophetic ministry is a common feature in the OT (cf. Exod 3–6; Isa 6; Jer 1); the characterization of persons as being "false" in 2:4, 6, 11–14 occurs often in the OT (e.g., Jer 6:13; 26:7–16; 27:9; 28:1; 29:1, 8); the recital of Israel's history beginning with Abraham is, of course, frequent in the OT (cf. Josh 24:2–3; Neh 9:7–8; Isa 5:2); and the quotation of divine oracles and the precepts of wise men, as in 3:6–14, is an OT commonplace. And all this has not even touched on the many parallels that can be drawn from Paul's Pharisaic background, as codified later in the Talmud and Midrashim, which we intend to highlight in the commentary proper. In sum, therefore, Betz's use of the parallels drawn from classical forensic rhetoric to demonstrate only genealogical relationships is somewhat wrong-headed. David E. Aune is much closer to the mark to see in Galatians "an eclectic combination of various rhetorical techniques and styles of diverse origin which are nevertheless welded together in a new and distinctive literary creation" ("Review of H. D. Betz, *Galatians*," *RSR* 7 [1981] 323).

Furthermore, Betz can be faulted for relating Galatians to the classical forms of forensic rhetoric in too scholastic and rigid a manner. Indeed, as himself a member of the Greco-Roman world, Paul may be assumed to have been influenced at least to some extent by classical rhetoric. Martin Hengel has demonstrated that "'Palestinian' Judaism also shared in the 'religious *koine*' of its Hellenistic environment" (*Judaism and Hellenism*, 1:312). And it should not be surprising that a Jew

of Tarsus, who trained under Gamaliel at Jerusalem, became a convert to the rising
messianic movement called Christianity, took leadership in the extension of that
gospel among Gentiles, and wrote pastorally to converts in Asia Minor, would use
in Galatians many literary and rhetorical conventions then current in the Greco-
Roman world. "Even if," as G. A. Kennedy observes, "he had not studied in a Greek
school, there were many handbooks of rhetoric in common circulation which he
could have seen. He and the evangelists as well would, indeed, have been hard put
to escape an awareness of rhetoric as practiced in the culture around them, for the
rhetorical theory of the schools found its immediate application in almost every
form of oral and written communication" (*New Testament Interpretation through
Rhetorical Criticism*, 10; cf. idem, *The Art of Persuasion in Greece*, 7–8; see also D. Daube,
HUCA 22 [1949] 239–64; R. M. Grant, *ATR* 34 [1952] 223–26). The forms of
classical rhetoric were "in the air," and Paul seems to have used them almost
unconsciously for his own purposes—much as he used the rules of Greek grammar.

Paul's argument in Galatians, therefore, cannot be judged simply as a replica of
some classical model. It reflects certain features of classical forensic rhetoric,
particularly in its first two chapters, and Betz has made a significant contribution
to the study of Galatians in pointing these features out. But Betz must be faulted
for (1) trying to make all of Galatians fit the model of forensic rhetoric or conform
to the genre of "apologetic letter," (2) drawing hard genealogical lines between
this one model and Galatians, without taking sufficiently into account other
epistolary and rhetorical influences on Paul, and (3) understanding the impact of
classical rhetoric on Paul in too scholastic and rigid a fashion. It would seem far
more appropriate to use the parallels Betz has highlighted as one set of descriptive
tools or influences to be taken into account along with others for interpreting
Paul's letter to the Galatians.

Much the same can be said with regard to the rhetorical use of chiasmus (i.e.,
the literary pattern A-B-B-A) by Paul in Galatians. John Bligh has argued that all
of Galatians must be seen as having been carefully structured in terms of chiasmus
(*Galatians: A Discussion of St. Paul's Epistle*). He begins with the chiastic structure that
J. B. Lightfoot long ago observed in 4:4–5 (cf. Lightfoot's *Galatians*, 168), goes on
to expand that into what he calls the "Central Chiasm" of 4:1–10, and then builds a case
for the "Symmetrical Structure of Galatians" wherein everything that precedes
4:1–10 can be matched with everything that follows in chiastic fashion (Bligh,
Galatians, 37–42, passim). Thus he lays out the structure of the letter as follows:

A   Prologue, 1:1–1:12;
B   Autobiographical Section, 1:13–2:10;
C   Justification by Faith, 2:11–3:4;
D   Arguments from Scripture, 3:5–3:29;
E   *Central Chiasm*, 4:1–4:10;
D¹ Argument from Scripture, 4:11–4:31;
C¹ Justification by Faith, 5:1–5:10;
B¹ Moral Section, 5:11–6:11;
A¹ Epilogue, 6:12–6:18

Bligh, however, fails to take into account anything having to do with an
epistolary analysis of Galatians, which would give just as reasonable a rationale for

many of the parallels he sees (e.g., between the prologue and the epilogue and between the Abraham accounts of 3:6–9 and 4:21–31) and which would provide far more objective controls for his understanding of the letter's structure. And Bligh fails to take into consideration other types of rhetorical analysis, either of a diachronic variety (as Betz's) or of a synchronic variety (as will be treated in what immediately follows).

So while it cannot be denied that chiasmus is a factor in Galatians and must be treated seriously in the exegesis of at least some portions of the letter (e.g., 1:1; 4:4–5, 25–26), it must not be treated in too hamfisted a manner and cannot be understood in any scholastic or rigid fashion. Chiasmus was one of many rhetorical tools lying at hand for Paul's use. It probably reflects, in large measure, the *parallelismus membrorum* of Jewish thought generally and Israelite poetry in particular. Yet other rhetorical tools were also at hand, and to them we must now turn.

4. Synchronic Rhetorical Analysis

"Rhetorical study, in its strict sense," Aristotle said, "is concerned with the modes of persuasion" (*Rhetoric* 1.1)—that is, not just with what is said (content) but how it is said (form). As Aristotle continues, "it is not enough to know what we ought to say; we must also say it as we ought." Furthermore, Aristotle defined rhetoric as "the faculty of observing *in any given case* the available means of persuasion" (ibid. 1.2; emphasis his, though, of course, italics mine), thereby understanding rhetoric in its synchronic dimension as not confined to any particular art, science, or subject matter, but applicable to "almost any subject presented to us" (ibid.).

Paul's letter to the Galatians is, of course, the "given case" at hand, and it is just as open to a synchronic rhetorical analysis as it is to a diachronic rhetorical analysis. In fact, more so! For the more unified we see the letter the more necessary it is for us to undertake such a compositional analysis. And the less reliance we place on diachronic exemplars for a full description of the course of Paul's argument, the more important become the synchronic features of that argument for interpretation.

Aristotle grouped all of the modes of rhetorical persuasion under three basic headings—viz., ethos, pathos, and logic:

> Of the modes of persuasion furnished by the spoken word there are three kinds. The first kind depends on the personal character of the speaker [ethos]; the second on putting the audience into a certain frame of mind [pathos]; the third on the proof, or apparent proof, provided by the words of the speech itself [logic] (ibid. 1.2).

Cicero's summation of the process of rhetorical composition has five parts:

> [The orator] must first hit upon what to say; then manage and marshall his discoveries, not merely in an orderly fashion but with a discriminating eye for the exact weight . . . of each argument; next go on to array them in adornments of style; after that keep them guarded in his memory; and in the end deliver them with effect and charm (*De Oratore* 1.31.142).

Within such generalized summaries were developed a number of categories of persuasion that were used widely by speakers and writers in the Greco-Roman world of Paul's day. Indeed, those who based themselves directly on Aristotle (*Rhetoric*), Cicero (*De Inventione* and *De Optimo Genere Oratorum*), and the anonymous writer of *Rhetorica ad Herennium* developed their categories almost ad infinitum, for rhetoricians delight in classifying and subdividing matters. A catalogue of specific rhetorical categories used in antiquity goes far beyond our present controls—certainly beyond our present interests. But certain rhetorical categories were generally current in Paul's day. And a number of these can be seen in Paul's Galatians argument.

A major category for ancient rhetoricians was that of *ethos*, or proof deriving from the character of the speaker himself. Aristotle began his discussion of rhetorical categories here and saw the speaker's personal character as constituting just about the most effective means of proof:

Persuasion is achieved by the speaker's personal character when the speech is so spoken as to make us think him credible. We believe good men more fully and more readily than others; this is true generally whatever the question is, and absolutely true where exact certainty is impossible and opinions are divided. . . . It is not true, as some writers assume in their treatises on rhetoric, that the personal goodness revealed by the speaker contributes nothing to his power of persuasion. On the contrary, his character may almost be called the most effective means of persuasion he possesses (*Rhetoric* 1.2).

And this emphasis continued unabated in Paul's day, as in Quintilian's repeated stress on an orator's virtue as having the greatest evidential value (e.g., *Institutio Oratoria* 12.1.3: "I do not merely assert that the ideal orator should be a good man, but I affirm that no man can be an orator unless he is a good man"). This form of proof appears in both forensic and deliberative rhetoric—as when a satirist offers an apologia for his life and writings and then asks his audience for the right to continue vexing and mending the world.

Paul, too, appeals to *ethos*. In fact, he uses it in Galatians as a platform for his entire argument. It is because of his character as (1) an apostle commissioned by Jesus Christ and God the Father (1:1), (2) a servant of Christ (1:10), (3) one who received from Christ the message he proclaims (1:11–12), and (4) one who was set apart and called by God from birth to his ministry (1:13–17) that his addressees are to believe him. It is because of his faithfulness to the gospel amidst fluctuating approval and deviation on the part of other Christian leaders (1:18–2:14) that his addressees are to have confidence in him. And it is because of his adherence to "the truth of the gospel" in his life as well as in his preaching (2:19–20; 6:14–15), even in the face of persecution (5:11; 6:17), that his authority is invulnerable. Thus because of his character, he has the right to establish the canon for "the Israel of God" (6:16).

Of the various logical categories of rhetoric in antiquity, much was made of *enthymeme*, or proof based on a deduction from a major or minor premise to a conclusion. Aristotle called it a "rhetorical syllogism" and insisted that "everyone who effects persuasion through proof uses either enthymemes or examples—there is no other way" (*Rhetoric* 1.2). In actual practice, an enthymeme may run from premise to conclusion or from conclusion to premise. When the former, such words as "therefore," "hence," "thus," or "which show that" appear; when the latter, such words as "since," "for," "because," or "for the reason" that are used.

Often, though not always, Paul's use of γάρ (thirty-five times) and ὅτι (nine times) in Galatians signals the presence of enthymemes in his argument. For example, his claim that his preaching is the standard by which to measure any other message (1:6–9) is deduced from the fact that his gospel was received by divine revelation (1:11–12). The implicit major premise is that all messages received by revelation from God have ultimate authority, which is the premise that shapes the entire argument of Galatians. The autobiographical section of the letter (1:13–2:10) develops further that premise by providing evidence that Paul's gospel came to him not through human tradition but by divine revelation. Likewise, the argument from Scripture (3:6–14) builds on the premise of divine revelation, and so lends authority to his message. And from this premise, Paul concludes that the message of the Judaizers is under a curse since it contradicts what he proclaimed (1:8–9).

Paired with enthymeme in the rhetorical handbooks was proof by *example*. Whereas enthymeme argues from a premise to a conclusion or vice versa, argument by example seeks to persuade by appealing to a specific person, thing, or situation to establish or illustrate a general concept, principle, or truth. Of these two rubrics, Aristotle wrote:

> In some oratorical styles, examples prevail; in others, enthymemes. In like manner, some orators are better at the former and some at the latter. Speeches that rely on examples are as persuasive as the other kind, but those which rely on enthymemes excite the louder applause (*Rhetoric* 1.2).

In Galatians Paul puts forward Abraham as an example for his converts. He does this first by citing Abraham's faith (3:6–9) to confirm the principle that righteousness comes by faith and not by keeping the law. So he links the Galatians' experience of the Spirit (3:1–5) with Abraham's faith, thereby providing double support for the "rule of faith." Implicit as well in his argument is the appeal to imitate Abraham, "the man of faith," by continuing to live a life of faith. Then he focuses on Abraham in the Hagar-Sarah allegory (4:21–31) to make the point that just as Abraham obeyed God and got rid of Hagar and her son, so the Galatian Christians are to get rid of the Judaizers. As well, by setting out the accounts of his own loyalty to "the truth of the gospel" (1:13–2:21) in roughly parallel fashion to that of Abraham's loyalty to God (see the commentary proper), Paul positions himself alongside Abraham as a model for his converts to emulate. He even begins his appeal by calling on his converts to "become like me" (4:12). Thus as Abraham exemplified the truth of the gospel, so does Paul. The argument of Galatians, in fact, is structured in terms of these two parallel models or examples.

Ancient rhetoricians also made much of *argument by definition*. And Paul's Galatian letter is no exception. One of the most important terms in Galatians is "the gospel," which Paul defines as to its uniqueness in 1:6–9, as to its source in 1:11-12, and as to its content in 1:13ff. He uses the phrase "the truth of the gospel" in 2:5, 14 as a sort of catch phrase or caption for this content, with that content then further expressed in what appear to be five confessional portions (1:4; 3:1, 13, 27–28; 4:4–5) and a "sayings" statement (3:26) drawn from the proclamation of the early church (see comments in the commentary proper on these verses). At 3:8 Paul links the gospel (note the verbal form προευηγγελίσατο, "proclaimed the gospel . . . in advance") with the promise given to Abraham, and thereafter drops the term "gospel" and develops a definition of the promise (cf. 3:14–29; 4:23, 28). Since, however, the gospel is identified with the promise, defining the promise is actually a continuation of the process of defining the gospel. Thus just as the gospel has direct benefits for Gentiles, so the promise pertains to Gentiles as well (cf. 3:8,14, 29; 4:28).

Closely related to the argumentative use of definition is *argument by dissociation of ideas*. When the process of dissociation is developed into a series of antithetical pairs, the technique of dissociation lends structure to the argument. And this is what occurs in Paul's Galatian argument, as in his antithetical pairings of blessing versus curse, faith versus works, spirit versus flesh, freedom versus slavery, the free woman versus the slave woman, the free woman's son versus the slave woman's son, and "Jerusalem that is above" versus "the present city of Jerusalem." These antithetical pairs elaborate the distinction between "the gospel of Christ" and "the other gospel" of the Judaizers, and so serve to provide a framework for Paul's argument.

Argument by dissociation of ideas also involves, of course, a dissociation of individuals or a group from those offending ideas, and so *argument by the severance of a group and its members* was used by ancient rhetoricians. Some commentators on Galatians treat Paul's converts and the Judaizers as one. Bernard Brinsmead, for example, writes, "The Galatians are in an important sense the offending party, and the whole letter is written because of their espousal of an offending theology . . . There is no division into heresies of the intruders and heresies of the Galatians" (*Dialogical Response*, 69; which assumption allows Brinsmead to treat all of Paul's statements as countering both the Judaizers and the Galatian Christians, and so not impede his own excessive use of mirror reading or his understanding of all of Galatians as a "dialogical response to opponents"). Now, certainly, Paul's anguish over the Galatian situation was not just because the Judaizers were present but because his converts were responding favorably to their enticements. In that sense they were united. Yet Paul also makes a clear distinction between his converts and the troublemakers, and the entire Galatian letter elaborates this distinction and uses it rhetorically in support of its argument. Thus, though the Galatian Christians are in the process of deserting (note the present tense of μετατίθεσθε, "you are deserting," in 1:6) because of being bewitched (3:1) and hindered (5:7), they are not the ones causing the trouble or trying to distort the gospel (1:7)—they are not the leaven in the lump that needs to be removed (5:9) or the slave woman's son who needs to be expelled (4:30). Paul, in fact, is confident that his Galatian converts will agree with him (5:10a). The Judaizers, on the other hand, are the offending party, and he is sure that they "will pay the penalty" for their teachings (5:10b).

This dissociation of the Galatians ("you") from the Judaizers ("they") is an important feature in the structure of Paul's argument. Indeed, Paul rebukes his converts. But he also dissociates them from the opponents. The Judaizers who come from outside the congregation are the troublemakers and the perverters of the gospel (1:7); they are under a curse (1:8–9); they are guilty of witchcraft (3:1); they are not truly seeking the Galatians' good (4:17); they are children of the slave woman Hagar (4:29); they are obstructing the Christians' progress (5:7) and are leaven in the dough (5:9); they will bear their own judgment (5:10); they only seek to circumcise the Galatians so that they can boast about it and thereby avoid persecution because of the cross of Christ (6:12); they do not, in fact, keep the law themselves (6:13). So Paul urges his converts to exercise their proper role as the true sons of Abraham, the true beneficiaries of the Spirit's activity, the true heirs of the promise, and the true children of the free woman and the heavenly Jerusalem, and so expel those troublemakers (4:30).

Other ancient logical categories of persuasion can be discerned in Paul's Galatian letter as well. For example, argumentation was often structured to enhance the value of something by showing how it was the means to something of even greater value. Or, conversely, something may be devalued by showing how it was the means to a debased end. Paul uses a *means-end argument* when he links the gospel and the promise (3:8) and then shows that through that association the blessing given to Abraham comes to the Gentiles (3:9, 14). The cross of Christ and faith are also presented as the means of obtaining the Abrahamic blessing (3:6–14). Conversely, the law and one's keeping of the law cannot be the means of obtaining life or righteousness, since the law brings God's curse and imprisons mankind under sin (3:10, 21–24). Furthermore, the *argument of direction*, which attempts to show how a step taken will lead to a "slippery slope" that allows no stopping and ends in total capitulation, is used by Paul when he argues that acceptance of circumcision results in the necessity to keep the whole law, in losing Christ, and in falling from divine grace (5:2–4). Likewise, Paul uses the *argument by repetition and amplification*, by which a speaker draws attention to his central themes by repeating certain key words and building on them, particularly in his repetition and treatment of the terms "faith" and "promise." In 3:6-14, πίστις, "faith," or πιστεύειν, "to believe," appear eight times; in 3:14 ἐπαγγελία, "promise," is used, and then repeated seven times more in 3:15–22; in 3:22 πίστις occurs again, and then is repeated seven times more in 3:23–29. Thus Paul's repetition and amplification of key terms in 3:6–29 serves rhetorically to carry the movement and highlight the emphases of the argument.

In addition to proof derived from a speakers' character and proof based on the demonstration of a case by means of argument—that is, in addition to *ethos* and *logic*—ancient rhetoricians looked on *pathos* as an important form of persuasion and used it to their advantage in argumentation. By *pathos* they meant the emotions induced in an audience, with the purpose of eliciting a favorable response to the speaker's words. Peter Dixon speaks of the rhetorical function of *pathos* as follows:

> The audience begins to feel that the speaker must be right, and is won over to his side. The skilful rhetorician will put the hearers into a receptive frame of mind and then proceed to play upon their feelings, arousing delight or sorrow, love or hatred, indignation or mirth. It follows that the orator must understand the complexities of the human heart in order to gauge the probable responses of his audience, and to work successfully on their attitudes and foibles (*Rhetoric*, 25).

And this is exactly what Paul does throughout Galatians in alternating expressions of sternness and tenderness, wherein the whole gamut of astonishment, irony, sarcasm, threat, promise, affection, wise counsel, and Christian concern is run. For example, Paul begins the body of his letter with an expression of astonishment and perplexity ("I am astonished," 1:6). Then he threatens his opponents with damnation ("Let him be eternally condemned!" 1:8–9), going on to speak of their misguided zeal (4:17), their coming judgment (5:10b), their unworthy motivations (6:12), and their duplicity (6:13). He even in caustic sarcasm—in what must be the crudest of all Paul's extant, written statements—says of his knife-wielding, circumcising opponents: "I wish they would go the whole way and emasculate themselves!" (5:12).

With irony he refers to the Jerusalem apostles as "those who seemed to be important" and "those reputed to be pillars" (2:6, 9). With evident agitation he addresses his converts as "You foolish Galatians!" (3:1), though also with affection as "brothers" (1:11; 3:15; 5:13; 6:1, 18). In his appeal he reminds his converts of their great concern for him at an earlier time (4:13–15), and he speaks of his concern for them under the metaphor of a mother in the pains of childbirth (4:19). Throughout his exhortations of 5:1– 6:10 the tone and feeling of *pathos* prevail. And his closing remarks in the subscription, "See what large letters I use as I write to you with my own hand!" (6:11) and "Finally, let no one cause me trouble, for I bear on my body the marks of Jesus" (6:17), reverberate with emotion, as we will attempt to explicate in commenting on these portions later.

The persuasive modes of the classical rhetorical handbooks had become the common coinage of the realm in Paul's day. One did not have to be formally trained in rhetoric to use them. Nor did rhetoricians have proprietory rights on them. In his Galatian letter (as elsewhere in his writings), Paul seems to have availed himself almost unconsciously of the rhetorical forms at hand, fitting them into his inherited epistolary structures and filling them out with such Jewish theological motifs and exegetical methods as would be particularly significant in countering what the Judaizers were telling his converts. All this he did in order to highlight his essential message: "Christ gave himself for our sins" (1:4), "Christ crucified" (3:1), "Christ redeemed us from the curse of the law" (3:13), Christians being "all sons of God through faith in Christ Jesus" (3:26), Christians being "all one in Christ Jesus" (3:27–28), and Christians having "the full rights of sons" before God apart from the law (4:4–5)—the five basic confessional portions (1:4; 3:1,13, 27–28; 4:4–5) and the one "sayings" statement (3:26) that Paul draws from the proclamation of the early church. It is, in fact, this combination of Hellenistic epistolary structures, Greco-Roman rhetorical forms, Jewish exegetical procedures, and Christian soteriological confessions—together, of course, with Paul's own revelational experiences and pastoral concerns—that makes up Paul's letter to the Galatians. It is our hope to spell out all of these features in the exegetical studies that follow.

I. Salutation (1:1–5)

Bibliography

Barrett, C. K. *The Signs of an Apostle.* ———. *"Shaliah* and Apostle." In *Donum Gentilicium.* FS D. Daube, ed. C. K. Barrett, E. Bammel, and W. D. Davies. London: Oxford University Press, 1978. 88–102. **Bauckham, R. J.** "Barnabas in Galatians." *JSNT* 2 (1979) 61–70. **Berger, K.** "Apostelbrief und apostolische Rede: Zum Formular frühchristlicher Briefe." *ZNW* 65 (1974) 190–231. **Burton, E. deW.** "Αἰών and Αἰώνιος" and "'Ενεστώς." In *Galatians,* 426–33. **Deissmann, A.** *Light from the Ancient East,* 224–46. **Doty, W. G.** *Letters in Primitive Christianity.* **Fridrichsen, A.** *The Apostle and His Message.* **Friedrich, G.** "Lohmeyers These über 'Das paulinische Briefpräskript' kritisch beleuchtet." *ZNW* 46 (1955) 272–74. **Lightfoot, J. B.** "The Name and Office of an Apostle." In *Galatians* (1890), 92–101. **Lohmeyer, E.** "Probleme paulinischer Theologie: I. Briefliche Grussüberschriften." *ZNW* 26 (1927) 158–73. **Lohse, E.** "Ursprung und Prägung des christlichen Apostolats." *TZ* 9 (1953) 259–75. **Rengstorf, K. H.** "ἀπόστολος." *TDNT* 1:407–45. **Schmithals, W.** *The Office of Apostle in the Early Church.* **Schnider, F.,** and **Stenger, W.** *Studien zum neutestamentlichen Briefformular.*

Translation

¹*Paul, an apostle—not from men nor through any man, but through Jesus Christ and [from] God the Father,ᵃ who raised him from the dead—²and all the brothers with me. To the churches of Galatia.*

³*Grace and peace to you from God ourᵇ Father and the Lord Jesus Christ, ⁴who gave himself forᶜ our sins in order that he might rescue us from the present evil age, according to the will of our God and Father, ⁵to whom be glory for ever and ever. Amen.*

Notes

ᵃMarcion omitted καὶ θεοῦ πατρός, "and [from] God the Father" (and so probably read αὐτόν, "himself," for αὐτόν, "him").

ᵇInstead of πατρὸς ἡμῶν καὶ κυρίου, "our Father and the Lord" (as in ℵ A 33 81 et al.), P⁴⁶ P⁵¹ᵛⁱᵈ B D G H Byzantine vg syr copˢᵃ read πατρὸς καὶ κυρίου ἡμῶν, "our Father and Lord." There is some evidence for the text without any personal pronoun: πατρὸς καὶ κυρίου, "Father and Lord," 1877 Pelag Chrys Aug; less evidence for two personal pronouns: πατρὸς ἡμῶν καὶ κυρίου ἡμῶν, "our Father and our Lord," copᵇᵒ eth.

ᶜInstead of ὑπέρ, "for" (as in P⁵¹ B H 33 TR), P⁴⁶ᵛⁱᵈ ℵ* A D G et al. read περί, "for."

Form/Structure/Setting

Greek letters began with a formulaic salutation or prescript: "A to B," or at times "To B from A," with the greeting χαίρειν (lit. "rejoice"; colloquially, "greetings," "welcome," "hello"). So in line with the conventions of his day, Paul begins his Galatian letter with his name (v 1), an identification of his addressees (v 2), and a greeting (v 3). He also refers to those who join him in sending the letter (v 2), expands the greeting by the insertion of what appears to be an early Christian confession (v 4), and adds a doxology (v 5). More importantly, Paul goes beyond the epistolary conventions of his day by pouring into his salutation (1) affirmations

regarding his apostleship (v 1) and Christ's salvific work (v 4), and (2) allusions to
God the Father's activity and will (vv 1b, 4b) and his converts' salvation (v 4)—
thereby highlighting at the very beginning the central themes of his letter. In the
process, two rather typical Pauline methodological features appear: (1) that of
"going off at a word" (cf. the elaborations on "apostle," "God the Father," and "the
Lord Jesus Christ") and (2) that of chiasmus (cf. "not *from* men nor *through* any
man, but *through* Jesus Christ and [*from*] God the Father").

Comment

1 Παῦλος, "Paul," is a Greek name that means "little." As a Jew of the tribe of
Benjamin (cf. Phil 3:5), he proudly bore the name of Israel's first king, the
Benjamite Saul. As a Roman citizen (cf. Acts 16:37–38; 25:10–12), he would have
had three names: a clan or family *nomen*, preceded by a personal *praenomen* and
followed by a more commonly used *cognomen*. Greeks and other provincials who
gained Roman citizenship kept their Greek names as cognomens, to which they
added Roman nomens and praenomens—usually those of the ones to whom they
owed their citizenship. Neither Paul's nomen nor his praenomen appears in the
NT. As a Jewish Christian missioner to Gentiles, he seems to have used only his
Greek name Paul, which, as a Roman cognomen, would have been acceptable to
both Greeks and Romans without bringing in any nuance as to status.

ἀπόστολος, "apostle," is the term Paul uses in Galatians, as well as in all his letters,
to epitomize his consciousness of having been commissioned by God to proclaim
with authority the message of salvation in Jesus Christ. In the NT the noun
ἀπόστολος connotes personal, delegated authority; it speaks of being commissioned to represent another. It is used broadly of anyone sent by another (cf. John
13:16, "an ἀπόστολος is not greater than the one who sent him"), of Christian
brothers sent from Ephesus to Corinth (cf. 2 Cor 8:23, "They are ἀπόστολοι of the
churches"), of Epaphroditus sent by the Philippian church to Paul (cf. Phil 2:25,
"he is your ἀπόστολον"), and even of Jesus sent by God (cf. Heb 3:1, "the
ἀπόστολον and high priest whom we confess"). More narrowly, it is used of a group
of believers in Jesus who had some special function (e.g., Luke 11:49; Acts 14:4, 14;
Rom 16:7; Gal 1:19; Eph 3:5; Rev 18:20), with particular reference to the twelve
disciples (Matt 10:2; Mark 3:14 [א B et al.]; Luke 6:13; 9:10; 17:5; 22:14; Acts 1:2,
26; passim). This narrower usage is how the term is usually used in its approximately seventy-six occurrences in the NT, and that is how Paul uses it of himself in
all his letters: one with personal, delegated authority from God to proclaim
accurately the Christian gospel.

This is not, however, the way in which ἀπόστολος was commonly understood by
either Greeks or Hellenistic Jews of the day. Classical Greek writers usually used the
term in an impersonal way, most often to refer to a naval expedition for military
purposes—even, at times, of the boat used to transport such an expedition.
Josephus' one clear use of ἀπόστολος in *Ant.* 17.300 (the occurrence in *Ant.* 1.146
is textually uncertain) carries the verbal sense of "to send out" (πρεσβεία is the noun
in this passage for "delegation"). In fact, there are only a few references in all the
extant Greek and Jewish Greek writings from the fifth century B.C. through the
second century A.D. where the term means, or could be taken to mean, something
like "envoy," "messenger," or "delegate," and so to signal the idea of personal,

delegated authority (cf. Herodotus 1.21; 5.38; *Corpus Hermeticum* 6.11–12; POxy 1259.10; *SbGU* 7241.48; 3 Kgdms 14:6 LXX[A]; Isa 18:2 Symm.).

Karl Rengstorf has pointed out that though the NT's use of ἀπόστολος cannot be readily paralleled in the Greek and Hellenistic Jewish writings of the day, it is comparable to the Jewish institution of the *šālîaḥ* as found in the Talmud (*TDNT* 1:414–20). For in these codifications, שליח (*šālîaḥ*) has an assured place as a noun meaning "envoy" or "messenger" and carries the notion of delegated authority—as in, for example, the oft-repeated dictum: "A man's *šālîaḥ* is as the man himself" (*m. Ber.* 5.5; *b. Ned.* 72b; *b. Nazir* 12b; *b. Qidd.* 43a; *b.B.Qam.* 113b; *b. B.Meṣ.* 96a; passim). According to rabbinic sources, a man could appoint a *šālîaḥ* to enter into an engagement of marriage for him (*m. Qidd.* 2.1; *b. Qidd.* 43a), to serve a notice of divorce for him (*m. Giṭ.* 3.6; 4.1; *b. Giṭ.* 21a–23b), to perform ceremonial rituals on his behalf (e.g., the heave offering, *m. Ter.* 4.4), to act as his agent in economic matters (*b. B. Qam.* 102a, b), and so on. In fact, the authority of the sender was thought of as so tied up with the *šālîaḥ* that even if the *šālîaḥ* committed a sacrilege, so long as he did not exceed the bounds of his commission, it was the sender and not the *šālîaḥ* who was held responsible (*m. Meg.* 6.1–2; *b. Ketub.* 98b).

Rengstorf further argues (1) that the Jewish institution of the *šālîaḥ* served as the model for Jesus in calling his disciples and sending them out on his behalf (*TDNT* 1:424–37), and (2) that it was on the basis of Jesus' usage that the early Christian church used this concept for its own purposes and translated שליח by the relatively rare Greek term ἀπόστολος, probably first at Syrian Antioch (*TDNT* 1:420–24, 437–45). And Rengstorf has largely carried the day for the linguistic relation of ἀπόστολος to שליח (cf. 3 Kgdms 14:6 LXX[A], where the passive participle שליח is treated as a noun and translated ἀπόστολος) and for an early date for the origin of the *šālîaḥ* institution in Judaism.

There are, however, certain significant differences between the rabbinic idea of a *šālîaḥ* and the Christian concept of an apostle. In the first place, the appointment of an agent in Judaism was always a temporary matter; when the task was completed, his commission was over. The rabbis did not think of a *šālîaḥ* as having a life-long calling, as is taken for granted of an apostle in the narrower sense of that term in the NT. More importantly, the *šālîaḥ* was not viewed in a religious context or as a religious office, except in the sense that law and religion were inseparably intertwined in Judaism. The term, however, was never used of missionaries, proselytizers, or prophets. So while the concept of the *šālîaḥ* in Second Temple Judaism provides to some extent a reasonable background for the use of the term ἀπόστολος in the NT, it falls short of fully explicating that background or adequately highlighting some of the most important features of an apostle in early Christianity. For such matters, we must look as well to ideas that developed within Israel's religion having to do with a prophet (cf. *Comment* on 1:15–16) and to Jesus' reconstruction of both the *šālîaḥ* concept and traditional prophetology.

Playing on the inadequacy of the Jewish *šālîaḥ* concept to explain fully the NT's use of ἀπόστολος, Walter Schmithals has argued for a gnostic origin of the term (see his *The Office of Apostle in the Early Church*). In support, he cites various patristic references that use ἀπόστολος of the gnostic teachers (e.g., Origen, *Comm. on John* 2.8; Eusebius, *Eccl. Hist.* 4.22 and 23.12; Tertullian, *De Praesc.Haer.* 30; Ps.-Clem., *Hom.* 11.35). In none of these passages, however, is it directly said that the Gnostics used the term in designation of themselves. Rather, every reference can be read as a Christian use of the expression "false apostle" (also "false prophet" and "false Christ") to characterize the Gnostics—which, of course, hardly proves that the NT usage was rooted in gnostic nomenclature.

οὐκ ἀπ᾽ ἀνθρπώπων οὐδὲ δι᾽ ἀνθρώπου, "not from men nor through any man," together with its accompanying positive assertions, is unique to the salutation of Galatians. In the salutations of his other letters, of course, Paul habitually identifies himself as an apostle (e.g., Rom 1:1; 1 Cor 1:l; 2 Cor 1:1, etc.; though in Phil 1:1 only as a δοῦλος, "slave" [together with Timothy; cf. the use of δοῦλος in Rom 1:1 as well], and in Philem 1 as a δέσμιος, "prisoner"). In none of his other salutations, however, does he take pains to emphasize, first negatively and then positively, how he came to be an apostle. It is in these negative and positive parenthetical statements that we have both apology (defensive response) and polemic (aggressive explication) at their height. So by a process of "mirror reading," we can say with some confidence that Paul's converts had undoubtedly been given by the agitators at Galatia an account of his apostleship quite different from what he told them or what they had been led to believe by his early evangelistic preaching—an account which claimed that, despite what he asserted, Paul had actually received his authority from certain Christian leaders before him.

The authority of both a šālîah and an apostle stemmed from the one who commissioned him. So Paul affirms at the very beginning of his letter, in evident opposition to the claims of his opponents, that his apostleship was not derived from any human source (οὐκ ἀπ᾽ ἀνθρώπων) nor received through any human agency (οὐδὲ δι᾽ ἀνθρώπου). Others may have been appointed by one or the other of the then-existing congregations (cf. his later mention of such appointments in 2 Cor 8:23 and Phil 2:25). The source of his apostleship, however, was not any such body of Christians, whether at Damascus, Jerusalem, or Syrian Antioch. Nor was it received through the mediation of Ananias (cf. Acts 9:10–19; 22:12–16), Barnabas (cf. Acts 9:27; 11:25–26; 13:1ff.), Peter, James, or any other apostle. The double genitival use of ἄνθρωπος is undoubtedly generic, first in the plural with ἀπό to denote source and then in the singular with διά to refer to agency. It is not hard, however, to believe that behind these qualitative uses we should understand some particular church and some particular Christian leader or leaders as being in mind. And by the way Paul narrates events in 1:17–2:14, probably it was the Jerusalem church and the Jerusalem apostles who were being pointed to by the opponents— and who were being denied by Paul.

ἀλλὰ διὰ ᾽Ιησοῦ Χριστοῦ καὶ θεοῦ πατρος, "but through Jesus Christ and [from] God the Father," sets out the converse to Paul's denials with a positive statement as to the origin of his apostleship. Some find it strange that διά, "through," is used as the preposition before both ᾽Ιησοῦ Χριστοῦ and θεοῦ πατρός, for, they believe, Paul would hardly have thought of either Jesus Christ or God the Father as an intermediary; so διά should be seen here more in terms of ultimate source than agency (e.g., Burton, Galatians, 5–6; Bruce, Galatians, 72–73, citing Rom 11:36; 1 Cor 1:9; Heb 2:10). Stranger still is the fact that the order here is first "Jesus Christ" and then "God the Father," which is a reversal of Paul's usual order when referring to God and Christ together (cf. the bipartite references of Rom 1:7; 1 Cor 1:3; 2 Cor 1:2; Eph 1:2; Phil 1:2; 1 Thess 1:1; 2 Thess 1:1; 1:12; 1 Tim 1:2; 2 Tim 1:2; Titus 1:4 [perhaps also 2:13]; Philem 3; though, of course, the tripartite "grace" of 2 Cor 13:14 has Christ first)—with that usual order reappearing almost immediately after this variant in the salutation of Galatians at v 3: "Grace and peace to you from God our Father and the Lord Jesus Christ." John Bligh argues that in the denials and affirmations of Gal 1:1 we have "a neat chiasm," which, he insists, explains the reversal of order in the second part and allows us to understand ἀπό, "from," as the proper, though unstated, preposition for θεοῦ πατρος (*Galatians*, 62). And while admittedly there is much in Bligh's work—particularly his seeing all of Galatians in terms of one large chiasmus—that can legitimately be called arbitrary, speculative, and even eccentric, his drawing attention to the chiastic nature of v 1 is, I believe, valid and to be applauded.

Indeed, Christ is no intermediary like Moses, as Paul labors to point out in Gal 3:19–20. Neither is he to be thought of in terms comparable to any human agency, as the strong adversative ἀλλά, "but," makes clear. Rather, he is to be seen as associated with God the Father—here as the agent in Paul's commissioning as an apostle (on Christ as God's agent in Pauline thought, cf. 2 Cor 5:19; 1 Tim 2:5–6), with that appointment having its source in God himself. Probably Paul had in mind his Damascus road experience when referring to Jesus Christ as the agent in his apostleship, for it was the risen and exalted Jesus who commissioned him to be God's missioner to the Gentiles (cf. Acts 9:15–16; 22:21; 26:16–18).

τοῦ ἐγείραντος αὐτὸν ἐκ νεκρῶν, "who raised him from the dead." As a Jew, Paul needed no arguments for theism, no arguments for God's concern as Creator for his creation, and certainly no arguments for God's redemptive interests in his people. Furthermore, as a Jew he thought of God more in terms of function than ontology. Having been confronted by Christ, however, Paul came to think of God principally in relation to what he accomplished redemptively through the work of Jesus Christ. So here when he speaks of God the Father, he speaks of him not in ontological terms but in categories more functional, redemptive, and Christocentric in nature: he is the one "who raised him [Jesus Christ] from the dead."

2 καὶ οἱ σὺν ἐμοὶ πάντες ἀδελφοί, "and all the brothers with me." The salutations of several of Paul's letters include one or more names of persons associated with him in sending the letter in question: Sosthenes (1 Cor 1:1), Timothy (2 Cor 1:1; Phil 1:1; Col 1:1; Philem 1), and Silas and Timothy (1 Thess 1:1; 2 Thess 1:1). These were probably those who served as Paul's secretaries (see *Introduction*, "Amanuensis") and when known to the recipients were mentioned by name (cf. also Rom 16:22). The phrase οἱ σὺν ἐμοὶ ἀδελφοί, "the brothers with me," occurs in Phil 4:21, identifying not amanuenses who aided in writing that letter but rather those who joined with Paul in sending greetings and who may be presumed to endorse what is said. And it is this latter nuance of endorsement that is probably to the fore here—i.e., though they were unknown to the recipients personally, those associated with Paul at the time of writing add their endorsement to what he says. In fact, by the use of the emphatic πάντες, "all," Paul wants to suggest that he has solid support for what he writes.

Just who πάντες ἀδελφοί, "all the brothers," refers to depends largely on what is thought as to provenance and date. If the letter was written at Syrian Antioch to believers in the southern part of the Roman province of Galatia, shortly after Paul and Barnabas returned from evangelizing in that area and before the Jerusalem Council, as we believe (see *Introduction*, "Addressees" and "Date"), then we should think of these "brothers" as the leaders of the church there at Antioch. Barnabas is not singled out, which may seem at first glance somewhat strange, particularly because of his prominent role in the evangelization of Galatia. Perhaps, however, that omission is because of Paul's disappointment over Barnabas' behavior as narrated in 2:11–13 and the Judaizers' use of that incident as an implied endorsement of their activity (cf. R. J. Bauckham, *JSNT* 2 [1979] 61–70). Likewise, the one who served as Paul's secretary for Galatians is not named, nor are any of the other leaders of the church at Antioch. But that is probably because none of them was personally known to the addressees. Of course, if we date Galatians later in the Pauline mission, with its place of writing correspondingly viewed with more uncertainty, the impulse grows to see Paul's reference here being to "fellow missionaries known to the Galatians, and not to the whole church from where he sent the letter" (so Betz, *Galatians*, 40; see also those he cites in support).

ταῖς ἐκκλησίαις τῆς Γαλατίας, "to the churches of Galatia." Paul's address in Galatians is exceedingly brief, without the epithets and compliments found in the addresses of all his other letters. Together with the absence of a thanksgiving section (see *Comment* below), this rather matter-of-fact address serves to signal Paul's agitation and indignation over the situation faced and to set a tone of severity that permeates the entire letter. The address is also somewhat different from those in Paul's other letters in its exclusively local use of ἐκκλησία— comparable to, though not the same as, "to the church of the Thessalonians in God the/our Father and the Lord Jesus Christ" of the Thessalonian letters (1 Thess 1:1; 2 Thess 1:1) and "to the church of God at Corinth" of the Corinthian letters (1 Cor 1:2; 2 Cor 1:1), but certainly much more locally constrained than the universalistic use of ἐκκλησία in the Prison Epistles (see *Introduction*, pp. lxxxv–lxxxvi). Also, of course, Paul's address here differs in its plural ταῖς ἐκκλησίαις, "the churches," which raises questions regarding how many congregations there were, how they were related geographically, how they were made up ethnically, and how they were organized. The answers to many of these matters depend to an extent on how one understands provenance and date. We have opted for a South Galatian destination and early date (see *Introduction*, "Addressees" and "Date"), and so view these churches as assemblies of believers scattered in the cities and towns of the missionary outreach recorded in Acts 13:14–14:25, as ethnically diverse, and as probably only functionally related (cf. Acts 14:23). Yet many of these questions, on whatever understanding of provenance and date, cannot be answered precisely. All that seems evident from the address itself is that Galatians was meant as a circular letter to various Gentile Christian congregations somewhere in the Roman province of Galatia. Its reference to "large letters" at 6:11 also suggests that it circulated among the churches not in various copies, but only in the one form in which it was sent, for Paul's point has to do with the impression that his own large handwriting in the subscription should make on the consciousness of all his readers (see *Comment* on 6:11).

3 Χάρις ὑμῖν καὶ εἰρήνη, "grace and peace to you," may seem to be nothing more than the union of Greek and Hebrew forms of address. One could expect such from a man of Paul's background, for χαίρειν, "greetings," is common in the Greek nonliterary letters of the day and שׁלום (*šālôm*), "peace," was a common epistolary greeting among the Jews (cf. Str-B 1:154; 2:94–95; 3:1, 25; attributed also to Nebuchadnezzar in Dan 4:1 and expanded to εἰρήνη καὶ ἔλεος, "peace and mercy," in 2 *Apoc. Bar.* 78.2 [note Gal 6:16]; see also K. Berger, *ZNW* 65 [1974] 193–95, on the letters of Simeon ben Kosebah/bar Kokhbah). For Paul, however, "grace" and "peace" had great theological meaning, as his addition "from God our Father and the Lord Jesus Christ" makes evident. In Rom 5, for example, "peace" is what characterizes (or should characterize, if the verb of v 1 is subjunctive and not indicative) the believer's life (5:1–11) because of the "grace" brought by Christ (5:12–21). So "grace" and "peace," whether joined or mentioned separately, appear frequently in the blessings of Paul's letters, as well as in those of other NT letters (e.g., Rom 15:33; 16:20 [perhaps also v 24]; 1 Cor 16:23; 2 Cor 13:11, 14; Gal 6:16, 18; Eph 6:23–24; Phil 4:9, 23; Col 3:15; 4:18; 1 Thess 5:23, 28; 2 Thess 3:16,18; Heb 13:20–21, 25; 1 Peter 5:14; etc.). In fact, "grace" and "peace" seem to be Paul's (and the NT's) shorthand way of epitomizing the essence of the gospel, with particular reference to its cause and its effect.

ἀπὸ θεοῦ πατρὸς ἡμῶν καὶ κυρίου Ἰησοῦ Χριστοῦ, "from God our Father and the Lord Jesus Christ." "Grace" and "peace" have their origin in God and Christ. In fact, throughout Paul's letters God and Christ are presented as completely at one in mankind's salvation. In Galatians, for example, the grace which undergirds salvation is called indiscriminately both "the grace of God" (2:21; cf. 1:15) and "the grace of Christ" (1:6), while elsewhere in Paul's writings the peace which grace effects is called both "the peace of God" (Phil 4:7) and "the peace of Christ" (Col 3:15). Such a joining of Christ with God is a reflection of the exalted place that the risen Christ had in Paul's thought. And while this almost unconscious association of Christ with God is here principally functional in nature, it very soon begins to assume a more elevated and Christocentric focus in Paul's other letters (cf. esp. the bipartite reference of 1 Thess 1:12 and the tripartite reference of 2 Cor 13:14)—which, of course, furnished important data for the Church's later trinitarian creeds.

4 τοῦ δόντος ἑαυτὸν ὑπὲρ τῶν ἁμαρτιῶν ἡμῶν, "who gave himself for our sins." When Paul speaks of Jesus Christ, he immediately thinks in functional terms of Christ's redemptive work: he "gave himself" (cf. 2:20; also Eph 5:2, 25; 1 Tim 2:6; Titus 2:14)—or alternatively, was given by God (cf. Rom 4:25; 8:32)—"for our sins." Both of the expressions "to give himself" (δοῦναι ἑαυτόν) and "for our sins" (ὑπὲρ τῶν ἁμαρτιῶν ἡμῶν) are rooted in Jesus' statement, as later recorded in Mark 10:45, about the purpose of his mission: "to give his life (δοῦναι τὴν ψυχὴν αὐτοῦ) a ransom for many (λύτρον ἀντὶ πολλῶν)." In turn, Jesus' statement seems to have been derived from Isaiah's fourth Servant Song (cf. esp. Isa 53:5–6, 12), which he used to highlight his own consciousness of being God's Righteous Servant.

Here in this verse we have what appears to be an outcropping of one of the early confessions of the Christian church. It begins with the adjectival, substantival participle τοῦ δόντος (as does, of course, v 1b in its use of τοῦ ἐγείραντος, which may also be a reflection of early Christian language about "God the Father"). It highlights the affirmation "Christ gave himself for our sins," which is both similar to the confession "Christ died for our sins" (cited by Paul in 1 Cor 15:3 as being part of early Christian preaching) and different from Paul's usual way of identifying the referents of Christ's death (cf. Rom 5:6–8; 14:15; 1 Cor 1:13; 11:24; Col 1:21–22). Furthermore, the verb ἐξέληται ("he might rescue") is a Pauline *hap. leg.* (Paul uses σώζω, ῥύομαι, ἐλευθερόω, or [ἐξ]αγοράζω elsewhere as verbs of deliverance), though it is common in the LXX in this sense and is reported by Luke in Acts to have been used in the early church (by Stephen quoting Scripture in 7:10, 34; by Peter in 12:11; by the Roman commander in 23:27; and by the exalted Jesus in 26:17). Likewise, the phrase ὁ αἰὼν ὁ ἐνεστώς ("the present age"), which is the equivalent of the

Jewish expression *hā'ōlām hazzeh* (ὁ αἰὼν οὗτος, "this age") as contrasted to *hā'ōlām hābba'* (ὁ αἰών ὁ ἐρχόμενος or ὁ αἰὼν ὁ μέλλων, "the age to come"), is a NT *hap. leg.* And though the evil character of this age is implied in Rom 12:2 (cf. 1 Cor 1:20) and assumed in all Paul's writings, it is only here that the adjective πονηρός is directly attached to αἰών. Richard B. Hays has drawn attention to the very real possibility that underlying Paul's theological arguments of 3:1–4:11 is a Jesus narrative drawn from the confessions and preaching of the early church, which "while not all-determinative, is integral to Paul's reasoning" (see his *The Faith of Jesus Christ*, 85–137, citing particularly 3:13–14, 21–22; 4:3–6). And here, too, it seems we have some such narrative substructure or confessional bit (the two being integrally intertwined), which Paul, knowing well the preaching of the early church (cf. 1 Cor 15:11), almost unconsciously includes when speaking about Jesus Christ.

Whether ὑπέρ (P⁵¹ B H 33 TR) or περί (P⁴⁶ᵛⁱᵈ ℵ* A D G et al.) is to be preferred is difficult to determine from the manuscript evidence alone. Likewise, it is difficult to determine from Paul's usage elsewhere, for he uses both prepositions with the genitive to mean both "concerning" and "on behalf of"—though with περί most often signaling the former and ὑπέρ most often the latter. And this same interchangeability of prepositions appears in the extant Koine Greek materials outside the NT. Nevertheless, preference here should probably be given to ὑπέρ, principally because of (1) the use of ὑπέρ in the confession of 1 Cor 15:3 to which we have compared this affirmation (Χριστὸς ἀπέθανεν ὑπὲρ τῶν ἁμαρτιῶν ἡμῶν), and (2) the parallel use of ὑπέρ in Gal 3:13 (γενόμενος ὑπὲρ ἡμῶν κατάρα) on which we must comment later—with the vicarious idea of "in place of" being connoted in all these passages.

ὅπως ἐξέληται ἡμᾶς, "in order that he might rescue us." The conjunction ὅπως signals purpose ("in order that"), and so interprets the functional Christology of v 4a ("Christ gave himself for our sins") soteriologically ("in order to rescue us"). The verb ἐξέληται, as in Luke's reporting of its use in the early church (Acts 7:10, 34; 12:11; 23:27; 26:17, where the emphasis is on the idea of rescue), denotes not removal but rescue from the power of. So the deliverance spoken of here is not a removal from the world but a rescue from the evil that dominates it.

ἐκ τοῦ αἰῶνος τοῦ ἐνεστῶτος πονηροῦ, "from the present evil age." The distinction between "this age" and "the age to come" was common in Second Temple Judaism. 4 Ezra 7:50 only makes explicit what was widely accepted, that "the Most High has made not one age but two." The Sadducees, of course, did not hold such a view, for they tended to see their times—i.e., since the Maccabean rebellion and the reign of the great Hasmonean priest-king Simeon—as the Messianic Age inchoate. But the Pharisees looked on "this age" as coming to a climax in a period of awful "messianic travail," which would usher in "the age to come" and/or "the Messianic Age." The apocalyptic writers of the day likewise viewed the present age as "already grown old, ... already past the strength of youth" (4 Ezra 5:55). Because of Adam's sin, "the ways of this world," as they viewed matters, "became narrow and sorrowful and painful, and full of perils coupled with great toils ... but the ways of the future world are broad and safe, and yield the fruit of immortality" (4 Ezra 7:12–13). More particularly, because of mankind's continued wickedness, "the world lies in darkness, and the dwellers therein are without light" (4 Ezra 14:20). The literature from Qumran parallels this attitude at many places, often speaking of the current age as the "epoch of wickedness" (e g., 1QpHab 5.7–8) during which Belial, who opposes the will of God, has free rein. Another parallel, this time from an early Christian source, appears in the so-called Freer Logion that was sometimes appended to Mark's Gospel, where the disciples say, "This age (ὁ αἰὼν οὗτος) of lawlessness and unbelief is subject to Satan" (Mark 16:14 W).

The expression τοῦ αἰῶνος τοῦ ἐνεστῶτος, "the present age," is paralleled in meaning, if not precisely in word, by Paul's exhortation of Rom 12:2 not to be conformed "to this age" (τῷ αἰῶνι τούτῳ). Paul also uses κόσμος as a synonym for αἰών to denote not just the present period of world history but also the way of life that characterizes it (cf. 1 Cor 1:20; 2:12; 3:19; 7:31), as does also John (cf. John 17:15; 1 John 2:15–17). The climactic position of the adjective πονηρός, "evil," at the end of the phrase gives it special emphasis, undoubtedly reflecting the attitude of the earliest Christians—in line with that of religiously sensitive, nonconformist Jews generally—toward attitudes and events of their day. Paul's use here of this confessional portion (if, indeed, that is what it is), with its stress on Christ's having rescued us from this present *evil* world, is, in fact, particularly relevant to his argument in Galatians, for later he makes the point that the law to which his converts are being urged to submit belongs to this present age and so can be characterized as one of "the weak and miserable elementary principles of the world" (4:3, 9).

κατὰ τὸ θέλημα τοῦ θεοῦ καὶ πατρὸς ἡμῶν, "according to the will of our God and Father," may be seen as referring only to δόντος, "who gave," or to ἐξέληται, "he might rescue." Probably, however, it has both Christ's giving of himself and our rescue in view, and so proclaims that both were "according to the will of our God and Father." The phrase, then, underscores the fact that Christ's redemptive work and mankind's salvation are to be understood in the context of God's will and fatherly concern.

5 ᾧ ἡ δόξα εἰς τοὺς αἰῶνας τῶν αἰώνων, ἀμήν, "to whom be glory for ever and ever, Amen." Only here among the letters of Paul is there a doxology at the end of a salutation, which may indicate that the confession of v 4 originally included the doxology of v 5 as well. The language of the doxology suggests that it originated in the liturgical worship of a Jewish-Christian community (cf. Rev 1:5b–6), with roots in the OT and Second Temple Judaism. The relative pronoun ᾧ, "to whom," undoubtedly has as its antecedent τοῦ θεοῦ καὶ πατρὸς ἡμῶν, "of our God and Father." The use of the article in ἡ δόξα, "glory," signals "the glory of the God of Israel" (probably not Christ's work referred to in v 4, as Burton argues [*Galatians*, 16], though Paul would not have been averse to such an inclusion)—i.e., the praise and worship of God by his creatures, of which he alone is worthy (cf. Pss 29:2; 96:8). The phrase εἰς τοὺς αἰῶνας τῶν αἰώνων (lit. "unto the ages of the ages") is a more emphatic way of expressing the common Septuagintalism εἰς τὸν αἰῶνα τοῦ αἰῶνος (lit. "unto the age of the age"), and so highlights unlimited extent. To this praise and worship the early Christians, like their forefathers at the end of each of the first four books of Israel's psalter (Pss 41:13; 72:19; 89:52; 106:48), added their ἀμήν, "Amen." Paul, too, joins in this "Amen," for his gospel is epitomized in the early Christian confession of v 4: "Christ gave himself for our sins in order to rescue us from the present evil age, according to the will of our God and Father." All that Paul desires to add to that in light of the issues facing his converts in Galatia is what to him seems obvious: that our deliverance is apart from any "works of the law."

Explanation

Paul's letter to his converts in Galatia begins (vv 1–3) like the normal Greek letter of his day: the sender's name, an identification of the addressees, and a greeting. Into this conventional epistolary form, however, Paul inserts a vigorous defense of his apostleship (v 1), and so highlights at the very start one of the important themes of his letter vis-à-vis his opponents' charges—i.e., the legitimacy of his apostleship. He also includes greetings from those with him (v 2), thereby suggesting, it seems, their endorsement of what he writes. Furthermore, he expands the greeting to read "grace and peace" (v 3), thereby epitomizing the essence of the Christian gospel.

To this standard, though enriched, opening, Paul adds what appears to be a portion of an early Christian confession (v 4), which speaks of Christ's work and the purpose of that work for mankind's salvation. In so doing, he highlights a further important theme of the letter—i.e., the full sufficiency of Christ's work for mankind's salvation, apart from any works of the Mosaic law. In v 5 Paul then closes with a doxology in praise to God, which may have been a part of the confession he quotes or may be his own. The doxology itself is unique among the salutations of Paul. But whatever its immediate source, it seems rooted ultimately in Jewish Christian worship (in which, of course, both the earliest believers in Jesus and Paul participated) and is used to give praise to God for the complete sufficiency of Christ's work for mankind's salvation.

So in the salutation of Galatians, Paul sets out the two main issues dealt with in the letter: the nature of his apostleship and the nature of the Christian gospel. And against those who were stirring up his converts to think otherwise, he enlists the support of, first, "all the brothers with me" (v 2), and then a confession drawn from the liturgy of the early church (v 4).

Also to be noted in this salutation is the more functional (as distinguished from more speculative or ontological) nature of Paul's statements. For when speaking of God, there is no treatment of his person or attributes. Rather, the stress is entirely on God as the source of Paul's apostleship (v 1), on God as having raised Jesus Christ from the dead (v 1), on God as the source of the Christian's "grace and peace" (v 3), on God's will and fatherly concern as the basis for Christ's work and mankind's salvation (v 4), and on praise and worship as being God's due (v 5). Likewise when speaking of Jesus Christ, his function as the agent of Paul's apostleship (v 1) and his redemptive self-giving receive emphasis (v 4), rather than who he is or his person. And when using the word ἐκκλησία, it is "the churches in Galatia" in a localized sense that are referred to (v 2) and not the universal Church (though Paul uses the term in both senses later, cf. 1:13, 22). Yet while set in functional contexts, it is noteworthy as well the way in which Paul associates Jesus Christ with God in this salutation, for they are spoken of as standing together behind Paul's apostleship (v 1) and as together being the source of the Christian gospel (vv 3–4). Such statements relating Jesus Christ to God (as found also throughout Paul's letters) are truly astonishing—particularly so when we stop to realize that they were written by a monotheistic Jewish Christian with reference to one who had lived on earth within recent memory.

II. Rebuke Section (1:6 – 4:11)

The first major section of Galatians is introduced by the word θαυμάζω ("I am astonished"), which was a conventional expression in Greek letters from the third century B.C. through the fourth century A.D. to signal astonishment, rebuke, disapproval, and disappointment—even at times irony and irritation. The θαυμάζω sections of the Greek papyrus letters often included such features as: (1) a statement as to the cause of the astonishment and rebuke; (2) a reminder of previous instructions not carried out; (3) rebukes for foolishness, negligence, or change of mind; (4) expressions of distress; (5) rebuking questions put directly to the addressees; and (6) a summons to a given responsibility. These θαυμάζω sections were then customarily followed by a request to remedy the disappointing, distressing situation, and this request was sometimes followed by further instructions.

The rebuke section of Paul's letter to the Galatians conforms quite closely in its epistolary structure to the θαυμάζω sections of Greek letters of the day. It begins, as we noted, with a conventional expression of rebuke ("I am astonished," 1:6a); it states the cause for this rebuke ("you are deserting the one who called you by the grace of Christ and are turning to a different gospel," 1:6b); and it reminds us of previous instruction ("as we have already said, so now I say again," 1:9). Later it restates the original rebuke in the form of a series of questions (3:1–5; 4:8–10), with appended rebukes for foolishness (3:1, 3) and for negligence in not being true to knowledge already possessed (4:9). It closes with an expression of distress ("I fear for you, that somehow I have wasted my efforts on you," 4:11), with then a further expression of distress interjected into the request section at 4:20.

Even the various stages within the development of Paul's rebuke section in Galatians are fairly well set off by certain rather conventional epistolary expressions, which tend to be grouped at the start of each new subsection in the argument or to bring matters to a close. For example, the rebuke formula of 1:6 (θαυμάζω ὅτι, "I am astonished that") and the reminder of past teaching at 1:9 (ὡς προειρήκαμεν καὶ ἄρτι πάλιν λέγω, "as we have said before, so now I say again") serve as the epistolary pegs for 1:6–10. Likewise, the disclosure formulae of 1:11 (γνωρίζω δὲ ὑμῖν, "I want you to know") and 1:13 (ἠκούσατε γὰρ, "for you have heard") serve as the beginning points for their respective sections, 1:11–12 and 1:13–2:21—with these two subsections being closely related, the first as the thesis for what immediately follows and the second as an autobiographical elaboration in support of that thesis. So too the rebuke for foolishness of 3:1 (ὦ ἀνόητοι Γαλάται, "you foolish Galatians") and the rebuking questions of 3:1–5 hold these five verses together as an epistolary unit, as do also the rebuking questions of 4:8–10 for those three verses. Also to be observed is the fact that the disclosure formula of 3:7 (γινώσκετε ἄρα ὅτι, "you know, then, that"), which draws a conclusion from the quotation of Gen 15:6 in 3:6, provides a transition to the extended argument from Scripture in 3:6–4:10. Finally, the expression of distress at 4:11 (φοβοῦμαι ὑμᾶς, "I fear for you") serves to bring the rebuke section to a formal close.

Surveying the material in terms of its rhetorical genre, 1:6–4:11 has many of the characteristics of forensic rhetoric, at least up through the early part of chap. 3. Paul defends himself against accusations (1:10), yet also takes the offensive in accusing his opponents of perverting the Christian proclamation (1:7). His vehement denials of any dependence on human authority (1:11–12, 16–17, 19–20, 22; 2:5–6) and the setting out of his experiences in support of those denials (1:13–2:14) make the courtroom scene a feasible backdrop for this section of the letter. So while we must later insist that at 4:12 a major rhetorical shift takes place in the letter, 1:6–4:11 may appropriately be categorized as to its rhetorical genre as a type of forensic rhetoric. Indeed, Paul seems to have used the basic features of Greco-Roman forensic rhetoric for his own purposes, filling out those structures with his own content, particularly in 1:6–3:7 and 4:8–11. The structures and modes of forensic rhetoric were "in the air," and Paul seems to have used them simply because they were a part of his way of thinking and served his purposes well. We need, therefore, to recognize these features in Paul's presentation, and may properly call them as they were known by their Latin names: *exordium* (1:6–10), *narratio* (1:11–2:14), *propositio* (2:15–21), and *probatio* (3:1–4:11).

A. Occasion for Writing/Issues at Stake (Exordium) (1:6–10)

Bibliography

Behm, J. "ἀνάθεμα, ἀνάθημα, κατάθεμα." *TDNT* 1:354–55. Burton, E. deW. *Galatians*, also Appendix V: "'Ετερος and 'Άλλος," 420–22. Dahl, N. A. "Paul's Letter to the Galatians: Epistolary Genre, Content, and Structure." Unpublished SBL Paul Seminar paper, 1974. Elliott, J. K. "The Use of ἕτερος in the New Testament." *ZNW* 60 (1969) 140–41. Maurer, C. "μετατίθημι." *TDNT* 8:161–62. Mullins, T. Y. "Formulas in New Testament Epistles." *JBL* 91 (1972) 380–90. O'Brien, P. T. *Introductory Thanksgivings*. Ramsay, W. M. *Galatians*, 249–69. Schubert, P. *Pauline Thanksgivings*. White, J. L. *The Form and Function of the Body of the Greek Letter*.

Translation

⁶*I am astonished that you are so quickly deserting the one who called you by the grace of Christ* ᵃ *and are turning to a different gospel—* ⁷*which is not at all the same gospel, except that some people are confusing you and desiring to pervert the gospel of Christ.* ⁸*But even if we or an angel from heaven should preach a gospel* ᵇ *other than the one we preached to you, let him be accursed!* ⁹*As we have said before,* ᶜ *so now I say again: If anybody is preaching to you a gospel other than what you accepted, let him be accursed!*

¹⁰*Am I now seeking the approval of men, or of God? Or am I trying to please men? If I were still trying to please men, I would not be a servant of Christ.*

Notes

ᵃ The inclusion of Χριστοῦ is supported by P⁵¹ ℵ A B Byzantine vg syrᵖᵉˢʰ copᵇᵒ; Ἰησοῦ Χριστοῦ by D 326 itᵈ˒ᵉ syrʰᵉˡ; Χριστοῦ Ἰησοῦ by itᶻ copˢᵃ. Apparently the Chester Beatty papyrus (P⁴⁶ᵛⁱᵈ) omits Χριστοῦ (and variants), as do also G Hᵛⁱᵈ itᵃʳˑᵍ Mcion Tert Cyp Ambst Ephr Pel. There is also some evidence for θεοῦ in place of Χριστοῦ (327 Orˡᵃᵗ).

ᵇ The MS evidence is fairly mixed as to whether we should read ὑμῖν εὐαγγελίζηται (P⁵¹ᵛⁱᵈ B), or εὐαγγελίζηται ὑμῖν (Dᶜ), or εὐαγγελίζεται ὑμῖν (K P Byzantine), or εὐαγγελίσηται ὑμῖν (ℵᶜ A), or εὐαγγελίσηται (it⁹).

ᶜ The reading προείρηκα appears in ℵ* syrᵖᵉˢʰ instead of προειρήκαμεν.

Form/Structure/Setting

Paul's letters usually have a thanksgiving (εὐχαριστῶ, "I give thanks") section that immediately follows the salutation (cf. Rom 1:8ff.; 1 Cor 1:4ff.; Phil 1:3ff.; Col 1:3ff.; 1 Thess 1:2ff.; 2 Thess 1:3ff.; 2 Tim 1:3ff.; Philem 4ff.; see also Eph 1:15ff., though here the thanksgiving is separated from the salutation by an extensive quasi-doxology). In these thanksgiving sections Paul takes the occasion to commend his addressees for whatever he can find to commend them and to highlight the nature of his prayers for them. The thanksgiving sections of Paul's letters also serve, as Paul Schubert points out, "to focus the epistolary situation, i.e., to introduce the vital theme of the letter" (*Pauline Thanksgivings*, 180) — or, as Robert Funk puts it, they "tend to 'telegraph' the content of the letter" (*Language, Hermeneutic, and Word of God*, 257).

In Galatians, however, there is no thanksgiving section. This omission reflects Paul's agitation and indignation over the situation faced. It further highlights the severity of tone and urgency of purpose that is carried on throughout the letter. For though he refers to his Galatian converts with affection as "brothers" (1:11; 3:15; 4:12, 28, 31; 5:11, 13; 6:1, 18) and expresses his concern for them everywhere in the letter (particularly in his appeals), Paul evidently could not think of anything to commend them for, and so enters directly into the issues at hand. He had just received, it seems, news of their impending defection, and he reacts to that news on the spot. So θαυμάζω, "I am astonished," takes the place of εὐχαριστῶ, "I give thanks," in Galatians, and the *exordium* of 1:6–10 takes the place of a thanksgiving section in setting the theme for the letter.

In stating his occasion for writing, and so setting out the issues at stake, Paul begins with a conventional expression of rebuke (v 6a, θαυμάζω ὅτι, "I am astonished that"), which is followed by a statement as to the cause for that rebuke (v 6b, "you are so quickly deserting the one who called you by the grace of Christ and are turning to a different gospel"). He then disassociates the gospel from the message of the errorists (vv 6b–7a, theirs is "a different gospel—which is not at all the same gospel") and defines the true gospel in terms of its relational uniqueness (vv 7b–9, it is "of Christ," what "we preached to you," and "what you accepted"). In the process, Paul pronounces a double curse on anyone—himself or "an angel from heaven" included—who would preach otherwise (vv 8–9, "let him be accursed!") and reminds his converts of his previous instruction to this effect (v 9, "as we have said before, so now I say again"). Finally, probably in contradistinction to the assertions of his opponents, he disclaims any attempt to seek merely human approval in this matter and insists that as "a servant of Christ" his only desire is to please God (v 10).

Comment

6 θαυμάζω ὅτι, "I am astonished that," is a conventional epistolary rebuke formula, which, as we have proposed, signals the start of a major section in the Galatian letter. T. Y. Mullins argues that in antiquity a letter writer who uses θαυμάζω "is rebuking, even scolding the addressee. He is not really astonished, he is irritated" (*JBL* 91 [1972] 385). So Mullins speaks of Paul's "ironic rebuke" and depreciates the element of astonishment here (ibid.). But while Mullins is able to point to some ancient letters where a writer in using θαυμάζω appears more irritated than surprised, there are others where the word is used with genuine surprise as well as displeasure (e.g., POxy 3063:11–16). It is more accurate, therefore, to call θαυμάζω ὅτι an "astonishment-rebuke" formula. Paul is certainly displeased with his converts, as the lack of a thanksgiving section in Galatians clearly indicates. But the note of astonishment in his rebuke seems more prominent than the note of irony.

One reason for Paul's astonishment is that his converts had "so quickly" (οὕτως ταχέως) come to the verge of abandoning the gospel that he had preached to them and they had received. The expression οὕτως ταχέως has, of course, often been used as an index to provenance and date (see *Introduction*, p. lxiv). Yet "so quickly" is a somewhat relative temporal expression, and so fails to provide any precise indication as to how long it was between the Galatians' conversion and Paul's hearing about their impending defection. It may very well be, in fact, as Franz Mussner suggests (*Galaterbrief,* 53), that by the use of this particular expression Paul meant to suggest a correlation between his converts' impending apostasy and Israel's defections (1) in the case of the golden calf (cf. Exod 32:8 LXX, "They have turned *quickly from the way* [ταχὺ ἐκ τῆς ὁδοῦ] that you commanded them") and (2) during the period of the judges (cf. Judg 2:17 LXX, "They would not listen to their judges because they prostituted themselves to other gods and worshiped them and made the Lord angry. And they fled *quickly from the way* [ταχὺ ἐκ τῆς ὁδοῦ] in which their fathers had walked"). Particularly suggestive are these parallels when it is remembered that "the Way" (ἡ ὁδός) was the earliest self-designation of those who believed in Jesus (cf. Acts 9:2; 19:9, 23; 22:4; 24:14, 22). So then, οὕτως ταχέως may be more rhetorical than chronological in nature—though, of course, the shorter the interval between the Galatians' conversion and their defection, the more apt the parallels with Israel's apostasies and the more pointed Paul's drawing attention to the temporal factor.

A further reason for Paul's astonishment is that the Galatian Christians were "deserting the one who called [them] by the grace of Christ" (μετατίθεσθε ἀπὸ τοῦ καλέσαντος ὑμᾶς ἐν χάριτι Χριστοῦ). The middle form of μετατίθημι has the special sense of "change over," "turn away from," "fall away," "desert," and "become apostate," being used in this manner in secular Greek (Herodotus 7.18.3; Plato, *Republic* 1.345b; Polybius 24.9.6), the LXX (Sir 6:9; 2 Macc 7:24), and by Josephus (*Ant.* 20:38; *Life* 195). The substantival participle ὁ μεταθέμενος, in fact, meant in the world of Hellenistic philosophy one who leaves one school of thought for another (cf. Diogenes Laertius 7.1.37; 4.166). "The present tense of the verb μετατίθεσθε," as Burton points out, "indicates clearly that when the apostle wrote, the apostasy of the Galatians was as yet only in process. They were, so to speak, on the point, or more exactly in the very act, of turning" (*Galatians,* 18–19)—which is what is reflected in 4:9–10 and 5:2–4 as well.

The focus of Paul's astonishment, however, appears to be on the substantival participle τοῦ καλέσαντος, "the one who called you," whom they were deserting. It could, of course, be argued that Paul had himself in mind, for he was the Christian missioner who first brought the gospel to them. Or it could be argued that Christ is in view as "the one who called you by grace" (as Luther, Calvin, Bengel, and many since have thought), particularly if p⁴⁶ᵛⁱᵈ, G, Hᵛⁱᵈ, Marcion, Tertullian, Ambrosiaster, et al. are right in their reading of the text (i.e., omitting Χριστοῦ). But Paul's reference elsewhere in Galatians to God as the one who calls (cf. 1:15, "the one who called me by his grace"; 5:8, "the one who calls you") and his continuance of this practice in his other letters (cf. Rom 4:17; 8:30; 9:12, 24; 11:29; 1 Cor 1:9, 26; 7:15, 17–24; Eph 1:18; Phil 3:14; 1 Thess 2:12; 4:7; 5:24; 2 Thess 1:11; 2:14; 2 Tim 1:9)—with never, except in cases of someone "naming" or "inviting to a feast," anyone else in view—make it reasonably certain that he is here referring to God. And this being so, Paul is astonished that his converts in their pious attempt to be rigorously scrupulous are actually turning away from God, "the one who called you by the grace of Christ." This was a shocking state of affairs. For by their turning away from "the truth of the gospel" (2:5,14), Paul's converts were in actuality recapitulating the scenarios of Israel's apostasies and rebuffing the very One whom they professed to be attempting to worship more adequately.

ἐν χάριτι Χριστοῦ should probably be taken as a dative of means with a possessive genitive (i.e., "by the grace of Christ"), equivalent to διὰ τῆς χάριτος αὐτοῦ of 1:15 ("by his [God's] grace"). Indeed, ἐν Χριστῷ ['Ιησοῦ], "in Christ [Jesus]," appears in Gal 1:22; 2:4, 17; 3:26, 28 (and with increasing frequency in Paul's later letters) with local significance as a description of the situation of believers before God. Here, however, the preposition ἐν with the dative χάριτι highlights the means by which the Galatians were first brought to God—i.e., by God's unmerited benevolence ("grace"), as contrasted to their "works of the law." In 1:15 (cf. 2:21) it is God (αὐτοῦ) who is referent; here, however, the better texts read Christ (Χριστοῦ). But just as in the letter's salutation God and Christ are presented as completely at one in mankind's salvation, so in these texts they are presented interchangeably as the source of redemptive grace.

6b–7a εἰς ἕτερον εὐαγγέλιον, ὃ οὐκ ἔστιν ἄλλο, "to a different gospel—which is not all the same gospel." The spiritual direction in which Paul's converts were moving is depicted in the words εἰς ἕτερον εὐαγγέλιον, which are then qualified by the expression οὐκ ἔστιν ἄλλο. Generally speaking, ἕτερον and ἄλλος are synonyms, with both words usually denoting an enumerative sense ("an additional one") rather than a differentiative sense ("another of a different kind"). In the LXX and the NT, however, as Burton points out, "in so far as there is a distinction between the two words ἄλλος is enumerative and ἕτερος differentiative" (*Galatians*, 421; see also J. K. Elliott, *ZNW* 60 [1969] 140–41). Usually Paul does not distinguish between ἕτερος and ἄλλος (cf. 1:19; also 1 Cor 15:39–41; 2 Cor 11:4). Yet here in context there seems little doubt that he means to suggest a qualitative difference, with ἕτερος signaling "another of a different kind" and ἄλλος "another of the same kind." In all likelihood the errorists were claiming that their message and activity should be seen as complementary to Paul's preaching and ministry. As Paul viewed matters, however, theirs was "a different gospel—which is not at all the same gospel."

7b εἰ μή τινές εἰσιν οἱ ταράσσοντες ὑμᾶς καὶ θέλοντες μεταστρέψαι τὸ εὐαγγέλιον τοῦ Χριστοῦ, "except that some people are confusing you and desiring to pervert the gospel of Christ." The idiomatic use of εἰ μή ("except that"; cf. πλὴν ὅτι of Acts 20:23) suggests that no one would ever think of calling the Judaizers' message a "gospel" *except* with the intention of confusing the Christians of Galatia. The plural τινές ("some people") indicates a plurality of errorists in Galatia, not a single person (as the singular τις of Col 2:8 suggests was true at Colossae; the τις of Gal 1:9 is generic). The present tense of the verbs and participles points up the fact that these errorists were still in Galatia when Paul was writing this letter, and that he wrote with the intention of stopping them in the very midst of their activities. The characterization of the errorists as οἱ ταράσσοντες ὑμᾶς ("those confusing you") and οἱ θέλοντες μεταστρέψαι τὸ εὐαγγέλιον τοῦ Χριστοῦ ("those desiring to pervert the gospel of Christ") is, of course, from Paul's perspective and not how the Judaizers would have spoken of themselves. The verb ταράσσω ("disturb," "unsettle," "confuse") was used in the Greco-Roman world of political agitators who caused confusion and turmoil, but appears in the NT in a figurative sense to describe mental and spiritual agitation. It is the word used to describe the Judaizers and their work again in 5:10 and 6:17 (cf. Acts 15:24), and may very well be an allusion to Achar "the troubler of Israel" (cf. 1 Chr 2:7). The verb μεταστρέφω ("change," "alter," "pervert") was also originally a political term, having revolutionary action particularly in view— though it is used here and elsewhere in the NT (cf. Acts 2:20; Jas 4:9) more figuratively.

Paul's characterization of his message as τὸ εὐαγγέλιον τοῦ Χριστοῦ ("the gospel of Christ") appears a number of times elsewhere in his letters as well (cf. Rom 15:19; 1 Cor 9:12; 2 Cor 2:12; 4:4; 9:13; 10:14; Phil 1:27; 1 Thess 3:2; see also 2 Thess 1:8), being used synonymously with τὸ εὐαγγέλιον τοῦ θεοῦ ("the gospel of God"; Rom 1:1–3; 15:16; 1 Thess 2:2, 8–9; 1 Tim 1:11). The genitive τοῦ Χριστοῦ is undoubtedly both objective (referring to Christ as its content) and subjective (referring to Christ as its source). While the other genitive forms of Χριστοῦ in Galatians may very well be taken syntactically in other ways (see comments on 1:6; 2:16; 3:22; 5:24), the formula τὸ εὐαγγέλιον τοῦ Χριστοῦ here and elsewhere in Paul must be taken in the same way as in Mark 1:1: the gospel which has Jesus Christ (and God through Christ) as its focus and God (together with Christ) as its source.

8 ἀλλὰ καὶ ἐὰν ἡμεῖς ἢ ἄγγελος ἐξ οὐρανοῦ ὑμῖν εὐαγγελίζηται παρ' ὃ εὐηγγελισάμεθα ὑμῖν, "but even if we or an angel from heaven should preach a gospel other than the one we preached to you." The antithesis expressed by ἀλλά, "but," a strong adversative, is probably between what Paul suspects his converts feel as to the Judaizers' message—i.e., it is complementary to what they originally accepted—and Paul's own conviction as to the serious difference between their preaching and his. The καί, "even," is intensive, signaling the extreme nature of the supposition to follow.

The protasis of this verse is in the form of a third class "future more probable" condition, where what is expressed is a matter of some doubt but with the possibility of realization. The protasis of v 9 that follows is a first class "simple" condition, which assumes the reality of what is stated. Such a pairing of first and third class conditions is fairly common in Koine Greek, with some distinction between the two in view (cf. John 10:37–38; 13:17; Acts 5:38–39; 1 Cor 10:27–28). Here the subjunctive mood is used because Paul is making a statement that is somewhat doubtful, though theoretically possible, about the preaching of heresy by either himself or a heavenly being. It is the message of the gospel that is all important and not Paul's authority or anyone's status, however exalted. Of course, the authority and character of the preacher are important, as Paul has asserted of himself in 1:1 and will continue to assert throughout the autobiographical section of 1:11–2:14 (cf. also 2 Cor 10:1–12:10; Phil 3:4–21; 1 Thess 2:1–12). Their importance, however, is secondary to that of the gospel itself.

The reference to ἄγγελος ἐξ οὐρανοῦ, "an angel from heaven," carries a note of irony. Probably it is in response to the Judaizers' claim either (1) to have impeccable credentials as members in good standing in the Jerusalem church, or (2) to have the authority of the Jerusalem apostles supporting them—or both (cf. Paul's rather ironic references to the Jerusalem apostles in 2:6–10 and his opposition to Peter in 2:11–14). Paul saw the preacher's authority as derived from the gospel, and not vice versa. So he was not prepared to allow any change in the focus or content of that gospel on the basis of someone's credentials or by an appeal to some more imposing authority.

ἀνάθεμα ἔστω, "let him be accursed!" The apodosis of both the future more probable condition of v 8 and the simple condition of v 9 is the solemn imprecation: "Let him be accursed!" The noun ἀνάθεμα is a Koine variant of the classical ἀνάθημα, with both meaning (1) something dedicated or consecrated to God, and so (2) something delivered over to divine wrath for destruction. It is the regular translation of חרם (ḥērem), "ban," in the LXX (e.g., Lev 27:28–29; Deut 7:26; 13:17; Josh 6:17–18; 7:11–13, 15), where what is under the ban is removed from ordinary circulation and given over to destruction. In the NT ἀνάθημα is used in Luke 21:5 in the sense of something dedicated or consecrated to God. Paul, however, uses ἀνάθεμα here and in Rom 9:3; 1 Cor 12:3; 16:22 (cf. Acts 23:14; also the intensified κατάθεμα of Rev 22:3) along the lines of the LXX emphasis on destruction. The basic idea in Paul's usage, as Johannes Behm points out, is "delivering up to the judicial wrath of God" (TDNT 1:354). Furthermore, as Behm continues to observe, "We can hardly think of an act of Church discipline [as later expressed by the Church against heretics, invoking the anathema formula of Gal 1:8–9 and 1 Cor 16:22], since the apostle uses the phrase ἀπὸ τοῦ Χριστοῦ (R. 9:3) and also considers that an angel from heaven (Gl.1:8) or even Jesus Himself (1 C. 12:3) might be accursed" (ibid., 354–55).

9 ὡς προειρήκαμεν, καὶ ἄρτι πάλιν λέγω, "as we have said before, so now I say again," is a typical Hellenistic epistolary formula used to remind readers of past instruction. Elsewhere in his letters Paul frequently reminds his readers of what he taught them before and repeats that instruction for emphasis (e.g., 1 Cor 15:3; 2 Cor 7:3; 13:2; Gal 5:3, 21; 1 Thess 4:1, 6; 2 Thess 2:5). In many cases it is clear that he is referring to some teaching he gave his converts while with them personally and which he is now repeating by letter. Here, however, it is not clear whether he means instruction given on a previous visit (so BAG, s.v. προεῖπον, 2a; W. Schmithals, Paul and the Gnostics, 18–19; et al.) or instruction given previously in the same document (so Chrysostom; Schlier, Galater, 40; Bruce, Galatians, 84; et al.). Gal 5:3 and 21 lean in the direction of a former visit, and that is probably how we should understand matters here as well. All that can be said with certainty is that "the two curses are related in such a way that the second actualized the first" (Betz, Galatians, 54).

εἴ τις ὑμᾶς εὐαγγελίζεται παρ' ὃ παρελάβετε, ἀνάθεμα ἔστω, "if anybody is preaching to you a gospel other than what you accepted, let him be accursed!" Whatever the temporal relationship between the two curses, Paul here repeats ἀνάθεμα ἔστω, "let him be accursed," in order to impress it forcibly on his converts' minds. No longer is the protasis in the subjunctive mood but in the indicative, thereby stressing the reality of the situation. The singular τις, "anybody," is generic. The use of παρελάβετε, "you accepted," signals the passing on of an authoritative tradition (cf. 1 Cor 11:23; 15:3; Gal 1:12; 1 Thess 2:13; 2 Thess 3:6), which Paul had received "by revelation from Jesus Christ" (1:12) and proclaimed to the Galatians. If, then, anyone proclaims something different, he comes under the judicial wrath of God!

10   ἄρτι γὰρ ἀνθρώπους πείθω ἢ τὸν θεόν, "am I now seeking the approval of men, or of God?" The relation of this verse to what precedes and what follows has been extensively debated. Is it part of the paragraph that begins at v 6 (so Souter, JB, Wey, Lightfoot, Duncan, et al.)? Does it introduce what follows (so WH, Nestle, Moffatt, AmT, Berkeley, et al.)? Does it serve along with v 11 as a literary transition from the *exordium* of 1:6–9 to the *narratio* of 1:12–2:14 (so Betz)? Or should it be seen as standing alone as something of an emotional outburst? Most recent translators and commentators treat v 10 as an emotional outburst that is to be related in some manner to the curses of vv 8–9, yet to be set off as a separate paragraph (so UBSGT, RSV, NEB, NIV, Burton, Bruce, et al.) or by parentheses in the same paragraph (so Phillips).

ἄρτι, "now," picks up the ἄρτι of v 9, and so refers us back to the strong language of vv 8–9. The postpositive γάρ would be expected to have a causal or explanatory force, but probably should be taken here in more an illative or asseverative sense (cf. Phil 1:8; Acts 16:37). πείθω means "seek the favor or approval of," with the suggestion of "conciliate" (cf. 2 Macc 4:45; Matt 28:14; Acts 12:20). Evidently the Judaizers were claiming that Paul only presented half a gospel in his evangelistic mission in Galatia, purposely trimming his message so as to gain a more favorable response. They might, in fact, have applied to him such epithets as ὁ ἄρεσκος ("the man pleaser") and ὁ κόλαξ ("the flatterer"), so comparing him to the common rhetoricians of the day who sought to gain influence over others for their own ends (cf. Paul's assertions to the contrary in 1 Cor 10:33; 1 Thess 2:4–5). It seems, therefore, that Paul's response here "is as if one reproved for undue severity should reply, 'My language at least proves that I am no flatterer,' the answer tacitly implying that this fact justified the severity" (Burton, *Galatians*, 31).

ἢ ζητῶ ἀνθρώποις ἀρέσκειν, "or am I trying to please men?" repeats the thought just expressed a bit more distinctly, with ζητῶ ἀρέσκειν taking the place of πείθω to signal more directly the idea of attempt. The Judaizers, it seems, had told the Galatians that Paul really did believe in and preach the necessity of circumcision (5:11)—at least, he preached it elsewhere in his mission. Undoubtedly, therefore, they were saying that his failure to do so to Gentiles in Galatia was because he did not want to offend them, but rather wanted to win their favor. Paul, of course, does not deny that he himself continued as a Christian to live a basically Jewish lifestyle (cf. 1 Cor 9:19–23), or that he saw it as legitimate for Jewish believers in Jesus to continue to express their faith in the traditional forms of Judaism (cf. 1 Cor 7:17–20). But he made a distinction between Jewish Christians and Gentile Christians with regard to the Mosaic law. And so, he insists, he was attempting no subterfuge by not bringing in the law in his Galatian mission, either as a means of acceptance before God or as the normative expression of the Christian life.

εἰ ἔτι ἀνθρώποις ἤρεσκον, Χριστοῦ δοῦλος οὐκ ἂν ἤμην, "if I were still trying to please men, I would not be a servant of Christ." This last part of v 10 is an implied answer to the questions of the first part. The sentence is in the form of a second class "contrary to fact" conditional sentence, which assumes the condition to be untrue. Paul is here not speaking against being pleasing to others for the sake of the gospel (cf. 1 Cor 10:33, "I try to please everybody in every way; for I am not seeking my own good but the good of many, so that they may be saved"), but against gaining the favor of others for one's own advantage and as the motivation and goal of Christian ministry. Furthermore, his words are not to be taken in an absolute sense, as though renouncing all desires to please others under any circumstance, but in a comparative sense to mean the disavowal of pleasing others in preference to God. Paul recognizes the incongruity of trying to be both a "servant of Christ" and a "man pleaser." The errorists, of course, were minimizing his claim to be Christ's servant. But he asserts it and bases his whole ministry on that premise (cf. 1:1). So he tells his Galatian converts that his own consciousness of apostleship ("servant of Christ") would not have allowed the motivation ascribed to him by others.

Explanation

Paul's designation of himself as an apostle in 1:1 goes far beyond statements as to his apostolic status found elsewhere in his letters, and so suggests at the outset that apostolic authority will be an important feature in his Galatians argument. Yet 1:6–9 is not, as might have been expected, a direct development of Paul's claim to apostolic authority. Instead, Paul moves to an analysis of the problem at Galatia and a definition of the gospel that excludes any possible alternative version. He then subordinates all authority and status—including his own and that of even an "angel from heaven"—to the one true gospel. So Paul responds to the judaizing threat among his converts by setting out as the touchstone for all Christian thought and life the gospel of Christ, which he preached and which they received. In fact, if any one preaches another gospel, insists Paul, he forfeits his claim to authority and comes under God's curse.

After the twice-repeated *anathema*, Paul rather emotionally interjects two somewhat defiant questions, which may be paraphrased as follows: "Now, does that sound like the language of one whose main concern is to gain the favor of others?" He then asserts that knowing himself to be a servant of Christ, the stance of a "man pleaser" would be impossible.

Paul's statement as to the occasion for writing Galatians is forceful and unyielding. His setting out of the issues is pointed and his initial response emotional. Many have noted elsewhere in his letters attitudes of openness, tolerance, and accommodation to issues in his churches (e.g., 1 Cor 7–14, passim) and a breadth of spirit (e.g., Phil 1:15–18; 4:8–9), and have contrasted those features to what we find here. Yet Paul seems able to be magnanimous with regard to certain matters (the so-called *adiaphora*) only because he knows what the fundamental issues are. Where, however, foundational matters are at stake, he is prepared, without hesitation, to draw clear lines and to speak with fervor in defense of "the truth of the gospel" (2:5, 14). And that is what he does here, as well as elsewhere in his letters where the gospel itself is at stake (cf. 2 Cor 11:13–15; Col 2:8).

B. Autobiographical Statements in Defense (Narratio) 1:11–2:14

After the *exordium* of 1:6–10, Paul uses two common epistolary disclosure formulae. The first (γνωρίζω δὲ ὑμῖν, "I want you to know") introduces the thesis statement of 1:11–12 regarding the nature and origin of the gospel he proclaims. The second, which is a formulaic use of the verb of hearing (ἠκούσατε γάρ, "for you have heard"), introduces the autobiographical presentation that runs from 1:13 through 2:14 in support of that thesis. Taken together, the thesis statement of 1:11–12 and the autobiographical material of 1:13–2:14 make up Paul's *narratio*—i.e., the "statement of facts" as to what has occurred of relevance to the case.

1. Thesis Statement (1:11–12)

Bibliography

Bornkamm, G. "The Revelation of Christ to Paul on the Damascus Road and Paul's Doctrine of Justification and Reconciliation: A Study in Galatians I." Tr. J. M. Owen, in *Reconciliation and Hope*. FS L. L. Morris, ed. R. Banks. Exeter: Paternoster, 1974, 90–103. **Dahl, N. A.** "Paul's Letter to the Galatians: Epistolary Genre, Content, and Structure." Unpublished SBL Paul Seminar paper, 1974. **Dupont, J.** "The Conversion of Paul and Its Influence on His Understanding of Salvation by Faith." In *Apostolic History and the Gospel*. FS F. F. Bruce, ed. W. W. Gasque and R. P. Martin. Exeter: Paternoster, 1970, 176–94. **Jeremias, J.** "Chiasmus in den Paulusbriefen." *ZNW* 49 (1958) 145–56. **Menoud, P. H.** "Revelation and Tradition: The Influence of Paul's Conversion on His Theology." *Int* 7 (1953) 131-41.

Translation

[11]*I want you to know,[a] brothers, that the gospel I preached to you is not simply human.* [12]*I did not receive it from any man, nor[b] was I taught it; rather, I received it by revelation from Jesus Christ.*

Notes

[a] The reading γάρ, "for," after γνωρίζω, "I want . . . to know," appears in B D* G it cop^sa. The better reading, however, is probably δέ, "but," which is supported by P^46 ℵ A Byzantine syr cop^bo.

[b] The MS evidence is almost equally divided as to the negative conjunction before ἐδιδάχθην, "was I taught": οὔτε in P^46 B Byzantine, or οὐδέ in ℵ A D* G et al. There is, however, no difference of meaning, for both are translated "nor."

Form/Structure/Setting

JoachimJeremias viewed 1:11–12 as the first part of an extended chiasmus that runs throughout the entire body of Galatians (*ZNW* 49 [1958] 152–53). As Jeremias understood the letter's structure, κατὰ ἄνθρωπον, "human," of v 11 and παρὰ ἀνθρώπου, "from any man," of v 12 are spelled out in reverse order throughout the rest of the body of the letter: first in 1:13–2:21, with its elaboration of the theme that the gospel is not παρὰ ἀνθρώπου; then in 3:1–6:10, where it is stressed that it is not κατὰ ἄνθρωπον. So as Jeremias saw it, Galatians is a carefully constructed chiasmus wherein Paul's defense of the divine origin of his message in the autobiographical section of 1:13–2:21 elaborates παρὰ ἀνθρώπου of 1:12 and his theological arguments drawn from his biblical exposition of 3:1– 6:10 pick up on κατὰ ἄνθρωπον of 1:11.

Franz Mussner explicitly uses Jeremias' chiastic analysis in his 1974 Galatians commentary, structuring his treatment of the letter as follows:

I.   The Pauline gospel not παρὰ ἀνθρώπου (1:13–2:21);
II. The Pauline gospel not κατὰ ἄνθρωπον, but κατὰ τὴν γραφήν (3:1–6:10)
(*Galaterbrief*, vii–viii, 77).

Likewise, Jeremias' analysis is reflected in J. Christiaan Beker's 1980 magnum opus, where in speaking of the literary structure of Galatians Beker says:

The theme, which is subsequently unfolded chiastically, is stated in Gal. 1:11–12: "The gospel which was preached by me is not man's gospel (*kata anthrōpon*). For I did not receive it from man (*para anthrōpou*), nor was I taught it, but it came through a revelation about (of?) Jesus Christ."
   1. *"The apostle": Gal 1:13–2:21.* Paul's gospel does not derive "from a human source" (*para anthrōpou*); to the contrary, it is directly from God, and this constitutes his apostleship.
   2. *"The gospel": Gal 3:1–5:25.* Paul's gospel is not "according to human standards" (*kata anthrōpon*); to the contrary, it is according to Scripture (*kata graphēn*, Gal. 3:1–4:31) and verified by the Spirit (Gal 5:1–15)" (*Paul the Apostle*, 44–45).

The attempt to see the body of Galatians as one large chiasmus, however, falters on several grounds: (1) the inability of its proponents to identify significant repetitions within its parts; (2) the difficulty of laying out a well-balanced structure between its parts; and (3) uncertainties as to where one theme ends and another begins (cf. N. A. Dahl, "Paul's Letter to the Galatians," 76–77). It can even be debated, in fact, whether κατὰ ἄνθρωπον and παρὰ ἀνθρώπου are really set out by Paul in balanced fashion, or whether the latter is not an explication of the former and to be paired with ἐδιδάχθην that immediately follows (see *Comment* on v 12). Indeed, Paul's autobiographical presentation of 1:13–2:14 is, as Jeremias insists, a defense of the divine origin of his message. But it is also an introduction to the essential nature of his gospel, and is probably best seen coming to a climax in the *propositio* of 2:15–21.

There are, of course, common themes that run throughout 1:11–2:21. Yet the structure of this material seems better highlighted by the two epistolary disclosure formulae of 1:11 and 1:13, and better described by rhetorical argumentative modes of *narratio* (1:11–2:14) and *propositio* (2:15–21). So we conclude that 1:11–12 functions as the thesis statement for the autobiographical elaboration that follows in 1:13–2:14.

Comment

11 γνωρίζω δὲ ὑμῖν, ἀδελφοί, "I want you to know, brothers." Whether γάρ, "for," or δέ, "but," should be read as the postpositive conjunction is difficult to determine from the MS evidence alone. B D G et al. read γάρ, and so WH, Souter, Burton, RSV, UBSGT³, Betz, and others favor that; P⁴⁶ ℵ A et al., however, read δέ, which has been accepted by UBSGT² and other interpreters (also Lightfoot somewhat cautiously). The issue is of some importance, since γάρ as an explanatory conjunction suggests that v 11 should be seen as summarizing or concluding what has gone before, whereas δέ as a resumptive and/or mildly adversative conjunction would indicate that Paul meant to begin a new section in his argument at v 11— which as resumptive picks up the themes of 1:1–5 and as adversative stands in contrast to 1:6–10. In addition to the slight tipping of the scales in favor of δέ in the MS evidence (esp. P⁴⁶ and ℵ), the issue is influenced by an epistolary analysis of Galatians. For if Paul's disclosure formulae of vv 11 and 13 introduce his *narratio* (as we have argued), then δέ is much to be preferred. Furthermore, though Paul can use the disclosure formula γνωρίζω ὑμῖν ὅτι without any conjunction (cf. 1 Cor 12:3), elsewhere in his letters where he begins a new section with such a formula the conjunction is δέ (cf. 1 Cor 15:1; 2 Cor 8:1: γνωρίζω [ʼομεν] δὲ ὑμῖν, ἀδελφοί).

The verb γνωρίζω, as we have seen, was part of a common disclosure formula in Hellenistic letters (for papyri references, see MM, 129). Paul also uses it to introduce somewhat formal and solemn assertions (cf. 1 Cor 12:3; 15:1; 2 Cor 8:1). Here, as Burton points out, "the assertion that follows is in effect the proposition to the proving of which the whole argument of 1:13–2:21 is directed" (*Galatians*, 35).

The ἀδελφοί, "brothers," of 1:2, whether leaders of the church at Syrian Antioch or Paul's fellow missionaries, were mainly, if not entirely, Jewish Christians. Here, however, the ἀδελφοί are Gentile Christians who were being enticed into apostasy. Jews spoke of other Jews as brothers (Lev 19:17; Deut 1:16; 2 Macc 1:1; Acts 7:2; Rom 9:3); likewise, members of Hellenistic religious communities designated each other as brothers (see MM, 9). The practice of calling one another "brothers" in the early church may have derived, in part, from both such usages—though probably it stemmed principally from Jesus' having called his disciples "brothers" because of their relationship to him and their doing the Father's will (cf. Matt 23:8; Mark 3:31–35). Paul, too, views Christians as brothers because of their common relationship to Christ (cf. Rom 8:29; see also vv 16–17). And from this basis of shared relationship he goes on in his use of "brothers" to stress the fraternal, affectionate, mutually helpful attitude of Christians to one another (Rom 14:10, 13, 15; 1 Cor 5:11; 6:5–8; 8:11–13; 15:58; 2 Cor 1:1; 2:13). So in Galatians even amidst tones of sternness and severity Paul speaks of his wayward converts as "brothers" (see also 3:15; 4:12, 28, 31; 5:11, 13; 6:1, 18)—in effect, therefore, reminding them of his and their fraternal relationship, even though they were beginning to forget it.

τὸ εὐαγγέλιον τὸ εὐαγγελισθὲν ὑπ᾽ ἐμοῦ, "the gospel I preached to you," is Paul's somewhat cumbersome way of identifying his message preached at Galatia, which he calls more concisely "my gospel" (τὸ εὐαγγέλιόν μου) in Rom 2:16 and 16:25. His preaching, of course, focused on "Christ crucified" (3:1). More particularly, however, it laid stress on Gentiles who believed in Christ being accepted by God apart from any Jewish rituals and living before God apart from a Jewish lifestyle. For Paul, "Christ crucified" meant a proclamation completely different from that of the Judaizers, simply because nothing could be added to what Christ had already done. Indeed, in its focus on the redemptive work of Christ, Paul's preaching was identical to that of the Jerusalem apostles (cf. 1 Cor 15:1–11). It was, however, distinctly Paul's gospel ("the gospel I preached to you" or "my gospel") because of his clear recognition of its law-free nature. It was, therefore, not his preaching of "Christ crucified" that was being called into question by the Judaizers in Galatia, but the implications which Paul drew from that regarding God's acceptance of Gentile believers apart from their conformity to the Mosaic law.

ὅτι οὐκ ἔστιν κατὰ ἄνθρωπον, "is not simply human." The aorist adjectival participle εὐαγγελισθέν, "preached," of the previous clause referred the reader back to what Paul preached in his original mission among the Galatians. Here, however, ἔστιν, "is," suggests that Paul's gospel is always the same. This converse use of aorist and present tenses occurs with similar effect in 2:2, ἀνεθέμην αὐτοῖς τὸ εὐαγγέλιον ὃ κηρύσσω ἐν τοῖς ἔθνεσιν, "I set before them the gospel that I preach among the Gentiles."

οὐκ κατὰ ἄνθρωπον, "not simply human," is Paul's basic negative statement, in line with οὐκ ἀπ᾽ ἀνθρώπων οὐδὲ δι᾽ ἀνθρώπου, "not from men nor through any man," of v 1a, and will be spelled out more fully in v 12a. The preposition κατά means "according to" or "after the manner of," and connotes "stemming from the will or authority of." The noun ἄνθρωπον conveys simply the thought of "human" without any more exact discrimination. The complete phrase κατὰ ἄνθρωπον suggests both source and agency (as do its parallels in v 1a), but these ideas are left to be elaborated in the statements of v 12a.

12 οὐδὲ γὰρ ἐγὼ παρὰ ἀνθρώπου παρέλαβον αὐτό, οὔτε ἐδιδάχθην, "I did not receive it from any man, nor was I taught it." The explanatory γάρ, "for," signals that this sentence with its two negatives is meant to be an elaboration and clarification of οὐκ ἔστιν κατὰ ἄνθρωπον, "is not simply human." The preposition παρά is often used in the NT in the sense of ultimate source, with ἀπό and παρά appearing indistinguishably in parallel accounts (cf. Mark 5:35 and Luke 8:49; Matt 12:28 and Luke 11:16). The noun ἀνθρώπου, "any man," is generic, as used before. So it seems we should understand οὐδὲ παρὰ ἀνθρώπου, "not from any man," here as equivalent to οὐκ ἀπ᾽ ἀνθρώπων, "not from men," of v 1a, with both expressions referring to source and denying that Paul's law-free gospel had its origin in any human tradition. Likewise, οὔτε ἐδιδάχθην, "nor was I taught it," should probably be paralleled with οὐδὲ δι᾽ ἀνθρώπου, "nor through any man," of v 1a, with both referring to agency and denying that Paul's law-free gospel came to him by means of any human instruction.

ἀλλὰ δι᾽ ἀποκαλύψεως Ἰησοῦ Χριστοῦ, "rather . . . by revelation from Jesus Christ." The οὐκ . . . οὐδὲ . . . οὔτε . . . ἀλλά construction of vv 11–12 corresponds to the οὐκ . . . οὐδὲ . . . ἀλλά construction of v 1, which necessitates that we interpret the two sets of statements in similar fashion. Likewise, just as the negatives are to be taken as parallels, so we should interpret δι᾽ ἀποκαλύψεως Ἰησοῦ Χριστοῦ in line with the positive affirmation of v 1b. Admittedly, most commentators take Ἰησοῦ Χριστοῦ as an objective genitive and so understand Jesus Christ as the content of the revelation, mainly because of v 16a (see also 2:20a) where Paul says that God's purpose in calling him was "to reveal his Son in me (ἀποκαλύψαι τὸν υἱὸν αὐτοῦ ἐν ἐμοί) so that I might preach him among the Gentiles" (so Burton, Duncan, Betz, Bruce, et al.). But just as Paul viewed the preaching of "Christ crucified" to entail a law-free gospel, so he understood a Gentile mission as involved in God's sending of his Son. The word ἀποκαλύψεως, "revelation," may signify either content or means. With the preposition διά, "by," and in parallel with Paul's statement of v 1b, it is probably best seen here in the sense of means. The question Paul faced at Galatia was where his message of a law-free gospel came from. His assertion in v 1, as we have seen, is: Jesus Christ is its agent and God the Father its source. So here too we should probably understand δι' ἀποκαλύψεως in the sense of means and Ἰησοῦ Χριστοῦ as a subjective genitive (so Bring; cf. Rev 1:1). Paul's thesis, therefore, in line with his affirmation of 1:1, is that he received authority for preaching Christ in law-free terms to Gentiles by means of a revelation of which Jesus Christ was the agent. In all probability he had his encounter with Christ on the Damascus road in mind, with that revelation including (at least embryonically) a mission to Gentiles.

Explanation

Questions as to Paul's dependence and independence vis-à-vis early Christian tradition have always been of concern to interpreters, with some stressing dependence and others independence. The issue comes to the fore particularly here in the thesis statement of 1:11–12 and in the autobiographical section of 1:13–2:14 that follows. In fact, there appears to be a direct contradiction in Paul's disavowal here of having "received" (παρέλαβον) his message from others and his various acknowledgements elsewhere in his letters of having "received" (παρέλαβον) the central kerygmatic traditions from those who preceded him in the Christian faith (e.g.,1 Cor 11:23–26; 15:3–11).

It is a mistake, however, to read such statements apart from their contexts, or to set them in rather wooden opposition to one another. Paul's gospel given him by revelation was not a message that differed in kerygmatic content from that of the early church. Rather, it was a message that included a new understanding of what might be called the "redemptive logistics" for these final days—i.e., (1) a direct outreach to Gentiles apart from Judaism's rituals, (2) authentic Christian living for Gentiles apart from a Jewish lifestyle, and (3) the equality of Jewish and Gentile believers in the Church. As for the basic content of the gospel, Paul was dependent on those who were his Christian predecessors, as his repeated use of early Christian confessional materials indicates (for such materials in Galatians, see R. B. Hays, *The Faith of Jesus Christ*; for a survey of such materials elsewhere in Paul's letters, see A. M. Hunter, *Paul and His Predecessors*). However, as for Gentiles being accepted by God and living as Christians apart from the regulations of the Mosaic law—and so, as for the legitimacy of a Gentile mission apart from the Jewish law—Paul saw this as a "mystery" (μυστήριον) enigmatically rooted in the prophetic Scriptures but now made known to him by revelation (cf. Rom 16:25–26; Eph 3:2–10; Col 1:26–27), and so uniquely his.

The Judaizers in Galatia were not arguing against the Church's basic kerygmatic confessions. What they opposed were the implications Paul drew from these confessions for a law-free gospel among Gentiles. Paul, however, saw in the proclamation of full salvation in Christ the attendant truth of acceptance and life for Gentiles apart from the Mosaic law. This is what he calls "the gospel I preached to you" (1:11) or "my gospel" (Rom 2:16; 16:25; see also 2 Tim 2:8; and "our gospel" at 2 Cor 4:3; 1 Thess 1:5; 2 Thess 2:14). And this is what he asserts in 1:11–12 did not come to him from any human source or through any human agency, but rather was received "by revelation" (the means) "through Jesus Christ" (the agent).

Paul could not claim the usual apostolic qualifications as expressed in John 15:27 and Acts 1:21–22. He was dependent on those who were believers before him for much in the Christian tradition, as his letters frankly indicate. But he had been confronted by the exalted Lord, directly commissioned an apostle by Christ himself, and given the key to the pattern of redemptive history in the present age. The Jerusalem apostles had the key to many of the prophetic mysteries and were the living canons of the data in the gospel proclamation. He, however, had been entrusted with a further aspect of that message, which came to him "by revelation through Jesus Christ" and so was uniquely his. Together, the apostolic kerygma and the mystery revealed to Paul regarding a law-free gospel for Gentiles combined to enhance the fullness of the Christian message.

2. Early Life, Conversion and Commission (1:13–17)

Bibliography

Bruce, F. F. "Further Thoughts on Paul's Biography: Galatians 1:11–2:14." In *Jesus und Paulus*. FS W. G. Kümmel. Tübingen: Mohr-Siebeck, 1975. 21–29. **Donaldson, T. L.** "Zealot and Convert: The Origin of Paul's Christ-Torah Antithesis." *CBQ* 51 (1989) 655–82. **Dupont, J.** "La Revelation du Fils de Dieu en faveur de Pierre (Mt 16, 17) et de Paul (Gal 1, 16)." *RSR* 52 (1964) 411–20. **Holmberg, B.** *Paul and Power.* **Longenecker, R. N.** *Paul, Apostle of Liberty,* 33–36 (Paul's persecution of the Church) and 160–70 ("in Christ"). ———. "The Acts of the Apostles." In *The Expositor's Bible Commentary,* Vol. 9. Ed. F. E. Gaebelein. Zondervan, 1981, 367–79. ———. *The Christology of Early Jewish Christianity,* 93–99 ("Son of God"). **Martyn, J. L.** "A Law-Observant Mission to Gentiles: The Background of Galatians." *MQR* 22 (1983) 221–36.

Translation

[13]For you have heard of my previous way of life in Judaism, how intensely I persecuted the church of God and tried to destroy it. [14]I was advancing in Judaism beyond many Jews of my own age, being far more zealous for the traditions of my fathers. [15]But when the One who set me apart from birth and called me by his grace was pleased[a] [16]to reveal his Son in me so that I might preach him among the Gentiles, I did not immediately thereafter consult

with anyone; [17]*nor did I go up*[b] *to Jerusalem to see those who were apostles before me, but I went away into Arabia and returned again to Damascus.*

Notes

[a]The reading εὐδόκησεν (or ηὐδόκησεν) ὁ θεός appears in ℵ A D Byzantine syr[hel] cop[sa, bo] et al., so making explicit by the addition of ὁ θεός what is plainly to be understood. However, εὐδόκησεν alone, as in P[46] B G, is to be preferred.

[b]The majority of MSS (ℵ A et al.) read ἀνῆλθον ("went up") εἰς ʼΙεροσόλυμα, though ἀπῆλθον ("went away") appears in P[51] B D G and ἦλθον ("went") in P[46vid].

Form/Structure/Setting

In support of his claim that "the gospel I preached to you is not simply human— I did not receive it from any man, nor was I taught it" (1:11–12), Paul sets out in 1:13–2:14 a number of incidents having to do with his life in Judaism, his conversion to Christ, his commission to minister among Gentiles, his visits to Jerusalem, and his contacts with the Jerusalem apostles. The section begins with the epistolary disclosure formula ἠκούσατε γάρ ("for you have heard"), which directly introduces the statements about his life in Judaism of 1:13–14, though probably it is meant as well to stand over all the autobiographical narration from 1:13 through 2:14. For while it may be assumed that Paul, when with them, had told his converts something about many, if not all, of these incidents, his opponents evidently had another version and had circulated that version among the Galatian churches. Thus Paul feels compelled to rehearse the incidents in question, setting matters right and so elaborating on the thesis of 1:11–12.

Here in 1:13–17 he speaks of his life in Judaism, his conversion to Christ, and his commission to a Gentile mission, obviously rebutting rumors to the contrary. As for his life in Judaism (vv 13–14), he denies that he was in any way prepared for preaching a law-free gospel to Gentiles. Far from it! Rather, he was a faithful and zealous observer of the Jewish religion and way of life, even to the point of persecuting Christians and trying to destroy "the church of God."

We know from some second-, third-, and fourth-century writings that opposition to Paul among Jewish Christians was often bitter and intense. The *Ascension of James*, whose author probably lived in or near Pella and wrote sometime after the middle of the second century, speaks of Paul's law-free approach as reducing the number of Gentiles who came to Christ through the outreach of Jewish Christians and characterizes Paul as follows:

Paul was a man of Tarsus—indeed, a Hellene [Greek], the son of a Hellenist mother and a Hellenist father. Having gone up to Jerusalem and having remained there a long time, he desired to marry a daughter of the (high) priest and on that account submitted himself as a proselyte for circumcision. When, however, he did not obtain the girl, he became furious and began to write against circumcision, the sabbath, and the law (cf. Epiphanius, *Panarion* ["Medicine Chest"] or *Adv. Haer.* 30.16; see also 30.25).

The late-second-century *Kerygmata Petrou* "Preachings of Peter" repeatedly refers to Paul as "the enemy man" who proclaimed a "lawless and absurd doctrine."

Comment 27

Likewise, the third- and fourth-century pseudo-Clementine *Homilies* and *Recognitions*, in addition to accusing Paul of short-circuiting the Jewish Christian mission to the entire world, vehemently discredit him under the cover figure of Simon Magus, who is constantly opposed by Peter and James.

It is impossible, of course, to be certain that such attacks against Paul were explicitly mounted by any branch of Jewish Christendom during the first century A.D. Yet they undoubtedly had roots in earlier times, and so it may be assumed that Paul's opponents in Galatia were insinuating something of the kind. And it is against any such suggestion as to the inferiority of his experience in Judaism that Paul speaks in vv 13–14.

As for his conversion to Christ and his commission to minister among Gentiles, Paul seems to be rebutting in vv 15–17 certain suggestions to the effect (1) that his Christian profession can be explained along the lines of human motivations and events, and (2) that his subsequent activity included instruction under the Jerusalem apostles, from whose teaching he then deviated. To such assertions, Paul answers that it was God who called him in prophetic fashion to minister to Gentiles and that he had no contact with his Christian predecessors at Jerusalem until much later.

Comment

13 ἠκούσατε γὰρ τὴν ἐμὴν ἀναστροφήν ποτε ἐν τῷ 'Ιουδαϊσμῷ, "for you have heard of my previous way of life in Judaism." The force of the explanatory γάρ, "for," extends, in effect, through 2:14, since the argument of the *narratio* is cumulative. So too ἠκούσατε is probably meant to stand over all the autobiographical narration of 1:13–2:14. Paul's evangelistic practice, it seems, included certain of his own experiences in proclaiming the gospel, though these were twisted by his opponents for their own purposes.

The noun ἀναστροφή among classical authors meant "return," but it became in Koine Greek a locution for "behavior," "conduct," or "way of life" (see the inscriptional evidence cited by MM, 38; also Polybius 4.82; Tob 4:14; 2 Macc 3:23; Eph 4:22; 1 Tim 4:12; Heb 13:7; Jas 3:13; 1 Peter 1:15, 18; 2:12; 3:1, 2, 16; 2 Peter 2:7; 3:11). It is not found in the canonical writings of the LXX or in the papyri, which may only mean that it was not current in Egypt.

'Ιουδαϊσμός, meaning "the Jewish religion and way of life," appears in the NT only here and at v 14. It may originally have been coined by Gentiles as a term of contempt (similar to believers in Christ being called Χριστιανός). However, its use in 2 Macc 2:21; 8:1; 14:38; 4 Macc 4:26 for the Jewish religion and way of life as contrasted to Seleucid Hellenism indicates that, whatever its origin, it became for Jews an honored title.

ὅτι καθ᾽ ὑπερβολὴν ἐδίωκον τὴν ἐκκλησίαν τοῦ θεοῦ καὶ ἐπόρθουν αὐτήν, "how intensely I persecuted the church of God and tried to destroy it." Elaborating exegetically on τὴν ἐμὴν ἀναστροφήν, "my previous way of life," Paul gives two examples of pertinence for his argument: (1) his intense persecution of Christians (v 13), and (2) his extreme zeal for everything Jewish (v 14). καθ᾽ ὑπερβολήν, "intensely," is a classical comparative that signals an excess of either quality or character (or both) over what might be expected. It appears in the NT only in Paul's letters (cf. Rom 7:13; 1 Cor 12:31; 2 Cor 1:8; 4:17). The imperfect verbs ἐδίωκον and ἐπόρθουν, with their connotations of past repeated action, highlight the continuance of Paul's earlier persecuting activity. πορθέω, the latter of these verbs, was used from Homer on to mean "devastate," "sack", or "destroy" cities, and so intensifies the verb διώκω, "persecute" (cf. v 23; see also Acts 8:3).

Paul's use of τὴν ἐκκλησίαν τοῦ θεοῦ, "the church of God," is especially interesting, particularly since it signals a more elevated understanding of "church" than appears in the localized uses of 1:2 and 22 (cf. 1 Thess 1:1; 2 Thess 1:1; 1 Cor 1:2; 2 Cor 1:1). In context, "the church of God" stands in opposition to "Judaism," and so the more universal sense of ἐκκλησία may be claimed to have arisen from the need for Christian self-definition vis-à-vis Judaism. In his earlier letters (including Galatians, as we have argued), Paul usually thinks of churches as local communities of Christians. His use here, however, indicates that he also, when defining his position vis-à-vis Judaism, began to think more universally of all such communities as making up the one church of God. Furthermore, it should be noted that "the church of God" here, while referring directly to Jewish Christians, has relevance to Paul's Gentile converts as well, so indicating in Paul's thinking the union of Jewish and Gentile believers in Christ. Yet, as Burton points out, "inasmuch as the church which Paul persecuted was a Jewish church, not only in that it was composed of Jews, but probably mainly of those who still observed the Jewish law, his characterisation of it as the church of God shows how far he was from denying the legitimacy of Jewish Christianity in itself" (*Galatians*, 45–46).

Commentators have frequently seen in Paul's persecution of the Christian church an attempt to slay externally the dragons of doubt that he could not silence within his own heart and to repress "all humaner tendencies in the interests of his legal absolutism" (C. H. Dodd, *The Mind of Paul: Change and Development*, 36; see also his *The Mind of Paul: A Psychological Approach*, esp. 12–13). But the day of the psychological interpretation of Paul's conversion appears to be over, and deservedly so. It is probable that Paul took up his task of persecution with full knowledge of the earnestness of his opponents, the stamina of martyrs, and the agony he would necessarily cause. Fanaticism was not so foreign to Palestine as to leave him unaware of such things, and it is quite possible that he was prepared for the emotional strain involved in persecuting those he believed to be dangerous schismatics within Israel.

More important, however, in days when the keeping of the Mosaic law was considered by Pharisaic Jews to be the vitally important prerequisite for the coming of the Messianic Age (cf. *b. Sanh.* 97b–98a; *b. B. Bat.* 10a; *b. Yoma* 86b), Paul could very well have validated his actions against Christians by reference to such godly precedents as (1) Moses' slaying of the immoral Israelites at Baal-peor (cf. Num 25:1–5); (2) Phinehas' slaying of the Israelite man and Midianite woman in the plains of Moab (cf. Num 25:6–15); and (3) the actions of Mattathias and the Hasidim in rooting out apostasy among the people (cf. 1 Macc 2:23–28, 42–48). Perhaps even the divine commendation of Phinehas' action in Num 25:11–13 rang in his ears:

Phinehas son of Eleazar, the son of Aaron, the priest, has turned my anger away from the Israelites; for he was as jealous as I am for my honor among them, so that in my zeal I did not put an end to them. Therefore tell him I am making my covenant of peace with him. He and his descendants will have a covenant of a lasting priesthood, because he was zealous for the honor of his God and made atonement for the Israelites.

2 Macc 6:13 counsels that "it is a mark of great kindness when the impious are not let alone for a long time, but punished at once." The DSS define a righteous man as one who "bears unremitting hatred toward all men of ill repute" (1QS 9.22). They speak of unswerving allegiance to God and his laws as alone providing a firm foundation for the Holy Spirit, truth, and the arrival of Israel's hope (1QS 9.3–4, 20–21) and call for volunteers who are blameless in spirit and body to root out apostasy in the final eschatological days (1QM 7.5; 10.2–5). The Qumran psalmist, in fact, directly associates commitment to God and his laws with zeal against apostates and perverters of the law when he says:

> The nearer I draw to you, the more am I filled with zeal against all that do wickedness and against all men of deceit. For they that draw near to you cannot see your commandments defiled, and they that have knowledge of you can brook no change of your words, seeing that you are the essence of right, and all your elect are the proof of your truth (1QH 14.13–15).

With such precedents and parallels, coupled with the rising tide of messianic expectation within Israel, Paul may well have felt justified in mounting a persecution against Jewish Christians. Probably he reasoned that in light of Israel's rising messianic hopes the nation must be unified and faithful in its obedience to the law and kept from schism or going astray. And in this task he doubtless expected to receive God's commendation.

14 καὶ προέκοπτον ἐν τῷ Ἰουδαϊσμῷ ὑπὲρ πολλοὺς συνηλικιώτας ἐν τῷ γένει μου, "I was advancing in Judaism beyond many Jews of my own age," continues Paul's epexegetical elaborations on his earlier ἀναστροφή, "way of life," in Judaism. The verb προκόπτω, which seems to have been originally a nautical term for "make headway in spite of blows," came to connote in the philosophical and religious writings of the Hellenistic world "the process of moral and spiritual development" in an individual (cf. G. Stählin, "προκοπή, προκόπτω," TDNT 6:704–7). It is used in this way by Josephus of his own "great progress in education" (Life 8), by Luke of Jesus' growth "in wisdom and stature, and in favor with God and men" (Luke 2:52), and in the Pauline letters some eight times total (here and at Rom 13:12; Phil 1:12, 25; 1 Tim 4:15; 2 Tim 2:16; 3:9, 13). Its imperfect form (προέκοπτον), in line with the two imperfects of v 13, lays stress on the past durative idea—i.e., that there was a continuing process of moral and spiritual development throughout Paul's life in Judaism.

συνηλικιώτας, which appears in the NT only here, is a Hellenistic term for "a person of one's own age" or "a contemporary" (cf. ἡλικία, "age"). γένος ("race," "family," "class"), particularly in tandem with Ἰουδαϊσμός, refers to the Jewish nation without any further discrimination (so also 2 Cor 11:26; Phil 3:5; cf. Acts 7:19; 13:26). Thus the comparison is with other Jews of Paul's age generally, without any attempt to rank his progress among Pharisees specifically.

περισσοτέρως ζηλωτὴς ὑπάρχων τῶν πατρικῶν μου παραδόσεων, "being far more zealous for the traditions of my fathers." Paul uses the comparative adverbs περισσοτέρως ("far more," 2 Cor 1:12; 7:13, 15; 12:15) and ὑπερβαλλόντως ("to a much greater degree," 2 Cor 11:23) synonymously. Here the comparison is with "many Jews of my own age." Contrary to Lightfoot, who understood Paul to mean that he "belonged to the extreme party of the Pharisees" and so was what later became known as a Zealot (*Galatians*, 81–82), ζηλωτής here should be taken only as "an ardent observer of Torah"—as it appears also in Acts 22:3 in one of Paul's defenses (cf. Josephus, *Ant.* 12.271, of Mattathias; Acts 21:20 of Jewish Christians at Jerusalem; see also 1 Macc 2:26–27, 50; 2 Macc 4:2; 4 Macc 18:12; Philo, *Spec. Leg.* 1.30; 2.253; *Abr.* 60; *Virt.* 175). τῶν πατρικῶν μου παραδόσεων, "for the traditions of my fathers," refers to (1) the teachings and practices developed in the Pharisaic schools of Second Temple Judaism, which later became codified in the Mishnah, Palestinian and Babylonian Gemaras, Midrashim, and the various individual halakic and haggadic collections of rabbinic lore, and (2) the interpretations of a more popular nature that arose within the synagogues of Paul's day, as represented in the extant Targumim. What Paul is insisting on is that as far as his standing in Judaism is concerned, his credentials are impeccable (cf. Acts 22:3; Phil 3:5–6). Or, as Betz puts it, "As a Jew he had no reason to leave Judaism" (*Galatians*, 68).

15 ὅτε δὲ εὐδόκησεν ὁ ἀφορίσας με ἐκ κοιλίας μητρός μου καὶ καλέσας διὰ τῆς χάριτος αὐτοῦ, "But when the one who set me apart from birth and called me by his grace was pleased." The crux of Paul's argument in vv 15–17 comes near the end: "I did not consult immediately thereafter with anyone; nor did I go up to Jerusalem to see those who were apostles before me" (vv 16b–17a). He prepares for these assertions, however, by first setting out in positive fashion the bases for his ministry—i.e., God's good pleasure (εὐδόκησεν), ordination (ἀφορίσας), and call (καλέσας).

The subject of the substantival participles ἀφορίσας and καλέσας is clearly God (cf. 1:6; 2:8; 3:5; 5:8; also Rom 8:11; Phil 1:6; 1 Thess 5:24), so that the addition of ὁ θεός in ℵ A D et al. is uncalled for. ὁ ἀφορίσας με ἐκ κοιλίας μητρός μου, "the One who separated me/set me apart from birth," is an expression rooted in the call of certain OT prophets (cf. Jer 1:5) and that of the Servant of Yahweh (cf. Isa 49:1–6). Its use by Paul of his own apostleship—with evident intent (cf. Rom 1:1, ἀφωρισμένος εἰς εὐαγγέλιον θεοῦ, "having been set apart for the gospel of God")—suggests that he thought of his apostleship not just along the lines of a Jewish understanding of *šalîaḥ* (i.e., representative messenger or envoy; cf. *Comment* on 1:1), but also in terms of Israelite prophetology. ἐκ κοιλίας μητρός μου, "from my mother's womb," is a Septuagintalism that may mean either "from my birth" or "from before my birth," with its specific temporal determination being heavily dependent on context. It is probably best, however, as with any idiomatic expression, to allow a measure of ambiguity and to translate it here simply "from birth."

καλέσας διὰ τῆς χάριτος αὐτοῦ, "called ... by his grace," completes the couplet "set apart" and "called." There is no necessary logical or chronological order in Paul's mind as to God's ordination and call, as his reversal of these ideas in Rom 1:1 shows (κλητὸς ἀπόστολος, ἀφωρισμένος εἰς εὐαγγέλιον θεοῦ, "called an apostle, set apart for the gospel of God"). What Paul is stressing, without any thought expended as to logical or chronological relationships, is that his apostleship stems from God's good pleasure, ordination, and call. As a dative of means with a possessive genitive, the expression διὰ τῆς χάριτος αὐτοῦ, "by his grace," is equivalent to ἐν χάριτι Χριστοῦ, "by the grace of Christ," of v 6. The interchange of God (αὐτοῦ) and Christ (Χριστοῦ) in the phraseology highlights the fact that Paul thought of God and Christ as completely at one in mankind's salvation.

16 ἀποκαλύψαι τὸν υἱὸν αὐτοῦ ἐν ἐμοί, "to reveal his Son in me." The language of v 16a raises a number of difficult questions and has caused a great deal of speculation. The Christological title "Son of God," "his [God's] Son," or simply "the Son" appears in Paul's writings fifteen times ("Son of God": Rom 1:4; 2 Cor 1:19; Gal 2:20; "his Son" or "the Son": Rom 1:3, 9; 5:10; 8:3, 29, 32; 1 Cor 1:9; 15:28; Gal 1:16; 4:4, 6; 1 Thess 1:10), which warrants Werner Kramer's comment: "In comparison with the passages in which the titles Christ Jesus or Lord occur, this is an infinitesimally small figure" (*Christ, Lord, Son of God*, 183). Furthermore, in that all of these fifteen instances are in Paul's earlier letters (i.e., the *Hauptbriefe* and 1 Thessalonians, but none in the Prison or Pastoral Epistles), it can be argued that "Son of God" as a Christological title was derived by Paul from his Jewish Christian heritage (cf. ibid., 185).

During the first half of the twentieth century, of course, scholars influenced by G. H. Dalman and W. Bousset tended to separate "Son of God" from its Jewish roots and to see it as a Hellenistic epiphany accretion. Of late, however, the title is being increasingly related to Jewish messianology (cf. 4QFlor on 2 Sam 7:14; 4 Ezra 7:28–29; 13:32, 37, 52; 14:9) and seen as a feature of early Jewish Christian Christology (cf. my *The Christology of Early Jewish Christianity*, 93–99). In Galatians the title "Son of God" or "his Son" appears elsewhere at 2:20 and 4:4, 6, with each of these occurrences situated in a confessional or quasi-confessional portion (see *Comment* on these verses). So it may be claimed that "Son of God" is a title carried over from both Paul's Jewish and his Christian past, and that he uses it here as a central Christological ascription because (1) it was ingrained in his thinking as a Jewish Christian, and (2) it was part of the language of his opponents, who were also Jewish Christians.

Paul's use of ἀποκαλύψαι, "to reveal," raises the question as to exactly what form of revelation he had in mind, for the term carried a number of nuances in both Hellenism and Judaism (cf. A. Oepke, "ἀποκαλύπτω, ἀποκάλυψις," *TDNT* 3:563–92). Most commentators compare his words here with those of 1 Cor 9:1 ("have I not seen Jesus our Lord?") and 1 Cor 15:8 ("last of all he appeared to me"), and view these latter passages as alluding to Christ's encounter with Paul on the road to Damascus (cf. Acts 9:1–19; 22:3–16; 26:12–18). But the verb used in 1 Corinthians is ὁράω, "see," rather than ἀποκαλύπτω, "reveal"— first in the active (9:1, ἑώρακα) and then in the passive (15:8, ὤφθη). ὁράω suggests an external vision whereas ἀποκαλύπτω has been taken to signify an internal experience (cf. A. Wikenhauser, *Pauline Mysticism*, 134–36). However, to quote H. D. Betz: "We should not suppose that Paul feels he contradicts himself in Gal 1:16 and 1 Cor 9:1; 15:8. Apparently for him the two forms of visions (external and internal) are not as distinct as they may be for some commentators" (*Galatians*, 71).

The accusative τὸν υἱὸν αὐτοῦ, "his Son," is the direct object of the verb ἀποκαλύψαι, and so cannot be taken as anything other than the content of what was revealed to Paul on the Damascus road. The usage here, however, is not determinative for whether Ἰησοῦ Χριστοῦ of v 12 is an objective genitive (specifying content) or a subjective genitive (specifying agent), even though most have so concluded (see *Comment* on 1:12). What Paul received by revelation on his way to Damascus was (1) a new understanding of Jesus Christ, which he shared with others who had come in contact with the resurrected Lord, and (2) a new understanding of God's strategy of redemption (or, God's "redemptive logistics") for this final age, which included his law-free mission to Gentiles, but which he found was not always appreciated by others. These two features of that one revelation always went together in Paul's mind, though at times depending on context he emphasized one over the other. Thus in Galatians, where issues relating to both justification by faith in Christ and the legitimacy of a law-free mission to Gentiles are intertwined, Paul speaks of Jesus Christ as (1) the content of the Damascus road revelation (here and passim), as well as (2) the agent of that revelation on which he bases his ministry to the Gentiles (1:1, 12).

The expression ἐν ἐμοί, "in me," corresponds to "Christ lives in me" of 2:20 and "God sent the Spirit of his Son into our hearts" of 4:6, with all three of these passages pointing to the inward reality of Christian experience. Christ "in me" is the flip side of the Christian being "in Christ Jesus" (see 3:26, 28, and *Comment* there).

ἵνα εὐαγγελίζωμαι αὐτὸν ἐν τοῖς ἔθνεσιν, "so that I might preach him among the Gentiles." In being confronted by Christ while traveling to Damascus, Paul was both converted and commissioned (cf. Rom 1:5, "Through him and for his name's sake, we received grace and apostleship to call people from among all the Gentiles to the obedience that comes from faith"). So having spoken of the content of that revelation ("his Son"), he goes on to speak of its purpose: "so that [ἵνα] I might preach him among the Gentiles." We need not suppose that Paul immediately grasped all that was either stated or implied in that encounter—i.e., that he fully understood in a moment everything pertaining to "his Son" or everything pertaining to preaching Christ "among the Gentiles." Paul's own letters suggest that his understanding of Christ developed throughout his life as a Christian, and the Acts of the Apostles indicates that there were stages in his comprehension of what a mission to Gentiles involved. In good Semitic fashion, Paul speaks in ultimates without any attention to stages or progression of thought (cf. Acts 26:16–23). As F. F. Bruce aptly says: "Indeed, the logic of 'the gospel according to Paul' was implicit in his Damascus-road experience. Paul grasped this in essence there and then, although the fuller implications of the experience became plain to him more gradually" (*Galatians*, 93).

The phrase εὐαγγελίζωμαι αὐτόν, "that I might preach him," is somewhat remarkable, for elsewhere in Galatians Paul speaks of preaching "the gospel" (τὸν εὐαγγέλιον, cf. 1:8, 9, 11; 2:2; 4:13) or "the faith" (τὴν πίστιν, cf. 1:23). In his other letters, however, Paul easily equates "the gospel," "the faith," and "Christ," for the content of the Christian gospel and of the Christian faith is Jesus Christ (cf. Rom 15:18–20; 2 Cor 1:19; 4:5; Phil 1:15–18; Col 1:28)—or more precisely, "Christ crucified" (cf. 1 Cor 1:23; 2:2; Gal 3:1) and "Christ raised from the dead" (cf. 1 Cor 15:3–12). The present tense of εὐαγγελίζωμαι, particularly following the aorists ἀφορίσας ("set apart"), καλέσας ("called"), and ἀποκαλύψαι ("to reveal"), lays stress on Paul's continued preaching of Christ (i.e., "the gospel" or "the faith") among the Gentiles, as based on God's ordination, call, and revelation. The preposition ἐν ("among") indicates the sphere and scope of his mission—i.e., the regions of the Gentiles and all who lived in those areas (cf. 2:2, 8). And while in Paul's quotation of the Abrahamic blessing ἔθνη means "nations" in a general sense (3:8b), elsewhere in Galatians it uniformly means "Gentiles" as distinguished from Jews (cf. 2:2, 8, 9, 12, 14, 15; 3:8a, 14).

16b–17a εὐθέως οὐ προσανεθέμην σαρκὶ καὶ αἵματι, οὐδὲ ἀνῆλθον εἰς Ἱεροσόλυμα πρὸς τοὺς πρὸ ἐμοῦ ἀποστόλους, "I did not immediately thereafter consult with anyone; nor did I go up to Jerusalem to see those who were apostles before me." The crux of Paul's argument in vv 15–17, as we noted above, comes in this statement. So despite the versification, we must treat vv 16b and 17a together.

Commentators differ as to whether εὐθέως ("immediately") should go with the negative assertions here (so Zahn, Schlier, Mussner, Betz; cf. Luther, KJV, Knox, Berkeley) or with the first of the affirmative clauses to follow, "I went into Arabia" (so Lightfoot, Burton, Bruce; cf. Moffatt, JB, NEB, GNB, NIV)—or, in fact, should be seen only as an enthusiastic particle (similar to the extensive use of εὐθύς in Mark 1–2, passim) and not to be translated at all (so RSV, Phillips). The strongest argument for taking εὐθέως as modifying not the two immediately following negative clauses (οὐ προσανεθέμην . . . οὐδὲ ἀνῆλθον, "I did not consult . . . nor did I go up") but the affirmative clause which they lead up to (ἀλλ' ἀπῆλθον, "but I went away") is that "by its meaning εὐθέως calls for an affirmation, not simply a statement of non-action" (Burton, *Galatians*, 53–54). Indeed, it may seem somewhat strange that Paul focuses first on what he did *not* do, rather than affirm what he did (as in Acts 26:20, "first [πρῶτον] to those in Damascus"). Yet the issue at Galatia had to do with where Paul got his message and how he received certification as an apostle, with his opponents claiming that he was dependent on and subordinate to the apostles at Jerusalem. So it is understandable that the thrust of his argument in these verses should be on the negative aspects of his thesis statement of 1:11–12—as it is, in fact, throughout the remainder of his autobiographical *narratio*. In this context, then, εὐθέως makes eminent sense at the beginning of his negative assertions. It should probably be translated "immediately thereafter," so tying together Christ's revelatory encounter (vv 15–16a) and the crux of the polemic of this passage (vv 16b–17a).

προσανατίθημι in the middle voice means "betake oneself to," and so connotes "consult," "confer" or "communicate with." It appears in the NT only here and at 2:6— the first as a first person singular, aorist, indicative, middle verb (προσανεθέμην) suggesting the purpose of obtaining instruction (cf. Diodorus Siculus 17.116, where it is used in the context of consulting soothsayers); the second as a third person plural, aorist, indicative, middle verb (προσανέθεντο) suggesting the purpose of giving instruction. In both cases, however, Paul denies (οὐ, οὐδέν) that he received or was given such instruction. σάρξ καὶ αἷμα is a metonymy for "mankind in its finitude and frailty" or "humanity as temporally and corporeally conditioned," in contrast to beings of a higher order, especially God (cf. Sir 14:18; 17:31; Matt 16:17; 1 Cor 15:50; Eph 6:12; Heb 2:14). Its use here is general ("anyone"), though expressing the same concerns as in 1:1a, 11–12. The prefix ἀνά ("up") of the aorist verb ἀνῆλθον conforms to the expression εἰς Ἱεροσόλυμα (see also v 18), for one regularly "goes up" to Jerusalem (cf. 2 Sam 8:7; Ezra 1:3; 7:7; 1 Esd 2:5; 1 Macc 4:36–37; 3 Macc 3:16; Mark 10:32–33; Luke 2:42; John 2:13; 5:1; Acts 11:2; 18:22; 21:12, 15; 24:11; 25:1, 9). Probably the reading ἀπῆλθον (P⁵¹, B, D, G) came about by assimilation to ἀπῆλθον εἰς Ἀραβίαν ("I went away into Arabia") of v 17b.

Paul's use of Ἱεροσόλυμα, "Jerusalem" (cf. also 1:18; 2:1), may raise questions, particularly when compared with his use of Ἱερουσαλήμ at 4:25–26. NT references to Jerusalem, however, are almost equally divided between Ἱερουσαλήμ, the Hebraic and LXX name with sacred connotations, and Ἱεροσόλυμα, the profane designation used more by Gentile writers and Jews addressing a Greek-speaking audience. The former appears seventy-six times in all in the NT; the latter sixty-three times. The authors of Hebrews and Revelation, of course, always use Ἱερουσαλήμ, for they are speaking of the heavenly and eschatological city. Mark and John, on the other hand, never use the more sacred form. Luke in his Gospel usually reworks Mark's Ἱεροσόλυμα to Ἱερουσαλήμ (using Ἱεροσόλυμα only four

times and Ἰερουσαλήμ twenty-six times), and he continues to use Ἰερουσαλήμ
throughout Acts 1–7 (with 1:4 being an exception). From Acts 8 onward, however,
he uses both forms without much distinction. So too Paul refers to Jerusalem in
Galatians using both forms. If any difference of meaning is to be seen, it is probably
that in 1:17–18 and 2:1 he has simply the geographical site in mind, whereas in
4:25–26 his emphasis is more on the religious significance of the city.

The ἀπόστολοι, "apostles," at Jerusalem included Peter and "the Twelve" (1 Cor
15:5), and also James (cf. v 19) and others (cf. 1 Cor 15:7; see also Rom 16:7 for a
wider use of ἐν τοῖς ἀποστόλοις, "among the apostles"). πρὸ ἐμοῦ, "before me,"
is temporal, and so not to be taken as denoting precedence of status. The whole phrase
πρὸς τοὺς πρὸ ἐμοῦ ἀποστόλους, "to those who were apostles before me," on the
one hand, involves Paul's recognition of the apostolic status of the Twelve and
implies that he regarded his apostleship as of the same essential character as theirs.
On the other hand, however, set as it is as evidence for his assertion in 1:11–12, it
culminates the claim of this section that his gospel did not originate with them.

ἀλλὰ ἀπῆλθον εἰς Ἀραβίαν, "but I went away into Arabia," is somewhat vague,
for it neither specifies exactly where Paul went nor for what purpose. The Nabatean kingdom of Arabia was a rather large and somewhat amorphous geographical
entity in Paul's day. It lay to the east of the Jordan valley rift, and traditionally
extended from the Red Sea on the southwest to the Euphrates River on the
northeast. Its main cultural centers were Petra in the south and Bostra in the north,
but it included at various times also some of the Decapolis cities of eastern Syria (e.g.,
Damascus) and the Transjordan (e.g., Philadelphia/Amman; Gerasa/Jerash). It was
ruled from 9 B.C. to A.D. 40 by Aretas IV, with Damascus being a part of the Nabatean
kingdom at certain periods during his reign (cf. 2 Cor 11:32). Its exact borders,
however, seem to have shifted at various times, and it may be assumed from Paul's
statement, "I went away [from Damascus] into Arabia," that when Galatians was written
(c. A.D. 49?) Damascus was no longer included within Arabia.

Except that it was away from Damascus, we have no way of telling exactly where
Paul went in Arabia. He refers in 4:25, of course, to Mount Sinai as being in Arabia,
and from that some have thought that it was to the Sinai peninsula that he went.
But Paul seems to mean by Arabia only the Nabatean kingdom, and the boundaries
of that kingdom were near at hand. In fact, as Burton points out: "There is nothing
to necessitate the supposition that he went far from Damascus, nor anything to
exclude a far-distant journey except that if he had gone far to the south a return to
Damascus would perhaps have been improbable" (Galatians, 58). Nor can we tell
from Paul's brief statement why he went to Arabia. Many have supposed that it was
for the purpose of missionary outreach. But it could just as well be argued that it
was principally for solitude to rethink his life and learning from the perspective of
Christ's revelatory encounter, away from Jewish jurisdiction and pressures.

καὶ πάλιν ὑπέστρεψα εἰς Δαμασκόν, "and returned again to Damascus," is an
indirect confirmation of Acts that Paul's conversion and commission took place at
Damascus (cf. Acts 9:1–22; 22:5–16; 26:12–20a). Damascus was a large and thriving
commercial center at the foot of the Anti-Lebanon mountain range. Since 64 B.C.
it had been officially part of the Roman province of Syria and was granted certain
civic rights by Rome as one of the ten cities of the Decapolis. Its architecture and
inscriptions show that during Paul's day it was extensively influenced by Hellenism
(cf. F. V. Winnett and W. L. Reed, *Ancient Records from North Arabia*). It had, how-

ever, a large Arab population and was even included at certain times under Nabatean rule. It also had a large Jewish population, 10,500 of whom Josephus reports were killed by the people of Damascus at the outbreak of Jewish-Roman hostilities in A.D. 66 (cf. *J. W.* 2.561; though the figure is 18,000 in *J. W.* 7.368). To this city Paul went with Sanhedrin authority to persecute Jewish believers in Jesus; on the way to this city he was confronted by the resurrected, ascended Christ; here he first preached that "Jesus is the Christ, the Son of God" (Acts 9:20–22); and it was to this city that he returned after living for a time in Arabia. Neither Arabia nor Damascus, however, were places where Paul would have been in contact with the Jerusalem apostles, and that is his point in referring here to these locations.

Explanation

Paul presents in 1:13–17 a brief account of his great reversal from a zealous proponent of the traditions of Judaism (vv 13–14) to a proclaimer of the Christian gospel that has as its content God's Son and as its legitimate sphere of outreach the Gentiles (vv 15–16a). Both his life in Judaism and his life as a Christian are viewed as having been under God's sovereignty, for he was "set apart from birth." But it was the call of God and the encounter by Christ which together formed the basis for Paul's proclamation of God's Son to the Gentiles. No claim can be made for his dependence on the Jerusalem apostles, for, as Paul takes pains to emphasize (vv 16b–17), he had no contact with them in the period of time immediately following his Damascus-road encounter.

Though referring to his past life in Judaism (cf. Phil 3:4–6; also Acts 22:3; 26:5) and setting out the basis for his Christian conversion and commission, the crux of Paul's argument in these verses is in vv 16b–17a: "I did not immediately thereafter consult with anyone; nor did I go up to Jerusalem to see those who were apostles before me." His defense here is a type of "alibi-reasoning ('I was not there')," as B. Holmberg calls it (*Paul and Power*, 15). This type of defense is continued in 1:18–24.

Why does Paul feel it necessary to make these statements of denial? Evidently, because the Judaizers in Galatia were asserting that he was really dependent on and subordinate to the Jerusalem apostles. Their accounts of his early life, conversion, and commission were undoubtedly different, with suggestions of deviation, dependence, and subordination included. So Paul speaks here in explication of his contention in 1:11–12 and to counter the Judaizers' innuendoes.

3. First Visit to Jerusalem (1:18–24)

Bibliography

Bammel, E. "Galater 1:23." *ZNW* 59 (1968) 108–12. **Bauernfeind, O.** "Die Begegnung zwischen Paulus und Kephas, Gal 1, 18–20." *ZNW* 47 (1956) 268–76. **Brown, R. E.; Donfried,**

K. P.; Fitzmyer, J. A. and **Reumann. J.**, eds. *Mary in the New Testament: A Collaborative Assessment by Protestant and Roman Catholic Scholars.* Philadelphia: Fortress; New York: Paulist, 1978. 65–72, 270–78. **Howard, G.** "Was James an Apostle? A Reflection on a New Proposal for Gal. i.19." *NovT* 19 (1977) 63–64. **Kilpatrick, G. D.** "Galatians 1:18 ΙΣΤΟΡΗΣΑΙ ΚΗΦΑΝ." In *New Testament Essays.* FS T. W. Manson, ed. A. J. B. Higgins. Manchester: University of Manchester Press, 1959, 144–49. **Lightfoot, J. B.** "The Brethren of the Lord." In *Galatians* (1890), 252–91. **Longenecker, R. N.** "Christianity in Jerusalem." In *Paul, Apostle of Liberty,* 271–88. **Sampley, J. P.** "'Before God, I Do Not Lie' (Gal. I.20): Paul's Self-Defence in the Light of Roman Legal Praxis." *NTS* 23 (1977) 477–82. **Trudinger, L. P.** "'ΕΤΕΡΟΝ ΔΕ ΤΩΝ ΑΠΟΣΤΟΛΩΝ ΟΥΚ ΕΙΔΟΝ ΕΙ ΜΗ ΙΑΚΩΒΟΝ: A Note on Galatians 1:19." *NovT* 17 (1975) 200–202.

Translation

[18]*Then after three years, I went up to Jerusalem to get acquainted with Cephas[a] and stayed with him fifteen days.* [19]*I did not see any of the other apostles—only James, the Lord's brother.* [20]*I assure you before God that what I am writing you is no lie.* [21]*After that I went into the districts of Syria and Cilicia.[b]* [22]*I remained personally unknown to the churches of Judea that are in Christ.* [23]*They only kept hearing, "The one who formerly persecuted us is now preaching the faith he once tried to destroy."* [24]*And they praised God because of me.*

Notes

[a]Κηφᾶν is supported by P[46,51*] ℵ* A B syr[pesh, hel.mg] cop[sa, bo]; Πέτρον by ℵ[c] D F G Byzantine lat syr[hel]. See also 2:9, 11, 14.

[b]Only ℵ* and the Greek minuscules 33 (9th cent.) and 1611 (12th cent.) omit the article τῆς before Κιλικίας.

Form/Structure/Setting

The structure of 1:18–2:10 is governed by the adverb ἔπειτα ("then," "next") at 1:18, 21; 2:1, with these three occurrences introducing a series of events that stem from Paul's Damascus-road experience but are not a part of that experience or of Paul's immediate reaction to it. The events introduced by ἔπειτα are clearly meant to be taken in successive order. Their precise temporal relations, however, particularly vis-à-vis the Damascus-road experience, depend heavily on how one interprets μετὰ τρία ἔτη ("after three years") of 1:18 and διὰ δεκατεσσάρων ἐτῶν ("after fourteen years") of 2:1—i.e., (1) whether Paul's primary referent is the Damascus-road experience or his later return to Damascus; (2) whether Paul is using the enumeration "three" and "fourteen" in consecutive or concurrent fashion; and (3) whether Paul means by "years" full years or is using a method of computation wherein parts of years are counted as complete years.

The Judaizers were evidently claiming that Paul was dependent on and subordinate to the apostles at Jerusalem. Paul's defense is to lay out an account of his career since Christ's encounter with him on his way to Damascus, with particular attention to his contacts with the Jerusalem leaders. So in the narrative of 1:18–2:10 he uses ἔπειτα to assure his readers that there are no gaps in his account. And so in 1:18–24 he tells of his first visit to Jerusalem as a Christian (vv 18–20) and of his return thereafter to Syria and Cilicia (vv 21–24), continuing the alibi type of argument ("I was not there") begun in vv 16b–17.

Comment

18 ἔπειτα μετὰ τρία ἔτη, "then after three years." The adverb ἔπειτα, "then," appears frequently in Koine Greek (at times with its cognate εἶτα) in enumerations to denote chronological sequence or the logical succession of ideas (cf. 4 Macc 6:3; Josephus, *Ant.* 12.92; 1 Cor 15:5b–7) and is often contrasted with πρῶτον, "first" (cf. 1 Cor 15:46; 1 Thess 4:16b–17; Heb 7:2; Jas 3:17; see also the ἀπαρχή . . . ἔπειτα . . . εἶτα series of 1 Cor 15:23–24). Here it is contrasted with εὐθέως, "immediately thereafter," of v 16b. Therefore, just as "immediately thereafter" refers back to Paul's Damascus-road experience, so "after three years" has as its referent that same experience—i.e., the three years are not to be counted from the immediate antecedent, Paul's return to Damascus after residence in Arabia, but from the earlier antecedent of vv 15–16a, the crisis in Paul's life that occurred on his way to Damascus. The exact interval of time between this revelatory experience and his first visit as a Christian to Jerusalem, however, cannot be determined—and so the precise length of time spent in either Arabia or Damascus cannot be calculated—for "after three years" is probably to be understood in an inclusive manner to mean "in the third year" rather than "after three full years" (cf. μετὰ τρεῖς ἡμέρας, "after three days," of Mark 8:31; 10:34 par.).

ἀνῆλθον εἰς Ἱεροσόλυμα ἱστορῆσαι Κηφᾶν, "I went up to Jerusalem to get acquainted with Cephas." On the expression ἀνῆλθον εἰς and the form Ἱεροσόλυμα, see *Comment* on v 17 above. The verb ἱστορέω is used in classical Greek to mean "make inquiry of" or "inquire about." In 1 Esd 1:33 (twice) and 42 it is used in the sense of "narrate" or "report" (also in Aristotle and some later writers). There is as well, however, considerable evidence for ἱστορέω as meaning "get acquainted with (someone)" (cf. Josephus, *J.W.* 6. 81; Plutarch, *Theseus* 30, *Pompey* 40, *Lucullus* 2, *De Curiositate* 2; Epictetus, *Diss.* 2.14.28; 3.7.1). And this seems to be the sense in which Paul uses it here. The Western and Syrian MSS generally read Πέτρον, "Peter," which is probably a case of substituting the more familiar name of the apostle for the less familiar. But Paul regularly designates him Κηφᾶς (Aramaic כיפא, "rock" or "stone," with a Greek case ending), as in Gal 2:9, 11, 14 (see also 1 Cor 1:12; 15:5). Only in Gal 2:7–8 does Paul speak of him as Πέτρος. Outside of Paul's letters Κηφᾶς occurs in the NT only at John 1:42, but then with the explanation ὃ ἑρμηνεύεται Πέτρος, "which is translated Peter."

καὶ ἐπέμεινα πρὸς αὐτὸν ἡμέρας δεκαπέντε, "and stayed with him fifteen days." The preposition πρός with the accusative to mean "with" is probably a colloquialism of Koine Greek (cf. Mark 6:3, πρὸς ἡμᾶς, "with us"; John 1:1, πρὸς τὸν θεόν, "with God"; 1 John 1:2, πρὸς τὸν πατέρα, "with the Father"). "Fifteen days" with Peter is in contrast to "three years" absence from Jerusalem, thereby highlighting the comparatively short period of time and suggesting how impossible it is from that to conceive of Paul as a disciple of Peter. Certainly an informal visit with the foremost disciple of Jesus three years after Paul's dramatic conversion carries no idea of subordination or dependence. It is of itself quite understandable without any onerous implications for Paul's apostolic integrity. In fact, one could wonder why it did not happen sooner.

On the other hand, though Paul did not go up to Jerusalem διδαχθῆναι ("to be taught") by Peter, but ἱστορῆσαι Κηφᾶν, "to get acquainted with Cephas," that does not mean, as F. J. A. Hort concluded, that he only went to 'explore' St. Peter, to find out how he would be disposed to treat the persecutor now become a champion"

(*Judaistic Christianity*, 56). With Paul's stress on the unity of believers in Christ (cf. 3:26–29; see also 1 Cor 1:10ff.; 12:12ff., passim), it is quite understandable that he would at some time want to establish fellowship with Peter. The fact that he waited three years before making the attempt need not indicate either aloofness from or disagreement with Peter. As A. S. Peake observed: "Jerusalem would not be the safest place for Paul to visit after he had not merely failed to fulfill his commission from the High Priest but had gone over to the Christians" (*Paul and the Jewish Christians*, 8 n. 1). Furthermore, while being with the acknowledged leader among Jesus' earthly companions, Paul could not have failed to be interested in a firsthand account of Jesus' earthly life (cf. G. D. Kilpatrick, "Galatians 1:18 ΙΣΤΟΡΗΣΑΙ ΚΗΦΑΝ," 144–49). Certainly their fifteen days together were not spent "talking about the weather." They discussed, without a doubt, matters pertaining to their common commitment to Christ. And it is not beyond the range of reasonable probability to believe that such discussions included Peter's accounts of Jesus' ministry, and that from such accounts Paul learned much. But to learn about the details of Jesus' earthly life from Peter and to be subordinate to or dependent on Peter for his apostleship and Gentile mission are clearly quite different matters. Paul is willing to acknowledge the former, but he is adamant in his rejection of the latter.

19 ἕτερον δὲ τῶν ἀποστόλων οὐκ εἶδον, εἰ μὴ ᾽Ιάκωβον τὸν ἀδελφὸν τοῦ κυρίου, "I did not see any of the other apostles—only James, the Lord's brother." The major issue of v 19 is whether James is classed by Paul among the apostles (cf. v 17) or distinguished from them. The question has usually been discussed in terms of whether the idiomatic expression εἰ μή ("except," "only") which has exceptive force, refers to the whole clause, "I did not see any of the other apostles," or only to the verb, "I did not see." The latter is possible (cf. 2:16; also Matt 12:4; Luke 4:26–27; Rev 21:27). Yet as Lightfoot pointed out, "the sense of ἕτερον naturally links it with εἰ μή, from which it cannot be separated without harshness, and ἕτερον carries τῶν ἀποστόλων with it" (*Galatians*, 84–85). So with Lightfoot most have concluded: "It seems then that St James is here called an Apostle, though it does not therefore follow that he was one of the Twelve" (ibid., 85; cf. Acts 9:27).

L. P. Trudinger has argued that ἕτερον, "other," here has a comparative force that differentiates ("other than the apostles") and so excludes James from the apostles (*NovT* 17 [1975] 200–202). George Howard, however, observes that while such a use of ἕτερον is possible, the examples cited by Trudinger from classical literature to support his thesis actually compare persons or things of the *same* class; and he further rightly argues that if Paul wanted to distinguish James from the apostles, he would have written ἕτερον δὲ ἢ τοὺς ἀποστόλους, "other than the apostles," or used ἕτερον in combination with παρά, "than," or the dative case (*NovT* [1977] 63–64). Thus whatever ambiguity remains in this verse about James being classed among the apostles, it has to do with the referent of εἰ μή and not with the use of ἕτερος. And this being so, ἕτερον here should probably be seen as enumerative and not differentiative, εἰ μή as referring to the whole previous clause, and James as included among the apostles (also, then, among the τοὺς πρὸ ἐμοῦ ἀποστόλους, "apostles before me," of v 17).

James, τὸν ἀδελφὸν τοῦ κυρίου, "the Lord's brother," is in all probability the James named first among the four brothers of Jesus in Mark 6:3 (cf. Matt 13:55). He is not to be confused with Jesus' two disciples of the same name, James the son of Zebedee and James the son of Alphaeus (cf. Mark 3:17–18, par.; Acts 1:13; 12:2). During Jesus' ministry, James seems to have been skeptical of his brother's activities and so was not a follower of Jesus (cf. Mark 3:21, 31–35, par.; John 7:3–5). He was, however, converted by an appearance of the resurrected Christ (1 Cor 15:7), and along with others of Jesus' family became a member of the Jerusalem church (Acts 1:14). He rose to prominence quickly in the church (cf. Acts 15:13; 21:18–19; Gal 2:1–10), and after Peter's departure from Jerusalem (cf. Acts 12:17) became the leading figure within that church. It would be unfair to attribute his rank in the Jerusalem church simply to a veneration of one who was physically related to Jesus. Probably it is more accurate to say that his prominence came about as a result of the need for someone to lead the growing number of scrupulously minded Christians in the Jerusalem church, and that his physical relation to Jesus, his Davidic descent, and his personal qualities fitted him for the task (cf. R. N. Longenecker, "Christianity in Jerusalem," 272–73). His death as a martyr took place in A.D. 62 when the High Priest Annas, during an interim between two Roman governors, persecuted Christians in Jerusalem (cf. Josephus, *Ant.* 20.200; Hegesippus, in Eusebius *Eccl. Hist.* 2.23.10–18). He was known for his deep, ascetic piety, and so bore the title ὁ δίκαιος ("the Just"; cf. Hegesippus, in Eusebius *Eccl. Hist.* 2.23.4–7). Later the Ebionites (Symmachians) thought of him as the twelfth apostle (cf. Victorinus, *Marii Victorini Afri commentarii in epistulas Pauli,* 14 on Gal 1:19), which opinion may have been held by some Jewish Christians earlier.

There has been considerable discussion within the Church as to exactly how we should understand the NT references to Jesus' "brothers." Tertullian (c. A.D. 160–after 220), in what appears to be the standard view of his day, speaks of them as simply other sons of Joseph and Mary (*Adv. Marc.* 4.19; *De Car.* 7), which view was explicitly affirmed by Helvidius of Rome about A.D. 380. So this view is called Helvidian. The *Protevangelium of James,* however, whose roots may go back to about A.D. 150, takes them as sons of Joseph by a previous marriage (9:2), and this view was defended by Epiphanius (c. 315–403) in a letter subsequently incorporated into his *Panarion* or "Medicine Chest" (*Adv. Haer.* 78). So this view is called Epiphanian. In opposition to Helvidius, Jerome (c. A.D. 347–420) in A.D. 383 argued that Jesus' "brothers" were really first cousins, the sons of Alphaeus and Mary of Clopas—which Mary he inferred from John 19:25 to have been the virgin Mary's sister (cf. Mark 15:40)—and so sought to safeguard the perpetual virginity of Mary (*Adversus Helvidium de perpetua virginitate beatae Mariae*). And this view is called Hieronymian. The controversy obviously has been occasioned by doctrinal interests. Apart from such polemical considerations, there appears to be no reason to regard James as anything other than Jesus' uterine brother.

20 ἃ δὲ γράφω ὑμῖν, ἰδοὺ ἐνώπιον τοῦ θεοῦ ὅτι οὐ ψεύδομαι, "I assure you before God that what I am writing to you is no lie." Against the accusation that his is a second-hand gospel, being dependent on and subordinate to the apostles at Jerusalem, Paul has offered in vv 15–19 two lines of evidence: (1) that his authority and message stem from a prophetic ordination by God and a revelatory encounter with Christ (vv 15–16a; cf. 1:1, 12b), and (2) that his activities following his conversion show that he was not dependent on any sanction from Jerusalem (vv 16b–19; cf. 1:1, 11–12a). Here in v 20 he reinforces these lines of defense by an oath as to the truthfulness of what he has said. The phrase ἃ γράφω ὑμῖν, "what I am writing to you," therefore, refers to all that precedes in vv 15–19—perhaps even beginning at v 13 (so Burton, *Galatians*, 61; contra F. Sieffert, *Galater*, 71, who argues for vv 18–19 alone as the referent, and H. Schlier, *Galater*, 62, who sees it only as v 19).

Roman legal practice provided for the use of an oath as one way for a trial to be concluded short of running its full course, with oaths also being made outside of court proceedings to attest to veracity and to warn the other party that one was prepared to stand before a court of inquiry on the matter (cf. J. P. Sampley, *NTS* 23 [1977] 477–82). Since a broad knowledge of Roman law was common throughout the empire, it may be assumed that the use of oaths was part of the consciousness of both Paul and his Galatian converts. So in swearing that "before God what I am writing you is no lie," it may plausibly be concluded that, as J. P. Sampley puts it, Paul "not only reinforces the thrust of his two lines of defence but signals his readers that he is prepared to take the ultimate step that resolves a matter in the courts— even though we know from 1 Cor vi.1–8 that Paul thinks it wrong for Christians to take one another to court" (ibid., 481).

Elsewhere in Paul's letters there are similar affirmations that "before God" he is speaking the truth (cf. 2 Cor 1:23; 11:31; 1 Thess 2:5). His use of an oath here in Galatians suggests that his judaizing opponents were claiming in particular that it was during his first visit to Jerusalem that Paul both learned the gospel from the Jerusalem leaders and received his authority to be an apostle. Against such claims, Paul affirms in the strongest manner possible the surety of his two lines of defense and puts his readers on guard against any challenge to what he has said.

21 ἔπειτα ἦλθον εἰς τὰ κλίματα τῆς Συρίας καὶ τῆς Κιλικίας, "after that I went into the districts of Syria and Cilicia." The adverb ἔπειτα, "after that," introduces a further set of events after Paul's first visit as a Christian to Jerusalem, with the inference being that nothing intervened between that visit and what is now referred to. The word κλίματα should probably be rendered more generally as "districts" or "territories" in a nonpolitical sense (cf. Rom 15:23; 2 Cor 11:10), and not as "regions" which could connote administrative subdivisions of a Roman province (cf. W. M. Ramsay, *Galatians*, 278–80). The repetition of the article τῆς suggests that two geographical districts are in view: the district of Syria and that of Cilicia. From v 22 it seems evident that Paul does not regard Judea (here probably the Roman province of Judea, which included the districts of Judea, Samaria, and Galilee; cf. *Comment* on v 22) as part of Syria. So by the district of Syria he probably means the area around Antioch and by the district of Cilicia the area around his hometown of Tarsus (cf. Acts 9:30; 11:25–26).

What Paul did between his first postconversion visit to Jerusalem (1:18–20) and his second postconversion visit (2:1–10) can be inferred from the verb εὐαγγελίζεται ("he is preaching") of v 23. So it may be concluded that this was a period of evangelization, though probably not a full-blown Gentile mission as he later took up. Many, of course, have seen in v 21 an extensive missionary outreach that included Macedonia and Achaia as well (see *Introduction*, lxxv), agreeing with Johannes Weiss that "Gal. 1:21 cannot be taken to mean that for the fourteen years, he worked *only* in Syria and Cilicia. The statement merely indicates the point from which his work at that time began, but does not in any way describe this work as a whole" (*The History of Primitive Christianity* [New York: Wilson-Erickson, 1937] 1:204; cf. C. H. Buck and G. Taylor, *Saint Paul*, 251). But to include evangelistic missions to Macedonia and Achaia within the statements of 1:21–24 makes a mockery of language and discredits Paul's claim to truthfulness so fervently stated just above in v 20.

Comment

Some have speculated that a number of the hardships Paul mentions in 2 Cor 11:23–29 occurred during his early evangelizing in Syria and Cilicia, for they do not appear in the accounts of his later missionary activities in Acts—particularly his being lashed five times by the Jews and beaten three times by the Romans (cf. my *Paul, Apostle of Liberty,* 247–48). Indeed, he may have been witnessing about Christ within the synagogues of the Diaspora in such a manner as to bring about persecution from both the religious and the civil authorities, though that cannot be proven. "At any rate," as F. F. Bruce observes, "enough was happening for news of Paul's activity to get back to Judea" (*Galatians,* 103).

22 ἤμην δὲ ἀγνοούμενος τῷ προσώπῳ ταῖς ἐκκλησίαις τῆς Ἰουδαίας ταῖς ἐν Χριστῷ, "I remained personally unknown to the churches of Judea that are in Christ." The imperfect, periphrastic ἤμην δὲ ἀγνοούμενος emphasizes the continuance of the state described, and so suggests "I remained unknown." τῷ προσώπῳ ("by face") is a locution (both then and today) for "personally." ταῖς ἐκκλησίαις ... ταῖς ἐν Χριστῷ, "the churches ... that are in Christ," is a common way for Paul to designate locally gathered groups of believers who share an incorporative relation with the risen Christ (cf. the salutations of 1 Cor 1:2; Eph 1:1; Phil 1:1, Col 1:2; 1 Thess 1:1, 2 Thess 1:1). The phrase ἐν Χριστῷ, "in Christ," is a favorite of Paul's to signal the personal, local, and dynamic relation of the believer to Christ (cf. my *Paul, Apostle of Liberty,* 156–70). In Galatians it comes to expression a total of eight times (here, 2:4, 17; 3:14, 26, 28; 5:6, 10 [ἐν Κυρίῳ]), most significantly in 3:26–29. The expression ταῖς ἐκκλησίαις τῆς Ἰουδαίας ταῖς ἐν Χριστῷ is paralleled exactly in 1 Thess 2:14, where "the churches of God that are in Judea in Christ Jesus" are spoken of as having suffered persecution from their own countrymen. "Judea" in both Gal 1:22 and 1 Thess 2:14 probably denotes the whole of the Roman province of Judea, which included the districts of Judea, Samaria, and Galilee (cf. Acts 9:31)—and which, of course, included Jerusalem as well. Paul's purpose in speaking of his departure to Syria and Cilicia (v 21) and of his being unknown to the Judean churches (v 22) is undoubtedly to show that his work during the time between his two Jerusalem visits was not in such areas as would have been expected had he been under the supervision of the Jerusalem apostles.

23 μόνον δὲ ἀκούοντες ἦσαν ὅτι ὁ διώκων ἡμᾶς ποτε νῦν εὐαγγελίζεται τὴν πίστιν ἣν ποτε ἐπόρθει, "they only kept hearing, 'The one who formerly persecuted us is now preaching the faith he once tried to destroy.'" The neuter μόνον ("only") is used as an adverb to limit the previous clause of v 22, so indicating that what follows is the only exception to the ignorance referred to. The imperfect, periphrastic ἀκούοντες ἦσαν (as in v 22) lays emphasis on the continuance of the action, "they kept hearing"—with the subject being the Judean churches. The gender of the participle ἀκούοντες, however, is masculine (rather than feminine to agree with ταῖς ἐκκλησίαις), which is a construction *ad sensum*: that it was the members of the Judean churches who heard the reports about Paul's activities. ὅτι is recitative and not to be translated. It serves only to call attention to the quotation that follows and so functions like our quotation marks.

The latter part of v 23 is in the form of direct speech. Ernst Bammel sees this as a quotation from the Judean churches themselves, and so one of the oldest Christian statements (*ZNW* 59 [1968] 108–12). As Bammel views it, the quotation reflects an early Jewish-Christian provenance particularly in its non-Pauline use of πίστις, "faith," and its Jewish martyrological theme wherein the conversion of a persecutor comes about by a miraculous act of God. But while this may be so, it is necessary to point out that Paul also uses πίστις in Galatians in an absolute sense in 3:23, 25 to mean the content of the Christian gospel and in 6:10 as part of a descriptive phrase for Christians. Furthermore, a common *topos* in many martyrologies was that of the miserable end of the persecutor (e.g., 2 Macc 9:5–12, 28; Eusebius, *Eccl. Hist.* 8.16.3–5; Lactantius, *De Mortibus Persecutorum*), which, of course, is not the case here. Thus, without denying the possibility of a direct quotation, what we probably have here is a summation of reports that Paul heard were circulating about him among the Judean churches, the gist of which he presents in his own words in the form of direct speech.

Paul, of course, is the persecutor turned proclaimer, with the particle ποτέ, "formerly," and the adverb νῦν, "now," signaling the temporal shift. τὴν πίστιν, "the faith," is used absolutely as a synonym for the Christian gospel (cf. 3:23, 24; see also Phil 1:27). The same set of verbs, διώκω, "persecute," and πορθέω, "destroy," are used in v 13 and here of Paul's preconversion activities, though with different objects—in v 13, "the church of God"; here it is "us" and "the faith" (i.e., the Christian gospel). All of this suggests an easy association in Paul's mind of "the Church," "the faith," "the gospel," and Christians themselves. No account is taken, however, of any differences of content or emphasis between the gospel as the Judean Christians understood it and the gospel as Paul proclaimed it. The point made, in fact, is quite the reverse: Paul is now preaching the very same gospel that the Judean Christians held, which earlier he had opposed.

24 καὶ ἐδόξαζον ἐν ἐμοὶ τὸν θεόν, "and they praised God because of me." The dissatisfaction of the Judaizers with Paul is here dramatically contrasted with the satisfaction that the Judean Christians had in his earlier missionary activity. For whereas the opponents denigrated Paul's authority and message, "they praised God because of me." The use of ἐν (so "because of") as the ground or basis of an action is paralleled in Rom 1:24; 9:7 (based on Gen 21:12; cf. Heb 11:18) and 1 Cor 7:14. The thought and language of this verse are similar to God's statement regarding his Servant Israel in Isa 49:3 LXX: ἐν σοὶ δοξασθήσομαι, "because of you I shall be praised."

Explanation

Paul's remarks as to his first postconversion visit to Jerusalem and his preaching after that in Syria and Cilicia are brief, comprising only what is needed for the purpose of his defense. His use of an oath with respect to his activities during that first visit suggests that his opponents were claiming that it was particularly then that Paul both learned the gospel from the Jerusalem leaders and received his authority to be an apostle. Paul's insistence, however, is that such was not the case: (1) a fifteen-day visit with first Peter and then James is hardly sufficient to establish dependency or to suggest subordination (vv 18–19), and (2) his ministry thereafter in Syria and Cilicia, when he was personally unknown to the Judean churches, shows that he was hardly under the supervision of the Jerusalem apostles (vv 21–22). In fact, the response of the Judean Christians, including those at Jerusalem, to his early missionary activities was to give praise to God because of his preaching (vv 23–24), which is quite the opposite to the Judaizers' carping about his authority and message. This, in fact, as Paul sees it, gives the lie to the Judaizers' reconstruction of events.

4. Second Visit to Jerusalem (2:1–10)

Bibliography

Aus, R. D. "Three Pillars and Three Patriarchs: A Proposal Concerning Gal 2:9." *ZNW* 70 (1979) 252–61. **Barrett, C. K.** "Paul and the 'Pillar' Apostles." In *Studia Paulina*, FS J. de Zwaan, ed. J. N. Sevenster and W. C. van Unnik. Haarlem: Bohn, 1953, 1–19. ———. "Titus." In *Neotestamentica et Semitica*. FS M. Black, ed. E. E. Ellis and M. Wilcox. Edinburgh: T. & T. Clark, 1969, 1–14. **Bammel, E.** "πτωχός." *TDNT* 6:888–915. **Bauckham, R. J.** "Barnabas in Galatians." *JSNT* 2 (1979) 61–70. **Berger, K.** "Almosen für Israel: Zum historischen Kontext der paulinischen Kollekte." *NTS* 23 (1977) 180–204. **Filson, F. V.** *Three Crucial Decades.* **Foerster, W.** "Die δοκοῦντες in Gal 2." *ZNW* 36 (1937) 286–92. **Geyser, A. S.** "The Earliest Name of the Earliest Church." In *De Fructu Oris Sui.* FS A. van Selms, ed. I. H. Eybers et al. Leiden: Brill, 1971, 58–66. **Hall, D. R.** "St. Paul and Famine Relief: A Study in Galatians 2¹⁰." *ExpTim* 82 (1971) 309–11. **Hay, D. M.** "Paul's Indifference to Authority." *JBL* 88 (1969) 36–44. **Keck, L.** "The Poor among the Saints in the New Testament." *ZNW* 56 (1965) 100–29. ———. "The Poor among the Saints in Jewish Christianity and Qumran." *ZNW* 57 (1966) 54–78. **Longenecker, R. N.** "Christianity and Judaism." Appendix in *Paul, Apostle of Liberty*, 271–88. **Lührmann, D.** "Gal 2, 9 und die katholischen Briefe: Bemerkungen zum Kanon und zur *regula fidei*." *ZNW* 72 (1981) 65–87. **Munck, J.** "Paul, the Apostles, and the Twelve." *ST* 3 (1951) 96–110. **Orchard, B.** "The Ellipsis between Galatians 2, 3 and 2, 4." *Bib* 54 (1973) 469–81. **Pfitzner, V. C.** *Paul and the Agon Motif.* **Robinson, D. W. B.** "The Circumcision of Titus, and Paul's 'Liberty.'" *ABR* 12 (1964) 24–42. **Schmithals, W.** *Paul and James.* **Wilckens, U.** "στῦλος." *TDNT* 7:732–36.

Translation

¹ *Then fourteen years later I went up again*[a] *to Jerusalem with Barnabas, taking Titus along as well.* ² *I went up in response to a revelation. And I set before them the gospel that I preach among the Gentiles—only privately before those reputed to be important, lest somehow I should run or had run in vain.* ³ *Yet not even Titus, who was with me, was compelled to be circumcised, even though he was a Greek.* ⁴ *Now this happened because certain false brothers infiltrated our ranks, who intruded to spy out our freedom that we have in Christ Jesus and to make us slaves.*[b] ⁵ *We did not give in to them*[c] *in this matter even for a moment, so that the truth of the gospel might remain with you.*

⁶ *As*[d] *for those reputed to be important—whatever they were at one time makes no difference to me; God does not take into account human credentials—those seemingly important men added nothing to me.* ⁷ *On the contrary, when they saw that I had been entrusted with the task of preaching to the uncircumcised just as Peter was entrusted with preaching to the circumcised—* ⁸ *for the One who was at work in Peter as an apostle to the circumcised was also at work in my ministry to the Gentiles—* ⁹ *James, Cephas*[e] *and John (that is, those reputed to be "pillars"), knowing that divine grace had been given to me, gave me and Barnabas the right hand of fellowship, on the understanding that we should go to the Gentiles and they to the circumcised.* ¹⁰ *All they asked was that we should continue to remember the poor, which is what I have always been eager to do.*

Notes

ᵃπάλιν ἀνέβην, "I went up again," is widely supported by P⁴⁶ℵ A B, etc.; ἀνέβην πάλιν by D G it (except itᶜ) Pel Jerome; ἀνέβην alone by itᶜ copᵇᵒ Mcion Ir⁽ˡᵃᵗ⁾ Tert Ambst (Hilary). Also πάλιν ἀνῆλθον, "I went up again," by C.

ᵇκαταδουλώσουσιν, "they might make us slaves" (future indicative active), is well supported by ℵ A B* C D, etc.; καταδουλώσωσιν, "they might make us slaves" (aorist subjunctive active), appears in B² and G; καταδουλώσωνται, "they might make us slaves for themselves" (aorist subjunctive middle), in TR.

ᶜοἷς οὐδέ, "not . . . to them," is omitted in D* itᵈ,ᵉ Ir (or his Latin translator) and a number of Latin church fathers (e.g., Tert Ambst [Hilary] Vic Pel). It receives strong support, however, from the Greek uncial MS tradition (except D*), P⁴⁶, all the versions except itᵈ,ᵉ (even the vg), and the Greek church fathers (with the possible exception of Ir). The relative pronoun οἷς is omitted in a few texts that have οὐδέ and retained in some that omit οὐδέ, but generally the two are retained or omitted together.

ᵈMarcion omitted vv 6–9a (so Tert. *Adv. Marc.* 5.3).

ᵉΚηφᾶς is omitted in A; Πέτρος is read for Κηφᾶς in P⁴⁶ and itʳ; Πέτρος καὶ Ἰάκωβος for Ἰάκωβος in D G itᵃ,ᵇ Mcion Ambst (Hilary). See also 1:18; 2:11, 14.

Form/Structure/Setting

The adverb ἔπειτα ("then," "next") stands over all that Paul recounts in 2:1–10, identifying this as the third enumerated event following his time at Damascus (cf. 1:18ff. and 1:21ff. for the first two) and assuring his readers that there are no gaps in his narrative. Paul's emphasis in this section is on the fact that though he conferred with the apostles at Jerusalem (i.e., with those "pillars" of the Jerusalem church to whom the Judaizers appealed) he did not receive from them any reproof or orders. On the contrary, they acknowledged the validity of his ministry and considered it to be parallel to their own, asking only that he "continue to remember the poor." Paul's argument vis-à-vis the Judaizers' accusations highlights the following three points: (1) that though he met with Peter and James at Jerusalem three years after his conversion, a much longer period elapsed ("fourteen years later") before he met with the body of apostles and leaders at Jerusalem; (2) that he went to Jerusalem in response to a divine revelation and not at the request of the Jerusalem authorities or to submit himself to them; and (3) that the result of meeting with the so-called pillars of the Jerusalem church was their full recognition of the validity of his Gentile mission, which they accepted as parallel to their own Jewish mission.

The first half of this section (vv 1–5) deals with the events of pertinence themselves: Paul's coming to Jerusalem with Barnabas and Titus; the absence of pressure from the Jerusalem apostles to have Titus circumcised; and the opposition stirred up by certain "false brothers." Syntactically, Paul's narration of events is broken; contextually, it is also abrupt. For unless we accept the highly disputed Western reading for v 5, there is a grammatical anacoluthon at the beginning of v 4. Structurally, vv 3–5 are a parenthesis in the narration—perhaps, though less likely, a primary parenthesis (vv 3ff.) that contains a secondary parenthesis (vv 4–5). The second half of the section (vv 6–10) is one long, complex, and seemingly convoluted sentence that tells us of the Jerusalem apostles' response to Paul and his mission to Gentiles. There is in this latter section no hiding of the fact that there were differences between Paul and the Jerusalem leaders, principally as to the logistics of their respective missions. There was also, however, a basic unity between them, which was signaled by the Jerusalem apostles in their giving the "right hand of fellowship" to Paul and

Barnabas. On Paul's part this unity was to be expressed by his continuing "to remember the poor."

Comment

1 ἔπειτα διὰ δεκατεσσάρων ἐτῶν, "then fourteen years later." Having used the adverbs εὐθέως ("immediately," 1:16) and ἔπειτα ("then," "next," 1:18, 21) to mark off the successive stages of his *narratio*, Paul here begins the next episode in his account with ἔπειτα again. His purpose in the use of these temporal adverbs, as we have seen, is to lay out in successive fashion his contacts with the Jerusalem apostles and to assure his readers that he has omitted nothing. On the temporal use of διά with the genitive, see Mark 2:1 (δι' ἡμερῶν, "a few days later") and Acts 24:17 (δι' ἐτῶν . . . πλειόνων, "after several years"). The variation between μετά with the accusative (1:18) and διά with the genitive (2:1) is purely stylistic, reflecting (1) a Jewish mind-set that treats parallelisms in terms of verbal synonyms, and (2) a Greek linguistic facility that seeks to avoid monotony. The language and syntax of 2:1a do not, however, aid us in any direct manner in answering the question as to whether the fourteen years of Paul's second Jerusalem visit should be counted from his conversion (1:15) or from his first Jerusalem visit (1:18–20). The probability is that the three years of 1:18 and the fourteen years of 2:1 are to be understood concurrently, not consecutively—that is, that both are to be measured from Paul's conversion and not that the fourteen years are to be counted from his first Jerusalem visit. Determination of that matter, however, can only be made in connection with a number of other issues having to do with the addressees and date of the letter, and it is to those discussions that we must here direct the reader (see *Introduction,* "Addressees" and "Date").

πάλιν ἀνέβην εἰς Ἰεροσόλυμα, "I went up again to Jerusalem." While contextually the ἔπειτα, "then," of this verse follows on from the ἔπειτα of v 21 and Paul's time in Syria and Cilicia, historically πάλιν, "again," refers back to the ἔπειτα of v 18 and Paul's first visit to Jerusalem. So Paul speaks here of his second visit to Jerusalem as a Christian. The omission of πάλιν in a few versions (it^c cop^{bo}) and by Marcion, Irenaeus, Tertullian, and Ambrosiaster (Hilary) probably stems from attempts to square this second visit with Paul's Jerusalem Council visit of Acts 15, which in Acts is his third visit (or fourth, if εἰς Ἰερουσαλήμ of 12:25 is accepted). The use of ἀνῆλθον, "I went up," for ἀνέβην, "I went up," in C is probably by way of assimilation to ἀνῆλθον of vv 17 and 18, not realizing that the variation in the use of these two aorists is simply a stylistic feature. The prefix ἀνά ("up") of ἀνέβην conforms to the expression ἡ δὲ ἄνω Ἰερουσαλήμ, "the Jerusalem that is above," of 4:25–26 (see discussion at 1:17). Here, however, Paul simply has the geographical site of Jerusalem in mind, whereas in 4:25–26 his emphasis is more on the religious significance of the city.

μετὰ Βαρναβᾶ, "with Barnabas." Barnabas was a major figure in the early church. He appears in Acts a number of times as something of a bridge between the Christian mission to Jews and that to Gentiles (cf. 9:27; 11:22–30; 13:1–14:28; 15:2–4, 12, 22, 36–41). He is mentioned in Gal 2:1 for the first time in Paul's letters, and appears soon after in 2:9, 13 as well (also in 1 Cor 9:6). According to Acts, Joseph was his real name. The apostles, however, gave him the sobriquet Barnabas ("son of encouragement"), probably in description of his character and to distinguish him from others of the same name (cf. 1:23). He was a Levite from Cyprus who became a Christian while in Jerusalem and who supported the nascent church by selling a piece of land and giving the proceeds to the apostles (4:36–37). Later, he introduced Saul of Tarsus to the apostles and vouched for the genuineness of his conversion (9:27). He was sent by the Jerusalem church to Antioch of Syria to check out and then direct the Christian mission there, and into that ministry he brought Paul as an associate (11:22–26). During that ministry the Antioch Christians sent Barnabas and Paul to Jerusalem with a gift of money for the impoverished believers of Judea (11:27–30). Later they sent them out on a missionary journey that started on the island of Cyprus and extended into southern Galatia (13:1–14:28). Then, after their return, they sent them again to Jerusalem to discuss the vexing issue of Jewish-Gentile relations within the church, particularly the need for Gentiles to be circumcised (15:1–35). After the Jerusalem Council, Paul and Barnabas separated to carry on their own missions (15:36–41), though the tone of Paul's reference to Barnabas in 1 Cor 9:6 (perhaps also 2 Cor 8:18–19) suggests that they remained friends.

Acts 11:25–26, 30 implies that at the time of Paul's famine visit to Jerusalem (with which we have identified Gal 2:1–10) Barnabas was Paul's senior colleague, whereas Gal 2:1–10, particularly in its repeated use of the first person singular, reads as though Paul was the leader. Such a description fits well the situation of Acts 15:1–30. But it is also to be expected—at a time after the missionary party's return from southern Galatia when Paul was not only the chief speaker but also the leader *de facto*— that Paul would recount earlier events from such a perspective, particularly when, as he saw it, Barnabas had vacillated on the issue at hand (cf. Gal 2:13). The preposition μετά, "with," here, however, signals only association, without any necessary idea of inferiority or subordination, as does also the reference to "me and Barnabas" in 2:9.

συμπαραλαβὼν καὶ Τίτον, "taking Titus along as well." As for Titus, however, the situation was different. The participle συμπαραλαβών ("taking along"), combined with the adverbial use of καί ("as well"), suggests a distinctly subordinate status for him: one who was "taken along."

Titus was a Gentile (v 3) who seems to have been converted by Paul (cf. Titus 1:4) evidently at Syrian Antioch. The fact that he is mentioned in Galatians suggests that he was known to believers in Galatia, either personally or by name. Perhaps he had been with Paul and Barnabas on their first foray into the area. In 2 Cor 2:12–13; 7:5–16 he appears as Paul's representative to the Corinthian church, and in 2 Cor 8:6–24, 9:35; 12:18 as the chief organizer for the Jerusalem collection. Somewhat surprisingly, he is not referred to at all in Acts. William Ramsay and Alfred Souter postulated that Titus was Luke's brother and so was omitted by Luke from Acts, as is Luke himself (W. M. Ramsay, *St. Paul the Traveller*, 390; A. Souter, "A Suggested Relationship between Titus and Luke," *ExpTim* 18 [1906–7] 285; idem, "The Relationship between Titus and Luke," ibid., 335–36). More likely, Titus was omitted because of his close association with the Jerusalem collection, which, except for its mention at 24:17 in Paul's defense before Felix, also finds no place in Acts (cf. C. K. Barrett, "Titus," 2; also the comments on Luke's omission of the Jerusalem collection in my "Acts of the Apostles," 519). 2 Tim 4:10 speaks of Titus going to Dalmatia, the southern part of the Roman province of Illyricum; the letter to Titus presents him as Paul's delegate to Crete. On the basis of Titus 1:5, later tradition identified him as the first bishop of Crete.

With συμπαραλαβών, "taking along," of 2:1 being singular, it is implied that it was Paul who took the initiative to bring Titus along to Jerusalem. But just why he was brought along we are not told. Luther suggested that Paul was attempting to demonstrate his Christian liberty by bringing with him both Barnabas and Titus: "to make it clear that he was at liberty to be a Gentile with Titus and a Jew with Barnabas; thus proving the freedom of the gospel in each case, namely, that it is permissible to be circumcised and yet that circumcision is not necessary, and that this is the way one should think of the entire Law" (*Luther's Works*, 27:200). And many have seen Paul's purpose in bringing along Titus—particularly, indeed, if Gal 2:1–10 is Paul's account of the Jerusalem Council—as being something of a test case. Yet if Titus had accompanied Paul and Barnabas on their first missionary venture, it might not have been thought exceptional that he should also accompany them to Jerusalem, even though Gentile Galatia and Jewish Jerusalem were far different places. If this trip to Jerusalem was, in fact, the famine visit of Acts 11, then it may be assumed that issues were not at that time as clearly drawn or positions as firmly fixed as later. Furthermore, prior to the Judaizers' active opposition, Paul may not have been as aware of all the possible ramifications of bringing along Titus as he would have been later. It was probably, therefore, only from a later perspective—that is, after his mission to southern Galatia and the Judaizers' agitation both at Syrian Antioch and throughout southern Galatia—that Paul realized the full significance of events surrounding the presence of Titus at Jerusalem. And it is in that later light that he reports those earlier circumstances here.

2 ἀνέβην δὲ κατὰ ἀποκάλυψιν, "I went up in response to a revelation." In saying that he went to Jersualem "in response to a revelation" (κατὰ ἀποκάλυψιν), Paul wants to make clear that his visit did not stem from any human motivation, either on his part or that of the Jerusalem leaders, but must be seen in the same way as his call and commission (cf. 1:1, 12, 16). Revelations, of course, were of great significance to Paul (cf. 2 Cor 12:1)—not just as mystical experiences confirming a spiritual relationship, but also as giving directions for specific courses of action. Acts recounts a number of ways by which revelations came to Paul: by dream visions (16:9; 18:9–10; 23:11; 27:23–24), by ecstatic trances (22:17–21; cf. 2 Cor 12:2–4), by signs given by the Spirit in some manner (13:2; 16:6, 7; 20:22–23; 21:4), and by signs given by a prophet (11:28; 21:10–11). Which of these, if any, Paul has here in mind is impossible to say. It is tempting, however, along with W. M. Ramsay, (*St. Paul the Traveller*, 57), C. W. Emmet (*Galatians*, 13), G. S. Duncan (*Galatians*, 38), and a number of other "South Galatianists" (see *Introduction*, "Addressees"), to postulate that the "revelation" in view is that given by Agabus in Acts 11:28 which resulted in Paul's famine visit to Jerusalem.

καὶ ἀνεθέμην αὐτοῖς τὸ εὐαγγέλιον ὃ κηρύσσω ἐν τοῖς ἔθνεσιν, "and I set before them the gospel that I preach among the Gentiles." The pronoun αὐτοῖς, "them," without an expressed antecedent, may have in mind (by anticipation) the Jerusalem leaders referred to later in the sentence (also in vv 6–10). Probably, however, it refers to the Jerusalem Christian community generally. The verb ἀνατίθημι in the middle voice has the sense of "present" or "set out" a matter for consideration or "communicate" with a view to consultation. This is a meaning not found in classical Greek. But it is attested in later Greek writings (cf. Mic 7:5 LXX; 2 Macc 3:9; Acts 25:14, its only other occurrence in the NT).

Paul's use of τὸ εὐαγγέλιον, "the gospel," has already been commented on at
1:11–12. It has to do with the character and purposes of God, the work of Christ,
the nature of salvation being offered, and how this salvation is operative—particularly, how operative among the Gentiles. The present tense of κηρύσσω, "I preach,"
suggests that Paul, when writing, was still preaching the same gospel that he did
before going to Jerusalem. Use of the past tense ἐκήρυξα or (ἐκήρυσσον) would
imply that what he then preached he is no longer preaching. The phrase ἐν τοῖς
ἔθνεσιν, "among the Gentiles," is comparable to εἰς τὰ ἔθνη, "to the Gentiles," of
2:8, though here by "among the Gentiles" Paul seems to have in mind more his
preaching to people living in Gentile lands, whether Gentiles alone or also Jews,
whereas there "to the Gentiles" is distinguished from "to the circumcised."

κατ' ἰδίαν δὲ τοῖς δοκοῦσιν, "only privately before those reputed to be important." Paul may be speaking of two events in this verse: one when he appeared
before the Jerusalem Christian community in an open session (v 2b), and the other
when he met privately with the Jerusalem leaders (v 2c), either before or after the
open session. Such a scenario has frequently been postulated, particularly by those
who see 2:1–10 as Paul's account of the Jerusalem council. On the other hand, the
verse may be read simply as a general statement ("I set before them the gospel that
I preach among the Gentiles"), with succeeding amplifications as to (1) the
essentially private nature of the principal discussion (v 2c), (2) the identity and
character of those taking part (vv 2c, 6–9), and (3) the result and agreements
reached (vv 7–10). Undoubtedly on any visit to Jerusalem Paul would have met
others in addition to James, Peter, and John. But this verse need not be read as
telling us that. Rather, it focuses on Paul's private meeting with the three Jerusalem
leaders. So "those reputed to be important" should probably be understood as the
first of a series of descriptions amplifying αὐτοῖς, "them."

The expression οἱ δοκοῦντες ("those reputed to be important") was part of the
political rhetoric of the day, being used both positively and derogatorily or
ironically (cf. BAG 201; W. Foerster, ZNW 36 [1937] 286–92; C. K. Barrett, "Paul
and the 'Pillar' Apostles," 2–4; Betz, Galatians, 86–87). Plato's ironic use of τῶν
δοκούντων σοφῶν εἶναι ("those reputed to be wise men," Apology 21B; see also 21C,
D, E; 22A, B; 36D; 41E) is particularly apropos, recognizing, as it does, the claim
and yet distancing itself from it. So too Paul, probably in reaction to the Judaizers'
inflated adulation of the Jerusalem leaders (cf. Comment on v 9), recognizes in his
use of the expression the legitimate role of the Jerusalem apostles in the church,
yet without compromising his claim that his gospel stems from God and Christ
apart from any human authority (cf. 1:1, 12, 15–16). Contrary to many who deny
irony in Paul's usage (e.g., Lightfoot, Galatians, 103; Lietzmann, Galater, 9–10;
Burton, Galatians, 71; Mussner, Galaterbrief, 104–5; Bruce, Galatians, 109), it seems
hard to ignore at least a certain "dismissive" tone in Gal 2 (so J. Klausner, From Jesus
to Paul, 581; C. K. Barrett, "Paul and the 'Pillar' Apostles," 4; Betz, Galatians, 87; J.
D. G. Dunn, Unity, 408)—a dismissal, however, not of the Jerusalem apostles
themselves, but of the Judaizers' claims for them.

μή πως εἰς κενὸν τρέχω ἢ ἔδραμον, "lest somehow I should run or had run
in vain." The conjunction μή πως, "lest somehow," signals apprehension (cf. 4:11;
also 1 Thess 3:5). The expression εἰς κενόν, "in vain," always functions in Paul as an
adverb of result to mean "uselessly" or "without effect" (2 Cor 6:1; Phil 2:16; 1 Thess
3:5), as it usually does in the LXX (cf. Lev 26:20; Job 39:16; Isa 29:8; Mic 1:14, etc.).

The term τρέχω ("run") stems from the athletic imagery of the day (cf. V. C. Pfitzner, *Paul and the Agon Motif,* 99ff.) and appears elsewhere in Paul's letters as a metaphor for strenuous exertion in living the Christian life (Gal 5:7; Phil 3:14; 2 Tim 4:7; cf. Heb 3:1) and in carrying out his missions (1 Cor 9:24–27; Phil 2:16; cf. Pol. *Phil.* 9:2). The second appearance of the verb is certainly a second aorist indicative (ἔδραμον, "I had run"). Its first (τρέχω), however, may be either a present indicative ("I am running") or a present subjunctive used as a future ("I should run"). Understanding it here as a present indicative is possible. But in contrast with the past idea of ἔδραμον, the subjunctive used as a future seems more likely.

H. Schlier sees Paul here as recognizing the decisive authority of the earlier apostolate at Jerusalem and wishing to validate the genuineness of his mission by their acknowledgement (*Galater,* 67–69). Such an interpretation, however, reflects more Schlier's hierarchical view of church authority than sound exegesis, for Paul had divine assurance of the validity of his preaching and needed no human authorization for his mission (again, see 1:1, 11–12, 15ff.). Rather, as F. F. Bruce aptly puts it: "His commission was not derived from Jerusalem, but it could not be executed effectively except in fellowship with Jerusalem. A cleavage between his Gentile mission and the mother-church would be disastrous: Christ would be divided, and all the energy which Paul had devoted, and hoped to devote, to the evangelizing of the Gentile world would be frustrated" (*Galatians,* 111). Indeed, disapproval by the Jerusalem leaders could not invalidate his ministry or message, but it would to a serious degree make the outreach of the gospel difficult. In fact, any rupture between Paul and the Jerusalem apostles on the essentials of the gospel—as distinct from differing understandings of the logistics of Christian outreach—would be disastrous for both the mission to Jews and that to Gentiles. The unity of the church even amidst its diversity was of great importance to Paul, as his strenuous efforts with regard to the Jerusalem collection clearly indicate (cf. Rom 15:25–32; 1 Cor 16:1–3; 2 Cor 9:12–15). And it was for this unity that he feared, even while having no doubts about the divine origin of his Gentile mission or the truth of his own proclamation.

3 ἀλλ᾽ οὐδὲ Τίτος ὁ σὺν ἐμοί, Ἕλλην ὤν, ἠναγκάσθη περιτμηθῆναι, "Yet not even Titus, who was with me, was compelled to be circumcised, even though he was a Greek." Vv 3–5 function as an extended parenthesis within Paul's account of his second Jerusalem visit. Vv 1–2 and 6–10 carry the flow of the narration, with vv 3–5 interjected to highlight a situation that Paul sees as giving the lie to the Judaizers' claims. Perhaps there are two antithetical parentheses here, one referring to the case of Titus at Jerusalem (v 3) and another having the judaizing agitators of Galatia in mind (vv 4–5), as B. Orchard has repeatedly argued (see esp. his "The Ellipsis between Galatians 2, 3 and 2, 4," 469–81). More likely, vv 4–5 build on the idea of compulsion or pressure in v 3, and so refer to the same historical incident at Jerusalem. Orchard's attempt to save the Jerusalem apostles from being called "false brothers," while laudatory in its motivation and generally proper in its overall conclusion, is extreme in its handling of the specific exegetical data. It fails, therefore, to interpret properly the situation at Jerusalem.

That Titus was with Paul at Jerusalem has already been mentioned in v 1. Reference to him here is for argumentative purposes to emphasize that he was not circumcised. The strong adversative ἀλλά, "yet," is frequently used by Paul to set off a disavowal of some previous suggestion (cf. Rom 4:2, 5:14; 1 Cor 6:12 [twice]; and

13), and probably here has in view some assertion by his opponents to the effect that prior to the Galatian mission all believers in Christ had been circumcised. The negative conjunction οὐδέ ("not even") lays stress on the evidential value of Titus' case: if true for him, it is true in principle. Ἕλλην in NT usage always means a Greek of Gentile origin. Ἕλλην ὤν, "even though he was a Greek," like ὁ σὺν ἐμοί, "who was with me," adds a fact probably already known to the readers, but necessary to be kept in mind to appreciate fully the significance of what is about to be said.

Paul's statement that Titus was not "compelled to be circumcised" (ἠναγκάσθη περιτμηθῆναι) has within it a certain ambiguity, and so has been variously understood. Most see it as a direct affirmation that Titus was not circumcised (e.g., Lightfoot, Ramsay, Burton, Betz, Bruce). Others, however, interpret it to mean that he was circumcised, but not as a result of any compulsion from the Jerusalem leaders: he allowed himself to be circumcised voluntarily or at Paul's suggestion, apart from any pressure from those at Jerusalem (e.g., F. C. Burkitt, *Christian Beginnings*, 118; Duncan, *Galatians*, 41–44). This latter understanding lays stress on the word "compelled" and cites Paul's habit of making practical concessions for the sake of the gospel (cf. 1 Cor 9:19–23). Yet there is no syntactical reason to take ἠναγκάσθη as being emphatic. Rather, the emphasis in the sentence is on οὐδέ before Titus ("not even Titus"), which is more in line with the view that Titus was not circumcised. Furthermore, while Paul was indeed a master of practical concession without disturbing theological principles, it is extremely difficult to hear him say that "we did not give in to them even for a moment" (v 5a, note the discussion on οὐδέ) and that he had preserved "the truth of the gospel" for his Gentile converts (v 5b), if he had already — whether voluntarily or under duress — conceded the Judaizers' main point of the necessity of circumcision for Gentile believers. The view that Titus was circumcised but not because of any external compulsion, therefore, rightly deserves to be called "an artificial construction" (so Betz, *Galatians*, 89).

4 διὰ δὲ τοὺς παρεισάκτους ψευδαδέλφους, "now this happened because certain false brothers infiltrated our ranks." Unless we are prepared to accept the Western omission of οὐδέ in v 5 and so read v 5 as the delayed protasis of v 4 ("we gave in for a moment, because of certain false brothers"), v 4 begins with a grammatical anacoluthon — that is, its syntax is broken, being without a subject and principal verb. F. C. Burkitt, elaborating his view of Titus' situation (see above), once quipped: "Who can doubt that it was the knife which really did circumcise Titus that has cut the syntax of Gal. ii.3–5 to pieces?" (*Christian Beginnings*, 118). Probably, however, the subject of v 4 is implicit, carrying on the idea of pressure signaled in the verb ἠναγκάσθη, with the result that vv 4–5 should be seen as an elaboration of the historical incident alluded to in v 3 (contra B. Orchard). The verse, therefore, should probably be read in some such manner as follows: "Now this happened (i.e., pressure for Titus' circumcision) because certain false brothers infiltrated our ranks." Just who these "false brothers" were we are not told. By connecting v 4 to v 3, we are committed to the view that they were in some manner directly responsible for the agitation against Titus at Jerusalem. Probably, like the "false brothers" of 2 Cor 11:26, they were men who claimed to be genuine and devoted followers of Christ, but whose activities and message endangered Paul's mission. The adjective παρεισάκτους is used of spies or traitors who infiltrate an opposing camp (cf. 2 Peter 2:1; Jude 4), that camp being

here the Christian church. Paul, however, does not class these people with the Jerusalem apostles, though they may have been regarded by the apostles—particularly at a time before issues regarding Jewish-Gentile relations within the Church were clear—as legitimate members of the Jerusalem congregation. Nor should the passive force of παρεισάκτους be pressed to suggest that others, perhaps the apostles themselves, were more to blame for bringing in these intruders than the intruders themselves. Rather, their aims and actions seem to have been their own (i.e., "to spy out our freedom that we have in Christ Jesus and to make us slaves"). By the use of the definite article τούς, however, Paul implies that their aims and actions were the same as those of the agitators in Galatia who were trying to impose the Mosaic law on Gentile Christians.

οἵτινες, "who intruded." It was a common practice for writers of Koine Greek to use ὅστις in the nominative singular, or οἵτινες (as here) in the nominative plural, to take the place of the simple relative pronoun ὅς, and so to emphasize a characteristic quality by which a preceding statement is to be confirmed (cf. John 8:53; Acts 7:53; Eph 4:19; Phil 2:20; 1 Tim 1:4; Titus 1:11; Heb 8:5; 10:11; 13:7; 1 Pet 2:11; Rev 2:24). Thus οἵτινες here has as its antecedent the "false brothers" just mentioned, and does not have in mind any other group brought in by them. The false brothers not only "infiltrated" the church but also "intruded" (παρεισῆλθον) into its ministry. Such pejorative terms, of course, are Paul's, and not those of the agitators themselves. In their eyes—as also in the self-evaluation of the Galatian Judaizers, with whom Paul compares them—they were orthodox and conscientious Jewish Christians, who were concerned both for the purity of the Christian message amongst Gentiles and for the welfare of Jewish believers amidst the rising tide of Jewish nationalism (see *Introduction*, "Opponents and Situation"). For Paul, however, they were false brothers, since they could not accept Gentile Christians as true brothers apart from circumcision and so denied the universality of the gospel.

κατασκοπῆσαι τὴν ἐλευθερίαν ἡμῶν ἣν ἔχομεν ἐν χριστῷ Ἰησοῦ, "to spy out our freedom that we have in Christ Jesus." The verb κατασκοπέω is a NT *hap. leg.* but appears frequently in the LXX (also spelled κατασκοπεύω) to mean either "watch over" with protective interest (as Moses' sister watched over the basket containing her brother in the bulrushes, Exod 2:4) or "spy out" with sinister intent (as David's messengers to Anan the Ammonite were accused of doing, 2 Kgs 10:3; 1 Chr 19:3). Here the sinister nuance applies: these intruders were as spies in the Jerusalem church working on behalf of other interests and not those of Christ and the gospel. Freedom, of course, is a major theme of Galatians. The noun ἐλευθερία, "freedom," appears four times (here; 5:1; and 5:13 [twice]; cf. Rom 8:21; 1 Cor 10:29; 2 Cor 3:17); the adjectival and substantival uses of the adjective ἐλεύθερος, "free," appear six times (3:28; 4:22, 23, 26, 30, 31; cf. Rom 6:20; 7:3; 1 Cor 7:21, 22, 39; 9:1, 19; 12:13; Eph 6:8; Col 3:11); and the verb ἐλευθερόω, "set free," appears once (5:1; cf. Rom 6:18, 22; 8:1, 21)—with ἐξαγοράζω ("redeem") carrying the idea of freedom in 3:13 and 4:5 as well. The use of ἡμῶν ("our"; cf. also ἡμᾶς in the following clause) has in mind, in the first place, Paul and those who came with him to Jerusalem — including, of course, Titus. So it refers particularly to the Pauline party made up of Jewish Christians and an uncircumcised Gentile Christian. By extension, however, it also takes in all Jewish and Gentile believers in Christ who hold to "the truth of the gospel" (cf. the ὑμᾶς at the end of v 5; see also the discussions of ἡμεῖς at 2:15–16, 3:13–14, 3:23–25; 4:3–7). The phrase ἐν Χριστῷ ᾽Ιησοῦ, "in Christ Jesus," is Paul's favorite way of speaking of the believer's relation to Christ (cf. 1:22; 2:17; 3:14, 26, 28; 5:6, 10 [ἐν Κυρίῳ, "in the Lord"]). Here it connotes both instrumentality ("by" or "through" Christ Jesus) and locality ("in" Christ Jesus). Freedom for Paul results from both what Christ effects in our lives (instrumentality) and our being brought into personal union with Christ (locality).

ἵνα ἡμᾶς καταδουλώσουσιν, "and to make us slaves." There is no difference of meaning between the future indicative active καταδουλώσουσιν and the aorist subjunctive active καταδουλώσωσιν. The aorist subjunctive middle καταδουλώσωνται of the Textus Receptus, however, suggests that the false brothers wanted to bring Paul and his party into bondage to themselves. Reading the verb as a subjunctive probably came about because of ἵνα at the beginning of the clause, with the change to the middle voice brought about by conformity to classical usage where the subjunctive in the middle voice is common. But ἵνα with the indicative future occurs several times in the NT (cf. in Paul 1 Cor 9:21; also Phil 2:10, where ἵνα governs both a future indicative and an aorist subjunctive in the same sentence), sometimes even with the present indicative (cf. Gal 4:17). And the sense of the sentence requires reading the verb as active, not middle: the intruders wanted to bring Paul and his party under the regulations of the Mosaic law, not just under their authority. What they desired was to ensure that Gentile Christians lived a nomistic or Torah-centered lifestyle. Paul saw this, however, as a return to life under a "pedagogue" and enslavement to "the elements of the world," as he elaborates later in 3:23–4:11.

5 οἷς οὐδὲ πρὸς ὥραν εἴξαμεν τῇ ὑποταγῇ, "we did not give in to them in this matter even for a moment." The Western text, together with such church fathers as Tertullian (*Adv. Marc.* 5.3.3) and Irenaeus (*Adv. Haer.* 3.13.3), omits οἷς οὐδέ, thereby reading "we gave in for a moment." The omission may have been accidental at first, but soon became used to support the view that Titus was circumcised (see above on v 3). Marcion, of course, retained οὐδέ, but omitted οἷς, which conforms to his insistence that Paul never made any concession to anyone, either to false brothers or to the Jerusalem apostles—who in his view were much the same. Both omissions, however, seem tendentious, and so unable to overturn the negative reading οἷς οὐδέ that is attested by all the Greek uncial MSS (except D*), p⁴⁶, all the versions (except it^d,e), and all the Greek church fathers (except Irenaeus in Latin translation).

The expression πρὸς ὥραν is an idiom meaning "for a short time"—or more colloquially "for a moment." It appears elsewhere in Paul at 2 Cor 7:8, 1 Thess 2:17; Philem 15 (cf. John 5:35; *Mart. Pol.* 11:2; see also Matt 10:19 [Luke 12:12]; 26:40 [Mark 14:37]; 26:45 [Mark 14:41]; 26:55 for illustrations of the flexible use of ὥρα). The aorist εἴξαμεν with the negative states the simple fact of history, "we did not yield" or "give in" to them. The dative noun ὑποταγῇ ("by way of subjection") is somewhat redundant, amplifying as it does εἴξαμεν, and so perhaps unnecessary to translate. The article before ὑποταγῇ, however, suggests a particular subjection that was being demanded and that Paul refused, which calls for some such translation as "in this matter" in order to specify.

ἵνα ἡ ἀλήθεια τοῦ εὐαγγελίου διαμείνῃ πρὸς ὑμᾶς, "so that the truth of the gospel might remain with you." The expression ἡ ἀλήθεια τοῦ εὐαγγελίου ("the truth of the gospel") appears in Paul only here and at 2:14 (cf. ἀλήθεια Χριστοῦ, "the truth of Christ," of 2 Cor 11:10 and ἐν τῷ λόγῳ τῆς ἀληθείας τοῦ εὐαγγελίου, "in the word of the truth of the gospel," of Col 1:5). It means "the Gospel in its integrity" (Lightfoot, *Galatians*, 107) or "the truth contained in, and so belonging to, the gospel" (Burton, *Galatians*, 86). In particular, it has in mind the true gospel proclaimed by Paul as opposed to the false gospel advocated by the Judaizers (cf. 1:6–9)—i.e., the gospel that has as its consequence Gentile freedom. The verb διαμείνῃ, "might remain," implies that at the time of writing the addressees had previously responded positively to Paul's preaching and so were already in possession of "the truth of the gospel." The pronoun ὑμᾶς, "you," refers directly to Paul's Galatian converts, though by extension has all Gentile Christians in view as well. While the preposition πρός as meaning "with" is usually used by Paul directly in association with people (cf. Gal 1:18; 4:18, 20; 1 Thess 3:4; 2 Thess 2:5; 3:10), here it is used of the presence of the gospel with people. Paul's purpose in refusing to give in to the demands of the false brothers at Jerusalem was so that (ἵνα) the truth of the gospel might remain intact, particularly for the benefit of his Galatian converts.

6 ἀπὸ δὲ τῶν δοκούντων εἶναί τι, "as for those reputed to be important." Vv 6–10 appear to be one long, convoluted sentence. "Detailed analysis, however," as H. D. Betz notes, "reveals that the section is by no means carelessly composed. The enormous care which the author has apparently devoted to this section can only be explained if the event on which he reports constitutes the center of this 'statement of facts' " (*Galatians*, 92). Here in these verses Paul takes up again his account of meeting with the leadership of the Jerusalem church that he began in vv 1–2, but from which he moved away somewhat in detailing the case of Titus in vv 3–5. And here he demolishes the claim of the Galatian Judaizers that they represent the theology of the apostles at Jerusalem.

In context, the particle δέ, "as for," must be seen as continuative, not adversative. Its function is to reach back behind the ἀλλά, "yet," of v 3 to the narrative of vv 1–2, thereby setting up what follows as a continuation of that narrative. The οἱ δοκοῦντες εἶναί τι ("those reputed to be important"), as mentioned in v 2 and referred to explicitly by name in v 9, are the three "pillars" of the Jerusalem congregation, James, Cephas, and John. On οἱ δοκοῦντες and its being joined with στῦλοι, "pillars," see *Comment* on vv 2 and 9.

ὁποῖοί ποτε ἦσαν οὐδέν μοι διαφέρει· πρόσωπον ὁ θεὸς ἀνθρώπου οὐ λαμβάνει, "whatever they were at one time makes no difference to me; God does not take into account human credentials." The correlative pronoun ὁποῖοι is a qualitative word meaning "what kind of" or "what sort of." It may refer to a person's character (as Jas 1:24), but is also used by Paul of a Christian's work (1 Cor 3:13) and of his own reception by the Thessalonians (1 Thess 1:9). Here it refers to the rank or status of the Jerusalem "pillars" as claimed by the Galatian Judaizers. The enclitic ποτέ with a verb in the past tense (here the imperfect ἦσαν, "were") signals a particular past period of time (cf. 1:13, 23; also Rom 7:9), and so emphasizes the idea of "at one time" or "formerly." But what period of time does ποτέ have in mind? Many have seen it as having reference to the meeting narrated here in vv 1–10, whether that be understood as the famine visit or the Jerusalem Council (e.g., T. Zahn, *Galater*, 98; A. Oepke, *Galater*, 48). If that were so, however, we should expect τότε ("then") rather than ποτέ, for ποτέ points the reader back to an earlier time.

C. K. Barrett suggests that the term στῦλοι ("pillars") among Jewish Christians was originally strictly eschatological in meaning (cf. *Comment* on v 9), but all too soon at Jerusalem took on institutional significance (a development of which Paul disapproved)—and that ποτέ here refers to that time when eschatology became ecclesiasticism and James, Cephas, and John were looked to as the institutional leaders of the Christian Church, having therefore special prerogatives ("Paul and the 'Pillar' Apostles," 1–19). Thus Barrett understands Paul's remark of v 6 to mean: "They have their special [eschatological] place in the last days, but this gives them no exclusive [institutional] rights in the Church" (ibid., 19). Probably, however, Burton is closer to the truth in relating ὁποῖοί ποτε ἦσαν to "that standing which the three here referred to had by reason of their personal relation to Jesus while he was in the flesh, in the case of James as his brother, in the case of Peter and John as his personal followers" (*Galatians*, 87; see also Lightfoot, *Galatians*, 108). Probably, therefore, it was a veneration of such past relationships that the Judaizers were extolling and that Paul is reacting to here (cf. his opposition to any κατὰ σάρκα, "according to the flesh" perspective in 2 Cor 5:16).

An interesting feature of the parenthesis starting with ὁποῖοι is that while it contains the imperfect ἦσαν, the main statement οὐδέν μοι διαφέρει ("it makes no difference to me") is in the present tense—as is also the appositional statement πρόσωπον ὁ θεὸς ἀνθρώπου οὐ λαμβάνει (lit. "God does not accept the face of a man"). Furthermore, Paul's use of both διαφέρει, "makes a difference," and λαμβάνει, "accept," suggests that what we have here are what could be called "proverbial presents" (so Betz, *Galatians*, 94–95)—the first drawn from Stoic ideas of *adiaphora* or "matters of indifference" (cf. 1 Cor 1:26–29; 8:1–11:1; Phil 3:7–8, where Paul also seems to subscribe to a doctrine of *adiaphora*) and the second from OT teaching that "God is a judge who cannot be corrupted and has no regard for the status of persons" (cf. esp. the LXX πρόσωπον passages: Lev 19:15; Deut 1:17; 16:19; 2 Chr 19:7; Job 13:10; Ps 81:2; Prov 18:5; Mal 2:9). Both, indeed, seem to be proverbial statements, in which the theological nature of the latter buttresses the more philosophical cast of the former, with both used to "evaluate the past status of the Jerusalem apostles ('they were') as having no argumentative value in the present" (ibid., 95). So Paul's point in the parenthesis of v 6 is that one cannot be unduly influenced in the present theological discussions by past relationships or physical proximities, whatever they may have been. For to restate his theological axiom more colloquially, "God does not take into account human credentials."

ἐμοὶ γὰρ οἱ δοκοῦντες οὐδὲν προσανέθεντο, "those seemingly important men added nothing to me." The postpositive γάρ here is explicative, reaching back behind the parenthesis to the beginning of the sentence and signaling that what was said there will now be explicated more fully. The verb προσανέθεντο here in the middle voice has a transitive sense ("they added to"), in contrast to the intransitive usage of the same verb (προσανεθέμην, "consult with") in 1:16. What kind of addition does Paul have in mind? Certainly it is that advocated by both the false brothers at Jerusalem (vv 3–5) and the Judaizers of Galatia: that Gentile Christians must be circumcised and live a nomistic lifestyle in accordance with the Jewish Torah. Paul, however, reports that the Jerusalem apostles "added nothing to me" at this crucial meeting, and that ought to give the lie to the Judaizers' message.

7a ἀλλὰ τοὐναντίον ἰδόντες, "on the contrary, when they saw." Having stated what the Jerusalem apostles did not do, Paul now turns in vv 7–10 to their positive reception of him and his mission. The idiom ἀλλὰ τοὐναντίον signals a strong reversal from what was previously stated (cf. 2 Cor 2:7; 1 Peter 3:9), with τοὐναντίον being a crasis (i.e., a contraction of two words that omits an unstressed vowel, so contracting τὸ ἐναντίον) meaning "that which is opposite." The aorist participle ἰδόντες ("having seen") is paralleled by the aorist participle γνόντες ("having known") of v 9a, with both participles combining to give the reason for the Jerusalem leaders' acceptance of Paul and Barnabas in vv 9b–10. As a temporal participle, ἰδόντες ("when they saw") is comparable to the finite verbal construction ὅτε εἶδον ("when I saw") of 2:14, so suggesting more theological insight than visual perception. The question, however, arises as to when they "saw": Was their recognition of the validity of Paul's Gentile mission based on his account of how he received his commission (cf. 1:11ff.), or on what they heard about his activities (cf. 1:23–24), or on what he argued before them in private as to the content of his preaching (cf. 2:2)? While impossible to say with certainty, probably such an insight was the result of all of the above, as brought together under the Spirit's direction.

    7b–8 ὅτι πεπίστευμαι τὸ εὐαγγέλιον τῆς ἀκροβυστίας καθὼς Πέτρος τῆς περιτομῆς, ὁ γάρ ἐνεργήσας Πέτρῳ εἰς ἀποστολὴν τῆς περιτομῆς ἐνήργησεν καὶ ἐμοὶ εἰς τὰ ἔθνη, "that I had been entrusted with the task of preaching to the uncircumcised just as Peter was entrusted with preaching to the circumcised—for the One who was at work in Peter as an apostle to the circumcised was also at work in my ministry to the Gentiles." This is what the Jerusalem apostles came to recognize. The perfect passive verb πεπίστευμαι ("I was entrusted") is a common Pauline expression (cf. Rom 3:2; 1 Cor 9:17; 1 Thess 2:4; 1 Tim 1:11; Titus 1:3). There are, however, two features of language in this statement that appear somewhat non-Pauline: (1) the references to a "gospel to the uncircumcised" and another gospel "to the circumcised," which seem at variance with the insistence on only one gospel in 1:6–9, 2:11–16, passim, and (2) the use of "Peter" rather than "Cephas," which occurs in Paul's letters only here (contra P[46] A D G etc.; for Paul's use of "Cephas," see Gal 1:18; 2:9, 11, 14; 1 Cor 1:12; 3:22; 9:5; 15:5). Furthermore, the material between the participles ἰδόντες, "when they saw," of v 7a and γνόντες, "knowing," of v 9a—which appears to be introduced by a ὅτι recitativum (i.e., a "that" which introduces a cited portion)—can be abstracted from its context without destroying the sentence.

    Now it is possible, of course, to lay too much weight on the difference between two kinds of gospels here and Paul's insistence elsewhere that there is only one gospel, for the point here is not with regard to content but audience and type of outreach. And it may, indeed, be that Paul used "Cephas" and "Peter" rather indifferently, with their easy interchangeability evident only here in his writings. Yet such linguistic and structural features as cited above suggest the possibility that Paul here is using expressions and words of others for his own purposes, as he frequently does elsewhere in his letters.

    Oscar Cullmann proposed that Paul "here cites an official document, in the Greek translation in which the form *Petros* was used" (*Peter*, 20; idem, *TDNT* 6:100). And Eric Dinkler, in support of Cullmann, has attempted to reconstruct that official document, assuming that at the Jerusalem Council an official decree was issued in both Aramaic and Greek and that Paul is here quoting verbatim the Greek version to buttress his argument (*VF* 1–3 [1953–55] 182–83). Such a reconstruction of events and documents, however, is somewhat hypothetical, particularly on a "South Galatian" view of provenance. Betz's evaluation of the matter, whether with reference to the Jerusalem Council or some earlier meeting, is much to be preferred: (1) that "the non-Pauline notions of the 'gospel of circumcision' and 'of uncircumcision' as well as the name 'Peter' may very well come from an underlying official statement," but (2) that "rather than 'quoting' from the written protocol, Paul reminds the readers of the agreements by using terms upon which the parties had agreed" (*Galatians*, 97).

9 καὶ γνόντες τὴν χάριν τὴν δοθεῖσάν μοι, "knowing that divine grace had been given to me." In v 9 we come to the nerve center of Paul's debate with the Galatian Judaizers: the Jerusalem apostles' formal recognition of Paul's Gentile mission. The participle γνόντες ("knowing") catches up the ἰδόντες ("when they saw") of v 7, with what follows being a summation with significant additions of the substance of vv 7–8. Reference to χάριν ("grace") is articular, signifying in its specificity not just grace generally but "divine grace" in particular. Some see reference here to "the grace of the apostolic office" (so Schlier, *Galater*, 78; Mussner, *Galaterbrief*, 118; Bruce, *Galatians*, 121). Yet in the traditionally based wording of vv 7–8, which we have taken to have some basis in an agreement reached between Paul and the Jerusalem apostles, Paul is not expressly called an apostle; and though Paul certainly believes himself to be an apostle and sees his apostolic office as given him by God, there is no evidence that the Jerusalem leaders expressly said such things of him. So one should not read Paul as though he claims that they did. Rather, what they recognized was that Paul had been graced by God for an effective ministry among Gentiles, just as Peter "as an apostle" (εἰς ἀποστολήν) was graced by God to work among Jews (cf. vv 7b–8 above). Thus τὴν χάριν should be understood here simply as "divine grace," with the aorist passive adjectival participle δοθεῖσαν ("had been given") signaling God as the subject and Paul as the object.

Ἰάκωβος καὶ Κηφᾶς καὶ Ἰωάννης, οἱ δοκοῦντες στῦλοι εἶναι, "James, Cephas, and John (that is, those reputed to be 'pillars')." Having previously spoken of certain men of eminence (οἱ δοκοῦντες), "those reputed" with whom he met privately during his visit to Jerusalem (v 2), Paul now for the first time names them: James, Cephas, and John. The order, of course, differs from that given in 1:18–19, as well as that implied in vv 7–8 above. That is probably because in 1:18–19 Paul has in mind the apostles as canons of the truth, in which function Peter took precedence over James, while the statement of vv 7–8 concerns missionary outreach, which again was preeminently Peter's domain (cf. Acts 2–12; 1 Peter 1:1). In matters of ecclesiastical polity and administration, however, James seems to have become increasingly influential—even dominant—in the Jerusalem congregation, as Paul's reference to "certain ones from James" and Peter's deference in 2:12 clearly suggest (cf. also Acts 15:13ff. and 21:18ff.). On James "the Lord's brother," see *Comment* at 1:19. The "James" of 2:9 is certainly the same as the one of 1:19.

Peter and John are frequently mentioned together in early Christian tradition, with Peter always referred to first (cf. Matt 17:1; Mark 3:17; 9:2; 10:35–45; 14:33; John 21:2; Acts 1:13; 3:1–11; 4:13–20, 23; 8:14–25; note Luke's order of "Peter and John and James" in 8:51 and 9:28, which probably results from his constant grouping of Peter and John in Acts). From the canonical Gospels we learn that John was the son of Zebedee and a (younger) brother of James (cf. Matt 4:21; 10:2; Mark 1:19–20; 3:17; 10:35; Luke 5:10). Acts 12:2 records the death of James the brother of John at the hands of Herod Agrippa I, probably in the spring of A.D. 44 (or late A.D. 43). John's death as a martyr is an inference drawn from Mark 10:39. Traditionally, John has been identified as "the Beloved Disciple" of the Fourth Gospel (cf. John 13:23; *passim*) and the author of the Johannine corpus (the

Gospel, three epistles, and the Apocalypse). Here in Gal 2:9 is the only place in Paul's letters where he, or any other John, is mentioned.

The expression οἱ δοκοῦντες has been used three times before by Paul in his narrative of his second Jerusalem visit (see *Comment* on vv 2 and 6). Now it occurs a fourth time explicitly with the names "James and Cephas and John." Its repeated use itself suggests something of a note of irony. And when one compares the use of δοκέω ("think," "seem") in Phil 3:4, where a similar situation is in view, such a suggestion of irony is strengthened.

More significantly, οἱ δοκοῦντες is here joined by the word στῦλοι ("pillars"). στῦλος was a common Greek architectural term for a supporting column. It appears in this way always in Josephus, and it is the usual translation of עמוד (*'ammûd*), "pillar," "column," in the LXX. As well, there are many examples from Greek literature of its use in a purely metaphorical sense (e.g., Aeschylus, *Agamemnon* 898: "I would hail my lord here as the watchdog of the fold, the savior forestay of the ship, the firm based pillar [στῦλος] of the lofty roof, the one and only son to a father"; Euripides, *Iphigeneia in Taurica* 57: "the pillars [στῦλοι] of a house are its sons"). More particularly, however, in the Talmud the patriarchs Abraham, Isaac, and Jacob are called the three "pillars" (עמודים, *'ammûdîm*) of Israel, upon whom were established not only the covenant community of Israel but also the whole world (cf. *Exod. Rab.* 15.7). There are other rabbinic statements that speak of twelve pillars supporting the world, or of seven, or of only one. And there are references to various prominent rabbis (e.g., Joh. b. Zakkai in *b. Ber.* 28b and *'Abot R. Nat.* 25.1) and the righteous generally (cf. *b. Ketub.* 104a) as being "pillars." But the earliest and most persistent tradition within Second Temple Judaism, as R. D. Aus points out, is that which identifies Israel's three patriarchs as the supporting "pillars" (or "tent pegs," "foundations") of the nation and the world (cf. *ZNW* 70 [1979] 252–61).

While, therefore, a metaphorical use of στῦλος was widespread in the ancient world, it may be surmised from early Christianity's most immediate ideological milieu that the identification of James, Cephas, and John as "pillars" stemmed from "a deliberate selection by the Aramaic-speaking Jerusalem church of three disciples/apostles as community leaders on the basis of the model of the three Patriarchs, Abraham, Isaac and Jacob, thought of in rabbinic sources as the three pillars of Israel, indeed, of the entire world" (ibid., 255). Thus, as Aus goes on to say, "as God once 'established the world,' the covenant community of Israel, on the basis of the three Patriarchs, so in the messianic period, inaugurated by the resurrection of Jesus from the dead, God was thought of by Jewish Christians as having 'established the world' anew, the new covenant community, the 'Israel of God,' to employ Paul's phrase from Gal 6.16, on the basis of three new pillars" (ibid., 256–57). "The same thought," observes Ulrich Wilckens, "surely stands behind the saying to Peter in Mt 16:18: The rock on which the Church is to be built holds up the house or temple of the ἐκκλησία and thus has the same function as is denoted by στῦλος in Gl. 2" ("στῦλος," *TDNT* 7:735).

The ironic or dismissive tone in Paul's usage need not, however, be viewed as stemming from either (1) a feeling that to call the Jerusalem apostles "pillars" devalued his own apostleship (so Wilckens) or (2) a theology of merit being so bound up with the pillars of Israel that to call the Church's leaders by a title associated with them would only tend to confuse the gospel (so Aus). Rather, while the Jewish Christians of Jerusalem had legitimately, from their perspective, applied the term "pillars" to their three leaders, the Judaizers, it seems, were using that attribution for their own purposes. So we may believe that Paul had no objection to the title in its original Christian context (cf. *1 Clem.* 5, where the title is applied to both Peter and Paul), connoting, as it did, a theology and ecclesiology with which he agreed. What he seems to be opposed to is the Judaizers' inflated adulation of the Jerusalem leaders and their use of the title, setting both them and it against Paul.

δεξιὰς ἔδωκαν ἐμοὶ καὶ Βαρναβᾷ κοινωνίας, "gave me and Barnabas the right hand of fellowship." "To give the right hand(s)" (δεξιὰς δοῦναι; conversely, "to receive the right hands[s]," δεξιὰς λαβεῖν) was an idiom of the day for pledging friendship and acknowledging agreement (cf. Josephus, *J.W.* 6.318–20, 345, 356, 378; *Ant.* 8.387; 18.328; 20.62; see also the Greek writings cited by Lightfoot, *Galatians,* 110, and Burton, *Galatians,* 95–96). The expression has only limited usage in the OT (Ezra 10:19; perhaps 2 Kgs 10:15). And judging by Josephus' account of the Parthian king Artabanus' conciliatory actions toward the Jewish brothers Asinaeus and Anilaeus (*Ant.* 18.328–29: "He offered his right hand [τὴν δεξιὰν ἐδίδου], and this is for all the barbarians of those parts the highest assurance of security in making visits. For no one would ever prove false when he had given his right hand [δεξιῶν ὑπ᾽ αὐτοῦ δόσεων] . . . "), it was not an idiom indigenous to the Jews (the OT idiom "to give the hand," while signaling accord, also often implied submission of the inferior; cf. 1 Chr 29:24; 2 Chr 30:8; Ezek 17:18; Lam 5:6). Through Persian influence, it seems, "to give the right hand(s)" and "to receive the right hand(s)" became idiomatic expressions among Jews of the Second Temple period (in addition to the Josephus references above, see 1 Macc 6:58; 11:50, 62, 66; 13:50; 2 Macc 11:26; 12:11; 13:22), without any necessary idea of either surrender or submission. Yet Paul's inclusion here of κοινωνίας ("fellowship") is not superfluous, for remnants of the OT idiom "to give the hand" undoubtedly lingered in some Jewish minds when the Persian-Greek idiom "to give the right hand(s)" was heard—with, for some, ideas of inferiority and subjection continuing to resonate. Paul's point, however, has to do with the mutual fellowship and partnership existing between himself and the leaders at Jerusalem, which they overtly signaled by giving "me and Barnabas the right hand of fellowship."

ἵνα ἡμεῖς εἰς τὰ ἔθνη, αὐτοὶ δὲ εἰς τὴν περιτομήν, "on the understanding that we should go to the Gentiles and they to the circumcised." The conjunction ἵνα functions here like the classical ἐφ᾽ ᾧτε ("on condition that," "on the understanding that"), so introducing two differing missionary strategies amidst an acknowledged doctrinal unity. The pronouns ἡμεῖς ("we") and αὐτοί ("they") stand in antithesis to one another, with the particle δέ making the latter somewhat emphatic but not intensive. Some such verb as ἔλθωμεν or πορευθῶμεν ("we should go") or εὐαγγελιζώμεθα ("we should preach") must be supplied in the first part, with a corresponding verb with αὐτοί in the second. The omission of a verb in Paul's sentences, however, is not uncommon (e.g., 2:10, 5:13b), particularly after ἵνα (cf. Rom 4:16; 1 Cor 1:31; 2 Cor 8:13). The phrase εἰς τὰ ἔθνη ("to the Gentiles") picks up the identical phrase in v 8b, while εἰς τὴν περιτομήν ("to the circumcised") parallels the genitive τῆς περιτομῆς ("of" or "to the circumcised") of v 8a—with both sets of expressions to be treated alike.

The question arises, however: Do the accusatives with the preposition εἰς of v 9b describe two different geographical spheres of labor (territorial) or two different racial audiences (ethnographical)? Burton (*Galatians,* 97–99) has mounted a case for the former based on linguistic grounds (the expression is εἰς τὰ ἔθνη, ἐν τοῖς ἔθνεσιν) and contextual data (in 1:16; 2:2 Paul speaks of his ministry in territorial fashion as being to people living in Gentile lands; see *Comment* at those verses). Yet τὰ ἔθνη ("the Gentiles") and ἡ περιτομή ("the circumcised") more appropriately designate people rather than territories (so W. Schmithals, *Paul and James*, 45–46; cf. Mussner, *Galaterbrief*, 122; Betz, *Galatians*, 100). Furthermore, the expression ἐν τοῖς ἔθνεσιν of 1:16; 2:2, while comparable, is not identical to εἰς τὰ ἔθνη of 1:8–9. In all likelihood, however, the issue of territory *or* race was not so sharply differentiated in the minds of early Jewish Christians as it is by commentators today. There could have been considerable overlapping between the two spheres. Jewish colonies existed in most Gentile cities of the eastern Mediterranean world and Acts tells us that Paul began his Gentile mission in those cities by speaking in the Jewish synagogues (cf. Acts 13:5, 14ff.; 14:1; 16:13, 16; 17:1ff., 10; 18:4, 19; 19:8), whereas a Christian outreach from Jerusalem to diaspora Jews certainly took place in Gentile lands (cf. Acts 11:19–21; Jas 1:1; 1 Peter 1:1).

10 μόνον τῶν πτωχῶν ἵνα μνημονεύωμεν, "all they asked was that we should continue to remember the poor." The adverb μόνον ("only") serves to separate what follows from what has just been said; yet at the same time it ties in to what has been said by way of a concession. In effect, by its use Paul is saying: "Only this one request was made in addition to the agreement referred to above, but that request was not related to the point at issue and so is immaterial to the conflict stirred up by the Judaizers in Galatia." The placing of the adverb first in the sentence is for emphasis. Some such verb as ἠτήσατο ("they asked") or ἐθέλησαν ("they desired") needs to be supplied after the adverb, but, as we have seen (cf. v 9b above), such an omission is not uncommon for Paul (cf. 6:12 and 2 Thess 2:7 for the omission of a verb after μόνον, with a similar derangement of order for the sake of emphasis).

The expression τῶν πτωχῶν ("the poor"), which here is a genitive of reference and the true predicate of the sentence, has also been moved forward for emphasis. Its articular form signals its absolute use: either (1) those financially impoverished (cf. Josephus, *J.W.* 569–70, where οἱ ἄποροι, "the lower classes," equals οἱ πτωχοί, "the poor"), or (2) those adhering to a special kind of Jewish piety (so-called *anawim* piety from the Hebrew adjective עָנִי, '*anî*), where "poor" suggests not only economic impoverishment but also carries honorific nuances of "humility," "obedience," and "piety" before God (cf. the consciousness of the Dead Sea covenanters, among whom "the community of the poor" seems to have been a favorite self-designation [see esp. 1QH 5.1, 21; 18.14; 1QM 14.7; 1QpHab 12.3, 6, 10]; also *Pss.Sol.* 5.2, 13, where πτωχός is used synonymously with εὐσεβής, "the pious"). Jewish Christians not only referred to themselves as "those of the Way" (cf. Acts 9:2; 19:9, 23; 22:4; 24:14, 22), but also, it seems, as "The Poor" (so, e.g., H. Lietzmann, *A History of the Early Church*, 62; H. Schlier, *Galater*, 80; A. S. Geyser, "The Earliest Name of the Earliest Church," 58–66; though see also L. Keck, *ZNW* 56 [1965] 100–29; idem, "The Poor among the Saints in Jewish Christianity and Qumran," 54–78)—signaling thereby both economic status and religious piety, though with an emphasis on the latter. Hence the later self-designation "Ebionites," from אביונים ('*ebyônîm*), "poor ones," by one branch of Jewish Christians.

Exactly how those who thought of themselves as "the Poor" related economic and spiritual factors in their self-understanding will probably continue to elude modern-day commentators (for a review of the biblical data, see E. Bammel, "πτωχός," *TDNT* 6.888–915). All that can be said with certainty is that here in v 10 the Jewish Christians of Jerusalem are principally in view, as is true as well in Rom 15:26 (εἰς τοὺς πτωχοὺς τῶν ἁγίων τῶν ἐν ᾽Ιερουσαλήμ, "for the poor among the saints in Jerusalem"). Probably πτωχοί here in 2:10 is a shortened form of the formula οἱ πτωχοὶ τῶν ἁγίων τῶν ἐν ᾽Ιερουσαλήμ as used in Rom 15:26, with the wording of that formula emanating from the Jerusalem church itself.

The auxiliary verb μνημονεύωμεν, being present subjunctive, points to a desired ongoing activity, and so is best translated "we should continue to remember." Almost all commentators assume that the request "to remember the poor" has principally to do with money — or, as H. D. Betz speaks of it, "a specific, ongoing financial subsidy" (*Galatians*, 102). And most see it as having been made at the Jerusalem Council (Acts 15) and as the basis for Paul's collection from his Gentile churches for Jewish believers at Jerusalem. The verb "to remember," however, in Greek as well as in English, means not just "to bring a gift," but more basically "to keep (someone) in mind as worthy of affection or recognition." It may be, therefore, that commentators have assumed too quickly that the thrust of the request had to do primarily with monetary support.

Understood more broadly, what the Jerusalem apostles seem to have asked for is that Paul, in exercising his freedom to carry on an independent strategy for the evangelization of Gentiles, "continue to keep the welfare of the Jerusalem believers in Jesus also in mind"— i.e., that he do nothing in the exercise of his freedom that would impede their outreach to Jews and that he take into consideration the special circumstances of their Jewish mission, supporting them whenever possible. "To remember the poor," therefore, seems to be something of an idiomatic expression or *Stichwort* meant to signal the special relationship that existed between Gentile churches and the Jewish Christian congregation at Jerusalem which both parties recognized. It undoubtedly included Paul's later collection of money from his churches for the Jewish believers of Jerusalem, which Paul meant to be a concrete expression on his part of that special relationship. But it cannot be confined to such a monetary gift, either on the part of the Jerusalem apostles or Paul.

ὃ καὶ ἐσπούδασα αὐτὸ τοῦτο ποιῆσαι, "which is what I have always been eager to do." The neuter relative pronoun ὃ ("which") picks up the whole idea of its immediate antecedent, "to remember the poor." The intensive pronoun αὐτό ("very") strengthens the neuter demonstrative pronoun τοῦτο ("this thing") to read (literally) "this very thing." The verb ἐσπούδασα, from σπουδάζω meaning "be eager" or "make diligent effort" (cf. Jdt 13:1, 12; 1 Thess 2:17), is particularly interesting because of both its singular pronominal suffix and its aorist tense. In fact, how we interpret the number and tense of the verb makes all the difference as to how we understand Paul here.

Burton has argued (1) that the aorist tense of σπουδάζω implies that Paul is not here referring to his present state of mind on the matter, for that would require an imperfect tense in Greek, and (2) that the singular pronominal suffix in the verb supports neither a past nor a present situation, since reference to either would have called for a plural suffix to include Barnabas. So he concludes that v 10b must be taken as "a reference to Paul's subsequent diligence in fulfilling the stipulation" made by the Jerusalem apostles, viz. the collection for believers at Jerusalem (*Galatians*, 99–100). Yet while the plural μνημονεύωμεν ("we should continue to remember") of v 10a assuredly refers to Barnabas along with Paul (not Paul and the Jerusalem apostles as

Marcion evidently believed, having first omitted 2:6–9a from the text of Galatians; cf. Tertullian, *Adv. Marc.* 5. 3), Paul's habit in 2:1–10, even when speaking of events where Barnabas was present, is to refer primarily to himself (cf. the first person singulars of vv 1–3 and 6–9a). And this is particularly the case when he speaks about matters having to do with perspective and leadership (cf. *Comment* above on v 1b).

The use of the first person singular in ἐσπούδασα, therefore, has little if anything to do with whether Paul was here thinking of the past, the present, or the future. Rather, it is his use of the aorist tense in the verb that is significant, for the Greek historical aorist implies completed action and corresponds to an English pluperfect (cf. D. R. Hall, *ExpTim* 82 [1971] 309–11). So, as F. F. Bruce says: "Paul means not only that he henceforth adopted this policy, but that he had already done so—he thinks of the famine relief which he and Barnabas brought to Jerusalem from Antioch, according to Acts 11:30" (*Galatians*, 126). In the translation, therefore, we have tried to highlight this feature of Paul's thought by the use of the word "always": "which is what I have always been eager to do."

Explanation

In his account of his third visit to Jerusalem after becoming a Christian, Paul lays emphasis on the following points (1) that there are no gaps in his narration of visits to Jerusalem, contrary to what the Judaizers of Galatia might have claimed; (2) that it was not until fourteen years after his conversion that he met with the body of apostles and leaders at Jerusalem, which hardly supports any claim for his dependence on them; (3) that his going to Jerusalem was in response to a divine revelation, not at the request of the Jerusalem apostles or to submit himself to them; (4) that the Jerusalem apostles accepted the validity of his Gentile mission, viewing it as parallel to their own Jewish mission; and (5) that the Jerusalem apostles asked only that the needs and circumstances of the Jerusalem church be kept in mind in any outreach to Gentiles. As Paul saw it, the "false brothers" of Jerusalem and the Judaizers of Galatia had the same agenda and a similar program, and so his addressees could learn from how he handled the former as to how they ought to respond to the latter. In both cases, however, their assertions were invalid. For though there were, indeed, differences between Paul and the Jerusalem apostles, principally as to the logistics of their respective missions, they were at one in the essentials of the gospel.

Shortly after writing his Galatian converts, the issues raised by the "false brothers" at Jerusalem and then by the Judaizers in Galatia received a more extensive hearing at the first ecumenical council at Jerusalem (so Acts 15). Here in Galatians, however, with that council yet in the future (as we believe), Paul cites only his earlier contacts with the Jerusalem apostles—particularly his meeting with them on his third visit to the city. His argument is that though there was opposition to his ministry and message (such as was also being carried on in the churches of Galatia), the Jerusalem apostles recognized the theological validity of his ministry and message, and that he reaffirmed his practical concern for their needs and circumstances.

There is much in this account of significance for Christians today, living, as we do, in a pluralistic society and amidst many representations of the Christian faith. "False brothers" and "Judaizers" of all sorts abound, who, motivated by their own agenda, attempt to conform the gospel to their own vision and purposes. Christians today need to be discerning. Furthermore, we need to appreciate how various practical concerns and speculative ideologies can distort "the truth of the gospel," whether they be those of others or ourselves. But Christians today also need to understand that there can be differences among true believers, and that such differences—particularly when involving differing understandings of redemptive logistics or differences of culture—need not tear us apart. Indeed, where there exists a basic agreement in the essentials of the gospel, Gal 2:1–10 sets before us a prototype of mutual recognition and concern for one another, despite our differences. It teaches us, in fact, something of how to distinguish between things that really matter and things of lesser importance (the so-called *adiaphora*), where to stand firm and where to concede, and even when to defy people and pressures and when to shake hands and reciprocate with expressions of mutual concern.

5. The Antioch Episode (2:11–14)

Bibliography

Antioch on the Orontes

Committee for the Excavation of Antioch and Its Vicinity. *Antioch-on-the-Orontes.* I: *The Excavations of 1932,* ed. G. W. Elderkin. Princeton, NJ: Princeton University Press, 1934; II: *The Excavations, 1933–1936,* ed. R. Stillwell. Princeton, NJ: Princeton University Press, 1938; III: *The Excavations, 1937–1939,* ed. R. Stillwell. Princeton, NJ: Princeton University Press, 1941; IV, Part 1: *Ceramics and Islamic Coins,* ed. F. O. Waage. Princeton, NJ: Princeton University Press, 1948; IV, Part 2: *Greek, Roman, Byzantine and Crusaders' Coins,* ed. D. B. Waage. Princeton, NJ: Princeton University Press, 1952. **Downey, G.** *A History of Antioch.* ———. *Antioch in the Age of Theodosius the Great.* ———. *Ancient Antioch.* **Liebeschuetz, J. H. W. G.** *Antioch.* **Longenecker, R. N.** "Antioch of Syria." In *Major Cities of the Biblical World,* ed. R. K. Harrison. Nashville: Nelson, 1985, 8–21. **Metzger, B. M.** "Antioch-on-the-Orontes." *BA* 11 (1948) 69–88.

Jews and Christians at Antioch

Bauer, W. *Orthodoxy and Heresy,* 61–76. **Brown, R. E.,** and **Meier, J. P.** *Antioch and Rome.* **Grant, R. M.** "Jewish Christianity at Antioch in the Second Century." In *Judéo-Christianisme.* FS J. Daniélou. *RSR* 60 (1972) 97–108. **Johnson, S. E.** "Asia Minor and Early Christianity." In *Christianity, Judaism, and Other Greco-Roman Cults.* FS M. Smith, ed. J. Neusner. 4 vols. Leiden: Brill, 1975, 2:77–145. **Kraeling, C. H.** "The Jewish Community at Antioch." *JBL* 51 (1932) 130–60. **McCullough, W. S.** *A Short History of Syriac Christianity.* **Meeks, W. A.,** and **Wilken, R. L.** *Jews and Christians in Antioch.* **Pieper, K.** "Antiochien am Orontes in apostolischen Zeitalter." *TGl* 22 (1930) 710–28. **Wallace-Hadrill, D. S.** *Christian Antioch.*

Exegesis of Galatians 2:11–14

Aurray, P. "S. Jerome et S. Augustin—La controverse au sujet de l'incident d'Antioche." *RSR* 29 (1939) 594–610. **Bacon, B. W.** "Peter's Triumph at Antioch." *JR* 9 (1929) 204–23.

Bauckham, R. J. "Barnabas in Galatians." *JSNT* 2 (1979) 61–70 **Carrington, P.** "Peter in Antioch." *ATR* 15 (1933) 1–15. **Cullmann, O.** *Peter,* 40–55. **Dix, G.** *Jew and Greek.* **Dunn, J. D. G.** *Unity,* 253–54. ———. "The Incident at Antioch (Gal 2:11–18)." *JSNT* 18 (1983) 7–11. **Dupont, J.** "Pierre et Paul à Antioche et à Jérusalem." *RSR* 45 (1957) 42–60, 225–39. **Féret, H. M.** *Pierre et Paul à Antioche et à Jérusalem.* **Gaechter, P.** "Petrus in Antiochia (Gal 2, 11–14)." *ZKT* 72 (1950) 177–212. **Kilpatrick, G. D.** "Gal 2, 14 ὀρθοποδοῦσιν." In *Neutestamentliche Studien. BZNW* 21. FS R. Bultmann, ed. W. Eltester. Berlin: Töpelmann, 1957, 269–74. **Reicke, B.** "Der geschichtliche Hintergrund des Apostelkonzils und der Antiochia-Episode." In *Studia Paulina,* FS J. de Zwaan, ed. J. N. Sevenster and W. C. van Unnik. Haarlem: Bohn, 1953. **Richardson, P.** "Pauline Inconsistency: 1 Cor 9:19–23 and Gal 2:11–14." *NTS* 26 (1980) 347–61. **Roberts, C. H.** "A Note on Galatians 2:14." *JTS* 40 (1939) 55–56. **Wiles, M. F.** *The Divine Apostle,* 19–25. **Winter, J. G.** "Another Instance of ὀρθοποδεῖν." *HTR* 34 (1941) 161–62.

Translation

[11]*But when Cephas[a] came to Antioch, I opposed him to his face because he stood condemned.* [12]*For before certain men[b] came from James, he used to eat with Gentile believers. When they arrived,[c] however, he began to draw back and separate from them, because he was afraid of the Jews.* [13]*And the rest of the Jewish believers[d] joined him in playing the hypocrite—so that even Barnabas was led astray by their hypocrisy.* [14]*But when I saw that they were not acting in line with the truth of the gospel, I said to Cephas[e] in the presence of them all: "If you, a Jewish believer, can live like a Gentile and not like a Jew,[f] how can you compel Gentile believers to become Jews?"*

Notes

[a]Κηφᾶς is well supported by ℵ A B C H P vg syr[pesh] etc.; Πέτρος appears in D F G TR Mcion Vict Chrysostom etc. See also 1:18; 2:9, 14.

[b]By far the better reading is τινάς (masc. accus. pl.), supported by ℵ A B C D G etc.; the reading τινά (masc. accus. sing. or neut. nom. pl.) is supported by P[46vid], some lat MSS (it[d, e, r]), and Ir. Probably τινά is an accommodation to ἦλθεν of the latter half of v 12 (see below), which appears to be an early scribal error.

[c]ἦλθον ("they came") is attested by A C D[c] it[r] vg syr[pesh, hel] cop[sa,bo] etc., but ἦλθεν ("he came") is better supported by P[46vid] ℵ B D* G etc. Despite the weight of external evidence for the latter, ἦλθον is probably to be preferred for internal reasons.

[d]καί ("also," after αὐτῷ) is supported by ℵ A C D F G etc., though omitted by P[46] B vg and Or. While neither external nor internal evidence is decisive, it seems easier, particularly on such a minor matter, to accept its original inclusion and later deletion (whether inadvertently or believing it to be superfluous) than its original omission and later addition.

[e]Κηφᾶ is well supported by P[46] ℵ A B C vg syr[pesh] cop[sa, bo] etc.; Πέτρῳ— appears in D F G TR lat Ambst (Hilary). See also 1:18; 2:9, 11.

[f]οὐχὶ Ἰουδαϊκῶς is supported by ℵ[c] B D* etc.; οὐκ Ἰουδαϊκῶς by ℵ* A C P etc. It seems easier to believe that οὐχί was original (cf. Acts 2:7; Rom 3:27) and οὐκ a corruption by the accidental dropping of the iota than vice versa.

Form/Structure/Setting

The Antioch episode of 2:11–14 is the last account in Paul's *narratio* of 1:11–2:14. It is not introduced by the adverb ἔπειτα ("then," "next"), as are the three preceding stages of Paul's defense (cf. 1:18ff.; 1:21ff.; 2:1ff.), but by the indeterminate particle ὅτε ("when"). This has led a number of commentators to postulate that the Antioch episode is not related in its true historical order, but must be seen as having taken place before the meeting narrated in 2:1–10 (so Augustine, *Epistulam ad Galatas* on 2:11; T. Zahn, *Galater*, 110–11; J. Munck, *Paul and the Salvation of Mankind*, 74–75, 100–103; H. M. Féret, *Pierre et Paul à Antioche et à Jérusalem*; though for a penetrating critique of this position, see J. Dupont, *RSR* 45 [1957] 42–60, 225–39). It is most natural, however, to take the Antioch episode of 2:11–14 as having occurred after the meeting narrated in 2:1–10. And that is how the vast majority of commentators have taken it, whether they see the meeting of 2:1–10 as being the famine visit of Acts 11 or the Jerusalem council of Acts 15.

There is much in 2:11–14 that we are not told about the situation at Antioch, and much of what we are told is mostly by way of allusion. What complex of events led up to Paul's rebuke of Peter? What was the Antioch church like before this incident? When and why did Peter come to Antioch? What issues were at stake—not only from Paul's perspective, but also from Peter's and those Christians of Antioch who joined him in his withdrawal? How did Barnabas view matters? Who really "won" in the dispute? And what was Antioch Christianity like after this episode? Indeed, as James Dunn rightly observes, "Here is one of the most tantalizing episodes in the whole of the NT. If we could only uncover the full picture of what happened here, what led up to it and what its sequel was, we would have gained an invaluable insight into the development of earliest Christianity" (*Unity*, 253).

The importance of the Antioch episode for an understanding of the development of early Christianity is highlighted by the many diverse interpretations given it during the first five centuries of Christian history. The Ebionites, for example, made it the basis for an attack on Paul (cf. *Ps.-Clem. Hom.* 17.19). Marcion, on the other hand, used it to attack Peter and to prove the direct antagonism of Christianity to everything Jewish (so Tertullian, *Adv. Marc.* 1.20; 5.3; idem, *De Praesc. Haer.* 23; Irenaeus, *Adv. Haer.* 3.12.15). And early critics of Christianity, such as Celsus (late second century) and Porphyry (c. 230–305), seem to have frequently used this incident to assail the Christian faith itself, impugning the characters of both Paul and Peter for their shameful quarreling (on Celsus, see Origen, *Contra Celsum* 5.64; on Porphyry, see Jerome, *Epistulam ad Galatas* on 2:1ff.).

Within the mainstream of Gentile Christendom, Tertullian, arguing against the Marcionites, took the rebuke of Peter to be an overreaction on Paul's part (*Adv. Marc.* 1.20; 5.3; *De Praesc. Haer.* 23); Clement of Alexandria asserted that "Cephas" here was not Cephas the apostle, the one called by Jesus "Peter," but one of the seventy apostles bearing the same name (cf. Eusebius, *Eccl. Hist.* 1.12, referring to Clement's *Hypotyposes* 5); while Origen, Chrysostom, and Jerome saw it as a staged event concocted between Peter and Paul in order to bring the issues out into the open and so to condemn the Judaizers more effectively (Origen, *Stromateis* 10 [though not in his later *Contra Celsum* 2.1]; Chrysostom, *Commentary on the Epistle to the Galatians* on 2:11–12; idem, *In illud, in faciem Petro restiti* [Latin title of *PG* 51:371ff.]; Jerome, *Epistulam ad Galatas* on 2:11 [though abandoned in his later *Adv. Pelagium* 1.22]). Augustine, however, in direct opposition to Jerome, interpreted it as a case of the higher claims of truth over rank and office—of Peter's error despite his primacy, of Paul's rightful rebuke and defense of the gospel, and of Peter's humility in accepting correction from an inferior in both age and standing (*Epistulam ad Galatas* on 2:11ff.; for the relevant correspondence between

Augustine and Jerome, see Augustine, *Epp.* 28.3; 40.3f.; 82.4ff.; Jerome, *Ep.* 112.4ff.). And many of these views continue in one form or another today.

Five stages in the development of the plot at Antioch are identifiable in Paul's account: (1) Peter's practice of eating with Gentile believers *before* a delegation from Jerusalem arrived; (2) Peter's withdrawal from table fellowship with Gentile believers *after* the delegation from Jerusalem arrived; (3) the separation of Jewish believers from Gentile believers as a result of Peter's withdrawal, with "even Barnabas" joining in that separation; (4) Paul's evaluation of the situation, crediting Peter's withdrawal as an act of hypocrisy based on fear and Barnabas's action in following Peter's example as based on irrational emotion; and (5) Paul's open denunciation of Peter. The account stands in apparent contrast to the affirmations of unity in 2:7–10, particularly "the right hand of fellowship" extended in v 9. Its purpose, however, is the same as all the other accounts of the *narratio*— to demonstrate Paul's lack of dependence on the Jerusalem apostles, particularly Peter, while at the same time affirming his essential agreement with them.

The Antioch of 2:11–14 is unquestionably the famous Syrian city located on the Orontes River, which was the third largest city of the Roman Empire at that time, after Rome and Alexandria. To appreciate more fully Paul's account, it is necessary, therefore, to know something about the history and circumstances of this famous city, particularly (1) its history under first the Seleucids and then the Romans, and (2) the circumstances of both Jews and Christians in this great metropolis.

Excursus: Antioch on the Orontes

Antioch of Syria was founded about 300 B.C. by Seleucus I Nicator ("The Conqueror"), who named it after either his father or his son, both of whom bore the name Antiochus. It was situated at the foot of Mt. Silpius on the Orontes River about three hundred miles north of Jerusalem and twenty miles east of the Mediterranean at the joining of the Lebanon and Taurus mountain ranges where the Orontes breaks through and flows down to the sea. To distinguish it from fifteen other Asiatic cities built by Seleucus and also named Antioch, it was commonly called "Antioch on the Orontes"—also "Antioch the Great," or "Antioch the Beautiful," or "Antioch by Daphne" (alluding to its celebrated suburb five miles to the south). Because of its strategic location, political importance, and great beauty, it was frequently given the epithet "Fair Crown of the Orient" or "The Queen of the East." During the first century it was, after Rome and Alexandria, the third largest city of the Roman Empire, with a population of over 500,000. In A.D. 540 after a catastrophic fire (A.D. 525) and two major earthquakes (A.D. 526 and 528) in which over 360,000 of its inhabitants perished, Antioch was sacked by the Persians, who took most of the remaining people to Mesopotamia as slaves. Those who remained suffered the terrible plague of A.D. 542. By the time the Arabs captured it in A.D. 637, Antioch was not much more than a frontier fortress. Today Antakiya (Antioch) is a sleepy, rather dingy town of about 35,000 inhabitants, part Turkish and part Arab.

Seleucid Antioch

After defeating his rival Antigonus at the battle of Ipsus in 301 B.C., and thereby winning full control of Syria for himself, Seleucus founded four "sister cities" in northwestern Syria: Antioch and its port city Seleucia Pieria; Apamea and its port city Laodicea of the Sea. These cities were founded in order to play a primary role in the subjugation of the conquered territory and were settled by Macedonians and Greeks in order to assure the transplantation of Greek culture onto Semitic soil. Seleucia

Pieria, named for Seleucus himself, was built first and was originally meant to be the capital city of the Seleucids because of its highly defensible position. Before long, however, principally because of its better location on the inland trade routes, Antioch eclipsed Seleucia Pieria in importance, as it did also the other cities of the Seleukis (i.e., the quadruplet of cities founded by Seleucus in northwestern Syria). Soon after Seleucus' death in 280 B.C., Antiochus I Soter (280–261 B.C.), his son, established Antioch as the Seleucid royal city and capital.

Seleucid Antioch was built by the architect Xenarius, with elephants from Seleucus' army stationed to mark the location of towers in the city wall and wheat used to lay out the streets. The city was laid out in an oblong plan of about 555 acres (slightly less than a square mile) between the river to the west and the main trade route to the east, being set far enough away from Mt. Silpius (farther to the east) so as not to be inundated by sediment and gravel brought down from the mountain by the winter rains. Like many other Greek cities, Seleucid Antioch was constructed on the Hippodamus plan, with streets crossing each other at right angles and buildings placed in the rectangles formed by the streets. The city was laid out to make the best use of the sun in both winter and summer, and so that the winds that blew up the Orontes valley from the sea could penetrate all its sections. The *agora*, or market, was situated along the east side of the river and probably was about eight city blocks in size. A citadel for protection was located to the east at the top of Mt. Silpius.

Five miles to the south on an elevated plateau with flowing springs and lush vegetation was the small town of Daphne. Though it was located on a site too small for a city, Daphne's amenities attracted many residents and visitors, and it soon became a flourishing suburb of Antioch. Royalty spent their summers at Daphne, enjoying its scenery, cool air, and clear, clean water. The wealthy built villas, private baths, and pleasure houses there. The famous Temple of Apollo was erected in the most beautiful part of Daphne, near the constantly flowing springs that were diverted into two streams around the shrine. Ordinary people took their pleasures in the precincts of the Temple of Apollo, in the public baths, and in the restaurants and colonnades where refreshment and entertainment were provided. There was also a large and fine theater located on the western slope of the Daphne plateau, which was built to take advantage of the contours of the land.

The original population of Antioch was made up of retired Macedonian soldiers of Seleucus' army, of Athenians who had been transferred from Antigonia (Antigonus's capital) and resettled at Antioch, of Jews who had served as mercenaries in the Seleucid army, and of slaves of diverse origins. In addition, there were native Syrians who were assigned a separate section in the city. Altogether, from various records and the excavations conducted from 1932–39, it seems fair to say that the free population of Antioch during its early Seleucid days numbered somewhere between 17,000 and 25,000—plus slaves and native Syrians, who were not counted.

Antiochus I enlarged Antioch to include a sizable second quarter east of the main trade route and up to the base of Mt. Silpius, a new section which he protected from the wash down the mountain by diverting the waters around the city. After his death, the Ptolemies of Egypt controlled northern Syria and the city of Antioch for about two decades. Taking the city back again, Seleucus II Callinicus (246–226 B.C.) enlarged Antioch by building a third quarter northwest of the existing city on a large island in the middle of the Orontes River (the island was completely wiped away by the earthquakes of the sixth century A.D.). The greed of Antiochus III "the Great" (223–187 B.C.), however, brought him into conflict with Rome, with the result that he was defeated at the battle of Magnesia (190 B.C.) and lost all of his empire beyond the Taurus range to the Romans or to kingdoms allied with the Romans (like Pergamum). This was a turning point in the history of the Seleucid empire, though not the end of the fame and fortunes of Antioch.

Antiochus IV Epiphanes (176–163 B.C.) was the last of the great Seleucid rulers. Under his reign the broad slope of Mt. Silpius became the fourth and main quarter of the city, meriting the title "Tetrapolis" or "Fourth City." In this new section of the city Antiochus IV built a new senate house and several new temples. After Antiochus IV, however, bloody internal struggles for the throne exhausted the economy of the Seleucids, and Antioch never regained its former splendor until the Romans came.

Roman Antioch

In 64 B.C. Pompey put an end to the Seleucid dynasty and annexed Syria to the Roman empire. And Antioch, because of its location on the most important trade routes, served as the capital of the Roman province of Syria throughout its history as a Roman city, except for a brief period when it fell out of favor with Septimius Severus (A.D. 193–211). Under Rome the city gained new vigor. Soon it came to reflect in its life, thought, and physical appearance the quintessence of Roman splendor, power, and pettiness. Greek institutions continued to exist, but they were now under Roman control and gradually transformed to serve Roman ends.

In the civil war between Julius Caesar and the Roman Senate that began in 49 B.C., Antioch sided with Caesar and rebuffed Pompey after his defeat at Pharsalus in 48 B.C. In 47 B.C. Caesar visited Antioch and conferred on it freedom (presumably in terms greater than the "freedom" previously conferred by Pompey). He also rewarded the city by restoring its Greek Pantheon and by building a new theater, amphitheater, aqueduct, and public bath. To cap off his building projects at Antioch, Julius Caesar also ordered the construction of a splendid basilica, which he called after his own surname the Caesareum. The imperial favor shown by Caesar continued under other Roman emperors as well, with each succeeding emperor (with a few exceptions) adding to the magnificence and beauty of the city. Particularly under Augustus (31 B.C.–A.D. 14) and Tiberius (A.D. 14–37), with the cooperation of Herod the Great and Agrippa I, the city was transformed into one of the most splendid and imposing cities of antiquity.

Probably the most noteworthy architectural feature of first-century Antioch was the great colonnaded street which ran northeast to southwest along the line of an earlier Seleucid street and formed the main street of the Roman city. It was two miles long, about 31 feet wide, and had flanking porticoes that were each about 32 feet wide. Its more than 3,200 columns supported the porticoes on each side and the vaulted stone roofs at each intersection, with these structures being highly ornamented. The surface of the road was paved with marble. Some of the porticoes led to the entrances of public buildings; some to homes of the wealthy. Others protected shoppers and a variety of merchants whose booths were set up between the columns. There was, in fact, no other city in the world where one could walk for two miles in such splendor under porticoes.

A major event begun at Antioch under Augustus was the founding of the local Olympic Games, which in time became one of the most famous festivals of the Roman world. At first the games were held every four years for thirty days during the month of October and were not specifically called Olympic Games. Later, after falling into disrepute through mismanagement, they were reorganized by Claudius (A.D. 41–54) to include theatrical, dramatic, and musical events, in addition to the athletic contests and races in the hippodrome. Under Claudius they became known as the Olympic Games (in continuity with the earlier Greek Olympic Games) and were held every five years, though later, because of wars, earthquakes, fires, or other public calamities, they were sometimes held at intervals of fifteen or twenty years.

Antioch was visited by almost everyone of prominence in their day, with many Roman nobles and their families living at one time or another in the city or its elegant suburb Daphne. Mark Anthony and Cleopatra, for instance, were probably married at

Antioch and spent their first winter there. The city was also noted for its philosophers, the most famous of whom was Libanius (A.D. 314–93) who taught in Antioch during the last forty years of his life and included among his students such later Christian leaders as Basil the Great, John Chrysostom, Theodore of Mopsuestia, and Gregory of Nazianzus. The city, however, was not only known for its grandeur, sophistication, and culture, but also for its vices. The beautiful pleasure park at Daphne was a center for moral depravity of every kind, and the expression *Daphnici mores,* "Daphnean customs," became a proverb for depraved living. The Roman satirist Juvenal (A.D. 60–140) aimed one of his sharpest gibes at his own decadent Rome when he said that the Orontes had flowed into the Tiber (*Satirae* 3.62), meaning by that that Rome had become flooded by the superstition and immorality of the East.

Jews at Antioch

Jews were among the original settlers in the city founded by Seleucus I about 300 B.C. Antioch's proximity to Palestine, its importance as the administrative center of so much of the Orient, and its commercial prosperity made it attractive to many Jews. For most of the Seleucid period Jews at Antioch seem to have been free to follow their own customs and to carry on their own affairs without governmental interference. Only during the reign of Antiochus IV Epiphanes, when repressions in Palestine seriously affected Jews in Syria as well, was the peace and tranquillity of the Jewish population in Antioch broken. Generally, however, under the Seleucid monarchs the Jewish community at Antioch grew and prospered.

Josephus summarizes the situation of Jews at Antioch during the first century as follows:

> The Jewish race, densely interspersed among the native populations of every portion of the world, is particularly numerous in Syria, where intermingling is due to the proximity of the two countries. But it was at Antioch that they especially congregated, partly owing to the greatness of that city, but mainly because the successors of King Antiochus [i.e., Antiochus I Soter] had enabled them to live there in security. For, although Antiochus surnamed Epiphanes sacked Jerusalem, and plundered the temple, his successors on the throne restored to the Jews of Antioch all such votive offerings as were made of brass, to be laid up in their synagogue, and, moreover, granted them citizen rights on an equality with the Greeks. Continuing to receive similar treatment from later monarchs, the Jewish colony grew in numbers, and their richly designed and costly offerings formed a splendid ornament to the temple. Moreover, they were constantly attracting to their religious ceremonies multitudes of Greeks, and these they had in some measure incorporated with themselves (*J. W.* 7.43–45, tr. H. St. J. Thackeray, LCL).

Rome's capture of Antioch in 64 B.C. did little to diminish the economic and social status of Jews in the city. Rather, in many ways it proved highly beneficial, at least for the next one hundred years. In the first century of Roman domination, in fact, the Jewish community of Antioch reached its greatest numerical strength, numbering somewhere around 65,000 or about one-seventh of the city's entire population. Few Jews, however, except for some mercenaries discharged from the Roman army and a few merchants, were Roman citizens, for that usually required sacrificing their Jewish religious and national identity. So as foreigners and a distinguishable minority they lived in three or more separate settlements in and around the city. Probably one such settlement was to the southwest of the city, near Daphne; another, northeast of the city in the Plain of Antioch; a third, in the city proper; with smaller enclaves possibly elsewhere.

There may not have been genuine legal equality between Jews and their Gentile neighbors at Antioch. Yet Rome for purposes of its own encouraged a state of toleration between various peoples of unequal station. So it was that there were no strong antagonistic feelings on the part of Greeks and Romans against Jews at Antioch during the first century or so of Roman rule. Likewise, the Jews of Antioch seem not to have been split into rival parties as they were in Palestine or antagonistic to Gentiles as they were in Jerusalem. As relatively wealthy inhabitants of a foreign land, who possessed almost all of the privileges of full citizenship, they were cooperative with their Gentile neighbors and willing to compromise with the Roman authorities. Many Gentiles, in fact, became attracted to the monotheism and ethics of Judaism, and so attended its synagogues as "God Fearers" or "Proselytes of the Gate."

The period of acceptance and prosperity that Antiochene Jews enjoyed, however, came to an end toward the middle of the first century. In A.D. 40, mobs were organized in Antioch to attack the Jews; they burned their synagogues and killed many of them. This took place in the third year of the reign of Caligula (A.D. 37–41), who in the winter of A.D. 39–40 had ordered a statue of himself erected in the temple precincts of Jerusalem. So while details of this mob action at Antioch are obscure, it seems safe to posit that such action should be seen in the context of Caligula's totally insane program of self-aggrandisement and antagonism against Jews generally (as also at Alexandria and Jerusalem), which Claudius (A.D. 41–54), on becoming emperor, put an end to.

The greatest crisis for Jews at Antioch, however, came during the Palestinian Jewish revolt against Rome in A.D. 66–70. Josephus tells us that although there were massacres of Jews throughout Syria in reprisal, the Jews of Antioch, Sidon, and Apamea were at first shielded to a great extent from the people's rage by the Roman authorities. But this did not last for long, for shortly after Vespasian's arrival in Syria, a Jew named Antiochus, who was the son of the leader of the Jewish community and who evidently thought of himself as no longer Jewish, turned the pagan population of Antioch against the Jews with a story of how the Jews were planning to burn the city down to the ground in one night. As a result, an intense persecution of Jews broke out, with Jewish leaders burned to death in the theater, sabbath privileges revoked, demands made on Jews to sacrifice to pagan deities, and wholesale massacres. Added to all this, a fire of extensive proportions did, indeed, break out in Antioch during the winter of A.D. 69–70, which, of course, was immediately blamed on the city's Jews, and so became the occasion for further persecutions and massacres.

The rage of the city's pagan population against Jews during the latter 60s was largely unchecked, since during these years there was no resident governor and no effective garrison at Antioch. Vespasian had sent Mucianus, the governor of Syria from A.D. 67 to 69, off with an army to the west to oppose Vitellius; Titus was in Caesarea making preparations for the siege of Jerusalem; and Vespasian himself was in Alexandria. With the arrival of Caesennius Paetus as governor of Syria in A.D. 70, however, the persecutions were halted and the Jews' legal rights restored. Yet the civic standing of Jews at Antioch was no longer what it had been, and thereafter the Jewish role in the life of the city was greatly diminished.

Jews at Antioch were further discredited by the imposition of the *fiscus Iudaicus* (Jewish poll tax) of Domitian (A.D. 81–96) and the decrees of Hadrian (A.D. 96–138) penalizing circumcision. They were also seriously affected by the active interests of Domitian, Hadrian, and their successors in prosecuting charges of "atheism" against all infidels and monotheists, which, of course, effectively put an end to Jewish proselytism and so severed the strongest tie existing between Jews and pagans. To shame the Jews further, Hadrian erected over a western gate of Antioch the Cherubim that had been taken from the Jerusalem temple in A.D. 70. Thus while they continued to live in the city and their legal status remained officially unchanged, the civil status of Jews in Antioch after the Palestinian uprisings of A.D. 66–70 (and again those of A.D. 132–35) was considerably lowered—almost, in fact, to the point of insignificance. Thereafter when the pagans of Antioch needed a scapegoat for their disaffections, they turned on the Christians.

Christians at Antioch

Apart from Jerusalem, no city of the Roman Empire played as large a part in the early life and fortunes of the Christian church as Antioch of Syria. The Acts of the Apostles tells us that it was Hellenistic Jewish Christians who, on fleeing Jerusalem, first brought the gospel to Antioch, preaching first only to Jews, but soon including Gentiles within their outreach as well. With the increase of believers at Antioch, the Jerusalem church sent Barnabas to check on the situation. And it was through his efforts, Acts tells us, that the Christian community at Antioch was joined to the Christian community at Jerusalem, thereby preventing any possible alienation or split because of Antioch Christendom's rather unusual beginnings. Furthermore, it was through Barnabas's efforts that Saul of Tarsus became involved in the ministry at Antioch.

First-century Antioch was a hotbed for various philosophies, cults, and religions. It was a city that prided itself on its toleration, with even its Jewish population more open to Gentiles than anywhere else in the Jewish diaspora (and certainly more open than in Palestine). Yet many Antiochenes were looking for a more significant religious experience and more meaning to life than paganism offered. Many Gentiles, in fact, were associated in one way or another with the Jewish synagogues of the city, being impressed by the monotheism and ethics of Judaism. So when the Christian gospel came to Antioch, it was received not only by Jews but also by Gentiles who had been mentally and spiritually prepared by Judaism.

A great number of people at Antioch, Acts tells us, accepted the gospel message and committed themselves to Jesus. Since, however, this group was made up of both Jews and Gentiles, the city's population had to find a name for them that would distinguish them from Jews and from all the devotees of the various pagan religions of the city. So they nicknamed them "Christians," which means literally "Christ Followers" or "People of Christ." And it is this name, rather than the earlier "Those of the Way," that stuck, simply because it was seen by the Christians themselves to be highly appropriate.

During a particularly severe famine that ravished Palestine in A.D. 45–47 (cf. Josephus, *Ant.* 20.51–53; possibly also *Ant.* 3.320–21)—with sporadic bad harvests and famine conditions occurring elsewhere throughout the empire during Claudius's reign (cf. Suetonius, *Vita Claudius* 18.2; also Tacitus, Dio Cassius, and Orosius)—the Christian community at Antioch, after only a year or so in existence, was strong enough and wealthy enough to send aid to Christians at Jerusalem in distress. Furthermore, it was the Christian community at Antioch that responded to God's call to send out missionaries to other Gentile cities, and so Antioch became the birthplace of the Church's foreign missions program. Throughout Paul's missionary journeys, it was Antioch, in fact, that was the apostle's home base. In addition, Antioch was the place where controversy between Jewish believers and Gentile believers first erupted within the Christian church (as we believe, following our "South Galatian" hypothesis), with that eruption being ultimately the occasion for the first ecumenical church council at Jerusalem.

Acts tells us nothing further about Antioch on the Orontes, for Luke's concern is with the forward movement of the Christian mission until it comes to Rome. That should not be taken, however, as suggesting that Antioch was no longer important as a Christian center. On the contrary, throughout the succeeding centuries Antioch played a significant role in the history of the Christian church (contra W. Bauer, *Orthodoxy and Heresy*, 63), and Antiochene Christianity was an important factor in the history of civilization within the Roman Empire. (For more on Christianity at Antioch during the succeeding centuries, see the latter part of my article "Antioch of Syria" in *Major Cities of the Biblical World*; also, more importantly, see the works by R. E. Brown and J. P. Meier, R. M. Grant, S. E. Johnson, W. S. McCullough, W. A. Meeks and R. L. Wilken, K. Pieper, and D. S. Wallace-Hadrill in the *Bibliography* above.)

Comment

11 ὅτε δὲ ἦλθεν Κηφᾶς εἰς Ἀντιόχειαν, "but when Cephas came to Antioch." The temporal particle ὅτε ("when") is indeterminate. Some have proposed that the episode of 2:11–14 should be seen as occurring historically before the events of 2:1–10, and that such a displacement of events is signaled by Paul's use of ὅτε rather than ἔπειτα as in 1:18, 21 and 2:1 (see above on *Form/Structure/Setting*). Most, however, take the Antioch episode as historically following the events described in 2:1–10, whether those verses be understood as Paul's version of the Jerusalem Council (so "North Galatianists") or his account of the earlier famine visit (so contemporary "South Galatianists"). In our view (see *Introduction*, lxvii–lxxxvii), the Antioch episode most likely took place *after* Paul and Barnabas returned to Syrian Antioch from their mission to Cyprus and southern Galatia as recorded by Luke in Acts 13:4–14:25, *during* the time when "they stayed there [at Antioch] a long time with the disciples" as told us in Acts 14:26–28, and *before* the Jerusalem Council of Acts 15:1–29. The postpositive δέ functions here both as a mild adversative and as a continuative particle, for it (1) signals a contrast between the unity of 2:7–10 and the confrontation of 2:11–14, yet also (2) continues the narrative as to Paul's nondependence on, but underlying agreement with, the Jerusalem apostles.

Clearly, Cephas's arrival at Antioch occurred before Paul's rebuke of him. Just when he came, however, whether before or after Paul and Barnabas first returned from southern Galatia, we are not told. Nor are we told why Cephas came to Antioch. There is a tradition dating from at least the third century that Peter was the first bishop of Antioch (cf. Origen, *Homily on Luke*, VI.C [*PG* 13:1814ff.]; Eusebius, *Eccl. Hist.* 3.22, 36; idem, *Chronicorum Canonum* on A.D. 44 ["Petros apostolus primus posuit fundamenta ecclesiae Antiochenae"]; Chrysostom, *Homily on Ignatius* [*PG* 50:591]; Jerome, *Epistulam ad Galatas* on Gal 2:1 [*PL* 26:340]; idem, *De viribus illustribus* [*PL* 23:637]). But that tradition, while polemically useful, is historically suspect. For though the Antioch church certainly began before Paul (cf. Acts 11:19–26) and had Jewish believers in it in Paul's day (else the Antioch episode would hardly have taken place), Acts views it as home base for Paul's Gentile outreach and the letters of Ignatius assume its Christianity to be Pauline in character. (W. Bauer, of course, disputed the portrayals of Antiochian Christianity in Acts and Ignatius, arguing instead for the earliest form of "Christianity" at Antioch as being a "Gnostic syncretism" [*Orthodoxy and Heresy*, 63–67]. But Bauer's treatment is tendentious.)

"When Cephas came to Antioch" implies a well-known visit of Cephas to the city—not a return of its first bishop, but a visit known to both Paul and his Galatian addressees. Jews frequently traveled between Jerusalem and Antioch (see C. H. Kraeling, *JBL* 51 [1932] 130–60), and Jewish Christians did likewise (see Acts 11:19–26, 30; 15:1–4, 22, 30; 18:22). Was, then, Cephas's visit something of an occasional visit? Was it a stopover on his way to somewhere else? Or was it where he went to escape persecution at Jerusalem (cf. Acts 12:17, "then he left [Jerusalem] for another place")? We just do not know, though by the way Paul alludes to the visit, we may believe that both Paul and his addressees did. (On Paul's habitual use of "Cephas," see 1:18; 2:9, 14. On his one use of "Peter" in all of his letters, see *Comment* at 2:7-8.)

Furthermore, while Luke tells us how the church at Antioch was founded (cf. Acts 11:20-26), we know very little about its character and nothing of its physical circumstances. Was it one congregation made up of both Jewish and Gentile believers? Were there two congregations, one Jewish and the other Gentile? Or were there a number of congregations meeting at various places in the city, some ethnically mixed and others not? The impression given by Paul is of one group composed of both Jews and Gentiles, and such an impression seems in line with what we know of Jewish-Gentile relations at Antioch at the time (see *Excursus* above, particularly "Jews at Antioch"). Yet it could just as well be that there were a number of groups of believers at Antioch, with some of mixed ethnic character and others not, and that what took place in one of the groups affected them all.

κατὰ πρόσωπον αὐτῷ ἀνέστην, "I opposed him to his face." The idiom κατὰ πρόσωπον ("to the face") does not of itself necessarily imply hostility, but only direct encounter (cf. Acts 25:16; 2 Cor 10:1). It is, rather, the verb ἀνέστην ("I stood against," "I opposed") that signals Paul's initiative and active opposition (cf. Mark 3:26; Acts 6:9). The object of his opposition is Cephas, whose conduct is described in v 12.

ὅτι κατεγνωσμένος ἦν, "because he stood condemned." Paul's judgment on Cephas's conduct is exceedingly severe: "he stood condemned" (so RSV). The verb καταγινώσκω means, as Ulrich Wilckens points out, "be condemned before God" (see *TDNT* 8:568 n. 51), and not just "be blamed" (KJV), "in the wrong" (JB, NEB, NIV), or even "self-condemned by the inconsistency of his own actions" (as Lightfoot, *Galatians*, 111; Burton, *Galatians*, 103; Bruce, *Galatians*, 129; et al.). Josephus regularly used καταγινώσκω to mean "condemned to death" before God or a tribunal (cf. esp. *J.W.* 1.635: "I stand condemned before God and before you . . . to die"; *J.W.* 7.154: "condemned to death"; *J.W.* 7.327: "doomed to perdition" [as Thackeray, LCL, translates it]). And that is exactly how the Ebionites understood the term when they used Gal 2:11 to attack Paul, placing in the mouth of Peter the retort: "You have opposed me as though I stood condemned [κατεγνωσμένος]. If, however, you call me condemned, you accuse God who revealed Christ to me" (*Ps.-Clem. Hom.* 17.19). The verb ἦν is an imperfect, which, joined to the perfect participle κατεγνωσμένος, reads like a pluperfect and heightens the idea of a past existing state.

12 πρὸ τοῦ γὰρ ἐλθεῖν τινας ἀπὸ Ἰακώβου μετὰ τῶν ἐθνῶν συνήσθιεν, "for before certain men came from James, he used to eat with Gentile believers." The explanatory conjunction γάρ ("for") signals that what follows gives the reason why Cephas, in Paul's view, stood condemned before God. The first half of v 12 (here commented on) sets the scene; the second half tells of Cephas's action and specifies why he acted as he did.

The masculine plural indefinite pronoun τινάς ("certain men") is well supported externally and much to be preferred internally. Probably the singular ἦλθεν ("he came") in the latter half of v 12 (see below) came about because of an early scribal error, and τινά a masculine singular ("a certain man") was then accommodated to it. "James" here is "James, the Lord's brother," who seems to have become the leading administrative figure in the Jerusalem church from sometime in the late 40s until his martyrdom in A.D. 62 (see *Comment* on James at 1:19 and 2:6-10).

Just who the "certain men from James" were, however, is a matter of some dispute. There is no evidence that they are to be equated with the "false brothers" of 2:4–5 or were Judaizers in the same sense as those who troubled the believers in Galatia (see *Introduction*, "The Identity of the Opponents"), though Paul seems to imply a parallel between their coming to Antioch and the Judaizers' arrival in Galatia. All that the evidence warrants is that a delegation from the Jerusalem church arrived at Antioch, probably sent by James to express certain practical concerns of Jerusalem believers regarding the expression of the Christian faith at Antioch, and that the arrival of these men and their statement of the Jerusalem church's concerns served to trigger Peter's withdrawal from table fellowship with Gentile believers at Antioch.

The articular τῶν ἐθνῶν here undoubtedly refers to "Gentile believers," as does τὰ ἔθνη of v 14b. The verb συνήσθιεν ("he used to eat") probably has in mind ordinary meals with Gentile believers (so Burton, *Galatians*, 104), though it may have reference to only the Lord's Supper (so Schlier, *Galater*, 83) or to both (so Bruce, *Galatians*, 129). The imperfect tense of the verb suggests that Cephas ate with Gentile believers repeatedly or habitually, and not just once—which is a picture consistent with what we know of him in Acts after he learns not to call anything that God has cleansed unclean (Acts 10:9–23) and during his visit with Cornelius at Caesarea (Acts 10:24–11:18).

ὅτε δὲ ἦλθον, ὑπέστελλεν καὶ ἀφώριζεν ἑαυτόν, φοβούμενος τοὺς ἐκ περιτομῆς, "when they arrived, however, he began to draw back and separate from them, because he was afraid of the Jews." The crux of Paul's account of what happened at Antioch appears here in the latter half of v 12: "When they came . . . he began to draw back and separate . . . because he was afraid of the Jews." And the *crux interpretum* is how one understands τοὺς ἐκ περιτομῆς whom Cephas feared. If one takes the preposition ἐκ to signal separation, then the expression means "converts *from* Judaism" (so Lightfoot, *Galatians*, 112). If, however, one takes it to signal standing or character—as in οἱ ἐκ πίστεως (cf. Gal 3:7, 9; Rom 3:26; 4:16) or οἱ ἐκ νόμου (cf. Gal 3:10; Rom 4:14)—then it means simply "the circumcised" or "the Jews" (so Burton, *Galatians*, 107–8). The latter is contextually preferable.

But taking περιτομή in this latter sense requires still further clarification, for a definition in terms of standing or character has a number of possibilities. Does it mean (1) Jewish Christians who held a particular partisan view of circumcision, i.e., the Judaizers; (2) Jewish Christians in a nonpartisan sense; (3) non-Christian Jews; or, though far less likely, (4) Gentile Christians enamored by Judaism who had taken on a Jewish perspective and lifestyle, either wholly or in part? The debate has been extensive and often highly convoluted (for representative views, see G. Dix, *Jew and Greek*, 43ff.; J. Munck, *Paul and the Salvation of Mankind*, 106–9; W. Schmithals, *Paul and James*, 66–68). We believe, however, that the most important data have to do with the way ἡ περιτομή is used in the immediately preceding episode of Paul's *narratio*, i.e., in 2:7–9, where it appears three times—once in contrast to ἡ ἀκροβυστία ("the uncircumcised") and twice in contradistinction to τὰ ἔθνη ("the Gentiles"). Certainly in 2:7–9 ἡ περιτομή refers simply to Jews and not to Jewish Christians or to Gentiles who had assumed Jewish ideas and ways. And that is how Paul usually, if not always, uses περιτομή in his letters, whether in an anarthrous or an articular fashion (see Rom 3:30; 4:9, 12; 15:8; Eph 2:11; Col 3:11; 4:11; Titus 1:10).

Most commentators have taken τοὺς ἐκ περιτομῆς whom Cephas feared as "manifestly those Jewish Christians who came from James" (so Burton, *Galatians*, 107, who, while translating περιτομή as "the circumcised" or "the Jews," goes on to assert that the term "is probably not used here as above [i.e., in 2:7–9]" because of "the presence of the article there and its omission here" [p. 108]—a distinction that cannot be supported by Paul's mixture of anarthrous and articular forms of περιτομή in Rom 3:30; 4:9, 12; 15:8; etc., all with reference to non-Christian Jews). On such a reading, the question arises: Why did Cephas fear a delegation from James and the Jerusalem church, when he himself was one of the "pillars" of that church? Were they Judaizers? Was James, who sent them, himself a Judaizer? Or if not Judaizers, did they represent some conservative faction within the Jerusalem church that frightened Cephas by threatening to break off fellowship with Antioch Christians if their counsel was not heeded—counsel having to do with the need for Gentile believers at Antioch to observe the fourfold decree of Acts 15:20–21, 28–29 (assuming a North Galatian provenance), or having to do with the extension of the Jerusalem church's authority over Antiochian Christianity, or having to do with Peter's sphere of apostolic authority even at Antioch, or some combination of the above? In such a scenario, Cephas's fear and withdrawal were theologically motivated, even though Paul called it hypocrisy. And in such a scenario, Cephas was, in fact, attempting to avert a break between the Jerusalem church and the community of believers at Antioch, even though Paul interpreted his action as doing just the opposite.

If, however, τοὺς ἐκ περιτομῆς means simply "Jews" in the sense of "non-Christian Jews," as we propose, then the scenario at Antioch works out differently. Accepting Robert Jewett's thesis that "Jewish Christians in Judea were stimulated by Zealot pressure into a nomistic campaign among their fellow Christians in the late forties and early fifties" (*NTS* 17 [1971] 205 [further on Jewett's thesis, see *Introduction*, xci–xciii, xciv]; cf. also the thrust of G. Dix, *Jew and Greek*), what seems to have concerned believers at Jerusalem vis-à-vis Gentile believers was the rising tide of Jewish nationalism in Palestine and its growing antagonism directed against any Jew who had Gentile sympathies or who associated with Gentile sympathizers. Such a concern seems to have been shared by all Jewish believers at Jerusalem—by James, Cephas, and John, the three "pillars" of that church; by the "false brothers" of Gal 2:4–5 who agitated for the circumcision of Titus; by the delegation from James to Antioch; and by the Judaizers who came to Galatia. Yet though they shared a common concern as to how their nation would respond to the gospel's Gentile outreach, there seem to have been distinct differences between Jerusalem believers as to how to express that concern. For the Jerusalem leaders and those standing with them, this was a matter of great practical concern and they tried to take measures to keep Gentile Christians from needlessly offending Jewish sensibilities, but they were not prepared to make Gentiles Jews (so the decision and decrees of the later Jerusalem Council of Acts 15:1–29). The "false brothers" referred to in Gal 2:4–5 and the Judaizers who invaded the churches of Galatia, however, turned this practical concern into a theological issue, and so tried to impose a Jewish lifestyle on all Gentile converts.

Taking, then, such a background for the problems Paul faced alike at Jerusalem, Antioch, and Galatia, we can understand better how Paul in Galatians can parallel, at least implicitly, the situations at Jerusalem (2:1–5) and Antioch (2:11–14) with that at Galatia, without, however, saying that they were identical. And building on such a background, we can posit a somewhat different scenario for the Antioch episode than is usually assumed: when the delegation from James came (ἦλθον) with this practical concern of how unrestricted table fellowship of Jews and Gentiles within the Christian community at Antioch would appear to non-Christian Jews of Palestine, Cephas began to draw back (ὑπέστελλεν) and to separate (ἀφώριζεν) from Gentile believers because he feared (φοβούμενος) the reaction of those more zealot-minded Jews and the effects of their antagonism toward the Jerusalem church in allowing Jewish believers at Antioch to fraternize with Gentiles.

The verb ὑποστέλλω ("draw back") with the reflexive pronoun ἑαυτοῦ ("oneself")—for ἑαυτόν is the object of both of the main verbs in the sentence—suggests a retreat or shrinking back due to caution (cf. Polybius 1.16.10; 7.17.1). The expression ἀφώριζεν ἑαυτόν ("he began to separate himself") probably derives from Jewish terminology for cultic separation from the "unclean" (cf. H. D. Betz, "2 Cor 6:14–7:1: An Anti-Pauline Fragment?" *JBL* 92 [1973] 96). The use of the imperfect tense here signals that Cephas's separation from Gentile believers was gradual and step by step, and not immediate on the arrival of the delegation from James.

The picture thus presented in v 12b is that of a misguided tactical maneuver made under pressure—the action of one whose convictions were proper, but who became confused under pressure, could not bring himself to express his true convictions, and so found himself retreating from what he knew to be right. Fearing the reaction of zealot-minded Jews and the difficulties they could make for the Jewish Christian mission when it was known back in Palestine that one of the "pillars" of the Jerusalem church ate with Gentiles at Antioch in an unrestricted manner, Cephas "began to draw back and separate himself" from Gentile believers. He had no theological difficulties with such table fellowship himself. But when confronted by the practical concerns of James and the delegation he sent, Cephas seems to have become confused. And in his endeavors to deal with this extremely important practical concern of the Jerusalem church, he took a course of action that, in effect, had dire theological consequences: that there could be no real fellowship between Jewish believers and Gentile believers in Jesus unless the latter observed the dietary laws of the former. Such a tenet, of course, would have serious implications for the proclamation of the gospel to Gentiles and for a doctrine of the oneness of the body of Christ. But Cephas seems not to have realized all of this at the time, being more conscious of the Jewish zealot pressures on the Jerusalem church and its mission to Jews.

13 καὶ συνυπεκρίθησαν αὐτῷ καὶ οἱ λοιποὶ Ἰουδαῖοι, "and the rest of the Jewish believers joined him in playing the hypocrite." "The rest of the Jews" [οἱ λοιποὶ Ἰουδαῖοι] clearly refers to the Jewish believers at Antioch. Whether they were really convinced by the logic of the case presented by the delegation from Jerusalem or simply conformed to their wishes out of deference to Cephas, there is no way of knowing for sure. Probably it was more the latter than the former. For as Antiochian Jews their relations with Gentiles were probably freer than those of Jerusalem Jews, and they would probably have felt less threatened by nationalistically minded Zealots than Palestinian Jews. Furthermore, as Jewish believers in Jesus, their practice, like that of Cephas, had been to fellowship with Gentile believers on a nonrestrictive basis. Now, however, with Cephas responding to the issues raised by the Jerusalem delegation as he did, they followed suit. They seem, like him, to have held proper convictions, but without having thought them out to any great extent, and so to have been confused with respect to the matters raised by the delegation from James. Thus they conformed to Cephas's course of action and "joined him in playing the hypocrite."

The verb ὑποκρίνομαι means literally "answer from under," and so "interpret," "explain," or simply "answer." It came to connote, however, the concealing of one's true character, thoughts, or feelings under a guise implying something quite different. Thus the noun ὑποκριτής in antiquity meant "actor." The compound συνυποκρίνομαι appears only here in the NT, though it is fairly common in both classical and Koine Greek meaning "join [someone] in hypocrisy" or "join [someone] in playing the hypocrite" (cf. Polybius 3.52.6; 3.92.5; etc.; Plutarch, *Marius* 14.8, 413A; 17.3, 415B; *Ep. Arist.* 267; Josephus, *J. W.* 1.569; 5.321).

ὥστε καὶ Βαρναβᾶς συναπήχθη αὐτῶν τῇ ὑποκρίσει, "so that even Barnabas was led astray by their hypocrisy." The conjunction ὥστε ("so that") introduces a result of what went on at Antioch that was particularly painful to Paul personally: "even Barnabas" became confused and took the same course of action. The pathos that reverberates in the expression καὶ Βαρναβᾶς ("even Barnabas") is gripping, for Barnabas had been Paul's advocate at Jerusalem (cf. Acts 9:26–28), mentor at Antioch (cf. Acts 11:25–30), and esteemed colleague in the evangelization of Cyprus and southern Galatia (cf. Acts 13:2–14:26). Barnabas, in fact, was the last person of whom such action would have been expected (on Barnabas, see *Comment* at 2:1; also 2:9). He certainly was in favor of the gospel going directly to Gentiles apart from any Jewish restrictions, as his past ministry clearly demonstrates. And on the basis of such a track record, who could doubt that he would stand with Paul on the matter raised at Syrian Antioch? Yet it seems somehow he too became confused, being torn between what he knew to be right and his sympathies for the plight of the Jerusalem church under Jewish nationalistic pressures. Thus Barnabas too capitulated, being "led astray by their hypocrisy."

The verb συναπάγω ("lead away/astray" or "carry off with") often appears in Koine Greek with a nuance of irrationality (cf. 1 Cor 12:2; 2 Peter 3:17; Josephus, *J. W.* 1.493; *Ant.* 18.344). Its use here suggests that it was irrational emotion that carried Barnabas away. The aorist passive συναπήχθη ("was led astray"), the instrumental dative τῇ ὑποκρίσει ("by hypocrisy"), and the possessive pronoun αὐτῶν ("their") all point to the fact that Paul credited Cephas and the other Jewish believers with being the agents of Barnabas's defection, and that he viewed Barnabas as only following along. Nevertheless, Barnabas did defect from what he knew to be right, and for Paul that was a blow of great personal magnitude. Though Barnabas later evidenced, at least in Paul's eyes, a similar irrational emotion in his desire to include John Mark again among the members of their missionary team (cf. Acts 15:36–39), it was this act of desertion at Antioch that seems to have rankled Paul the most. In effect, it put an end to their close association, probably causing Paul to speak somewhat reticently about Barnabas in Gal 2:1–10 and ultimately leading to their separation (Acts 15:39–41), even though the tone of Paul's reference to Barnabas in 1 Cor 9:6 (perhaps also 2 Cor 8:18–19) suggests that they remained friends (cf. R. J. Bauckham, *JSNT* 2 [1979] 61–70).

14 ἀλλ᾽ ὅτε εἶδον ὅτι οὐκ ὀρθοποδοῦσιν πρὸς τὴν ἀλήθειαν τοῦ εὐαγγελίου, "but when I saw that they were not acting in line with the truth of the gospel." The strong adversative ἀλλά ("but") signals that here in v 14 we have a direct contrast to what is narrated in vv 12–13. The aorist εἶδον ("I saw") coupled with the temporal particle ὅτε ("when")—particularly when contrasted with the imperfect verbs of v 12 ("he used to eat . . . he began to draw back . . . he began to separate")—suggests that it was only after the process of Jewish Christian withdrawal had gone on for some time that Paul intervened to confront Cephas directly. The question, of course, arises: Why did Paul allow such a process to go on for so long, whatever the length of time, before intervening? Was Paul himself unclear at first as to the implications involved, or perhaps unwilling to voice his opposition openly—or was he unable, for some reason, to speak freely? Or was Paul absent from Antioch during the early part of Cephas's visit, and only knew what was going on when he returned? The text simply does not tell us. The latter, however, seems more likely. For, as Burton points out, if the former were true then "Paul himself was involved only less deeply than Peter in the latter's confusion of thought and it is therefore hardly likely that he would have spoken in the words of sharp condemnation of Peter which he employs in v. 11 and in this verse" (*Galatians*, 110).

The verb ὀρθοποδέω is the basis for our English term "orthopedics" and means "walk straight or upright" (as opposed to limping), "go straight toward a goal," or "proceed on the right road" (cf. G. D. Kilpatrick, "Gal 2:14 ὀρθοποδοῦσιν," 269–74; see also C. H. Roberts, *JTS* 40 [1939] 55–56; J. G. Winter, *HTR* 34 [1941] 161–62, citing an occurrence in a third-century A.D. papyrus [No. 337] in the Michigan collection). In the present context it denotes upright, unwavering, sincere conduct, in contrast to the hypocritical, wavering, and more-or-less insincere course being followed by Cephas, the Jewish believers at Antioch, and Barnabas. The present tense of the phrase οὐκ ὀρθοποδοῦσιν describes matters at Antioch in terms of Paul's original perception: "they are not acting straightforwardly" (indirect discourse in Greek retains the form of the direct statement). The preposition πρός may mean either "in relation to" (so limiting the verb, as in Gal 6:10; 2 Cor 1:12; Col 4:5) or "in conformity with" (so extending the verb epexegetically, as in Luke 12:47; 2 Cor 5:10; Eph 3:4). Either way, the translation "in line with" is appropriate. The expression τὴν ἀλήθειαν τοῦ εὐαγγελίου ("the truth of the gospel") appears in Paul only here and at 2:5. It means "the Gospel in its integrity" (Lightfoot, *Galatians*, 107) or "the truth contained in, and so belonging to, the gospel" (Burton, *Galatians*, 86), which the Jewish Christian withdrawals at Antioch were perverting (see *Comment* at 2:5).

εἶπον τῷ Κηφᾷ ἔμπροσθεν πάντων, "I said to Cephas in the presence of them all." Paul was terribly disappointed over the withdrawal of the Antiochian Jewish believers from table fellowship with their Gentile colleagues. More than that, he was crushed by Barnabas's desertion. But his argument was really with Cephas, whose action as a leading apostle had precipitated all that transpired. So he confronted Cephas publicly (ἔμπροσθεν πάντων, "in the presence of them all") as well as directly (cf. v 11, "to his face"). (On Paul's habitual use of "Cephas," see 1:18; 2:9, 11; on his one use of "Peter" in all of his letters, see *Comment* at 2:7–8.)

The anarthrous form of πάντων ("all") suggests that Paul's rebuke of Cephas occurred before all the members of the Antioch church in open session (cf. 1 Cor 11:18; 14:23; 1 Tim 5:20) and not just before the Jewish believers referred to above. The aorist tense of the verb (εἶπον) alerts us to the fact that this confrontation took place at a certain specific time, i.e., it was not something that Paul by argumentation or advice gradually built up to.

Εἰ σὺ ᾽Ιουδαῖος ὑπάρχων ἐθνικῶς καὶ οὐχὶ ᾽Ιουδαϊκῶς ζῆς, πῶς τὰ ἔθνη ἀναγκάζεις ᾽Ιουδαΐζειν, "if you, a Jewish believer, can live like a Gentile and not like
a Jew, how can you compel Gentile believers to become Jews?" The protasis of the
sentence is cast in the form of a first class condition, which assumes the truth of
what is stated: Cephas, a Jewish believer in Jesus, lives like a Gentile and not like
a Jew. ᾽Ιουδαῖος is here contrasted with τὰ ἔθνη in the apodosis of the sentence,
with the context demanding that these terms be read as "a Jewish believer" and
"Gentile believers" respectively (cf. also τῶν ἐθνῶν of v 12). The terms ἐθνικῶς and
᾽Ιουδαϊκῶς refer to living according to Gentile and Jewish customs, particularly
here with respect to the observance of the Jewish dietary laws—the former
ignoring and the latter observing them. The present tenses of ὑπάρχων and ζῆς
point up Cephas's habit of life: as a Jewish believer in Jesus he "lived (regularly)
like a Gentile and not like a Jew." So the present tenses of the protasis imply that,
as Paul saw it, Cephas had not abandoned a nonlegal lifestyle on any permanent
basis, but only temporarily as a matter of expediency.

The apodosis of the sentence opens with the interrogative particle πῶς
("how"), which expresses all of the emotions of surprise, displeasure, and
agitation. The verb ἀναγκάζεις, being in the present tense, is certainly conative in
force, and so refers not to an accomplished result but to the intention or tendency
of Cephas's action ("how can you compel").

᾽Ιουδαΐζειν is probably the most crucial term of this sentence for an understanding of Paul's rebuke of Cephas. It does not appear anywhere else in the NT,
and it is not quite the same as ᾽Ιουδαϊκῶς ("to live like a Jew") of the sentence's
protasis, though obviously there must be some overlap of meaning. The term
appears elsewhere in roughly contemporary Greek writings, however, with the
meaning "to embrace the Jewish faith" or "to become a Jew." Josephus, for
example, writes that a Roman officer named Metilius promised Eleazar, his Jewish
captor, that he would "become a Jew" (᾽Ιουδαΐσειν, or "turn Jew" as Thackeray,
LCL, translates it), and so saved his life (J.W. 2.454; cf. Plutarch, Cicero 7.5, 864C;
Esth 8:17 LXX; Ignatius, Magn. 10.3; see also Josephus, J.W. 2.463). It seems, then,
that Paul's use of ᾽Ιουδαΐζειν must be read with a slightly more Jewish nuance than
his use of ᾽Ιουδαϊκῶς earlier, even though the terms may be considered generally
synonymous—i.e., "to become a Jew" rather than just "to live like a Jew."

In attempting to be considerate of the Jerusalem church in its existence under
zealot-nationalistic pressures, and so to preserve the integrity of the Jewish
Christian mission, Cephas had actually, even though inadvertently, destroyed the
integrity of Gentile Christians. Instead of treating them as true believers in Jesus
and full members of the Christian church, his action would have resulted in their
becoming converts to Judaism. Cephas's action, Paul points out, was inconsistent
with his own habitual practice. Worse than that, however, it was disastrous for the
cause of the gospel, for Gentile Christians would have had to become Jews for full
acceptance within the church.

Explanation

There is much we are not told in Paul's account of the Antioch episode, and
what Paul does give us is often quite allusive. We could wish, for example, that we
had parallel accounts from Peter and Barnabas, each with its author's own

perspective and rationale. Without such accounts, however, we are left to infer that behind their actions were concerns over rising Zealot pressures on the Jerusalem church and that what they did in withdrawing from fellowship with Gentile believers at Antioch was done for the sake of the gospel's outreach to Jews. Their motives, probably, were worthy, even though the course of action they took was confused. Paul, however, saw their withdrawals as not only confused but also hypocritical. More than that, such withdrawals were disastrous for the outreach of the gospel to Gentiles and for the unity of the Church. What he did was for the sake of the gospel's outreach to Gentiles and the oneness of all believers in Christ.

Yet the sharpness of Paul's public rebuke of Peter has always stood as a major problem for interpreters of the Antioch episode. Though in the right, did Paul have to be so quarrelsome, even vitriolic? Where in Paul's reaction is the spirit of Jesus, who said that quarrels between believers should be dealt with first privately and with the hope of winning over the other (cf. Matt 18:15ff.)? Or, for that matter, where in Paul's reaction can we find exemplified his own counsel regarding the restoration of others in a spirit of gentleness and humility (cf. Gal 6:1) or tolerance toward others in matters pertaining to culture and secondary concerns (cf. 1 Cor 9:19–23). Paul is certainly neither gentle nor tolerant in his confrontation of Peter here!

As something of a partial answer, it must simply be said that for Paul the issues raised at Antioch were not of the nature of *adiaphora* ("matters of secondary importance"). They might have been more cultural and strategic of nature when voiced by the delegation from James. But Peter's withdrawal of fellowship turned them into matters of great theological import. And so Paul dealt with Peter's action not as an incidental or secondary difference between believers but as a direct threat to "the truth of the gospel," whether so intended by Peter or not. In the heat of confrontation, there may, of course, have been some overstatements on Paul's part (to sound somewhat like Tertullian, though without agreeing with him), e.g., the denunciation of Peter as "condemned (before God)" and the assertion that Peter's action would "compel Gentile believers to become Jews" (though history has shown the latter not to be too far beyond the range of possibility). In the main, however, Augustine seems to have been right in his interpretation of Gal 2:11–14: here is a case of the higher claims of truth over rank or office, and Peter was dreadfully wrong and Paul right in his rebuke and his defense of the gospel.

Yet while we may believe that Paul's case was right in the conflict at Antioch, we do not know how the situation was actually resolved in the church there. Paul tells us what he said to Peter (see also the discussion of 2:15–21 to follow), but he does not tell us how Peter, Barnabas, or the Antioch church reacted to what he said. If the matter had been amicably resolved by the time he wrote Galatians, we would have expected him to say so. Furthermore, it would have been a very significant point to make in his argument against the Galatian Judaizers to say that the outcome of the episode was that Peter recanted and the Antioch church as a whole supported him, but he does not. The omission of such statements in Paul's account has led many to conclude that actually Paul lost and Peter triumphed at Antioch (e.g., B. W. Bacon, *JR* 9 (1929) 204–23; H. Koester, *HTR* 58 [1965] 286; J. D. G. Dunn, *Unity*, 254; J. P. Meier, in Brown and Meier, *Antioch and Rome*, 39–40). It may very well have been the case that at the time Paul wrote Galatians the Antioch church was siding more or less with Peter rather than Paul, and so Paul could only report what he said and the logic of his case. But from the high regard evidenced for Paul in Acts and the letters of Ignatius, it is difficult to believe that such continued to be true for long.

The juxtaposition of Paul's accounts in 2:1–5 and 2:11–14 makes an obvious point: just as Paul withstood the pressures of the "false brothers" at Jerusalem, so Peter should have withstood those exerted by the delegation from James. There may have been a common practical concern behind such pressures. But to turn that concern into a theologically based call for Gentile Christians to practice a Jewish lifestyle was tantamount to a denial of the Christian gospel. Paul saw this clearly at Jerusalem; Peter should have seen it as well at Antioch. And the same is true for Gentile believers of Galatia.

C. The Proposition of Galatians (propositio) (2:15–21)

An examination of Gal 2:15–21 immediately presents at least three questions or problems. First, there is the question of the immediate context. What is the relation of this passage to Paul's confrontation with Peter in 2:11–14 and to the theological argumentation of 3:1ff.? Second, while the passage presents itself as a connected, logical argument, it is notoriously difficult to trace out its line of thought. And third, while it is obvious that very important theological themes are introduced in 2:15–21, the highly compressed language of the passage makes it difficult to determine precisely what is being affirmed.

Interpreters have long been uncertain regarding the function and placement of 2:15–21. Is it a summary of what Paul said to Peter at Antioch, and so to be taken as a part of the Antioch episode? Or is it a précis of Paul's theological argument to the Galatians, and so to be seen as an introduction to 3:1–4:11? Most modern scholars take a middle position and suggest something along the lines of Paul here addressing Peter formally and the Galatians materially—i.e., Paul begins with the personal occasion (*Individualgeschichte*) and moves on to universal principles (*Weltgeschichte*) (e.g., Lightfoot, *Galatians*, 113–14; Burton, *Galatians*, 117–18; Schlier, *Galater*, 87–88, 104; Bruce, *Galatians*, 136–37; cf. W. G. Kümmel, "'Individualgeschichte' und 'Weltgeschichte' in Galater 2, 15–21," in *Christ and Spirit in the New Testament*. FS C. F. D. Moule, ed. B. Lindars and S. S. Smalley [Cambridge: Cambridge University Press, 1973] 157–73, responding to G. Klein, "Individualgeschichte und Weltgeschichte bei Paulus," a 1963 article now included in his *Rekonstruktion und Interpretation: Gesammelte Aufsätze zum Neuen Testament* [BEvT 50; Munich: Kaiser, 1969] 180–224).

In our view, Hans Dieter Betz has gone a long way toward resolving this dilemma in proposing that 2:15–21 is in reality the *propositio* of Galatians, which "sums up the *narratio*'s material content" and "sets up the arguments to be discussed later in the *probatio*" (*Galatians*, 114). So it should not be considered just as part of Paul's speech to Peter, though it springs immediately from that, but as the summary of all that Paul has argued in 1:11–2:14 and as the introductory transition to 3:1–4:11.

Furthermore, as Betz argues, the line of thought in the *propositio* of 2:15–21 can be clarified by comparing what Paul says here with what Aristotle, Cicero, Quintilian, and other ancient rhetoricians (e.g., the anonymous author of *Rhetorica ad Herennium*) have said about the nature and function of a *propositio*. For example, the *Rhetorica ad Herennium* tells us that a *propositio* should have two parts, a statement of facts agreed on and a laying out of what remains contested (1.10.17; cf. Cicero, *De Inventione* 1.22.31). And most ancient rhetoricians have insisted that *brevitas* ("brevity"), *absolutio* ("completeness"), and *paucitas* ("conciseness") should characterize a *propositio* (so Cicero, *De Inventione* 1.22.32; *Rhetorica ad Herennium* 1.10.17; Quintilian, *Institutio Oratoria* 4.5.26–28).

Betz's thesis also gives guidance as to how the compressed language of Paul's *propositio* should be treated. For if the *probatio* contains the proofs or arguments introduced by the *propositio*, then we must look to Paul's *probatio* of 3:1–4:11 for an understanding of how to unpack the terms of the *propositio* of 2:15–21. It is, of course, in unpacking the compressed language of Paul's *propositio* that scholars differ with one another. Our differences with Betz in understanding exactly what Paul is saying in 2:15–21, for example, will be evident at various places in our exegetical comments. Nonetheless, Betz's treatment of 2:15–21 as the *propositio* of Galatians is highly significant, and it is this approach to the passage that we will take, at least in the main, in what follows.

Bibliography

Barth, M. "The Kerygma of Galatians." *Int* 21 (1967) 131–46. ———. "The Faith of the Messiah." *HeyJ* 10 (1969) 363–70. **Dunn, J. D. G.** "The New Perspective on Paul." *BJRL* 65 (1983) 95–122. ———. "Works of the Law and the Curse of the Law (Galatians 3.10–14)." *NTS* 31 (1985) 523–42. **Hays, R. B.** *The Faith of Jesus Christ*, 139–91. **Hooker, M. D.** "ΠΙΣΤΙΣ ΧΡΙΣΤΟΥ." *NTS* 35 (1989) 321–42. **Howard, G.** "Notes and Observations on the 'Faith of Christ.'" *HTR* 60 (1967) 459–65. ———. "The 'Faith of Christ.'" *ExpTim* 85 (1974) 212–15. ———. *Paul: Crisis in Galatia*, 46–65. **Hübner, H.** *Law in Paul's Thought*, 15–50. **Lambrecht, J.** "The Line of Thought in Gal. 2.14b–21." *NTS* 24 (1978) 484–95. **Longenecker, R. N.** *Paul, Apostle of Liberty*, 149–52. **Räisänen, H.** *Paul and the Law*. ———. "Galatians 2.16 and Paul's Break with Judaism." *NTS* 31 (1985) 543–53. **Sanders, E. P.** *Paul, the Law, and the Jewish People*, 17–27. **Tyson, J. B.** "'Works of Law' in Galatians." *JBL* 92 (1973) 423–31. **Westerholm, S.** *Israel's Law and the Church's Faith*, esp. Part Two, 105–222. **Ziesler, J. A.** *The Meaning of Righteousness in Paul*.

Translation

[15]*We who are Jews by birth and not "sinners of the Gentiles,"* [16]*and[a] who know that a person is not justified by the works of the law but only by the faithfulness of Jesus Christ, even we have believed in Christ Jesus in order that we might be justified on the basis of the faithfulness of Christ and not on the basis of the works of the law. Because on the basis of the works of the law shall no one be justified.*

[17]*But if, while we are seeking to be justified by Christ, we are found to be sinners, does that mean that Christ is a minister of sin? Absolutely not!* [18]*For if I build again those things that I destroyed, I show myself to be a lawbreaker.* [19]*For through the law I died to the law*

in order that I might live to God. I have been crucified with Christ. [20]No longer do I live, but Christ lives in me. And the life I now live in the body, I live by faith in the Son of God,[b] who loved[c] me and gave himself for me. [21]I do not nullify the grace of God. For if righteousness is through the law, then Christ died for nothing!

Notes

[a]The particle δέ is omitted in P[46] A TR syr[hel] cop. Nestle [26] doubts its authenticity, though probably it should be retained and treated as a simple conjunction without negative import.

[b]The expression υἱοῦ τοῦ θεοῦ ("Son of God") is well supported by אּ A C D[c] and almost all the versions and patristic witnesses, though θεοῦ καὶ Χριστοῦ ("God and Christ") receives support from P[46] B D* G it[d, g] M Vict Pel. The latter, however, never appears elsewhere in Paul as the object of a Christian's faith, and so on the basis of internal evidence must be judged an early scribal error.

[c]The reading ἀγοράσαντος ("who bought" or "redeemed") for ἀγαπήσαντος ("who loved") is supported by Marcion (so Tert) and Rufinus, but only by them. It may be derived from ἐξηγόρασεν "redeemed" of Gal 3:13.

Form/Structure/Setting

In a typical apologetic letter, the *narratio*, which follows the salutation, is the first major section. It is essentially a "brief, clear and plausible" statement of the facts that are relevant to the charge addressed in the apology (cf. Betz, *Galatians*, 58–62). The *probatio* is the most important part of an apologetic letter, for it contains the proofs or arguments designed to establish the credibility of the case (ibid., 128). Between the *narratio* and the *probatio* is the *propositio*. It contains two main parts: a statement of the points on which there is agreement and a statement of the points that are contested. These points are set out briefly, completely, and concisely (cf. ibid., 114). Finally there appears a concluding statement, which functions as the refutation of what has been charged (cf. ibid., 126).

While Galatians may not conform in its entirety to the genre of an apologetic letter (see *Introduction*, cviii–cxi), in its first two chapters and the opening part of its third chapter it does. In particular, 2:15–21 should be seen as Paul's *propositio* that "sums up the *narratio*'s material content" and "sets up the arguments to be discussed later in the *probatio*" (so Betz, *Galatians*, 114). The points of agreement are given in vv 15–16: no one is justified "on the basis of the works of the law," but only "on the basis of the faith/ faithfulness of [Jesus] Christ." The points of disagreement are set out in vv 17–20, first negatively and then positively. Negatively, Paul argues against (1) any charge that Christian freedom encourages libertinism, and (2) any attempt to put Christian living on a legal basis (vv 17–18). Positively, he insists that the Christian life is to be characterized by the axiom "Christ lives in me" (vv 19–20). Then in v 21 he presents a final statement meant to bring his whole argument to a conclusion: his gospel does not nullify God's grace, but focuses on "Christ crucified" for righteousness.

So then, in 2:15–21 Paul lays out two major arguments that he will later develop in 3:1–4:11. The first in vv 15–16, which he believes is agreed to by all true believers, is that the law plays no positive role in becoming a Christian (contra "legalism"). And this finds explication in 3:1–18, first by way of an appeal to his converts' experience (vv 1–5), then by the exegesis of certain crucial and debated passages of Scripture (vv 6–14), and finally by means of *ad hominem* theological arguments (vv 15–18). The second is in vv 17–20, where he argues that the law plays no positive role in Christian living (contra "nomism") but rather that the Christian life is lived "in Christ." And this finds explication in 3:19– 4:7, with expressions of Paul's concern for his Galatian converts appended in 4:8–11. Finally, there is in v 21 a direct statement refuting the charge made against Paul, with an added explanatory sentence that identifies the crux of the matter.

Thus rather than 2:15–21 being simply a continuation of Paul's rebuke of Peter that has in some way universal application, the passage should be viewed as the propositional statement of Galatians that then is unpacked in the arguments that follow. While often largely ignored in the exposition of Galatians, this passage in reality is not only the hinge between what has gone before and what follows but actually the central affirmation of the letter.

Comment

15 ἡμεῖς φύσει 'Ιουδαῖοι καὶ οὐκ ἐξ ἐθνῶν ἁμαρτωλοί, "we who are Jews by birth and not 'sinners of the Gentiles.'" Paul begins the *propositio* of Galatians by stating in vv 15–16 what he believes is assuredly held in common between himself and Jewish Christianity. In these two verses, in fact, we have what Betz calls "a 'self-definition' of Jewish Christians" (*Galatians*, 115)—first in terms of race (v 15) and then in terms of theological commitment (v 16).

The pronoun "we" (ἡμεῖς), like its pronominal counterpart and the verbal suffixes of v 16b, has in mind all Jewish Christians, whether at Jerusalem, Antioch, or Galatia. The use of φύσει (literally, "by nature") highlights the fact that Jewish Christians are defined first of all by the circumstance of birth: they are "Jews" ('Ιουδαῖοι). "Sinners of the Gentiles" (ἐξ ἐθνῶν ἁμαρτωλοί) seems to be a colloquialism used by Jews with reference to Gentiles (cf. *Jub.* 23.23–24; on "sinners" as a synonym for Gentiles, see Isa 14:5; 1 Macc 2:44; *Pss. Sol.* 1.1; 2.1; Matt 26:45; Luke 6:32–33). While the expression itself reflects a rising Jewish antagonism toward Gentiles, Paul's use here probably carries with it a note of irony (so Lightfoot, *Galatians*, 115).

16 εἰδότες δὲ ὅτι οὐ δικαιοῦται ἄνθρωπος ἐξ ἔργων νόμου ἐὰν μὴ διὰ πίστεως 'Ιησοῦ Χριστοῦ, "and who know that a person is not justified by the works of the law but only by the faithfulness of Jesus Christ." The postpositive δέ is one of the most commonly used Greek particles, which often sets up some contrast between clauses but also is used simply as a connective without contrast. Here it appears simply as a conjunction ("and"), merging with the participle it follows. The perfect participle εἰδότες functions as an adverbial participle of attendant circumstance ("circumstantial participle") and so adds an associated fact or conception to what was stated in v 15. It is best translated as a coordinate verb with καί ("and we know"). Its use here suggests that what follows is commonly held knowledge. In fact, the appearance of ὅτι, which is probably a ὅτι *recitativum*, signals that what follows could even be set in quotes as something widely affirmed. The use of ἄνθρωπος is indefinite, meaning simply "a person," "anyone," or "someone," as it does elsewhere in Galatians (cf. 1:10, 11, 12; 2:6; 3:15; 5:3; 6:1, 7; see also Rom 3:28; 1 Cor 4:1; 11:28).

The contracted conjunction ἐάν (the conditional εἰ and the particle ἄν) with the negative μή is properly exceptive in force (cf. 1:19), though it can at times be used in an adversative fashion (cf. 1 Cor 7:17; also Matt 12:4; Luke 4:26–27). As an exceptive, ἐὰν μή introduces a qualification either (1) to the whole preceding statement ("a person is not justified by the works of the law *except*... "), or (2) to its principal part ("a person is not justified *except*... "). The former is linguistically possible and has been read here by many (so, e.g., J. D. G. Dunn, *BJRL* 65 [1983] 112–13). It yields the idea that one *can be* justified by the works of the law (understood not as "good works" but simply as circumcision and the Jewish dietary laws) *if* these "badges of Jewish covenantal nomism" are accompanied by faith in Jesus the Messiah (cf. ibid.). Such a reading, however, is totally contrary to what Paul says elsewhere about the relation of faith and the law—even contrary to what he says in the latter half of this same verse (as acknowledged by Dunn, who rather lamely suggests that "in v 16 Paul pushes what began as a qualification on covenantal nomism into an outright antithesis," ibid., 113). So if ἐὰν μή is exceptive, the latter reading must be the case: "a person is not justified *except*...." Yet since in English "except" always is taken to qualify the whole of what precedes, we must here resort to some such paraphrastic translation as "but only" (so Burton, *Galatians*, 120–21) or read ἐὰν μή simply as an adversative (so H. Räisänen, *NTS* 31 [1985] 547), the former being preferable.

The really crucial features of v 16, however, have to do with four matters: (1) Paul's use of the δικαι- cluster of words, with the verb δικαιόω ("justify," "make righteous") appearing three times in this verse and once in v 17 and the noun δικαιοσύνη ("justification," "righteousness") taking center stage in the conclusion of v 21; (2) Paul's understanding of νόμος ("law"), which he contrasts in some manner with Jesus Christ; (3) what Paul means by ἔργων νόμου ("the works of the law"); and (4) what he means by πίστεως ᾽Ιησοῦ Χριστοῦ ("faith in Jesus Christ" or "the faith/faithfulness of Jesus Christ"). If, as we believe, 2:15–21 serves as the propositional statement of Galatians—and, further, if v 16 expresses what Paul and all Jewish believers held in common—then it becomes vitally important to have some appreciation of what Paul means by these terms and expressions. The language here, of course, is considerably compressed, requiring help from Paul's arguments in 3:1–4:11 to unpack its meaning. Yet, while reserving discussion of what Paul says in his *probatio* for later, some preliminary treatment of these four crucial matters is necessary here.

The history of discussion on Paul's use of the δικαι- cluster of words has been extensive and complex. Set out in broad terms, the question is: When Paul speaks of δικαιόω ("justify," "make righteous"), δικαιοσύνη ("justification," "righteousness") and δίκαιος ("just," "righteous") does he have in mind a status conferred (i.e., a declaratory, forensic relationship) or a quality of life lived (i.e., an effective, ethical renewal)? Traditionally, Roman Catholics have tended to lay stress on the noun (δικαιοσύνη) and the adjective (δίκαιος) and to interpret the verb (δικαιόω) by them, concluding that δικαιοσύνη means both acquittal from past sins and "a making righteous" in the full ethical sense—but that a final declaration of "righteousness" awaits the last judgment. Protestants, on the other hand, have laid stress on the verb (δικαιόω) as being forensic in character and so interpret the δικαι- cluster of words in terms of "a right relationship" (declaratory or "imputed") rather than "an ethical uprightness" (effective or "real"). Or to put the question in more modern form: Is Paul's use of the δικαι- cluster of words to be understood as "transfer terminology" (so E. P. Sanders, *Paul and Palestinian Judaism*, esp. 470–72; idem, *Paul, the Law, and the Jewish People*, passim) or as applicable to "the day-to-day conduct of those who had already believed" (so J. D. G. Dunn, *BJRL* 65 [1983] 121)?

In our judgment, J. A. Ziesler has largely resolved this dilemma in demonstrating that the verb δικαιόω in Paul's letters is used forensically and relationally, but that the noun δικαιοσύνη and adjective δίκαιος have also behavioral nuances—thereby showing how Paul joins forensic and ethical categories in his understanding of righteousness, with the one always involving the other (see his *The Meaning of Righteousness in Paul*). And this convergence of categories appears as well in the *propositio* of Gal 2:15–21. For while the aorist ἐπιστεύσαμεν ("we have believed") of v 16 refers to a once-for-all response that results in a transfer of status (cf. ἵνα δικαιωθῶμεν), the four uses of the verb in vv 16–17 and the noun in v 21 cannot be treated as simply "transfer terms" when the issue at both Antioch and Galatia had to do with the lifestyle of those who were already believers in Jesus. So here in 2:15–21, as well as throughout Galatians (and Paul's other letters), we must treat the δικαι- cluster of words as having both forensic and ethical significance, though, as will be argued later, over all such terms stands the relational, participatory concept of being "in Christ."

The second of the four above-mentioned crucial features of v 16, that of Paul's understanding of the law, has also been extensively and variously debated. Indeed, there are a number of places where the law is extolled in the Pauline letters (e.g., Rom 7:12, "the law is holy, and the commandment holy, righteous, and good"; Rom 7:14, "the law is spiritual"; 1 Tim 1:8, "the law is good if one uses it properly"). In such passages Paul seems to be referring to the Mosaic law in its function as the *revelational standard* of God. There are many other places, however, where Paul depreciates and even attacks the law, setting it in antithesis to the work of Christ. And that is how he speaks of it here in v 16, contrasting Christ ("Jesus Christ" or "Christ Jesus") to it. In this sense, Paul seems to have in mind the Mosaic law as a *religious system* associated in some manner with righteousness (cf. *Comment* on 3:19ff. regarding the purposes and functions of the law).

The watershed in all discussions regarding Paul and the law has to do with Paul's view of the Mosaic law as a religious system. And the principal question here is: Is Paul's polemic directed against the law itself or against a particular attitude toward the law that sees the law as a means of winning favor with God (i.e., "legalism")? The Alexandrian fathers and the Antiochian fathers found themselves on opposite sides of this question (see *Introduction*, pp. xlvi–lii). And it continues to be a question that divides scholarship today (for presentations arguing that Paul opposed legalism and not the law per se, see, e.g., C. E. B. Cranfield, *SJT* 17 (1964) 43–68; C. F. D. Moule, "Obligation in the Ethic of Paul," 389–406 [though see Moule's retraction cited below]; D. P. Fuller, *Gospel and Law: Contrast or Continuum?*; F. F. Bruce, *Galatians*, 137–39; and (basically) J. D. G. Dunn, *BJRL* 65 [1983] 103–18; for presentations arguing that Paul directed his attack in some manner against the law itself, see, e.g., C. A. A. Scott, *Christianity According to St. Paul*, 41–6; C. F. D. Moule, *NTS* 14 (1968) 293–320 [which is Moule's retraction of his earlier view]; R. Bring, *Christus und das Gesetz*; J. C. Beker, *Paul the Apostle*, 235–54; H. Räisänen, *Paul and the Law*; and S. Westerholm, *Israel's Law and the Church's Faith*). My own understanding of Paul at this point is that Paul directs his attack not just against legalism, which the Old Testament prophets and a number of rabbis of Judaism denounced as well, but against even the Mosaic religious system, for he saw all of that as preparatory for and superseded by the relationship of being "in Christ." I must, however, leave the defense of such a position for my comments on the *probatio* of 3:1– 4:11, for that is where Paul deals specifically and at length with the Mosaic law vis-à-vis faith in Christ.

But what does Paul mean by the expression "the works of the law" (ἔργων νόμου)? Does he mean "good works" in the sense of mankind's striving for self-achievement apart from God—i.e., a person's attempt to have something worthy to present before God that he can call his own? Or does he mean observances of the Mosaic law that seek to earn God's favor? Or is his reference more restricted and less prejudicial to mean simply the distinctive Jewish identity markers of circumcision, dietary regulations, and sabbath observance, which were viewed more as "badges of Jewish covenantal nomism" than meritorious acts?

To be sure, as E. P. Sanders has rightly reminded us (cf. his *Paul and Palestinian Judaism*, Part One: "Palestinian Judaism," 33– 428), the "covenantal nomism" of first-century Judaism understood Torah observance not as merit-amassing, but as a gladsome response to a loving God who had acted on his people's behalf and who asked that they in turn identify themselves as his people by keeping his ordinances (see also my *Paul, Apostle of Liberty*, Chap. 3: "The Piety of Hebraic Judaism," 65–85). First-century Judaism was not fundamentally legalistic. Even Josephus, whose piety may at times be suspect, asserts in recounting Solomon's prayer that "it is not possible for men to return thanks to God by means of works [ἔργοις], for the Deity stands in need of nothing and is above any such recompense" (*Ant.* 8.111). And it is just such an understanding that Paul builds on in 2:16 when he says with confidence that "Jews by birth . . . know that a person is not justified by the works of the law." As Jewish Christians, of course, James, Peter, and other Jews had also come to believe in Jesus as Israel's promised Messiah. So they were able to blend their Jewish convictions regarding the nature of faith and their Christian convictions as to the content of faith in a complementary fashion.

Yet while not "legalistic" (i.e., attempting to gain favor with God by means of Torah observance), first-century Jewish Christians were certainly "nomistic" (i.e., expressing their Christian convictions in their lifestyle in ways compatible with Jewish traditions). Complementary relations between their Jewish identity and their Christian convictions were what they appreciated and wanted to continue. When, however, such a nomistic stance was foisted on Gentile Christians— whether consciously as in the Judaizers' activities or inadvertently by Peter's withdrawal from table fellowship—relations between the Mosaic law and the message of the gospel became antithetical, with legalism the result. So Paul here in 2:16 uses ἔργων νόμου not just to refer to "the badges of Jewish covenantal nomism," though that may have been how other Jewish believers thought of them, but as a catch phrase to signal the whole legalistic complex of ideas having to do with winning God's favor by a merit-amassing observance of Torah. Paul takes pains to point out, however, that such a legalistic use of the Mosaic law was not a tenet of true Jews, whether Jewish Christians or (by implication) non-Christian Jews (cf. E. P. Sanders, *Paul and Palestinian Judaism*, 519: "the general conception that one is saved by faith was completely common in early Christianity"; see also J. Jeremias, *The Central Message of the New Testament*, 70). And on this, Paul believes, he and all other Jewish believers in Jesus are in agreement.

The fourth of the above-mentioned crucial features of v 16, that regarding what Paul means by πίστεως (or πίστις in the nominative) 'Ιησοῦ Χριστοῦ, has been, particularly of late, a hotly debated issue. The generally accepted view has been that 'Ιησοῦ Χριστοῦ is assuredly an objective genitive, and so the expression must be read as "faith in Jesus Christ" (e.g., Burton, Galatians, 121, considered it "too clear to be questioned"; C. E. B. Cranfield, The Epistle to the Romans [ICC; Edinburgh: T. & T. Clark, 1975], 1:203 n. 2, calls the suggestion that it is a subjective genitive "altogether unconvincing"; Betz, Galatians, 118, speaks of a subjective genitive understanding as ambiguous and false). Nevertheless, a number of scholars have argued that πίστις 'Ιησοῦ Χριστοῦ should be read as a subjective genitival expression referring to the "faith or faithfulness of Jesus Christ" (so J. Haussleiter, Der Glaube Jesu Christi und der christliche Glaube; idem, "Was versteht Paulus unter christlichen Glauben?" in Theologische Abhandlungen, FS H. Cremer [Gütersloh: Bertelsmann, 1895] 159–81; G. Kittel, TSK 79 [1906] 419–36; K. Barth, The Epistle to the Romans, tr. E. C. Hoskyns [New York: Oxford, 1933] 41, 96; A. G. Hebert, Th 58 [1955] 373–79; T. F. Torrance, ExpTim 68 [1957] 111–14; E. Fuchs, "Jesu und der Glaube," ZTK 55 [1958] 170–85; P. Vallotton, Le Christ et la foi: Etude de theologie biblique [Geneva: Labor et Fides, 1960], 41–144; R. N. Longenecker, Paul, Apostle of Liberty, 149–52; H. Ljungmann, Pistis, 38–40; G. M. Taylor, JBL 85 [1966] 58–76; K. Kertelge, Rechtfertigung bei Paulus [Münster: Aschendorff, 1967] 162–66; J. Bligh, "Did Jesus Live by Faith?" Hey J 9 [1968] 418–19; M. Barth, Hey J 10 [1969] 363–70; G. E. Howard, HTR 60 [1967] 459–65; D. W. B. Robinson, RTR 29 [1970] 71–81; H. Lührmann, "Pistis in Judentum," ZNW 64 [1973] 28; R. N. Longenecker, "The Obedience of Christ in the Theology of the Early Church," in Reconciliation and Hope. FS L. L. Morris, ed. R. Banks [Exeter: Paternoster, 1974] 142–52; G. E. Howard, ExpTim 85 [1974] 212–15; M. Barth, Ephesians, 2 vols. [AB; Garden City, NY: Doubleday, 1974] esp. 1:224, 347; G. E. Howard, Paul: Crisis in Galatia, esp. 57–59, 95 n. 191; and lately M. D. Hooker, NTS 35 [1989] 321–42).

The expression πίστις 'Ιησοῦ Χριστοῦ appears in Paul's letters only seven times (in addition to twice here at 2:16, see Gal 3:22 [also 3:26 in P⁴⁶]; Rom 3:22, 26; Eph 3:12; Phil 3:9). It is admittedly a difficult expression. But when πίστις is understood in terms of the Hebrew term אֱמוּנָה, ʾĕmûnâ, which means both "faith" and "faithfulness," then it is not too difficult to view Paul as using πίστις 'Ιησοῦ Χριστοῦ much as he uses πίστις τοῦ θεοῦ ("the faithfulness of God") in Rom 3:3 and πίστις 'Αβραάμ ("the faith of Abraham") in Rom 4:16 (so even the KJV reads "the faith of Jesus Christ" and "the faith of Christ" here at 2:16, and treats Gal 3:22, Rom 3:22, Eph 3:12, and Phil 3:9 similarly).

In effect, then, Paul uses πίστις 'Ιησοῦ Χριστοῦ in his writings to signal the basis for the Christian gospel: that its objective basis is the perfect response of obedience that Jesus rendered to God the Father, both actively in his life and passively in his death. Thus in three places by the use of πίστις 'Ιησοῦ Χριστοῦ Paul balances out nicely the objective basis for Christian faith ("the faith/faithfulness of Jesus Christ") and mankind's necessary subjective response ("by faith"): Rom 3:22, "this righteousness of God is διὰ πίστεως 'Ιησοῦ Χριστοῦ ('through the faith/faithfulness of Jesus Christ') εἰς πάντας τοὺς πιστεύοντας ('to all who believe')"; Gal 3:22, "so that the promise, ἐκ πίστεως 'Ιησοῦ Χριστοῦ ('which is based upon the faith/faithfulness of Jesus Christ') δοθῇ τοῖς πιστεύουσιν ('might be given to those who believe')"; and Phil 3:9, "a righteousness τὴν διὰ πίστεως Χριστοῦ ('that is based upon the faith/faithfulness of Christ') and τὴν ἐπὶ τῇ πίστει ('that depends upon faith')." These are not just redundancies in the Pauline vocabulary, as so often assumed, but Paul's attempts to set out both the objective and the subjective bases for the Christian life.

The prepositions ἐκ and διά are used interchangeably throughout v 16, as also in the other passages cited above—with ἐξ ἔργων νόμου and διὰ πίστεως ᾽Ιησοῦ Χριστοῦ appearing in the traditional formulation of v 16a, though only ἐκ in both cases thereafter. The contrast being made is between righteousness "based upon the works of the law" (ἐξ ἔργων νόμου) and righteousness "based upon the faith/ faithfulness of Jesus Christ" (διὰ/ἐκ πίστεως ᾽Ιησοῦ Χριστοῦ), which contextually and conceptually is probably best translated "the faithfulness of Jesus Christ." And on this point, too, Paul believes that he and all other Jewish Christians are agreed.

καὶ ἡμεῖς εἰς Χριστὸν ᾽Ιησοῦν ἐπιστεύσαμεν, ἵνα δικαιωθῶμεν ἐκ πίστεως Χριστοῦ καὶ οὐκ ἐξ ἔργων νόμου, "even we have believed in Christ Jesus in order that we might be justified on the basis of the faithfulness of Christ and not on the basis of the works of the law." The explicative use of καὶ ("even") makes the pronoun ἡμεῖς ("we") emphatic and serves to recall the beginning of the sentence in v 15, "we who are Jews by birth." The historical aorist ἐπιστεύσαμεν ("we believed") signals a once-for-all response, which in tandem with εἰς ("into," "in") expresses in its fullest and most definitive form the act of Christian faith, i.e., commitment of oneself to Christ. The purpose of their act of commitment is stated in the ἵνα clause that follows: "in order that we might be justified [forensically, with ethical implications] on the basis of the faithfulness of Christ [ἐκ πίστεως Χριστοῦ] and not on the basis of the works of the law [ἐξ ἔργων νόμου]." On the meaning of the individual words and expressions in this purpose clause, see Comment on v 16a above. No material difference is to be seen in Paul's use of "Christ," "Christ Jesus," and "Jesus Christ." For though Paul seldom uses "Jesus" alone (only some six times or so in quoted confessional material), variations on "Christ" are common in his letters.

ὅτι ἐξ ἔργων νόμου οὐ δικαιωθήσεται πᾶσα σάρξ, "because on the basis of the works of the law shall no one be justified." The conjunction ὅτι here has a causal function ("because") and also serves as a ὅτι recitativum to introduce quoted material. The quotation is from Ps 143:2 (142:2 LXX): ὅτι οὐ δικαιωθήσεται ἐνώπιόν σου πᾶς ζῶν (lit.: "because every living being shall not be justified before you"), though it is interpretatively quoted by Paul (cf. Rom 3:20 for the same quotation in a similar context). Paul uses πᾶσα σάρξ ("all flesh") for πᾶς ζῶν ("every living being"), for "the works of the law" are done by people of "flesh" and the flesh cannot be justified by its own efforts. "Works of the flesh" (ἔργα τῆς σαρκός) are equivalent to "works of the law" (ἔργα νόμου), and likewise to be condemned (cf. 5:19–21).

17 εἰ δὲ ζητοῦντες δικαιωθῆναι ἐν Χριστῷ εὑρέθημεν καὶ αὐτοὶ ἁμαρτωλοί, ἆρα Χριστὸς ἁμαρτίας διάκονος; μὴ γένοιτο, "but if, while we are seeking to be justified by Christ, we are found to be sinners, does that mean that Christ is a minister of sin? Absolutely not!" From the statement of agreement in vv 15–16, Paul now turns in vv 17–20 to those matters where there is disagreement. He is not here dealing with the basis of justification and so speaking against "legalism," as in vv 15–16, but with the implications of justification by Christ for the lifestyle of Gentile believers and so countering the necessity of Jewish "nomism." As Paul sees it, the implications of the Christian doctrine of justification show what the doctrine really means. Thus, to deny the latter is to deny the former as well.

Verse 17 is complex and has been variously interpreted. It involves three propositions: (1) "we are seeking to be justified by Christ"; (2) "we are found to be sinners"; and (3) "Christ is a minister of sin." The questions that arise are: Is the entire sentence a factual statement or a question? Are all of the sentence's propositions presented as being true, or just the two contained in the sentence's premise or protasis—or perhaps just the first of these two? Is Paul here responding to a charge made by his opponents? If so, what is the truth of their claim and what does Paul counter? How can it be said, on whatever basis, that "Christ is a minister of sin" or "promotes sin"?

The protasis of the sentence contains the first two propositions, both of which are governed by the conditional particle εἰ ("if"). The sentence is a first class conditional sentence, which grammatically assumes all of the protasis to be true. Obviously, the first proposition of the protasis is true, as clearly stated in vv 15–16 already: "we are seeking to be justified by Christ." The phrase ἐν Χριστῷ appears frequently in Paul's letters to signal the sphere within which the believer lives and the intimacy of personal fellowship that exists between the believer and Christ (see also 1:22; 2:4; 3:14, 26, 28; 5:6, 10). While often the local idea in the phrase is emphasized, here, in parallel with and reflecting the expressions διὰ πίστεως Ἰησοῦ Χριστοῦ and ἐκ πίστεως Χριστοῦ of v 16, its dynamic factor ("by Christ") comes to the fore.

The crucial question for the interpretation of v 17, however, is, What does Paul mean by the second proposition of the protasis, "we are found to be sinners"? The addition of καὶ αὐτοί ("even ourselves") in connection with ἁμαρτωλοί ("sinners") carries the thought back to ἐξ ἐθνῶν ἁμαρτωλοί ("sinners of the Gentiles") in v 15, and so requires picking up that idea in some way. Does Paul here mean that justification by Christ causes one to fall back into sin, and so become a sinner again (which seems hardly likely)? Or does he mean that justification by Christ apart from the law results in one being able to claim no better status than that of Gentiles (which could be said by either Paul or his opponents, though with differing connotations)? Or is Paul here responding to a charge of his judaizing opponents that ran something like this: "If you do not live according to the Mosaic law, then you have no way to check licentious living. And if Torah does not govern your Christian life, then Christ is responsible for your ethical failures. Indeed, without legal regulations, Christ himself, being alone responsible for morality, becomes a minister of sin. In fact, since libertinism is an obvious problem among believers in Galatia, this is the conclusion that Paul's lawless theology must bring you to: you are left by his gospel to live a lifestyle no better than that of Gentile sinners, and so a doctrine of justification by Christ alone becomes in actuality an encouragement to sin"?

In the discussion of the "Opponents and Situation" in the *Introduction*, we have argued that Paul faced two problems in Galatia: (1) that brought about by the Judaizers, who argued for the necessity of Gentile Christians living according to the Jewish law, and (2) that arising from among the Galatian believers themselves, who tolerated libertinism. And in attempting to gather up the diverse features of the Judaizers' message, we have suggested that on a purely practical basis they laid stress on the Torah as the divinely appointed way to check libertinism within the

Christian church—i.e., they offered a rather straightforward and seemingly God-honoring solution to libertinism within Paul's congregations: accept a Jewish nomistic lifestyle and you will have clear guidance as to what is right and wrong, and so be able to live a life that pleases God (see *Introduction*,xcvi–xcvii). In line with such an interpretation, it is not too difficult to suppose that in saying "we are found to be sinners" Paul is responding to a charge of his opponents and granting the truth of their underlying observation: that Christians, though claiming a higher standard for living, yet sin. For while forensic righteousness and ethical righteousness are intrinsically part and parcel of one another, the latter, sadly, is not always worked out in life as it should be. The premise of the sentence, therefore, is true in both its parts—the first in what it proclaims; the second in what it acknowledges.

The conclusion that "Christ is a minister of sin" and so actually "promotes sin" or "furthers sin's interests," however, is assuredly not true. Later in 5:13–26 Paul will deal directly with the libertinism of his Galatian converts, showing how ethical perversions are not corrected by the application of more laws but by the acceptance of the Spirit's direction in their lives. Here, however, he answers emphatically and emotively μὴ γένοιτο, "Absolutely not!" (lit.: "let it not be," though that translates only the words and not the emotion).

The interrogative particle ἆρα: ("does that mean") sets up the apodosis of the sentence as being a rhetorical question. And this conforms to the use of μὴ γένοιτο in Paul, which regularly follows such rhetorical questions (cf. Gal 3:21; see also Rom 3:4, 6, 31; 6:2, 15; 7:7, 13; 9:14; 11:1, 11; 1 Cor 6:15; note as well Gal 6:14 where the expression is not used in an absolute fashion, though it still functions to set off a sharp contrast; outside of Paul's letters, the expression occurs in the NT only at Luke 20:16; R. Bultmann, *Der Stil der paulinischen Predigt*, 33, 68, has shown that this use of the negative μή with the optative of γίνομαι was common in the diatribe of the Greeks).

18 εἰ γὰρ ἃ κατέλυσα ταῦτα πάλιν οἰκοδομῶ, παραβάτην ἐμαυτὸν συνιστάνω, "for if I build again those things that I destroyed, I show myself to be a lawbreaker." The postpositive γάρ ("for") is to be taken in association with μὴ γένοιτο and introduces why Paul says "Absolutely not!" to the charge that Christ promotes sin. For, Paul insists, to go back to the law (as a Christian) after having been done with the law (for both acceptance before God and living a life pleasing to him) is what really makes one a lawbreaker—which, of course, sounds paradoxical, but is what happens if one rejects legalism but still espouses nomism.

The argument here is a type of contrary reasoning: "If I do what I shouldn't, then I am." The sentence is cast in the form of a first class conditional sentence, not a second class contrary-to-fact condition, probably because Paul has in mind Peter and certain other Jewish Christians who in one way or another seemed intent on doing just that, even though terribly inconsistent in so doing. The use of the first person singular suffix ("I") in the three verbs of the sentence (cf. also the reflexive pronoun ἐμαυτόν, "myself"), as opposed to the first person plural ("we") of v 17 (cf. also the plural intensive pronoun αὐτοί), is a rhetorical feature that allows Paul to make his point in more diplomatic fashion—i.e., by applying to himself a charge really directed against others.

The phrase ἃ κατέλυσα ταῦτα ("those things that I annulled/annihilated/destroyed") refers to the law as both the basis for justification and a necessary form of life. The aorist tense of the verb, as a historical aorist, has in mind a past, once-for-all act—that time of conversion when one ceased to rely on the Mosaic law for either justification or the supervision of life, but turned to Christ for both acceptance before God and the pattern for living. The verb οἰκοδομέω ("build") was used widely in classical and Koine Greek both literally and figuratively (cf. O. Michel, "οἰκοδομέω," *TDNT* 5:136–44; for rabbinic parallels, see Str-B, 3:537–38). Its use here, of course, is metaphorical, standing for the establishment or strengthening of the law. The term παραβάτης ("violator of the law," "law-breaker") is a synonym of ἁμαρτωλός ("sinner"), but is doubtless used here in order to get away from the pejorative use of "sinner" in vv 15 and 17. It has to do with not just breaking a specific statute of the law but with setting aside the law's real intent (cf. Rom 2:25, 27; Jas 2:9, 11; Josephus, *Ant.* 3.318; 5.112; 8.129). The verb συνιστάνω, which is a later variant of συνίστημι (literally: "set together" or "bring together"), means in the active voice "demonstrate," "show" or "bring out" something. So here in v 18 Paul insists that to revert to the Mosaic law as a Christian is what really constitutes breaking the law, for then the law's true intent is nullified.

19 ἐγὼ γὰρ διὰ νόμου νόμῳ ἀπέθανον ἵνα θεῷ ζήσω, "for through the law I died to the law in order that I might live to God." In vv 19–20 Paul presents in encapsulated form the essence of his own theology vis-à-vis Jewish nomism: (1) the law's purpose was to work itself out of a job and point us beyond itself to a fuller relationship with God; (2) Christ's death on the cross and our spiritual identification with his death effects freedom from the jurisdiction of the Mosaic law; and (3) the Christian's focus is to be on Christ, who lives within us and to whom we look for direction in life. In effect, while Jews and Christians deny the validity of a legalistic use of the law, Jews hold to a nomistic or Torah-centered lifestyle in expressing their faith and Christians are to be Christ-centered in expressing theirs.

Much of what this all means will be spelled out in Paul's treatment of the law and the Christian life in 3:19–4:7. Here in the first part of v 19 (see *Comment* on "I have been crucified with Christ" in v 19b) Paul simply says that it was the intention of the Mosaic law (διὰ νόμου) to bring us to a place of being no longer dependent on its jurisdiction for the living of our lives (νόμῳ ἀπέθανον) in order that we might be more alive to God in a personal, nonlegal fashion (ἵνα θεῷ ζήσω).

The use of the first person singular, which in v 18 was unemphatic because Paul was applying to himself a charge that was really directed against others, is here emphatic by the placement of the pronoun ἐγώ ("I") as the first word of the sentence. Its use is gnomic, referring to all who by an act of personal commitment ("faith") have based their hopes on Christ ("the faithfulness of Christ") and not on the law ("the works of the law"). The use of γάρ ("for") sets up both vv 19 and 20 as Paul's positive rationale for his claim that to revert to the Mosaic law in living one's Christian life is to nullify the law's own intent (cf. v 18). In Pauline usage, "to die to" something is to cease to have any further relation to it (cf. Rom 6:2, 10–11; 7:2–6). Conversely, "to live to" someone means to have a personal, unrestricted relationship with that one (cf. Rom 6:10–11; 14:7–8; 2 Cor 5:15). Just as believers in Christ have "died to sin," "died to self," and "died to the world," so they have "died to the law" (cf. Rom 7:2–6), the purpose being not just negation, but that they might "live to God" (on the relational use of the expression ζῆν τῷ θεῷ, see 4 Macc 7:19 and 16:25; also Luke 20:38 on ζῶσιν αὐτῷ).

Χριστῷ συνεσταύρωμαι, "I have been crucified with Christ." The death of Christ was the focus of early Christian preaching (cf. the preaching recorded in Acts; also the passion narratives of the Gospels), and it is that as well throughout Galatians (cf. 1:4; 3:1, 13; 6:12, 14). Later in Galatians Paul will speak of Christ's death as redeeming us from "the curse of the law" (see also Col 2:14) and from "the world" (see also Col 2:20), and elsewhere in his letters he emphasizes Christ's death as saving us from our sins (esp. Rom 3:23–26; 5:9–10, 18–19; 6:1–7) and from ourselves (esp. Rom 7:14–25). Here, however, Paul speaks of Christ's death and our spiritual identification with that death as releasing believers from the jurisdiction of the Mosaic law—much as he does later in the somewhat garbled illustration of Rom 7:1–6 which concludes: "So, my brothers, you also died to the law through the body of Christ, that you might belong to another. . . . Now, by dying to what once bound us, we have been released from the law so that we might serve in the new way of the Spirit, and not in the old way of the written code."

The σύν prefix of the verb συνεσταύρωμαι highlights the believer's participation with Christ in his crucifixion. Paul is undoubtedly not here thinking of a literal physical death on the part of the Christian, but of his or her spiritual identification with Christ's death on the cross. The perfect tense of the verb signals the believer's once-for-all act of commitment, with that act having results and implications for the present.

The versification of the KJV has accustomed Protestants to read "I have been crucified with Christ" as the beginning of v 20, and that tradition has been followed by many modern Protestant translations (so ASV, RSV, NIV). Critical editions of the Greek text, however, are almost unanimous in placing Χριστῷ συνεσταύρωμαι with the material of v 19. And if that be its rightful place, as we believe it is, then Paul's argument in this verse as to believers being released from the jurisdiction of the Mosaic law is fourfold: (1) that it was the law's purpose to bring about its own demise in legislating the lives of God's people; (2) that such a jurisdictional demise was necessary in order that believers in Christ might live more fully in relationship with God; (3) that freedom from the law's jurisdiction is demanded by the death of Christ on the cross; and (4) that by identification with Christ we experience the freedom from the law that he accomplished.

20 ζῶ δὲ οὐκέτι ἐγώ, ζῇ δὲ ἐν ἐμοὶ Χριστός, "no longer do I live, but Christ lives in me." Crucifixion with Christ implies not only death to the jurisdiction of the Mosaic law (v 19), but also death to the jurisdiction of one's own ego. The "I" here is the "flesh" (σάρξ) of 5:13–24, which is antagonistic to the Spirit's jurisdiction. So in identifying with Christ's death, both the law and the human ego have ceased to be controlling factors for the direction of the Christian life. Instead, Paul insists, the focus of the believer's attention is to be on the fact that "Christ lives in me."

The first δέ (untranslated) of the sentence is continuative, expressing another aspect of the rationale begun in v 19. It is certainly not adversative (contra KJV). The second δέ ("but"), however, is adversative, contrasting the jurisdiction of Christ in the believer's life to that of one's ego. The expression ἐν ἐμοί ("in me"), together with its converse ἐν Χριστῷ ("in Christ," cf. 1:22; 2:4; 3:14, 26, 28; 5:6, 10), suggests what may be called "Christian mysticism." Mysticism, of course, frequently conjures up ideas about the negation of personality, withdrawal from objective reality, ascetic contemplation, a searching out of pathways to perfection, and absorption into the divine—all of which is true for Eastern and Grecian forms of mysticism. The mysticism of the Bible, however, affirms the true personhood of people and all that God has created in the natural world, never calling for negation or withdrawal except where God's creation has been contaminated by sin. Furthermore, the mysticism of biblical religion is not some esoteric searching for a path to be followed that will result in union with the divine, but is always of the nature of a response to God's grace wherein people who have been mercifully touched by God enter into communion with him without ever losing their own identities. It is, as H. A. A. Kennedy once called it, "that contact between the human and the Divine which forms the core of the deepest religious experience, but which can only be felt as an immediate intuition of the highest reality and cannot be described in the language of psychology" (*The Theology of the Epistles*, 122).

In Pauline parlance, that reality of personal communion between Christians and God is expressed from the one side of the equation as being "in Christ," "in Christ Jesus/Jesus Christ," "in him," or "in the Lord" (which complex of expressions, as Adolf Deissmann once counted, appears 164 times in Paul's letters apart from the Pastoral Epistles [*Die neutestamentliche Formel "In Christo Jesu"*])—or, at times, being "in the Spirit" (cf. Rom 8:9). Viewed from the other side of the equation, the usual way for Paul to express that relation between God and his own is by some such phrase as "Christ by his Spirit" or "the Spirit of God" or simply "the Spirit" dwelling "in us" or "in you," though a few times he says directly "Christ in me" (as here in 2:20; cf. Col 1:27, 29; see also Eph 3:16–17) or "Christ in you" (cf. the interchange of expressions in Rom 8:9–11).

ὃ δὲ νῦν ζῶ ἐν σαρκί, "and the life I now live in the body." The postpositive particle δέ ("and") here is continuative (like that at the beginning of v 20), expressing a further feature of the rationale begun in v 19 and clarifying in an epexegetical manner what Paul means by "Christ lives in me." The relative pronoun ὃ ("that," "what") is an accusative of content (cf. Rom 6:10). It can be taken simply as a substantival synonym for "life" (so, e.g., Burton, *Galatians*, 138, and most commentators; see also KJV, RSV, NEB, NIV), or as limiting and qualifying mankind's present physical life (i.e., "that life") in contrast to the fuller life of eternity to come (so Lightfoot, *Galatians*, 119), or as defined by the phrase ἐν πίστει ("by faith") that immediately follows (so, BAG on ὅς, 7c). The decision is difficult, though probably viewing it as a substantive for the content of the verb ζῶ ("I live") is simplest and all that is required. The adverb νῦν ("now") refers to a time subsequent to the change expressed in the phrases "I died to the law" and "I have been crucified with Christ," and is contemporaneous with "Christ lives in me." It identifies the believer's Christian existence in contrast to that of his or her pre-Christian life (cf. 3:3; 4:9, 29). ἐν σαρκί, while often used by Paul in an ethical sense (cf. 3:3; 5:13, 16–17, 19–21, 24; 6:8), here means just "flesh" in the sense of "the mortal body." Yet as Betz points out: "This statement, simple as it is, may be polemical. It rejects widespread enthusiastic notions, which may have already found a home in Christianity, according to which 'divine life' and 'flesh' are mutually exclusive, so that those who claim to have divine life also claim that they have left the conditions of mortality" (*Galatians*, 125).

ἐν πίστει ζῶ τῇ τοῦ υἱοῦ τοῦ θεοῦ τοῦ ἀγαπήσαντός με καὶ παραδόντος ἑαυτὸν ὑπὲρ ἐμοῦ, "I live by faith in the Son of God, who loved me and gave himself for me." The Christian life is a life lived "by faith." Its basis is "the faith/

faithfulness of Jesus Christ" (διὰ/ἐκ πίστεως Ἰησοῦ Χριστοῦ, v 16); its response
is that of a commitment of belief (καὶ ἡμεῖς εἰς Χριστὸν Ἰησοῦν ἐπιστεύσαμεν,
v 16); and its atmosphere is one of wholehearted faith or trust (ἐν πίστει). The
object of Christian faith is here expressed by the dative article τῇ followed by a
Christological title in the genitive and by qualifying adjectival phrases also in the
genitive.

The variant reading θεοῦ καὶ Χριστοῦ ("God and Christ") receives support
from such excellent external sources as P⁴⁶ and B (also D* G and two Old Latin
manuscripts). As well, it certainly is the "harder reading," for nowhere else in
Paul's writings is God spoken of expressly as the object of Christian faith. Yet the
fact that it is a *hap. leg.* in Paul makes it probable that υἱοῦ τοῦ θεοῦ ("Son of God")
contained in ℵ A C and almost all versions and patristic witnesses was original. On
the Christological title "Son of God," see *Comment* at 1:16.

Qualifying "Son of God" are two adjectival phrases dominated by two substantival participles that express the essence of Christ's work: "who loved me and gave
himself for me." Both expressions characterizing the work of Christ appear
elsewhere in Paul's letters, either together (cf. Eph 5:2, 25) or separately (cf. esp.
1:4 on "gave himself"; also Rom 4:25; 8:32; 1 Cor 11:23–24; Phil 2:6–8; 1 Tim 2:6;
Titus 2:14; on "loved us," see Rom 8:37; 2 Thess 2:16, etc.). As Morna Hooker
observes, when Paul describes what God has done in the redemption of mankind
"Jesus' own role is understood as less passive and more active: he is not only 'given
up' by God on our behalf (Rom. viii.32) but 'gives himself up' for our sakes"
("Interchange and Atonement," *BJRL* 60 [1978] 480).

While using the gnomic "I" and "me" in vv 19–20, there also reverberates in
Paul's words his own intense personal feeling (cf. Rom 7:7–25 for a similar gnomic
treatment with intense personal identification). "It was," as F. F. Bruce comments,
"a source of unending wonder to him 'that I, even I, have mercy found'"
(*Galatians*, 146). So Paul closes his statement as to the essence of the gospel here
in 2:20 with an emphasis on Christ's love and sacrificial self-giving, much as he
began the Galatian letter in 1:4—which, of course, highlights what gripped his
own heart when he thought of the work of Christ.

21 οὐκ ἀθετῶ τὴν χάριν τοῦ θεοῦ, "I do not nullify the grace of God." The
final bit of a typical ancient *propositio* was a statement that flatly refuted what was
charged. So Paul concludes his *propositio* with a direct statement refuting his
opponents' charge against him, and then adds an explanatory sentence that
identifies the crux of the matter.

The sentence of refutation is introduced abruptly without any linguistic connective, for it is the final statement of Paul's *propositio* and conforms to that rhetorical
style. The verb ἀθετέω (here contracted) means "nullify," "declare invalid," or "set
aside." It is a rather strong term that has legal overtones, usually in connection with
invalidating a "treaty," "will," or "covenant" (cf. 1 Macc 11:36; 2 Macc 13:25; Gal
3:15; Ignatius, *Eph.* 10.3; see also Destinon's emendation to Josephus, *J.W.* 1.646).
The expression τὴν χάριν τοῦ θεοῦ ("the grace of God"), as interpreted by the
explanatory sentence that follows with its reference to the Mosaic law, means here
God's special grace to Israel in giving them the law (cf. Rom 3:1–2, 31).

Probably the Judaizers were picking up on one of Paul's favorite terms, "grace,"
and turning it against him, asserting that his doctrine of grace apart from law was
really a denial of God's grace to the nation Israel. Such a charge, however, Paul

answers by a direct denial, which he sustains in compressed fashion in the next sentence and will elaborate on more fully in his *probatio* of 3:1–4:11.

εἰ γὰρ διὰ νόμου δικαιοσύνη, ἄρα Χριστὸς δωρεὰν ἀπέθανεν, "for if righteousness is through the law, then Christ died for nothing!" The postpositive γάρ ("for") introduces an explanatory sentence in support of Paul's statement of denial. The protasis of the sentence is in the form of a first class condition, which linguistically assumes the truth of the statement. Paul, however, obviously sees such a supposition as false, as he says clearly in v 16 above. So the form of the sentence, like that of v 18 above, must be because Paul is here paraphrasing his opponents' theology, which claimed such a proposition to be true. The phrase "through the law" (διὰ νόμου) is to be equated with "the works of the law" in vv 16–17, which are in opposition to "the faith/faithfulness of Christ." The noun "righteousness" (δικαιοσύνη) picks up the forensic sense of the verb "justify" (δικαιόω) in vv 15–16 *and* the ethical sense of the discussion in vv 17–20, so suggesting that for neither status nor lifestyle does the Christian depend on the law.

The inferential particle ἄρα ("then") turns the argument of the sentence into a *reductio ad absurdum*: "then Christ died for nothing!" The accusative of δωρεά ("gift") is here used as an adverb to mean "in vain," "to no purpose," or "for nothing." Such a usage is to be found only here in the NT, though it sometimes appears elsewhere in late Greek (cf. Job 1:9 and Ps 34 [35]:19 in the LXX).

The central proclamation of the gospel concerns the atoning efficacy of the death of Christ. To argue for righteousness as being "through the law," therefore, whether that righteousness is understood forensically (2:15–16) or ethically (2:17–20), is to call into question the necessity of Christ's death; and, conversely, to base one's life on "Christ crucified" is to put an end to attempts to be righteous by observing the law (as Paul argues immediately following in 3:1). So just as "the works of the law" and "the faith/faithfulness of Christ" are to be seen as antithetically related (2:16), also "through the law" and "Christ crucified" are noncomplementary. To affirm the one is to deny the other, and vice versa.

Explanation

Gal 2:15–21 is the *propositio* of Paul's letter to the Galatians, which, as H. D. Betz observes, "sums up the *narratio*'s material content" and "sets up the arguments to be discussed later in the *probatio*" (*Galatians*, 114). The points of agreement between Paul and concerned Jewish Christians are given in vv 15–16; the points of disagreement between Paul and the Judaizers are set out in vv 17–20; and the refutation of a specific charge against Paul is stated in v 21. The language of the passage is considerably compressed, but that language will be unpacked in Paul's arguments of 3:1–4:11 and his exhortations of 4:12–6:10.

Of particular significance is the fact that in 2:15–21 Paul deals with both "legalism" (i.e., the attempt to gain favor with God by means of Torah observance) and "nomism" (i.e., the response of faith to a God who has acted on one's behalf by living a life governed by Torah). In 2:15–16 Paul presents in abbreviated form the case against the former; in 2:17–20 he deals with the latter, with 2:21 being a summary conclusion incorporating both. So in reading his *probatio* of 3:1–4:11 we must be guided by such a twofold argument and not just take it that only one point is being made (as commentators usually assume). Likewise in reading Galatians for spiritual profit, we need to recognize that both "legalism" and "nomism" are being dealt with—mainly the latter, though with implications for the former—and not assume only the former (as is usually done). Otherwise, we fall into the trap of being "half-Judaizers" in practice and possibly worse in theory.

97

D. Arguments in Support (probatio) (3:1–4:11)

In speeches of antiquity, as H. D. Betz points out, "the *probatio* section is the most decisive of all because in it the 'proofs' are presented. This part determines whether or not the speech as a whole will succeed. *Exordium* and *narratio* are only preparatory steps leading up to this central part" (*Galatians*, 128). So, likewise, the *probatio* of Galatians (also rhetorically called the *argumentatio* or *confirmatio*) is the most important argumentative section of Paul's letter, for here Paul moves beyond the negative arguments of the *narratio* of 1:11–2:14 to take the offensive by spelling out positive arguments in support of the *propositio* of 2:15–21.

Analyzed in terms of letter structure, the *probatio* of Galatians opens at 3:1 with an expression typical of a Hellenistic letter of rebuke, "You foolish Galatians" (ὦ ἀνόητοι Γαλάται). It closes at 4:11 with an expression of distress also commonly found in rebuke-type letters, "I fear for you" (φοβοῦμαι ὑμᾶς). And it contains two sets of rebuking questions, those of 3:1–5 and those of 4:8–10, which together form an *inclusio* and so signal the section's beginning and end. Thus by means of a rudimentary epistolary analysis one is able to determine in fairly clear fashion both where this new section of Galatians begins and where it ends.

Rhetorically, Paul here continues generally the forensic type of rhetoric begun at 1:6. At least in 3:1–5, where *interrogatio* conventions dominate, such a type of rhetoric seems fairly clear. An analysis of 3:6–4:11 in terms of Greco-Roman rhetorical conventions, however, is, as Betz admits, "extremely difficult" (ibid., 129). Only the *exemplum* type of argument at 3:6a and the resumption of the *interrogatio* method at 4:9 can be related directly to classical forensic rhetoric. Betz attributes this lack of rhetorical clarity to Paul's skill in diversifying his arguments so as to be more effective and not boring, in line with Quintilian's advice to "diversify by a thousand arguments" (Quintilian 5.14.32). More to the point is the fact that Paul in 3:6–4:11 seems much more heavily influenced by Jewish forms of argumentation and Jewish exegetical practices, and so drifts somewhat away from those Greco-Roman rhetorical conventions used earlier.

Thematically, the *probatio* of 3:1–4:11 sets out the proofs or arguments introduced by the *propositio* of 2:15–21. It is structured, in line with the structure of the *propositio*, into two main parts: (1) arguments having to do with matters on which there is agreement, and (2) arguments having to do with matters that are contested. The first part, that of 3:1–18, sets out experiential, scriptural, and theological arguments in support of the thesis that the law plays no positive role in becoming a Christian (contra "legalism"), explicating the affirmations of 2:15–16 in the *propositio*. The second, that of 3:19–4:7, argues that the law plays no positive role in Christian living (contra "nomism"), explicating the affirmations of 2:17–20 and the conclusion of 2:21. Appended to these two main parts are statements found in 4:8–11 expressing Paul's concern for his Galatian converts.

Here, then, in 3:1–4:11 the central affirmations of the *propositio* of 2:15–21 are unpacked—usually in ways more Jewish than Greco-Roman in styling and often in quite *ad hominem* fashion. Here, in fact, Paul moves beyond the more negative argumentation of Greco-Roman forensic rhetoric found extensively in the *narratio* to take the offensive by means of positive arguments that follow or more Jewish procedural norms.

1. Righteousness Apart from the Law: Against Legalism (3:1–18)

Gal 3:1–18 is one of the most familiar and closely studied portions of Paul's letters. That is so because of its concentration of themes central to the Christian gospel, its attack against legalism, and the complexity of Paul's arguments in support of a law-free gospel. Three sets of arguments are mustered in support of the thesis of 2:15–16 that the law plays no positive role in becoming a Christian: (a) arguments from experience (vv 1–5); (b) arguments from Scripture (vv 6–14); and (c) ad hominem theological arguments (vv 15–18).

(a) Arguments from Experience (3:1–5)

Bibliography

Betz, H. D. "Geist, Freiheit und Gesetz: Die Botschaft des Paulus an die Gemeinden in Galatien." *ZTK* 71 (1974) 78–93 ["Spirit, Freedom, and Law: Paul's Message to the Galatian Churches." *SEÅ* 39 (1974) 145–60]. ———. "In Defense of the Spirit: Paul's Letter to the Galatians as a Document of Early Christian Apologetics." In *Aspects of Religious Propaganda in Judaism and Early Christianity,* ed. E. Schüssler Fiorenza. Notre Dame: University of Notre Dame Press, 1976, 99–114. **Clark, K. W.** "The Meaning of ἐνεργέω and καταργέω in the New Testament." *JBL* 54 (1935) 93–101. **Hanson, A. T.** *The Paradox of the Cross.* **Hays, R. B.** *The Faith of Jesus Christ,* 143–49, 196–98. **Käsemann, E.** "The Pauline Theology of the Cross." *Int* 24 (1970) 151–77. **Lull, D. J.** *The Spirit in Galatia,* 54–58. **Lütgert, W.** *Gesetz und Geist.* **Weder, H.** *Das Kreuz Jesu bei Paulus.* **Williams, S. K.** "The Hearing of Faith: ΑΚΟΗ ΠΙΣΤΕΩΣ in Galatians 3." *NTS* 35 (1989) 82–93.

Translation

¹*You foolish Galatians! Who bewitched you,ᵃ before whose eyes Jesus Christ was clearly portrayedᵇ as having been crucified?* ²*Only this I want to learn from you: Did you receive the Spirit on the basis of the works of the law or on the basis of believing what you heard?* ³*Are you so foolish? Having begun with the Spirit, are you now trying to attain perfection*

by human effort? *⁴Have you experienced so much for nothing—if, indeed, it really was for nothing?* *⁵Did God, then, give you his Spirit and work miracles among you on the basis of the works of the law or on the basis of believing what you heard?*

Notes

ᵃ τῇ ἀληθείᾳ μὴ πείθεσθαι ("not to obey the truth") is added to τίς ὑμᾶς ἐβάσκανεν ("who bewitched you?") by C D² TR vg^cl syr^hel and most minuscules, evidently influenced by 5:7.
ᵇ ἐν ὑμῖν ("among you") is added to προεγράφη ("clearly portrayed") by D G TR vg^cl syr^hel and most minuscules.

Form/Structure/Setting

Paul's Galatians *probatio* begins with arguments drawn from his converts' experience, calling on them to recall what took place in their lives when they first responded to the proclamation of the gospel and thereafter, but before the Judaizers arrived on the scene. Paul is convinced that if the Galatian Christians would only make the connection between his preaching and God's blessings in their lives, the Judaizers would have no opening and matters would be settled. For if God had so evidently honored Paul's preaching of a law-free gospel and they had so evidently been blessed by God in responding to such a message, what more could they possibly want?

Gal 3:1–5 is loaded with rhetorical features assimilated from the preachers, teachers, and writers of the day (see Betz, *Galatians*, 128–31, and the extensive literature cited). The *interrogatio* method is prominent with six questions appearing in these five verses. Likewise, these six rebuking questions reflect a common Greco-Roman diatribe form of argumentation, which Paul seems fond of as well (cf. esp. Rom 3:1–9, 27–31; 4:1, 9–10; 6:1–3, 15–16; 7:1, 7; 8:31–35). Even the biting and rather insulting address with which the section opens, "You foolish Galatians" (v 1; see also v 3), reflects common rhetorical practice among the diatribe preachers of Paul's day. Thus in addressing his Gentile converts in Galatia, Paul begins the major argumentative section of his letter by making use of such Greco-Roman rhetorical techniques as he found useful and as his converts would have understood.

Comment

1 Ὦ ἀνόητοι Γαλάται, "you foolish Galatians!" Not since 1:9 has Paul mentioned the situation in Galatia itself and not since 2:5 has he referred to the Galatians directly, so intent has he been on demonstrating his own apostleship and defending the "truth of the gospel." The twice repeated ἀνόητοι, "foolish" (here and v 3), highlights the sharpness of Paul's address. It is, indeed, biting and aggressive in tone. Yet more than just a reprimand, it expresses Paul's deep concern, exasperation, and perplexity (cf. 4:11, 20). It is not a lack of intelligence on their part that grieves Paul but a failure to exercise even a modicum of spiritual discernment. The passion manifest in the *propositio* (esp. 2:21) carries over here at the start of the *probatio*.

Addressing readers in the vocative during the course of writing is common for
the Pauline letters (cf. 2 Cor 6:11, Κορίνθιοι; Phil 4:15, Φιλιππήσιοι; 1 Tim 6:20,
ὦ Τιμόθεε). The addition of the adjective ἀνόητοι (also in the vocative) together
with the emotive particle ὧ (or ὦ as some want to accent it, making it more an
exclamation than an interjection), however, appears only here in Paul, though ὦ
as an emotional interjection is common in Koine Greek and the NT with all sorts
of other vocatives and/or nominatives used as vocatives (cf. Matt 15:28; Mark 9:19
par.; Acts 13:10; Jas 2:20), as well as in Paul (cf. Rom 2:1, 3; 9:20; 1 Tim 6:20). The
closest parallel to Paul's use here is in Luke 24:25, where ὦ ἀνόητοι καὶ βραδεῖς
τῇ καρδίᾳ ("you foolish and slow of heart") is the expression used to stress lack
of discernment regarding the prophetic word. In Rom 1:14 ἀνόητοις is contrasted
with σοφοῖς ("wise ones"), and may there be seen as a locution for "barbarians."
But Paul is not here calling his Galatian converts barbarians, but rather those who
lack spiritual discernment.

τίς ὑμᾶς ἐβάσκανεν, "who bewitched you." The verb βασκαίνω, which appears
in the NT only here, was commonly used in the Greek world in a figurative sense
to mean "fascinate by casting an evil eye" or "bewitch" (see Betz, *Galatians*, 131,
for references and quotations from Plato, Demosthenes, Libanius, Philostratus,
Lucian, Philo, and Hesychius). It was part of the rhetoric of the day for
characterizing opponents and their strategies. H. Schlier thinks that Paul here
assumes that his Galatian converts had fallen into the hands of some magician and
were being influenced by his demonic spells (*Galater,* 119). Burton, however,
recognizing the term as a rhetorical expression, is undoubtedly more to be
believed when he says: "It would be overpressing the facts to infer from Paul's use
of this word that he necessarily believed in the reality of magical powers, and still
more so to assume that he supposed the state of mind of the Galatians to be the
result of such arts. It is more probable that the word, while carrying a reference
to magical arts, was used by him tropically, as we ourselves use the word 'bewitch,'
meaning 'to pervert,' 'to confuse the mind'" (*Galatians,* 144).

The clause τῇ ἀληθείᾳ μὴ πείθεσθαι ("not to obey the truth"), which appears
after ἐβάσκανεν in some Greek MSS (see *Note* a), evidently came about under the
influence of 5:7. It is a correct understanding of what Paul means in 3:1, but it is
not supported by our better manuscripts and is unnecessary, being obvious.

οἷς κατ' ὀφθαλμοὺς Ἰησοῦς Χριστὸς προεγράφη, "before whose eyes Jesus
Christ was clearly portrayed." The verb προγράφω may mean either "write beforehand" (the προ- being temporal) or "show forth" or "portray publicly" as on
a placard (the προ- being locative). It was used in both ways by Greek writers of
the day (e.g., Josephus used it temporally of what was written or appointed earlier
in *Ant.* 11.283 and 12.30, but locatively in the sense of a public announcement in
Ant. 12.33; cf. also BAG and MM). In Rom 15:4 it refers to what was written in the
past (so also probably Jude 4) and in Eph 3:3 to what the author himself had
written earlier. Here in 3:1, however, it probably has a locative sense, for to take
it in a temporal sense as referring to OT prophecy—which, it is true, would not
be inconsistent with either Paul's theology generally or current usage—seems
excluded by κατ' ὀφθαλμούς ("before your eyes"). Rather, the meaning "clearly
portray" as on a public placard seems most congruous with the imagery "before
your eyes." It is best, therefore, to understand Paul here as describing his
preaching to the Galatians under the figure of a public announcement or

placarding of Jesus before them. What he had preached to them was so openly and clearly proclaimed that Paul is at a loss to know how his converts could ever have failed to see its significance or to appreciate its implications for the question at hand. The phrase ἐν ὑμῖν ("among you") of the TR (see *Note* b) is a redundant statement of the obvious.

The participle ἐσταυρωμένος, being in the perfect tense, lays emphasis on the crucifixion as an accomplished fact with present results, and so should be translated "having been crucified." The phrase "Christ crucified" was on Paul's lips an abbreviated form of the gospel (cf. 1 Cor 1:23; 2:2; also 1 Cor 1:13; 2:8; 2 Cor 13:4); by metonymy such associated terms as "cross" and "death" also were used to represent the basic Christian kerygma (cf. 1 Cor 1:17–18; 15:3; Gal 5:11; 6:12, 14; Phil 2:8; 3:18; Col 1:20; 2:14–15). Underlying these expressions and that basic kerygma, however, as R. B. Hays has shown, was a narrative substructure that recounted the redemptive ministry of Jesus of Nazareth (see his *The Faith of Jesus Christ*). And it is that narrative substructure that Paul alludes to and recalls to his converts' minds by speaking of "Jesus Christ having been crucified."

For Paul, the gospel of Christ crucified so completely rules out any other supposed means of being righteous before God that he finds it utterly incomprehensible for anyone who had once embraced such a gospel ever to think of supplementing it in any way. To hold before one's eyes "Jesus Christ having been crucified" is to put an end to all forms of Jewish legalism, for "Christ crucified" is not only the central kerygma of the Christian gospel but also the tenet of that gospel that most clearly distinguishes Christians from Jews. That was axiomatic for Paul, though his Galatian converts had to be told it again.

2 τοῦτο μόνον θέλω μαθεῖν ἀφ᾽ ὑμῶν, "only this I want to learn from you." In v 2 (together with its parallel of v 5) we have Paul's central argument of this section, for here he appeals directly to the Galatians' own experience of having received the Spirit and asks on what basis that experience came about. Paul wants to hear it from the Galatians themselves. He is convinced that if they would but recall their own experience of having received God's Spirit at the time when they accepted Paul's proclamation of the gospel, then no further argument from him would be necessary and no enticement from the Judaizers would be possible. So he begins the second rhetorical question of this section — the question that calls for the one item of evidence on which Paul is willing to rest his entire case — with a common dialogical device: "only this I want to learn from you" (see Betz, *Galatians*, 132, for parallels from antiquity).

ἐξ ἔργων νόμου τὸ πνεῦμα ἐλάβετε ἢ ἐξ ἀκοῆς πίστεως, "did you receive the Spirit on the basis of the works of the law or on the basis of believing what you heard?" Much that has been written on Galatians has tended to ignore the central place of the Spirit in Paul's argumentation throughout his Galatian letter. J. B. Lightfoot actually omitted any reference to the Spirit (except by way of translating Paul's words) in his comments on 3:1–5, and in dealing with 5:13–26 only tells us that πνεύματι of v 16 is a dative of rule or direction and that the statement "we live by the Spirit" of v 25 speaks of "an ideal rather than an actual life" (see his *Galatians*, 133–36, 209, 214). C. K. Barrett says that here in 3:1–5 Paul "momentarily turns aside . . . to use a pragmatic argument" (*The Holy Spirit and the Gospel Tradition*, 2), and John W. Drane calls 3:1–5 a "brief interlude" in Paul's Galatian argument (*Paul, Libertine or Legalist?* 24). Even when it is seen that Paul's reference to the Spirit in 3:2–5 is part of "a forcible appeal to the experience of the Galatians" (to quote Burton, *Galatians,* 147), there is usually no attempt on the part of commentators to show any continuity of Paul's argument here with the rest of Galatians which would take into account the work of the Spirit (so, e.g., Burton, Bruce, and even Betz, who though his 1976 article highlights the place of the Spirit in Paul's explicit references to the Spirit in Galatians, fails to work out in his 1979 commentary the relation of the Spirit to Paul's arguments and exhortations elsewhere).

Admittedly, reference to the Spirit does not appear in Galatians until about one third of the way into the letter. Yet there are two clusters of verses in Galatians where Paul refers directly to the Spirit, the first being here at the start of his *probatio* in 3:2–5 and the second being in his exhortations to those with libertine tendencies in 5:13–26. Although it never becomes a topic on its own, Paul's consciousness of the Spirit underlies and ties together all that he says in Gal 3:1– 6:10 by way of both argumentation and appeal.

Believers in Galatia had received the Spirit at the time of their conversion to Christ. That is evident by the use of the participle ἐναρξάμενοι ("having begun") in v 3 (see *Comment* there) and by the fact that Paul's whole argument hinges on their reception of the Spirit prior to the Judaizers' intrusion. Just how the Spirit's presence was manifest in their lives is uncertain from our vantage point, though, of course, it was well known both to them and to Paul. From 3:4–5, however, we may infer that there were outward signs of some sort (see *Comment* there), and from 6:1 that some of Paul's Galatian converts thought of themselves as "pneumatics" (see *Comment* there).

Paul does not argue as to whether or not his converts had received the Spirit. His reference to their reception of the Spirit is stated in such an absolute manner as to signal a shared familiarity of that fact on the part of both him and them. Paul's argument, rather, has to do with the basis for their reception of the Spirit, whether on the basis of ἔργων νόμου ("works of the law") or on the basis of ἀκοῆς πίστεως ("believing what you heard")—the antithesis which is picked up from 2:15–16 and which becomes dominant in Paul's argumentation down through 3:18.

ἐξ ἔργων νόμου ("on the basis of the works of the law"), as we argued earlier (see *Comment* on the phrase's three appearances in 2:16), is Paul's catch phrase to signal the whole legalistic complex of ideas having to do with winning God's favor by a merit-amassing observance of Torah. Paul said in the first part of the *propositio* (2:15–16) that true Jews, both Christian and non-Christian, knew that such a legalistic use of the Mosaic law was invalid. Now he makes that same point to Gentile Christians who are being enticed to take on certain aspects of the Jewish law. That Paul places ἐξ ἔργων νόμου first (for emphasis) in the sentence—before the subject, verb, and object of the sentence and separated from its coordinate predicate phrase ἐξ ἀκοῆς πίστεως—highlights the fact that his major concern in v 1–5 (as well as thereafter through v 18) is with countering legalism.

The meaning of ἐξ ἀκοῆς πίστεως, however, is somewhat more difficult to fathom. In that ἐξ ἔργων νόμου was contrasted in 2:16 with ἐκ πίστεως Χριστοῦ (or διὰ πίστεως Ἰησοῦ Χριστοῦ), we may assume that its contrast here with ἐξ ἀκοῆς πίστεως has something of a similar significance for Paul.

The preposition ἐκ denotes source or basis for, in this case the source or basis for justification (as in 2:16). But what does the noun ἀκοή mean here? It could mean "the faculty or organ of hearing," or "the act of hearing," or "the content of what is heard" (so LSJ, BAG, et al.), though obviously Paul does not have the first meaning in mind and so only the latter two are relevant here. What does the noun πίστις mean here? It could mean either "faith" or "faithfulness," or both (cf. *Comment* on 2:16), though here without Jesus Christ as its referent (as in 2:16). Taking the two words together, if ἀκοή means here "the act of hearing," then Paul was thinking about either "hearing about faith" (in contrast to doing the law) or "a faithful hearing" (in contrast to legalistic works). But ἀκοή was also used in classical and Koine Greek to denote "the content of what is heard" (cf. Thucydides, *History of the Peloponnesian War* 1.20.1, passim). And that is probably how it should be translated here: "believing what you heard"—i.e., the gospel as proclaimed by Paul, which focused on the faith/faithfulness of Christ apart from the Jewish law (cf. JB: "believed what was preached to you"; NEB: "believing the gospel message"; E. P. Sanders: "'believing what was heard', i.e. believing the gospel" [*Paul and Palestinian Judaism,* 482]).

3 οὕτως ἀνόητοί ἐστε, "are you so foolish?" Paul's third question of this section repeats the biting attack with which the section began: "Are you so foolish?" (cf. v 1). Paul speaks so scathingly because of his converts' lack of spiritual discernment in not perceiving the contradiction and imminent disaster of their own situation.

ἐναρξάμενοι πνεύματι νῦν σαρκὶ ἐπιτελεῖσθε, "having begun with the Spirit, are you now trying to attain perfection by human effort?" Two antitheses are set out in Paul's fourth question: that of beginning and completing (or perfecting), and that of the Spirit versus the flesh (or human effort). Instead of speaking of "the faith/faithfulness of Christ" (as in 2:16) or "believing what you heard" (as in 3:2) versus "the works of the law" (as in both 2:16 and 3:2), Paul here speaks of "the Spirit" versus "the flesh" or "human effort," which he evidently sees as a synonymous way of expressing matters and which he highlights (though in a somewhat different fashion) in his exhortations of 5:16–26. In Paul's mind, therefore, two sets of ideas stand in antithetical relation to one another: (1) the complex of ideas having to do with "the faith/faithfulness of Christ," "believing what you heard" (i.e., what Paul preached to them), and "the Spirit," on the one hand, over against (2) "the works of the law" and "the flesh" (whether "flesh" signifies "human effort," as with the Judaizers, or "sinful passions," as with the libertines).

The adverbial participle ἐναρξάμενοι ("having begun"), being both aorist and temporal, "cannot refer," as J. D. G. Dunn rightly asserts, "to anything other than the moment of becoming a Christian" (*Baptism in the Holy Spirit,* 108). It does not have in mind anything consequent to the beginning of the believer's new life, but rather takes it for granted that the beginning of the Christian life and the reception of God's Spirit are coterminous. The present infinitive passive verb ἐπιτελεῖσθε with the adverbial particle νῦν stresses the Galatian Christians' present orientation: "now trying to attain perfection." One may debate whether the datives πνεύματι and σαρκί are to be taken as "the manner in which" or "the instrument by which" (cf. Schlier, *Galater,* 123). As F. F. Bruce says, "the distinction is more grammatical than substantial" (*Galatians,* 150). The main point of Paul's rhetorical question here, however, has to do with the incongruity of beginning one's Christian life on one basis ("with the Spirit") and then shifting somewhere in progress to another basis ("by human effort"). What Paul wants his converts to see is that the Christian life is one that starts, is maintained, and comes to culmination only through dependence on the activity of God's Spirit (cf. 5:25; also see Phil 1:6, where the same verbs ἐνάρχομαι and ἐπιτελέω appear and where the point is made that completion of the Christian life comes about on the same basis as its inception, viz. by God's working).

4 τοσαῦτα ἐπάθετε εἰκῇ εἴ γε καὶ εἰκῇ, "have you experienced so much for nothing—if indeed, it really was for nothing?" The appeal to experience is renewed in the question of v 4 (wherever we understand the question mark itself should be placed), with the words suggesting some ongoing experiences beyond the time of conversion. The crucial term here is the verb πάσχω, which always in the LXX and elsewhere in the NT (some forty-one times in addition to Gal 3:4) is used in the unfavorable sense of "experience suffering" (e.g., Luke 22:15; 24:46; Acts 1:3; 3:18; 17:3; 1 Cor 12:26; Heb 2:18; 9:26; 1 Peter 2:20, 23; 3:17). So most have understood ἐπάθετε here *sensu malo* as in some way relating to persecution on account of the gospel (so Chrysostom, Augustine, Luther, Lightfoot, Zahn, Lütgert, Duncan, and Bruce, to name only a few). W. Michaelis, in fact, argues that when πάσχω is used absolutely it always implies suffering, except where the context suggests it should be understood *sensu bono* (*TDNT* 5:905–23). On the other hand, there are instances in Greek writings where πάσχω is used of favorable experiences (cf. BAG, though Josephus, *Ant.* 3.312 is disputed). So some recent interpreters have taken ἐπάθετε here to refer to positive experiences of the Spirit, either referring back to "having begun with the Spirit" of v 3 or forward to the statements about God giving his Spirit and working miracles among them of v 5—or both (so Lietzmann, Bligh, Mussner, and Betz). Others, however, take a middle course and give the appearance of πάσχω here a neutral sense (so probably Burton, Schlier, and apparently Michaelis himself: Gal 3:4 "refers to the violent and beneficial experiences implied by the τοσαῦτα, though πάσχω itself is not used in a good sense" [*TDNT* 5:912]).

The interpretation of v 4 is notoriously difficult. If one gives attention only to etymology and frequency of usage, then a meaning *sensu malo* must prevail. It is possible, however, indeed even likely, that if context is given primary importance, then a meaning *sensu bono* would appear more likely. For in the wider context of the letter there is no suggestion that the Galatian Christians had ever actually suffered any form of external persecution, though 6:12 intimates that the errorists themselves were fearful of such (see *Comment* there). More pertinently, v 4 is set in the immediate context of vv 3 and 5, where God's giving of his Spirit and God's working of miracles in the midst of the Galatians are highlighted. So τοσαῦτα ἐπάθετε ("have you experienced so much") should probably be taken as a recollection of the Galatian believers' past, positive spiritual experiences—perhaps even should be translated "have you had such remarkable experiences" (so BAG), or at least understood as "the great experiences through which the Galatians had already passed in their life as Christians" (so Burton, *Galatians*, 149, though Burton ends up speaking of πάσχω as a neutral term and actually translates it on p. 142 as "suffer").

The adverb εἰκῇ ("in vain," "to no avail") expresses futility. Paul's question is: Are all your past, positive spiritual experiences of no significance to you when faced with the option of going on with the Spirit or turning to the Jewish law? The added words εἴ γε καὶ εἰκῇ ("if, indeed, it really was for nothing") are of the nature of a parenthetical exclamation, expressing the hope that the situation is not yet irretrievable. As Lightfoot notes: "The Apostle hopes better things of his converts. Εἴ γε leaves a loophole for doubt, and καί widens this, implying an unwillingness to believe on the part of the speaker" (*Galatians*, 135).

5 ὁ οὖν ἐπιχορηγῶν ὑμῖν τὸ πνεῦμα καὶ ἐνεργῶν δυνάμεις ἐν ὑμῖν ἐξ ἔργων νόμου ἢ ἐξ ἀκοῆς πίστεως, "did God, then, give you his Spirit and work miracles among you on the basis of the works of the law or on the basis of believing what you heard?" This sentence brings to an end Paul's rhetorical queries of vv 1–5 and asks directly again the question of v 2, though here that question is asked in light of all Paul has referred to regarding his converts' experiences in vv 2–4. The postpositive οὖν ("then") signals the fact that Paul is here concluding in summary fashion his arguments from experience. Probably he is doing so by highlighting (1) what he has said about his converts' initial reception of the Spirit at the time of their conversion in vv 2–3 ("having begun with the Spirit"), and (2) what he has alluded to as to their ongoing spiritual experiences beyond the time of their conversion in v 4 ("have you experienced so much"), followed then by the fundamental antithesis that is first stated in v 2 but which dominates all of Paul's argumentation through v 18: Was all this on the basis of a merit-amassing observance of the Mosaic law or on the basis of a believing response to the gospel as Paul preached it?

The two substantival participles ἐπιχορηγῶν ("the one who gives") and ἐνεργῶν ("the one who works") are governed by one article (ὁ), and so refer to the same person (the unexpressed θεός, "God") and describe related activities affecting the same persons (ὑμῖν ... ἐν ὑμῖν, "you ... among you"). The verbs of the sentence are unexpressed, but evidently, since v 5 is summarizing what has been said in vv 2–4, to be understood as aorists in line with ἐλάβετε ("did you receive") of v 2 and ἐπάθετε ("you experienced") of v 4.

The phrase ὁ ἐπιχορηγῶν ὑμῖν τὸ πνεῦμα ("did God ... give you his Spirit") undoubtedly refers to the Galatians' initial reception of the Spirit at the time of their conversion (see *Comment* at vv 2–3). Probably [ὁ] ἐνεργῶν δυνάμεις ἐν ὑμῖν ("work miracles among you") has in mind and expands on the allusion in v 4 to the Galatian Christians' ongoing spiritual experiences beyond the time of their conversion. δυνάμεις ("miracles") refers to outward manifestations of the Spirit's presence such as enumerated in 1 Cor 12:7–11 (note the use of ἐνεργήματα δυνάμεων ["workings of miracles"] in v 10) and 2 Cor 12:12 (where σημείοις ["signs"], τέρασιν ["wonders"] and δυνάμεσιν ["miracles"] appear as synonyms). The expression ἐν ὑμῖν, as contrasted with the simple dative ὑμῖν of the preceding phrase, undoubtedly means "among you" (so Burton, Schlier, Mussner, Betz, et al., contra Lightfoot, *Galatians*, 136; cf. ἐν τοῖς ἔθνεσιν ["among the Gentiles"] of 1:16 and 2:2), and so identifies the Galatians themselves as the recipients of the Spirit's charismatic activities. It is true, of course, that 2 Cor 12:12 speaks of miracles as one of the signs of an apostle, and it might be argued from that that Paul has in mind here the miracles he performed as an apostle while evangelizing Galatia. As Shirley Jackson Case, however, once noted: "It is possible, so far as the mere wording of the passage goes, to affirm that Paul is here referring simply to his own performance of miracles while among the Galatians. But such an interpretation is quite unnatural; it certainly was God, or the exalted Christ, who supplied the Spirit and also made possible the working of miracles, and since the primary endowment is not confined to Paul there is no real reason for restricting the latter to him. In fact,

if this restriction were made, his argument would lose its natural force" (*The Evolution of Early Christianity* [Chicago: University of Chicago Press, 1914] 149 n. 1).
ἐξ ἔργων νόμου ἢ ἐξ ἀκοῆς πίστεως ("on the basis of the works of the law or on the basis of believing what you heard") repeats the fundamental antithesis first set out in 3:2, but which is coordinate with ἐξ ἔργων νόμου or ἐκ/διὰ πίστεως ['Ιησοῦ] Χριστῷ of 2:16 and σαρκί or πνεύματι of 3:3. It is this antithesis that dominates all of Paul's argumentation in the first half of his *probatio* (3:1–18) against legalism.

Explanation

The Judaizers in Galatia, it seems, claimed not to be opposing Paul but to be supplementing his message, and so to be bringing his converts to perfection (cf. *Introduction*, "Opponents and Situation"). One evidence of this attitude on their part is Paul's response in 3:3, which suggests, as Betz puts it, "that Paul's missionary efforts were taken as merely the first step, and that the opponents claimed to provide the necessary and final measures to bring salvation to completion and perfection" (*Galatians*, 136). So the strategy of the Judaizers was not to deny the importance of faith in Christ for salvation, but to affirm the necessity for Gentiles to accept at least the minimal requirements of the Mosaic law for filling out their commitment to God and perfecting their Christian lives. It was not, therefore, an overt advocacy of legalism per se, but a call for Gentile believers to accept a lifestyle of Jewish nomism (cf. *Comment* on 2:16 for the distinction between "legalism" and "nomism"). As such it combined faith in Christ for initial acceptance before God and a nomistic lifestyle for true holiness, thereby claiming to work out in full the meaning of righteousness.

Paul, however, was not content to allow any supplement to the work of Christ, either for one's initial acceptance before God or for one's life as a Christian. For him, to start talking about supplements was to bring matters back to square one and the issue of legalism, even if it be claimed that nomism alone was the question. So though the Judaizers would have insisted that faith in Christ versus legalism was not at issue, Paul deals with both legalism and nomism, dealing first in 3:1–18 with matters on which there was theoretic agreement (i.e., legalism), but which Paul considered were being undercut in practice, then treating in 3:19–4:7 those matters directly contested (i.e., nomism). And in 3:1–5 he begins his arguments against "the works of the law" by appeals to the Galatian Christians' own spiritual experiences.

Paul's tone of address in 1:6 was intense, but restrained; in 1:11 very earnest. In 3:1, however, after the emotionally charged recital of events in 1:13–2:14, Paul bursts out with a biting, even rather insulting, form of address: "You foolish Galatians!" We may surmise that it was only because Paul was personally and affectionately known to the Galatians that he could hope to make a convincing case before his readers by so blunt an accusation.

Then Paul goes on to make his appeal to his readers, first by way of arguing from their own experience. The appeal in this first set of arguments in 3:1–5 is impelled by two certainties: first, that Christ's death had obliterated all forms of legal righteousness before God, whether having to do with initial acceptance or lifestyle (2:21); and second, that Christ as crucified had so been preached to the Galatians that no doubt concerning "the truth of the gospel" could remain in their minds (3:1b). The appeal is worked out in the form of six rhetorical questions in as many sentences. The first, "Who bewitched you?" is left suspended, and, in fact, is not the important question of the lot. The second, found in v 2, "Did you receive the Spirit on the basis of the works of the law or on the basis of believing what you heard?" is the important one. It is introduced by a common rhetorical dialogical device, "only this I want to learn from you." All the questions that follow in this first section of Gal 3, in fact, turn on this second question, with the final question of v 5 expanding it somewhat.

Paul's argument in vv 2–5 has to do with the Galatian Christians' reception of the Spirit at the time of their conversion and their continuing experiences of the Spirit in their lives thereafter. The experience of the Spirit in their lives, both at conversion and thereafter, is the reality on which he builds. But Paul's chief point of emphasis, as his twice-repeated antithesis of ἐξ ἔργων νόμου ἢ ἐξ ἀκοῆς πίστεως, "on the basis of the works of the law or on the basis of believing what you heard" (vv 2 and 5), clearly reveals, is on the role of faith in responding to the gospel as Paul proclaimed it, apart from any merit-amassing use of the Mosaic law.

(b) Arguments from Scripture (3:6–14)

Bibliography

Barrett, C. K. "The Allegory of Abraham, Sarah, and Hagar in the Argument of Galatians." In *Rechtfertigung*. FS E. Käsemann, eds. J. Friedrich, W. Pohlmann, and P. Stuhlmacher. Tübingen: Mohr-Siebeck, 1976, 1–16, esp. 6–8. **Bruce, F. F.** "The Curse of the Law." In *Paul and Paulinism*. FS C. K. Barrett, ed. M. D. Hooker and S. G. Wilson. London: SPCK, 1982, 27–36. **Davies, W. D.** "Paul and the Law: Reflections on Pitfalls in Interpretation." In *Paul and Paulinism*. FS C. K. Barrett, ed. M. D. Hooker and S. G. Wilson. London: SPCK, 1982, 4–16. **Donaldson, T. L.** "The 'Curse of the Law' and the Inclusion of the Gentiles: Galatians 3.13–14." *NTS* 32 (1986) 94–112. **Dunn, J. D. G.** "Works of the Law and the Curse of the Law (Galatians 3.10–14)." *NTS* 31 (1985) 523–42. **Foerster, W.** "Abfassungszeit und Ziel des Galaterbriefes." In *Apophoreta*. FS E. Haenchen, ed. W. Eltester and F. H. Kettler. Berlin: Töpelmann, 1964, 135–41. **Gutbrod, W.** "νόμος." *TDNT* 4:1022–85. **Hansen, G. W.** *Abraham in Galatians*, 97–139, 167–215. **Hill, D.** "Salvation Proclaimed: IV. Galatians 3:10–14: Freedom and Acceptance." *ExpTim* 93 (1982) 196–200. **Hübner, H.** *Law in Paul's Thought*. **Longenecker, R. N.** *Biblical Exegesis in the Apostolic Period*, 19–50, 104–32. ———. "The 'Faith of Abraham' Theme in Paul, James, and Hebrews: A Study in the Circumstantial Nature of New Testament Teaching." *JETS* 20 (1977) 203–12. **Räisänen, H.** *Paul and the Law*. **Sanders, E. P.** *Paul, the Law, and the Jewish People*, 17–29. **Schoeps, H. J.** *Paul*, 168–218. **Tyson, J. B.** "'Works of Law' in Galatians." *JBL* 92 (1973) 423–31. **Wilcox, M.** "'Upon the Tree'—Deut 21:22–23 in the New Testament." *JBL* 96 (1977) 85–99.

Translation

[6]*Take Abraham as the example:*[a] *"He believed God, and it was credited to him as righteousness."* [7]*You know, then, that those who rely on faith are the sons*[b] *of Abraham.*

⁸The Scripture foresaw that God would justify the Gentiles by faith and proclaimed the gospel to Abraham in advance, saying, "All nations shall be blessed in you." ⁹So those who rely on faith are blessed with Abraham, the man of faith.ᶜ

¹⁰For all who rely on the works of the law are under a curse, for it is written, "Cursed is everyone who does not continue inᵈ all the things written in the book of the law to do them." ¹¹Clearly, however, no one is justified before God by the law, because, "The righteous shall live by faith." ¹²But the law is not based on faith; rather, "The oneᵉ who does these things shall live by them." ¹³Christ redeemed us from the curse of the law by becoming a curse for us, for it is written, "Cursed is everyone who is hanged on a tree"—¹⁴in order that the blessing given to Abraham might come to the Gentiles through Christ Jesus and in order that we might receive the promiseᶠ of the Spirit by faith.

Notes

ᵃγέγραπται ("it is written") is added to καθώς by G vgᶜˡ Ambst, so understanding καθώς as an abbreviated introductory formula (needing expansion) rather than an *exemplum* reference.

ᵇυἱοί appears after εἰσίν in ℵᶜ A C D G TR, so bringing υἱοὶ Ἀβραάμ together as a unit; the reading υἱοί εἰσιν Ἀβραάμ, however, has better external support in ᵖ⁴⁶ ℵ* B etc. and is the more difficult reading, and so is to be preferred.

ᶜMarcion omitted vv 6–9 (cf. Tertullian, *Adv. Marc.* 5.3), being opposed to any relation between what is Jewish and what is Christian.

ᵈἐν is added to ἐμμένει by ℵᶜ A C D TR to read ἐμμένει ἐν ("continue in"), so strengthening the prepositional prefix of the verb and conforming to the LXX of Deut 27:26.

ᵉἄνθρωπος is added to αὐτά by TR Clement to read ὁ ποιήσας αὐτὰ ἄνθρωπος ("the man who does these things"), so conforming to the LXX of Lev 18:5.

ᶠἐπαγγελίαν ("promise") is well supported by ℵ A B C D² etc., though εὐλογίαν ("blessing") receives support from ᵖ⁴⁶ D* G Mcion Ambst Ephr.

Form/Structure/Setting

The second section of Paul's Galatians *probatio* is 3:6–14. It consists of arguments from Scripture and is in two parts: the first highlights significant features of God's covenant with Abraham, citing in particular Gen 15:6 and the "Blessing of Abraham" section of that covenant (vv 6–9); the second deals with three pivotal passages and then a fourth of great significance, setting out the argument in terms of the polarities between law and curse, on the one hand, and faith, righteousness, and blessing, on the other.

In terms of epistolary conventions, this second section has near its beginning the standard disclosure formula γινώσκετε ἄρα ὅτι, "you know, then, that" (v 7), which draws a conclusion from the citation of Gen 15:6 and introduces Paul's arguments to follow. Rhetorically, the section starts out with Abraham as the exemplar of faith. But it soon moves away from a Greco-Roman *exemplum* type of argument to arguments based on Scripture that follow more Jewish exegetical norms.

Structurally, after focusing on Abraham's faith and blessing in vv 6–9, the movement of the argument in vv 10–12 rests on three sets of particles, each of which introduces a statement and then a biblical text in support: γὰρ ... γὰρ (v 10); δὲ ... ὅτι (v 11); and δὲ ... ἀλλά (v 12). This is then followed by an asyndeton (i.e., an omission of a conjunction from a construction where one would normally be used) that serves to highlight what appears to be a pre-Pauline, Jewish Christian confession in v 13 and Paul's application of the truth of that confession for the situation at hand in v 14.

It has appeared to some that 3:6–14 is only rather tenuously related thematically to 3:1–5 and that with v 6 Paul makes a decided shift in his argumentation, one that introduces a more important and more compelling set of arguments than previously given (so Schlier, *Galater*, 126; Mussner, *Galaterbrief*, 211). But while there is assuredly a shift in the type of argument Paul mounts (i.e., from those based on experience to those based on Scripture), one should not attempt to drive too great a wedge between these two sections. For after the last citation of Scripture in v 13b and a concluding reference to Abraham in v 14a, Paul returns in 14b to the theme of the Spirit in such a way as to connect quite closely this section with the previous one. In fact, Paul brings the arguments of vv 6–14 to a climax not by way of an appeal to justification by faith, as one would expect from his discussion of Abraham as the prototype and exemplar of faith, but by a renewed focus on the Spirit and the Galatians' experience. Thus while in vv 2–5 the reception of the Spirit is presented as a past fact, in v 14b it is presented as the divine purpose, thereby moving from the fact of the known and experienced to the rationale for that experience as based in Scripture and the redeeming death of Christ.

The connection between vv 1–5 and vv 6–14 is furnished linguistically by the word πίστις, "faith" (or πιστεύω, "believe," as in the quotation from Gen 15:6 in v 6). The argument of vv 2–5 was focused on the means by which the Spirit entered the lives of believers, with the twice-stated antithesis ἐξ ἔργων νόμου ἢ ἐξ ἀκοῆς πίστεως, "on the basis of the works of the law or on the basis of believing what you heard," leaving no doubt that faith is that means and not "the works of the law." Here in vv 6–14 it is also faith—specifically faith as exercised by Abraham—that carries the argument forward. Every theme in vv 6–14, in fact, is brought to the test of faith, with no statement (except the two adverse quotations of vv 10 and 13) lacking a reference to πίστις.

The argument of vv 6–14 contains themes that are both old and new. The theme of justification by faith that was stressed in the *propositio* (cf. 2:16, "even we have believed in Christ Jesus") is continued and expanded in vv 6, 8, 11, and 13; likewise, as noted above, also the receiving of the Spirit in v 14b (cf. again vv 2 and 5). New themes, however, are brought forward, such as being true sons of Abraham (v 7), the justification of Gentiles as having been foretold in the promise to Abraham (v 8), the curse of the Mosaic law (vv 10, 13), and redemption from the law's curse by Christ's death (v 13). The leading theme of this section, however, is that of the blessing of Abraham (vv 8, 9, 14), particularly the Abrahamic blessing as including Gentiles.

Although addressing Gentile Christians, much of what appears in this section was undoubtedly influenced by Paul's desire to meet the arguments of the Judaizers and outclass them on their own grounds. Indeed, Abraham was the exemplar for Jews in all sorts of ways, and so might be expected to be appealed to in any argument involving Jews. But evidently the Judaizers had told the Gentiles of Galatia that in order to be true children of Abraham they had to be circumcised, as Abraham himself was and as he was commanded in the covenant given him by God (cf. Gen 17:9–14). In presenting his case, therefore, Paul seeks to "put the record straight" regarding Abraham in vv 6–9, highlighting what was really the situation and refuting the Judaizers' claims. Likewise it may be assumed that in vv 10–14 Paul conditions his exegesis of Scripture in light of how the Judaizers had represented these same passages, and so speaks in these verses as well in ad hominem and circumstantial fashion. As C. K. Barrett says of vv 10–14: "Paul's words can be best explained if we may suppose that he is taking up passages that had been used by his opponents, correcting their exegesis, and showing that their Old Testament prooftexts were on his side rather than on theirs" ("The Allegory," 6).

Before we comment directly on vv 6–14, however, the obvious must be said: Paul's exegesis of Scripture in these verses (and throughout the rest of chaps. 3 and 4) goes far beyond the rules of historico-grammatical exegesis as followed by biblical scholars today. That is a fact that everyone recognizes, though it is not explained by everyone in the same way. Yet understood in terms of his own presuppositions and inherited exegetical procedures (cf. my *Biblical Exegesis in the Apostolic Period*, 19–50, 104–32), Paul's arguments from Scripture are understandable and cogent (cf. Betz, *Galatians*, 138: keeping in mind his inherited exegetical method, "it can be shown that Paul's argument is consistent"). Furthermore, assuming that his exegesis here (and throughout the rest of chaps. 3 and 4) is also circumstantial gives us a greater appreciation of what Paul is about in these verses.

Excursus: Abraham's Faith and Faithfulness in Jewish Writings and in Paul

The esteem with which Abraham was held and the role he played in Jewish thought is clearly set out in Sir 44:19–21: "Abraham, the father of a multitude of nations, tarnished not his glory; who kept the commandment of the Most High and entered into covenant with Him: in his flesh He engraved him an ordinance, and in trial he was found faithful. Therefore with an oath He promised him 'to bless the nations in his seed', to multiply him 'as the dust of the earth', and to exalt his seed 'as the stars'; to cause them to inherit 'from sea to sea, and from the River to the ends of the earth'" (tr. G. H. Box and W. O. E. Oesterley in *APOT* 1:483). Cf. *Jub.* 23.10: "For Abraham was perfect in all his deeds with the Lord, and well-pleasing in righteousness all the days of his life" (tr. R. H. Charles in *APOT* 2:48); 1 Macc 2:52: "Was not Abraham found faithful in temptation, and it was reckoned unto him for righteousness?" (tr. W. O. E. Oesterley in *APOT* 1:74).

In rabbinic writings, Abraham is often affectionately called "a bag of myrrh," for "just as myrrh is the most excellent of spices, so Abraham was the chief of all righteous men" (*Cant. Rab.* 1.13). As early as Shemaiah and Abtalion, the immediate predecessors to Hillel and Shammai in the line of rabbinical succession in *m. 'Abot* 1.10–12, questions as to the nature of Abraham's faith and the relation of merit to that faith were being discussed among the Pharisees.

Two emphases with regard to Abraham are constantly made in the literature of Judaism: (1) that Abraham was counted righteous because of his faithfulness under testing; and (2) that Abraham's faith spoken of in Gen 15:6 must be coupled with his acceptance of circumcision as referred to in the covenant of Gen 17:4–14. The tests, or trials, of Abraham are usually considered to be ten in number, but there is no agreement in the various passages as to exactly what these ten were (though the tenth is always the " *'Aqēdâ* Isaac" or "Binding of Isaac"). Furthermore, Abraham's faithfulness under testing is always presented as being meritorious, both for Abraham himself and for his posterity.

In *Exod. Rab.* 44.4 (on Exod 32:13), for example, there is a long parable attributed to Rabbi Abin in the name of Rabbi Aha that well illustrates the Jewish attitude toward the merit of Abraham's faithfulness. It is a tale about a king whose friend deposited with him ten pearls and afterwards died. After his friend's death the king married the man's only daughter, making her his chief lady and giving her a necklace of ten pearls. But alas, the lady later lost the pearls, and the king in his anger sought to banish her from his presence. Her best friend, however, came to plead her cause before the king; and when he saw how adamant the king was, he reminded him of the ten pearls the father had left with the king and suggested that they be accepted in place of those the lady lost. The spiritual application of the story is then spelled out by Rabbi Abin:

> So, when Israel sinned, God was angry with them and said: "Now, therefore, let Me alone, that My wrath may wax hot against them, and that I may consume them" [Exod 32:10]. But Moses pleaded: "Lord of the Universe! Why art Thou angry with Israel?" "Because they have broken the Decalogue," He replied. "Well, they possess a source from which they can make repayment," he urged. "What is the source?" He asked. Moses replied: "Remember that Thou didst prove Abraham with ten trials, and so let those ten [trials of Abraham] serve as compensation for these ten [broken commandments]."

Admittedly, the parable cited comes from a time later than the NT period, for both Rabbi Abin and Rabbi Aha were fourth-generation Amoraim. Nevertheless, though the story itself is later than Paul's day, the conviction it carries as to the meritorious character of Abraham's faith has roots that go back to a much earlier time (cf., e.g., Sir 44:19–21 and 1 Macc 2:52 cited above).

Likewise, in Jewish writings there is the repeated insistence that Abraham's faith referred to in Gen 15:6 must always be coupled with Abraham's acceptance of circumcision in the covenant of Gen 17:4–14, so that the two matters of believing and keeping the covenant must be constantly brought together when one speaks of the righteousness of Abraham. There is in Judaism the motif of truth appearing in two forms, an elemental form and a developed form, and that only when one brings the two together can one come to understand truth in its fullness (cf. D. Daube, "Public Retort and Private Explanation," in *The New Testament and Rabbinic Judaism*, 141-50). Abraham, therefore, can certainly be spoken of as being righteous by faith in Gen 15:6, but that is only the elemental statement of the matter. It is in Gen 17:4–14, with its explicit insistence by God himself that "my covenant shall be in your flesh an everlasting covenant; any uncircumcised male who is not circumcised in the flesh of his foreskin shall be cut off from his people, he has broken my covenant," that the full nature of Abraham's righteousness is proclaimed.

For Judaism, then, trust in God and obedience to the law were inseparable. And though Abraham lived before the actual giving of the Mosaic law, he anticipated the keeping of that fuller expression of God's Torah in his acceptance of circumcision and in his offering of a ram in the *'Aqēdâ* Isaac ("Binding of Isaac") on Mt. Moriah. *Lev. Rab.* 2.10 (on Lev 1:12), therefore, argues that "Abraham fulfilled [in anticipation] the whole of the Torah, as it is said, 'Because that Abraham hearkened to My voice and kept My charge, My commandments, My statutes, and My laws' (Gen 26:6), and 'he offered a ram as a sacrifice.'"

When Paul, however, speaks of Abraham, he lays all of the emphasis on Abraham as being righteous by faith in response to the promise of God, apart from any effort of his own to keep the law. Thus in Galatians Paul takes pains to point out: (1) that the righteousness credited to Abraham in Gen 15:6 is associated solely with God's promise and the patriarch's faith (3:6, "he believed God, and it was credited to him as righteousness"); (2) that the principle of righteousness by faith was expressed in Abraham's life long before the Mosaic law was given (430 years before, says Paul), without being supplemented or abrogated by that later law (3:15–18); (3) that the promise given Abraham was, indeed, meant for the patriarch and his posterity, but the true "seed" of Abraham is Christ *and* all who belong to Christ (3:16, 29); and (4) that since righteousness in the divine economy is based on God's promise and mankind's response of faith, the Judaizers' attempted imposition of the law on Gentile believers should be treated in the same way as God told Abraham to treat his mistress Hagar and her son: "Get rid of the slave woman and her son, for the slave woman's son will never share in the inheritance with the free woman's son" (4:30).

Paul's use of the "faith of Abraham" theme, therefore, stresses entirely the patriarch's trust and commitment in response to God, and not Abraham's faithfulness under trial as a precondition to being considered righteous by God—or even his faithfulness to the Mosaic law as an expression of his faith. In fact, faithfulness to the custodial requirements of the Mosaic law in the expression of one's faith, Paul insists, was only begun with Moses and was meant to end with Christ (3:19–4:7). Later in Galatians, of course, Paul insists that true faith will express itself in loving service to others (5:6, 13–15), and he exhorts his converts to "do good to all people, especially to those who belong to the family of believers" (6:10). So we cannot say that the apostle was not interested in a faithful expression of a living faith that results in the good of others. But his emphasis in treating Abraham in Galatians (as well as in Romans) is entirely on the acceptance of Abraham as righteous before God on the basis of faith, apart from any works of the law.

Comment

6 καθὼς ᾿Αβραάμ, "take Abraham as the example." The adverb καθώς is often used in Greek writings and the NT to set off a comparison ("just as," "as . . . so"). Also, it frequently appears with γέγραπται as part of an introductory formula introducing a citation from Scripture ("as it is written"; so, e.g., Matt 26:24; Mark 1:2; 14:21; Luke 2:23; Acts 15:15; Rom 1:17; 2:24; 3:10; 4:17; 8:36; passim). Its absolute use, however, is rare, appearing only here in Paul. Almost all commentators have taken καθώς here as an abbreviated introductory formula introducing the quotation of Gen 15:6 (so explicitly G vg^cl Ambst, who add γέγραπται). A number of translators, however, have begun to treat καθώς here as an *exemplum* reference more than a quotation formula, and so translate καθὼς ᾿Αβραάμ as "take Abraham for example" (JB), "look at Abraham" (NEB), or "consider Abraham" (NIV). And that is, in our opinion, how it ought to be seen, translating it something along the lines of "take Abraham as the example." The fact that καθώς has such a broad semantic range as to include use as a comparative, use with γέγραπται as an introductory formula, and use as an *exemplum* reference allows Paul to use it in a bridging fashion, signaling directly an *exemplum* argument but also setting up arguments from Scripture. It is, in fact, at this point that Paul seems to shift in his *probatio* from more Greco-Roman types of rhetorical arguments to arguments more heavily influenced by Jewish procedural norms. For while he starts in v 6 with the exemplar of Abraham, and while the overtones of that *exemplum* type of argument continue to reverberate throughout the rest of chaps. 3 and 4, the structure of his argumentation after the words καθὼς ᾿Αβραάμ is strongly Jewish.

ἐπίστευσεν τῷ θεῷ καὶ ἐλογίσθη αὐτῷ εἰς δικαιοσύνην, "he believed God, and it was credited to him as righteousness." This is Paul's first quoted passage in his series of arguments from Scripture in vv 6–10. It is an almost exact quotation of Gen 15:6 LXX, though without the name ᾿Αβραάμ after ἐπίστευσεν (cf. Rom 4:3 and Jas 2:23 where the quotation conforms exactly). No doubt the Judaizers were citing Abraham as the great example of faith plus circumcision (even keeping the Mosaic law before it was actually given), probably using Gen 17:4–14 in support. Paul, however, does not attempt to interact with their treatment of Gen 17 (though in Rom 4 he shows his awareness of that chapter's relevancy by citing Gen 17:5 at 4:17), but rather focuses entirely on Gen 15:6 and its unitary statement regarding Abraham's faith and its efficacy. It would have been difficult to refute the Judaizers on the basis of an exegesis of Gen 17:4–14, for vv 10–14 are particularly plain as to the necessity of being circumcised in order to be accepted by God and remain in covenant relation with him. So Paul focuses on Gen 15:6 in an attempt to highlight the larger and underlying issue, apart from any further regulations or conditions given later.

Abraham's faith was not specifically faith in Jesus Christ, but faith in God and his promise. Some have distinguished between Abraham's faith as "faith in the promise" and Christian faith as "faith in fulfillment of that promise" (e.g., H. Schlier, *Galater*, 141; H. Boers, *Theology Out of the Ghetto: A New Testament Exegetical Study concerning Exclusiveness* [Leiden: Brill, 1971] 80). But such a distinction has more appearance than reality. For as H. D. Betz notes, "the faith of the Christians also remains faith in a promise (Gal 5:5)" and "both Abraham and the Christians believe in God who makes the dead alive" (*Galatians*, 153 n. 141). Abraham's faith was, for Paul, qualitatively like that called for in the Christian gospel, and so stands as the prototype of human response to God and his activity on behalf of humanity, however that activity is expressed throughout the course of redemptive history. The verb λογίζομαι appears in Greek writings and the NT in a variety of ways: "reckon" or "calculate"; "evaluate" or "estimate"; "think about" or "consider." In the LXX λογίζομαι is the translation of חשׁב, *hāšab*, which means "think" but also "account" or "credit" (in addition to Gen 15:6, see Ps 105 [106]:31 and 1 Macc 2:52). And it is in this latter sense that the word is used here in quoting Gen 15:6 (cf. Rom 4:3, 5, 9, 10, 22; 2 Cor 5:19).

Jews of Paul's day also, of course, used Gen 15:6 when speaking about Abraham. In many Jewish references, however, Abraham's faith is set in the context of his righteous deeds, with the result that the faith of Abraham in Gen 15:6 becomes the faith of one already righteous before God because of his previous works of righteousness. The Aramaic Targums, for example, which represent interpretive readings of Scripture that were prevalent in the synagogues of Palestine during (roughly) Paul's day, speak of Gen 15:6 in the context of Abraham's merits before God in rescuing Lot and his family from the four northern kings in Gen 14 (see *Tg. Ps.-J., Tg. Neof., Tg. Onq.*). J. A. Fitzmyer's comment in contrasting the treatment of Gen 15:1 in the Dead Sea *Genesis Apocryphon* (which, sadly, is broken off toward the end of v 4 and so does not include v 6) and in the Targums is apropos here:

> In the *Genesis Apocryphon* God's words to Abram make no allusion to the subject matter of Gn 14, his victory over the four kings. God merely recalls his own favor and benevolence toward Abram and promises him further wealth. How different these few lines are from the lengthy insertion which one finds in the Targums at this point. The latter try to establish Abram's merit before God, so that he will have some basis for the declaration of uprightness in Gn 15:6 (*The Genesis Apocryphon of Qumran Cave I: A Commentary,* BibOr 18 [Rome: Biblical Institute Press, 1971] 182).

So the paraphrase of Gen 15:6 in *Tg. Ps.-J.*: "He [Abraham] believed in the Lord and had faith in the Word of the Lord, and He credited it to him for righteousness, *because he parlayed not before him with words* [but with deeds]" (italics and brackets mine). And this same understanding is carried on by Philo (cf. *Abr.* 262–74, which stresses that Abraham's faith "is a little thing if measured by words, but a very great thing if made good by actions"; *Praem.* 27: "He [Abraham] received for his reward belief in God") and the rabbinic Midrashim (e.g., *Exod. Rab.* 3.12; 23.5; *Cant. Rab.* 4.8). But Paul cites Gen 15:6 without any reference to Abraham's meritorious deeds of Gen 14 as a basis for his reception by God or to Abraham's acceptance of circumcision in Gen 17 as a condition. His emphasis, as even his contextual omissions reveal, is on faith alone, apart from righteous deeds or circumcision.

7 γινώσκετε ἄρα ὅτι οἱ ἐκ πίστεως, οὗτοι υἱοί εἰσιν Ἀβραάμ, "you know, then, that those who rely on faith are the sons of Abraham." The verb γινώσκετε is either indicative ("you know") or imperative ("recognize," "consider"). Most have taken it as an imperative since it is in a teaching section and "conforms to the parallels in didactic literature" (so Betz, *Galatians*, 141, et al.). Yet γινώσκετε ἄρα ὅτι is a typical disclosure formula in ancient Hellenistic letters that serves more to remind readers of what is known than to exhort. So it should be read in the indicative mood, "you know, then, that." The particle ἄρα ("then") marks this statement of v 7 as the logical consequence of the quotation of v 6. The preposition ἐκ denotes source or basis for, as in 2:16 ("by [ἐκ] works of the law" or "by [ἐκ] the faith/faithfulness of Christ") and 3:2, 5 ("on the basis of [ἐκ] works of the law" or "on the basis of [ἐκ] believing what you heard"). Here, however, the word πίστις ("faith") signals a subjective response to the objective factors of what Christ has done and the proclamation of that message. Being, therefore, set in a subjective context, ἐκ here should be taken as "rely on," for faith is not the objective basis for human redemption but man's subjective response to what has been done by Christ and proclaimed by his messengers.

The expression υἱοὶ Ἀβραάμ ("sons of Abraham") is probably to be seen as polemically based. The Judaizers' message undoubtedly focused on being rightly related to Abraham and God's covenant with Israel (cf. *Comment* on "Abraham's seed" at 3:16, 29, the Hagar-Sarah allegory of 4:21–31, and "the Israel of God" of 6:16). Paul's habit in addressing Gentiles was not to commend Christ to them on OT grounds or to explain how they were related to Abraham and the Jewish nation (cf. esp. 1 & 2 Corinthians, Philippians, Colossians, 1 & 2 Thessalonians; the argument of Romans may be explained in other ways). That was, however, the Judaizers' approach, and so the Jewish question as to who really were "sons of Abraham" was probably often on their lips (cf. W. Foerster, "Abfassungszeit und Ziel des Galaterbriefes," 139). Likewise Paul's use of the phrase οἱ ἐκ πίστεως ("those who rely on faith") in all likelihood arises from and counters the Judaizers' call for Gentile Christians to be "those who rely on the law" (οἱ ἐκ νόμου) for perfection in their lives. In answering his opponents' propaganda, therefore, Paul is here, it seems, using expressions that he had picked up from them and then adjusted for his own purposes.

8 προϊδοῦσα δὲ ἡ γραφὴ ὅτι ἐκ πίστεως δικαιοῖ τὰ ἔθνη ὁ θεὸς προευηγγελίσατο τῷ Ἀβραὰμ ὅτι Ἐνευλογηθήσονται ἐν σοὶ πάντα τὰ ἔθνη, "the Scripture foresaw that God would justify the Gentiles by faith and proclaimed the gospel to Abraham in advance, saying, 'All nations shall be blessed in you.'"

The postpositive particle δέ (here untranslatable) connects v 8 to v 7, which in turn was deduced from v 6. Here is Paul's answer to the Judaizers' insistence that if all nations are to be blessed in Abraham, then the Galatian Christians must be related to Abraham—i.e., be his descendants by becoming circumcised. They quoted the last part of the Abrahamic covenant, the "Blessing of Abraham" section that appears in the LXX in a number of forms (cf. Gen 12:3; 18:18; 22:18; 26:4; 28:14; Ps 71:17; Sir 44:21). Their emphasis undoubtedly was on being related to Abraham—i.e., on the synonymous expressions "in you" (Gen 12:3), "in your seed" (Gen 22:18; 26:4), "in you . . . even in your seed" (Gen 28:14), and "in him [Abraham]" (Gen 18:18). Paul's emphasis, however, is on the fact that "all the nations of the earth" (Gen 18:18; 22:18; 26:4) or "all the tribes of the earth" (Gen 12:3; 28:14) are included in that foundational blessing.

The singular ἡ γραφή ("the Scripture") refers to a particular portion of Scripture (cf. Rom 9:17; 10:11; 11:2; see also Luke 4:21; John 19:36–37; Acts 8:35), viz., the last part of the Abrahamic covenant, the "Blessing of Abraham" section that is repeated a number of times in the OT (see passages above). The aorist adverbial participle προϊδοῦσα is probably circumstantial in function, and so sets out an additional statement to that of the sentence's main verb (i.e., "foresaw . . . that God would justify"). The attributing of foresight to Scripture is a figure of speech for the divine foresight expressed in Scripture, comparable to the rabbinic personification of Torah in the statement, "What has the Torah seen?" (cf. Str-B, 3.538). The finite verb δικαιοῖ ("would justify") is third person, present, indicative, active, but functions as a future as demanded by προϊδοῦσα. The expression τὰ ἔθνη here means "the Gentiles" whose righteousness is under question, with πάντα τὰ ἔθνη [τῆς γῆς] (cf. Gen 18:18; 22:18; 26:4) to be read more inclusively as "all the nations [of the earth]" (parallel to πᾶσαι αἱ φυλαὶ τῆς γῆς of Gen 12:3 and 28:14). The verb προευηγγελίσατο is found nowhere else in the NT, LXX, or Jewish apocryphal writings, but does appear in Philo and Sophist materials to mean "to proclaim good news in advance" (cf. BAG and MM)—with that "good news" here meaning, of course, the gospel as proclaimed apart from law. The central phrase of the verse, ἐκ πίστεως, being parallel with ἐκ πίστεως of v 7, certainly refers to the human response of trust and commitment "by faith."

9 ὥστε οἱ ἐκ πίστεως εὐλογοῦνται σὺν τῷ πιστῷ Ἀβραάμ, "so those who rely on faith are blessed with Abraham, the man of faith." Paul found Gentiles at the very heart of the Abrahamic covenant. In fact, as Rom 15:9–12 shows (citing Ps 18:49; 2 Sam 22:50; Deut 32:43; Ps 117:1; Isa 11:10), Paul found God's saving purpose toward Gentiles everywhere in the Old Testament. His missionary experiences of God's direct, redemptive dealings with Gentiles, of course, had sensitized him to reading Scripture with Gentiles in mind. And he wants his Gentile converts to know that they were in the mind and purpose of God when God gave his covenant to Abraham.

Here ὥστε ("so") introduces a concluding statement that stresses result. The emphasis in this statement is on οἱ ἐκ πίστεως ("those who rely on faith") as against οἱ ἐκ νόμου ("those who rely on the law"), οἱ ἐξ ἔργων νόμου ("those who rely on the works of the law"), or οἱ περιτετμημένοι ("those who are circumcised") whom the Judaizers claimed were alone eligible for full inheritance of the blessings of the Abrahamic covenant. Clearly, "those who rely on faith" is equivalent to "sons of Abraham" of v 7 and in line with "blessed with Abraham" here in v 9. The preposition σύν lays stress on the believer's vital connection "with" Abraham. ἐν could have been used just as well, but that seems to have been the grammatical form the Judaizers were using with reference to Abraham (see *Comment* on ἐν σοί of v 8) and Paul may have purposely steered clear of it here. The adjective πιστῷ is to be taken in its active sense, as required by ἐπίστευσεν of v 6. The translation "believing" more exactly expresses its meaning (certainly not "trustworthy" as in Sir 44:20 or "faithful" as in KJV and NEB). But such a translation tends to subjugate the adjective to its noun and not highlight its alignment with οἱ ἐκ πίστεως. So some such translation as "Abraham who had faith" (RSV) or "Abraham, the man of faith" (JB, NIV) is better.

Burton proposed that Paul's use of εὐλογοῦνται ("they are blessed") rather than δικαιοῦνται ("they are justified") here "is doubtless due to the fact that he is still using the language of his opponents" (*Galatians*, 162; see also P. Bonnard, *L'Épître de Saint Paul aux Galates*, 67). That may be so. Yet it may be as well that Paul found the term "blessed" congenial with the next movement of his argument wherein he sets out proofs from Scripture for the antithesis of law and curse versus faith, righteousness, and blessing. So in reinterpreting the "Blessing of Abraham" portion of the Abrahamic covenant for his Gentile converts (contra the Judaizers' treatment) he is able also to set up in the strongest terms the contrast between what the gospel actually bestows and what the errorists of Galatia were offering.

10 ὅσοι γὰρ ἐξ ἔργων νόμου εἰσὶν ὑπὸ κατάραν εἰσίν, "for all who rely on the works of the law are under a curse." The second part of Paul's argument from Scripture is introduced by the postpositive γάρ ("for"), which suggests that what follows in vv 10–14 is meant to be explanatory of the dichotomy implicit in vv 6–9 between relying on faith for righteousness and relying on one's own observance of the law. Here in these verses Paul mounts a direct and vigorous attack against the Judaizers' claims, showing how in two passages that speak of the law (Deut 27:26; Lev 18:5)—passages which, it may be assumed, the Judaizers were citing to Paul's converts—there is no reference to faith, righteousness, or blessing, but rather only curse. On the other hand, another passage of great significance for the issues at hand (Hab 2:4) associates righteousness only with faith, and still another that seems so troublesome for belief in Jesus as Israel's Messiah (Deut 21:23) actually should be read as meaning that the curse of the law has been borne entirely by Christ, and so now only faith remains as the prerequisite to receiving the Abrahamic blessing and God's Spirit.

The absolute use of ὅσοι ("all who") coupled with ἐξ ἔργων νόμου ("rely on the works of the law") marks out a particular group of people in contrast to those designated in v 9 as οἱ ἐκ πίστεως ("those who rely on faith"). The combined phrase is expressive, for it denotes "a specific mode of existence," one that views observance of Torah as obligatory for God's people (cf. J. B. Tyson, *JBL* 92 [1973] 430). By so distinguishing this group from "those who rely on faith," Paul removes all who adhere to the observance of the Mosaic law for righteousness before God from the "mode of existence" conditioned by faith. For by taking up "the works of the law" they have placed themselves ὑπὸ κατάραν ("under a curse").

The preposition ὑπό is connected with the law, either directly or indirectly, a total of ten times in Galatians. In each occurrence it expresses a situation of being under the authority or power of that which it modifies: "under sin" (3:22), "under the law" (3:23; 4:4, 5, 21; 5:18), "under a pedagogue" (3:25), "under guardians and trustees" (4:2), and "under the basic principles of the world" (4:3). Here in 3:10 it is being "under a curse," which Paul associates with the law. The Judaizers, of course, did not view being "under the law" in any pejorative sense. Much like Josephus, they probably invited their Gentile hearers in some such words as follows: "To all who desire to come and live under the same laws with us [ὑπὸ τοὺς αὐτοὺς ἡμῖν νόμους], he [Moses] gives a gracious welcome, holding that it is not family ties alone that constitute relationship, but agreement in the principles of conduct" (*Ag. Ap.* 2.210). Paul, however, wants his Galatian converts to know that if they insist on taking up the requirements of the law they will bring themselves under a curse. And he appeals to Deut 27:26 in support for that association of law and curse.

The words of Deut 27:26 constitute the last of the twelve curses pronounced by the Levites on Mt. Ebal in Israel's annual renewal of the Mosaic covenant, and in many ways they serve to summarize the curses of the covenant: "Cursed is everyone who does not continue in all the things written in the book of the law to do them." Undoubtedly the Judaizers had quoted this passage as being decisive. Paul also knew these words well, not only from his Jewish training but also from the five times he received "forty lashes minus one" at the hands of certain synagogue authorities (cf. 2 Cor 11:24). For if the detailed instructions for synagogal lashings given in *m. Mak.* 3.10–14 were carried out those five times in Paul's experience—instructions which include provisions for a reader to read intermittently the curses prescribed in the Mosaic law, specifically Deut 28:58–59 (which speaks explicitly of curses for not doing "all" the words of this law) but also "returning again to the beginning of the passage"—then it could be said that such words, indeed, had been duly impressed on Paul's memory. Israel had willingly placed herself under the stipulations of the covenant (cf. Exod 24:3, 7), and in so doing had accepted the threat of being cursed for nonfulfillment (cf. Josephus, *Ant.* 4.302, 307). Coming under a curse was therefore inextricably bound up with receiving the law, and Paul seeks to make that point explicit in his treatment of Deut 27:26.

γέγραπται γὰρ ὅτι Ἐπικατάρατος πᾶς ὃς οὐκ ἐμμένει πᾶσιν τοῖς γεγραμμένοις ἐν τῷ βιβλίῳ τοῦ νόμου τοῦ ποιῆσαι αὐτά, "for it is written, 'Cursed is everyone who does not continue in all things written in the book of the law to do them.'" Deut 27:26 is introduced by Paul's usual introductory formula γέγραπται ("it is written"). The text of the citation, however, does not agree fully with any extant MT or LXX version, though it comes close to LXX[A]—departing only in the omission of ἄνθρωπος ("man") after πᾶς ("every"), the dropping of ἐν ("in") before πᾶσιν ("all the things"), and the change of λόγοις τοῦ νόμου τούτου ("the words of God's law") to γεγραμμένοις ἐν τῷ βιβλίῳ τοῦ νόμου ("written in the book of the law"). Paul may be quoting from a version then in circulation but now lost, or quoting freely from memory, or making intentional changes for his own purposes. At any rate, none of the changes affect materially the sense of the passage as found in the LXX, though πᾶσιν ("all") in all the extant LXX readings goes beyond what is found explicitly in the MT, even though implied.

The Judaizers had evidently focused on the words ποιῆσαι αὐτά ("to do them"). Paul, however, seems to be more concerned to stress πᾶσιν ("all"), which is his emphasis again in 5:3 (cf. also 6:13). Thus those listening favorably to the Judaizers' arguments must realize the full consequences of what they are about to accept, for they are obligating themselves not just to a few legal observances but to "all the things written in the book of the law to do them."

We may assume that the premise of the Judaizers' argument was that one who faithfully observes the Mosaic law will live a full and acceptable life before God, which is what is stated as the principle of the law in v 12 quoting Lev 18:5: "The one who does these things shall live by them" (see *Comment* at v 12). Paul's premise, however, though unstated, is that no one is capable of keeping all the law (so Burton, *Galatians,* 164–65; H. Lietzmann, *Galater,* 11; H. J. Schoeps, *Paul,* 176–77; A. Oepke, *Galater,* 72; F. Mussner, *Galaterbrief,* 224–26; contra Betz, *Galatians,* 145–46). And such an understanding, while not a common Jewish view (cf. W. Gutbrod on rabbinic writings: "In the main it is asserted in principle that the Law can be fulfilled" [*TDNT* 4:1058]), was present in a number of rabbis and Jewish writers of Paul's day (cf. H. J. Schoeps, *Paul,* 177; R. N. Longenecker, *Paul, Apostle of Liberty,* 40–43,120, 124).

11 ὅτι δὲ ἐν νόμῳ οὐδεὶς δικαιοῦται παρὰ τῷ θεῷ δῆλον, "clearly, however, no one is justified before God by the law." While γάρ at the start of v 10 was explanatory, here δέ is adversative (contra Betz, *Galatians,* 146). Used in the same sentence with the adverb δῆλον ("clear," "plain," "evident"), the antithetical nature of vv 10 and 11 is heightened (so "it is evident, however" or "clearly, however"). By means of the antithesis presented in these two verses, in fact, Paul sets out his biblical evidence in support of what he said in 2:15–16 of the *propositio* and what he said about his converts' experience and Abraham in the *probatio*— i. e., that Scripture in those pivotal passages under dispute associates curse with law and righteousness with faith. And it is this dichotomous categorization of the biblical texts that Paul wants to highlight against the Judaizers' claims.

The expression ἐν νόμῳ ("by the law") corresponds to ἐξ ἔργων νόμου ("by the works of the law") used earlier (cf. 2:16; 3:2, 5 and 10); after the use of the fuller phrase in v 10, ἐν νόμῳ here suffices to express the same idea (cf. Phil 3:6). There is here no change of reference from the Mosaic law to "law" in some universal sense, as many have supposed (contra Mussner, *Galaterbrief,* 228). The passive construction of δικαιοῦται ("is justified") emphasizes righteousness as bestowed by another rather than as achieved by one's own effort, which is Paul's usual mood for the verb throughout Galatians and Romans (cf. Gal 2:16, 17; 5:4; Rom 2:13; 3:20, 24, 28; 4:2; 5:1; though active in Rom 3:30; 4:5; 8:30). The phrase παρὰ τῷ θεῷ ("before God") is used figuratively of God's estimation or judgment (cf. Rom 2:13; 1 Cor 3:19; 2 Thess 1:6; also Job 9:2; Jas 1:27; 1 Peter 2:4, 20; 2 Peter 3:8; Josephus, *Ant.* 6.205). It highlights a significant point that Paul wants to make: "that as over against the verdict of law set forth in the preceding sentence he is now speaking of the actual attitude of God" (Burton, *Galatians,* 165).

ὅτι Ὁ δίκαιος ἐκ πίστεως ζήσεται, "because, 'The righteous shall live by faith.'" In support of the association of faith with righteousness, Paul cites Hab 2:4. He does not introduce this biblical text by his usual introductory formula "it is written" (though he does in Rom 1:17), but the γέγραπται ("it is written") of v 10 makes it clear that he is continuing to quote from Scripture in all the material cited in conjunction with the quotation in v 10.

Hab 2:4 was understood by Jews in Paul's day in various ways. The MT reading וצדיק באמונתו יחיה (*wĕṣadîq beʾĕmûnātô yihyeh,* "the righteous shall live by his faith/ faithfulness") evidently raised uncertainties as to how to understand the pronominal suffix "his" and the word אמונה *ʾĕmûnâ,* "faith/faithfulness"). The LXX, for example, reads the text in two ways: either ὁ δίκαιος ἐκ πίστεώς μου ζήσεται ("the righteous shall live on the basis of my [God's] faithfulness," so LXX[B]) or ὁ δίκαιός μου ἐκ πέστεως ζήσεται ("my righteous one shall live on the basis of faith/faithfulness," so LXX[A]). The rabbis seem to have coupled Hab 2:4 with Gen 15:6 as two important *testimonia* having to do with the nation's inheritance of Abraham's meritorious faith (cf. *Exod. Rab.* 23.5), viewing Hab 2:4 in particular as the summation of the whole Mosaic law in one principle—i. e., faithfulness rewarded by faith (cf. *Mid. Ps.* 17A.25 and *b. Mak.* 24a, where David is said to have summed up the law in eleven principles [Ps 15], Isaiah in six [Isa 33:14–16], Micah in three [Mic 6:8], Isaiah again in two [Isa 56:1], Amos in one [Amos 5:4], and Habakkuk in one [Hab 2:4]). The Dead Sea covenanters applied Hab 2:4 to their own situation, understanding it in terms of observing the Mosaic law and trusting the guidance of their founding teacher: "This concerns all those who observe the law in the house of Judah, whom God will deliver from the House of Judgment because of their suffering and because of their faith in the Teacher of Righteousness" (1QpHab 7.14–8.3).

C. H. Dodd has argued that Hab 2:4 was probably an early Christian *testimonium* used in support of salvation by faith in Christ, since it appears in Gal 3:11 in an ad hominem manner (presupposing its acceptance by both Paul's converts and the Judaizers) and since it evidences textual fluctuation in its use by Paul in Gal 3:11 and Rom 1:17 and the writer of Hebrews in Heb 10:38 (cf. *According to the Scriptures* [London: Nisbet, 1952] 50–51). George Howard, however, asserts that Paul's use of Hab 2:4 in Gal 3:11 should not be seen in terms of Christian soteriology, and thus not reflective of a common Christian use, since there is no reference in the immediate context to faith in Christ and since a Christian soteriological understanding clashes with the statement of v 12 (cf. *Paul: Crisis in Galatia,* 63). But Howard's reasoning is weak, for while Abraham's faith of Gen 15:6 was not specifically Christian in content, it yet served for Paul as the prototype of Christian faith in vv 7–9. And the conflict between v 11 and v 12 would be damaging to such a view only if one treated these passages as if there should be none, but there is (see *Comment* below). There is, therefore, much to be said in favor of Dodd's hypothesis that Hab 2:4 was used widely by Christians and that Paul is here reinterpreting this passage in ad hominem fashion for his Galatian converts in contradistinction to how the Judaizers were using it.

In Paul's use of Hab 2:4 he drops the whole discussion regarding how to read the pronominal suffix "his" of the MT or the personal pronoun "my" of the LXX. His emphasis is entirely on ἐκ πίστεως ("by faith"). And the point he is making here is that righteousness in this pivotal text is associated with faith alone—not with the law! Paul may himself have read the text "the one who is righteous by faith shall live" (as the close association of ὁ δίκαιος and ἐκ πίστεως in the word order might suggest) or "the righteous one shall live by faith" (which is the more traditional reading, both then and today). Either way, however, in v 11 Paul sets up a sharp antithesis to v 10: righteousness is to be associated with faith alone; curse is the result of trying to observe the law in order to gain righteousness.

12 ὁ δὲ νόμος οὐκ ἔστιν ἐκ πίστεως, "but the law is not based on faith." The postpositive δέ here, particularly in association with ἀλλά that follows, is adversative ("but"), just as it is in v 11—thereby setting v 12 in sharp contrast to v 11, just as v 11 is in sharp contrast to v 10 (contra Betz, *Galatians,* 147; Howard, *Paul: Crisis in Galatia,* 63–64). So vv 10 and 12 are lined up on the one side, that of law and curse, with v 11 on the other, that of faith and righteousness.

Here in v 12 Paul sets out his thesis in as abbreviated a form as possible: νόμος ("law") and πίστις ("faith") are mutually exclusive as bases for righteousness. Paul does not attempt to give reasons; his intention is only to enunciate the principle and cite Lev 18:5 in support. In his further discussion of the law in 3:19–25, however, he sets out several reasons that apply here as well: (1) the law was given in salvation history to uncover sin, at times even by rousing it to action, and so functions for another purpose and on a different level than faith (3:19, 22; cf. Rom 5:20; 7:7–12); (2) the law has no power to make alive (3:21), a statement indirectly presupposing the spiritual death of all mankind (cf. Rom 5:12, 17–18; 8:3); and (3) the redeeming work of Christ is God's answer for sin-enslaved mankind (3:22, 24).

ἀλλ' Ὁ ποιήσας αὐτὰ ζήσεται ἐν αὐτοῖς, "rather, 'the one who does these things shall live by them.'" The quotation of Lev 18:5 is introduced by the strong adversative ἀλλά ("on the contrary," "rather") and not Paul's usual introductory formula "it is written," though here again (as with v 11) the γέγραπται of v 10 makes it evident that Paul is continuing to quote Scripture in all the citations brought forward in conjunction with that of v 10. His point in quoting Lev 18:5 is obvious: the law has to do with "doing" and "living by its prescriptions" and not with faith. So this fundamental passage of Jewish religion cannot just be Christianized and used to urge Gentile Christians to observe the Mosaic law, as the Judaizers were doing. Rather, in its basic principles Lev 18:5 must be seen to line up with Deut 27:26, for it refers to law and to doing but not to faith.

In the targumic tradition arising out of the synagogues of Palestine, Lev 18:5 is seen as having reference to the life of the age to come, which is the reward of obedience to the Torah: "And you shall keep my statutes and my judgments, which if a man do he shall live by them an everlasting life" (Tg. Onq.); "And you shall keep my statutes, and the order of my judgments, which if a man do he shall live in them, in the life of eternity, and his position shall be with the just" (Tg. Ps-J.). In rabbinic thought that represents more the scholastic tradition of Judaism, "The Torah," as W. Gutbrod aptly states, "may be summed up in two inwardly related principles: 1. God has revealed Himself once and for all and exclusively in the Torah; 2. man has his relationship with God only in his relationship with Torah" ("νόμος," TDNT 4:1055). "The aim of the Torah," as Gutbrod continues, "is to show man what he should do and not do in order that, obedient to the Torah, he may have God's approval, righteousness, life, and a share in the future world of God" (ibid., 4:1058). So in Judaism there is an emphasis not only on knowing the law but more importantly on doing the law (cf. the texts supplied by Gutbrod, ibid., 4:1058, and Str-B 4:6). It is this emphasis that is captured in the Jewish use of Lev 18:5, "the one who does these things shall live by them," to which Paul objects so much.

Paul's quotation of Lev 18:5 in Gal 3:12 leaves out the word ἄνθρωπος ("man") that is included in all extant LXX versions, translating הָאָדָם (hā'ādām) of the MT. One tradition of talmudic lore that goes well back into the Tannaitic period lays stress on the fact that the general term "man" appears in Lev 18:5 and draws from that the conclusion that even a Gentile may be regarded in God's sight as a high priest if he observes the law. So, for example, Rabbi Meir (second generation Tannaim) is cited in b. Sanh. 59a as saying:

Whence do we know that even a Gentile who studies the Torah is as a High Priest? From the verse "[Ye shall therefore keep my statutes and my judgments,] which if a man do, he shall live in them" [Lev 18:5]. Priests, Levites, and Israelites are not mentioned, but "men"; hence thou mayest learn that even a Gentile who studies the Torah is as a High Priest" (cf. *b. B. Qam.* 38a; *Midr.Ps.* 1.18; *Num. Rab.* 13.15–16, where the same tradition appears).

In omitting ἄνθρωπος from the quotation, therefore, Paul may even have been implying that Lev 18:5 should be withdrawn from the category of passages having relevance to pious Gentiles. The Judaizers may have been so using the passage, and he wanted to undercut that specific usage; or Paul may have known generally of such a usage and therefore could not bring himself to include ἄνθρωπος in the text (contra all the textual traditions of the MT, LXX, and Targums). Be that as it may, however, in Gal 3:12 Paul sees Lev 18:5 as devoid of the principle of faith and so lines it up with Deut 27:26 in the category of law and curse.

13 Χριστὸς ἡμᾶς ἐξηγόρασεν ἐκ τῆς κατάρας τοῦ νόμου γενόμενος ὑπὲρ ἡμῶν κατάρα, "Christ redeemed us from the curse of the law by becoming a curse for us." In v 13 Paul breaks away quite abruptly from his depiction of mankind's position under a curse in vv 10 and 12 to introduce the idea of deliverance through Christ's redemption. The asyndeton (absence of a connective where one would normally be expected), particularly after the consistent use of connecting particles in vv 10–12, lends rhetorical force to the change of subject (cf. *Comment* at 4:10). The verb ἐξαγοράζω ("redeem") is new to the discussion, though the idea of deliverance is not (cf. 1:3b–4, Ἰησοῦ Χριστοῦ τοῦ δόντος ["Jesus Christ who gave"]; see later 4:5, ἵνα τοὺς ὑπὸ νόμον ἐξαγοράσῃ ["in order that he might redeem those under the law"]). The aorist tense of ἐξηγόρασεν ("redeemed") signals the historical event of Christ's death on the cross, which is then further referred to as his γενόμενος ὑπὲρ ἡμῶν κατάρα ("becoming a curse for us"). The thought involved here is that of "an exchange curse" (*ein Tauschgeschäft*, as Klaus Berger calls it; "Abraham in den paulinischen Hauptbriefen," *MTZ* 17 [1966] 52; or more expansively, M. Luther: "Thou Christ art my sin and my curse, or rather, I am thy sin, thy curse, thy death, thy wrath of God, thy hell; and contrariwise, thou art my righteousness, my blessing, my life, my grace of God and my heaven"; *Galatians*, 283). The explicit phrase "the curse of the law" occurs only here in Paul, though the concept appears earlier in v 10 where Deut 27:26 pronounces a curse on everyone who accepts the obligations of the law but "does not continue in all the things written in the book of the law to do them."

Two striking features about v 13a are (1) its conciseness in stating what Christ accomplished redemptively, and (2) its use of the first person plural pronoun ἡμεῖς, which in Galatians often refers to Jewish Christians (see esp. 2:15; 3:23–25; 4:5) and here certainly has in mind those "under the law," yet refers to Gentiles who as yet had not submitted to circumcision. (L. Gaston's position that "Paul so identified with his readers that the first person plural actually means 'we Gentiles'" and that ὑπὸ νόμον "seems to have been used by Paul to designate the Gentile situation" ["Paul and the Torah," 62] is impossible to maintain.) Also of note is the fact that the imagery of v 13a is pregnant with meaning, though not spelled out: "redemption" as a commercial metaphor used in a religious setting and "becoming a curse for us" as language stemming from the sacrificial cultus. All of this, it seems, suggests that what we have here is a pre-Pauline, Jewish Christian confessional statement regarding Jesus' death as a redeeming and atoning self-sacrifice (cf.

Betz, *Galatians*, 149–51, citing Gal 1:4 and 2:20 as parallels; for the view that both v 13 and v 14 constitute a fragment of a Jewish Christian midrash based on the *'Aqēdâ* Isaac and here taken over by Paul, see N. A. Dahl, "The Atonement—An Adequate Reward for the Akedah? (Rom. 8.32)," 23–24; idem, *Studies in Paul*, 133–34; M. Wilcox, *JBL* 96 [1977] 99)—a confession Paul quotes as a powerful reason why the Galatians need not and should not place themselves under the Mosaic law.

ὅτι γέγραπται, Ἐπικατάρατος πᾶς ὁ κρεμάμενος ἐπὶ ξύλου, "for it is written, 'Cursed is everyone who is hanged on a tree.'" In support of what appears to be an early Jewish Christian confession, the central portion of Deut 21:23 is here quoted, being introduced by Paul's customary introductory formula γέγραπται ("it is written"). Deut 21:22–23 originally had reference to the exposure of the body of a criminal after his execution: "If a man guilty of a capital offense is put to death and his body is hung on a tree, you must not leave his body on the tree overnight. Be sure to bury him that same day, because cursed is everyone who is hanged on a tree. You must not desecrate the land the Lord your God is giving you as an inheritance." Originally, therefore, these verses pertained to the practice of hanging the dead bodies of criminals or enemies on a tree or pole for added insult or as a public warning (cf. Num 25:4; Josh 10:26–27; 2 Sam 21:6–9). In the NT period, however, Deut 21:22–23 was applied both to the exposure of a dead corpse on a tree or pole and the impalement or crucifixion of a living person (cf. J. A. Fitzmyer, "Crucifixion in Ancient Palestine, Qumran Literature, and the NT," *CBQ* 40 [1978] 493–513). So, for example, in 11QTemple 64.6–13 regulations are given for hanging the corpse of a man executed "on a tree" and hanging a living man "on a tree that he may die," with both forms of hanging related to Deut 21:22–23 and the phrase "cursed by God" expanded to "cursed by God and men."

Paul's quotation of Deut 21:23 differs from all extant LXX readings. He writes ἐπικατάρατος ("cursed") rather than κεκαταραμένος ("having been cursed," or κεκατηραμένος in LXX[A, F]), probably by way of assimilation (intentional or otherwise) to ἐπικατάρατος of Deut 27:26 quoted in v 10 (cf. M. Wilcox, *JBL* 96 [1977] 87). Also he omits ὑπὸ θεοῦ ("by God") after ἐπικατάρατος, either to avoid saying directly that Christ was cursed by God—though, of course, "the curse of the law" is another way of saying "cursed by God"—or to highlight the absolute nature of the curse itself. It may be, in fact, as Max Wilcox proposes, that the underlying text-form used here by Paul was not that of any of the LXX versions as we know them, but a Hebrew version akin to the tradition of interpretation found in the *Temple Scroll* from Qumran (ibid.).

For Jews, the proclamation of a crucified Messiah was scandalous (cf. 1 Cor 1:23; Gal 5:11), "a blasphemous contradiction in terms" (Bruce, *Galatians*, 166). Undoubtedly the central problem for all Jewish Christians was how to understand Jesus as God's Messiah and yet as cursed by God, with the magnitude of the problem only heightened by the pronouncement of Deut 21:23. The process as to how early Christians came to understand Jesus as both Messiah and accursed may be obscure, but their conclusion is clear: the curse of the cross was "an exchange curse" wherein Christ became a curse for us (cf. esp. 2 Cor 5:21). And it is just such an assertion that appears in 3:13a, which we believe is probably an early Christian confession used by Paul.

If, then, v 13a is a pre-Pauline, Jewish Christian confessional statement that epitomizes the work of Christ in terms of "an exchange curse," the quotation of Deut 21:23 in apparent support probably stems from early Jewish Christianity as well, whether joined to the confession from the start or not. In all likelihood, therefore, what Paul is doing here in v 13 is citing a traditional confessional portion, presumably known to his Galatian converts (also to the Judaizers, though they may not have used it themselves), to show how Christ's bearing of mankind's curse nullifies all thoughts of legalism and to set up his conclusion regarding the blessing of Abraham and the promise of the Spirit in v 14.

14 ἵνα εἰς τὰ ἔθνη ἡ εὐλογία τοῦ Ἀβραὰμ γένηται ἐν Χριστῷ Ἰησοῦ, ἵνα τὴν ἐπαγγελίαν τοῦ πνεύματος λάβωμεν διὰ τῆς πίστεως, "in order that the blessing given to Abraham might come to the Gentiles through Christ Jesus and in order that we might receive the promise of the Spirit by faith." Paul's arguments from Scripture in 3:6–14 conclude with two ἵνα clauses that bring to a climax in somewhat intertwined fashion the two main themes of both this section and the previous one: (1) the blessing of Abraham given to Gentiles, and (2) the promise of the Spirit received by faith. Structurally, the two clauses are coordinate, and the second is not subsidiary to the first (contra G. S. Duncan, *Galatians,* 103; et al.). Grammatically, the two clauses are pure purpose clauses. Yet, as C. F. D. Moule has observed, "the Semitic mind was notoriously unwilling to draw a sharp dividing-line between purpose and consequence" (*An Idiom-Book of New Testament Greek,* 1st ed. [Cambridge: Cambridge University Press, 1953] 142).

In the first clause concerning "the blessing of Abraham" Paul highlights two phrases: εἰς τὰ ἔθνη ("to the Gentiles") and ἐν Χριστῷ Ἰησοῦ ("in/through Christ Jesus"). "To the Gentiles" receives the main emphasis, for the inclusion of the Gentiles is Paul's chief point throughout his Galatian letter. "In/through Christ Jesus," however, is Paul's whole gospel *in nuce,* which is not so much argued as presupposed (cf. the other seven occurrences of the "in Christ" expression in Galatians at 1:22; 2:4, 17; 3:26, 28; 5:6, 10). Positively, "being in Christ" is the connection between Abraham and Gentile Christians; conversely, it is the reality that absolutely negates the Judaizers' attempt to relate Gentile Christians to Abraham by means of Torah observance.

The second clause regarding "the promise of the Spirit" highlights the expression "by faith" that has appeared repeatedly throughout Paul's *probatio* so far. While Paul has not mentioned the Spirit in vv 6–14a, the fact that he began his *probatio* with appeals to his converts' reception of the Spirit and now ends his proofs from Scripture by speaking of "the promise of the Spirit" suggests that lying close to the surface in all of his thought was a consciousness of God's Spirit as indwelling and directing. The phrase "receive the promise of the Spirit" connotes acceptance by God, with the denotation being the reception of the Spirit itself as promised. So Paul stresses, against the Judaizers, that acceptance by God as signaled in receiving God's Spirit depends entirely on faith apart from any merit-amassing attitude toward the Jewish law.

It seems, therefore, that v 14 functions in two ways: first of all as the conclusion to Paul's arguments from Scripture, but also as the conclusion to all Paul has presented so far in his *probatio.* It brings together in somewhat intertwined, though climactic, fashion (1) "the blessing of Abraham that is given to Gentiles" theme (v 14a) that was argued in vv 6–13, and (2) "the promise of the Spirit that is received by faith" theme (v 14b) that was set out in vv 2–5 when dealing with the

Galatians' experience and argued throughout vv 2–13 in asserting the centrality of faith.

Explanation

Gal 3:6–14 has often been seen as "a maze of laboured exegesis, puzzling illustration, and cryptic theological shorthand" (T. L. Donaldson's apt phraseology in *NTS* 32 [1986] 94). It deals with themes that are at the very heart of the Christian gospel. It also has a proportionately greater use of OT passages than elsewhere in Paul's letters, with those passages being the pivotal passages for Christianity vis-à-vis Judaism and with their use in these verses highly influenced by Paul's polemical concerns. Thus vv 6–14 have been the focus of a great deal of study, with widely divergent interpretations common.

The first section (vv 6–9) of Paul's argument from Scripture deals with how one should understand the Abrahamic covenant, against how the Judaizers were asking the Galatians to understand it. Here Paul focuses on the connection of faith and righteousness in Gen 15:6 and the centrality of the Gentiles in the "Blessing to Abraham" portion of that covenant. Abraham is the prototype and exemplar of faith. He believed in God and was blessed; Christians believe and are blessed with Abraham. The link is not natural generation, or circumcision, or the merit of Abraham's observance of the law. Rather, it is faith in the sense that Paul preached it—that is, faith in what Christ has accomplished redemptively (cf. "the faithfulness of Christ" of 2:16 and Christ being "cursed" for us of 3:13) and so being "in Christ" (cf. 3:14a and presupposed throughout). Already the Galatian Christians are sons of Abraham by faith; already they have been blessed by God, as foreseen in the Abrahamic covenant itself. Thus by faith they are joined to Abraham, "the man of faith," and so need no further teaching from the Judaizers as to how to enter, maintain, or perfect that relationship.

The second section (vv 10–14) of Paul's argument from Scripture deals with four important biblical passages—three that evidently the Judaizers had used in support of their message (Deut 27:26; Hab 2:4; Lev 18:5), which Paul reinterprets in rather *ad hominem* fashion for his converts, and a fourth that appears to have been part of an early Jewish Christian confession (Deut 21:23), which Paul cites as having put an end to questions about legalism. In treating the three passages used by his opponents, Paul sets them out in terms of opposing categories: those having to do with law and curse (Deut 27:26 and Lev 18:5) and another having to do with faith and righteousness (Hab 2:4). Here the radical nature of Paul's understanding of the relation of faith and law (or, "gospel and law") comes to the fore, for in dealing with these passages he sharply distinguishes between them—not in what we know as a Marcionite type of distinction, but in seeing that they operate on different levels and for different purposes (so the Antiochian interpreters, contra the Alexandrian interpreters; see Part I of the *Introduction* and *Comment* on 3:19–4:11). In presenting the fourth passage of this second section (Deut 21:23), Paul reiterates the important point made at the beginning of his *probatio*: acceptance of Christ's death for us puts an end to all legalistic enticements (cf. 3:1). Paul's theology is a theology of the cross, of the Spirit, of faith, and of being "in Christ." All these elements reverberate throughout Paul's *probatio*, but he begins at v 1 with the cross and in v 13 lays stress on it again.

The conclusion of Paul's arguments from Scripture brings this section to a close in saying that Christ redeemed us "in order that the blessing given to Abraham might come to the Gentiles through (*or*, in) Christ Jesus," but it also ranges more widely in bringing all of Paul's presentation in the *probatio* so far to a close in the words "in order that we might receive the promise of the Spirit by faith" (v 14). The reference to "the promise" sets up the presentations of 3:15–4:31, for hereafter it is the word "promise" that dominates in the discussions, being used synonymously with "gospel" and "blessing," but with these previously used favorite words no longer appearing in Paul's Galatian letter.

(c) Ad Hominem Theological Arguments (3:15–18)

Bibliography

Bammel, E. "Gottes ΔΙΑΘΗΚΗ (Gal. III.15–17) und das jüdische Rechtsdenken." *NTS* 6 (1960) 313–19. **Cosgrove, C. H.** "Arguing like a Mere Human Being: Galatians 3:15–18 in Rhetorical Perspective." *NTS* 34 (1988) 536–49. **Daube, D.** *The New Testament and Rabbinic Judaism*, 438–44. **Hübner, H.** *Law in Paul's Thought.* **Kreller, H.** *Erbrechtliche Untersuchungen.* **Räisänen, H.** *Paul and the Law.* **Sanders, E. P.** *Paul, the Law, and the Jewish People.* **Schoeps, H. J.** *Paul.* **Taubenschlag, R.** *The Law of Greco-Roman Egypt*, 109–207. **Taylor, G. M.** "The Function of ΠΙΣΤΙΣ ΧΡΙΣΤΟΥ in Galatians." *JBL* 85 (1966) 58–76. **Wilcox, M.** "The Promise of the 'Seed' in the New Testament and the Targumim." *JSNT* 5 (1979) 2–20. **Yaron, R.** *Gifts in Contemplation of Death in Jewish and Roman Law.* Oxford: Clarendon, 1960.

Translation

[15] *Brothers, let me take an example from everyday life: No one annuls or adds to a human covenant once it has been established, and so it is in this case.* [16] *Furthermore, the promises were spoken to Abraham and to his seed. It does not say "and to seeds," as though to many, but "and to your seed," as though to one, who* [a] *is Christ.* [17] *So this I say: The law that appeared 430 years later does not annul the covenant previously established by God,* [b] *to do away with the promise.* [18] *For if the inheritance is based on the law, then it is no longer based on promise. But God graciously gave it to Abraham by promise.*

Notes

[a] ὅ (neuter relative pronoun referring to neuter noun "seed") is read by D* Ir[lat] Tert Ambst Aug, though ὅς (masculine relative pronoun "who") is well supported by P[46] ℵ A B C et al. οὗ (genitive of ὅς, "of whom") is read by F G.

[b] εἰς Χριστόν is added after θεοῦ by D G TR Chr Theodore[lat] Thret and most minuscules; ἐν Χριστῷ by lat syr[pesh,harcl] Ambst Pel. These readings seem influenced by 3:24–28, where εἰς Χριστόν and ἐν Χριστῷ are used interchangeably. θεοῦ alone, however, is well supported by P[46] ℵ A B C et al.

Form/Structure/Setting

In Gal 3:15–18 Paul constructs an argument based on two factors: (1) that the covenant with Abraham represents God's pristine and irrevocable will, and (2) that the promise of the Abrahamic covenant has a singular recipient in mind, viz., Christ. In effect, Paul is here going behind the teaching of his opponents to remind his converts that God's promise was given long before the Mosaic law appeared and to assert that it was given not to observers of that law but to Christ (and, as he says later, to those who are Christ's own, cf. v 29). If Paul is to be charged with denigrating the law, his opponents are to be charged, he insists, with denigrating God's promise, the inheritance of that promise, Christ, and the Spirit—for these are matters associated with the Abrahamic covenant long before and apart from the law. Thus the law has no part in their receiving the inheritance promised to Abraham.

Two common epistolary conventions appear in vv 15-18 and serve to signal the movement of the argument in this section. The first is the vocative address ἀδελφοί ("brothers") coupled with a "verb of saying" construction at the start of v 15, which indicates a new feature in the argument and introduces the two arguments of vv 15-16 on the irrevocable nature of the Abrahamic covenant and the true recipient of its promise. The second is the "verb of saying" construction τοῦτο δὲ λέγω ("but this I say") at the start of v 17 which sets off Paul's conclusion of vv 17-18 drawn from the two arguments above. Rhetorically, *ad hominem* arguments are very much to the fore—not arguments that attack persons rather than ideas, but arguments that build on the premises of opponents and seek to refute them on their own grounds. For it may be assumed that the Judaizers were teaching (1) that the Mosaic law was meant by God to be a fuller expression of and a supplement to the Abrahamic covenant, and (2) that the promise to Abraham had in view as its recipients only Abraham's biological descendants and those related to the Jewish nation by Torah observance.

Paul is not in vv 15-18 putting forward a new set of arguments in contradistinction to what he has argued before in his *probatio*. Rather, here he spells out in ad hominem fashion the theological implications he sees as a Christian in the Abrahamic covenant. Thus as Paul ended v 14 with reference to receiving "the promise of the Spirit by faith"—a phrase which nicely served to epitomize all he had said up to that point in the *probatio*—so now he picks up on the word "promise" to speak about how that promise relates to the law and how the inheritance referred to in that promise should be understood. There is much more that he will say regarding the purpose and function of the law in 3:19-4:7 when he asks, "Why, then, the law?" Here, however, his point is that the law is not a supplement to faith for righteousness before God or for receiving the promised inheritance of the Abrahamic covenant.

Comment

15 Ἀδελφοί, κατὰ ἄνθρωπον λέγω, "brothers, let me take an example from everyday life." On Paul's affectionate use of "brothers" in such a severe letter as Galatians, see *Comment* at 1:11. The vocative ἀδελφοί appears almost always in Galatians in the epistolary seams: at the start of a major section (1:11; 4:12; 5:13), at the start of a subunit within a section (here; 6:1), at the end of a unit of material (4:31; 5:11), or as the final word of the entire letter (6:18, not counting ἀμήν). So except for its use at 4:28, ἀδελφοί functions as an epistolary convention signaling certain breaks in the letter structure of Galatians, as well as expressing Paul's sincere affection.

The phrase κατὰ ἄνθρωπον λέγω is somewhat difficult to interpret since it appears in Paul's letters only four times (here; Rom 3:5; 6:19 [variant form]; and 1 Cor 9:8), and nowhere else in the NT, the LXX, or other Greek literature. Nor can it be paralleled to date by any Hebrew or Aramaic expression. In Paul's other uses it suggests an implication (Rom 3:5) that goes beyond the express statements of Torah (1 Cor 9:8), which Paul brings forward in a somewhat condescending manner (Rom 6:19). And all of these features seem to be involved here, for in vv 15–18 Paul draws certain theological implications that are not expressly based on Scripture but which he believes he can still deduce from Scripture in an ad hominem fashion. The practical question, of course, is how to translate the phrase. Literally it means "I am speaking as a man," though in context it connotes taking an example from everyday human life and suggests an *ad hominem* use of that example. So it should be rendered something like "let me take an example from everyday life." "Speaking as a man," however, should not be taken as implying a difference in authority as though between God and Paul as a man, or between Christ and Paul as an apostle (cf. 1 Cor 7:12), or between Paul as an apostle and Paul as a mere man. As Burton rightly points out, such a distinction "is improbable here, both because there is no suggestion of it in the context and because the depreciation of the value of the argument which such a reference would imply is uncalled for and without value for the apostle's purpose" (*Galatians*,178).

ὅμως ἀνθρώπου κεκυρωμένην διαθήκην οὐδεὶς ἀθετεῖ ἢ ἐπιδιατάσσεται, "no one annuls or adds to a human covenant once it has been established, and so it is in this case." The adverb ὅμως coupled with the generic use of ἄνθρωπος in the genitive identifies Paul's example as an *a minori ad maius* argument—that is, an argument from what occurs in the human sphere to what is true in the divine economy. Linguistically, ὅμως ("nevertheless," "yet," "at the same time") may mark an antithesis between κατὰ ἄνθρωπον λέγω and what follows, and so be read: "Though I am speaking as a man, nevertheless what follows is true: No one annuls or adds to a human covenant once it has been established." More likely, however, ὅμως should be understood as setting up a comparison between ἀνθρώπου and what follows, and so understood to mean: as with a human covenant, "so it is in this case" of God's covenant with Abraham. This would mean that ὅμως is displaced in the sentence, not where expected before the second member of the comparison but before the first. That is how it appears in its only other occurrence in Paul's letters, that of 1 Cor 14:7, where ὅμως at the beginning of the sentence sets up a relationship between φωνὴν διδόντα ("giving a sound") and ἐὰν διαστολήν ("if a distinction"), not between τὰ ἄψυχα ("inanimate things") and φωνὴν διδόντα that immediately follows. Furthermore, since in 1 Cor 14:7 ὅμως introduces a comparison (cf. the οὕτως that follows in 14:9), it seems best to treat ὅμως here as influenced by the older ὁμῶς ("equally," "likewise") and so read Gal 3:15 in terms of comparative relations rather than antithetical relations (cf. BAG), though without attempting to accent ὅμως to read ὁμῶς.

The tense and mood of the participle κεκυρωμένην, from the verb κυρόω ("establish," "confirm," "ratify," or "validate"), highlight the features of irrevocability (perfect tense) and unilateralness (passive mood) that Paul wants to stress in the case of the Abrahamic covenant. The transitive use of ἀθετέω ("declare invalid," "nullify," "set aside") is common in Greek literature and in Paul (cf. 2:21; see also 1 Cor 1:19). The verb ἐπιδιατάσσομαι ("add a codicil"), however, appears nowhere else in the NT or other extant Greek writings, though διατάσσω ("order," "direct," "arrange") is frequent in both Greek literature and the NT (e.g., in Paul Gal 3:19; 1 Cor 7:17; 11:34).

The introduction of διαθήκην ("covenant") here at v 15 has not been unprepared for. It is clear that Paul had the Abrahamic covenant in view from v 6 on, even though he did not use the term itself. Yet here he inserts διαθήκη by way of an example or illustration drawn from human affairs, and the common understanding of the term in the ancient world was that of "testament" or "will." Josephus, for example, who was both a man of his day and one trained in Jewish thought, always uses διαθήκη to mean "testament" or "will," and never in the thirty-two appearances of the term in his writings to mean "covenant" (e.g., J. W. 1.451, 573, 588, 600, passim; Ant. 13.349; 17.53, 78, 146, passim). On the other hand, the LXX's constant translation of the theologically significant term ברית (běrît "covenant") by διαθήκη—with 270 of the 286 occurrences of ברית in the MT translated by διαθήκη in the LXX—was most available to Paul and seems ultimately to have controlled his use of the term (cf. 4:24, where Hagar and Sarah are said to represent δύο διαθῆκαι). It appears, therefore that in developing his *a minori ad maius* type of argument, Paul has both secular and theological connotations for διαθήκη in mind and that he is working from that of "testament" or "will" to that of "covenant."

More difficult to ascertain, however, is the legal situation presupposed by Paul's argument. William Ramsay argued that Greek jurisprudence modified by local usage was the secular background for Paul's illustration, particularly with regard to the irrevocable character of a father's will where the inheritance of sons is concerned (*Galatians*, 349–70). His argument was largely based on the supposition that Paul's Galatian converts would have been conversant with Greek law but not Roman law, since they resided in southern Galatia and were not ethnically Gauls (ibid., 370–75). Others, assuming Paul's converts to have been "eastern Gauls" of northern Galatia, have argued that Roman law was the background for Paul's thought (for bibliographical references on the debate up through the late 1950s, see E. Bammel, *NTS* 6 [1960] 313–19; see also G. M. Taylor, *JBL* 85 [1966] 58–76, who argues for a Roman legal background). Both the advocates of Greek jurisprudence and of a Roman background, however have been influenced by their understanding of the provenance of Galatians and have gone beyond the evidence in attempting to prove instances of irrevocability with regard to inheritance in the respective bodies of law.

The disposition of one's goods at death by means of a will or testament was a legal practice of long standing in the Greco-Roman world, with the term διαθήκη being often used for such a legal instrument. It was always possible however, both in Greek and in Roman jurisprudence, for the testator to revoke or alter his will. As early as 1921 Burton could say with assurance, "it is now well established that both Greek and Roman wills were revocable by the maker" (*Galatians*, 504). And this was true in Egypt as well, where our knowledge from the papyri as to customs and laws governing everyday life in the Greco-Roman world is more extensive. As Raphael Taubenschlag points out:

Greco-Egyptian testaments were revocable. The right to revoke a will was provided by the insertion of a special clause. The first testament could not be revoked by the drawing up of a new one. The revocation of the first had to be made either in the form of a special clause in the new testament, or by a separate legal act, or by the withdrawal of the document from the notaries (*The Law of Greco-Roman Egypt*, 204; cf. the more amply documented work of H. Kreller, *Erbrechtliche Untersuchungen*).

Several examples of official documents dealing with the revocation of a will are, in fact, extant in the papyri—chiefly POxy 106, 107, and 601, which date from the early part of the second century A.D.

There was, however, another means for the disposition of property within the family in the Greco-Roman world, the *donatio mortis causa*, in which ownership was transferred while the donor was still alive, though the donor retained usufruct ("the right of use and enjoyment") until his death. Since this type of disposition was considered to be a gift, it was assumed to be irrevocable unless explicit mention was made of revocability, even though the recipient did not gain actual possession of the property until the death of the donor (cf. R. Taubenschlag, *The Law of Greco-Roman Egypt*, 204–7). Reuven Yaron has cited BGU 993 (127 B.C.) as evidence that this practice was known in pre-Christian Egypt and presumably widely practiced throughout the Roman empire, and that irrevocability was assumed. For, as he says in describing this papyrus: "The donor is Psenthotes, a priest of Isis; he transfers all his property to his daughter and his wife. The irrevocability of the disposition and the immediate passing of ownership to the donees are conclusively proved by the fact that transfer-taxes are paid at the time of the execution of the document" (*Gifts in Contemplation of Death in Jewish and Roman Law*, 46). Furthermore, as Yaron points out, this type of transaction "is characterized by the use of the formula μετὰ τὴν τελευτήν ["after death"]; this implies that usufruct remains with the donor" (ibid.).

As for Jewish jurisprudence, Yaron has shown how at least by the time of the Tannaim (mid-second century through third century A.D.) Judaism had taken over both the διαθήκη type of testamentary disposition of property and the μετὰ τὴν τελευτήν type of gift. In so doing, the Jewish leaders were able to fill a vacuum in the inheritance laws of Scripture and make the disposition of property within the family much more flexible: the former, the testamentary type of disposition that took effect at death, was revocable by the testator during his life but could not be drawn up in a way to circumvent the inheritance laws of the Torah; the latter, the gift type of disposition that took effect immediately after being attested, was irrevocable, but also was not bound by Torah legislation at the testator's death. The reason for the Jewish acceptance of this latter type of instrument was, no doubt, precisely because of its ability to circumvent the inheritance laws of the Torah, even though it irrevocably bound the donor. Important rabbinic texts spelling out the distinction between these two types of inheritance laws are *m. B. Bat.* ("The Last Gate") 8.5–7; *t. B. Bat.* 8.9–11; *b. B. Bat.* 135b, 136a–b.

Building on Yaron's work, Ernst Bammel has highlighted the distinction in rabbinic writings between inheritance *dĕyāytîqî* (דייתיק׳) laws, which take effect at the death of a testator but are revocable prior to his death, and *mattĕnat bārî'* (מתנת בריא) inheritance laws, which take effect immediately during a donor's life and are irrevocable. Bammel proposes that Paul's use of διαθήκη in Gal 3:15 really has in mind the Jewish legal instrument *mattĕnat bārî'* (*NTS* 6 [1960] 313–19). But this suggestion, while well supported, is not without its difficulties for the interpretation of Paul. The major problem is not that the concept of an irrevocable disposition of property may not have been widely enough known to be relevant to Paul's Gentile readers in Galatia (contra Betz, *Galatians*, 155), for Taubenschlag and Yaron have shown otherwise. Rather, the problem is that Paul seems to be using the term διαθήκη in a manner at variance with the terminology of both Greco-Roman and Jewish inheritance legislation, for a διαθήκη could be revoked or changed by its testator, whereas it was the Greek μετὰ τὴν τελευτήν, the Roman *donatio mortis causa*, or the Jewish *mattĕnat bārî'* that was irrevocable.

Perhaps one could explain this discrepancy by positing that the annulment or alteration Paul had in mind had to do with an attempt made by a party not involved in the original drafting of the διαθήκη. It might be argued, for example, that Paul thought of the angels as a third party, who were not able to alter a legal disposition of inheritance once it had been ratified—i.e., using the tradition of the angels' involvement in the giving of the law (cf. 3:19) and playing on the dual meaning of the word διαθήκη as both "will" and "covenant," without really intending to suggest the logical conclusion that the angels were then acting apart from God. But such an explanation, though not entirely impossible, is rather flimsy. Or perhaps one could argue that Paul knew of and was referring to the tradition incorporated only in *t. B. Bat.* 8.11 that the *dĕyāytîqî* of a dying man was revocable only if he recovered (which, at first glance, seems rather obvious). But the otherwise universal understanding of a διαθήκη as able to be revoked or amended makes this unlikely.

On the basis of our present knowledge of inheritance laws in the Greco-Roman and Jewish worlds, it seems, therefore, that Paul's use of of διαθήκη in 3:15 is not exactly in accord with the legal situation of the day. It may be that we lack sufficient data. Or it may be that Paul felt no compulsion to speak in precise legal parlance, and that his readers would have felt the same. We today often use terms pertinent to a particular discipline with less precision than purists rightly call for, even though we might know better. Nonetheless, despite such imprecision of language—or perhaps despite scholarship's inability to discover true parallels—the point of Paul's example in its application is clear: that God established his covenant with Abraham in an irrevocable manner, so it can never be annulled or added to.

16 τῷ δὲ Ἀβραὰμ ἐρρέθησαν αἱ ἐπαγγελίαι καὶ τῷ σπέρματι αὐτοῦ, "furthermore, the promises were spoken to Abraham and to his seed." The fact that vv 15–18 are structured in terms of a "verb of saying" construction at the start of v 15 and another "verb of saying" construction at the start of v 17 suggests that vv 15–16 should be seen as setting forth Paul's argumentation and vv 17–18 as spelling out his conclusions drawn from that argumentation. The postpositive δέ, therefore, is probably to be taken as a coordinating conjunction, thereby relating the two statements of vv 15–16 as complementary arguments: the first of v 15 supplemented by the second of v 16 (so our translation "furthermore"), with the implications of these two arguments then highlighted in vv 17–18.

Paul's reference to "the promise of the Spirit" in 3:14 brought to a climax his arguments from experience and Scripture in 3:1–14. It also, however, set up the presentations of 3:15–4:31, for thereafter it is the word "promise" (here and at 3:17, 18, 21, 22, 29; 4:28) that dominates the discussions, taking the place of the terms "gospel" (1:7–9, 11; 2:2, 5, 7, 14; 3:8) and "blessing" (3:8, 9, 14) used before and giving rise to the treatments of "inheritance" (3:18; 4:1–7, 21–31) that follow. Paul usually uses the singular ἐπαγγελία ("promise") when referring to God's covenant with Abraham (so vv 17, 18, 22, 29; also Rom 4:13, 14, 16, 20), though also at times the plural ἐπαγγελίαι ("promises") without any difference of meaning (so here and v 21; also Rom 9:4). Jews frequently spoke of God's promises of care and blessing given to Moses at Sinai (e.g., Josephus, *Ant.* 3.24, 77) as well as of God's promises given to Abraham (e.g., Josephus, *Ant.* 1.236), but Jewish writings never set up the dichotomy implicit here between "promises to Abraham" and "law to Moses." In all the Genesis accounts of the Abrahamic covenant, reference is made not only to Abraham but also to Abraham's "seed" as recipients of God's promises (12:2–3, 7; 13:15–16; 15:4–6, 18; 17:4, 7–8; 22:17–19; 24:7). And that dual referent is carried on in all Jewish writings whenever the Abrahamic covenant is referred to (e.g., Sir 44:21; *Jub.* 24.10–11; *b. Yebam.* 42a; *Num. Rab.* 12.4, to cite only a few passages from various kinds of material).

οὐ λέγει, Καὶ τοῖς σπέρμασιν, ὡς ἐπὶ πολλῶν, ἀλλ' ὡς ἐφ' ἑνός, Καὶ τῷ σπέρματί σου, ὅς ἐστιν Χριστός, "it does not say, 'and to seeds,' as though to many, but 'and to your seed,' as though to one, who is Christ." The verb λέγει ("it says") is without an expressed subject, but there is no doubt that "God" is implied (cf. 2 Cor 6:2). That ὁ θεός is the understood subject is confirmed by ὑπὸ τοῦ θεοῦ ("by God") of v 17. The preposition ἐπί with the genitive to mean "in respect to" or "as though to" is a NT *hap. leg.*, but it occurs commonly in classical Greek. The most distinctive feature of v 16, however, is Paul's treatment of the noun σπέρμα ("seed"); he points out that it is singular and then argues that the singular has reference to Christ as the true recipient of God's promise to Abraham.

"Seed" in the Abrahamic promise is a generic singular that was always understood within Judaism to refer to the posterity of Abraham as an entity, excluding only the descendants of Abraham through Ishmael ("for in Isaac shall thy seed be called") and those born of Esau (cf. *b. Sabb.* 146a; *b. Pesah.* 56a, 119b; *b. Ned.* 31a; *Gen. Rab.* 4.5), though also those who "have forfeited their share in the world to come" by such things as denying the resurrection, reading the heretical books, pronouncing the sacred name of God, and being unmerciful to others (cf. *m. Sanh.* 10.1; *b. 'Erub.* 19a; *Lev. Rab.* 9.1; *Exod. Rab.* 19.14). Jews, of course, prided themselves on being "true sons of Abraham," and therefore on being the recipients of the promises made to Abraham. The Targums, in fact, take this corporate understanding of the promise so much for granted that they uniformly and unequivocally cast the expression into the plural: "and to your sons" (cf. M. Wilcox, *JSNT* 5 [1979] 2–20). Paul, however, for whom physical descent was no guarantee of spiritual relationship (cf. Rom 9:6b–7a), and with a possible swipe at the targumic plural, argues that Christ is the "seed" in view in the Abrahamic covenant, and then goes on in v 29 to speak of those "in Christ" (or "of Christ") as also being "Abraham's seed and heirs according to the promise."

Paul Billerbeck (Str-B, 3:553) has cited three places in the Talmud where certain rabbis based their arguments on the plural or singular forms of a noun in the biblical text: on "seeds" and "seed" (*m. Sabb.* 9.2, "seeds planted in the earth") and on "bloods" and "blood" (*m. Sanh.* 4.5; *Gen. Rab.* 22.9). But these passages say very little about Paul's treatment here, except to illustrate a type of atomistic exegesis presumably known to Paul as well. David Daube has shown how some rabbis, in an endeavor to solve the discrepancy between Gen 15:13 ("four hundred years") and Exod 12:40 ("430 years") regarding the length of Israel's Egyptian captivity, took the thirty years' difference as the time between God's giving the covenant to Abraham and the birth of Isaac, and so understood the "seed" of Gen 15:13 ("know for certain that your seed will be strangers in a country not their own, and they will be enslaved and mistreated four hundred years") as a specific singular, meaning Isaac (*The New Testament and Rabbinic Judaism*, 440–44, citing *S.ʿ Olam Rab.* 3; *Pesiq. R.* 42.3; *Gen. Rab.* 44.18). And from this Daube concludes (1) that at least some rabbis understood Abraham's "seed" as a specific singular, having Isaac in mind, and (2) that this haggadic tradition must be seen as a source for Paul's argument here.

But while both Billerbeck and Daube, each in his own way, have demonstrated to an extent how one trained in rabbinic exegetical methods could treat the text as Paul does in v 16, the parallels they cite do not force us to believe that Paul understood "seed" here as a specific singular rather than a generic singular. Later in v 29 Paul treats "seed" as a collective, as he does also in Rom 4:13–18. So, it seems that Paul is here invoking a corporate solidarity understanding of the promise to Abraham wherein the Messiah, as the true descendant of Abraham and the true representative of the nation, is seen as the true "seed" of Abraham—as are, of course, also the Messiah's own, as v 29 insists.

The Judaizers in Galatia were undoubtedly proclaiming that God's promises were given only to Abraham and his "seed," the Jewish people (understood as a generic singular), or possibly, as Daube suggests, to Abraham and his "seed" Isaac (understood as a specific singular). Some of the Galatian Christians seem to have been taken in by their argument. Paul, however, in what appears to be an argument directly *ad hominem* in nature, "deliberately furnishes them with a deeper application" of the promise of God made to Abraham and his "seed" (D. Daube, *The New Testament and Rabbinic Judaism*, 441). Based, it seems, on a corporate solidarity understanding of relationships in the divine economy, and coupled with the previous argument of v 15, Paul's point here is that not only was the promise to Abraham established on the principle of faith before the law was introduced but also that God had in mind in the Abrahamic promise not those who observe the law but primarily Christ (and, as we shall see in v 29, Christ's own).

17 τοῦτο δὲ λέγω· διαθήκην προκεκυρωμένην ὑπὸ τοῦ θεοῦ ὁ μετὰ τετρακόσια καὶ τριάκοντα ἔτη γεγονὼς νόμος οὐκ ἀκυροῖ, εἰς τὸ καταργῆσαι τὴν ἐπαγγελίαν, "so this I say: the law that appeared 430 years later does not annul the covenant previously established by God, to do away with the promise." The relation of v 17 to vv 15–16 has been viewed in various ways by commentators. Most see v 17 as resumptive—that is, picking up the thought of v 15 and arguing it in more detail, either after the "parenthesis" of v 16 (so Burton, *Galatians*, 182) or after the "application" of the argument of v 15 in v 16 (so Betz, *Galatians*, 156). Some, however, see v 17 as the conclusion to what has been argued in vv 15–16 (so Mussner, *Galaterbrief*, 240). If, as we have proposed, the two "verb of saying" constructions at the beginning of v 15 and at the beginning of v 17 serve to signal an argumentative section and a conclusion section respectively, then we must agree with those who take v 17 as Paul's conclusion to this unit of material. The postpositive δέ, therefore, should probably be seen as a transitional particle that serves in connection with τοῦτο λέγω to alert the reader to an immediately following concluding statement ("so this I say").

As a concluding statement, v 17 contains a number of terms that are either the same as or synonymous with those used in vv 15–16. The nouns διαθήκη (vv 15, 17) and ἐπαγγελία (vv 16, 17) are the most obvious: the first covering the whole semantic range from a human "will" to a divine "covenant," with diverse applications depending on context; the second, whether plural or singular, having reference to God's promise to Abraham. The verb προκυρόω ("establish [previously]") also appears in both sections as a perfect passive participle and functions similarly in both, though in v 17 the prefix προ- is added to make clear the temporal relation between the covenant and the law. And though the verbs ἀθετέω of v 15 and ἀκυρόω of v 17 are manifestly different, they mean the same ("annul").

The phrase ὑπὸ τοῦ θεοῦ ("by God") identifies God as not only the giver of the Abrahamic covenant but also the one who attested or established it. The use of γίνομαι to mean "appear in history" can be paralleled in Mark 1:4; John 1:6, 17; and 1 John 2:18. As a perfect participle it identifies the law as having both a past and a present existence. The preposition εἰς with the articular infinitive τὸ καταργῆσαι speaks of purpose ("to do away with").

The most perplexing feature of v 17 is the statement that the law appeared in history "430 years" after God's covenant with Abraham. The exact figure, of course, whether 430 years or 400 years, is of no great importance for Paul's argument, though, of course, the impact would be slightly increased with the larger number. Yet it has often seemed strange to many that in working extensively from the Genesis accounts, Paul should speak of 430 years from Abraham to Moses, which is the figure given in Exod 12:40 for Israel's captivity in Egypt, whereas Gen 15:13 has 400 years for that same period of enslavement.

The rabbis found the difference between Gen 15:13 ("400 years") and Exod 12:40 ("430 years") somewhat perplexing as well, and there are many places in their writings where the matter is dealt with. Usually they solved the problem by taking 430 years as the time between God's covenant with Abraham and Moses' reception of the law and 400 years as the period Israel spent in Egypt (cf. Str-B, 2:670, citing such diverse references as *Tg. Ps.-J.* on Exod 12:40; *Mek.* on Exod 12:40; *Gen. Rab.* 44.18; *Exod. Rab.* 18.11; *S.ʿ Olam Rab.* 3; etc.). And Josephus handles the time spans in much the same way: 400 years for Israel's sojourn in Egypt (*Ant.* 2.204; *J.W.* 5.382) and 430 years from Abraham's entrance into Canaan to Moses' leading the people out of Egypt (*Ant.* 2.318). It seems, therefore, that this was the traditional way in Paul's day of treating the discrepancy between Gen 15:13 and Exod 12:40 and of understanding the respective time spans. And so Paul here is probably not relying on Exod 12:40 versus Gen 15:13, but only repeating the traditionally accepted number of years for the time span between the Abrahamic covenant and the Mosaic law.

Jewish tradition viewed Abraham as having kept the entire Mosaic law even though that law was not given until much later (cf. Str-B, 204–6). His acceptance of circumcision in Gen 17:10–14, in effect, signaled for Jews his acceptance of all the Mosaic law. Furthermore, Judaism, with its view of truth as coming first in an elemental form and then in a developed form, understood the Mosaic law as simply the developed form of the Abrahamic covenant. Paul, however, elaborating further on his *a minori ad maius* argument of v 15 and in line with Hillel's seventh exegetical rule *dābār hallāmēd mēʿinyāynô* (i.e., a word established by its context), argues for the precedence of the Abrahamic covenant with its promise over the Mosaic law with its prescriptions, insisting that the purpose of the law of Moses had nothing to do with either annulling or adding to what God had covenanted with Abraham.

18 εἰ γὰρ ἐκ νόμου ἡ κληρονομία, οὐκέτι ἐξ ἐπαγγελίας· τῷ δὲ 'Αβραὰμ δι' ἐπαγγελίας κεχάρισται ὁ θεός, "for if the inheritance is based on the law, then it is no longer based on promise. But God graciously gave it to Abraham by promise." The γάρ ("for") of v 18 is explanatory and so sets up the real reason for Paul's conclusion of v 17: that promise and law are diametrically opposed to one another when thought of in terms of acceptance before God. This is in line with the dichotomous sets of categories that Paul has set up from 2:15 through 3:18. For in the *propositio* he distinguishes between "the works of the law" and "the faith/faithfulness of [Jesus] Christ" (2:16); in the first part of the *probatio* between "the works of the law" and "believing what [i.e., the message that] you heard" (3:2, 5); in the second part of the *probatio* between "all who rely on the works of the law" and "those of faith," and then between law and curse, on the one hand, and faith, righteousness, and blessing, on the other (3:6–14); and throughout he rings the changes on the Spirit, the Abrahamic covenant, the promises and blessings of that covenant, and Christ as set in opposition to the Mosaic law. Indeed, as Paul will tell us in what immediately follows (3:19–4:7), the law had proper purposes and functions in the divine economy (and by implication may still have such in some measure). But when speaking of acceptance before God and the reception of God's benefits, Paul insists that law and promise must be kept separate, for they operate on entirely different planes. To bring them together as equals, in fact, is to destroy all that God has graciously established by promise. So on the question of acceptance before God, Paul is radically opposed to any mingling of God's promise and grace with the Mosaic law.

"Inheritance" is introduced by Paul into the discussion here for the first time, though subsequently it plays a major role (κληρονομία, "inheritance," here; κληρονόμος, "heir," at 3:29; 4:1, 7; κληρονομέω, "inherit," at 4:30; 5:21; with the idea being prominent in the illustration of 4:1–7, the allegory of 4:21–31, and the blessing of 6:16). It stems, of course, from references to the promise(s) contained in the Abrahamic covenant of vv 16–17. The inheritance promised in the Abrahamic covenant had principally to do with territorial, material possessions (cf. Gen 13:14–17; 15:7, 18–21; 17:3–8), but since these were expressions of God's favor they easily became spiritualized as well (cf. 2 Chr 6:27; *Pss. Sol.* 7.2; 9.2; 14.3; 17.26). The territorial and material features of the Abrahamic inheritance are not mentioned here by Paul, for in Christian thought "inheritance" had become thoroughly spiritualized (cf. 5:21; also Acts 2:32; 1 Cor 6:9–10; Eph 5:5; Col 3:24) and Paul's opponents would undoubtedly have thought along such lines as well. The verb χαρίζομαι ("graciously give") lays stress on the character of the inheritance given—that is, it was an expression of God's grace and not a commercial transaction. The perfect tense (κεχάρισται) identifies the inheritance as still being in force, so bringing to the fore Paul's underlying argument throughout vv 15–17.

Explanation

Paul's experiential, biblical, and theological arguments in the first half of his *probatio* (3:1–18) develop what he said in brief in the first half of his *propositio* (2:15–16). They are directed against all attempts to use the Mosaic law as a means to gain acceptance before God, i.e., "legalism." The Judaizers of Galatia themselves might have claimed that this was not the thrust of their endeavors; that all they wanted was for Gentile Christians to supplement their faith in Christ with Torah observance, just as God directed Abraham to do and so to experience a more perfect Christian life. For Paul, however, any mingling of faith and law, even if it is claimed that this has only to do with a proper lifestyle and not justification, is a discrediting of the Abrahamic covenant, the work of Christ, the ministry of the Spirit, and the principle of faith, and so brings one right back to the issue of legalism. In 3:19–4:7 Paul will speak to the question of "nomism" and so deal directly with the Judaizers' message. Here in 3:1–18, however, he has dealt with what he sees to be the implications of their message. And seeing it to be ultimately a question of the gospel of Christ versus legalism, he speaks out in ways that set up dichotomous categories of thought and draw sharp lines of distinction. For he is convinced that neither a true Jew (cf. 2:15) nor a true Christian can embrace legalism and still be acceptable before God.

2. The Believer's Life not "under Law" but "in Christ": Against Nomism (3:19–4:7)

Gal 3:19–25 is usually treated as a digression (i.e., an excursus that strays from the main subject) in Paul's Galatian argument against legalism (cf. Betz, *Galatians*, 163: "an extremely concise 'digression' [*digressio*]; most commentators agree, though without the use of Betz's rhetorical parlance). And 3:26–28 together with 4:1–7 (though not 3:29, which is commonly related to 3:16) are often taken to be rather incidental to the polemic of Galatians, even though they may be interesting and theologically significant of themselves (cf. L. H. DeWolf, *Galatians*, 48, on 3:26–27: "This statement sends Paul's thought ranging far beyond the issues immediately involved in the controversy among the Galatian churches"). Many treatments of Paul and the law, in fact, practically ignore 3:19–4:7, evidently believing that in treating 3:1–18 they have dealt with the heart and core of what Paul has to say on the subject in Galatians. But it is a serious mistake to treat 3:19–4:7 in this manner, either in whole or in its respective parts of 3:19–25, 3:26–29, and 4:1–7.

If, as we have argued (see *Introduction*, "Opponents and Situation"), the Judaizers of Galatia were not presenting themselves as opposing Paul's message of faith in Christ (i.e., not overtly advocating "legalism"), but rather claiming to be complementing his proclamation so as to bring his converts to perfection (i.e., advocating Jewish "nomism"), then Paul's treatments of (1) the purpose and function of the law (3:19–25, particularly the law as a *paidagōgos* in the supervision of one's life of faith), (2) the new relationship established by God of being "in Christ" (3:26–29), and (3) how relationships under the supervision of the law and being "in Christ" are to be seen (4:1–7) are directly related to issues in the churches of Galatia. Paul, of course, saw that what the Judaizers claimed to be only a matter of lifestyle (i.e., nomism) really struck at the heart of the Christian gospel (i.e., legalism), and so he began his *probatio* by dealing with legalism itself in 3:1–18. But all of that was only in preparation for his discussion of the issues as directly raised by the Judaizers that we find in 3:19–4:7. Furthermore, if, as we have argued (see *Comment* on 2:15–21), the *propositio* of Galatians states in brief the points of agreement in 2:15–16, which are explicated in 3:1–18, and subsequently the points of disagreement in 2:17–20, which are explicated in 3:19–4:7, then 3:19–4:7 can hardly be described as a digression in Paul's argument, as incidental material, or as unrelated to the issues at hand. In actuality, here Paul comes to the heart of his differences with the Judaizers.

(a) The Purpose and Function of the Law (3:19–25)

Bibliography

Belleville, L. L. "'Under Law': Structural Analysis and the Pauline Concept of Law in Galatians 3.21–4.11." *JSNT* 26 (1986) 53–78. **Callan, T.** "Pauline Midrash: The Exegetical Background of Gal 3:19b." *JBL* 99 (1980) 549–67. **Donaldson, T. L.** "The 'Curse of the Law' and the Inclusion of the Gentiles: Galatians 3.13–14." *NTS* 32 (1986) 94–112. **Goldin, J.** "Not by Means of an Angel and Not by Means of a Messenger." In *Religions in Antiquity*. FS E. R. Goodenough, ed. J. Neusner. *Numen* Supplements 14. Leiden: Brill, 1968, 412–24. **Gordon, T. D.** "A Note on ΠΑΙΔΑΓΩΓΟΣ in Galatians 3.24–25." *NTS* 35 (1989) 150–54. **Hübner, H.** *Law in Paul's Thought.* **Longenecker, R. N.** *Paul, Apostle of Liberty,* 122–55. ———. "The Pedagogical Nature of the Law in Galatians 3:19–4:7." *JETS* 25 (1982) 53–61. **Lull, D. J.** "'The Law Was Our Pedagogue': A Study in Galatians 3:19–25." *JBL* 105 (1986) 481–98. **Räisänen, H.** *Paul and the Law.* **Sanders, E. P.** *Paul, the Law, and the Jewish People,* 65–70. **Westerholm, S.** *Israel's Law and the Church's Faith,* esp. 174–222. **Young, N. H.** "*Paidagōgos* : The Social Setting of a Pauline Metaphor." *NovT* 29 (1987) 150–76.

Translation

[19] *Why, then, the law* [a] *? It was added* [b] *because of transgressions until the Seed for whom the promise was intended should come. And it was ordained through angels by means of a mediator.* [20] *A mediator, however, does not represent just one party; but God is one!* [21] *Is the law, then, opposed to the promises of God* [c] *? By no means! For if a law had been given that could give life, then righteousness would certainly have been on the basis of law.* [d] [22] *But the Scripture confined everyone without distinction under sin, so that the promise that is based on the faithfulness of Jesus Christ might be given to those who believe.* [23] *Before this faith came, we were kept in custody under the law, being confined until this coming faith should be revealed.* [24] *The law, therefore, was* [e] *our supervisory guardian until Christ came, in order that we might be justified by faith.* [25] *But now that this faith has come, we are no longer under a supervisory guardian.*

Notes

[a] ὁ νόμος τῶν πράξεων ("the law of actions") appears in P[46] G Ir[lat] Ambst, but this is certainly an expanded reading.

[b] ἐτέθη ("was placed," "was set up") after χάριν appears in D*G Ir[lat] Ambst, though προσετέθη ("was added") is well supported by P[46] ℵ A B C et al.

^cτοῦ θεοῦ ("of God") is omitted by P⁴⁶ B lat^{d,e} Ambst Vic, but included by ℵ A C D TR et al. (also G, though without the article).

^dἐκ νόμου ᾽ἀν ἦν ("would have been based on the law"), which is supported by A C et al., appears in a number of other roughly synonymous forms: ᾽ἀν ἐκ νόμου ἦν in D² TR et al.; ἐκ νόμου ἦν ἄν in ℵ et al.; ἐκ νόμου ἦν in D* et al.; ἐκ νόμου in G; ἐν νόμῳ ἦν ἄν in P⁴⁶; and ἐν νόμῳ ᾽ἀν ἦν in B.

^eἐγένετο (second aorist, "it was") appears in P⁴⁶ and B, so reading the otherwise well-supported perfect γέγονεν as a historical aorist.

Form/Structure/Setting

Gal 3:19–25 is structured in three parts: a major question that asks regarding the purpose and function of the Mosaic law; a supplementary question that asks regarding the relation of the law to the promises of God; and then a final paragraph that speaks directly to the issue being debated within the churches of Galatia. The two questions are rhetorical in nature and similar in form: "Why, then, the law?" (v 19) and "Is the law, then, opposed to the promises of God?" (v 21). They arise from Paul's put-down of legalism in 3:1–18. More importantly, they are the questions that cry out for an answer, if the Judaizers' call for a nomistic Christian lifestyle is to be dealt with effectively.

Each of the two questions is introduced rather abruptly without any connecting particle, and then answered somewhat briefly and cryptically, though also pointedly for the issue at hand. Vv 23–25 are joined to the two questions and their answers by the connective particle δέ (untranslated), which serves to set off this final portion as being climactic in nature. In this final statement Paul brings his argument against nomism to a focus. His main expression here is "under the law" (ὑπὸ νόμον); the thrust of his argument is what it meant to live "under the law"; and the analogy he uses to express his thought is that of a *paidagōgos* in a patrician family.

Though sadly often treated as an addendum to Paul's earlier discussion of legalism, or worse yet ignored, 3:19–25 is the *crux interpretum* for Paul's response to the problems in Galatia. Here Paul lays out a Christian understanding of the purpose and function of the Mosaic law vis-à-vis the Judaizers' nomistic message. It is not, of course, a complete discussion of every aspect of the law, to be treated as though what we have here is all that Paul has to say on the subject. Rather, here Paul speaks circumstantially in countering the Judaizers' call for a nomistic lifestyle. Yet what Paul says, though directed to the situation he then faced, is vitally important for Christians today, particularly as we encounter similar questions as to how to live our lives vis-à-vis the God-given Mosaic law of the Old Testament.

Comment

19 τί οὖν ὁ νόμος, "why, then, the law?" Paul frequently uses τί adverbially to mean "why" (cf. 5:11; also Rom 3:7; 14:10; 1 Cor 4:7; etc.), though not elsewhere with οὖν ("then"). With the transitional conjunction οὖν, the interrogative pronoun τί usually is translated "what is" or "what signifies" (cf. Rom 3:1, 9; 4:1; 6:1, 15; etc.). There is here, however, no decisive consideration to enable us to decide between "Why the law?" and "What is the significance of the law?" And there is no real difference of meaning. Of the two translations, probably the former is to be preferred simply because of its crispness and therefore greater rhetorical impact.

οὖν connects this question to what precedes, for Paul's arguments of 3:1–18 seem to have left the law without any function. The ellipsis of the verb is as common in Greek as in English, often being omitted for rhetorical effect. ὁ νόμος is certainly the Mosaic law, the article specifying that law which has repeatedly been referred to in the immediate context and earlier: "the law that appeared 430 years" after the Abrahamic covenant (3:17); the law whose curse "Christ redeemed us from" (3:13); and that law which was the focus of the Judaizers' message (1.6ff.).

τῶν παραβάσεων χάριν προσετέθη, ἄχρις οὗ ἔλθῃ τὸ σπέρμα ᾧ ἐπήγγελται, διαταγεὶς δι' ἀγγέλων ἐν χειρὶ μεσίτου, "it was added because of transgressions until the Seed for whom the promise was intended should come. And it was ordained through angels by means of a mediator." Paul's answer to the question "Why the law?" is expressed in terms of five emphases: (1) "it was added"; (2) "because of transgressions"; (3) "until the Seed to whom the promise was given should come"; (4) "it was ordained through angels"; and (5) "by the hand of a mediator." Each feature or clause needs to be treated separately, though with an eye always to their cumulative impact.

The first feature to be noted in Paul's answer is the aorist passive verb προσετέθη ("it was added"), which carries in its suffix the singular subject "it" corresponding to "the law." It introduces an important temporal point: the Mosaic law was brought into effect by God subsequent to his covenant of promise. The fact that the augmented προστίθημι ("add" to something already present) appears in the text and not the simple verb τίθημι ("place," "set up") signals a nuance of disparagement and suggests that the law was not of the essence of God's redemptive activity with humankind, which undoubtedly is why D G Irenaeus (in Latin) and Ambrosiaster seem to have felt uncomfortable with προσετέθη and so read ἐτέθη. Or as Burton aptly puts it: "προσετέθη marks the law as supplementary, and hence subordinate to the covenant" (*Galatians*, 188).

The second emphasis in Paul's answer, "because of transgressions" (τῶν παραβάσεων χάριν), has usually been found more difficult to understand than the first. The prepositional use of χάριν, which almost always appears after the word it governs, may be understood as either cognitive in function (i.e., "to bring about a knowledge of" or "point out" transgressions) or causative in function (i.e., "to cause" or "increase" transgressions). The noun παράβασις has the sense of "deviation from a standard or norm," or of "neglecting an obligation." Thus the phrase "because of transgressions" may mean either that the law was given to bring about a knowledge of sin (cf. Rom 3:20) by identifying it as transgression before God (cf. Rom 4:15; 5:13; 7:7), or that the law was given to increase and multiply sin (cf. Rom 5:20). Both the immediate context and Paul's usual way of speaking about the function of the law favor a cognitive interpretation, that the law was given to bring about a consciousness of sin in sin-hardened humanity. For although "because of transgressions" can be understood in a causal fashion, "to bring about or multiply sin" makes little sense of the following temporal clause "until the Seed to whom the promise was given should come." For why should God want an increase of sin building up to the coming of Christ? Furthermore, "to bring about a knowledge of sin" fits the contextual imagery of a supervisory custodian (the παιδαγωγός of 3:24–25 or the ἐπίτροποι and οἰκονόμοι of 4:2) and provides an answer to why being ὑπὸ νόμον ("under law") results in being ὑπὸ κατάραν ("under a curse") in Paul's earlier discussion at 3:10.

Nonetheless, deciding definitively what Paul meant here by χάριν is exceedingly difficult, for both a cognitive (more probable) and a causative (less probable) interpretation are possible. It may be, in fact, that Paul had no intention of being as precise as commentators would like to make him. In all likelihood, all Paul wants to say here is that the Mosaic law's God-given purpose had to do with "transgressions" and not with making anyone righteous (as in legalism) or with bringing anyone to perfection (as in nomism) by its observance. Probably the phrase "because of transgressions" is to be understood broadly to include all such matters as signaled in both the cognitive and the causative understandings of the purpose of the law, but also, as we shall see later in this section, in the law's condemnatory and supervisory functions.

The third point made in Paul's answer lays stress again on a temporal factor: "until the Seed for whom the promise was intended should come." Without a doubt, "seed" is to be given the same sense that Paul insisted it be given in 3:16b, viz., the Christ, though here Paul uses the term as a title (and so it is capitalized in the *Translation*). The perfect tense of the deponent verb ἐπαγγέλλομαι ("promise") signals a past action with present results, thereby suggesting that the promise is still in effect. The whole clause beginning with the temporal conjunction ἄχρι "until" (ἄχρις before a vowel) sets the *terminus ad quem* for the law, just as προσετέθη set its *terminus a quo*. Thus the Mosaic law, for Paul, was intended by God to be in effect for God's people only up until the coming of Christ. Or stated more positively and comprehensively, as Burton does: "Thus the covenant of promise is presented to the mind as of permanent validity, both beginning before and continuing through the period of the law and afterwards, the law on the other hand as temporary, added to the permanent covenant for a period limited in both directions" (*Galatians*, 189).

Paul's view here, of course, deviates widely from that of Judaism. Wis 18:4, for example, speaks of the "imperishable light of the law"; Josephus states that if not their wealth and their cities, at least the law given the Jews remains immortal (*Ag. Ap.* 2.277); and Philo echoes this sentiment in speaking of the changelessness of the law for as long as sun, moon, heavens, and the earth continue to exist (*Vit. Mos.* 2.14). The apocalyptic writings also emphasize the eternal and immutable character of the law (e.g., *Jub.* 1.27; 3.31; 6.17). It would, in fact, be difficult to find any Jew who thought otherwise. Certainly the Judaizers of Galatia argued along these lines. Viewing matters from a Christocentric perspective, however, Paul thought otherwise, and here he makes his point as to the law's intended duration.

Paul's fourth emphasis, that the law was "ordained through angels," needs to be understood both as to the history of the phrase and as to Paul's use here. The MT has no explicit reference to angels being present in the giving of the law at Mt. Sinai. Exod 19:18 portrays God as descending on Mt. Sinai "in fire" accompanied by smoke and the quaking of the mountain. Deut 33:2, however, says that the Lord came to Sinai "from myriads of holiness" (or "with myriads of holy ones") and "with a fiery law," while Ps 68:18 (LXX 67:18) refers poetically to an accompanying retinue of chariots in the giving of the law, but not directly angels. The first explicit association of angels with the giving of the law came about, it seems, with the LXX's translation of the textually ambiguous phrase אֵשְׁדָּת לָמוֹ, ('*ēšdāt lāmô*, "with a fiery law'') of Deut 33:2 as ἐκ δεξιῶν αὐτοῦ ἄγγελοι μετ᾽ αὐτοῦ ("angels from his right hand were with him"). In later rabbinic thought Ps 68:18 (LXX 67:18) was even more important than Deut 33:2 for the association of angels with the giving of the law, for, as Terrance Callan points out, the chariotry of God mentioned there was "regularly understood as a reference to a large number of angels accompanying God at Sinai" (cf. *JBL* 99 [1980] 551; the talmudic references and bibliography cited in notes 6–10). And it was such an understanding of angels as being present at the giving of the Mosaic law that seems to have been the dominant tradition in Paul's day, as in *Jub.* 1.27–29; Acts 7:38, 53; Heb 2:2; Philo, *Somn.* 1.140–44; and Josephus, *Ant.* 15.136 (though for the view that ἄγγελοι in this text does not refer to angels but to prophets or priests, see W. D. Davies, *HTR* 47 [1954] 135–40; F. R. Walton, *HTR* 48 [1955] 255–57). Aquila's more rigidly literal rendering of the final phrase of Deut 33:2 as πῦρ δόγμα αὐτοῖς ("a fiery teaching for them") and Symmachus' translation of the same as πύρινος νόμος ("a fiery law") may represent another tradition, either current in Paul's day or later.

Such a mediatorial role for angels in the giving of the law seems to have been part of the widespread attempt in early Judaism to assign a role for angels in all the major revelatory and redemptive events of Scripture. In rabbinic Judaism, however, there was a rather strong reaction to seeing angels intervening at the critical moments in Israel's history, with many rabbis arguing that it was God alone who acted for the nation at these times (cf. L. Finkelstein, "The Oldest Midrash: Pre-Rabbinic Ideals and Teaching in the Passover Haggadah," *HTR* 31 [1938] 290–92). After the close of the NT period efforts were made within certain circles of rabbinic Judaism to belittle the role of angels at Sinai in order to counter the Christian claim that the law was an inferior revelation because of its mediation by angels (cf. W. D. Davies, *HTR* 47 [1954] 140 n. 17).

By itself, of course, Paul's reference to angels at the giving of the law does not necessarily carry any depreciatory connotations. As H. J. Schoeps points out, "The presence of angels at the event of the giving of the law was a favourite bit of embroidery in rabbinic tradition, and was meant to enhance the glory of Sinai" (*Paul*, 182). Yet from the context of what was said earlier in v 19a and what follows in vv 19b–20, it is almost impossible to read "ordained through angels" in any other way than with the intent "to depreciate the law as not given directly by God" (so Burton, *Galatians*, 189; and so the vast majority of scholars, whether they agree with Paul or not). It was probably the case that the Judaizers were citing the angels' presence at Sinai as evidence of the law's glory and God's approval. Paul, however, turns this tradition in *ad hominem* fashion against them.

The final feature of Paul's answer to the question "Why, then, the law?" is the phrase ἐν χειρὶ μεσίτου (lit.: "in the hand of a mediator"). ἐν χειρί is a Hebraism that means simply "by means of" (cf. C. F. D. Moule, *An Idiom-Book of New Testament Greek*, 184; note also Acts 11:30). The implied subject of the phrase is certainly Moses, though Origen, Chrysostom, Jerome, Luther, Calvin, et al. understood it to be Christ, being influenced by such texts as 1 Tim 2:5 and Heb 8:6; 9:15; 12:24. In the LXX ἐν χειρί is regularly used of Moses in his role as God's spokesman (cf. A. Vanhoye, "Un médiateur des Anges en Ga 3, 19–20," *Bib* 59 [1978] 403). In particular, it is the law and the commandments of God that are said in the LXX to have been given ἐν χειρὶ Μωϋσῆ (cf. Lev 26:46; Num 4:37, 41, 45, 49; 9:23; 10:13; 15:23; 17:5; 33:1; 36:13; Josh 21:2; 22:9; Judg 3:4; 1 Chr 16:40; 2 Chr 33:8; Ps 76:21; 2 *Apoc. Bar.* 2.28). Yet in the biblical accounts ἐν χειρὶ Μωϋσῆ does not lay stress so much on the role of Moses as a mediator as it does on the act of transmission itself.

In the Judaism of Paul's day, however, the title μεσίτης ("mediator") was commonly assigned to Moses. Philo in *Vit. Mos.* 2.166, describing Moses' intercession on behalf of Israel, explicitly refers to him as μεσίτης καὶ διαλλακτής ("mediator and reconciler"); and *As. Mos.* 1.14 (cf. 3.12) portrays Moses as saying that God destined him from the foundation of the world to be ὁ μεσίτης τῆς διαθήκης αὐτοῦ ("the mediator of his covenant"). More implicit, yet just as significant, is the understanding of Moses as God's mediator in the giving of the law in Philo, *Somn.* 1.142–43 and Heb 8:6. Saul Lieberman also cites the Samaritan *Marqah* where the title Mediator is used of Moses (see his *Hellenism in Jewish Palestine*, 81–82).

While the phrase ἐν χειρὶ μεσίτου appears in the NT only here at v 19, it may nevertheless be assumed from the number and diversity of references cited above that "Paul draws upon a common tradition in calling Moses *mesitēs*" (so T. Callan *JBL* 99 [1980] 555). Paul's reference to Moses as a mediator of itself, of course, carries no necessary nuance of disparagement, either directed against Moses or against the Mosaic law. But his comments on this tradition in v 20 certainly do.

20 ὁ δὲ μεσίτης ἑνὸς οὐκ ἔστιν, ὁ δὲ θεὸς εἷς ἐστιν, "a mediator, however, does not just represent one party; but God is one!" "This verse," Terrance Callan tells us, "is one of the most obscure in the letters of Paul" (*JBL* 99 [1980] 549). Lightfoot reports that in his day "the number of interpretations of this passage is said to mount up to 250 or 300" (*Galatians*, 146), though he gives us none but his own; and Albrecht Oepke continues the hyperbole in speaking of 430 interpretations (*Galater*, 117), though obviously that number is taken from Gal 3:17 and not based on research. The most complete survey of interpretations of v 20a is to be found in Callan's unpublished Yale dissertation "The Law and the Mediator: Gal 3:19b–20."

In v 20 Paul tells us what it is about mediation that reflects negatively on the law: that the presence of a mediator implies a plurality that stands in contrast to the oneness of God. But how this plurality is to be defined is problematic. Of all the claimed hundreds of interpretations, three are most likely:

1. That the plurality signaled in ἑνὸς οὐκ ("not one") has to do with *a duality of parties* involved in a mediated arrangement, God on the one hand and the Jewish people on the other (so J. B. Lightfoot, *Galatians*, 146–47; E. deW. Burton, *Galatians*, 191–92);

2. That the plurality signaled in ἑνός οὐκ has to do with *a plurality of persons*, though with the persons understood as being groups rather than individuals, and that since a whole group cannot easily engage in a transaction with another group, a mediator is required to act as a go-between—in this case between the angels, through whom the law was ordained, and the Jewish people (so H. Lietzmann, *Galater* [1923], 21–22; A. Oepke, "μεσίτης," *TDNT* 4:619);

3. That *the concept of a mediator itself* implies a plurality, which stands in contrast to the oneness of God—the assumption being that any transaction in which a mediator is involved is inferior to one in which God acts directly (so H. D. Betz, *Galatians*, 171–73; T. Callan, *JBL* 99 [1980] 555–67).

It is extremely difficult to determine exactly what Paul meant when he said, "A mediator, however, is ἑνὸς οὐκ." Is the plurality that of two parties (God and the Jewish people), or of two groups (angels and the Jewish people), or implied simply because of the inferiority of a mediator who must always work as a go-between?

Of the three positions, the latter two seem more tenuous than the first. The second falters because angels were never thought of in Judaism as being the principal cause or originators of the Torah, even though the tradition arose as to their being an efficient cause or agents of what took place at Sinai. Furthermore, the second view makes Moses only a functionary of the angels, which seems hard to countenance not only for Jews but also for Christians. The third view also seems tenuous because in all of the Jewish texts about Moses as a mediator of the Torah, nowhere does the fact of his being a mediator carry a negative connotation or reflect badly on the law itself. And while it can be argued that Paul here, as has been his pattern, "once again gives the tradition an unexpected twist in somehow viewing the fact that it was mediated by Moses as a point against the law" (T. Callan, *JBL* 99 [1980] 555), yet because Paul's arguments throughout the *probatio* of Galatians are mounted directly against the law itself, in both its legalistic and nomistic forms, one wonders why he would now change the focus of that polemic to attack Moses directly and the law only as a result of its association with Moses. The first position, while not without difficulties, at least keeps the focus of attention on the inferiority of the law itself without deflecting attention first to either angels or Moses. Its point has to do with the inferiority of the law because of its indirect introduction into the people's experience. That is certainly a different understanding than Judaism had of what went on at Sinai, but at least it is not first a put-down of the angels or Moses in order then to put down the law.

The second part of v 20 is a citation of the quintessential confession of all Jews: the great Deuteronomic utterance, known as the Shema, that "God is one!" (Deut 6:4). The point Paul seems to be making in citing this confession is, as Betz says, that "the process of divine redemption requires conformity to the oneness of God" (*Galatians*, 172–73; see also Rom 3:30 where a similar implication is drawn from God's oneness). So just as ἑνός οὐκ in the first part of the verse drew attention to the law's indirect and contractual nature, here εἷς ἐστιν ("is one") draws attention to the fact that God's true redemptive activity is always direct and unilateral in nature. To desire the former, therefore, is to desire the inferior, whereas God wants to deal with his people directly.

A further strand of tradition in early Judaism saw mediation of any kind as being inferior and stressed God's direct dealing with his people. This tradition appears as early as the LXX's translation of Isa 63:9: "Not an elder [πρέσβυς] nor an angel [ἄγγελος] saved them, but he himself [the Lord] saved them"—translating the MT's "the angel of his presence saved them." And the tradition seems to appear widely in such diverse writings as:

Sipre Deut. 42 (on 11:14): "Then will I give: I—not by the hands of an angel, and not by the hands of a messenger."
Sipre Deut. 325 (on 32:35): "I personally will exact retribution from them, not by means of an angel and not by means of a messenger."
'*Abot R. Nat.* B 2: "Moses received Torah from Sinai. Not from the mouth of an angel, and not from the mouth of the Seraph, but from the mouth of the King over the king of kings, the Holy One, blessed be He."
1QH 6.13–14 (based on the reconstruction of G. Vermes and M. Mansoor): "There shall be no mediator to [invoke Thee] and no messenger [to make] reply."

Josephus, *Ant.* 3.89: "He [Moses] made the people advance with their wives and children, to hear God speak to them of their duties, to the end that the excellence of the spoken words might not be impaired by human tongue in being feebly transmitted to their knowledge."

Philo, *Quaest. Gen.* 1.55: "Moreover, he [God] did not use any intermediary [μεσίτης] to urge him or exhort him to give others a share of incorruptibility."

Thus running parallel to the tradition that Moses acted as a mediator in the giving of the law at Sinai, there was also another tradition that stressed God's direct dealing with his people over anything mediated (for discussions of the above references, see J. Goldin, "Not by Means of an Angel and Not by Means of a Messenger," 412–24; T. Callan, *JBL* 99 [1980] 556–58). And this tradition may very well have been in the back of Paul's mind when he argued here in v 20 that the circumstances involved in the giving of the law at Sinai only serve to point up the inferiority of that law, whereas God's redemptive activity is always direct and unilateral in nature, reflecting the oneness of his person.

21 ὁ οὖν νόμος κατὰ τῶν ἐπαγγελιῶν τοῦ θεοῦ, "is the law, then, opposed to the promises of God?" Having argued for the disjunction of the Mosaic law and the Abrahamic promise in 3:15–18, and then the inferiority of that law to God's direct redemptive activity in 3:19–20, Paul now asks whether the logical conclusion of all this is that the law must be seen as standing in opposition to the promise. It is a supplemental question to that of v 19, but just as vital. For Paul must now protect his readers from any Marcionite type of thinking and at the same time clarify relationships between the God-given law of Moses and the God-given promise to Abraham. The inclusion of the possessive τοῦ θεοῦ ("of God") could be debated, for the sentence is equally clear, more terse, and more in line with Paul's usual manner of referring to the promise (or promises) without these two words. Yet the manuscript evidence is too strong to permit deleting them.

μὴ γένοιτο, "by no means!" Paul's immediate reaction to any claim that the law and the promise are in principle opposed to one another is the emotionally charged optative expression μὴ γένοιτο, which may be literally rendered "Let it not be!" but more evocatively translated "By no means!" or "Absolutely not!" (KJV's "God forbid!" captures the emotional quality of the expression but translates none of the words.) How could the law and the promise be inherently opposed? For God is the originator of both. After this exclamation, Paul goes on in characteristic fashion to state his reason (cf. 2:17; also Rom 6:1, 15; 7:7).

εἰ γὰρ ἐδόθη νόμος ὁ δυνάμενος ζῳοποιῆσαι, ὄντως ἐκ νόμου ἂν ἦν ἡ δικαιοσύνη, "for if a law had been given that could give life, then righteousness would certainly have been on the basis of law." The postpositive γάρ ("for") sets off this sentence and the next as the explanatory reason for Paul's strong negative exclamation. This first sentence of Paul's explanation is in the form of a second class "contrary to fact" condition (εἰ with a past tense in the protasis; ἄν with a past tense in the apodosis), which assumes the condition to be untrue (cf. 1:10b; see also 1 Cor 2:8; 1 John 2:19). The aorist passive ἐδόθη ("had been given") coupled with the anarthrous νόμος signals the idea of "any God-given law." The adjectival participial phrase ὁ δυνάμενος ζῳοποιῆσαι ("which is able to give life") goes grammatically with νόμος, but the form of the sentence shows plainly that the association of "law" and "life" is for Paul a false one. "Life" in Paul's thought

is "spiritual life" (cf. Rom 8:11; 1 Cor 15:22, 36; 2 Cor 3:6; see also John 6:63),
which stands in antithesis to "death" with which the law is associated.

The apodosis of the sentence completes the hypothetical character of the
statement, but its conclusion is patently false: "then righteousness would certainly
have been on the basis of law." "Being made alive," "being in Christ," "being led
by the Spirit," and "being righteous (both forensically and ethically)" are for Paul
cognate expressions (cf. 2:20; 5:16, 25). The phrase ἐκ νόμου indicates source (cf.
2:16; 3:2, 5), and so "on the basis of law." Paul, however, insists that no law can give
life, and so righteousness in whatever its dimension, whether forensic or ethical,
cannot be based on any law.

22 ἀλλὰ συνέκλεισεν ἡ γραφὴ τὰ πάντα ὑπὸ ἁμαρτίαν, "but the Scripture
confined everyone without distinction under sin." The second sentence of Paul's
explanation starts with the strong adversative particle ἀλλά ("but"), which marks
a contrast between the unreal hypothesis of v 21 and the actual situation as here
stated. The use of ἡ γραφή ("the Scripture") as the subject of the sentence, rather
than ὁ νόμος as in the first sentence, has raised all sorts of questions as to what
exactly Paul had in mind. Is ἡ γραφή to be identified with ὁ νόμος (so, e.g., A.
Oepke, Galater, 119; F. F. Bruce, Galatians, 180) or to be differentiated from ὁ νόμος
(so, e.g., H. Schlier, Galater, 164–65; H. Betz, Galatians, 175)? And if it is to be
differentiated, does it refer to Scripture generically (so, e.g., G. S. Duncan,
Galatians, 118; R. A. Cole, Galatians, 106; so also JB, NEB, NIV), to Scripture as a
metonomy for God himself (so, e.g., B. B. Warfield, The Inspiration and Authority of
the Bible [Philadelphia: Presbyterian & Reformed, 1948] 299–348), or to a more
generalized conception akin to the Greek idea of "Fate" (so, e.g., H. D. Betz,
Galatians, 175)? Or, as Lightfoot and Burton have argued, does Paul here have in
mind a particular passage of Scripture that he has cited earlier, either Ps 143:2,
possibly alluded to in 2:16, or Deut 27:26, quoted in 3:10 (cf. Lightfoot, Galatians,
147–48; Burton, Galatians, 195–96)? Paul's normal use of the singular γραφή (see
Comment and passages cited at v 8 above) and the presence of the article ἡ (so "the
Scripture" as KJV, RSV, GNB) suggest that he had a particular passage in mind,
probably the more immediate antecedent of 3:10, i.e. Deut 27:26—a passage he
learned from his rabbinic training but one also probably vividly impressed on
him from his synagogal beatings (see Comment on 3:10). That he had in mind Deut
27:26 rather than Ps 143:2 is made more probable by the fact that the function of
the law is under discussion, and so a passage from the Pentateuch would be most
appropriate. Furthermore, such an implied reference would then make ὑπὸ ἁμαρτίαν
("under sin") to be equivalent to ὑπὸ κατάραν ("under a curse") of 3:10, which is
not at all unlikely and would bring matters into perspective.

The verb συγκλείω means figuratively "confine," "hem in," or "imprison." The
neuter τὰ πάντα (lit.: "all things") used of people has the effect of obliterating
every distinction and referring to all humanity as an entity (so "all people" or
perhaps better "everyone without distinction"; cf. Eph 1:10; Col 1:20, though in
these passages the expression is used even more broadly). Accepting ὑπὸ ἁμαρτίαν
as here equivalent to ὑπὸ κατάραν (assuming Deut 27:26 to be in mind), Paul is
then saying that a primary function of the Mosaic law was to bring all humanity
under the curse of the law. So reaching back to the expression "because of
transgressions" in v 19 and combining that with the statement "confined all things
under sin" here in v 21, we can say that Paul saw the law functioning in a negative

Comment

fashion vis-à-vis God's promise: it brought about a knowledge of sin, perhaps even an intensified knowledge by actually increasing sin, and it brought condemnation by bringing all humanity under its curse. In effect, it was, as Lutheran theologians often call it, "God's strange work" instituted in order to bring us to "God's proper work." It was not opposed to God's promises, for it operated in the economy of God on a different level or plane than did God's promises.

ἵνα ἡ ἐπαγγελία ἐκ πίστεως Ἰησοῦ Χριστοῦ δοθῇ τοῖς πιστεύουσιν, "so that the promise that is based on the faithfulness of Jesus Christ might be given to those who believe." On the expression ἐκ πίστεως Ἰησοῦ Χριστοῦ, see the *Comment* on 2:16. Paul saw two strands of God-given material running throughout the Scriptures: (1) the law of God, which was given to highlight the true nature of sin and so bring sinful humanity under its curse; and (2) the promises of God, which have always called for a response of faith and are now focused in the faithfulness or obedience of Jesus Christ. In terms of how these two strands operate in our standing before God: the one brings us down; the other raises us up. Ultimately, the strands are united in a common, overall purpose. They cannot be pitted against each other, as Marcion later asserted. Yet because they function on different levels in the divine economy or "operate in different spheres" (Burton, *Galatians*, 193), they cannot be treated as though they are basically the same, or supplementary to each other, or simply to be amalgamated, as the Alexandrian Fathers tried to do.

23 πρὸ τοῦ δὲ ἐλθεῖν τὴν πίστιν ὑπὸ νόμον ἐφρουρούμεθα συγκλειόμενοι εἰς τὴν μέλλουσαν πίστιν ἀποκαλυφθῆναι, "before this faith came, we were kept in custody under the law, being confined until this coming faith should be revealed." In some respects, v 23 is remarkably parallel to v 22. Both have the verb συγκλείω ("confine," "hem in," "imprison"), with the aorist form of the verb appearing in v 22 and the present passive adverbial participle in v 23; and both refer to the Christian gospel as the culmination of the purposes of the law, with the expression "the faithfulness of Jesus Christ" in v 22 and the term "the faith" in v 23 used in parallel fashion to signal that gospel. The verses, however, differ in their subjects and in their depictions of the functions of the law. For while v 22 portrays "everyone without distinction" (τὰ πάντα used of people) as under the law's curse, v 23 portrays Jews (note the first person plural suffix "we" of the verb ἐφρουρούμεθα and the participle συγκλειόμενοι) as having been under the law's guardianship. In speaking of these two functions of the Mosaic law, one condemnatory and the other supervisory, Paul uses the one verb συγκλείω, because in both cases the feature of constraint is prominent—i.e., condemning sin with respect to "everyone without distinction" (v 22), while supervising life with respect to Jews (v 23). By definition, of course, Jews are included among "everyone without distinction," and so the Mosaic law exercises its condemnatory function in their case as well. But Jews also lived "under the law" in a special way distinct from all others, which Paul will clarify in his analogy of the *paidagōgos* in vv 24–25.

By τὴν πίστιν ("the faith") and τὴν μέλλουσαν πίστιν ἀποκαλυφθῆναι ("the coming faith to be revealed") Paul means not faith generically, but the particular faith referred to in v 22b that has to do with "the faithfulness of Jesus Christ" and humanity's response of faith. The use of the article makes the expressions here definite and serves to signal that what is in mind is that which has just been stated in the final clause of v 22. Likewise, the prepositional phrase πρὸ τοῦ ἐλθεῖν ("before the coming") and the present adjectival participle μέλλουσαν ("about to be") mark off this faith spoken of here as something that followed the supervisory reign of the law. Paul could not have spoken of faith in qualitative terms as only recently come about in the course of salvation history, since, as he has argued from 3:6 on, faith is at least as old as Abraham, the man who epitomized faith qualitatively.

The central idea of vv 23-25 is signaled by the phrase ὑπὸ νόμον ("under the law"), with the imperfect passive verb ἐφρουρούμεθα ("we were confined/kept in custody") and the present passive participle συγκλειόμενοι ("being confined") stating the nature of that relationship. But what did Paul have in mind here in v 23 in saying that Jews were "kept in custody under the law, being confined" until the gospel should come? Fortunately, we don't have to guess, for Paul tells us more exactly what he means by the use of the analogy of a *paidagōgos* in a patrician family.

24 ὥστε ὁ νόμος παιδαγωγὸς ἡμῶν γέγονεν, "the law, therefore, was our supervisory guardian." The particle ὥστε followed by an independent clause signals the result or consequence of what has just been stated ("so," or more formally "therefore"). The perfect γέγονεν (lit.: "it has been") is used here like a historical aorist to mean simply "it was" (so ἐγένετο as read by P⁴⁶ and B). Paul's use of the term παιδαγωγός has often puzzled commentators. For while today we think of pedagogues as teachers, in antiquity a *paidagōgos* was distinguished from a *didaskalos* ("teacher") and had custodial and disciplinary functions rather than educative or instructional ones.

Plato (427–347 B.C.) in *The Republic* speaks of "pedagogues [παιδαγωγῶν], nurses wet and dry, beauticians, barbers, and yet again cooks and chefs" as part of the retinue of Greek patrician households (373C), and characterizes pedagogues as "not those who are good for nothing else, but men who by age and experience are qualified to serve as both leaders and custodians of children" (467D). In chap. 4 of *Lysis* he provides us with a fascinating glimpse into the rearing of a son in a Greek family, from which the following dialogue between the boys, Socrates (who begins the dialogue), and Lysis is an excerpt:

> Do they [i.e., Lysis's father and mother] let you control your own self, or will they not trust you in that either?
> Of course they do not, he replied.
> But someone controls you?
> Yes, he said, my παιδαγωγός here.
> Is he a slave?
> Why certainly; he belongs to us, he said.
> What a strange thing, I exclaimed: a free man controlled by a slave! But how does this παιδαγωγός exert his control over you?
> By taking me to the teacher (εἰς διδάσκαλον), he replied (208C).

And in *Laws* Plato writes of children:

> Just as no sheep or other witless creature ought to exist without a herdsman, so children cannot live without παιδαγωγῶν, nor slaves without masters. And of all wild creatures, the child is the most intractable; for insofar as it, above all others, possesses a fount of reason that is yet uncurbed, it is a treacherous, sly and most insolent creature. Wherefore the child must be strapped up, as it were, with

many bridles—first, when he leaves the care of nurse and mother, with παιδαγωγοῖς to guide his childish ignorance, and after that with διδασκάλοις of all sorts of subjects and lessons, treating him as becomes a freeborn child. On the other hand, he must be treated as a slave; and any free man that meets him shall punish both the child himself and his παιδαγωγόν or his διδάσκαλον, if any of them does wrong (VII. 808D–E).

Aristotle (384–322 B.C.) alludes to such a custodial function of a pedagogue when he says that "the appetitive part of us should be ruled by principle, just as a boy should live in obedience to his παιδαγωγός (Nic. Ethics 3.12.8). And Xenophon (430–355 B.C.) writes: "When a boy ceases to be a child, and begins to be a lad, others release him from his παιδαγωγόν and from his διδάσκαλον ; he is then no longer under them, but is allowed to go his own way" (Laced. 3.1).

Reflecting more directly the NT period, Josephus (A.D. 37–100/110) uses παιδαγωγός six times in contexts having to do with biblical history (Ant. 1.56; 9.125; 10.186), with Greco-Roman households (Ant. 18.6.9; 20.8.10), and in speaking about his own son's pedagogue, who is described as "a slave, a eunuch" and who was punished by the emperor Domitian for an accusation made against Josephus (Life 76). Epictetus (first and second centuries A.D.) speaks of brothers having not only the same father and mother but also commonly the same παιδαγωγός (Diss. 2.22.26). He also tells of pedagogues cudgeling the family cooks when their charges would overeat, and exhorts them: "Man, we did not make you the cook's παιδαγωγός, did we? but the child's. Correct him; help him!" (Diss. 3.19.5). And in a late second or early third-century A.D. papyrus letter a mother, on hearing of the departure of her son's teacher, writes: "So, my son, I urge both you and your παιδαγωγόν that you go to a suitable διδάσκαλον," and then closes her letter with the words: "Salute your esteemed παιδαγωγός Cros" (POxy 6.930).

The pedagogue is frequently encountered in rabbinic writings, where the Hellenistic origin of the concept is shown by the fact that pĕdāgôg, is a Greek loanword. For the most part the term appears in parables that have to do with the household of a king where the prince is under custodial supervision. Gen. Rab. 29.6, for example, reads:

R. Judah said: This may be illustrated by the case of a king who entrusted his son to a pedagogue (pĕdāgôg) who led him into evil ways, whereat the king became angry with his son and slew him. Said the king, "Did any lead my son into evil ways save this man? My son has perished and this man lives!" Therefore [God destroyed] "both man and beast."

Or again, Gen. Rab. 31.7 reads:

It is as if a royal prince had a pedagogue (pĕdāgôg), and whenever he did wrong, his pedagogue was punished; or as if a royal prince had a nurse, and whenever he did wrong, his nurse was punished. Similarly, the Holy One, blessed be He, said, "Behold, I will destroy them with the earth!"

There are also several places in the Midrashim where Moses is depicted as Israel's pedagogue (e.g., Exod. Rab. 21.8; 42.9), or where Moses, Aaron, and Miriam are so presented (*Num. Rab.* 1.2), or Moses, David, and Jeremiah (*Deut. Rab.* 2.11). But there is no passage in the extant Jewish literature where the Mosaic law itself is spoken of as a pedagogue. 4 Maccabees comes close in referring in 1:17 to the law as bringing παιδεία ("instruction," "training," "discipline") and in speaking in 5:34 of the law as a παιδευτής ("instructor," "teacher"), yet without directly calling the law a παιδαγωγός.

From such a collection of Greek and Jewish references it seems evident that Paul's use of παιδαγωγός here in vv 24–25, though creatively applied, is not an isolated phenomenon. The παιδαγωγός, though usually a slave, was an important figure in ancient patrician households, being charged with the supervision and conduct of one or more sons in the family. He was distinguished from the διδάσκαλος, for he gave no formal instruction but administered the directives of the father in a custodial manner, though, of course, indirectly he taught by the supervision he gave and the discipline he administered. The characterization of the pedagogue as having "the bad image of being rude, rough, and good for no other business," one for whom "the public did not have much respect," and "a comic type" as Betz portrays him (*Galatians*, 177), arises from caricatures drawn by ancient playwrights. But such a characterization is itself a caricature and entirely ignores passages that speak of him as a trusted figure in antiquity who commanded respect and even affection. Plutarch (A.D. 46–120), in fact, considered the term appropriate for a good political leader when he wrote of Aratus: "And all the world thought that Aratus was a good παιδαγωγός for a kingdom no less than for a democracy, for his principles and character were manifest, like color in a fabric, in the actions of the king" (*Aratus* 48.3).

The depiction of the ancient pedagogue as a grim and ugly character is, indeed, a caricature, and must not be imported into Paul's analogy here. Yet, on the other hand, it is difficult to interpret vv 24–25 as assigning a positive preliminary or preparatory role to the law. The point of the analogy here is not that the Mosaic law was a positive preparation for Christ, though in terms of piety and education that cannot be doubted in other contexts. Rather, the focus here is on the supervisory function of the law, the inferior status of one under such supervision, and the temporary nature of such a situation in the course of salvation history.

εἰς Χριστόν, "until Christ came." The preposition εἰς, which signals motion into or toward something, has a wide variety of uses. Here it may be used in a pregnant sense to suggest a forthcoming result, with Paul understood to be saying that the law functions to bring forth Christ (cf. Rom 8:21, where "freedom from the bondage of decay" has the result of bringing one "into [εἰς] the glorious freedom of the children of God"). The last clause of v 24, "in order that we might be justified by faith," might suggest such a reading. Or it may be used in a telic sense to suggest that the purpose of being under the supervision of the Mosaic law was "to lead us to" Christ (so KJV, NIV). The analogy of a pedagogue who brings his young charge to a teacher might suggest this. Or εἰς may be used here in a temporal sense to mean that the law's supervisory reign over the lives of God's people was meant to be only until the coming of Christ (so JB, RSV, NEB, GNB). This would be in line with the use of εἰς in the immediately preceding clause of v 23b, "until [εἰς] this coming faith should be revealed." Taken on its own, theologically supported arguments for each of these three possibilities could be mounted.

Taken in context, however, only the temporal sense is possible. For the immediate context makes it clear that Paul is speaking of successive periods in salvation history, first that of the reign of the law and then that associated with the coming of Christ—with the first being displaced by the second (cf. vv 23 and 25). Furthermore, ὥστε ("therefore") at the start of the sentence ties v 24 directly to v 23 as the consequence of what was said immediately before. It is impossible, therefore, to understand εἰς Χριστόν here in any other way than temporally and so translate it by some such expression as "until Christ came" (RSV, GNB), "until the Christ came" (JB), or "until Christ should come" (NEB).

ἵνα ἐκ πίστεως δικαιωθῶμεν, "in order that we might be justified by faith." As a Jew, Paul usually speaks in ultimates, not in terms of mediate causation. So here he expresses the ultimate purpose of the law as a παιδαγωγός: "that we might be justified by faith." The law's other functions of bringing about a knowledge of sin, increasing sin, and condemning sin have this ultimate purpose in mind as well, and so serve this end among both Jews and Gentiles. Here, however, Paul has in mind the law in its custodial function in the experience of Israel, and so talks about being justified before God in the first person plural (note the verbal suffix "we"). "Justification by faith" is an emphasis made throughout the *propositio* and the *probatio* of Galatians. The aorist subjunctive passive form of δικαιωθῶμεν ("be justified") identifies God as the one who justifies (passive voice) and justification as an offer to be received. On ἐκ πίστεως, see *Comment* on 2:16 and 3:2, 5.

25 ἐλθούσης δὲ τῆς πίστεως οὐκέτι ὑπὸ παιδαγωγόν ἐσμεν, "but now that this faith has come, we are no longer under a supervising guardian." Here Paul delivers the *coup de grâce* to the Judaizers' argument for Gentile Christians to live a lifestyle governed by the Mosaic law. For with the coming of the Christian gospel (τῆς πίστεως) as effected by Christ, the law no longer has validity as a παιδαγωγός regulating the life of faith. One may, of course, as a Jew continue to live a Jewish nomistic lifestyle for cultural, national, or pragmatic reasons. To be a Jewish believer in Jesus did not mean turning one's back on one's own culture or nation. Yet no longer could it be argued that circumcision, Jewish dietary laws, following distinctly Jewish ethical precepts, or any other matter having to do with a Jewish lifestyle were requisite for the life of faith. Certainly not for Gentile Christians in any sense, though Paul and the Jerusalem apostles for cultural, national, and/or pragmatic reasons allowed Jewish believers in Jesus to live a Jewish lifestyle, but not as required spiritually (cf. the author's *Paul, Apostle of Liberty*, 245–88).

Explanation

Gal 3:19–25 is the first part of Paul's answer to the Judaizers' call for Gentile Christians to live their lives under the prescriptions of the Mosaic law. Here Paul sets out a Christian understanding of that law, highlighting in vv 19–20 its relation to God's redemptive promises, in vv 21–22 its condemnatory purpose, and in vv 23–25 its supervisory function. As given by God to reveal sin and condemn the sinner, it operates in the divine economy on a different level or in a different sphere than God's promises. So while it is, indeed, "God's strange work" instituted to bring us to "God's proper work," it in no way can be said to be a supplement to God's grace. Rather, it stands over all human endeavor, whether Jewish or Gentile, showing God's attitude toward sin, thereby bringing us down that we might then by faith look up. As given by God to supervise the lifestyle of his people Israel, its function as a supervisory custodian has come to an end with the work of Christ. To go back, then, to living a life regulated by law, even though motivated by a fervent piety, is to live a sub-Christian life—in effect, to renounce Christ in our actions.

The Christian church today has many who formally oppose legalism but hold firmly to nomism. Theirs is a religion of piety that they believe to be God-honoring. What they fail to realize, however, is that in many ways they are recapitulating the error of the Judaizers. More importantly, they fail to appreciate Paul's words regarding the purpose and function of the law here in 3:19–25, often preferring to dwell on his words of 3:1–18. Furthermore, they fail to appreciate the full import of what it means to be "in Christ" as presented in 3:26–29 that follows.

(b) New relationships "in Christ" (3:26–29)

Bibliography

Best, E. *One Body in Christ.* Byrne, B. *"Sons of God" —"Seed of Abraham."* Hester, J. D. *Paul's Concept of Inheritance.* Longenecker, R. N. *Paul, Apostle of Liberty,* 156–80. ———. *New Testament Social Ethics for Today.* Oepke, A. "βάπτω, βαπτίζω." *TDNT* 1:529–45. ———. "ἐν." *TDNT* 2:537–43. "ἐνδύω." *TDNT* 2:319–20.

Translation

[26] *For, you see, "You are all sons of God through your faith[a] in[b] Christ Jesus." [27]For, "As many of you as have been baptized into Christ have clothed yourselves with Christ. [28]There is neither[c] Jew nor Greek, slave nor free,[d] male nor female, for you are all one[e] in Christ[f] Jesus." [29]If you belong to Christ, then you are Abraham's seed and heirs according to the promise.*

Notes

[a] διὰ πιστεως appears in P[46] P Cl Cyr, but διὰ τῆς πίστεως is otherwise well supported.

[b] Χριστοῦ Ἰησοῦ ("of Christ Jesus") rather than ἐν Χριστῷ Ἰησοῦ ("in Christ Jesus") is read by P[46] and the 10th-century minuscule 1739 (with 1739 also reversing the order of the names), evidently by assimilation to 2:16 and 3:29.

[c] οὐκέτι ... οὐκέτι[(vid)] ... (lacuna), "no longer ... no longer ... (lacuna)," appears in P[46] for the thrice repeated οὐκ ἔνι, "there is neither," that is otherwise well supported.

[d] ἡ ἐλεύθερος ("the free") appears in D* for οὐδὲ ἐλεύθερος ("nor free"), which is otherwise well supported.

[e] ἔν (neuter "one") appears in G and the 9th-century minuscule 33 (see also lat) for εἷς (masculine "one"), which is otherwise well supported.

[f] ἐστὲ Χριστοῦ ("you are of Christ") appears in P[46] ℵ* A, evidently by assimilation to Χριστοῦ of v 29.

Form/Structure/Setting

The structure of Gal 3:26–29 is fairly complex. First there is what appears to be a "sayings" statement regarding the status of "all" believers as being "sons of God" because they are "in Christ" (v 26); then there is what is probably a confessional portion used in support of that statement and highlighting the new relationships that exist "in Christ" (vv 27–28); and finally there is a concluding statement as to what all this means for the issue raised by the Judaizers regarding Gentile Christians' relationship to Abraham (v 29). The "sayings" statement of v 26 and the confessional portion of vv 27–28 probably stem from the early church, being quoted here by Paul; the concluding statement of v 29 is in Paul's own words in application of these early Christian affirmations to the question at hand. Such a hypothesis seems to go far in explanation of (1) the three connecting particles γάρ . . . γάρ . . . ἄρα ("for . . . for . . . then") that introduce each of these three elements of the section, and (2) the somewhat diverse wording of the central concepts in these verses, which have been features that have troubled copyists, translators, and commentators down through the centuries. Within the confessional portion of vv 27–28 are three parallel couplets, with only the first being of pertinence to Paul's Galatian argument; the second and third evidently are included only by way of completing the confession. The main expression of this section is "in Christ Jesus" (ἐν Χριστῷ Ἰησοῦ, vv 26, 28), with "baptized into Christ" (εἰς Χριστὸν ἐβαπτίσθητε, v 27), "clothed with Christ" (Χριστὸν ἐνεδύσασθε, v 27) and "[being] of Christ" (Χριστοῦ, v 29) used in synonymous fashion. The polemical thrust of Paul's words here is indicated by the emphasis on "all" (πάντες), which is the first word of the section, and on being Abraham's "seed" by relation to Christ, which is the final sentence of the section. For Paul, it is the participationist soteriology of being "in Christ" that bridges the expanse between Abraham and the Gentile world, and not Torah observance as the Judaizers argued.

Whereas 3:19–25 dealt in negative fashion with why the Mosaic law could neither justify nor perfect—i. e., because its condemnatory purpose operates on a different plane than God's promises and because its supervisory functions have come to an end—3:26–29 sets out the positive reason for Christian living being apart from a nomistic lifestyle: because both Jewish and Gentile believers (πάντες) have been brought into a new spiritual experience as true "sons of God" (υἱοὶ θεοῦ) because of their oneness "in Christ," which means, in particular, that the life of God's people is now meant to be Christ-centered and not Torah-centered.

Comment

26 πάντες γὰρ υἱοὶ θεοῦ ἐστε διὰ τῆς πίστεως ἐν Χριστῷ Ἰησοῦ "for, you see, 'You are all sons of God through your faith in Christ Jesus.'" The postpositive γάρ here has both explanatory and continuative functions, and so is probably to be translated "for, you see," (cf. Rom 7:2; also Matt 12:40; 23:3; 24:38; Mark 7:3; Luke 9:14; John 3:16; 4:8, 9; Heb 3:4; 2 Peter 2:8). That πάντες ("all") is meant to be emphatic is indicated not only by its position at the beginning of the sentence but also by the emphases on universality in vv 27–28 and on Gentile Christians as "Abraham's seed" in v 29. The expression υἱοὶ θεοῦ ("sons of God") appears only here in Galatians, though the sonship of which it speaks is treated further in 4:6–7.

Somewhat jarring is the second person plural ἐστέ ("you are"), which shifts the perspective from Jews and Jewish believers ("we were . . . our . . . we might . . . we are") in vv 23–25 to a more inclusive reference. Likewise, somewhat strange is the appearance of the article τῆς ("the") when referring to "faith in Christ Jesus," for it is not the same as τὴν πίστιν or τῆς πίστεως found in the immediately preceding vv 23 and 25 that have the content of the Christian gospel in view, though it is like διὰ τῆς πίστεως of 3:14 earlier. The article here may specify the human response of trust and commitment that Paul spoke about throughout 3:1–14, so functioning as it does in 3:14; or it may serve in place of a possessive pronoun, and so be taken simply as "your faith" (cf. 2 Cor 1:24). Burton argues, "The latter is more probable because of the personal character of the statement as against the impersonal, historical, character of vv 23, 25" (*Galatians*, 203).

The differences of language in v 26 from Paul's usual ways of expressing himself are admittedly not great. Certainly "through faith in Christ Jesus" is typically Pauline, whatever might be thought about the inclusion and function of the article. Paul may very well be seen as simply changing his focus now from Jews and Jewish Christians in vv 23–25 to all believers in Jesus, both Jews and Gentiles, in vv 26–29 (so the change from "we" to "you"). And the use of "sons of God" and the article with "faith" as a human response need not appear too startling. On the other hand, it may be that these slight differences signal Paul's use of a "sayings" statement drawn from the early church (cf. the five "trustworthy sayings" of the Pastorals: 1 Tim 1:15, "Christ Jesus came into the world to save sinners"; as well as 1 Tim 3:1; 4:9; 2 Tim 2:11; Titus 3:8). If it is a "trustworthy saying" (πιστὸς λόγος) of the early church, the statement would have been a general affirmation: "You are all sons of God through your faith in Christ Jesus." As such it could have been used in a number of ways depending on the particular situation: the inclusive stress on πάντες ("all") wherever there was division in the church, without any necessary thought regarding Gentiles; the imagery of being υἱοὶ θεοῦ ("sons of God") to raise perspectives, without any necessary thought as to how Gentiles are to be seen as related to Abraham; the use of τῆς πιστεως to highlight the importance of personal faith ("your faith"), without any necessary thought as to how Torah observance and faith are to be related; and the use of ἐν Χριστῷ Ἰησοῦ ("in Christ Jesus") to signal the distinctive object of that faith vis-à-vis Judaism generally. The statement itself, then, may have stemmed from early Jewish Christianity—even the wording "through (the) faith in Christ Jesus" —and be quoted here by Paul in secondary fashion to counter the Judaizers' claims. I myself think that plausible, though admittedly such a hypothesis is more conjectural than proven. Nevertheless, whether the wording stems from the early church or is entirely Paul's own, the sentence is Paul's thesis statement of vv 26–29: "in Christ Jesus" there is a new universality of oneness and a new relationship of being God's children.

The phrase "in Christ" (and cognates) is a favorite with Paul to signal the personal, local, and dynamic relation of the believer to Christ. To say that it is a favorite of Paul's is not, however, to rule out its use by the early church as well, which seems to be the case, if v 26 is taken as an early Christian "sayings" statement and vv 27–28 as a portion of an early Christian confession (see later *Comment* on vv 27–28). The "in Christ" phraseology in its various forms appears a total of 164 times in the Pauline writings apart from the Pastorals (cf. A. Deissmann, *Die neutestamentliche Formel "in Christo Jesu"*; though Deissmann's count includes some debatable inclusions, such as Tertius's statement of having written ἐν κυρίῳ in Rom 16:22) and another eight times in the Pastorals (all being ἐν Χριστῷ Ἰησοῦ; see 1 Tim 1:14; 3:13; 2 Tim 1:1, 9; 2:1, 10; 3:12, 15). Variant phraseology for this idea includes: ἐν Χριστῷ (Gal 1:22; 2:17, and twenty-four times elsewhere in Paul's other letters); ἐν Χριστῷ Ἰησοῦ (Gal 2:4; 3:14, 26 [here], 28; 5:6, and thirty-seven more times in the Pauline writings); ἐν κυρίῳ (Gal 5:10, and another forty-six times elsewhere in Paul); ἐν αὐτῷ (nineteen times elsewhere in Paul); ἐν ᾧ (nine times, all in Ephesians and Colossians); with also such other variations as ἐν τῇ ζωῇ αὐτοῦ (Rom 5:10), ἐν Χριστῷ Ἰησοῦ τῷ κυρίῳ ἡμῶν (Rom 6:23), ἐν τῷ Χριστῷ (1 Cor 15:22), ἐν κυρίῳ Ἰησοῦ (Phil 2:19), and ἐν τῷ Ἰησοῦ (Eph 4:21).

Compared to what can be found in his other letters, Paul's use of the "in Christ" theme in Galatians appears to be somewhat elemental, stemming, it seems, from an elemental use of the theme in the early church. The expressions "in Christ [Jesus]" and "of Christ" (τοῦ Χριστοῦ of 3:29) at this stage in Paul's development are used somewhat interchangeably, without, it seems, any great preference as to which is used. Of the eight appearances of the "in Christ" motif in Galatians, one designates a corporate group of believers in their relation to the risen Christ (1:22, "the churches of Judea that are in Christ"), three are used instrumentally (2:17; 3:14; 5:10; i.e., "by/through Christ [Jesus]/the Lord"), while the other four reflect more a local sense (2:4; 3:26, 28; 5:6, "in Christ Jesus"). And this same semantic range in the motif continues in Paul's other letters, with at times "in Christ" meaning simply "Christians" or those who "belong to Christ" (as τοῦ Χριστοῦ of 3:29 and the reference to "the churches of Judea that are in Christ" of 1:22; note esp. the salutations of 1 Cor 1:2; Eph 1:1; Phil 1:1; Col 1:2; 1 Thess 1:1; 2 Thess 1:1), or with the phrase signifying at times the instrumental idea of "by" or "through Christ" (so, e.g., Rom 5:10; 14:14; 2 Cor 3:14; Phil 4:13), or with the phrase connoting at other times the local and personal sense of the believer being "in Christ" (so, e.g., Rom 8:1; 2 Cor 5:17, 19; Phil 3:9; Eph 1:20).

The use of "in Christ" as a locution for "Christian" or in an instrumental sense is not too difficult to understand. But how can Paul speak of the believer being "in Christ" (and its converse, of Christ—either directly or by his Spirit—being in the believer) in a local and personal sense? Deissmann proposed the analogy of a person being in air and air in a person, and so postulated that believers at conversion actually come to live in the ethereal Spirit and pneumatic Christ (*Die neutestamentliche Formel "in Christo Jesu"*, 92, 98). But such an analogy is not Pauline, for it breaks down the personality of both Christ and the Spirit. Rather, as Albrecht Oepke notes, Paul thought more of Christ as a "universal personality" ("ἐν," *TDNT* 2:542) than of Christ as ethereal or pneumatic (cf. Col 1:16–17, 19; Eph 1:10). Furthermore, as the OT can say that Abraham "trusted *in* Yahweh" (Gen 15:6—nine times using the preposition בְּ (*bĕ*) with the *hipʿîl* form of the verb when its object is God (cf. 2 Kgs 18:5–6; Ps 78:21–22; Prov 28:25–26; Isa 50:10; Jer 17:5–7; Nah 1:7; Zeph 3:2, 12), and as Jesus is reported to have spoken of his relationship with the Father as being "*in* the Father" (John 10:38; 14:10, 11, 20; 17:21), all without diminishing the concept of the real personality of God, so Paul with his high Christology could speak of being "in Christ" without softening or dissolving the fixed outlines of personality for either Christ or the Christian. To have been forced to give a definite psychological analysis of this relationship would have left Paul speechless. But he was convinced that he had experienced just such an intimacy with Christ, and he was also sure that his converts had experienced the same as well.

Of course, in positing a local and personal flavor for the phrase "in Christ" one is acknowledging a mystical mode of thought in Paul. But this need not be abhorred if we mean by the term *mysticism* "that contact between the human and the Divine which forms the core of the deepest religious experience, but which can only be felt as an immediate intuition of the highest reality and cannot be described in the language of psychology" (H. A. A. Kennedy, *The Theology of the Epistles*, 122). It is not a mysticism of absorption, for the "I" and the "Thou" of the relationship retain their own identities. Nor is it something separate from forensic righteousness before God, as though open to and experienced by only those who have been initiated into the more developed stages of the Christian life. "In Paul," as A. Oepke points out, "there is no suggestion of cleavage between a forensic and a mystical mode of thought. Forensic justification leads to pneumatic fellowship with Christ" ("βάπτω, βαπτίζω," *TDNT* 1:541). Being "in Christ" is, for Paul, communion with Christ in the most intimate relationship imaginable, without ever destroying or minimizing—rather, only enhancing—the distinctive personalities of either the Christian or Christ. It is "I-Thou" communion at its highest (cf. further my *Paul, Apostle of Liberty*, 160–70).

27 ὅσοι γὰρ εἰς Χριστὸν ἐβαπτίσθητε, Χριστὸν ἐνεδύσασθε, "for 'as many of you as have been baptized into Christ have clothed yourselves with Christ.'" In Koine Greek, as BAG (151, col. 1) tells us, γάρ ("for") is sometimes repeated either "to introduce several arguments for the same assertion" (so 1 Cor 16:7; 2 Cor 11:19–20; see also Sir 37:13–14; 38:1–2; Wis 7:16–17; John 8:42) or "to have one clause confirm the other" (so Rom 6:14; 8:2–3; see also Jdt 5:23; 7:27; 1 Macc 11:10; Matt 10:19–20; Luke 8:29; John 5:21–22; Acts 2:15). The latter, it seems, is what is taking place here: the thesis statement (whether an early church "sayings" statement or Paul's own composition) of v 26 is now confirmed by the confessional portion of vv 27–28.

Heinrich Schlier in 1949 first proposed that Gal 3:27–28 was a confessional portion, either whole or in part, drawn from the baptismal liturgy of the early church and used by Paul here in support of his statement of 3:26 (cf. *Galater*, 174–75). Structurally, one can go from v 26 to v 29, omitting vv 27–28, without noticing any break in Paul's logic or grammar. Furthermore, the last clause of v 28 clearly parallels v 26 (with the exception of the phrase διὰ τῆς πίστεως of v 26), which suggests that the γάρ of v 27 introduces a statement in support of the affirmation of v 26. Likewise, the ὅσοι ("as many as") that starts v 27 parallels the πάντες ("all") that starts v 26, not only being synonymous with that term but also clarifying its meaning. As for content, only the first pair of coordinates in v 28 ("neither Jew nor Greek") is directly relevant to Paul's argument in Galatians. Later in the letter, of course, Paul speaks of slavery and freedom. But his argument there in chaps. 4 and 5 concerns spiritual freedom as opposed to spiritual slavery, whereas here "neither . . . slave nor free" concerns social status; and his words there depend on the reality of the distinction, whereas here they proclaim its abolition. Likewise, Paul has not dealt at all with the relation of the sexes in arguing against the Judaizers in Galatia. Yet here we have the statement that "in Christ Jesus" there is "neither . . . male nor female."

These same pairings are to be found in either abbreviated or expanded form and in the same order at other places in Paul's letters, which suggests a degree of fixity for the pattern, at least in Paul's mind and probably as well in the early church. 1 Cor 12:13 reads: "For we were all baptized by one Spirit into one body—whether Jews or Greeks, slave or free—and we were all given the one Spirit to drink." Col 3:11

says that in the Christian life "there is no Greek or Jew, circumcised or uncircumcised, barbarian, Scythian, slave or free, but Christ is all, and is in all." Likewise, the exhortations of 1 Cor 7:17–28 as to being circumcised or uncircumcised (vv 17–19), slave or free (vv 21–23), and concerning marriage (vv 25–28) are structured in the same order. Furthermore, it should be observed that the pairings of Gal 3:28 and 1 Cor 12:13 appear explicitly in conjunction with the mention of baptism, and those of Col 3:11 are inferentially associated with baptism as well (cf. 2:12; 3:9–10), yet baptism as such is not discussed in any of these contexts. This suggests that these pairings were originally formulated in a baptismal liturgy of the early church.

There is much, therefore, to be said for the view that vv 27–28 were originally part of a baptismal confession of early Christians that Paul uses in support of his thesis statement of v 26. H. D. Betz, in particular, has argued for such a view (cf. *Galatians*, 181–85). And Betz cogently proposes the following two-strata understanding of the material of vv 27–28: "In the liturgy, the saying would communicate information to the newly initiated, telling them of their eschatological status before God in anticipation of the Last Judgment and also informing them how this status affects, in fact changes their social, cultural, and religious self-understanding, as well as their responsibilities in the here-and-now" (ibid., 184); whereas, "in the context of the [Paul's] present argument it serves as a 'reminder' and as the cardinal proof," for here Paul activates "the Galatians' situation of eye-witnesses: they themselves know the things of which Paul is reminding them; they have heard them before and have agreed to them in the decisive ceremony which had made them members of the Christian church" (ibid., 185).

The masculine plural ὅσοι ("as many as") is equivalent to the masculine plural πάντες ("all") of the preceding statement (v 26), with the clause it introduces serving to identify more precisely those referred to: "as many of you as have been baptized into Christ." The verb ἐβαπτίσθητε ("you have been baptized") undoubtedly refers to Christian baptism, i.e., immersion in water, for this is the uniform meaning of the term in Paul (cf. Rom 6:3; 1 Cor 1:13–17; 12:13; 15:29), with the single exception being his reference to the Israelites as "baptized into Moses [εἰς τὸν Μωϋσῆν ἐβαπτίσθησαν] in the cloud and in the sea" (1 Cor 10:2), though even there the term is used of something that is similar in character and significance to Christian baptism. The passive form of the verb (the middle is used in the NT only in Acts 22:16) suggests action done by another, certainly those baptizing but more importantly God himself (or Christ, as in Eph 5:26). The phrase εἰς Χριστόν is to be taken in the sense of "with reference to Christ" (cf. Rom 6:3, εἰς Χριστὸν Ἰησοῦν εἰς τὸν θάνατον αὐτοῦ, "with reference to Christ Jesus with reference to his death"; 1 Cor 1:13, 15, εἰς τὸ ὄνομα Παύλου, "with reference to the name of Paul"; 1 Cor 10:2, εἰς τὸν Μωϋσῆν, "with reference to Moses"), and so equivalent to εἰς τὸ ὄνομα [Χριστοῦ], "with reference to the name [of Christ]" (cf. Matt 28:19; Acts 8:16; 19:5), which parallels the Hebrew לְשֵׁם, *lĕšēm*. "with regard to the name."

The parallelism of πάντες in v 26 and ὅσοι in v 27 sets up a parallelism of what is said in each sentence as well. So "through your faith in Christ Jesus" is paralleled by "you have been baptized into Christ." The close association of faith and baptism in Paul (and throughout the NT), however, must never blind us to the fact that these are two distinct features of the one complex of Christian initiation. Each has its particular function in becoming a Christian, without ever being amalgamated or confused, as though, for example, baptism serves the same function as faith and so makes faith unnecessary, or conversely faith serves the same function as baptism and so makes baptism unnecessary. The two in Paul's mind are always related, though never thought of as identical or as supplements to one another. Faith in Christ is that which results in acceptance before God and the gift of God's Spirit (cf. 3:1–5); baptism is the outward sign and heavenly seal of that new relationship established by faith. In quoting an early Christian confession (as we believe), Paul is not simply replacing one external rite (circumcision) by another external rite (baptism). If that were so, i.e., if he viewed baptism as a supplement to faith in much the same way that the Judaizers viewed circumcision as a supplement to faith, he could have simply settled the dispute at Galatia by saying that Christian baptism now replaces Jewish circumcision. He would certainly have saved himself a great deal of argument. But Paul saw baptism in no such light. Rather, while faith and baptism are part and parcel of becoming a Christian, they are always to be distinguished. Each has its own function, with baptism never to be viewed as having *ex opere operato* efficacy or as being a supplement to faith.

The figurative use of ἐνδύω ("put on" or "clothe") with a personal object means to take on the characteristics, virtues, and/or intentions of the one referred to, and so to become like that person. Thus ἐνεδύσασθε as a second person plural, aorist, indicative (not here imperative), middle verb, with Χριστόν as the accusative of reference, means "you clothed yourselves with Christ"—i.e., you took on yourselves Christ's characteristics, virtues, and intentions, and so became like him. In the LXX there are frequent references to being clothed with righteousness, salvation, strength, and glory (cf. 2 Chr 6:41; Job 29:14; Ps 131[132]:9, 16, 18; Prov 31:25; Isa 51:9; 52:1; 61:10; Zech 3:3–5) or being clothed with shame (cf. Job 8:22; Ps 131[132]:18; 1 Macc 1:28). And this metaphor of clothing appears elsewhere in Paul's letters, running the gamut from clothing one's self with inner virtues (Col 3:12; 1 Thess 5:8) to putting on spiritual armor (Rom 13:12; Eph 6:11–17) to being clothed with immortality at Christ's coming (1 Cor 15:53–54). It may be as well that the metaphorical sense of clothing one's self with Christ was suggested to early Christians by baptismal candidates divesting themselves of clothing before baptism and then being reclothed afterwards (cf. C. F. D. Moule, *Worship in the New Testament*, 52–53; J. D. G. Dunn, *Baptism in the Holy Spirit*, 110; though C. J. Ellicott, *Galatians*, 89, argued against such an allusion).

28   οὐκ ἔνι Ἰουδαῖος οὐδὲ Ἕλλην, οὐκ ἔνι δοῦλος οὐδὲ ἐλεύθερος, οὐκ ἔνι ἄρσεν καὶ θῆλυ, "'there is neither Jew nor Greek, slave nor free, male nor female.'" After the events of vv 26–27, old divisions and inequalities have come to an end and new relationships have been established. The first half of v 28 speaks negatively of what has been eliminated; the second half, positively of what has been established. The thrice-repeated οὐκ ἔνι, "there is neither," contains the subject and verb of the main clause. Originally ἔνι was but an expanded form of the preposition ἐν. It came, however, to be used as a variant of ἔνεστιν ("it is possible"), and so it appears, for example, in 1 Cor 6:5 and 4 Macc 4:22. Yet it also was used as an emphatic equivalent for ἐστίν ("it is," "there is"), particularly when a strong negation was in view (cf. Col 3:11; Jas 1:17; also Sir 37:2, though not negated in this latter case). And that is how it is used here in v 28.

Three couplets representing three areas of inequality are set out in v 28, with the inequalities of each of these areas emphatically stated as having come to an end for believers in Christ. The first is the one particularly relevant for Paul's Galatians argument: "neither Jew nor Greek." Ἕλλην in the NT always means a Greek of Gentile origin (cf. 2:3). The second and third couplets have no relevance for Paul's immediate argument, though, of course, all three are highly significant as signposts that point the way toward a more Christian personal and social ethic (cf. my *New Testament Social Ethics for Today*, which builds extensively on these three couplets). They are quoted here only to complete the confession in which they are found. The third couplet reads οὐκ ἔνι ἄρσεν καὶ θῆλυ, differing only slightly in construction from the first two by the use of καί ("and") rather than οὐδέ ("nor"). This construction probably reflects the reading of Gen 1:27, ἄρσεν καὶ θῆλυ ἐποίησεν ("he made them male and female"), but it implies no real change in meaning.

Just why these three couplets, and not others, were incorporated into the confession of early Christians is impossible to say. Perhaps their inclusion was a conscious attempt to counter the three *běrākôt* ("blessings," "benedictions") that appear at the beginning of the Jewish cycle of morning prayers: "Blessed be He [God] that He did not make me a Gentile; blessed be He that He did not make me a boor [i.e., an ignorant peasant or a slave]; blessed be He that He did not make me a woman" (cf., e.g., *The Authorised Daily Prayer Book of the United Hebrew Congregations of the British Commonwealth of Nations*, tr. S. Singer, 2nd rev. ed. [London: Eyre & Spottiswoode, 1962] 6–7). These three *běrākôt* are credited to R. Judah ben Elai (c. 150 A.D.) in *t. Ber.* 7.18 and *j. Ber.* 13b, but to R. Meier (his contemporary) in *b. Menaḥ.* 43b. Analogous expressions of "gratitude" appear in Greek writings as well; for example, "that I was born a human being and not a beast, next, a man and not a woman, thirdly, a Greek and not a barbarian" (attributed to Thales and Socrates in Diogenes Laertius' *Vitae Philosophorum* 1.33, but to Plato in Plutarch's *Marius* 46.1 and Lactantius' *Divine Institutes* 3.19.17). So it may be surmised that in conscious contrast to such Jewish and Greek chauvinistic statements, early Christians saw it as particularly appropriate to give praise in their baptismal confession that through Christ the old racial schisms and cultural divisions had been healed.

Taking Gal 3:27–28 to be a pre-Pauline Christian confession, either in whole or in part, we may say, then, that when early Christians spoke of being "baptized into Christ" they also spoke of the old divisions between Jew and Gentile, slave and free, and male and female having come to an end. Certainly the proclamation of the elimination of divisions in these three areas should be seen first of all in terms of spiritual relations: that before God, whatever their differing situations, all people are accepted on the same basis of faith and together make up the one body of Christ. But these three couplets also cover in embryonic fashion all the essential relationships of humanity, and so need to be seen as having racial, cultural, and sexual implications as well. And that is, as I have argued elsewhere, how the earliest Christians saw them—admittedly, not always as clearly as we might like, but still pointing the way toward a more Christian personal and social ethic (cf. my *New Testament Social Ethics for Today*).

πάντες γὰρ ὑμεῖς εἷς ἐστε ἐν Χριστῷ Ἰησοῦ, "'for you are all one in Christ Jesus.'" The second half of v 28 sets out in positive fashion the basis for the new relationships that have been established: oneness (εἷς) in Christ Jesus (ἐν Χριστῷ Ἰησοῦ). Not only can γάρ in Koine Greek occur twice in one context, either "to introduce several arguments for the same assertion" or "to have one clause confirm the other" (see *Comment* on v 27a, citing BAG), it also can appear three times in the same presentation (cf. Wis 9:13–15; 14:27–29; Matt 16:25–27; Luke 9:24–26; Rom 4:13–15; 2 Cor 3:9–11), four times (Mark 8:35–38; Rom 1:16–18), and even five times (1 Cor 9:15–17). Here in vv 26a, 27a, and 28b we have a threefold use of γάρ: that of v 26a connecting vv 26–29 to vv 19–25 in explanatory and continuative fashion; that of v 27a used to confirm the thesis statement of v 26; and that of v 28b to confirm again that thesis statement by paralleling its terms and concepts, and so adding force to its words.

The words πάντες ("all"), ὑμεῖς ... ἐστέ ("you are"), and ἐν Χριστῷ Ἰησοῦ ("in Christ Jesus") are all familiar from the thesis statement of v 26, as is the concept of oneness implied in "all" being "sons of God." The only somewhat new features of v 28b are the explicit use of εἷς ("one") and the more direct correlation of εἷς to ἐν Χριστῷ Ἰησοῦ, but they are new only in focus and directness, for both are inchoate in v 26. In the "sayings" statement of v 26 and the confessional portion of vv 27–28, therefore, Paul finds the essence of the Christian proclamation: that "in Christ Jesus" there is a new "oneness" that breaks down all former divisions and heals injustices. The "in" of the equation is local and personal; "Christ Jesus" is viewed in universal and corporate terms; and "faith" and "baptism" describe the manner of entering into this state of being "in Christ" (cf. E. Best, *One Body in Christ*, 66–73).

29 εἰ δὲ ὑμεῖς Χριστοῦ, ἄρα τοῦ Ἀβραὰμ σπέρμα ἐστέ, κατ' ἐπαγγελίαν κληρονόμοι, "if you belong to Christ, then you are Abraham's seed and heirs according to the promise." Here Paul states his conclusion (note the εἰ ... ἄρα, "if ... then," construction), which, simply stated, is that relationship with Christ (Χριστοῦ) relates Gentile Christians directly to Abraham and God's covenantal promise. Having quoted what appears to be an early Christian "sayings" statement (v 26) plus an early Christian confessional portion (vv 27–28), Paul needs to mount no further argument. He evidently cites materials that his converts know already, and so needs only to draw out the implications inherent in those materials and state his conclusion.

The sentence is a first class conditional sentence, which assumes the truth of what is stated in the protasis. The protasis itself focuses on only one fact: relationship with Christ (ὑμεῖς Χριστοῦ, "you belong to Christ"; cf. οἱ τοῦ Χριστοῦ Ἰησοῦ, "those who belong to Christ Jesus," of 5:24), which has been affirmed earlier in the phrase "in Christ Jesus" of vv 26 and 28. In Paul's later letters this relationship will be spelled out more fully in the interplay between being "in Christ" and members of "the body of Christ" (see references cited at v 26; also Rom 12:5; 1 Cor 12:12, 27; Colossians and Ephesians passim). The apodosis of the sentence highlights the results of relationship with Christ: status as Abraham's "seed" (τοῦ Ἀβραὰμ σπέρμα ἐστέ, "you are Abraham's seed," which picks up ideas earlier expressed in 3:7, 9 and 16) and heirs of God's covenantal promise (κατ' ἐπαγγελίαν κληρονόμοι, "heirs according to the promise," which picks up ideas variously expressed in 3:14, 16–18, 19, 21–22). The Judaizers' call for a nomistic lifestyle on the part of Paul's Gentile converts, so that they might be related to Abraham and recipients of God's covenantal promise, is thus countered by the proclamation that it is being "in Christ" that brings about these results, and not observing the Torah. Or, as Burton aptly states matters, "the phrase 'seed of Abraham' is a synonym for objects of God's approval; the occasion of its employment was its use by those whose views and arguments Paul is opposing and the ground of its application to Gentiles is in their relation to Christ" (*Galatians*, 210).

Explanation

Gal 3:26–29 focuses on being "in Christ" and the new relationships that result from that status—new relationships spiritually ("sons of God," "clothed with Christ") and new relationships societally and culturally ("neither Jew nor Greek, slave nor free, male nor female"). Most importantly for his Galatians argument, Paul lays stress on the oneness that exists among "all" who have responded to Christ "through faith" and have been "baptized into Christ." For the ultimate answer to the Judaizers' call for Gentile Christians to observe Torah is not in setting out the God-intended purpose and functions of the Mosaic law, important as that discussion in 3:19–25 may be, but to assert that "in Christ" God has done something new that puts an end to the old. So while Paul's answer to the question "Why, then, the law?" concludes with a declaration that the law's function as a παιδαγωγός has come to an end with the coming of Christ, 3:20–29 declares why that is so: because God has done something new "in Christ." Being "under the law" (the theme of 3:19–25) has been replaced in the divine economy by being "in Christ" (the theme of 3:26–29).

It may seem strange to some that Paul's most conclusive point against the Judaizers' call for a nomistic lifestyle is presented very briefly—so briefly, in fact, that it is often overlooked or taken to be only a minor feature of Paul's overall argument. Paul does not argue in any extensive fashion his point of oneness and new relationships "in Christ"; rather, he just proclaims it and then draws the implication suitable for the situation at hand. In place of argument, Paul cites what appears to be an early Christian "sayings" statement in v 26 plus an early Christian confessional portion in vv 27–28. In so doing, he reminds his converts of what they affirmed in their conversion (probably at their baptism), evidently believing that recalling what they confessed in coming to Christ would be more convincing than any series of arguments. Paul's own words, however, are very brief, simply making the point that belonging to Christ is what relates Gentile believers to Abraham and God's covenantal promise (v 29).

Being "in Christ" is the essence of Christian proclamation and experience. One may discuss legalism, nomism, and even justification by faith, but without treating the "in Christ" motif we miss the heart of the Christian message. Likewise, Christians may live conscious of being "justified by faith" apart from legalism, but without being conscious of living "in Christ"; consequently, they often revert to some form of nomistic lifestyle. The climactic focus of Paul's Galatians argument (the *probatio*) is on being "in Christ," just as it is in the argument of his Romans letter, moving from justification-type arguments in 1:18–5:11 to incorporation-type arguments that climax with the "in Christ" motif in 5:12–8:39. And so the focus of Christians seeking to live out their commitments in a truly biblical fashion should be on being "in Christ," without reverting to some nomistic experience. Christians today can applaud Paul's antilegalist polemic of 3:1–18. Yet by ignoring his antinomist presentation of 3:19–29, which climaxes in the "in Christ" motif of vv 26–29, they may actually find themselves reproducing the Judaizers' error, despite protestations of piety and earnestness.

(c) An Illustration of Relationships (4:1–7)

Bibliography

Bandstra, A. J. *The Law and the Elements of the World: An Exegetical Study in Aspects of Paul's Teaching.* Kampen: Kok, 1964. 31–72. **Bertram, G.** "νήπιος." *TDNT* 4:912–23. **Calder, W. M.** "Adoption and Inheritance in Galatia." *JTS* 31 (1930) 372–74. **Dahl, N. A.** *Studies in Paul: Theology for the Early Christian Mission.* Minneapolis: Augsburg, 1977, 130–36, 171–72. **Delling, G.** "πληρόω, πλήρωμα." *TDNT* 6:286–306. ———. "στοιχέω, συστοιχέω, στοιχεῖον." *TDNT* 7:666–87. **Dunn, J. D. G.** *Christology in the Making.* London: SCM, 1980, 39–40. **Foerster, W.** "κληρονόμος." *TDNT* 3:767–85. **Hays, R. B.** *The Faith of Jesus Christ,* 85–137. **Hengel, M.** "Christologie und neutestamentliche Chronologie." In *Neues Testament und Geschichte: Historisches Geschehen und Deutung im Neuen Testament.* FS O. Cullmann, ed. H. Baltensweiler and B. Reicke. Zürich: Theologischer Verlag, 1972, 43–67 (ET in *Between Jesus and Paul* [Philadelphia: Fortress, 1983] 30–47). **Howard, G.** *Paul: Crisis in Galatia,* 66–82. **Kim, S.** *The Origin of Paul's Gospel,* 100–136, 258–60. **Kramer, W.** *Christ, Lord, Son of God,* 111–14, 187–89. **Longenecker, R. N.** "The Pedagogical Nature of the Law in Galatians 3:19–4:7." *JETS* 25 (1982) 53–61. **Lyall, F.** "Roman Law in the Writings of Paul—Adoption." *JBL* 88 (1969) 458–66. **Michel, O.** "οἰκονόμος." *TDNT* 5:149–51. **Reicke, B.** "The Law and This World According to Paul: Some Thoughts Concerning Gal 4:1–11." *JBL* 70 (1951) 259–76. **Reumann, J.** "'Stewards of God': Pre-Christian Religious Application of οἰκονόμος in Greek." *JBL* 77 (1958) 339–49. **Schweizer, E.** "Zum religionsgeschichtlichen Hintergrund der 'Sendungsformel' Gal 4,4f., Rm 8,3f., Joh 3,16f., 1 Joh 4,9." *ZNW* 57 (1966) 199–210. ———. "υἱός." *TDNT* 8:354–57, 363–92. ———. "υἱοθεσία." *TDNT* 8:399. ———. "Slaves of the Elements and Worshipers of Angels: Gal 4:3, 9 and Col 2:8, 18, 20." *JBL* 107 (1988) 455–68. **Stuhlmacher, P.** "Zur paulinischen Christologie." *ZTK* 74 (1977) 449–63 (ET in *Reconciliation, Law, and Righteousness* [Philadelphia: Fortress, 1986] 169–81). **Vielhauer, P.** "Gesetzesdienst und Stoicheiadienst im Galaterbrief." In *Rechtfertigung.* FS E. Käsemann, ed. J. Friedrich, W. Pohlmann, and P. Stuhlmacher. Tübingen: Mohr-Siebeck, 1976, 543–55.

Translation

[1]*What I am saying is this: As long as the heir is a minor, he is no different from a slave, even though he is the "young master" of all.* [2]*But he is under guardians and administrators until the time set by the father.* [3]*So also in our case, when we were minors, we were enslaved[a] under the basic principles of the world.* [4]*But, "When the fullness of time came, God sent his Son, born of a woman, born under the law,* [5]*in order that he might redeem those under the law, in order that we might receive the sonship."* [6]*And because you are sons, God[b] sent the Spirit of his Son[c] into our[d] hearts, crying, "Abba, Father."* [7]*Therefore you are no longer a slave but a son; and since a son, also an heir through God.[e]*

Notes

[a] ἦμεν δεδουλωμένοι (pluperfect periphrastic using the active [classical] form of εἰμί, "we were enslaved") appears in A B C TR and most manuscripts; ἤμεθα δεδουλωμένοι (pluperfect periphrastic using the middle [Hellenistic] form of εἰμί, "we were enslaved") in P⁴⁶ א D* G and the 10th-century

uncial 33. Though the MSS evidence is almost equally weighty, ἤμεθα is to be preferred since the natural tendency of scribes would have been to assimilate it to ἦμεν earlier in the sentence.

[b] ὁ θεός ("God") is omitted in B lat(t) cop^{sa} Tert and the 10th-century minuscule 1739.

[c] τοῦ υἱοῦ ("of his son") is omitted in P^{46} Mcion Aug.

[d] ὑμῶν ("your") appears in D^c K TR it vg syr^{pesh} cop^{bo} etc., evidently by assimilation with the verb ἐστέ ("you are") earlier in the verse; but ἡμῶν ("our") is well supported by P^{46} ℵ A B C D* G et al. and is the harder reading.

[e] διὰ θεοῦ ("through God") is well supported by P^{46} ℵ* A B C* etc., though a number of variants appear in the MSS as well: θεοῦ διὰ Χριστοῦ ("of God through Christ") in ℵ^c C^c D K P TR etc.; διὰ θεόν ("because of God") in G and the 14th-century minuscule 1881; as well as θεοῦ διὰ Ἰησοῦ Χριστοῦ ("of God through Jesus Christ"), or διὰ θεοῦ ἐν Χριστῷ Ἰησοῦ ("through God in Christ Jesus"), or μὲν θεοῦ συγκληρονόμος δὲ Χριστοῦ ("fellow heir of God and of Christ"), or simply θεοῦ ("of God").

Form/Structure/Setting

Having set out the diverse situations of God's people living "under the law" (3:23–25) but now living "in Christ" (3:26–29), Paul illustrates what he means in 4:1–7 by the use of the analogy of a son growing up in a patrician household. The language and imagery of the illustration are somewhat perplexing. For while the terms κληρονόμος ("heir"), νήπιος ("minor"), κύριος ("lord," "owner"), ἐπίτροπος ("guardian," "governor"), and perhaps οἰκονόμος ("administrator," "manager") of vv 1–2 all seem to be legal terms, it is uncertain what legal system Paul had in mind—whether Roman, Greek, Semitic, or some type of Greco-Roman-Seleucid hybrid used in the province of Phrygia—when he spoke of "the time set by the father" (v 2). Likewise, it is somewhat uncertain what Paul means by τὰ στοιχεῖα τοῦ κόσμου (lit.: "the elements of the world") and how ἡ υἱοθεσία (lit.: "the adoption") is used in v 5 and then commented on in v 7.

Even more difficult to ascertain are the structure and provenance of this section, particularly vv 4–5 and how they relate to their immediate context. These two verses have been widely recognized to be some sort of pithy kergymatic formulation. Within these verses appears some sort of "sending formula" and a chiastic construction. Furthermore, two expressions ("the fullness of time" and "born of a woman") seem to be unusual for Paul and to reflect early Jewish Christian interests. Do we have here a "sending formula" that arose originally within the Wisdom speculations of Hellenistic Judaism and then was applied to Christ as God's Son by Hellenistic Christians, and so taken over by Paul? Or is this Paul's own formulation drawn either from his Damascus-road experience or from the Church's witness that Jesus is the Father's "sent son"? Or is this Paul's retelling of the Church's Jesus story? Or is this a confessional portion drawn from the proclamation of the Church—with perhaps that confession itself based on the story told about Jesus by the early Christians—which Paul quotes here, either in whole or in part, because he knew his addressees would agree with such a generally acknowledged piece of tradition?

There is much that needs to be said regarding the form, provenance, meaning, and use of many of the individual items within this passage. But whatever one may conclude with regard to its details, Paul's overall meaning in the illustration is clear: the guardianship of the Mosaic law was meant to be for a time when God's people were in their spiritual minority; but now with the coming of Christ, the time set by the Father has been fulfilled and Christians are to live freely as mature sons "in Christ," not under the law's supervision.

Comment

1 λέγω δέ, ἐφ' ὅσον χρόνον ὁ κληρονόμος νήπιός ἐστιν, οὐδὲν διαφέρει δούλου κύριος πάντων ὤν, "what I am saying is this: As long as the heir is a minor, he is no different from a slave, even though he is the 'young master' of all." With the resumptive λέγω δέ ("what I am saying is this"; cf. 3:17; 5:16), Paul sets out an analogy meant to illustrate what he said in 3:23–25 about living "under the law" and in 3:26–29 about new relationships "in Christ." The picture he draws is of a boy in a home of wealth and standing who is legally the heir (ὁ κληρονόμος) and so the "young master" (κύριος, lit. "lord" or "owner") of the family estate, but who is still a minor (νήπιος) and so lives under rules very much like a slave (δοῦλος). The picture is that of a family, and so is a pleasant one overall—certainly not a bad situation per se, but one only judged to be an inferior relationship in comparison to adulthood.

In the Gospels νήπιοι are not only "children" (e.g., Matt 21:16) but also figuratively "disciples" to whom God gives revelation (cf. Matt 11:25//Luke 10:21). In Philo a νήπιος is a beginner or pilgrim on the journey from sense perception to virtue (cf. *Migrat.* 26–32, 46; *Prob.* 160; *Spec. Leg.* 2.32; *Congr.* 9–11; *Sobr.* 9). In Paul νήπιος usually signifies immaturity in the Christian life (cf. 1 Cor 3:1; 13:11; Eph 4:14; 1 Thess 2:7; see also Heb 5:13). Here, however, Paul uses νήπιος literally to mean an infant or minor (cf. Rom 2:20; see also Josephus, *Ant.* 6.262).

The temporal phrase ἐφ' ὅσον χρόνον ("as long as") is common in Greek literature to designate a period of time delimited by some temporary relationship (cf. Rom 7:1; 1 Cor 7:39; also Matt 9:15//Mark 2:19; 2 Peter 1:13). The words κληρονόμος ("heir"), νήπιος ("minor"), δοῦλος ("slave"), and κύριος ("lord," "owner"), while appearing frequently throughout the NT and Paul's letters in other contexts, are here used as legal terms, as they were also in the Greco-Roman world. Paul's statement that there is "no difference" between a young boy in the family and a slave is, of course, a hyperbole for the sake of the illustration. What he means is that they are alike in that they both live under rules and regulations. Looking back from the perspective of maturity, however, every adult acknowledges that in some ways minority status and slavery have much in common, whether the family experience was happy and beneficial or not. The participle ὤν is concessive in function ("even though"). The mundane use of κύριος in the sense of "owner" is unusual in the NT (cf. Matt 20:8; 21:40), though common in everyday parlance. The comparable English term for a boy in a family of wealth and standing, where (presumably) there exists a superior standard of upbringing, manners, and taste, is probably "young master," which connotes both minority position and status as heir.

2 ἀλλὰ ὑπὸ ἐπιτρόπους ἐστὶν καὶ οἰκονόμους ἄχρι τῆς προθεσμίας τοῦ πατρός, "but he is under guardians and administrators until the time set by the father." The terms ἐπίτροπος and οἰκονόμος have given rise to a good deal of discussion as to their precise meaning and what law Paul had in mind. There can be no doubt that they are meant to be synonymous with παιδαγωγός ("supervisory guardian"). This is particularly clear for ἐπίτροπος, which was a frequent term in Greek and became a loan word in Hebrew for the guardian of a minor (cf. Burton, *Galatians*, 212, for the Greek references; Str-B, 3:564–69, for rabbinic citations; see also Josephus, *J.W.* 1.49). There is, however, no certain instance of the use of

οἰκονόμος in the literature of antiquity for one who has charge of the person or estate of a minor, nor any case where the terms ἐπίτροπος and οἰκονόμος are used together. Yet οἰκονόμος appears frequently in Greek and as a loan word in Hebrew for one who acts as a steward or administrator for another (cf. O. Michel, "οἰκονόμος," *TDNT* 5:149–51; see also Josephus, *Ant.* 8.164, 308; 9.47; 11.138, 272; 12.199, 200, 205).

Many have argued from the appearance of these two terms together that Paul had in mind the Roman law *tutela impuberis* ("guardianship of a minor"), or more specifically *tutela testamentaria* ("guardianship established by testament"), where an heir was under the supervision of a tutor nominated by his father until fourteen years old and then under a curator appointed by the *praetor urbanus* until twenty-five (cf. Justinian, *Inst.* 1.22–23; see the literature cited by Betz, *Galatians*, 202 n. 6; also J. D. Hester, *Paul's Concept of Inheritance*, 18–19, 59; F. Lyall, *JBL* 88 [1969] 465). Others have proposed that Paul was here thinking in terms of Greek jurisprudence (so O. Eger, *ZNW* 18 [1917] 105–8; W. M. Calder, *JTS* 31 [1930] 372–74), and some have seen a Semitic background (so W. H. Rossell, *JBL* 71 [1952] 233–34; M. W. Schoenberg, *Scripture* 15 [1963] 115–23). But ancient inheritance laws— whether Roman, Greek, or Semitic—assumed the death of the testator before coming into effect, whereas Paul would hardly speak of the death of God before believers receive full sonship (though, of course, many modern theologians have said just that). Furthermore, Roman law (1) stipulated fixed times for an heir being first under a tutor and then under a curator, and (2) made the final appointments of these custodians the responsibility of the city administrator (the tutor being nominated by the father but not the curator), whereas Paul's illustration builds on the premises that the father himself appoints the supervisory guardian (or guardians) and for a period of time set by him alone.

William Ramsay argued for differences between Roman, Greek, and Greco-Phrygian (or Seleucid) inheritance laws, and held that Paul's references must be seen in light of the latter. For whereas in Roman law the periods of fourteen and twenty-five years for the maturity of an heir were strictly adhered to, "in pure Greek law" the legal periods for coming of age differed; and in Phrygian cities (i.e., those of South Galatia), where inheritance laws were neither purely Roman nor purely Greek but more influenced by Seleucid jurisprudence, they followed the practice of a father appointing both the child's tutor and his curator (cf. *Galatians*, 391–93). Thus while Roman law set out the provisions for a tutor nominated by a father in his will and a curator appointed by the city administrator, whose terms of office ended when their charges reached fourteen and twenty-five years respectively, Greek law allowed variations in these ages. More importantly, provincial law in the Phrygian cities of Asia Minor allowed the father to appoint both custodians and was flexible regarding not only the heir's age but also the custodian's functions.

One problem with most of these reconstructions is that the inheritance law cited dates from a time much later than Paul; Justinian jurisprudence was five hundred years after Paul's day (Justinian "the Great" was emperor during A.D. 527–65) and "the Syrian Law-book" on which Ramsay depends was also five hundred years after Paul's day. Furthermore, Paul's illustration does not quite conform to the specifics of any of these laws, for (1) he makes no mention of the death of the father for the inheritance to be received by the son, (2) he speaks of custodial supervision "until the time set by the father," and (3) he seems to use the terms ἐπίτροπος and οἰκονόμος synonymously.

Demosthenes (384–322 B.C.) in his oration *Against Nausimachus* used the double title ἐπίτροπος καὶ κηδεμών ("guardian and caretaker") for the one man Aristaechmus (*Naus.* 12.988), which, as Burton points out, "suggests that we should not seek to distinguish between the functions of the ἐπίτροπος and those of the οἰκονόμος, but regard οἰκονόμος as Paul's synonym for κηδεμών and, like that word, a further description of the ἐπίτροπος" (*Galatians*, 213). If this be so, then οἰκονόμος should be regarded as roughly synonymous with ἐπίτροπος, with the plural forms being qualitative plurals. It may even be, as Burton goes on to argue, that Paul had in mind more the situation described in 1 Macc 3:32–33; 6:17 and 2 Macc 10:11; 11:1; 13:2; 14:2 where Antiochus IV (Epiphanes) on leaving Syria appointed Lysias to be steward over the affairs of the Seleucid kingdom and the guardian of his son Antiochus V (Eupator) until his return, and to remain as guardian over his son if he should die and his son ascend the throne (ibid., 214).

It is difficult to determine exactly what legal system Paul had in mind when he said, "but he is under guardians and administrators until the time set by the father." It is entirely possible, in fact, that Paul, being more interested in application than precise legal details, made the specifics of his illustration conform to his purpose. No illustration is required to represent exactly every aspect of a situation in order to be telling or meaningful.

3 οὕτως καὶ ἡμεῖς, "so also in our case." The adverb οὕτως ("so") signals that the illustration of vv 1–2 is now to be applied. The phrase καὶ ἡμεῖς ("even we") is emphatic. Paul's use of the first person plural "we" in a letter addressed to Gentile Christians and where the second person plural "you" predominates is a phenomenon that has appeared a number of times already (cf. 2:15–16; 3:13–14, 23–25). And as in those earlier occurrences, so in 4:3–5 the use of the first person plural seems to carry greater significance than usually credited.

Almost all commentators today take the first person plural here to refer inclusively to all Christians, whether Jewish or Gentile (e.g., Lightfoot, *Galatians*, 166–67; Burton, *Galatians*, 215; Mussner, *Galaterbrief*, 268; Betz, *Galatians*, 204, et al.). Some, however, have interpreted it to have primary reference to Jewish Christians, with vv 6–11 then having Gentile Christians in view (so, e.g., Chrysostom; Ambrosiaster; T. Zahn, *Galater*, ad loc.; T. L. Donaldson, *NTS* 32 [1986] 95–98). Occasionally someone argues, based on Paul's evident concern for his Gentile converts, that "we" in Galatians means "Gentiles" with whom Paul identifies spiritually (so L. Gaston, "Paul and the Torah"). It may be that "we" is used here inclusively for both Jewish and Gentile believers. It is important to note, however, that in the three earlier passages where the first person plural occurs, it either (1) specifically refers to those who are Jewish (so 2:15–16, "we who are Jews by birth," and 3:23–25, "we . . . under the law"), or (2) can be read as a portion stemming from early Jewish Christianity, either in whole or in part (so 3:13–14). Likewise here, we believe, the first person plural of 4:3, as well as that of 4:5, ought to be understood as referring primarily to Jewish believers: in v 3 as Paul's application of his illustration of the Jewish experience under the custodianship of the law and in vv 4–5 as Paul's quotation of an early Jewish Christian confessional portion, with vv 6–7, then, applying the thrust of the confession cited in vv 4–5 to his Gentile converts' situation and therefore reverting back to his usual second person plural "you."

ὅτε ἦμεν νήπιοι, ὑπὸ τὰ στοιχεῖα τοῦ κόσμου ἤμεθα δεδουλωμένοι, "when we were minors, we were enslaved under the basic principles of the world." Paul's application repeats the basic components of his statement regarding the Jewish experience under the law in 3:23–25 and his illustration of that experience in 4:1–2: God's people in their minority ("minors") being kept under supervisory custody ("enslaved"). Though the textual evidence is almost equally divided, the (Hellenistic) imperfect middle ἤμεθα ("we were") at the end of the sentence, rather than the (classical) imperfect active ἦμεν ("we were"), is to be preferred simply because the natural tendency of scribes would have been to assimilate ἤμεθα to the earlier ἦμεν rather than to have retained it. The periphrastic pluperfect construction ἤμεθα δεδουλωμένοι ("we were enslaved") takes the place of the pluperfect verb ἐδεδουλώμεθα, and so emphasizes the state "we" were in "when we were minors." The pluperfect construction with its passive nuance carries the thought of another bringing about the enslavement—either the law itself or God, or both. The only new expression in this verse is ὑπὸ τὰ στοιχεῖα ("under the basic principles of the world"), which in context is certainly to be associated in some way with being "under the law" of 3:23, "under a supervisory custodian" of 3:24–25, and "under guardians and administrators" of 4:1–2, though exactly what is meant by the expression has been a subject of extensive debate.

The basic meaning of τὰ στοιχεῖα has to do with "elements that make up a series," "inherent components," or "members of a row"—being derived most probably from στοῖχος, which was originally a military term that meant "row," "rank," or "line" (cf. Burton, *Galatians,* 510–18; A. J. Bandstra, *The Law and the Elements of the World,* 31–46). The term, however, was "capable of taking on a wide variety of specific meanings as it was used in different spheres of ideas" (Bandstra, ibid., 46). Gerhard Delling lists six ways in which it was used outside of the NT (cf. "στοιχεῖον," *TDNT* 7:670–83):

1. Degrees on a sundial by which time is calculated;
2. Letters, syllables, or words of a sentence, or the sounds that they represent;
3. The basic elements of which the cosmos is composed, especially the four elements of earth, water, air, and fire;
4. The fundamental principles or rudimentary teachings of such subjects as, for example, music, mathematics, and child care;
5. The stars and other heavenly bodies, presumably because composed of the chief and finest of the elements, fire; and
6. The stellar spirits, gods, demons, and angels.

The first four of these uses appear in Greek writings before and during the NT period. The fifth does not appear in the literature until the middle of the second century A.D. The sixth use comes about only in the third or fourth century A.D.

"A man of NT days," Delling observes, "would take στοιχεῖα τοῦ κόσμου to refer to the 'basic materials' of which everything in the cosmos, including man, is composed" (ibid., 684; see esp. Josephus, *J.W.* 1.377; 6.47; *Ant.* 3.183). Paul, however, seems to have given this understanding a new twist. Building on the view of τὰ στοιχεῖα as being "first principles" or "elemental teachings," he asserts here in 4:3 that the Mosaic law comprised in the Jewish experience those "basic principles" given by God in preparation for the coming of Christ. His use of τοῦ κόσμου ("of the world") seems also somewhat unique. For while στοιχεῖα τοῦ κόσμου would have been taken by Greek writers cosmologically (e.g., the elements of the natural world), Paul takes κόσμος in an ethical sense to mean "worldly" with its synonym being "fleshly," as opposed to "spiritual" (cf. *Comment* on "flesh" and "spirit" in 5:13–26). Thus Jews under the law were "under the basic principles of the world," with τοῦ κόσμου used here in much the same way as it appears later in Heb 9:2 with reference to the tabernacle, which is called τὸ ἅγιον κοσμικόν ("a worldly sanctuary"). There is no doubt that the Mosaic law was given by God (as was the tabernacle for the writer of Hebrews). But God has moved forward in the explication of his redemptive activity, and now to return to life "under the law" is to return to living "under the basic principles of the world."

Such a use of τὰ στοιχεῖα τοῦ κόσμου might well have been coined by Paul himself, as Bo Reicke suggests (cf. *JBL* 70 [1951] 261). Thus when talking about the Jewish experience, it was the Mosaic law in its condemnatory and supervisory functions that comprised the Jews' "basic principles" of religion. Later in v 9 when talking about the Gentile experience, it was paganism with its veneration of nature and cultic rituals that made up the Gentiles' "basic principles" of religion. The use of τὰ στοιχεῖα τοῦ κόσμου in Col 2:8, 20 is to be distinguished from its use here in Gal 4:3 and that of τὰ ἀσθενῆ καὶ πτωχὰ στοιχεῖα ("the weak and miserable basic principles") in 4:9. For while Paul is speaking about first principles or rudimentary teachings in all four passages, his meaning varies in each of those passages in terms of the specific context (cf. also the use of τὰ στοιχεῖα in Heb 5:12 and 2 Peter 3:10, 12).

4 ὅτε δὲ ἦλθεν τὸ πλήρωμα τοῦ χρόνου, ἐξαπέστειλεν ὁ θεὸς τὸν υἱὸν αὐτοῦ, "but, 'When the fullness of time came, God sent his Son.'" When Paul speaks of Christ and redemption, he seems often to use confessional formulae or "sayings" statements drawn from the early church. We have already noted the probable presence of such materials at 1:4, 3:1, 13, 26, 27–28 (see *Comment* there). Such a portion appears to be incorporated here at 4:4–5 as well.

Structurally, vv 4–5 are complex. They begin with a temporal clause, "when the fullness of time came." Then there appears what many have taken to be a "sending formula," which seems to crop out also elsewhere in Paul and the Johannine writings (cf. Rom 8:3–4; John 3:16–17; 1 John 4:9 and 10): "God sent his Son . . . to redeem." Two participial clauses then follow that set out two features regarding the Son's person and work, with the section coming to a close with two ἵνα clauses that speak of the purpose (and/or result) of God's sending his Son on behalf of his people. Within this apparently carefully crafted formulation is a chiastic construction, as J. B. Lightfoot (*Galatians*, 168) long ago noted:

A   God sent his Son,
   B   born under the law,
   B¹   to redeem those under the law,
A¹   that we might receive our full rights as sons.

With regard to content, vv 4–5 begin with a phrase found only here in Paul's letters, "the fullness of time," and then include another Pauline *hap. leg.*, "born of a woman," with both phrases seeming to reflect the interests of early Jewish Christianity (see *Comment* later). Furthermore, only the second of the participial clauses, "born under the law," is really germane to the argument of Galatians; the first, "born of a woman," is never discussed in the letter. These features of structure and content, coupled with the appearance of the first person plural suffix in the verb λάβωμεν ("we might receive"; cf. *Comment* on the use of "we" at v 3 above), suggest that what we have here in vv 4–5 is a pre-Pauline confessional portion drawn from the proclamation of the early church—either in whole or in part, or at least echoing some of the language of such a portion—which Paul uses to support his emphases on sonship and freedom from the supervision of the law.

Eduard Schweizer has repeatedly argued that ἐξαπέστειλεν ὁ θεὸς τὸν υἱὸν αὐτοῦ ("God sent his Son") together with ἵνα ... ἐξαγοράσῃ ("to redeem") make up an early Christian "sending formula" that arose within the Torah-Wisdom-Logos speculations of Alexandrian Judaism and was taken over by Hellenistic Christians in application to Christ as God's Son (*ZNW* 57 [1966] 199–210; idem, *Jesus*, tr. D. E. Green [London: SCM, 1971] 81ff.; idem, "υἱός," *TDNT* 8:354–57, 363–92; idem, "Paul's Christology and Gnosticism," esp. 118–19). As Schweizer views the matter, the original formula was bifid: (1) God sending his pre-existent Wisdom or Logos or Son, so as (2) to redeem or save humanity. It probably originated among Alexandrian Jews, for "sending by God and the Son of God title are combined only in the realm of Egyptian Judaism" ("υἱός," *TDNT* 8:375). In the NT this sending formula appears in four passages: Gal 4:4–5, Rom 8:3–4, John 3:16–17, and 1 John 4:9 (also v 10). And "since [in the NT] the sending formula occurs only in Paul and John, who both presuppose an already developed christology in which the pre-existent Lord was depicted after the pattern of the logos or wisdom, the formula probably had its [Christian] roots in the same sphere" (ibid.).

Schweizer emphasizes the parallels between Wis 9:10–17 and Gal 4:4–7, for the verb used in the sending of both Wisdom and the Son is ἐξαποστέλλειν (Wis 9:10; Gal 4:4) and the sending of Wisdom/Son is followed in both passages by the sending of the Holy Spirit (Wis 9:17; Gal 4:7; though Wis 9:17 uses the verb πέμπειν). Parallels with Philo are also important for Schweizer, for in Philo we find a verb of sending with its object being the "son (of God)" (e.g., *Agric.* 51) and the idea that *the* son creates other sons (e.g., *Confus.* 145–48).

One need not doubt the influence of Wisdom speculations on either Paul or John (probably more on the latter than the former). Yet one can wonder (1) if the links drawn by Schweizer between Wisdom, Logos, and Son (of God) in Hellenistic Judaism are not somewhat tenuous (see esp. Schweizer's argument in *Jesus*, 81–82), and (2) if the parallels between the NT and Hellenistic Judaism are not somewhat few and disparate. Schweizer's view enables one to hold to a preexistent Son in the four NT passages cited and to escape problems of delimiting an original confession in Gal 4:4–5, for Schweizer sees these verses as Paul's own composition based on an early Jewish "sending formula" that was Christianized by certain branches of the early church. But one can wonder if preexistence is really to the fore in Gal 4:4–5 and if a better way of explaining the structure and content of these verses should not still be sought.

Scholarly study of Gal 4:4–5 (also, of course, of Rom 8:3–4, John 3:16–17, and 1 John 4:9, 10) has been greatly influenced by Schweizer's thesis, with many acknowledging it favorably (though few interact with it in any detail). Others, however, modify it extensively or reject it altogether. Seyoon Kim, for example, agrees that there is a sending formula in Gal 4:4–5 (and Rom 8:3–4) and that this formula can be paralleled with Jewish Torah-Wisdom-Logos speculations. But Kim does not share Schweizer's view that Wis 9:10–17 parallels Gal 4:4–5 or that it serves as a basis for Paul's reflections on Christ (see his *The Origin of Paul's Gospel*, 117–19). Nor does Kim agree that the sending formula is pre-Pauline, but rather insists that Paul himself drew the connection between Wisdom-Logos and the Son: that the sending formula of Gal 4:4–5 (and Rom 8:3–4), while reflective of Wisdom-Logos ideas (but not really paralleled by Wis 9:10–17), is Paul's own composition (not that of earlier Christians) inspired by Christ's encounter with him on his way to Damascus, for in the Damascus-road Christophany Jesus of Nazareth "was revealed to him as the exalted and enthroned Son of God" (ibid., 126). Having earlier subscribed to the Jewish notion that Torah is to be equated with Wisdom, Paul realized in that Damascus encounter that "Wisdom, the revelation of God, is found in him [Christ], and not in the Torah, as the Jews thought. . . . So Paul began to ascribe all the attributes and functions of the divine Wisdom to Christ: pre-existence and mediatorship in creation, revelation and salvation. Paul expressed these attributes and functions especially clearly through the [his own] formula of God's sending his Son into the world to save mankind (Rom 8.3; Gal 4.4)" (ibid., 258).

James D. G. Dunn also denies the relevance of Wis 9:10–17 for Gal 4:4–5 and disparages the pre-Pauline nature of the sending formula of Gal 4:4–5 and Rom 8:3 (see his *Christology in the Making*, 39–43). Rather than looking to the Wisdom-Logos speculations of Hellenistic Judaism, Dunn locates the language of the formula in "the more specific Christian tradition that Jesus both thought of himself as God's son [a point Dunn argued earlier] and spoke of himself as 'sent' by God (Mark 9.37 pars.; 12.6 pars.; Matt 15.24; Luke 4.18; 10.16)" (ibid., 39–40). In particular, the parable of the wicked tenants of Mark 12:1–12 (par.) is the most likely basis for the language and structure of Gal 4:4–7, for "here we have the father sending his son in what can fairly be called an eschatological act—Mark 12.6; last of all . . . (ἔσχατον)—just as in Gal. 4.4 God sends his son 'at the fullness of time'. Moreover, at the same point in the parable . . . we have a close conjunction of the ideas of sonship and inheritance—again, just as in Gal. 4.4–7" (ibid., 40).

Furthermore, whereas Schweizer understands Wisdom language as being present in Gal 4:4–5, Dunn sees Adam Christology-soteriology: "Jesus wholly shared man's frailty and bondage to the law, shared, that is, man's condition as a child of Eve, a descendant of fallen Adam, in order that through his death fallen man might come to share his liberation from the law and sin . . . might come to share the Spirit of his sonship" (ibid., 39). Paul in 4:4–5, therefore, has brought together two early Christian traditions. The first has to do with Christ as the sent Son, which goes back to Jesus' own self-consciousness as expressed most vividly in the parable of the wicked tenants (which consciousness and language Paul and John developed independently); the second is the understanding of Christ as the Last Adam.

For Dunn, then, "we cannot safely assume that Paul intended [in 4:4–5] an allusion to Christ as pre-existent Son or Wisdom of God" (ibid., 40). And even if we assume that Wisdom-Logos speculation does somehow impinge on Gal 4:4–5—a possibility that Dunn must allow, since the synoptic Gospels portray Jesus as not only a messenger of Wisdom (Q; Luke 11:49) but also as Wisdom itself (Matt 23:34)—this lends no weight to the view that the sending of the Son implies his preexistence. For Wisdom was never understood in Judaism as a literally preexistent being beside Yahweh. Rather, the "Wisdom of God" was simply a way of describing God-being-wise from all eternity, and language that seems to hypostasize Wisdom independently of God is really only a Hebraic way of personifying the wise action of God himself (ibid., 173–76).

The sending formula of Gal 4:4–5, therefore, as Dunn views it, says nothing as to Jesus' preexistence beside God. Instead, given the early Christian tradition that Jesus both spoke of himself as sent by God and as being God's Son—a tradition epitomized in the parable of the wicked tenants—"Paul and his readers in writing and reading [Gal 4:4–7] may well have thought only of the man Jesus whose ministry in Palestine was of divine commissioning and whose uniquely intimate relation with God was proved (and enhanced) by his resurrection, despite his rejection by the stewards of Israel's heritage" (ibid., 40). Jesus in his earthly life was God's Son not because of his preexistence but by virtue of his commissioning by God, which is what Paul learned from the early church and what he formulated in what we now have as Gal 4:4–5.

Most analyses of Gal 4:4–5 have focused on what structuralists call "surface structure," that is, the structure that is readily apparent and that may be compared to other texts that have a similar ordering of features. Richard B. Hays, however, has recently attempted to analyze 4:4–5 in terms of its substructure or underlying features that determine the ordering of the text (see his *The Faith of Jesus Christ*, esp. 85–137). These features, he believes, can be identified as narrative elements that follow the structure of an underlying story—a story about God's saving activity in the ministry of Jesus, which, though never fully articulated by Paul, lies behind all his thinking and orders the sequence of his argument as he speaks to various situations. In Galatians, Hays believes, while that story underlies Paul's argument throughout, partial summaries rise to the surface in more explicit form particularly at 3:13–14 and 4:3–6 (though Hays's central analysis of the latter focuses on vv 4–5).

By means of narrative analysis, Hays seeks to demonstrate that Paul's proclamation and teaching is shaped by the early church's story of how God's redemption of humanity took place "through the faith (or faithfulness) of Jesus Christ." Thus he sheds new light on the old exegetical conundrum of what Paul meant by ἐκ/διὰ πίστεως Ἰησοῦ Χριστοῦ (cf. 2:16 and 3:22). That, of course, is Hays's major point. On the way to establishing that point, however, Hays shows how 4:4–5 is integral to the story about Jesus that underlies Paul's message. And in laying stress on 4:4–5 as reflecting the early church's story about Jesus, Hays plays down the confessional or formulaic nature of the language in these verses, for, though the story itself stems from the early church, Paul's highlighting of certain features of that story are in his own words. Or as Hays states his view in an aside: "I began this study under the assumption that Gal 4:4–5 was in fact a fragment of pre-Pauline tradition; this investigation has substantially undermined my confidence in this assumption, as most of the features which have been thought to mark it off from the 'grain' of Paul's thought have been shown to be capable of explanation in other ways" (ibid., 135 n. 80).

There is much in Hays's analysis that is laudatory, particularly, as we have noted earlier, his treatments of 1:4 and 3:1 (perhaps also elsewhere) as outcroppings of the church's gospel story, of 3:13 (perhaps also v 14) as a confessional statement of early Christianity, and of the expression ἐκ/διὰ πίστεως Ἰησοῦ Χριστοῦ (2:16 and 3:22) as part and parcel of that story (cf. *Comment* at those verses). But so-called surface structure is still important in the analysis of any passage, including comparisons with similar passages, and Hays has given rather short shrift to such analyses. Both formal structures that immediately present themselves to the interpreter and underlying narrative structures are fit subjects for analysis. Hays himself, in fact, while stressing almost exclusively the narrative substructure of our passage, nonetheless inserts the following caveat: "Nothing in this analysis necessarily precludes the theory that 4:4–5 might originally have been a piece of independent tradition" (ibid., 119).

Gal 4:4–5 is admittedly notoriously difficult to analyze as to its structure and provenance. Our own evaluation of the data and weighing of the various hypotheses offered in explanation is that what we have here is an early Christian confessional portion that Paul has drawn, either in whole or in part, from the Church's proclamation—a confession which, as narrative analysis suggests (à la R. B. Hays), was based on the gospel story as told by the earliest Christians. And we will treat the material of these verses in this fashion, asking particularly how Paul uses that confessional portion to support his emphases on sonship and freedom from the supervision of the law.

The idea expressed in the clause "when the fullness of time came"—i. e., that the coming of Christ was fixed in the purpose of God—was common in early Jewish Christianity. It was part of Jesus' consciousness (cf. Mark 1:15; Luke 1:21), appears in the Church's early preaching (cf. Acts 2:16ff.; 3:18), and is particularly prominent in the Gospels of Matthew (cf., e.g., the evangelist's use of πληρόω, "fulfill," at 1:22; 2:15, 17, 23; 3:15; 4:14; 5:17; 8:17; 12:17; 13:35; 21:4; 27:9, ten of these being his distinctive introductory "fulfillment formulae") and John (cf., e.g., the evangelist's seven editorial quotations: 2:17; 12:15, 38, 40; 19:24, 36, 37). Paul shares in this understanding (cf. Acts 13:27; Rom 3:26; 5:6; Eph 1:10), though his usual way of expressing fulfillment to a Gentile audience is simpler, more direct, and without the word πληρόω (cf. G. Delling, "πληρόω," *TDNT* 6, esp. 296–97; note Paul's ten introductory formulae in Galatians: 3:6, 8, 10, 11, 12, 13, 16; 4:27, 30; 5:14, with πληρόω appearing in only the last one).

The expression "God sent his Son" may well have been understood by Paul to include the idea of the preexistence of the Son, as it does in Rom 8:3 (which parallels our verse here, though probably more in Paul's own words: ὁ θεὸς τὸν ἑαυτοῦ υἱὸν πέμψας, "God sent his own Son"). Certainly Paul believed in the preexistence of Christ (cf. 1 Cor 8:6b; 10:4; Col 1:15–17), however he came to that conviction—whether by the association of Wisdom with Christ (cf. 1 Cor 1:24, 30), with Wisdom understood as being preexistent, or in some other way. But if the statement "God sent his Son" is here part of an early Christian confession, the question may legitimately be asked: Did those who formulated this confession have preexistence in mind? If Eduard Schweizer is right, preexistence was always part of a traditional "sending formula." Both the formulators of this early confession (or those who formulated the sending formula within it) and Paul, therefore, may have had in mind the idea of preexistence. Yet that is not what is emphasized here. And it need not be claimed to be necessarily present. When considered part of a pre-Pauline confession, all that need be seen is a functional stress on God's commissioning of Christ to bring about the redemption of humanity. Likewise, Paul's use of the formula "God sent his Son," whatever its origin, need be viewed only functionally and not necessarily ontologically. Set in the context of a fulfillment motif, the statement tells us that Jesus, God's Son par excellence, is the culmination and focus of all of God's redemptive activity on behalf of humanity.

4b γενόμενον ἐκ γυναικός, γενόμενον ὑπὸ νόμον, "born of a woman, born under the law." The last part of v 4 consists of two parallel participial clauses that set out two features regarding the person and work of God's sent Son. The first, "born of a woman," emphasizes his true humanity and representative quality. The aorist middle use of γίνομαι ("be," "become") for γεννάω ("beget"; in the passive "be born") was common in Jewish circles (cf. Sir 44:9; 1 Esd 4:16; Tob 8:6; Wis 7:3; Rom 1:3 [an early Christian confessional portion]; John 8:58; Josephus, *Ant.* 2.216; 7.21; 16.382; echoing אשה ילוד yĕlûd 'iššâ, "born of woman"] of Job 14:1; 15:14; 25:4, as carried on in such passages as 1QH 13.14 and 1QS 11.21), with the participle γενόμενον used in synonymous fashion to the adjective γεννητόν ("begotten," "born"). The expression "born ἐκ γυναικός" has often been seen as implying a virgin birth. But ἐκ γυναικός is a Jewish locution for a human birth or idiom simply for being human—as, for example, Job 14:1, "For man born of woman [βροτὸς γεννητὸς γυναικός] is of few days and full of trouble"; Matt 11:11 / / Luke 7:28, "Among those born of women [ἐν γεννητοῖς γυναικῶν] there has not risen anyone greater than John the Baptist" (see also Josephus, *Ant.* 7.21; 16.382). It provides, therefore, no clue of itself as to whether either early Christians or Paul believed in, or even knew of, Jesus' virginal conception. Rather, as a qualitative expression "born of a woman" speaks of Jesus' true humanity and representative quality—i.e., that he was truly one with us, who came as "the Man" to stand in our place. Furthermore, as an elaboration of the formula "God sent his Son," it suggests that God's sending coincides with the Son's human birth, which is a notion comparable to the theme of God's call, commission, and sending of his prophetic servants from their birth that appears elsewhere in Scripture (cf. Isa 49:1, 5; Jer 1:5; and Paul's own consciousness in Gal 1:15).

The second participial clause at the end of v 4, "born under the law," lays stress on another factor involved in the representative work of "the Son." For it was not just that Christ came as "the Man" but also that he came as "the Jew" under obligation to God's Torah, so fulfilling the requirements of the law in his life (cf. Matt 5:17–18) and bearing the law's curse in his death (cf. Gal 3:13; Phil 2:8). The term νόμος here means not just legal requirements in general (contra Lightfoot, *Galatians,* 168, who based his view on the now discredited distinction between the articular and anarthrous use of νόμος) — and certainly not "legalism" as a misconception of Torah, as though Jesus in his life became a legalist—but law in the sense used throughout Galatians, viz., the Mosaic law with its regulations for life. In early rabbinic (Tannaitic) writings, the expressions "the yoke of the Torah" (עול תורה, ôl tôrâ), "the yoke of the kingdom heaven" (עול מלכות שמים, 'ôl malkût sāmayim), and "the yoke of the commandments" (עול מצות, 'ôl miṣwot) are synonyms for the idea of being in submission to the will of God as revealed through Moses (cf. Str-B, 1:608–10; K. H. Rengstorf, "ζυγός," *TDNT* 2:900–901). It was essential for Jews to be under "the yoke of the Torah"—in fact, being under "the yoke of the Torah" comprised the very meaning of existence for Jews. For Jews generally, this yoke was not felt to be a burden but a privilege. Jewish believers in Jesus, however, looking back from the perspective of their new relationship with Christ and having experienced Christ's "yoke," saw living under "the yoke of the Torah" to be both condemnatory and oppressive (cf. Matt 11:28–30). Thus in elaborating on the formulaic expression "God sent his Son," the early church spoke of Christ not only as being truly human and possessing a representative quality ("the Man") but also as "born under the law" to offer a perfect obedience to God the Father on behalf of those under the law ("the Jew").

5 ἵνα τοὺς ὑπὸ νόμον ἐξαγοράσῃ, ἵνα τὴν υἱοθεσίαν ἀπολάβωμεν, "'in order that he might redeem those under the law, in order that we might receive the sonship.'" Two ἵνα clauses present in this verse two purposes and/or results of God's sending his Son on behalf of his people. While the conjunction ἵνα denotes purpose, aim or goal, in Koine Greek its use was considerably increased so that "in many cases purpose and result cannot be clearly differentiated, and hence ἵνα is used for the result that follows according to the purpose of the subj. or of God" (BAG, 378). In fact, as BAG continues, "in Jewish thought, purpose and result are identical in declarations of the divine will" (ibid.). Many see these two clauses as sequential in nature, reflecting Paul's order of "Jew first and then Greek" (so Mussner, Galaterbrief, 270–71; Betz, Galatians, 208; Bruce, Galatians, 197). But such an understanding rests heavily on the assumption that "we" in vv 3 and 5 includes both Jewish and Gentile Christians, with the result that v 5a ("those under the law") has in mind Jewish believers but v 5b ("we") includes all Christians. If vv 4–5, however, are a confessional portion that stems from early Jewish Christendom, as we propose, then "those under the law" of v 5a and "we" of v 5b are to be seen in parallel fashion (cf. Comment on "we" at v 3), with the result that what is said about God's activity in these two cases should also be taken as roughly parallel. The statements, then, are probably to be interpreted as complementary facets of what Jewish believers in Jesus had experienced: (1) redemption from both the law's condemnation (cf. 3:13) and the law's supervision (cf. 3:23–25), and (2) reception of a new relationship with God, which involved primarily the enjoyment of full sonship rights.

The two ἵνα clauses spell out the purpose, and so the result, of the main verb ἐξαπέστειλεν ("sent"), with ὁ θεός ("God") being the subject, τὸν υἱὸν αὐτοῦ ("his Son") the agent, the two participle clauses beginning with γενόμενον ("born") indicating the means, and the substantival articular phrase τοὺς ὑπὸ νόμον ("those under the law") together with the verbal suffix -ωμεν ("we") designating the objects of the divine salvific activity. The verbs ἐξαγοράσῃ ("that he might redeem") and ἀπολάβωμεν ("that we might receive") highlight both God's purpose and the need for humanity's response, nicely balancing out the dual emphases of the gospel on (1) what God has done through Christ, and (2) humanity's need to respond by faith.

The term υἱοθεσία ("adoption," "sonship") does not occur in the LXX or in the non-Pauline writings of the NT. In Paul, however, it is used with various connotations depending on context: the Christian's present sonship (Rom 8:15); the Christian's future resurrection body (Rom 8:23); Israel's past special relationship with God (Rom 9:4); and that predestined by God for believers "through Jesus Christ" (Eph 1:5). It is a word unique to Paul's lips, as the above passages indicate, though it was probably also a word used within the Judaism of Paul's day and by Jewish Christians generally, as Paul's seemingly traditional recital of factors constituting the special status of Jews in Rom 9:4–5 (beginning with ὧν ἡ υἱοθεσία, "theirs is the sonship") seems to suggest. The article τήν is doubtless restrictive in function, pointing to the hope of Israel for the culmination of God's promises and to the time referred to in vv 1–2 when the boy reaches the age of maturity, "the time set by the father."

173

6 ὅτι δέ ἐστε υἱοί, ἐξαπέστειλεν ὁ θεὸς τὸ πνεῦμα τοῦ υἱοῦ αὐτοῦ εἰς τὰς καρδίας ἡμῶν, κρᾶζον, Ἀββα ὁ πατήρ, "and because you are sons, God sent the Spirit of his Son into our hearts, crying, 'Abba, Father.'" Commentators have been troubled by a certain awkwardness in the relation of vv 6–7 to what has preceded in Galatians, both as to what has immediately preceded and as to what appears in the broader context of Paul's *probatio*. There is, of course, the linguistic problem of the change from the first person plural "we" (vv 3–5) to the second person plural "you" (vv 6–7) mentioned earlier (see *Comment* at vv 3 and 5). Of greater theological significance (perhaps) is the fact that in the larger context of his *probatio* Paul has argued from his converts' reception of the Spirit (3:2–5, 14b) to their being "sons of God" (3:26), which is also the order of his presentation in Rom 8:15–17. Here, however, that relationship seems to be reversed in saying "because you are sons, God sent the Spirit of his son into our hearts" (4:6).

The argument as to whether the proper order is first sonship and then the gift of the Spirit, or first the reception of the Spirit and then sonship, has been fervent and heated (cf., e.g., J. B. Lightfoot, *Galatians*, 169; H. Schlier, *Galater*, 197; F. Mussner, *Galaterbrief*, 274–75; E. Schweizer, "πνεῦμα, πνευματικός," *TDNT* 6:420–28). As Betz points out, much of the discussion has been dominated by "dogmatic and philosophical categories" (*Galatians*, 209). If, however, we take 4:4–5 to be a confessional portion drawn from the early church that Paul quotes for his own purposes (see *Comment* at v 4), with vv 6–7 being Paul's application of that confession for the purposes at hand, much of the perceived awkwardness in relating vv 6–7 to what has gone before in the letter, we suggest, is dissipated or at least explainable. Certainly the change from "we" to "you" is understandable on this basis, and probably also the change in soteriological order from (1) the reception of the Spirit to sonship, as in 3:2–5, 14b and 26, to (2) sonship as the basis for receiving the Spirit, as here in 4:6.

For Paul, it seems, sonship and receiving the Spirit are so intimately related that one can speak of them in either order (cf. the almost free intertwining of categories in Rom 8:1–2 and 9–11), with only the circumstances of a particular audience, the issue being confronted, or the discussion that precedes determining the order to be used at any given time or place. So in 3:2–5 Paul begins his *probatio* by reminding his converts of their experiences as recipients of the Spirit in order then to lead them on to the climax of his argument as to their status as "sons of God" (3:26), with the conclusion being that they are therefore "Abraham's seed" and heirs of the promise given to Abraham (3:29). In vv 6–7, however, though building to the same conclusion, Paul is working from a Christological confession of the church and so speaks of sonship as the basis for God's gift of the Spirit.

Clearly, ὅτι here is causal ("because," "since"), building on the expressions υἱοὶ θεοῦ ("sons of God") of 3:26 and ἡ υἱοθεσία ("the adoption," "the sonship") of 4:5. The statement is declarative of the Christian's status: "You are sons" (ἐστὲ υἱοί). Also declarative is the statement "God sent the Spirit of his Son into our hearts" (ἐξαπέστειλεν ὁ θεὸς τὸ πνεῦμα τοῦ υἱοῦ αὐτοῦ εἰς τὰς καρδίας ἡμῶν). Paul is not here setting out stages in the Christian life, whether logical or chronological. Rather, his emphasis is on the reciprocal relation or correlational nature of sonship and the reception of the Spirit.

That is why, it seems, "the Spirit of his Son" (τὸ πνεῦμα τοῦ υἱοῦ αὐτοῦ) is used. The expression is unique for Paul in Galatians, for elsewhere in the letter πνεῦμα is used absolutely (for that reason τοῦ υἱοῦ is omitted by P⁴⁶, Marcion, and Augustine; see *Note* c). It also does not appear elsewhere in Paul's letters, though similar expressions do (cf. πνεῦμα Χριστοῦ, "Spirit of Christ," in Rom 8:9; πνεῦμα υἱοθεσίας, "Spirit of sonship," in Rom 8:15; τὸ πνεῦμα κυρίου, "the Spirit of the Lord," in 2 Cor 3:17; τὸ πνεῦμα Ἰησοῦ Χριστοῦ, "the Spirit of Jesus Christ," in Phil 1:19; see also Acts 16:7; Heb 9:14; 1 Peter 1:11). But it appears here evidently to highlight the integral nature of sonship and the reception of the Spirit—not as two stages in the Christian life, but as two mutually dependent and intertwined features in the subjective experience of salvation. The prepositional phrase εἰς τὰς καρδίας ἡμῶν ("into our hearts") is a collective synonym for ἐν ἐμοί ("in me"), as appears in 2:20. The use of καρδία ("heart") as the seat of a person's intellectual and emotional life generally (cf. Rom 9:2; 10:1; 1 Cor 2:9; passim) and as the center of one's moral and spiritual life in particular (cf. Rom 1:21, 24; 2 Cor 4:6; passim) is common in biblical thought (cf. J. Behm, "καρδία," *TDNT* 3:609–13). The appearance of the expression "into our hearts" shows that the verb ἐξαπέστειλεν ("he sent") here is not to be understood as a historical aorist (as in v 4, "God sent his Son"), and so seen as God's historical act of sending the Spirit at Pentecost, but as stating in punctiliar fashion what God did in the Galatians' experience when they responded to the gospel by faith and so became "sons of God." The reading ἡμῶν ("our") is well supported (see *Note* d). Here Paul identifies with his Gentile converts (not in the earlier use of "we" in v 5).

Paul has previously emphasized the importance of the Spirit in the Galatians' experience (cf. 3:2, 5, 14), and here he lays stress on the Spirit again. The primary function of the Spirit in one's life, however, is not to cause a believer in Jesus to become a "spiritual" or "charismatic" person, as is so often popularly assumed, but to witness to the filial relation of the believer with God that has been established by the work of Christ—a witness both to the believer (so 3:2, 5) and to God the Father (so here). The verb κράζω ("cry out," "call") is used in the NT for a loud or earnest cry (cf. Matt 9:27; Acts 14:14; Rom 9:27), though also often used in the LXX of prayer addressed to God (cf. Ps 3:4; 106 [107]:13). As a neuter participle κρᾶζον ("crying") agrees in gender with τὸ πνεῦμα ("the Spirit"), so identifying its subject. It is the Spirit who cries out to God the Father on behalf of the believer, though synonymously Paul can also say that the believer cries out to God the Father as energized by the Spirit (Rom 8:15).

The content of the cry or acclamation epitomizes the believer's new relationship with God: "Father." The use of both Ἀββᾶ (the Greek transliteration of the Aramaic אבא, 'abbā, which is the emphatic form of the Hebrew and Aramaic אב, 'āb) and πατήρ ("Father") reflects the bilingual character of the early church. Its retention in Christian thought evidently reflects Jesus' own filial use of the term (cf. J. Jeremias, *The Central Message of the New Testament*, 9–30; idem, *Abba: Studien zur neutestamentlichen Theologie und Zeitgeschichte*, 15–67 [ET in , *The Prayers of Jesus*, SBT 2:6 (London: SCM, 1967) 11–65]; idem, *New Testament Theology*, I: *The Proclamation of Jesus*, tr. J. Bowden [London: SCM, [1971] 61–68, 197). Many have assumed as well that the acclamation "Father" stems from a liturgical use of the invocation "Our Father" in the Lord's Prayer (cf., e.g., O. Cullmann, *The Christology of the New Testament*, 208–9; G. Kittel, "ἀββᾶ," *TDNT* 1:6; J. Jeremias, *New Testament Theology*, 1.191–97). That may be so, though probably the relationship between acclamation and invocation is more analogical than genealogical in nature: the acclamation "Father" stemmed primarily from Jesus' own consciousness and usage, with the early Christians' remembrance of Jesus' usage giving expression to their new realization of a more intimate relationship with God "in Christ"; the invocation "Our Father" was secondary, but certainly supportive. As those "in Christ," believers experience a more intimate and truly filial relationship with God the Father, one that displaces the legal relationship that existed earlier for God's own. Now God's own, as inspired by the Spirit, address God directly as "Father."

7 ὥστε οὐκέτι εἶ δοῦλος ἀλλὰ υἱός, "therefore you are no longer a slave but a son." With ὥστε ("so," "therefore") Paul concludes not only his illustration in 4:1–6 but also his presentation of new relationships "in Christ" in 3:26–29. In fact, it can be legitimately said that 4:7 brings to a conclusion all that Paul has argued throughout his *probatio* from 3:1 onwards, though here with special application to Gentile converts. The use of the second person singular εἶ ("you are") has the effect of bringing matters home to each individual person in view, without, of course, changing the persons designated (cf. 6:1 for a similar change from plural to singular persons, and for the same reason: ὑμεῖς οἱ πνευματικοι ... μὴ καὶ σὺ πειρασθῆς, "you [pl.] who are spiritual ... you [sing.] be not also tempted"). The expression οὐκέτι ("no longer") has played a prominent part in Paul's argument heretofore: in the second part of the *propositio* at 2:20 (with that second part of 2:17–21 setting out the thesis to be elaborated in 3:19–4:7); at the conclusion of the first half of the *probatio* at 3:18; and in the concluding statement regarding the law as a "supervisory guardian" (παιδαγωγός) at 3:25. With Christ's coming, "no longer" are believers in Jesus under slavery to whatever was preparatory in their religious lives, whether to the Mosaic law as Jews (so 3:23–25) or to pagan ideas and practices as Gentiles (anticipating 4:8–9). Rather, as Bruce rightly reads Paul, "believers are now full-grown sons and daughters of God; they have been given their freedom and the power to use it responsibly" (*Galatians*, 200). It is the status of being a son of God, as the Galatians themselves evidently affirmed when they repeated the "sayings" statement incorporated by Paul at 3:26 ("You are all sons of God through your faith in Christ Jesus"), that Paul wants his Galatian converts to hold on to and cherish. The contrast is between being a son and being a slave. And though the Judaizers tried to combine these categories (as do many earnest Christians today), Paul saw them as mutually exclusive.

εἰ δὲ υἱός, καὶ κληρονόμος διὰ θεοῦ, "and since a son, also an heir through God." The postpositive δέ ("and") is here continuative, so signaling a further explication of Paul's conclusion for the issues at hand. The sentence is in the form of a first class condition that assumes the truth of the statement (so "since"). The question raised by the Judaizers was: Who really is an heir of the promise God gave to Abraham—those who simply believe in Jesus, or those who also relate themselves to Abraham and national Israel by Torah observance? Paul's answer is straightforward: Being "in Christ" makes one a son of God, and so an heir of God! Later in Rom 8:17 Paul gives the same answer, though with a slight extension of thought: "If children, also heirs—indeed, heirs of God and co-heirs with Christ!" The addition of the prepositional phrase διὰ θεοῦ ("through God") serves the twofold purpose of (1) reminding Paul's readers that their status as heirs is entirely the result of God's grace, not of their works or merit, and (2) assuring them of the certainty of their possession of that status, since it is the result of God's work on their behalf and not their own endeavors.

Explanation

The second part of Paul's Galatian *probatio* (i.e., 3:19–4:7) explicates the second part of his earlier *propositio* (i.e., 2:17–21), with both sections dealing with the matter of disagreement between Paul and the Judaizers. In 4:1–7, having dealt with the purpose and function of the Mosaic law in 3:19–25 and then the new relationships that exist "in Christ" in 3:26–29, Paul brings his argument to a close with an illustration (vv 1–3), the quotation of an early Christian confession (vv 4–5), and an application to the situation at hand (vv 6–7). The thrust of all that he says in 3:19–4:7, particularly in 4:1–7, is that the believer's life is to be lived not "under the law" but "in Christ"—that it is to be lived in the full freedom of mature sonship, and not in slavery to a legal code.

Three points, briefly, need to be made by way of bringing all of this together and into perspective. In the first place, it needs to be said that Paul is not denying that God's self-revelation, be it identified as Torah or the Mosaic law, stands as the external standard for all human thought and action. He implies as much in 3:19 when he says that the law "was added because of transgressions," and he says it directly in 3:22 when he declares that "the Scripture confined everyone without distinction under sin." But while Paul holds to the eternal validity of God's law as the standard of righteousness that condemns sin and thereby brings us to an intelligent and realistic act of repentance, he sees that revelatory standard as having reached its zenith in the teachings and example of Jesus Christ. So later he tells his Corinthian converts that though he is "free" and "not under the law," yet he is "not free from God's law" because he is "under Christ's law" (1 Cor 9:19–21).

Second, it needs to be insisted that Paul was always against any idea of soteriological legalism—i.e., that false understanding of the law by which people think they can turn God's revelatory standard to their own advantage, thereby gaining divine favor and acceptance. This, too, the prophets of Israel denounced, for legalism so defined was never a legitimate part of Israel's religion. The Judaizers of Galatia, in fact, would probably have disowned "legalism" as well, though Paul saw that their insistence on a life of Jewish "nomism" for his Gentile converts actually took matters right back to the crucial issue as to whether acceptance before God was based on "the works of the law" or faith in what Christ had effected. Thus in his *propositio,* Paul says: "We who are Jews by birth and not 'sinners of the Gentiles' . . . know that a person is not justified by the works of the law" (2:15–16); and he concludes that section by saying: "I do not nullify the grace of God. For if righteousness is through the law, then Christ died for nothing!" (2:21). And so in 3:1–18 he explicates that first part of his *propositio* in the first part of his *probatio,* arguing from the Galatians' experience, from the Scriptures, and in an ad hominem theological fashion against the Judaizers' implicit soteriological legalism.

A third point, however, also needs to be emphasized—particularly because it is so often neglected—and that is that Paul not only opposes in Galatians a soteriological legalism but also the necessity for a nomistic lifestyle. The Jewish religion at its best was never legalistic in the sense we have defined that term above. The Decalogue, for example, was not understood as ten prescriptions for attaining God's favor, but as a declaration of God's personal relationship with his people and his salvific action on their behalf (so Exod 20:2: "I am the Lord your God, who brought you out of Egypt, out of the land of slavery"), with what follows being a list of statements as to how God's people were to live in response to such a relationship and act. Yet while not legalistic, the religion of Israel, as contained in the OT and all forms of ancient and modern Judaism, is avowedly "nomistic"— i.e., it views the Torah, both Scripture and tradition, as supervising the lives of God's own, so that all questions of conduct are ultimately measured against the touchstone of Torah and all of life is directed by Torah. Though the prophets denounced legalism, they never sought to set aside the custodial function of the law over God's people. The Mosaic law was for Israel, therefore, not only the standard by which righteousness was defined and sin denounced, it was also a system by which the lives of God's people were regulated. So the law, while it did not make people righteous, served (1) a condemnatory function as the revelatory standard of God, thereby bringing about an intelligent and realistic act of repentance, and (2) a custodial function as a religious system instituted by God until Christ should come, thereby supervising the lives of God's people as they responded by faith to divine mercy.

The Judaizers of Galatia were evidently urging on Paul's Gentile converts the necessity for both faith in Christ and obedience to the Jewish Torah. As they saw it, a lifestyle of Jewish nomism was necessary for full acceptance before God and true perfection in one's Christian life. What Paul saw, however, was that in their insistence on the necessity for Gentile Christians to live a Jewish lifestyle, they were actually reintroducing legalism—whether they would acknowledge it or not. Like the prophets of old, Paul denounces their legalism (so 2:15–16 and 3:1–18). But unlike the prophets and all forms of Judaism, Paul also denounces their nomism (so 2:17–21 and 3:19–4:7). For life controlled by law was instituted by God only for the period of his people's spiritual minority and until Christ should come. Now God's own "in Christ" are to live as mature "sons of God" and not in slavery to legal prescriptions.

God's purpose in redemption has always been to bring his people to a full realization of their personal relationship with him as sons and to a full possession of their promised inheritance. So with the coming of Christ, Paul insists that "we are no longer under a supervisory guardian" (3:25) and "no longer a slave but a son; and since a son, also an heir through God" (4:7). It is for this reason that Judaism speaks of itself as being Torah-centered and Christianity declares itself to be Christ-centered, for in Christ the Christian finds not only God's law as the revelatory standard preeminently expressed but also the law as a system of conduct set aside in favor of guidance by reference to Christ's teachings and example and through the direct action of the Spirit. So in Rom 10:4 Paul declares that "Christ is the end of the law in its connection with righteousness to everyone who believes," understanding the much discussed τέλος of that verse as properly "termination" and not just "goal." It is just such a concept that Paul has illustrated by his analogy of a son in a patrician household in 4:1–3 and has declared to be involved in the early church's confession quoted in 4:4–5. And it is just such a concept that Christians need to recapture today. Otherwise, we are in danger of repeating the Judaizers' error of arguing for the necessity of a nomistic lifestyle and so reverting in practice to legalism, whether overtly or inadvertently. Paul's argument of Gal 3:19–4:7, however, was made as a corrective to such thinking. It sets before us the central message of Galatians, which is vitally important for Christians today as we wrestle with issues having to do with "Gospel and Law" and "the Christian vis-à-vis the Mosaic law."

3. Paul's Concern for the Galatians (4:8–11)

Closing off his *probatio,* Paul once again addresses his Galatian converts directly, as he did in 3:1–5. The arguments against legalism (3:1–18) and nomism (3:19–4:7) have come to an end. Now Paul expresses his heartfelt concern for the Galatians, which includes a concern for the effectiveness of his ministry among them.

Bibliography

Bandstra, A. J. *The Law and the Elements of the World,* esp. 31–72. **Reicke, B.** "The Law and This World According to Paul: Some Thoughts Concerning Gal 4:1–11." *JBL* 70 (1951) 259–76. **Schweizer, E.** "Slaves of the Elements and Worshipers of Angels: Gal 4:3, 9 and Col 2:8, 18, 20." *JBL* 107 (1988) 455–68. **Vielhauer, P.** "Gesetzesdienst und Stoicheiadienst im Galaterbrief." In *Rechtfertigung.* FS E. Käsemann. Tübingen: Mohr-Siebeck, 1976, 543–55.

Translation

[8]Formerly when you did not know God, you were enslaved to those who in reality[a] are not gods. [9]But now knowing God—or, rather, being known by God—how can you turn back again to the weak and miserable basic principles? Do you want to serve[b] them all over again? [10]You are observing[c] days and months and seasons and years! [11]I fear for you, that perhaps I have worked hard[d] for you to no avail.

Notes

[a] φύσει ("by nature," "in reality") is omitted by K Ir[lat] Vict Ambst.

[b] The aorist infinitive δουλεῦσαι ("to serve") appears in ℵ B rather than the present infinitive δουλεύειν ("to be serving") that is supported by P[46] ACDG, etc., but the difference is inconsequential.

[c] The present (modal) participle παρατηροῦντες ("by observing") appears in P[46] rather than the present middle verb παρατηρεῖσθε ("you are observing"), thereby making v 10 part of the question (or questions) of v 9.

[d] The aorist ἐκοπίασα ("I worked hard") appears in P[46] and the minuscules 1739 (10th century) and 1881 (14th century) rather than the perfect κεκοπίακα ("I have worked hard"), though with no real difference of meaning.

Form/Structure/Setting

His arguments finished, Paul in 4:8–11 closes off his *probatio* with a direct word to his readers. In v 9 he uses once more the *interrogatio* method used in 3:1–5. In fact, 3:1–5 and 4:8–11 with their direct form of address and their *interrogatio* method of argumentation form an *inclusio* for all that is argued in the *probatio.* Paul's desire, of course, is to change his converts' minds and reverse their plans. Having argued at length, he now speaks personally and directly of his concern for them.

Comment

8 ἀλλὰ τότε μὲν οὐκ εἰδότες θεόν, "formerly when you did not know God." Speaking directly, Paul reminds his converts of what they were "formerly" (τότε). The adversative particle ἀλλά (untranslated) highlights the contrast between their status described in vv 6–7 and that now described in v 8. The phrase οὐκ εἰδότες ("not know"), as F. F. Bruce points out, "is a rare instance of the classical use of οὐ with the participle; in Hellenistic Greek there is a steady drift towards the use of μή, as in the following τοῖς φύσει μὴ οὖσιν θεοῖς (although there μή would be quite classical, since the sense is generic)" (*Galatians,* 201). Paul's usual practice is to use μή with both adjectival and adverbial participles (cf. 6:9; also Rom 1:28; 2:14; 4:17), except when quoting from the LXX (cf. Burton, *Galatians,* 229).

ἐδουλεύσατε τοῖς φύσει μὴ οὖσιν θεοῖς, "you were enslaved to those who in reality are not gods." Though the pre-Christian experiences of Jews and Gentiles were decidedly different, Paul thinks of both as times of enslavement. So he uses the illustration of vv 1–2 and the perfect passive participle δεδουλωμένοι ("enslaved") in v 3 of the Jewish experience; so likewise the noun δοῦλος ("slave") in v 7 and the aorist verb ἐδουλεύσατε ("you were enslaved") here in v 8 appear with respect to that of the Gentiles. Before coming to Christ, Gentiles offered worship "to those who by nature are not gods," though, of course, they then thought them to be divine beings. The noun φύσις, from the verb φύω ("grow up," "come up"), signifies the essential character or disposition of a person or thing. The adjectival phrase φύσει μὴ οὖσιν ("not being by nature") that qualifies τοῖς θεοῖς ("gods") should be read to mean that what the pagans think to be gods are not gods "in reality." Later in 1 Cor 8:5 Paul speaks of pagans worshiping "so-called gods" (λεγόμενοι θεοί), while in 1 Cor 10:20 he refers to pagan sacrifices as offerings "to demons, and not to God" (δαιμονίοις καὶ οὐ θεῷ). Some have seen Paul's outright rejection of the validity of pagan gods and yet his speaking of them as though they had a real demonic existence to be somewhat contradictory (cf., e.g., J. Weiss, *The History of Primitive Christianity,* tr. F. C. Grant et al. [London: Macmillan, 1937] 1:326; W. L. Knox, *St. Paul and the Church of Jerusalem,* 113 n. 13). Betz struggles to propose that perhaps Paul did not outrightly reject the existence of pagan gods, but viewed them as existing "only as inferior demonic entities" (*Galatians,* 214–15). Yet Paul's words here and in 1 Cor 8:5 seem to imply quite clearly that he saw no reality to the claimed existence of the pagan deities, even though human convention had set up many "gods" and many "lords" (so 1 Cor 8:6). At the same time, however, he says in 1 Cor 8:7 that "not everyone knows this," and so he often conditions his words and actions by that fact.

Paul's attitude toward pagan idolatry is paralleled by the engaging story told about Gamaliel (either Gamaliel I, Paul's teacher, or Gamaliel II, Paul's contemporary) in *m. 'Abod. Zar.* ("Idolatry") 3.4:

Proklos the son of Philosophos [perhaps originally "Proklos the philosopher"] asked Rabban Gamaliel in Acre while he was bathing in the Bath of Aphrodite, and said to him, "It is written in your Law, 'And there shall cleave nought of the devoted thing to thine hand'. Why then doest thou bathe in the Bath of Aphrodite?" He answered, "One may not make answer in the bath" [it is forbidden to speak words of the Law while naked]. And when he came out he said, "I came not within her limits; she came within mine! They do not say, 'Let us make a bath for Aphrodite', but 'Let us make an Aphrodite as an adornment for the bath'. Moreover if they would give thee much money thou wouldest not enter in before thy goddess naked or after suffering pollution, nor wouldest thou make water before her! Yet this goddess stands at the mouth of the gutter and all the people make water before her. It is written, 'Their gods' [Deut 12:3] only. Thus what is treated as a god is forbidden, but what is not treated as a god is permitted" (H. Danby's translation and footnotes in brackets).

9 νῦν δὲ γνόντες θεόν, μᾶλλον δὲ γνωσθέντες ὑπὸ θεοῦ, "but now knowing God—or, rather, being known by God." The temporal phrase νῦν δέ ("but now") contrasts with τότε ("formerly"), and so sets out the Galatians' present condition (in continuity with 3:26–29 and 4:6–7). The aorist participle γνόντες here has an inchoative or inceptive force signifying "having come to know" or "knowing" (the result of having come to know), and not the past historical idea of "having known." "To know" is not used in any mundane sense of either "to perceive" or "to acquire knowledge about," but in the biblical sense of "to experience." For in being "sons of God" (3:26) and having "the Spirit of his Son" (4:6), Galatian Christians had come to experience God in the intimacy of a family relationship. The phrase μᾶλλον δέ ("but rather," "or rather," or simply "rather") introduces a thought or statement that supplements and so corrects what has just been said (cf. Rom 8:34; 1 Cor 14:1, 5; Eph 4:28; 5:11; also 2 Macc 6:23; Wis 8:20). It transfers the emphasis from what has just been said to the superior significance of what is now being said, with the result that while still maintaining the reciprocal relation between the two statements, the latter is given greater prominence. Thus here, as elsewhere throughout Scripture, experiential relations between God and his people are set out in terms of God's initiative and mankind's response. Relationship with God does not have its basis in man's seeking (mysticism) or doing (legalism) or knowing (gnosticism), but it originates with God himself and is carried on always by divine grace.

πῶς ἐπιστρέφετε πάλιν ἐπὶ τὰ ἀσθενῆ καὶ πτωχὰ στοιχεῖα, "how can you turn back again to the weak and miserable basic principles?" "How can you turn back?" is a rhetorical question that puts before the Galatian Christians a dilemma: Knowing God the Father in the intimacy established by Christ and the Spirit, how is it possible for them to want any other relationship? The use of πῶς in such questions suggests "how is it possible that" (cf. 2:14; also Rom 3:6; 6:2). The verb ἐπιστρέφω ("turn around," "turn back") is a technical term for either religious conversion (cf. 1 Thess 1:9; also Luke 1:16; Acts 3:19; 9:35; 11:21; 14:15; 15:19; 26:18, 20; passim) or religious apostasy (cf. 2 Peter 2:21–22). Its use here in the present tense indicates that the Galatians' action of apostatizing was then in progress (cf. v 10; also *Comment* at 1:6 and 5:2–4).

The object of the Galatians' attention had become Torah observance, which Paul here calls "the weak and miserable basic principles"—carrying on the epithet τὰ στοιχεῖα ("basic principles") used for the Mosaic law in v 3 and adding the highly uncomplimentary adjectives ἀσθενῆ ("weak," "powerless," "feeble") and πτωχά ("poor," "beggarly," "miserable," "impotent"). The use of πάλιν ("again," "once more") that appears here and in the appended relative clause points up the fact that Paul lumped the pre-Christian religious experiences of both Jews and Gentiles under the same epithet, that of being τὰ στοιχεῖα or "basic principles." For though qualitatively quite different, both have been superseded by the relationship of being "in Christ."

οἷς πάλιν ἄνωθεν δουλεύειν θέλετε, "do you want to serve them all over again?" Appended to Paul's main rhetorical question is a relative clause that in effect becomes a supplementary question extending the impact of the main question: "Do you want to serve them all over again?" The positioning of the relative pronoun οἷς ("them") at the beginning of the sentence and the verb θέλετε ("do you want") at the end expresses in dramatic fashion the new focus of the Galatians (i.e., on "the basic principles" as taught by the Judaizers) and their inclination to leave the Pauline gospel. The verbs δουλεύειν ("to serve") and θέλετε ("desire," "want," "wish") are both in the present tense, again indicating matters in progress. The adverb ἄνωθεν (here "anew") coupled with πάλιν ("again," "once more") emphasizes the fact that by taking on Torah observance Gentile Christians would be reverting to a pre-Christian stance comparable to their former pagan worship (so the translation "all over again")—not, of course, that paganism and the Mosaic law are qualitatively the same, but that both fall under the same judgment when seen from the perspective of being "in Christ" and that both come under the same condemnation when favored above Christ.

Beyond question, Paul's lumping of Judaism and paganism together in this manner is radical in the extreme. No Judaizer would ever have accepted such a characterization of Torah observance; nor would those in Galatia who acceded to their message. By accepting circumcision and the observance of Torah that went with it, they had no thought of returning to paganism. Such a move, they believed, would bring them closer to perfection in their Christian lives. In fact, they might even have thought that obedience to the Jewish law was their only real protection against the ethical perversions associated with their former paganism. For Paul, however, whatever leads one away from sole reliance on Christ, whether based on good intentions or depraved desires, is sub-Christian and therefore to be condemned. Martin Luther (taking up the imagery of one of Aesop's fables) is true to Paul's thought here when he speaks of one who desires to supplement faith by works as being like "the dog who runs along a stream with a piece of meat in his mouth, and deceived by the reflection of the meat in the water, opens his mouth to snap at it, and so loses both the meat and the reflection" ("The Freedom of a Christian," *Luther's Works*, 31.356).

10 ἡμέρας παρατηρεῖσθε καὶ μῆνας καὶ καιροὺς καὶ ἐνιαυτούς, "you are observing days and months and seasons and years!" Although no particle connects v 10 to v 9, it seems clear, nonetheless, that the four terms enumerated here are cited as evidence that Gentile Christians of Galatia were in the process of taking up "the weak and miserable basic principles" referred to in v 9. p46 evidently wanted to make the connection explicit, and so has the participle παρατηροῦντες (present modal: "by observing") instead of the verb παρατηρεῖσθε, thereby making v 10 part of the question (or questions) of v 9. But while the absence of a connective in a language so rich in means of coordination as Greek is somewhat striking, asyndeton (absence of a connective), when it occurs, often signals in Koine Greek emotion, passion, liveliness of speech, or something to be highlighted (cf. 3:13). Thus the sentence here should probably be read as declarative with a nuance of rhetorical passion (so the exclamation mark in the translation).

Extensive debate has focused on what precisely Paul means by "days . . . months . . . seasons . . . years." That they all have to do with the Jewish cultic calendar in some way has seemed obvious, at least for most, from the context. Furthermore, though παρατηρέω ("watch," "observe") occurs nowhere else in the NT or LXX in a religious sense, its use by Josephus in contexts having to do with the observance of the Jewish law supports such a supposition (cf. *Ant.* 3.91; 11.294; 14.264; *Ag. Ap.* 2.282). But what exactly do the four terms themselves signify? ἡμέρας ("days") probably refers to sabbath days, but may also include special festivals of a day's duration. μῆνας ("months") may have reference to monthly recurring events (cf. Isa 66:23) or to the appearance of the new moon that marked the beginning of each month (cf. Col 2:16; also Num 10:10; 28:11; 1 Chr 23:31). καιρούς ("seasons") seems to have in mind the great feasts of the Jewish calendar, such as Passover and Tabernacles, that were not limited to one day. And ἐνιαυτούς ("years") could mean the recognition of sabbatical years, of the year of Jubilee, or of Rosh Hashanah, the start of the new year on the first day (or first and second days) of the month Tishri. Debate as to what each of these terms signifies seems endless. Burton, however, is probably closest to the truth in concluding: "Formal exactness in such matters is not characteristic of Paul. It is, indeed, most likely that, as used here, μῆνας is included in ἡμέρας, and ἐνιαυτούς in καιρούς or ἡμέρας, the four terms without mutual exclusiveness covering all kinds of celebrations of days and periods observed by the Jews" (*Galatians*, 234).

In the secular uses of παρατηρέω in the NT, the active and middle voices are used interchangeably with the same meaning, and that is how we should undoubtedly understand παρατηρεῖσθε here as well (i.e., middle in form but active in meaning). The present tense of the verb indicates that the Galatians had begun to observe Torah by keeping certain calendar prescriptions. Jost Eckert has argued that such a supposition does not square with v 9, where observance of the Jewish law is being contemplated but not as yet practiced, and so these four calendar matters must be viewed as typical ancient *topoi* of the kind of behavior that religiously scrupulous people engage in, behavior which Paul fears his Galatian converts will practice but which they have not as yet engaged in (cf. his *Die urchristliche Verkündigung*, 92–93, 126ff.). Eckert's view has been accepted by Mussner (*Galaterbrief*, 301–2) and Betz (*Galatians*, 217–18), who also cite Eckert's references from antiquity to the character of the δεισιδαίμων (the "religiously scrupulous" or "superstitious"). Betz concludes: "Therefore the description cannot be a summary of activities in which the Galatians are presently engaged, but in which they would be engaged once they took up Torah and circumcision. In fact, Paul describes the *typical* behavior of religiously scrupulous people" (*Galatians*, 217, italics his). It is, however, as Bruce observes, "more likely that Paul is referring to news which he has just received, to the effect that the Galatians were actually adopting the Jewish calendar" (*Galatians*, 205). While not, as yet, submitting to circumcision, Gentile Christians of Galatia seem to have begun to observe the weekly Jewish sabbaths, the annual Jewish festivals, and the Jewish

Explanation

183

high holy days—all, as they evidently were led to believe by the Judaizers, as a means of bringing their Christian faith to completion.

11 φοβοῦμαι ὑμᾶς μή πως εἰκῇ κεκοπίακα εἰς ὑμᾶς, "I fear for you, that perhaps I have worked hard for you to no avail." Paul's long rebuke section of 1:6–4:11 closes with an expression of distress: φοβοῦμαι ὑμᾶς, "I fear for you." The indicative is used because the Galatians' departure from the Pauline message had already begun, but the present tense indicates that its final result is as yet undetermined. The conjunction μή πως (or μήπως) after a verb of apprehension means "that perhaps" or "lest somehow" (cf. 2:2; 1 Thess 3:5). The verb κοπιάω ("work hard," "struggle," "toil") combined with the adverb εἰκῇ ("in vain," "to no avail") expresses the content of Paul's fear, with the adverb being emphasized by its position: "I have worked hard to no avail." The perfect tense of the verb refers to Paul's past ministry among them and its continuing result, which Paul here fears may, in fact, be without any continuing result (though see 5:10 for a more hopeful result). The prepositional phrase εἰς ὑμᾶς is a dative of advantage, "for you."

Explanation

In the *probatio* of his Galatian letter (3:1–4:11), Paul operates extensively in what may be called a "mode of recapitulation" (cf. R. B. Hays, *The Faith of Jesus Christ*, 85). He begins by recalling his converts' own experience of the Spirit (3:1–5); goes on to cite Abraham as the example of faith (3:6–9); turns then to the exegesis of a number of pivotal passages that were evidently being widely used among the believers of Galatia (3:10–14); and finally mounts a series of arguments, some ad hominem in nature (3:15–18) and others more direct (3:19–4:7), on the impossibility of legalism and the termination of nomism. Throughout "this argumentative recapitulation," as Hays points out (summarizing "a growing consensus among scholars"), Paul "employs several pithy kerygmatic formulations, some of which appear to be relatively fixed units of tradition that would have been known already to the Galatians and accepted by them as authoritative"—i.e., certain "christological confessional formulae" stemming from the proclamation of the pre-Pauline church (ibid.). These we have identified as found at 3:1, 13, 26 (a "sayings" statement), 27–28; 4:4–5. And on these Paul bases his major theological arguments, for, as Werner Kramer says:

> Evidently the primary consideration in Paul's mind when he adopted any formula was that his church would be bound to assent to it, simply because it represented a piece of tradition which was generally acknowledged. That is why he often uses formulae, either as the point of departure for his train of thought, or as the decisive argument in it, or as its climax (*Christ, Lord, Son of God*, 186, quoted in Hays, 85).

Having argued from (1) the Galatians' own experience, (2) the example of Abraham, (3) crucial biblical portions, and (4) traditional confessions and statements drawn from the proclamation of the early church, Paul concludes his rebuke section of Galatians (1:6–4:11) with an expression of concern for his Galatian converts. Matters were at a crisis point in his converts' spiritual experience, and Paul fears for their welfare and for the effectiveness of his ministry among them. With his arguments concluded, Paul now turns to the request section of his letter (4:12–6:10).

III. Request Section (4:12–6:10)

The second major section of Galatians opens with a series of personal appeals (4:12–20). Clustered among these appeals are five rather standard epistolary conventions: a request formula in v 12 (δέομαι ὑμῶν, "I plead with you"); two disclosure formulae in vv 13 and 15 (οἴδατε ὅτι, "you know that," and μαρτυρῶ ὅτι, "I testify that"); a vocative address in v 19 (τεκνία μου, "my children"), and a reference to a desired visit in v 20 (ἤθελον παρεῖναι πρὸς ὑμᾶς, "how I wish I could be with you"). Such a cluster of epistolary conventions, coupled with an expression of distress in 4:11 (φοβοῦμαι ὑμᾶς, "I fear for you") and the transitional use of a verb of saying in 4:21 (λέγετέ μοι, "tell me"), suggests that 4:12–20 should be understood as a significant turning point in the letter. For, as T. Y. Mullins has observed, where such epistolary formulae are found grouped together "they almost always punctuate a break in the writer's thought" (*JBL* 91 [1972] 387).

In the Greek papyri, as J. L. White and K. Kensinger note, "the body of the letter of request divides into two parts, the background and the request" (*SBLASP* 10 [1976] 85), with such epistolary conventions as disclosure formulae and "a wonder element (introduced by θαυμάζω, 'I am amazed')" being used in the background material to strengthen the request (ibid., 79, 90 n. 7). In most of Paul's letters there is an εὐχαριστῶ ("I am thankful")-παρακαλῶ ("I exhort") structure. In Galatians, however, the verbs θαυμάζω ("I am amazed/astonished") and δέομαι ("I plead") appear and serve a similar function. Following the sharp tone of rebuke set by θαυμάζω in 1:6, δέομαι in 4:12 seems far more appropriate than παρακαλῶ. The expressions θαυμαζω and δέομαι, in fact, reflect something of the tension and estrangement that existed between Paul's converts and himself when Galatians was written (cf. C. Bjerkelund, *Parakalō*, 177–78). So analyzing Galatians broadly in epistolary fashion, it is appropriate to view the entire first half of Paul's letter introduced by θαυμάζω ὅτι (i.e., 1:6–4:11) as the background to the request section that follows (i.e., 4:12–6:10), that latter request section starting out with γίνεσθε ὡς ἐγώ ("become like me"), which is the first imperative to appear in the letter to the Galatians, but headed by δέομαι ὑμῶν ("I plead with you"), which appears at the end of the sentence for emphasis.

Rhetorically, a major shift in Paul's argument occurs at 4:12. There are, of course, still elements of forensic rhetoric to be found in what follows, particularly in Paul's accusations against the errorists (4:17; 5:7–12; 6:12–13) and his statements of self-defense (4:13–16; 5:11; 6:14, 17). But the dominant tone from 4:12 onwards is that of deliberative rhetoric, not forensic rhetoric. Deliberative rhetoric, rather than taking a judicial or defensive stance, seeks to exhort or dissuade an audience regarding future actions by demonstrating that those actions are expedient or harmful (cf. Aristotle, *Rhetoric*, 1.3.5: "The end of the deliberative speaker is the expedient or harmful; for he who exhorts recommends a course of action as better, and he who dissuades advises against it as worse"). In 4:12ff. Paul is no longer so much concerned to accuse or defend as to persuade his Galatian converts to adopt a certain course of action.

Hans Dieter Betz has attempted to interpret all of Galatians in terms of forensic rhetoric. And, as we noted earlier, his treatment of the letter in these terms comes off fairly well in the *exordium* of 1:6–10, the *narratio* of 1:11–2:14, the *propositio* of 2:15–21, and at the beginning and end of the *probatio*—that is, the opening *interrogatio* of 3:1–5, the *exemplum* of 3:6–7, and the concluding *interrogatio* of 4:8–11. For most of chaps. 3–4, however, Betz is forced to say, "Admittedly, an analysis of these chapters in terms of [forensic] rhetoric is extremely difficult" (*Galatians*, 129). So he here speaks of Paul's skill "in disguising his argumentative strategy" and explains the "apparent confusion" of these chapters by Quintilian's advice "to diversify by a thousand figures" (ibid.). But that, we believe, is somewhat thin and a rather desperate justification for keeping Galatians as a whole within the bounds of classical forensic rhetoric. Likewise with regard to 5:1–6:10, which he identifies as Paul's *exhortatio*, Betz continues to experience some embarrassment, since exhortation, as G. A. Kennedy points out, "is not regarded as a part of judicial rhetoric by any of the ancient authorities" (*New Testament Interpretation through Rhetorical Criticism*, 145). Betz recognizes this, and so admits: "It is rather puzzling to see that paraenesis plays only a marginal [*sic*] role in the ancient rhetorical handbooks, if not in rhetoric itself" (*Galatians*, 254). And he laments the fact that Quintilian "has no special treatment of it" (ibid., n. 12).

George A. Kennedy, on the other hand, picking up on Betz's dilemma as to the lack of paraenesis in the forensic rhetoric of antiquity, asserts that "the exhortation of 5:1–6:10 is strong evidence that the epistle is in fact deliberative in intent" (*New Testament Interpretation through Rhetorical Criticism*, 145). Indeed, it is Kennedy's claim (1) that the paraenesis of chaps. 5–6 is the heart of the argument of Galatians ("Galatians, like other works intended to be heard, unfolds in a linear manner. What Paul is leading to in chapters 1–4 is the exhortation of chapters 5–6. That is the point of the letter"; ibid., 146), and (2) that Paul's intent in writing Galatians was not to defend his own stance, position, or preaching, but to challenge his converts to action in the immediate future ("The letter looks to the immediate future, not to judgment of the past, and the question to be decided by the Galatians was not whether Paul had been right in what he had said or done, but what they themselves were going to believe and to do"; ibid.). So Kennedy calls for Galatians to be seen as an example of deliberative rhetoric throughout, with all of the narration and doctrinal explication of chaps. 1–4 leading to the exhortation of chaps. 5–6. In so doing, Kennedy plays down the judicial features of Paul's argument in 1:6–3:7, which we believe (with Betz) are certainly present. His view of Galatians is based in the main on the ancient rhetoricians' understanding of a speech as being linear and cumulative in nature, and so allowing only one rhetorical genre per composition. Thus, if Galatians cannot be an example of forensic rhetoric, because of its *exhortatio*, and if the exhortations of 5:1–6:10 are central to the letter, then the letter must be an example of deliberative rhetoric throughout.

Galatians, however, appears to be a case of mixed rhetorical genres: Greco-Roman forensic rhetoric dominating in 1:6–3:7 and 4:8–11; Jewish rhetorical and exegetical conventions being introduced in the *exemplum* of 3:6–7 (see *Comment* on 3:6) and continuing on through 4:7; and Greco-Roman deliberative rhetoric being prominent in 4:12–6:10. One must not force Galatians (or any of Paul's letters) into one particular rhetorical mold. For, as Abraham Malherbe has argued, rhetorical conventions were simply part of the culture of ancient Greco-Roman society, which everyone, whether formally educated or simply exposed to the marketplace of ideas, was influenced by and used to his own advantage (cf. *Social Aspects*, 33–35, 41–45). So Paul, living amidst the overlapping of Greco-Roman and Jewish cultures, used, in what appears to be a largely unconscious fashion, the rhetorical conventions at hand for his own purposes, thereby fusing his Christian convictions with his inherited rhetorical conventions to produce the unique presentation of Galatians.

A. Exhortations against the Judaizing Threat (Exhortatio, Part I) (4:12–5:12)

While debate has been extensive as to whether Paul's exhortations in Galatians begin at 4:12, 4:21, 4:31, 5:1, 5:2, 5:7, or 5:13 (cf. O. Merk, *ZNW* 60 [1969] 83–104, who surveys opinion to his day and argues that the paraenesis commences at 5:13), in actuality, the first imperative of the letter—and so the first word of exhortation, with the carrying out of this request being the chief concern of the rest of the letter—appears at the start of 4:12: γίνεσθε ὡς ἐγώ, "become like me!" Four more imperatives appear in the Hagar-Sarah allegory at 4:27, 30 in quoting Isa 54:1 and Gen 21:10. The first three appear somewhat in passing: "be glad," "break forth," "cry aloud" from Isa 54:1; the fourth from Gen 21:10, however, epitomizes Paul's exhortations to his Galatian converts vis-à-vis the Judaizers: ἔκβαλε τὴν παιδίσκην καὶ τὸν υἱὸν αὐτῆς, "Cast out the slave woman and her son!" Thereafter both imperatives and hortatory subjunctives appear repeatedly throughout 5:1–6:10: imperatives at 5:1 (twice) 13, 14, 16; 6:1, 2, 6, 7; hortatory subjunctives at 5:25, 26; 6:9, 10. It is therefore necessary to insist that all of the request section of 4:12–6:10 is in effect the *exhortatio* of Paul's Galatian letter, for throughout all of this section Paul is pleading with his converts.

Earlier we proposed that Paul faced both a judaizing threat and libertine tendencies at Galatia, with the former brought in by certain Jewish Christian errorists from outside the church after Paul's deparature and the latter present in the church from its inception (cf. *Introduction*, xcvii–xcviii). Not that there were two separate or distinguishable parties among Paul's erring converts at Galatia, so that Paul faced opposition on two fronts. Rather, as Robert Jewett has argued, "Paul viewed the congregation as a more or less homogeneous unit capable of being swayed in this direction and that" (*NTS* 17 [1971] 209). For in countering the judaizing threat he seems to characterize all the Galatian Christians as "foolish Galatians" (3:1) and in speaking to the libertine tendencies he seems to assume that he is speaking to all the believers, as the equation of πνευματικοί with ἀδελφοί suggests (6:1). "The Hellenistic assumptions of this congregation," as Jewett goes on to argue, "were as susceptible to the propaganda of the agitators as to the lures of libertinism" (ibid.). So whereas the Judaizers' activity came about only after Paul's departure from Galatia, the libertine threat seems to have been a problem that Paul had to deal with from the very beginning, as his words of 5:21 suggest: "I warn you, *as I did before*, that those who live like this [in libertine fashion] will not inherit the kingdom of God."

In what follows, therefore, two distinctive theses will be proposed: (1) that the exhortatio of Galatians must be seen as comprising all of 4:12–6:10; and (2) that within this exhortation section Paul deals first with the immediate problem posed by the judaizing threat in 4:12–5:12 (the *exhortatio*, Part I) and then with the continuing problem of libertine tendencies in 5:13–6:10 (the *exhortatio*, Part II). Here in his "Exhortations against the Judaizing Threat" (4:12–5:12), Paul parallels in rough fashion the form and development of his earlier arguments in the rebuke section of 1:6–4:11: he begins with autobiographical statements in his personal appeals of 4:12–20 (cf. those of the *narratio* of 1:13–2:14); he moves on to the Hagar-Sarah allegory of 4:21–31 (cf. his use of Abraham and his biblical exegesis in the first part of the *probatio* of 3:6–18); and he concludes with specific exhortations regarding Christian freedom in 5:1–12, which include something of a précis of the Christian faith in vv 5–6 (cf. the doctrinal content that runs throughout the *propositio* of 2:15–21 and the *probatio* of 3:1–4:11). Paul's "Exhortations against Libertine Tendencies" will be treated later in discussing 5:13–6:10.

1. Personal Appeals (4:12–20)

Bibliography

Bjerkelund, C. *Parakalō.* **Funk, R. W.** "The Apostolic Parousia: Form and Significance." In *Christian History and Interpretation.* FS J. Knox, ed. W. R. Farmer, C. F. D. Moule, and R. R. Niebuhr. Cambridge: Cambridge University Press, 1967, 249–68. **Kennedy, G. A.** *New Testament Interpretation through Rhetorical Criticism,* esp. 144–52. **Malherbe, A. J.** *Social Aspects.* ———. *Moral Exhortation.* **Mullins, T. Y.** "Petition as a Literary Form." *NovT* 5 (1962) 46–54. ———. "Disclosure as a Literary Form in the New Testament." *NovT* 7 (1964) 44–50. ———. "Formulas in New Testament Epistles." *JBL* 91 (1972) 380–90. ———. "Visit Talk in the New Testament Letters." *CBQ* 35 (1973) 350–58. **White, J. L.** *The Form and Function of the Body of the Greek Letter.* **White, J. L., and Kensinger, K.** "Categories of Greek Papyrus Letters." *SBLASP* 10 (1976) 79–91.

Translation

[12]*I plead with you, brothers: Become like me, for I became like you! You did not wrong me.* [13]*You know that it was because of an illness that I first preached the gospel to you.* [14]*And though my illness was a temptation for you* [a] *[to reject me], yet you did not despise nor disdain* [b] *me. Rather, you welcomed me as if I were an angel of God, as if I were Christ Jesus himself.* [15]*Where,* [c] *then, is* [d] *your [former state of] blessedness? I testify on your behalf that, if you could have done so, you would have torn out your eyes and given them to me.* [16]*So, [it seems,] I have become your enemy because I am telling you the truth!*

[17]*[Those people] earnestly court you, but for no good. What they desire is to exclude you [from us], so that you would earnestly court them.* [e] [18]*But, "good is always to be courted* [f] *in a good way"—and not just when I am with you.*

[19]*My little children,* [g] *for whom I am once again in the pains of childbirth until Christ is formed in you—* [20]*how I wish I could be with you now and exchange my voice [for this letter], because I am perplexed about you!*

Notes

ᵃ τὸν πειρασμὸν ὑμῶν ("your temptation") appears in ℵ* A B C²ᵛⁱᵈ D* G vg Ambst Vic Jerome Augustine etc.; τὸν πειρασμόν μου ("my temptation") in P⁴⁶ C*ᵛⁱᵈ D² TR Chr Cyr Thoret etc.; τὸν πειρασμόν in ℵᶜ Bas Euthalius Theophylact etc.

ᵇ P⁴⁶ omits οὐδὲ ἐξεπτύσατε ("nor did you disdain").

ᶜ The interrogative adverb ποῦ ("where") is well attested by ℵ A B C etc., though τίς ("what") appears in D K L etc.

ᵈ Some witnesses add the understood verb ἦν ("was"; D G Byzantine etc.) or ἐστίν ("is"; 103 vg etc.) after οὖν.

ᵉ ἵνα αὐτοὺς ζηλοῦτε ("so that you would be zealous for them" or "earnestly court them") is well attested; D* G it Ambst, however, read ζηλοῦτε δὲ τὰ κρείττω χαρίσματα ("but be zealous for, or earnestly court, the better gifts"), evidently influenced by 1 Cor 12:31.

ᶠ The infinitive ζηλοῦσθαι ("to be zealous" or "to be earnestly courted") is supported by A and most MSS. The articular infinitive τὸ ζηλοῦσθαι, the article being a stylistic feature used to make the infinitive more adaptable to a preposition that follows, appears in D G Byzantine; while ℵ B vg Or read ζηλοῦσθε, which may be seen as another way of writing the infinitive or as an imperative (so vg).

ᵍ τέκνα (nom., accus., and voc. plural: "children") appears in ℵ* B D* G it Mcion; τεκνία (voc. plural with a diminutive nuance: "little children") in ℵᶜ A C Byzantine Cl.

Form/Structure/Setting

Commentators have often treated 4:12–20 as a passionate and emotional, though also somewhat erratic and irrational, outburst, which largely defies analysis. Burton begins his treatment of this section with the words: "Dropping argument, the resumption of which in vv 21–31 is probably an after-thought, the apostle turns to appeal, begging the Galatians . . . " (*Galatians*, 235). Schlier calls it "an argument of the heart" reflecting "strong pathos" and an "erratic train of thought" (*Galater*, 208). Mussner views Paul here as overcome with emotion and losing control of the argument, so that an intuitive grasping of what is being said is required (*Galaterbrief*, 304–5). And even Betz, who insists that 4:12–20 "is neither inconsistent nor lacking argumentative force," can justify Paul's presentation here only by a rather general reference to "Hellenistic style, which calls for change between heavy and light sections and which would require an emotional and personal approach to offset the impression of mere abstractions" (*Galatians*, 221).

Admittedly, 4:12–20 is a passionate and emotionally charged section. Likewise, because of the allusive nature of Paul's references, there is much that we have no way to ascertain but which his readers would probably have known. Nonetheless, these verses must not be treated as simply an erratic or irrational aside. Rather, here Paul begins the exhortation portion of his letter, principally by recalling his past relations with his converts and contrasting their past and present attitudes to him. Standing at the head of this section and epitomizing all that Paul wants to say in these verses is the first imperative of Galatians, which in effect is also the operative appeal of the entire letter: "become like me!" (4:12).

In the Pauline letters there frequently appears what has been called a travelogue or apostolic parousia section where Paul talks about being with his addressees in the future, either directly or through an emissary (e.g., Rom 15:14–32; 1 Cor 16:1–18; Phil 2:19–30). The closest thing we get to such talk about a visit in Galatians, however, is in 4:20, where Paul expresses a desire to be with his converts in the present. But a wish to be with his addressees in the present is hardly the same as announcing a planned visit for the future. Furthermore, unless one

connects 4:12–20 with 5:11–12 and/or 6:11 and takes them together as forming
a somewhat scattered surrogate for Paul's usual apostolic parousia section, it is
probably best to say that Galatians, in fact, has no formal apostolic parousia
section but only a wish to be present with the addressees in the present.

Comment

12 γίνεσθε ὡς ἐγώ, ὅτι κἀγὼ ὡς ὑμεῖς, "become like me, for I became like
you," is, on the face of it, somewhat enigmatic and paradoxical, at least in its
second part. "Become like me" looks back to the autobiographical accounts of
1:13–2:14, where Paul speaks of his own loyalty to the truth of the gospel, and to
the expositions of 2:15–4:11, where Paul sets out his arguments in defense of the
Christian gospel vis-à-vis the Jewish law, so calling on his Galatian converts
themselves to be loyal to the truth of the gospel (2:5, 14), dead to the law (2:19),
no longer under the law (3:25), living by faith in Christ (2:20; 3:26–29), and
therefore not nullifying the grace of God (2:21) but enjoying all the benefits of
the gospel by faith in Christ (3:6–4:7). The imperative γίνεσθε ὡς ἐγώ ("become
like me") assumes, of course, that the Galatian Christians were not like Paul, for
they were beginning to observe the Jewish calendar and dietary laws as necessary
for a proper Christian lifestyle and they were contemplating circumcision as
requisite for a true biblical faith (cf. 1:6–9; 4:9–10). Nonetheless, Paul still thinks
of them as Gentile Christians who have not as yet apostatized, as his reference to
his having become like them suggests.

The second part of the entreaty requires an understood verb, either the present
εἰμί ("I am") or the perfect γέγονα ("I became")—or perhaps the second aorist
middle ἐγενόμην read as a historical aorist ("I became"). Linguistically, εἰμί would
fit well, being parallel to ἐστέ ("you are") that must be supplied with ὑμεῖς. Either
the perfect γέγονα or the aorist ἐγενόμην, however, corresponds nicely with the
imperative γίνεσθε of the first part of the entreaty, setting up a balanced "You
become"—"I became" construction. Furthermore, either the perfect or the aorist
reading is in line with Paul's declaration of 1 Cor 9:20–21: "I became [ἐγενόμην]
... like one not having the law ... so as to win those not having the law." Yet if Paul
had meant to stress here only the past, he would probably not have used the aorist
ἐγενόμην but the imperfect ἤμην (so Chrysostom, Jerome, et al.). On the other
hand, if he had wanted to stress only the present, εἰμί would be fitting. His thought
throughout 4:12–20, however, concerns his past contacts with his Galatian converts
and the continuing results of those contacts at present, and so the perfect γέγονα
("I became," signifying both past action and present state) seems most appropriate.

ἀδελφοί, δέομαι ὑμῶν, "I plead with you, brothers." On Paul's affectionate use
of "brothers" in Galatians, see *Comment* at 1:11. On the vocative ἀδελφοί as signaling the beginning or the end of an epistolary unit, see *Comment* at 3:15. Here
ἀδελφοί occurs after the imperative, since Paul evidently wanted to head up all of
the hortatory material of 4:12–6:10 by the entreaty "Become like me!"

Yet while the imperative heads up the subject matter of 4:12–6:10, the
epistolary caption for all that follows is δέομαι ὑμῶν, "I plead with you." "Used by
itself," T. Y. Mullins asserts, "δεῖσθαι indicates a definite degree of dignity or of
formality beyond the other verbs of petition" (*NovT* 5 [1962] 48). So Mullins sees
δέομαι here as "probably to be interpreted as more forensic than fond" (ibid., 50).

Verbs of petition, however, were part of the common parlance of the day to be used by speakers or writers as each deemed most suitable. Furthermore, it is difficult to believe, particularly in its association with ἀδελφοί, that Paul here uses δέομαι in any stiff or formal manner, without tenderness or affection.

οὐδέν με ἠδικήσατε, "you did not wrong me," is susceptible to a number of interpretations. It could be read: (1) you did not wrong me when I was with you, but now you are treating me as your enemy (cf. v 16); (2) you did not wrong me, but have wronged Christ or God (cf. 1:6); or (3) you did not wrong me, but have wronged yourselves. It is more likely, as Burton suggests, for the statement to have "found its occasion in some word of theirs [the Galatian believers] than to have originated with Paul himself" (*Galatians*, 238)—a word of theirs to the effect that their proposed acceptance of a Jewish lifestyle must not be taken as a discrediting of Paul, to which Paul accedes; or perhaps a claim that their proposed action would indeed be a personal affront to Paul, which Paul denies. So here Paul should probably be understood as affirming: "I grant, whatever your views and proposed actions, that I have not been personally wronged by what has gone on among Christians in Galatia."

13 οἴδατε δὲ ὅτι δι᾽ ἀσθένειαν τῆς σαρκὸς εὐηγγελισάμην ὑμῖν τὸ πρότερον, "you know that it was because of an illness that I first preached the gospel to you." Following Paul's request to "become like me," two disclosure formulae appear: οἴδατε ὅτι, "you know that" (v 13), and μαρτυρῶ ὅτι, "I testify that" (v 15). It is not unusual in Paul's letters for a request formula to be followed immediately by a disclosure formula (cf. 1 Cor 16:15; I Thess 4:1-2). Here the disclosure formulae are used to remind the Galatians of the close relationship that they and Paul enjoyed when Paul was first with them.

ἀσθένεια ("weakness") is a term denoting any kind of weakness, as opposed to ἰσχύς ("strength"). Modified by τῆς σαρκός ("of the flesh"), however, it certainly refers to a physical weakness—i. e., a "sickness" or "illness." The preposition διά with the accusative ἀσθένειαν expresses the occasion of the preaching (i.e., "on the occasion of" or "because of an illness"), not the means (δι᾽ ἀσθενείας, "through an illness") or the limiting condition (ἐν ἀσθενείᾳ, "in illness"). The verb εὐαγγελίζω ("proclaim" or "preach") is common in Paul and throughout the NT as a locution for proclaiming the gospel, whether or not its content or its recipient(s) are mentioned (cf. 1:8, 9, 11, 16, 23 for a variety of uses in Galatians). In the NT εὐαγγελίζω usually appears in the middle voice, following classical usage; the active form was a later development in Greek, appearing in the NT only at Rev 10:7 and 14:6 (also Acts 16:17 in D). The adjective πρότερος in classical Greek functioned as a comparative (the "former" of two) in distinction from πρῶτος (the "first" of a series), but in Koine Greek πρότερος is often equivalent to πρῶτος. Paul's use of τὸ πρότερον may signal "the former of two visits," as has been argued by both North Galatian theorists (i.e., the visit of Acts 16:6, with that of Acts 18:23 being "the latter") and South Galatian theorists (i.e., the eastward journey from Pisidian Antioch to Derbe of Acts 13:14–14:20, with the westward retracing of the same route as mentioned in Acts 14:21 being "the latter"). In context, however, τὸ πρότερον here should probably be contrasted with the implied νῦν ("now") of v 16, thereby understanding the contrast throughout vv 13–16 as being between the Galatians' reception of Paul when he *first* proclaimed the gospel to them and their response to him *now* after the Judaizers' intrusion.

It was an illness, Paul tells us, that served as the occasion for his original ministry in Galatia, either by causing him first to go into the province or by detaining him there longer than he originally planned. Perhaps that illness was the result of one or more of the afflictions mentioned in 2 Cor 11:23–25: frequent imprisonments, severe floggings, exposure to death again and again, lashed five times by synagogal authorities, beaten three times by Roman authorities, etc.—if one or more of these took place before his evangelistic mission in Galatia. Or perhaps it is to be equated with his "thorn in the flesh" referred to in 2 Cor 12:7–10. Paul does not tell us, and so there is no way for us to know.

William M. Ramsay, rightly taking δι' ἀσθένειαν ("because of an illness") to signal the occasion for his ministry in Galatia, postulated that Paul contracted malaria in the marshes of Pamphylia and came to the plateau area of Pisidian Antioch at first only to recuperate (*St. Paul the Traveller*, 94–97). William Wrede (*Paul*, tr. E. Lummis [London: Green, 1907] 22–23), Joseph Klausner (*From Jesus to Paul*, tr. W. F. Stinespring [New York: Macmillan, 1943] 325–30), and others have viewed Paul's illness as epilepsy, based primarily on a literal rendering of οὐδὲ ἐξεπτύσατε, "you did not spit out," of v 14, which they saw as alluding to the practice of spitting to avert the evil eye or to exorcise an evil spirit, as in the case of epilepsy. And others more popularly, based on the statement "if you could have done so, you would have torn out your eyes and given them to me" of v 15, have supposed that Paul suffered from ophthalmia or some other affliction of the eyes. All of these suppositions are possible, as well as those referred to by Paul himself in 2 Cor 11:23–25 and 12:7–10. We are just too ill-informed to make any direct equation. And after all, as Franz Mussner observes, "for a man like Paul everything became a καιρός [i.e., a significant opportunity], when the gospel was to be proclaimed" (*Galaterbrief*, 307).

14 καὶ τὸν πειρασμὸν ὑμῶν ἐν τῇ σαρκί μου οὐκ ἐξουθενήσατε οὐδὲ ἐξεπτύσατε, "and though my illness was a temptation for you [to reject me], yet you did not despise nor disdain me." The phrase τὸν πειρασμὸν ὑμῶν ἐν τῇ σαρκί μου (lit., "your temptation in my flesh") is awkward grammatically, perhaps because it is idiomatic. Any easy translation is difficult, though its meaning is clear. As early as the third century there were those who tried to resolve the grammatical awkwardness by reading τὸν πειρασμόν μου, "my temptation" (so P[46], Chrysostom, et al.) or simply τὸν πειρασμόν, "the temptation" (see *Note* a). But τὸν πειρασμὸν ὑμῶν, "your temptation," is well attested externally and is certainly the "harder" reading, and therefore to be accepted. Evidently, Paul's illness would have been reason enough for the Galatians to have rejected him when he was first with them. Illness would probably have been interpreted by them as demonic in nature (cf. 2 Cor 12:7, where Paul calls his "thorn in the flesh" an ἄγγελος Σατανᾶ, "messenger of Satan"), and so they could easily have been tempted to dismiss both Paul and his message because of his illness. Thus while the grammar is awkward, perhaps because of the idiomatic nature of what we have in the first part of v 14, a sense translation would be something like: "Though my illness was a temptation for you [to reject me]."

The verb ἐξουθενέω ("despise," "disdain") is used also of Paul in 2 Cor 10:10, repeating the accusation of certain Corinthian Christians who thought of him more as a charlatan than an apostle: "his speaking is to be despised" (ὁ λόγος ἐξουθενημένος; cf. also Rom 14:3, 10; 1 Cor 1:28; 6:4; 16:11; 1 Thess 5:20). The verb ἐκπτύω ("spit out," "disdain") does not appear in the LXX and occurs only here in the NT, though it appears elsewhere in Greek writings from Homer on. Originally it meant "spit out," both as a gesture of disrespect and as a means of protection against the evil eye or demons. It came, however, to be used synonymously with ἐξουθενέω. So synonymous were these two terms, in fact, that P⁴⁶ omits the latter here, evidently believing it to be redundant (see Note b). Yet the Hellenistic Jewish religious romance *Joseph and Aseneth,* written at roughly the same time as Paul wrote his letters, uses them together in synonymous fashion (2.1). And Paul likewise uses them together to emphasize the point that the Galatians, at the time of their reception of the gospel, "did not despise nor disdain" him because of his illness, whatever its nature or its symptoms.

ἀλλὰ ὡς ἄγγελον θεοῦ ἐδέξασθέ με, ὡς Χριστὸν Ἰησοῦν, "rather, you welcomed me as if I were an angel of God, as if I were Christ Jesus himself." The adversative ἀλλά ("instead," "rather") sets up a strong contrast between how the Galatians could have received Paul and how they actually did. The particle ὡς ("as," "as if") appears twice to introduce two exaggerated comparisons that compare the Galatians' earlier reception of Paul to the reception they would have given "an angel of God" or even "Christ Jesus" himself. ἄγγελος is commonly used in the NT to mean "messenger" (cf. Matt 11:10; Luke 7:24, 27; Mark 1:2; Jas 2:25). Paul, however, usually uses ἀπόστολος for messenger (cf. 2 Cor 8:23; Phil 2:25), with ἄγγελος elsewhere in Galatians and Paul's other writings signifying an extraterrestrial, superhuman being (cf. 1:8; 3:19; also 1 Cor 4:9; 13:1; perhaps 2 Cor 12:7). And that is how it should be taken here. Likewise, elsewhere Paul views himself as identified with Christ (cf. Gal 2:20 and the many "in Christ," "in him," "in the Lord" expressions in his letters), an imitator of Christ (cf. 1 Cor 11:1; Phil 3:10–17; 1 Thess 1:6), and a representative of Christ (cf. 2 Cor 2:14–17; 5:18–20; 13:3–4; Eph 3:1–19; Col 1:23–2:5; 1 Tim 1:12–17), so that in a real sense those who welcome him also welcome Christ. Yet Paul is not saying here that he believed himself to be either "an angel of God" or "Christ Jesus" himself. The exaggerated comparisons are used to praise the Galatians with regard to their earlier response to Paul and his evangelistic ministry, and not to extol Paul himself.

15 ποῦ οὖν ὁ μακαρισμὸς ὑμῶν, "where, then, is your [former state of] blessedness?" While there is minor external support for reading τίς ("what") rather than ποῦ ("where") and for inserting either ἦν (3rd sing. imperf.) or ἐστίν (3rd sing. pres.) after οὖν, the preponderance of evidence calls for the adoption of ποῦ οὖν ("where then") and allowing some form of the verb εἰμί ("I am") to be understood (see Notes c and d). The question is rhetorical, implying that a former state had come to an end, but without good reason. The inferential particle οὖν ("then") looks back to those former days depicted in vv 13–14 when relations between Paul and his converts were joyous. The substantive ὁ μακαρισμός connotes a state of "blessedness," "happiness," or "joy." The pronoun ὑμῶν ("your") may be understood as either simple or reflexive; furthermore, it may be seen to function as a possessive genitive, a subjective genitive, or an objective genitive. A good case could be made for each of these possibilities. Yet the simplest and most direct way to take it is as a simple pronoun that is possessive in function, and so to read the question: "Where, then, is your [former state of] blessedness?"

μαρτυρῶ γὰρ ὑμῖν ὅτι εἰ δυνατὸν τοὺς ὀφθαλμοὺς ὑμῶν ἐξορύξαντες ἐδώκατέ μοι, "I testify on your behalf that if you could have done so, you would have torn out your eyes and given them to me." The second instance of a disclosure formula in this section, μαρτυρῶ γὰρ ὅτι, "I testify that," serves also to remind the Galatians of a past relationship (cf. v 13). The contracted form μαρτυρῶ (from μαρτυρέω) appears regularly in Hellenistic epistolary disclosure formulae (cf. POxy 105:13; PLond 1164; Rom 10:2; Col 4:13). The dative plural pronoun ὑμῖν in the formula may be seen as an indirect object denoting the persons who receive the testimony ("I testify to you that"; cf. Acts 15:8) or as a dative of advantage denoting those to whose credit the testimony is borne ("I testify on your behalf that"; cf. Acts 22:5; Rom 10:2; Col 4:13). Since the former is understood, and in light of the parallels with Rom 10:2 and Col 4:13, the latter is preferable.

The construction εἰ δυνατὸν . . . ἐδώκατέ μοι, "if you could have done so . . . you would have . . . given . . . to me," is a second class contrary-to-fact condition, with ἄν, which usually (but not always) occurs in the apodosis, being omitted. The expression εἰ δυνατόν ("if possible") saves what follows from being a hyperbole, for it is only "if you could have done so." The statement "you would have torn out your eyes and given them to me," while often popularly taken to suggest ophthalmia on Paul's part (see *Comment* on v 13), is probably an idiom that speaks of going to the extreme to provide for another's needs. The eyes in antiquity were considered the most precious of the body's parts (cf. "the apple of his eye" in Deut 32:10; Ps 17:8; Zech 2:8), and so "to tear out one's eyes for someone" is a graphic and significant idiom for going to the extreme for another's welfare. Certainly it is more telling than our modern idiom of "giving the shirt off one's back"!

16 ὥστε ἐχθρὸς ὑμῶν γέγονα ἀληθεύων ὑμῖν, "so, [it seems,] I have become your enemy because I am telling you the truth!" Elsewhere in the NT ὥστε ("therefore," "so") is always used at the beginning of independent clauses to draw an inference from what has just been stated (cf. Gal 3:9, 24; 4:7, etc.). Most commentators acknowledge this. Yet almost all critical texts, translations and commentaries treat v 16 as a rhetorical question (e.g., WH, Souter, Nestle, UBSGT, KJV, RSV, JB, NIV, Lightfoot, Lietzmann, Oepke, Schlier, Mussner, Betz, Bruce), despite demurrings to the contrary (cf. Betz, *Galatians*, 228: "The connection of ὥστε ["therefore"] is certainly loose"; ibid., 228 n. 97: "ὥστε ["therefore"] introducing a question is odd"). Nonetheless, linguistically speaking, Burton, Zahn, and Sieffert are right: v 16 must be read as an indignant exclamation that draws an inference from what is stated in vv 14–15; "the appropriate punctuation is, therefore, an exclamation point" (Burton, *Galatians*, 244–45). It is not, of course, Paul's own statement of relationships, but his evaluation of what seems to be his converts' attitude: "So, [it seems,] I have become your enemy because I am telling you the truth!"

ἐχθρός, "enemy," was the epithet given Paul by the later Ebionites (cf. *Ps.-Clem. Hom., Ep. Pet.* 2.3; *Ps.-Clem. Recog.* 1.70), though whether the Judaizers of Galatia ever used it of him is impossible to say. The modal present participial phrase ἀληθεύων ὑμῖν, "by telling you the truth," refers not to some past proclamation, but to the truth Paul is now telling the Galatians, which, of course, is what he told them when he was first with them and which then won such a favorable response from them.

17 ζηλοῦσιν ὑμᾶς οὐ καλῶς, ἀλλὰ ἐκκλεῖσαι ὑμᾶς θέλουσιν, ἵνα αὐτοὺς ζηλοῦτε, "[those people] earnestly court you, but for no good. What they desire is to exclude you [from us], so that you would earnestly court them." Paul's indignant exclamation of v 16 has broken the cadence of the litany of his remembrances of earlier times with his converts in vv 13–15. Now he launches into a biting attack against the judaizing errorists in vv 17–18. The errorists, of course, as elsewhere in the letter, are unnamed—here not even identified by a pronoun, but referred to only in the verbal suffix—but everyone knew who they were. The verb ζηλόω ("strive," "desire," "exert oneself") was used in the language of love and friendship to mean "take a personal interest in" or "earnestly court another's favor." Lightfoot has drawn attention to its use by Plutarch in *De Virtute Morali* 448E in contexts of courtship between men and women and friendship between teachers and students (*Galatians* [1890], 176–77). And that is how the verb is used here in v 17 as well: of the Judaizers who were trying to "earnestly court" the Galatian Christians' favor, and who desired that they would "earnestly court" them in return.

Paul's evaluation of the Judaizers' activity is that it was "for no good" (οὐ καλῶς) and that it sprang from a "desire to exclude you" (ἐκκλεῖσαι ὑμᾶς θέλουσιν). Later in 6:12–13 he speaks again of their motives, relating them there to the rising tide of Jewish nationalism and zealot opposition to Gentile sympathizers, which they wanted to placate (cf. *Introduction*, xci, xcii–xciv, and *Comment* at 6:12–13). Here, however, his evaluation is entirely on a personal basis with only personal motives in view. The verb ἐκκλείω means "shut off" or "exclude" in the sense of withdrawing from or forbidding fellowship with someone. Though the clause "they desire to exclude you" leaves it ambiguous "from what" or "from whom" this exclusion was desired, the context is entirely about whom the Galatians were going to follow and have fellowship with, Paul or the Judaizers. So it seems natural to interpret the desired exclusion as being one from Paul's leadership and fellowship ("from us"), which would also be, of course, at least in Paul's eyes, exclusion from Christ (cf. 5:4) and from God "who called" them (cf. 1:6).

18 καλὸν δὲ ζηλοῦσθαι ἐν καλῷ πάντοτε, καὶ μὴ μόνον ἐν τῷ παρεῖναί με πρὸς ὑμᾶς, "but 'good is always to be courted in a good way'—and not just when I am with you." The first part of this verse has every appearance of being an aphorism of the day, which Paul simply quotes for his own purposes when talking about ζηλόω: "good is always to be courted in a good way." Burton calls it "a general maxim" (*Galatians*, 247); Betz speaks of it as "a kind of definition" or a *sententia* (*Galatians*, 231). The verb ζηλοῦσθαι ("to be courted") was evidently understood by Paul as passive, not middle, since the other uses of the verb in the context are active, so that there is no reason to use the middle. The adverbial expressions ἐν καλῷ ("in a good way") and πάντοτε ("always") extend the meaning of the verb, with their presence probably being why Paul quotes this bit of tersely phrased ancient lore. For, as Paul sees it, the Judaizers' courting of his converts was hardly "in a good way." Furthermore, the Galatians' response to courting is to make sure that it is "always" carried on "in a good way"—that is, honestly, sincerely, and for the good of the recipients—both when Paul himself is with them as the one courting and when his absence allows others the opportunity to court them.

19 τεκνία μου, οὓς πάλιν ὠδίνω μέχρις οὗ μορφωθῇ Χριστὸς ἐν ὑμῖν, "my little children, for whom I am once again in the pains of childbirth until Christ is formed in you." An abrupt change of tone occurs as Paul finishes off this section in vv 19–20, for rather than the bitter and assured polemic of vv 17–18, these verses express deep affection, concern, and perplexity. Yet they must also be seen as tied in somehow to vv 17–18, for the words παρεῖναι . . . πρὸς ὑμᾶς ("am with you") of v 18 furnish the linguistic trigger for Paul's wish παρεῖναι πρὸς ὑμᾶς ("to be present with you") of v 20. Many have argued on a linguistic basis that vv 19–20 are part of the same paragraph or sentence as vv 17–18 (e.g., WH, Lightfoot, Burton, and many modern versions, particularly if in v 19 τέκνα ["children"] is accepted and treated as a nominative [so NEB, NAB] and if in v 20 δέ ["but"] is highlighted as a connective). Others, on the basis of tone, view vv 19–20 as a separate paragraph (e.g., Tisch., Schlier, Mussner). The arguments are closely balanced, though in such an emotionally charged portion tone is probably more conclusive.

Likewise, deciding between τέκνα μου ("my children") and τεκνία μου ("my little children") is difficult. τέκνα is better supported externally (see *Note* g). Internally it can be argued also that it is the better reading, for elsewhere in his letters Paul refers to his converts as τέκνα (cf. 4:28; also 1 Cor 4:14, 17; 2 Cor 6:13; 12:14; 1 Thess 2:7, 11; Philem 10), but never τεκνία. Nonetheless, the deeply affectionate tone of these verses suggests (1) that at the beginning of v 19 we have a vocative, not a nominative as τέκνα could be read, and (2) that the more appropriate vocative in context is τεκνία rather than τέκνα, even though supported only by some witnesses (see *Note* g). Additionally, it could be argued that τεκνία is the "harder" reading, since it occurs nowhere else in Paul and an early scribe might have wanted to conform it to Paul's usual practice. But the imagery of v 19 (i.e., of the apostle as a pregnant mother giving birth to converts) is not to be found elsewhere in Paul either, and with that unusual imagery the unusual expression τεκνία conforms nicely.

The masculine relative pronoun οὕς (accusative) after a neuter antecedent, rather than the neuter ἅ, is a case of *constructio ad sensum*. The expression πάλιν ("again," "once again," "anew") points to the need of returning to basics, repeating, as it were, the Galatians' conversion to Christ. The verb ὠδίνω ("suffer the pains of childbirth") presents imagery that is somewhat startling, for nowhere else in Paul's letters does he portray himself as a pregnant mother giving birth to his converts. Indeed, in 1 Thess 2:7 he compares himself to "a mother caring for her children," with that figure then coupled in 2:11 with that of a father dealing with his children. But elsewhere in his letters the birth simile is that of a father begetting children (cf. 1 Cor 4:15; Philem 10).

Yet while the imagery here is that of Paul as a pregnant mother, it is also that of the Galatians themselves bearing Christ as a fetus in their wombs and needing a further gestation period for that fetus to be fully formed. It, too, is rather unusual imagery, for rather than speaking of "Christ being formed in you" (μορφωθῇ Χριστὸς ἐν ὑμῖν), Paul usually speaks of Christians being conformed (σύμμορφος) to Christ (e.g., Rom 8:29) or conformed (συμμορφιζόμενος) to his death (e.g., Phil 3:10). The expression ἐν ὑμῖν ("in you") is taken by some to refer to "the body of Christ" or the Church, and so Paul's birth pangs are seen as having to do with forming again the body of Christ in a corporate sense in the Galatian community (so Schlier, *Galater*, 214). But "in you" is the converse of "in Christ," with both expressions having to do with a vital personal relationship between Christians and God through Christ by the Spirit (see *Comment* at 2:20 and 3:26). Thus, as Burton well expresses matters: "The reactionary step which the Galatians are in danger of taking, forces upon the apostle the painful repetition of that process by which he first brought them into the world of faith in Christ, and his pain, he declares, must continue till they have really entered into vital fellowship with Christ" (*Galatians*, 249).

20 ἤθελον δὲ παρεῖναι πρὸς ὑμᾶς ἄρτι καὶ ἀλλάξαι τὴν φωνήν μου, ὅτι ἀποροῦμαι ἐν ὑμῖν, "how I wish I could be with you now and exchange my voice [for this letter], because I am perplexed about you." The concerns of Paul in 4:12–20 come to a head in the emotionally charged words of v 20. The postpositive particle δέ (untranslated) seems not just to be a connective but to have the force of signaling a conclusion. The imperfect form of θέλω ("wish") should be viewed as a "potential" or "voluntative imperfect" expressing the desire for something in the present, with, of course, that wish unable to be realized, since "wishes about the present are naturally unattainable" (A. T. Robertson, *A Grammar of the Greek New Testament in the Light of Historical Research*, 2nd ed. [London: Hodder & Stoughton; New York: Doran, 1915] 886).

Letters in antiquity served as substitutes for one's personal presence, just as they do today. Paul, however, was unable for whatever reason to be with his Galatian converts at the time. So he sends this letter. But he sends it with the wish "to be with you now and exchange my voice [for this letter]." The expression παρεῖναι πρὸς ὑμᾶς ("to be with you"), as we noted in commenting on v 18, picks up the words at the end of v 18, and so lays emphasis on Paul's desire to be personally present with his Galatian converts—not present just by means of his letter or some emissary who might have brought the letter, but himself there with them. The adverb ἄρτι ("now") is often used to connote a more sharply defined present time than its synonym νῦν, and so should probably be understood to suggest "at this very moment." The phrase ἀλλάξαι τὴν φωνήν μου (lit.: "to exchange my voice") may be understood as expressing Paul's desire either to change the tone of his admonitions (so RSV, NEB, NIV) or to change their content (so JB). More likely, however, it has in mind the contrast between Paul's voice as expressed in a letter and Paul's voice as expressed in person, and so is to be understood as expressing Paul's desire to talk with his converts directly rather than through the substitute of a letter.

Paul's desire to be present with his converts is "because I am perplexed about you" (ὅτι ἀποροῦμαι ἐν ὑμῖν). The middle voice of the verb ἀπορέω relates the action intimately and directly to the subject ("be at a loss," "be in doubt," "be uncertain"), and so connotes the intensified state of "perplexity." ἐν ὑμῖν is either a dative of reference or a dative of advantage, with its function being to identify the objects of Paul's perplexity. Thus Paul begins his exhortations against the judaizing threat in Galatia with a section of personal appeals that closes on a note of perplexity regarding his converts. He does not, however, leave matters at that, but in the sections that follow he sets out his Hagar-Sarah allegory (4:21–31) and then directly exhorts to hold fast to the freedom found in the gospel (5:1–12).

Explanation

Gal 4:12–20 has often been treated as a somewhat erratic and irrational emotional outburst that has either been tacked on to the argumentation of chaps. 3–4 or serves as something of a lighter interlude between the argumentation of chaps. 3–4 and the exhortations of chaps. 5–6. In reality, however, as epistolary analysis suggests, at 4:12 begins the second main section of Paul's Galatian letter: the request section of 4:12–6:10, with γίνεσθε ὡς ἐγώ ("become like me!") introducing the key for all the exhortations that follow and δέομαι ὑμῶν ("I plead with you") serving as the section's epistolary caption. While later in this section there appear a few features characteristic of forensic rhetoric, as carried over from the rebuke section of 1:6–4:11, in the main, it need be noted, deliberative rhetoric dominates throughout 4:12–6:10—that is, rhetoric that seeks to exhort or dissuade an audience regarding future actions by demonstrating that those actions are expedient or harmful.

Paul begins his request section much as he did his rebuke section, viz., by setting out certain autobiographical matters in his personal appeals of 4:12–20 (cf. the *narratio* of 1:11–2:14). Here in 4:12–20 he appeals with passion to his converts, reminding them of their former warm response to his person and proclamation, even when they might have had reason to be antagonistic, and expressing his perplexity regarding their present disaffection. The appeals close with the somewhat surprising imagery of Paul as a pregnant mother giving birth again to his converts and of the Galatians themselves as needing a further gestation period for Christ to be fully formed in their spiritual wombs.

There is no doubt that 4:12–20 is filled with passion and emotion. The apostasy of his converts would have been horrendous, both for them and for him. Here, in fact, we get a glimpse into the heart of a true evangelist and pastor, for whom the waywardness and struggles of those committed to his charge are his agonies as well. While Paul himself could never be wronged by what they did or said about him (cf. v 12b), their welfare was his greatest concern and their struggles were his agonies.

2. The Hagar-Sarah Allegory (4:21–31)

Bibliography

Barrett, C. K. "The Allegory of Abraham, Sarah, and Hagar in the Argument of Galatians." In *Rechtfertigung*. FS E. Käsemann, ed. J. Friedrich, W. Pohlmann, and P. Stuhlmacher. Tübingen: Mohr-Siebeck, 1976, 1–16. **Bonsirven, J.** "Exégèse allegorique chez les rabbins tannaites." *RSR* 23 (1933) 522–24. ———. *Exégèse rabbinique et exégèse paulinienne*, 328–30. **Büchsel, F.** "ἀλληγορέω." *TDNT* 1:260–63. **Daube, D.** "Rabbinic Methods of Interpretation and Hellenistic Rhetoric." *HUCA* 22 (1949) 239–64. ———. "Alexandrian Methods of Interpretation and the Rabbis." In *Festschrift Hans Lewald*. Basel: Helbing & Lichtenbahn, 1953. 27–44. ———. *The New Testament and Rabbinic Judaism*. **Ellis, E. E.** *Paul's Use of the Old Testament*, 51–54. **Goppelt, L.** "τύπος." *TDNT* 8:246–59. **Hansen, G. W.** *Abraham in Galatians*, 141–54. **Hanson, A. T.** *Studies in Paul's Technique and Theology*, 67–103. **Hanson, R. P. C.** *Allegory and Event*, 11–96. **Kepple, R. J.** "An Analysis of Antiochene Exegesis of Galatians 4:24–26." *WTJ* 39 (1977) 239–49. **Lampe, G. W. H.** "The Reasonableness of Typology." In *Essays in Typology*, ed. G. W. H. Lampe and K. J. Woollcombe. London: SCM, 1957, 9–38. **Lauterbach, J. Z.** "Ancient Jewish Allegorists." *JQR* 1 (1911) 291–333, 503–31. **Longenecker, R. N.** *Biblical Exegesis in the Apostolic Period*, 45–48, 126–29. **McNamara, M.** " 'to de (Hagar) Sina oros estin en tē Arabia' (Gal. 4:25a): Paul and Petra." *MS* 2 (1978) 24–41. **Michel, O.** *Paulus und seine Bibel*, 109–111. **Mussner, F.** "Hagar, Sinai, Jerusalem." *TQ* 135 (1955) 56–60. **Woollcombe, K. J.** "Biblical Origins and Patristic Development of Typology." In *Essays in Typology*, ed. G. W. H. Lampe and K. J. Woollcombe. London: SCM, 1957, 39–75.

Translation

²¹ *Tell me, you who want to be under the law, Do you not hear ᵃ the law?* ²²*For it is written that Abraham had two sons, one by the slave woman and the other by the free woman.* ²³*Indeed,ᵇ the one by the slave woman was born according to the flesh but the one by the free woman was born as a result of promise.ᶜ*

²⁴ *These things are [now] being interpreted allegorically. The women represent two covenants. One, indeed, is from Mt. Sinai and bears children unto slavery, which is Hagar.* ²⁵*Nowᵈ Hagar ᵉ stands for Mt. Sinai in Arabia and corresponds to the present city of Jerusalem, because she is in bondage with her children.* ²⁶*But the Jerusalem that is above is free, and she is our mother.ᶠ* ²⁷*For it is written:*

Be glad, O barren woman, who bears no children;

break forth and cry aloud, you who have no labor pains.

Because more are the children of the desolate woman

than of her who has a husband.

²⁸*So you,ᵍ brothers, like Isaac, are children of promise.* ²⁹*And just as it was then, where the one born according to the flesh persecuted the one born according to the Spirit, so it is even now.* ³⁰*But what does the Scripture say? "Cast out the slave woman and her son, for the son of the slave woman will never share in the inheritance with the son of the free woman.ʰ"* ³¹*Therefore,ⁱ brothers, we are not children of the slave woman, but of the free woman.*

Notes

ᵃ ἀκούετε ("you are hearing") is well supported, though ἀναγινώσκετε ("you are reading") appears in D G it vg copˢᵃ, ᵇᵒ arm, perhaps influenced by Acts 8:30.

ᵇ The affirmative particle μέν ("indeed") is omitted by P⁴⁶ B vg.

ᶜ The anarthrous phrase δι᾽ ἐπαγγελίας ("through promise") is supported by P⁴⁶ ℵ A etc.; the articular διὰ τῆς ἐπαγγελίας ("through the promise") by B D G Byzantine.

ᵈ The particle δέ and the conjunction γάρ appear almost equally throughout the MSS: τὸ δὲ Ἁγάρ ("now Hagar") in A B D etc.; τὸ γὰρ Ἁγάρ ("for Hagar") in K L P Byzantine etc.; τὸ δὲ Σινᾶ ("now Sinai") in P⁴⁶ etc.; τὸ γὰρ Σινᾶ ("for Sinai") in ℵ G etc. There is, however, no difference of meaning between δέ as a simple connective without contrast and γάρ as a continuative conjunction.

ᵉ τὸ ... Ἁγὰρ Σινᾶ ὄρος ἐστίν ("Hagar is Mount Sinai") is supported by A B D K L Byzantine etc.; τὸ...Σινᾶ ὄρος ἐστίν ("Sinai is a mountain") by P⁴⁶ℵ C F G etc. The external evidence is almost equally divided, as have been text critics and commentators throughout history. The former reading, however, is more susceptible to scribal modification (i.e., the "harder reading") and therefore more likely the original, whereas there is nothing of either form or meaning in the latter to make its conversion into the former likely.

ᶠ μήτηρ ἡμῶν ("our mother") is well supported by P⁴⁶ ℵ* B C* D G it vg syrᵖ copˢᵃ, ᵇᵒ Mcion Ir Tert Or Chr Jerome et al., whereas μήτηρ πάντων ἡμῶν ("the mother of us all") is supported by ℵᶜ A C² K P Byzantine syrʰ, ᵖᵃˡ arm Irˡᵃᵗ Orˡᵃᵗ Eusebius Hilary Cyril Ambrose et al. The latter reading seems to be an attempt to highlight the inclusive nature of the personal pronoun, but that is textually unnecessary.

ᵍ ὑμεῖς ...ἐστέ ("you are") is supported by P⁴⁶ B D* G etc.; ἡμεῖς ...ἐσμέν ("we are") by ℵ A C Dᶜ K P Byzantine etc.

ʰ τοῦ υἱοῦ τῆς ἐλευθέρας ("the son of the free woman") is well supported, though τοῦ υἱοῦ μου Ἰσαάκ ("my son Isaac") appears in D* G Ambst.

ⁱ διό ("therefore") is supported by ℵ B D* etc., though variants appear in the textual tradition: ἄρα ("then") in P⁴⁶ Dᶜ K L etc.; ἄρα οὖν ("then, therefore") in G etc.; ἡμεῖς δέ ("but we") in A C P etc.; ἡμεῖς οὖν ("we, therefore") in syr Ephraem.

Form/Structure/Setting

Commentators have usually treated the Hagar-Sarah allegory of 4:21–31 as Paul's final argument from Scripture for the superiority of the new covenant over the old. Questions, of course, have often been raised by the commentators as to why Paul concludes his argumentation in this manner and as to what force he saw in this argument. Nonetheless, the dominant approach to this passage has been to see it as a "supplementary argument" that occurred to the apostle "apparently as an after-thought" to reinforce what he had argued earlier (quoting Burton, *Galatians*, 251; cf. also such commentators as Chrysostom, Luther, Lightfoot, Findlay, Duncan, Bruce, et al.), though some take it as a displaced portion of Paul's argument (so U. Luz, "Der alte und der neue Bund," *EvT* 27 [1967] 319; A. Oepke, *Galater*, 147; F. Mussner, *Galaterbrief*, 316–17). Betz, however, asserts that rhetorically this "sixth argument" of 3:1–4:31 is actually Paul's "strongest argument" and that the conclusion of 4:31 formulates "not merely the conclusion to the 'allegory' but to the entire *probatio* section" (*Galatians*, 238–40). Yet understood within its epistolaɪy and rhetorical contexts (see *Comment* above that introduce the request section), the Hagar-Sarah allegory of 4:21–31 should be seen not as part of Paul's argumentative *probatio* but as part of his appeals and exhortations headed by the imperative "become like me!" of 4:12.

The Hagar-Sarah allegory begins with the "verb of saying" λέγετέ μοι, "tell me" (v 21), and it includes two uses of the vocative: ὑμεῖς δέ ἀδελφοί, "now you, brothers" (v 28), and διό, ἀδελφοί, "therefore, brothers" (v 31). Its stress is on the four imperatives cited from two biblical passages: "be glad," "break forth," "cry aloud" (v 27, quoting Isa 54:1), and, in particular, "cast out the slave woman and her son" (v 30, quoting Gen 21:10). And as the second part of the request section of the Galatian letter, it sets up a rough parallel to Paul's treatment of Abraham and Scripture in his arguments of 3:6–14, with the immediately previous autobiographical portions of 4:12–20 being also roughly parallel to the *narratio* of 1:11–2:14.

Earlier we argued that throughout Galatians Paul seems to be interacting with a typically Jewish understanding that truth comes in two forms, an elemental and a developed form, and that in particular he is countering the Judaizers' application of this Jewish understanding to the effect that Paul's message was an elemental form of the gospel proclamation while theirs is the developed form (see *Introduction*, xcv–xcvi, passim). In explicating their position, the Judaizers undoubtedly claimed that Paul's preaching represented an "Ishmaelian" form of truth. Their argument probably was that while Ishmael was, indeed, the first son of Abraham, it was only Isaac who was considered the true son of Abraham, with the conclusion being that only as Paul's converts are related to Isaac and so the Jewish nation, and not Ishmael the non-Jewish representative, can they legitimately be called "sons of Abraham." In response, Paul sets out in allegorical fashion two rather traditional lines of contrast: the line of Hagar and Ishmael, which has to do with slavery and the natural process of procreation, and the line of Sarah and Isaac, which has to do with freedom and promise. But Paul's contemporization of the Hagar-Sarah story does not stop with these contrasts. He makes matters even more explicit by introducing two further dualities (one incomplete): Mount Sinai and the present city of Jerusalem in contrast to "the Jerusalem that is above" (with Mount Zion being understood as equivalent but not expressed).

Paul's allegorical treatment of the Hagar-Sarah story is for polemical purposes, countering, it seems, the Judaizers' own contemporization of that story in ad hominem fashion. In effect, he is saying that not his but their message is the Ishmaelian form of truth: it is Hagar, who has contacts with Mount Sinai (from whence came the law that the Judaizers so extol), who should be associated with the present city of Jerusalem, which explains the bondage of Jerusalem and her emissaries; while it is Sarah, Isaac, and spiritual Jerusalem who are involved in the promises of God, and we (Paul and his Gentile converts) are children of promise in association with them. The argument regarding faith and righteousness as exemplified by Abraham has been made in 3:6–9 of the *probatio;* the exhortation regarding freedom as exemplified by Sarah and Isaac is now made here.

Excursus: The Hagar-Sarah Story in Jewish Writings and in Paul

Paul was doing no injustice to the biblical text to focus attention on the contrasts and conflicts in the Hagar-Sarah story (Gen 16:1–16; 21:1–21), for those are the features on which the dynamic of the story depends. Nor was he unique in so doing. Many of the contrasts and conflicts he highlights were highlighted by other Jews as well.

The closest parallels between Paul and other Jewish writers are to be found in the materials stemming from what could be called mainline Second Temple Judaism or "formative" Judaism, both in its scholastic expressions as codified later in the Mishnah, the Palestinian and Babylonian Gemaras, the Midrashim, the Tosephta, and the numerous sayings collections of individual rabbis, and in its more popular synagogal expressions as found in the Targums. Prominent among these parallels are the many passages where a contrast is made between the slave status of Hagar and the free status of Sarah. Though late, *Pirqe R. El.* 30 is representative:

Rabbi Judah [the Prince] said: In that night the Holy One, blessed be He, was revealed unto him. He said to him: "Abraham! Dost thou not know that Sarah was appointed to thee for a wife from her mother's womb? She is thy companion, and the wife of thy covenant. Sarah is not called thy handmaid, but thy wife; neither is Hagar called thy wife, but thy handmaid."

The fact that Joseph was sold into slavery by the Ishmaelites (Gen 37:27) provided the basis for another comparison between the slave status of Hagar and the free status of Sarah in *Eccl. Rab.* 10.7:

"I have seen servants upon horses [i.e. the Ishmaelites] and princes walking as servants [i.e. Joseph]" (Eccl 10:7). R. Levi said: A servant [i.e. Potiphar] bought him, and the sons of a handmaid sold him [i.e. the Ishmaelites], and the sons of free men were sold to both of them.

The Targums also draw attention in various ways to Hagar's slave status; for example (italics mine):

Tg. Onq. Gen 16:2 (the words of Sarah to Abraham): "Behold, now, the Lord hath restrained me from bearing; go to my handmaid and *set her free;* perhaps I may be builded by her";

Tg. Ps.-J. Gen 21:14 (the action of Abraham in dismissing Hagar): "And he gave [bread and a skin of water] to Hagar to bear upon her shoulders and bound [a veil] to her loins, *to signify that she was a servant,* as also the child, and dismissed her with a letter of divorce" (cf. *Pirqe R. El.* 30: "And he took the veil, and he bound it around her waist, so that it should drag behind her to disclose that she was a bondwoman");

Tg. Ps.-J. Gen 22:1 (the imagined dispute between Isaac and Ishmael): "And it was after these things that Isaac and Ishmael contended. Ishmael said: 'It is right that I should inherit what is the father's, because I am his first-born son.' Isaac said: 'It is right that

I should inherit what is the father's, because I am the son of *Sarah his wife* and you are the son of *Hagar the handmaid* of my mother.'"

Though charges of idolatry and wickedness are often leveled in the rabbinic writings against Ishmael, the situation is more ambivalent with regard to Hagar. In an attempt to justify Sarah's treatment of Hagar, especially since it was Sarah who first suggested Abraham's sexual involvement with her, the Targums and early Midrashim claim that Hagar was the granddaughter of the impious King Nimrod who threw Abraham into the fiery furnace after Abraham destroyed his idols (cf. *Tg. Ps.-J.* Gen 16:1, 5; *Tg. Neof.* Gen 16:5; *Frg. Tg.* Gen 16:5; *Gen. Rab.* 45.1; see L. Ginzberg, *The Legends of the Jews*, tr. H. Szold [Philadelphia: Jewish Publication Society, 1937] 1:198–203). In a similar vein, *Gen. Rab.* 45.4 has it that Hagar told certain solicitous ladies that had Sarah been a righteous woman, she would have had no trouble conceiving. And in *Pirqe R. El.* 30 Hagar's expulsion by Abraham is justified on the basis of her idolatrous tendencies:

> By the merit of our father Abraham, the water did not fail in the bottle. But when she reached the entrance to the wilderness she began to go astray after the idolatry of her father's house, and forthwith the water in the bottle was spent.

But such accusations against Hagar are not common in the rabbinic materials. Usually she is elevated to the status of a daughter of Pharoah who was given by her father to Abraham as a servant in recompense for attempting to take Sarah into his harem and in acknowledgment of God's presence with Abraham (Gen 12:10–20), for, said Pharaoh, "Better let my daughter be a handmaid in this house than a mistress in another house" (*Gen. Rab.* 45.1; cf. *Tg. Ps.-J.* Gen 16:1; *Pirqe R. El.* 26).

Charges of idolatry and wickedness, however, are frequently leveled against Ishmael, often in explicit contrast to Isaac and, of course, with an implied polemic against the Arabs vis-à-vis the Jews. So, for example, when dealing with the question of why Abraham did not bless his children when God allowed him to bless whom he would (cf. Gen 12:2), *Num. Rab.* 11.2 reads:

> Nevertheless Abraham did not bless his children. Why was this? It may be illustrated by the parable of a king who possessed an orchard which he gave over to a tenant. Now in that orchard there was one tree which yielded a life-giving potion and another which yielded deadly poison. Said the tenant: "I shall just cultivate it and accomplish my task. Let the king do whatever he likes with his orchard." So here the king is the Holy One, blessed be He, and the orchard is the world. He handed it over to Abraham by saying to him: "Be thou a blessing." What did Abraham do? He had two sons, one righteous and one wicked, Isaac and Ishmael. Abraham thought: "If I bless Isaac, then Ishmael will wish to be blessed, and he is wicked. But I am God's servant; I am flesh and blood, and will be gone from this world tomorrow. Let the Holy One, blessed be He, do with this world of His as He pleases." When Abraham died, the Holy One, blessed be He, revealed Himself to Isaac and blessed him.

Likewise, when attempting to justify Abraham's expulsion of Hagar and Ishmael—which, on the face of it, appears to be a very callous act—the rabbis pointed to Ishmael's idolatry, wickedness, and mistreatment of Isaac as necessitating it, as in *Exod. Rab.* 1.1:

> Then why: "He that spareth his rod hateth his son"? To teach you that anyone who refrains from chastising his son causes him to fall into evil ways and so comes to hate him. This is what we find in the case of Ishmael, who behaved wickedly before Abraham his father; but he did not chastise him, with the result that he fell into evil ways so that he despised him and cast him forth empty-handed from his house. What did Ishmael do? When he was fifteen years old, he commenced to bring idols from the street, toyed with them as he had seen others do. So "when Sarah saw the son of Hagar the Egyptian, whom she had borne unto Abraham, making sport" (Gen 21:9) [מְצַחֵק (*mĕsaḥēq*), "making sport," here understood as idolatrous worship], she immediately "said unto Abraham: 'Cast out this bondwoman and her son'

(Gen 21:10) lest my son learn of his ways." Hence "and the thing was very grievous in Abraham's sight on account of his son" (Gen 21:11), because he had become depraved. . . . He hated Ishmael because of his evil ways and sent him together with his mother Hagar away empty-handed and expelled him from his house on this account. [For otherwise] do you really think that Abraham, of whom it is written: "And Abraham was very rich in cattle" (Gen 13:2), could send away his wife and son from his house empty-handed without clothes or means of livelihood? But this is to teach you that when Ishmael became depraved he ceased to think about him. What became of him in the end? After he had driven him out, he sat at the cross-roads and robbed and molested passers-by, as it is said: "And he shall be a wild ass of a man: his hand shall be against every man" (Gen 16:12).

So Ishmael is characterized in the literature of "formative" Judaism as "doing evil works" by being involved in "strange worship" (cf. *Tg. Ps.-J., Tg. Onq., Tg. Neof.,* and *Frg. Tg.* on Gen 21:9) and as persecuting his younger brother Isaac, often by "shooting deadly arrows at him" when out hunting birds (cf. *Pesiq. R.* 48.2; *Pirqe R. El.* 30). And to these passages that speak of Ishmael's wickedness, numerous others can be added (e.g., *Gen. Rab.* 53.4; 62.5; *Exod. Rab.* 3.2; *Deut. Rab.* 4.5).

In fact, Ishmael and Esau are viewed in the rabbinic writings as wicked anomalies in an otherwise righteous line. The Babylonian Gemara *Pesah.* 119b pictures Abraham at the banquet for the righteous refusing to take the cup of grace offered him and saying: "I cannot say Grace, because Ishmael issued from me." And this lament regarding Ishmael, together with Esau, appears a number of times in the writings of the rabbis; for example:

b. Pesah. 56a (credited to Rabbi Simeon ben Lakish): "Perhaps, heaven forbid, there is one unfit among my children, like Abraham from whom there issued Ishmael, or like my father Isaac, from whom there issued Esau."

b. Šabb. 146a (credited to Rabbi Aliba ben Kahana): "Until three generations the lustful [strain] did not disappear from our Patriarchs: Abraham begat Ishmael, Isaac begat Esau, [but] Jacob begat the twelve tribes in whom there was no taint whatsoever."

Lev. Rab. 36.5: "From Abraham sprang Ishmael and all the sons of Keturah; from Isaac sprang Esau and all the chiefs of Edom; but Jacob's bed was perfect, all his sons being righteous."

Num. Rab. 2.13 (answering the question, Why are the righteous in Dan 12:3 compared to the stars rather than to the sun or moon?): "For this reason: Abraham was compared to the sun, Isaac to the moon, and Jacob to the stars. In the Messianic era the sun and moon will suffer humiliation, as it is said 'the moon will be abashed, the sun ashamed' [Isa 24:23]. The stars, however, will not be humiliated. Thus it will be with Abraham and Isaac, whose faces in the hereafter will blanch on account of their children: Abraham's because of Ishmael and the sons of Keturah; Isaac's on account of Esau and his chiefs. And as the stars will suffer no humiliation, so also will Jacob suffer no humiliation, for he will not need to feel shame [all his children being righteous]."

The story of the '*Aqēdâ* Isaac ("Binding of Isaac") also became an occasion to draw contrasts between Isaac and Ishmael. It was, in fact, a discussion between Isaac and Ishmael over their comparative degrees of righteousness that was seen by some rabbis to have been the occasion for the '*Aqēdâ* in the first place. Two passages, one from a Babylonian Gemara and one from the Targums, are particularly significant here and deserve to be quoted in full:

b. Sanh. 89b (credited to Rabbi Levi): "Ishmael said to Isaac: 'I am more righteous than you in good deeds, for you were circumcised at eight days [and so could not prevent your circumcision], but I at thirteen years [and so accepted circumcision willingly].' 'On account of one limb would you incense me?,' he [Isaac] replied. 'Were the Holy One, blessed be He, to say unto me: "Sacrifice yourself before me," I would obey.' Straightway, 'God did tempt Abraham' (Gen 22:1)";

Tg. Ps.-J. Gen 22:1 (the first part of which has been cited above with regard to the
contrast between Hagar and Sarah): "And it was after these things that Isaac and
Ishmael contended. Ishmael said: 'It is right that I should inherit what is the
father's, because I am his first-born son.' Isaac said: 'It is right that I should inherit
what is the father's, because I am the son of Sarah his wife, and you are the son of
Hagar the handmaid of my mother.' Ishmael answered and said: 'I am more
righteous than you, because I was circumcised at thirteen years; and if it had been
my will to hinder, they should not have delivered me to be circumcised. But you were
circumcised a child of eight days; if you had knowledge perhaps they could not have
delivered you to be circumcised.' Isaac responded and said: 'Behold now, today I am
thirty and six years old; and if the Holy One, blessed be He, were to require all my
members, I would not delay.' These words were heard before the Lord of the
universe, and immediately, the word of the Lord tested Abraham, and said to him,
'Abraham,' and he said, 'Here am I.'"

Similar contrasts between Ishmael and Isaac appear further on in the *'Aqēdâ* Isaac
story. In rabbinic tradition it was believed that the two young men who accompanied
Abraham and Isaac on their journey to Mt. Moriah (Gen 22:3) were none other than
Ishmael and Eliezer (cf. *Tg. Ps.-J.* Gen 22:3; *Lev. Rab.* 26.7). When they approached Mt.
Moriah, its peak was enveloped in a cloud that was visible to Abraham and Isaac but not
to Ishmael and Eliezer (cf. *Lev. Rab.* 20.2; *Eccl. Rab.* 9.7; *Pirqe R. El.* 31). *Pirqe R. El.* 31
even adds that when Isaac was about to be offered, Ishmael and Eliezer engaged in the
following shameless dispute:

Ishmael said to Eliezer: "Now that Abraham will offer Isaac his son for a burnt
offering, kindled upon the altar, and I am his firstborn son, I will inherit [the
possessions of] Abraham." Eliezer replied to him, saying: "He has already driven
you out like a woman divorced from her husband, and he has sent you away to the
wilderness, but I am his servant, serving him by day and by night, and I shall be the
heir of Abraham." The Holy Spirit answered them, saying to them: "Neither this
one nor that one shall inherit."

There is, however, no way of determining just how much of this rabbinic tradition
regarding Hagar and Ishmael had been developed by Paul's day, though the Targumic
elaborations suggest that at least some of it had. Furthermore, given the fact that the
contrasts in the story are readily apparent to any reader, similarities between Paul and the
rabbis do not necessarily imply either familiarity or dependence. Still, it is useful to note
that interest in the contrast of status between Hagar and Sarah and the contrast of
righteousness between Ishmael and Isaac was not unique to Paul, and it is possible to
speculate that in these matters Paul was dipping into certain streams of tradition that
were already flowing within Judaism, possibly even into a stream of tradition that was
being used against him by his judaizing opponents at Galatia.

Yet Paul was not interested in the contrasts of the Hagar-Sarah story for their own
sakes. Rather, he used them in what appears to be an ad hominem fashion in his
exhortations to his Galatian converts against what they had heard from the Judaizers—
that is, to align the negative side of the contrasts with his judaizing opponents. This raises
the question of whether there are any parallels in Jewish tradition to the way in which Paul
uses this story in Gal 4:21–31: How was it "contemporized" in the Judaism of Paul's day?
The most extensive utilization of the Hagar-Sarah story for contemporary purposes, of
course, is to be found in the writings of Philo. Like other Jewish commentators, Philo was
drawn to the contrasts of slave and free and the conflicts that resulted in the banishment
of Hagar and Ishmael. His own allegorical interpretation of the story, however, depends
on a further observation: that Abraham was able to be fruitful with Sarah only after he
had first produced offspring with Hagar.

For Philo, Hagar the handmaid symbolizes the preliminary learning that can be
obtained in the schools, that is, "grammar, geometry, astronomy, rhetoric, music, and

all the other branches of intellectual study" (*Congr.* 11)—with the fruit of the mating of the mind with this "lower instruction" being sophistry (*Congr.* 12), or producing a man like Ishmael "with his pretense of excessive openmindedness and his love of arguing for arguing's sake" (*Fug.* 209). Sarah, the mistress of the house, on the other hand, exemplifies virtue, and her offspring is true wisdom. Just as Hagar conceived before Sarah, so the search for wisdom must begin with the "lower branches of school lore"; but just as Hagar was expelled at the command of Sarah, so it is necessary to move beyond mere sophistry and mundane learning if one wishes to attain wisdom and virtue.

The Hagar-Sarah story provides for Philo, in fact, the basis for an entire allegorical treatise, "On Mating with the Preliminary Studies" (*De Congressu Eruditionis Gratia*), and is a recurring feature in Philo's writings (cf. esp. *Cher.* 3–10; *Poster.* 130–31; *Mutat.* 261; *Somn.* 1.240; *Fug.* 209–13; *Sacrif.* 43–44; *Quaest. Gen.* 3.19–35). The following is a representative sample of such passages:

Congr. 9–10: "For we are not capable as yet of receiving the impregnation of virtue unless we have first mated with her handmaiden, and the handmaiden of wisdom is the culture gained by the primary learning of the school course. For, just as in houses we have outer doors in front of the chamber doors, and in cities suburbs through which we can pass to the inner part, so the school course precedes virtue; the one is a road which leads to the other";

Congr. 12: "What is meant [by Abraham's unions with Hagar and Sarah] is a mating of mind with virtue. Mind desires to have children by virtue, and, if it cannot do so at once, is instructed to espouse virtue's handmaid, the lower instruction";

Congr. 14: "'Go in, then,' she says, 'to my handmaid, the lower instruction given by the lower branches of school lore, that first you may have children by her,' for afterwards you will be able to avail yourself of the mistress's company to beget children of higher birth";

Congr. 23: "Sarah, virtue, bears, we shall find, the same relation to Hagar, education, as the mistress to the servant-maid, or the lawful wife to the concubine, and so naturally the mind which aspires to study and to gain knowledge, the mind we call Abraham, will have Sarah, virtue, for his wife, and Hagar, the whole range of school culture, for his concubine";

Cher. 9: "When all this is come to pass [i.e., the name changes that mean that Abraham and Sarah have achieved true wisdom], then will be cast forth those preliminary studies which bear the name of Hagar, and cast forth too will be their son the sophist named Ishmael";

Leg. All. 3.244: "The wise Abraham complies with her [Sarah/virtue] when she recommends the course to follow. For at an earlier time, when he had not yet become perfect but, before his name had been changed, was still only inquiring into supramundane things, being aware that he could not beget seed out of perfect virtue, she advises him to beget children out of the handmaiden, that is school-learning, even Hagar. This name means 'Sojourning,' for he that is studying to make his home in perfect virtue, before he is registered as a member of her city, sojourns with the subjects learned in the schools, that he may be lead by these to apply his unfettered powers to virtue";

Quaest. Gen. 3.19: "'Hagar' is interpreted as 'sojourning' and she is a servant, waiting on a more perfect nature. And she is very naturally an Egyptian by race. For she is the study of school disciplines, and being a lover of wide learning, is in a certain sense a servant waiting on virtue, since school studies are serviceable to him who needs help in receiving it, inasmuch as virtue has the soul as its place, while the school studies need bodily organs; and Egypt is symbolically the body, (wherefore Scripture) rightly describes the form of the school studies as Egyptian. Moreover, it also named her 'sojourning' for the reason that sophistry is a sojourner in comparison with native virtue which alone is at home and which is mistress of intermediate education and provides for us through the school studies" (*Philo* I–X, ed. F. H. Colson et al. [LCL; London: Heinemann, 1929–62]).

Philo's Hagar-Sarah allegory bears several striking surface similarities to Paul's in Gal 4:21–31. Both depend on similar elements in the story: the contrast between slave and free; the two sons; the banishment of Hagar and Ishmael in favor of Sarah and Isaac. In both, Hagar and Ishmael represent a preliminary and preparatory stage that is superseded by something greater, rather than a totally negative and wicked quantity as is the case in rabbinic tradition. Yet these similarities may have arisen quite naturally from the Genesis account itself and demonstrate nothing more than that Paul and Philo both read Scripture. Apart from their desire to contemporize the story and certain surface similarities, the allegorical interpretations of Paul and Philo are sufficiently divergent to suggest independence.

When one looks into the rabbinic traditions for a similar contemporization of the Hagar-Sarah story in which the interpreter's opponents are identified with Hagar and Ishmael and so denounced or marginalized, one finds the potential but not the reality— that is, one finds all the elements being present, but not, with only rare and generally late exceptions, being brought together for polemical purposes.

There was, of course, as noted above, an extant rabbinic tradition that drew from the Ishmael and Esau stories the theological conclusion that the salvation-historical line did not include all of Abraham's offspring. Particularly quotable here is *Pesiq. R.* 48.2:

The Holy One, blessed be He, says: "I always love the pursued and hate the pursuers, as when Ishmael pursued his brother Isaac"—"And Sarah saw the son of Hagar the Egyptian... making sport" [Gen 21:9]. Because Ishmael shot arrows at Isaac—"As one who makes sport by shooting deadly arrows, and said, Am not I in sport?" [Prov 26:18–19]—the Holy One, blessed be He, loved Isaac, saying to Abraham: "Take now thy son" [Gen 22:2]. Our father Abraham replied: "I have two sons; Thou hast given me Isaac and Ishmael." God said: "Thine only son." Abraham replied: "Both are only sons; Isaac is an only son to Sarah and Ishmael an only son to Hagar." God said: "Whom thou lovest." Abraham replied: "Are there different areas of love within a man—one of more love for one son and of less love for the other? I love both of them." God declared: "Even Isaac—for it is Isaac I love because he is pursued" (cf. also *b. Ned.* 31a; *Gen. Rab.* 55.7; *Deut. Rab.* 4.5).

Ishmael was frequently identified with various non-Jewish groups, particularly the Arabs (e.g., *Pesiq. R.* 21.2–3; *Pirqe R. El.* 41; *Lam. Rab.* 3.1; cf. also *Jub.* 20:13; Josephus, *Ant.* 1.221), sometimes Gentiles generally (e.g., *Gen. Rab.* 45.8), and once or twice a foreign king (e.g., Nebuchadnezzar in *Exod. Rab.* 27.1). But most of these identifications of Ishmael with the Arabs, the Gentiles, or a foreign ruler are stated in a more or less matter-of-fact manner, with no explicit polemical or contemporizing edge to them (though possibly such should be seen as implied).

Closer parallels to Paul's contemporization in Gal 4:21–31, however, can be seen in the Qumran *War Scroll*, where in 1QM 2.13 the battle plans for the ninth year include an attack on "the descendants of Ishmael and Keturah," for here Ishmael is seen as one of the progenitors of the "Sons of Darkness." Likewise in *Gen. Rab.* 45.9, in a discussion of the phrases "he shall dwell" (Gen 16:12) and "he fell" (Gen 25:17), Ishmael seems to be identified either with Aretas, the king of Nabatea who attacked Aristobulus and besieged Jerusalem (cf. Josephus, *Ant.* 14.19–21), or with the Arabian prince who joined Vespasian's army in the siege and destruction of Jerusalem, and so read from the perspective of a contemporary situation of opposition. As well, *Pirqe R. El.* 30 and 32 speak of "the children of Ishmael" (Arabs? Gentiles?) bringing about oppression in the land in the last days, for which reason, it is said, Hagar's son was called Ishmael.

Going beyond the confines of the Hagar-Sarah story itself, there are numerous parallels to Paul's contemporizing of Scripture in various Jewish writings. The targumic interpretations of the Cain and Abel story of Gen 4, for example, which view the dispute that led to that fatal confrontation as being over the doctrine of the resurrection, obviously have the Sadducees in mind when depicting the nefarious figure of Cain. And Scripture is handled in similar fashion at Qumran, particularly in the treatment of Hab 2:17 in 1QpHab 12.3–4 where "Lebanon" (etymologically "white") stands for the Communal Council (who dressed in white) and "wild beasts" for the simple minded Jews who carry out the law, as well as in the treatment of Num 21:8 ("The Song of the Well") in CD 6.3–11 where "well" stands for the law, the "princes" who dig it for the members of the community, the "sceptre" or "staff" with which it is dug for "the expositor of the law," and "the nobles of the people" for those who carry out his ordinances (cf. 1QpMic 8–10 and CD 7.9–20 for other allegorical contemporizations).

With respect to the specific Hagar-Sarah story, though there is enough interest in the contrasts and conflicts of the story in Jewish writings to suggest that Paul's use of it was not entirely unique, there is no evidence that his particular allegorical treatment of it was following any Jewish prototype, particularly in the identification he makes between Hagar, Ishmael, Mt. Sinai, and the present city of Jerusalem, and in the contrast he sets out between "the Jerusalem that is above" vis-à-vis Mt. Sinai and the present city of Jerusalem. To understand Paul's Hagar-Sarah allegory, therefore, it seems that at least four factors must be taken into account: (1) Paul's Jewish heritage, which was not averse to highlighting the contrasts and conflicts of the story; (2) tendencies within the various streams of Judaism generally to contemporize the persons and places of the biblical narrative for their own purposes, whether such contemporizations be understood as allegorical or typological treatments; (3) the Judaizers' contemporization of the story, with the polemics of their usage probably directed against Paul; and (4) Paul's own ad hominem use, with his polemics directed against the Judaizers.

Comment

21 λέγετέ μοι, οἱ ὑπὸ νόμον θέλοντες εἶναι, τὸν νόμον οὐκ ἀκούετε, "tell me, you who want to be under the law, Do you not hear the law?" Paul begins his Hagar-Sarah allegory with the epistolary "verb of saying" λέγετέ μοι, "tell me," which serves to signal the start of a new subsection in the hortatory portion of his letter and to knit this subsection together with what has gone before (see Introduction, ciii–cvii; also the introductory comments to 4:12–6:10). His address is to all those within the Galatian churches, as in 3:1 (ὦ ἀνόητοι Γαλάται), and not just to a group among them that was prepared to follow a judaizing line, as W. Lütgert proposed (cf. Gesetz und Geist, 11, 88). If Paul had had in mind only some of the believers of Galatia he would probably have used the pronoun ὑμεῖς ("you") to identify them more precisely (cf. H. Schlier, Galater, 216; F. Mussner, Galaterbrief, 317). Furthermore, his inclusive use of personal pronouns and verbal pronominal suffixes suggests that all the Galatian Christians are being addressed, and not, as in a "Two-Front Theory," only those belonging to one of two groups within the churches: "Jerusalem that is above . . . is our mother" (v 26); "Now you, brothers, like Isaac, are children of promise" (v 28); "we are not children of the slave woman, but of the free woman" (v 31, italics mine).

In speaking of his addressees as "those who want to be under the law," Paul implies that his converts had not yet fully adopted the Judaizers' nomistic principles and practices (cf. 1:7; 4:17), though they were beginning to observe the fasts and festivals of the Jewish calendar (cf. 4:10) and were at the point of going further in observing the Jewish law (cf. 1:6; 3:3; 4:11). The Galatians were not yet ὑπὸ νόμον ("under the law") but ὑπὸ νόμον θέλοντες εἶναι ("who want to be under the law"). The expression ὑπὸ νόμον here obviously has the same meaning as in 3:22 and 4:4, where it refers in context to the nomistic regulation of life by Mosaic legislation (both written Torah and oral Torah), but also suggests that since Christ's coming, such a reversion to law for the living of life would really be, at least for Gentile Christians, a retrogression to legalism. On the other hand, the expression τὸν νόμον in the latter part of the verse, by its association with v 22 and the introductory formula γέγραπται ("it is written"), refers to the Scriptures wherein that legislation as written is set forth.

Some MSS and versions read ἀναγινώσκετε ("Do you not read the law?") rather than ἀκούετε ("Do you not hear the law?"; see *Note* a). But hearing played a very important role in the Jewish community, with the Torah being read aloud in the synagogues every Sabbath (cf. Acts 15:21). Furthermore, "to hear" in Jewish thinking is not just a physical activity. For to hear God's word is to internalize that word, to understand it, and to obey it. So in Isa 1:10 and 6:9–10, for example, "seeing," "hearing," "understanding," and "repenting" are used synonymously as part and parcel of one process. Likewise, the foundational confession of Judaism, the Shema (Deut 6:4), articulates the response of God's own in terms of hearing: "Hear, O Israel: the Lord our God is one Lord; and you shall love the Lord your God with all your heart, and with all your soul, and with all your might." Similarly, rabbinic study of Torah is expressed in terms of hearing: "I hear; I understand" (cf. D. Daube, *The New Testament and Rabbinic Judaism*, 55–62; G. Kittel, "ἀκούω," *TDNT* 1:218). So Paul's challenge is that if the Galatians would really "hear" the law—that is, understand it fully and respond to it aright—they would not regress to Jewish nomism, for, as he argued earlier, the law's purpose as a pedagogue was to function until the coming of Christ (cf. esp. 3:23–25).

22 γέγραπται γὰρ ὅτι Ἀβραὰμ δύο υἱοὺς ἔσχεν, ἕνα ἐκ τῆς παιδίσκης καὶ ἕνα ἐκ τῆς ἐλευθέρας, "for it is written that Abraham had two sons, one by the slave woman and the other by the free woman." γέγραπται ("it is written") is a standard Pauline formula that usually introduces biblical quotations (cf. E. E. Ellis, *Paul's Use*, 48–49, 156–85). Here, however, what follows is not a direct quotation from the OT, but rather a statement summarizing the stories about Abraham as found in several chapters of Genesis. This departure from Paul's usual exegetical procedure, as C. K. Barrett points out ("The Allegory," 9), is one hint that Paul is here responding to the scriptural arguments of his opponents, for here "it is written" does not identify a specific text but rather it "allows the genuine Old Testament foundation of the Judaizers' argument" (ibid.). A second hint as to the ad hominem nature of Paul's use of Hagar and her son Ishmael vis-à-vis Sarah and her son Isaac is the fact that none of the principals are named as the story begins, and thereafter in the main only descriptive epithets are used in referring to them: "Hagar" appears first in vv 24b–25, but then only to make an etymological-geographical point; "Isaac" first in v 28, but only to recall the obvious; and neither "Sarah" nor "Ishmael" appears at all. "The wording," as Barrett observes, "implies that the story is already before the Galatians; they will know that the slave is Hagar, the free woman Sarah. The articles are anaphoric in this sense" (ibid.). The Judaizers had evidently contemporized the Hagar-Sarah story in their argument to prove that since the promises were made to Abraham and his seed, who was Sarah's son Isaac, Gentile Christians had no share in the promise unless they submitted to the Mosaic law given to Isaac's posterity and were circumcised. The feminine noun παιδίσκη properly refers to age and not status, and so originally signified only "young woman"; but it became in later Greek the term for a female slave, and is frequently used in the LXX in this way (note esp. its use with reference to Hagar in Gen 16:1 LXX).

23 ἀλλ' ὁ μὲν ἐκ τῆς παιδίσκης κατὰ σάρκα γεγέννηται, ὁ δὲ ἐκ τῆς ἐλευθέρας δι' ἐπαγγελίας, "indeed, the one by the slave woman was born according to the flesh but the one by the free woman was born as a result of promise." The adversative ἀλλά (untranslated) sets up a further antithesis. For now it is not just one of social caste, whether slave or free, but also one having to do with the manner of each son's birth: the first by the natural process of procreation; the second because of God's promise. The antithesis, of course, is not one of mutual exclusion, as though Isaac's birth "as a result of, or through, promise" meant that he was not born as a result of normal sexual relations between Abraham and Sarah—that is, a "virgin birth" (contra J. Bligh, *Galatians*, 398–400). Rather, it has to do with ultimate causation, not merely mediate causation, to highlight the fact that Isaac's birth must be understood primarily in terms of God's promise to Abraham that his heir would be the son of his aged, barren wife Sarah. So while Ishmael's birth can be understood simply in terms of κατὰ σάρκα, "according to the flesh," or the natural processes of procreation, Isaac's must ultimately be seen as δι' ἐπαγγελίας, "as a result of, or through, promise." The text has been read as both δι' ἐπαγγελίας ("through promise") and διὰ τῆς ἐπαγγελίας ("through the promise"), with the MSS about equally divided (see *Note* c). In either case, however, reference is to God's promise to Abraham in Gen 15:4–6 and 17:15–21.

The affirmative particle μέν ("indeed") is omitted by some excellent textual witnesses (see *Note* b). Yet if Paul's use of the Hagar-Sarah story is seen as ad hominem throughout, μέν here (and in v 24) fits in, acknowledging, as it would, his opponents' rightful emphasis on the differences between the births of the two sons. For they were "indeed" right in seeing the contrast between the two sons as being not only that of status but also that of the ultimate explanation for their births, though they were terribly wrong, as he will spell out allegorically in what follows, in how they lined up matters and in the implications they drew.

24 ἅτινά ἐστιν ἀλληγορούμενα, "these things are [now] being interpreted allegorically." The neuter plural relative pronoun ἅτινα ("these things") has in mind in summary fashion all that has been said regarding Abraham, Sarah, Hagar, and their two sons in vv 22–23. The compound ἅτινα has taken over the function of the simple neuter plural relative pronoun ἅ, as it does also in 5:19 (cf. Phil 3:7; Col 2:23). A parallel feature is the use of the compound ἥτις for the simple ἥ in vv 24b and 26. As Burton points out, "the use of the relatives in the Pauline letters seems to indicate both a preference for the longer form in the nom. plur. and an ignoring of the distinction between these and the shorter forms" (*Galatians*, 257).

The verb ἀλληγορέω ("speak allegorically" or "interpret allegorically") is a late Greek word not found in the LXX but appearing first in Philo (*Cher.* 25); the noun ἀλληγορία ("allegory") appears first in Cicero (*Orat.* 94). Plutarch says that ἀλληγορία in late Greek replaced ὑπόνοια, which came then to mean "suspicion" (cf. F. Büchsel, "ἀλληγορέω," *TDNT* 1:260). Paul's use of the participle ἀλληγορούμενα here is the only occurrence of this word in the NT.

Allegorical interpretation has had a long and varied history. In Paul's day it was well developed, with varying forms present (cf. esp. R. P. C. Hanson, *Allegory and Event*, 11–64). Much has been made of the parallels between Philo's allegorical method of interpretation and Paul's Hagar-Sarah allegory (e.g., H. A. A. Kennedy, *Philo's Contribution to Religion* [London: Hodder & Stoughton, 1919] 40–41; for a summary of Philo's interpretive methods, see my *Biblical Exegesis in the Apostolic Period*, 45–48). What has not always been taken into account, however, is, as R. P. C. Hanson observes, that "the practice of allegorizing was much more widespread among Rabbis trained in a Palestinian tradition in Paul's day than has hitherto been realized, or than later Rabbinic literature was willing to admit" (*Allegory and Event*, 80; cf. J. Z. Lauterbach, *JQR* 1 [1911] 291–333, 503–31; J. Bonsirven, *RSR* 23 [1933] 522–24; D. Daube, 239–64; idem, "Alexandrian Methods of Interpretation and the Rabbis," 27–44).

Indeed, Paul's treatment of the Hagar-Sarah story "is explicitly and undisguisedly allegorical" (R. P. C. Hanson, *Allegory and Event*, 80; cf. K. J. Woollcombe, "Biblical Origins and Patristic Development of Typology," 42; H. J. Schoeps, *Paul*, 234). Many, of course, have preferred to call Paul's use of Scripture here "typological" or "figurative" rather than "allegorical," since it differs from what we know of the allegorical treatments of the first-century Alexandrian Jew Philo and the late third- and early fourth-century Alexandrian Christian Origen (e.g., John Chrysostom, Theodore of Mopsuestia, and Theodoret of Cyrrhus, who opposed Alexandrian hermeneutics; also many contemporary scholars, such as O. Michel, *Paulus und seine Bibel*, 110, and A. T. Hanson, *Studies in Paul's Technique and Theology*, 95, who see real differences between Paul and Philo). But Paul's treatment here is in line with Palestinian allegorical exegesis (see the articles cited above by Lauterbach, Bonsirven, and Daube), and so merits the appellative that he himself gives it—i. e., "allegorical interpretation." It is certainly not, however, to be equated with Philonic allegorical exegesis. For, as R. P. C. Hanson aptly notes:

> Paul is not here trying to emancipate the meaning of the passage from its historical content and transmute it into a moral sentiment or a philosophical truth, which is the almost invariable function of Alexandrian allegory. . . . [Rather,] he is envisaging a critical situation which took place under the Old Covenant (or, to be strictly accurate, before it but in prefiguration of it) as forecasting and repeated by a situation under the New Covenant. The 'similar situation' typology has here been strained and distorted in an unconvincing but highly Rabbinic fashion into allegory; that is all (*Allegory and Event*, 82).

What, then, does Paul mean by his use of the participle ἀλληγορούμενα, for ἀλληγορεῖν may mean either (1) "to speak or write allegorically," and so refer to the original intent of the speaker or writer, or (2) "to explain or interpret allegorically," and so have in mind how a text is handled by an interpreter? If we view Galatians simply as a piece of Greek prose that expresses Paul's own preferred exegetical practices throughout, then the former may be what is meant. Philo certainly viewed Scripture in this way. And Paul's allegorical treatment of Deut 25:4 ("the muzzled ox") in 1 Cor 9:9–10 leans heavily in this direction. So by analogy it may be argued that this is what Paul meant with regard to the biblical accounts of Hagar and Sarah: the story was originally given as an allegory and meant by its original author to be treated as such.

If, however, we view Paul's use of the Hagar-Sarah story here as ad hominem in nature—that is, responding in kind to some treatment of the same story by his Galatian opponents—then we need not see Paul as saying that allegory was built into the biblical narrative itself but that the biblical narrative is now being treated by the interpreter (whether the Judaizers, or Paul, or both) in allegorical fashion. The present passive participle suggests this latter view: Paul is saying that "these things are now being interpreted allegorically" (on Paul's allegorical treatments, see my *Biblical Exegesis in the Apostolic Period*, 126–29; also, of course, O. Michel, *Paulus und seine Bibel*, 109–11; J. Bonsirven, *Exégèse rabbinique et exégèse paulinienne*, 328–30; E. E. Ellis, *Paul's Use*, 51–54; R. P. C. Hanson, *Allegory and Event*, 80–83). As we noted in commenting on 3:10–14, C. K. Barrett has proposed that Paul's exegetical practices throughout Galatians "can be best explained if we may suppose that he is taking up passages that had been used by his opponents, correcting their exegesis, and showing that their Old Testament prooftexts were on his side rather than on theirs" ("The Allegory", 6). In line with such a proposal, Barrett's further point here is apropos: "His [Paul's] so-called allegorical treatment of Abraham and the two women was evoked not by a personal love of fantastic exegesis but by a reasoned case which it was necessary that he should answer" (ibid., 13).

R. P. C. Hanson is quite right to bring his discussion of 4:21–31 to a close with the following statement:

> It seems reasonable to conclude, then, that St Paul was quite ready to use allegory, and even to use it in order to evacuate the ordinances of the Torah of their literal meaning on occasion, but that he employed this allegory in a Palestinian rather than an Alexandrian tradition, and that in practice the bent of his thought lay so much towards typology rather than what we should strictly call allegory that he had in the course of his extant letters few occasions to indulge in allegory. His motives for using it were, as far as we can discover, far from being those of the Alexandrians, and especially Philo, who wanted by allegory to avoid the necessity of taking historical narrative seriously; Paul on the contrary used allegory as an aid to typology, a method of interpreting the Old Testament which, however fanciful some of its forms may be, does at least regard history as something meaningful. It is significant that there is no typology in Philo whereas Paul is full of it (*Allegory and Event*, 82–83).

All that is necessary to add to such a statement is Barrett's thesis regarding the ad hominem character of Paul's use of Scripture here and throughout Galatians (perhaps also elsewhere in Paul's letters, particularly where allegorical exegesis appears), and so to clarify "his motives for using" such a "fanciful" exegetical practice here. αὗται γάρ εἰσιν δύο διαθῆκαι, μία μὲν ἀπὸ ὄρους Σινᾶ, εἰς δουλείαν γεννῶσα, ἥτις ἐστὶν Ἁγάρ, "the women represent two covenants. One, indeed, is from Mt. Sinai and bears children unto slavery, which is Hagar." The postpositive conjunction γάρ may be used either in an explanatory or a continuative fashion, with perhaps the latter more likely (and so untranslated). The feminine plural demonstrative pronoun αὗται ("these") used substantivally refers to the women mentioned in vv 22–23. The verb εἰσιν in allegorical, parabolic, or figurative contexts means in effect "represents" or "stands for" (e.g., Philo, *Cher.* 25; Matt 13:38; Mark 14:24). Paul has used διαθήκη ("covenant") in his arguments of 3:15–18 in both a secular and a theological fashion, arguing *a minori ad maius* from one to the other (see *Comment* on 3:15 and 17). Here, however, he uses the term solely in its theological sense, meaning something like "a world order decreed by divine institution" that "contains God's definition of the basis and purpose of human life" (so Betz, *Galatians*, 244, if that definition is not too fulsome). What he means by "two covenants," of course, are the Old Covenant that is Torah-centered, under which the Judaizers were attempting to subsume the faith of Galatian Christians, and the New Covenant that is Christ-centered, which Paul proclaimed.

The affirmative particle μέν ("indeed") probably operates here as in v 23—that is, to acknowledge the correctness of a statement before going on to draw different conclusions. If so, then Paul is here acknowledging a connection made by the Judaizers between Hagar, Mt. Sinai, and slavery, which was made in Jewish tradition when talking about the Ishmaelities (Hagar's posterity) and their settling in the desert regions to the south. But while acknowledging such a connection, Paul goes on in what follows to turn it to his own advantage.

Paul has no problem in saying quite directly that the one covenant represents Hagar ("this is Hagar"). He leaves, however, the other covenant unrepresented, though obviously it is epitomized by Sarah. The feminine participle γεννῶσα ("bearing") may modify either the one covenant in view or the one woman in view, or both. Applied to the covenant it identifies those under this covenant as slaves; applied to Hagar it signifies that her children share her status of slavery.

25 τὸ δὲ Ἁγὰρ Σινᾶ ὄρος ἐστὶν ἐν τῇ Ἀραβίᾳ, "now Hagar stands for Mt. Sinai in Arabia." The beginning of v 25 presents us with two very vexed questions: (1) whether "Hagar" is to be read in the text, and (2) the meaning of the text if "Hagar" is included. The MSS and the church fathers are divided as to the inclusion or omission of "Hagar" (see *Note* e), and so also are present-day critical editions of the text, translations, and commentaries. Omitting "Hagar," the text would be translated: "Now Sinai is a mountain in Arabia" or "Mt. Sinai is in Arabia." The question with such a reading is: Why would Paul have included such a seemingly mundane bit of geographical information in such a highly polemical passage? The best answer to that question, assuming the omission, is that Paul's purpose was to point out that Mt. Sinai is in pagan territory, outside the land of promise and the stage of sacred history (e.g., H. Schlier, *Galater*, 218–19). But that explanation, though not without its parallels (cf. Acts 7:2–36 with its recital of foreign locations, which is evidently meant to show how God's great redemptive acts have usually taken place outside the Holy Land), seems forced here. Rather, since the inclusion of "Hagar" in v 25a is more susceptible to scribal modification than its omission, it seems best to retain it, despite its difficulties of interpretation.

Accepting such a reading, the question then is: How can "Hagar" be identified with Mt. Sinai? Many scholars have worked from the name itself, so associating it with the Arabic word *hağar* ("rock" or "cliff") that was used with reference to mountains (cf. the various treatments of Burton, *Galatians*, 260; J. Klausner, *From Jesus to Paul*, 456; J. W. Doeve, *Jewish Hermeneutics in the Synoptic Gospels and Acts* [Assen: Van Gorcum, 1954] 202; A. T. Hanson, *Studies in Paul's Technique and Theology*, 95–96; Betz, *Galatians*, 245; et al.). The major problem with this approach is that the Arabic *h* does not correspond to the Hebrew ה (*h*), except only roughly in sound. But usually it is assumed, as Betz says, that this "would not bother a man who is absorbed with 'allegory' and who would be guided even by the most superficial similarities" (ibid., 245). More likely, however, Martin McNamara is right to insist: "An explanation of the connection would seem to lie not so much in the text of v. 25a itself as in the constellation of ideas that we can with some probability presume to have been in Paul's mind" (*MS* 2 [1978] 27).

It is McNamara's thesis, which he convincingly argues in some detail, that not only were "most of the significant episodes of the desert wanderings and of the further Jewish traditions" centered in and around the Nabatean capital Petra, but also that the giving of the law on Mt. Sinai was believed by some to have taken place in that region; and so Paul, who himself may have resided in this region during his postconversion sojourn in Arabia mentioned in Gal 1:17, perhaps had this constellation of ideas in mind when saying "Now Hagar is (or, 'represents') Mt. Sinai in Arabia" (ibid., 27–41). Basing his argument on Jewish tradition as drawn principally from the Targums, but also referring to Arabic place names and Paul's own word association, McNamara concludes:

> Hagar, in fact, would be a very suitable designation for Sinai, and would be all the more appropriate if Sinai were believed to be in the vicinity of Petra, associated in the Jewish interpreted Bible [the Targums] with the dwelling place of Hagar, the bondwoman, and her son Ishmael. There was also a place named Hagra or Hagar (with an initial *heth*) in that area, and this name may also have been read or pronounced as Hagra or Hagar [with an initial *he*]. In fact, it is quite conceivable that this very place, Hagar, was regarded in some sections of Jewish tradition as the mount of revelation. Hagar, in fact, may have been a designation for Mount Sinai in the vicinity of Petra and at the heart of Arabia (ibid., 36).

"One may legitimately ask," McNamara interjects, "if the Galatians can be expected to have understood such a reference to Jewish tradition" (ibid.). To this he replies: "They probably did not. But this would not weaken the strength of the argument, since at times, particularly in moments of heightened tension, Paul seems to have written from the abundance of his own mind rather than from what his readers would be expected to know" (ibid., citing his *The New Testament and the Palestinian Targum to the Pentateuch* [AnBib 27; Rome: Biblical Institute, 1966], 182–88, on 2 Cor 3:17). In addition to McNamara's reply, however, one need also observe that an ad hominem interpretation of Paul's use of the Hagar-Sarah story, which postulates that Paul's Galatian converts had heard much already from the Judaizers regarding Hagar and her associations, understands that it is the Judaizers' explication of the story that Paul here responds to. Thus, Paul's Galatian converts seem to have been caught in a cross-fire of interpreted associations, with Paul's identification of Hagar with Mt. Sinai being more understandable and meaningful to them than can be demonstrated from the text itself.

συστοιχεῖ δὲ τῇ νῦν Ἰερουσαλήμ, δουλεύει γὰρ μετὰ τῶν τέκνων αὐτῆς, "and corresponds to the present city of Jerusalem, because she is in bondage with her children." If, as we understand it, the Hagar-Sarah story is being used by Paul in ad hominem fashion, with certain points of agreement between his opponents and himself acknowledged, here in associating Hagar with Jerusalem Paul goes beyond anything the Judaizers would have told the Galatian Christians—in fact, here, if not earlier, he takes a quite different line in the interpretation of the story than theirs.

The verb συστοιχέω ("stand in the same line") was originally a military term for soldiers aligned in the same rank or file, but came to connote more generally the idea of "corresponds to" (cf. Burton, *Galatians*, 261–62; G. Delling, "συστοιχέω," *TDNT* 7:669). Being in form a third person, singular, present verb, its logical subject is "Hagar": "Hagar corresponds to the present city of Jerusalem." The spelling Ἱεροσόλυμα ("Jerusalem") appears in 1:17, 18; 2:1 when Paul refers to his early visits as a Christian to Jerusalem, while here the name of the city is spelled Ἱερουσαλήμ. The former is more the profane designation used simply to identify the city; the latter is the Hebraic and LXX name used often with sacred connotations (see *Comment* on 1:17). Evidently in 1:17–18 and 2:1 Paul had simply the geographical site in mind. Here, however, particularly in antithesis to ἡ ἄνω Ἱερουσαλήμ ("the Jerusalem that is above") of v 26, his emphasis is on the religious significance of the city: the present city of Jerusalem to which the Judaizers looked as the source and support of their gospel.

For Jews generally, the salvation-historical line of Scripture began with Abraham, Sarah, and Isaac, extended on through Moses and the Torah given at Mt. Sinai, and came to focus in the present city of Jerusalem as the epitome of Israel's hopes regarding the law, the land, and the temple (cf., e.g., Josephus on Abraham, Sarah, Hagar, and their two sons in *Ant.* 1.183–93, 213–19). This is how the Judaizers, evidently, set out associations as well. For Paul, however, slavery and freedom were the most important factors to be taken into consideration when asking how the various participants in salvation history were to be understood. So Paul, in what was undoubtedly a shocking realignment of personages and places in a Jewish understanding of salvation history, sets out the line of slavery as follows: Hagar and her son Ishmael, who have to do with Mount Sinai, are to be associated with the present city of Jerusalem and her children, from whence the Judaizers came. For, says Paul, Jerusalem, like Hagar, "is in slavery with her children."

26 ἡ δὲ ἄνω Ἱερουσαλὴμ ἐλευθέρα ἐστίν, ἥτις ἐστὶν μήτηρ ἡμῶν, "but the Jerusalem that is above is free, and she is our mother." Structurally, vv 25 and 26 together comprise two halves of a chiasm, though with a lacuna or anomaly in the second part:

> A   Hagar
>
> B   Mt. Sinai
>
> C   slavery
>
> D   the present city of Jerusalem
>
> D^1 the Jerusalem that is above
>
> C^1 freedom
>
> B^1 (Mt. Zion)
>
> A^1 our mother.

Each item of v 26 deserves comment, including the lacuna where a positive counterpart to Mt. Sinai would be expected.

The idea of a "heavenly Jerusalem" ("the Jerusalem that is above") has a rich Jewish background. The concept has to do with the culmination of God's redemptive purposes in human history, the realization of God's reign in its totality. As such, it is an eschatological concept that describes Jerusalem as it will be at the end of time, often in contrast to what the city is at present. References to a "heavenly Jerusalem" are to be found in embryonic form in the Jewish Scriptures (e.g., Ps 87:3; Isa 54 [the opening verse of which Paul quotes in 4:27]; Ezek 40–48), in Jewish wisdom literature (e.g., Sir 36:13ff.; Tob 13), and in more developed form in the apocalyptic writings of Second Temple Judaism (cf. *1 Enoch* 53.6; 90.28–29; *2 Enoch* 55.2; *Pss. Sol.* 17.33; 4 Ezra 7:26; 8:52; 10:25–28; *2 Apoc. Bar.* 4.2–6; 32.2; 59.4; also of relevance here are 1QM 12.1–2 and 4QShirShab, which speak of angelic ministry in a heavenly temple). The idea of a "heavenly Jerusalem" in contrast to the present Jerusalem appears a number of times in rabbinic literature as well (e.g., *b. Ta'an.* 5a; *b. Ḥag.* 12b; *Gen. Rab.* 55.7; 69.7; *Num. Rab.* 4.13; *Midr. Pss.* 30.1; 122.4; *Cant. Rab.* 3.10; 4.4; *Pesiq. R.* 40.6), though without reflecting negatively on Judaism itself. This concept of a "heavenly" or "new" Jerusalem also epitomized the hopes of Jewish Christians, as in Heb 11:10, 14–16; 12:22; 13:14; and Rev 3:12; 21:2, where the full realization of God's kingdom and Christ's reign is set out in terms of a "heavenly" or "new" Jerusalem that was looked forward to by the patriarchs and is now experienced by Christians in inaugurated fashion.

Paul's description of "the Jerusalem that is above" as being "free" is largely dependent on the statement "who is our mother." For although the "heavenly Jerusalem" may be presumed to be not in bondage but free, Paul's argument for the freedom of Christian believers has rested largely on the depiction of the status of Sarah "the free woman" in vv 22–23, who, though unnamed, is the spiritual mother of the Galatians and of all Christians.

There is, however, as noted above, a lacuna or anomaly in Paul's chiastic arrangement of correspondences, for there is in the second part of the chiasm no positive counterpart to Mt. Sinai. This is particularly striking when compared to the contrasts between Mt. Sinai and Mt. Zion set out by the writer to the Hebrews in Heb 12:18–24, where the second part of that depiction begins with the words, "But you have come to Mt. Zion, to the heavenly Jerusalem, the city of the living God" (v 22). As Terence L. Donaldson has shown, the contrast between Mt. Sinai as the mountain of revelation and Mt. Zion as the mountain of eschatological redemption was a rising phenomenon in Second Temple Judaism (cf. *Jesus on the Mountain: A Study in Matthean Theology* [JSNTSup 8; Sheffield: JSOT Press, 1985] 30–83). But Paul does not here set out such a contrast. This is probably, first of all, because of Mt. Zion's connections in many Jewish minds with only an earthly Jerusalem, but also because many Jews still tended to conflate the symbolism of Mt. Sinai and Mt. Zion. So it may be supposed that to set out in explicit fashion a Mt. Zion transcendental symbolism in contrast to a Mt. Sinai historical symbolism would have introduced an ambiguity in many minds that would have worked against Paul's purposes. The fact that Heb 12:22 and the First Gospel equate eschatological redemption with Mt. Zion symbolism probably reflects an established Christian tradition that builds on a developed "mountain theology" in Second Temple Judaism (cf. Donaldson, ibid., 87–213). For Paul, however, to refer to Mt. Zion in the context of his polemic with the Galatian Judaizers would probably only have introduced an element of ambiguity, since they seem to have thought more in historical than transcendental terms and since they undoubtedly equated Mt. Sinai (historical revelation) and Mt. Zion (eschatological redemption) in their understanding of salvation history.

The reference to "Jerusalem that is above" as being "our mother" also draws on a rich Jewish heritage. For example, Ps 87 is a song that praises Jerusalem (Zion) as the mother of God's own, while Isa 66:7–11 describes Jerusalem (Zion) as a mother in labor bringing forth a son (cf. also Isa 50:1). Furthermore, in 4 Ezra 10 Zion is called "the mother of us all" (v 7), represented in Ezra's vision as a barren woman who becomes the heavenly Jerusalem and finally gives birth to a son (vv 25–57). Here in his Hagar-Sarah allegory, therefore, Paul conflates two Jewish traditions: the first, that of Sarah, the barren freeborn wife of Abraham, who was destined to be the mother of nations; the second, that of the holy city Jerusalem, the eschatological Zion, who symbolically is the mother of God's own.

The possessive pronoun ἡμῶν ("our") refers to all believers in Christ, not just to one group of Christians in Galatia. The reading πάντων ἡμῶν ("of us all"; see *Note* f) is evidently an attempt to highlight the inclusive nature of the personal pronoun. But the inclusion of "all," while significant for showing us how the pronoun was understood by the church fathers, is textually unnecessary. On the compound ἥτις for the simple relative pronoun ἥ, see *Comment* on ἅτινα at v 24.

27 γέγραπται γάρ, Εὐφράνθητι, στεῖρα ἡ οὐ τίκτουσα, ῥῆξον καὶ βόησον, ἡ οὐκ ὠδίνουσα, ὅτι πολλὰ τὰ τέκνα τῆς ἐρήμου μᾶλλον ἢ τῆς ἐχούσης τὸν ἄνδρα, "for it is written: Be glad, O barren woman, who bears no children; break forth and cry aloud, you who have no labor pains. Because more are the children of the desolate woman than of her who has a husband." γέγραπται ("it is written") here, as is usually the case in Paul's letters, introduces a specific biblical quotation, viz., Isa 54:1, which was a prominent oracle in Jewish eschatological expectation that had to do with the future glory of Zion (cf. Str-B, 3.574–75). The conjunction γάρ is used in a confirmatory manner in support of the identification of Sarah with "the Jerusalem that is above" and the claim that all Christians (including Gentile believers) have as their mother both Sarah and the heavenly Jerusalem.

According to the second of the seven *middôt* or interpretive principles ascribed to Rabbi Hillel, when the same word occurs in two separate passages, then the considerations of the one can be applied to the other (*gĕzêrâ šāwâ*, or interpretation by verbal analogy). Here the fact that Sarah was barren (cf. στεῖρα in Gen 11:30 LXX) allows Paul to connect Sarah with Isa 54:1, which also contains the word "barren" (cf. στεῖρα in Isa 54:1 LXX). Thus the "barren one" is also the city of Jerusalem, who, though barren, is the wife of the Lord (54:5–8) and should rejoice because she will be rebuilt by the Lord (54:11–12; cf. Tob 13:16–18) and because her sons will be taught by the Lord (54:13). In *Tg. Isa.* on 54:1 the city in question is explicitly identified as being Jerusalem: "Sing praises, O Jerusalem, who was as a barren woman who bore not . . . for more shall be the children of desolate Jerusalem than the children of inhabited Rome" (cf. also *Cant. Rab.* 1.5; 4.4); while in *Pesiq. R.* 32.2 Sarah is associated with the rebuilding of Jerusalem and Isa 54:1 is cited in support.

In Paul's allegorical treatment of the Hagar-Sarah story, Sarah is spiritual mother to Gentile Christians in Galatia as well as Jewish Christians ("our mother"), for she as the freeborn wife of Abraham bears children who are born free because of God's promise to Abraham. In fact, as Paul's proof text states, her children will be more—i.e., include not only the believing Jews but also the believing Gentiles—than the one who has a husband, viz., Hagar. Moreover, Sarah is "our mother" because as "the Jerusalem that is above" she stands in direct contrast to "the present city of Jerusalem," whose children (like those of Hagar) are children of slavery. Since, therefore, "the Jerusalem that is above" is an eschatological term expressing a reality that will exist in the future, Paul's use of it here for the experience of the Galatian believers implies that, as Paul understood matters, the Galatian believers had come into the eschatological situation of already participating in that future reality, in that the promise made to Abraham was fulfilled in Christ (cf. 3:16; 5:1).

28 ὑμεῖς δέ, ἀδελφοί, κατὰ Ἰσαὰκ ἐπαγγελίας τέκνα ἐστέ, "so you, brothers, like Isaac, are children of promise." Having given biblical support, Paul now spells out the consequences of his argument as set out in vv 22–27. The postpositive particle δέ functions here as a consequential connective ("so"). The personal pronoun ὑμεῖς ("you") is not only well supported externally (see *Note* g) but also required by the thrust of Paul's argument. For against the Judaizers' claim, Gentiles "in Christ"—apart from any Jewish nomistic lifestyle—are true sons and daughters of Abraham's freeborn wife Sarah and true children of the heavenly Jerusalem through God's promise made to Abraham. They are represented by Isaac, not Ishmael. Therefore they are "brothers" with all who come to God by faith through Christ, both Jews and Gentiles (on Paul's use of ἀδελφοί in Galatians for Gentile believers, see *Comment* at 1:11; also 3:15; 4:12, 31; 5:11, 13; 6:1, 18).

29 ἀλλ᾿ ὥσπερ τότε ὁ κατὰ σάρκα γεννηθεὶς ἐδίωκεν τὸν κατὰ πνεῦμα, οὕτως καὶ νῦν, "and just as it was then, where the one born according to the flesh persecuted the one born according to the Spirit, so it is even now." The truth of the conclusion of v 28 is now confirmed by the experience of the Galatians themselves, which Paul sees as an antitype of Ishmael's persecution of Isaac. On the face of it, ἀλλά introduces a fact that is in contrast to the statement of v 28. Logically, however, it provides a transition to the sentence of v 29 (so "and") rather than a contrast with v 28. The particles ὥσπερ ("just as") and οὕτως ("so") serve to introduce the protasis and apodosis of the sentence, with their accompanying temporal adverbs τότε ("then") and νῦν ("now") being reflective of Paul's fundamental understanding of eschatological fulfillment.

The contrast between the one born "according to the flesh" (κατὰ σάρκα) and the one born "according to the Spirit" (κατὰ πνεῦμα) picks up the contrast between Abraham's two sons in v 23, with κατά here, as there, having to do with "cause" or "means." Two features, however, need to be noted, for they differ slightly from what was stated in v 23 and their presence is of some significance in Paul's argument. The first is that here the emphasis is on the two types of people the two sons represent, those who live out their lives in terms of legal ordinances and those who live their lives by the Spirit's direction. The second is that those "like Isaac" are referred to as born "according to the Spirit." Paul's arguments from the Galatians' experience and Scripture in 3:1–14 were interlaced with references to "the Spirit" (cf 3:2, 3, 5, 14), but thereafter the word "promise" (or "promises") dominated the discussion (cf. 3:16, 17, 18, 21, 22, 29; 4:28), taking the place not only of "Spirit" but also of "gospel" (1:7–9, 11; 2:2, 5, 7, 14; 3:8) and "blessing" (3:8, 9, 14), and laying the basis for treatments of "inheritance" (cf. 3:18; 4:1–7, 21–31). Here, however, Paul uses κατὰ πνεῦμα ("according to the Spirit") in roughly synonymous fashion with δι᾿ ἐπαγγελίας ("as a result of promise") in v 23 and ἐπαγγελίας τέκνα ("children of promise") in v 28, with references to the Spirit being dominant thereafter (cf. 5:5, 16–18, 22, 25; 6:8). In effect, then, all of Paul's previous references to the gospel, the Spirit, the promise, the blessings, and the inheritance become focused here and throughout the rest of the letter in terms of the Spirit's presence and guidance in a believer's life.

Paul, of course, presumes a more developed account of the story of Ishmael and Isaac than the one presented in Scripture, for the Old Testament does not record anything about Ishmael's persecution of Isaac. There are, however, various Jewish traditions in the Targums and rabbinic writings that either understand מצחק (*mĕsaheq*, "making sport") of Gen 21:9 in a hostile manner (e.g., *Tg. Ps.-J.* Gen 21:9–11; *Tg. Onq.* Gen 21:9; *t. Soṭa* 6.6; *Pesiq. R.* 48.2; *Pirqe R. El.* 30; cf. also Josephus, *Ant.* 1.215) or depict Ishmael and Isaac as arguing with one another over the inheritance and as to who was most righteous (see above "Excursus: The Hagar-Sarah Story in Jewish Writings and Paul"). Probably most significant of these latter traditions is the one represented in *Tg. Ps.-J.* Gen 22:1 (cf. also *b. Sanh.* 89b) that identifies such an argument as the occasion for the '*Aqēdâ* Isaac (for the text, see above pp. 198–204). Thus by reference to what he sees as a confirming historical parallel, Paul identifies the Judaizers with Ishmael, who is of "the flesh" and a persecutor, and the Gentile believers of Galatia with Isaac, who is of "the Spirit" and persecuted.

30 ἀλλὰ τί λέγει ἡ γραφή; Ἔκβαλε τὴν παιδίσκην καὶ τὸν υἱὸν αὐτῆς, οὐ γὰρ μὴ κληρονομήσει ὁ υἱὸς τῆς παιδίσκης μετὰ τοῦ υἱοῦ τῆς ἐλευθέρας, "but what does the Scripture say? 'Cast out the slave woman and her son, for the son of the slave woman will never share in the inheritance with the son of the free woman.'" The climax of Paul's Hagar-Sarah allegory comes in the exhortation of v 30. Here Sarah's uncharitable words in Gen 21:10 are applied to the situation in Galatia, though Paul attributes them not to Sarah but to "the Scripture" and adapts them to the Galatian context by changing "my son Isaac" (LXX: τοῦ υἱοῦ μου Ἰσαάκ) to "the son of the free woman" (τοῦ υἱοῦ τῆς ἐλευθέρας). Probably the Judaizers of Galatia had themselves used Gen 21:10 against Paul, whose theology in their view was an "Ishmaelian" form of truth and so should be "cast out." Paul, however, having re-allegorized the Hagar-Sarah story from his own perspective, now uses the same exhortation against them to "enshrine the basic gospel truth: legal bondage and spiritual freedom cannot coexist" (Bruce, *Galatians*, 225).

The directive of v 30 is not a broadside against all Jews or Judaism in general (contra Burton, *Galatians*, 262, 267–68; Betz, *Galatians*, 251; et al.). Nor is it a call for Gentile believers to rise up and expel their Jewish Christian brothers and sisters, whoever they might be (contra J. Bligh, *Galatians*, 390–409, though, of course, Bligh rather ingeniously sees the Hagar-Sarah allegory as the climax of Paul's reply to Cephas at Antioch, which, he holds, runs with some interruptions from 2:14b through 5:13a). Paul's attitudes as expressed in Rom 11:13–32 and 14:1–15:13 negate both such views, despite Betz's claim that in Rom 9–11 "Paul had revised his ideas as compared with Galatians" (*Galatians*, 251). Rather, here in v 30 Paul calls for the expulsion of the Judaizers who had come into the Galatian congregations from the outside. Indeed, they were Jewish Christians. But that does not mean that Paul saw all Jewish Christians or all Jews in the same light. What Paul is saying here is much more specific: contrary to how the Judaizers may have used Gen 21:10 against him, in an allegorical treatment of the passage its message is really to be seen as directed against the troublers of the Galatian believers, and so the Galatian believers should "cast out" the Judaizers and their influence from the Christian congregations of Galatia.

31 διό, ἀδελφοί, οὐκ ἐσμὲν παιδίσκης τέκνα ἀλλὰ τῆς ἐλευθέρας, "Therefore, brothers, we are not children of the slave woman, but of the free woman." The question that comes directly to the fore in Paul's use of Abraham in 3:6–9, and that underlies all of his argumentation thereafter in 3:10–4:11, is: Who are Abraham's true children and heirs? Likewise in his hortatory use of the Hagar-Sarah story in 4:21–31 it is this question that permeates all the discussion. So in concluding his allegorical reinterpretation of the Hagar-Sarah story Paul makes an affirmation that serves as the conclusion of 4:21–31 (so Lightfoot, *Galatians* [1890], 184–85; Burton, *Galatians*, 267–69; Schlier, *Galater*, 228; Mussner, *Galaterbrief*, 334; et al.; contra Zahn, Lagrange, Bousset, et al., who consider v 31 to be the beginning of a new hortatory section), but also sets up the exhortations of 5:1–12 by reiterating the key features of "slavery" and "freedom."

The inferential conjunction διό ("therefore"), which appears rather than such more common concluding expressions as ὥστε ("therefore"), ἄρα ("therefore"), or ἄρα οὖν ("therefore"), is well attested, though variants are to be found in the textual tradition (see *Note* i). Its use here, rather than a stronger inferential expression, probably signals the fact that Paul himself realized the conclusion to be somewhat redundant (cf. v 28), yet wanted to say it again both to give a formal conclusion to his allegorical treatment of 4:21ff. and to set up the exhortations of 5:1ff. As in the conclusion of v 28, so here in its repetition Paul speaks of his converts as "brothers" (cf. *Comment* at 1:11). On the other hand, whereas in the conclusion of v 28 he used the pronoun ὑμεῖς (plural "you"), here he speaks of "we" (verbal suffix of ἐσμέν), thereby including himself with his Gentile converts as children "of the free woman."

Explanation

The argument of the Judaizers at Galatia seems clear. It is summarized by C. K. Barrett as follows: "The true descendants of Abraham are the Jews, who inhabit Jerusalem. Here are the true people of God; and it will follow that Jerusalem is the authoritative centre of the renewed people of God, now called the church. Those who are not prepared to attach themselves to this community by the approved means (circumcision) must be cast out; they cannot hope to inherit promises made to Abraham and his seed" ("The Allegory," 10). In developing their argument, it may be postulated that the Judaizers themselves allegorized the Hagar-Sarah story (1) to demonstrate how truth comes in two forms, an earlier elemental form and a later developed form, (2) to acknowledge that Ishmael was the firstborn son of Abraham but to insist that the inheritance came only through Isaac the progenitor of the Jews, (3) to align Paul's preaching with that earlier elemental form of truth, and so identify it as an "Ishmaelian" gospel, and (4) to use the statement recorded in Gen 21:10, "Cast out the slave woman and her son," against Paul in some manner. So it seems the Judaizers set up the lines of correspondence as follows: Hagar, Ishmael, and Paul are related to Abraham in some tangential fashion, but Sarah, Isaac, the Jews, the Mosaic law, Mt. Sinai, Jerusalem, the mother church of Jerusalem, and the Judaizers themselves are directly associated with Abraham and the God-ordained channels for the reception of the Abrahamic promise.

In sharp contrast, Paul contemporizes the Hagar-Sarah story from his own perspective, setting out the following line in salvation history: (1) Sarah the free woman and wife of Abraham, (2) her son Isaac, who was born as a result of promise, (3) Jerusalem that is above, who is the true mother of all believers, (4) his own proclamation of the Christian gospel, which focuses on freedom and promise, and (5) Gentile Christians of Galatia as true sons and daughters of Abraham since they are children of promise and children of the free woman.

At least four matters of note must be kept constantly in mind when reading Paul's Hagar-Sarah allegory. The first is that the central question dealt with by Paul in his use of both the example of Abraham in 3:6–9 and the Hagar-Sarah story in 4:21–31 is one of self-identification: Who are Abraham's true children? On this matter the Judaizers and Paul were diametrically opposed. Second, Paul is using the Hagar-Sarah story in an ad hominem fashion, and so his purposes and procedures must be seen in that light and not treated as the climax of his argument or as his own preferred procedure. Third, Paul's words here are specific, being directed against the Judaizers' message and activities, and so are not to be taken as broadsides against all Jewish Christians or Jews. And fourth, what Paul says in contemporizing the Hagar-Sarah story is as an explication of his overall exhortation to his Galatian converts given in 4:12: "become like me!" For Paul, though himself a Jewish Christian, focused his thoughts and life on being "in Christ" (cf. 2:20), not on a nomistic Jewish lifestyle (cf. 3:23–25), and so experienced both freedom and the benefactions of God's promise to Abraham.

Paul's Galatian letter, it must always be remembered, is not concerned just with "legalism," even though sadly it is often understood only in those terms. Rather, Galatians is principally concerned with "nomism" or whether Gentiles who believe in Christ must also be subject to the directives of the Mosaic law. The *propositio* of 2:15–21 sets out the matters agreed on (i.e., the impossibility of legalism for righteousness before God) and the matters of disagreement (i.e., the necessity of Jewish nomism for a proper Christian lifestyle) between Paul and his Jewish Christian opponents (see *Comment* on 2:15–21 for issues and definitions). Indeed, any nomistic position can become a legalistic one, for matters easily become intertwined and confused. So Paul deals first with legalism in his argumentation of 3:1–18, but primarily so as to set the stage for his primary polemic against nomism in 3:19–4:7 (see *Comment* on these sections). And his exhortations against the Judaizers in 4:12–5:12, particularly his Hagar-Sarah allegory of 4:21–31, are focused on repelling the call of the Judaizers to view the Jewish law as a necessary appendage or addendum to the Christian faith.

Christians today often have difficulty in understanding their faith vis-à-vis the Mosaic law. Legalism is not too difficult to define and renounce. But nomism continues in large measure within the Christian church generally and the lives of many believers in particular. Galatians, however, sets out a mandate for freedom, not only with regard to access before God but also with regard to a Christian lifestyle. Paul's allegorical reinterpretation of the Hagar-Sarah story speaks specifically to every attempt to govern the life of faith by nomistic direction. In what Paul says by way of exhortation regarding the spheres of "the flesh" and of "the Spirit" in what follows, this antithesis between faith and law in the life of the believer will be sharpened and teaching regarding "life in the Spirit" will be given.

3. Holding Fast To Freedom (5:1–12)

Bibliography

Barrett, C. K. *Freedom and Obligation*, 53–70. **Bradley, D. G.** "The TOPOS as a Form in the Pauline Paraenesis." *JBL* 72 (1953) 238–46. **Deissmann, A.** *Light from the Ancient East*, 324–34. **DeVries, C. E.** "Paul's 'Cutting' Remarks about a Race: Galatians 5:1–12." In *Current Issues in Biblical and Patristic Interpretation.* FS M. C. Tenney, ed. G. F. Hawthorne. Grand Rapids: Eerdmans, 1975, 115–20. **Dibelius, M.** *A Fresh Approach.* **Longenecker, R. N.** *Paul, Apostle of Liberty.* **Macgregor, W. M.** *Christian Freedom.* **Malherbe, A. J.** *Moral Exhortation.* **Merk, O.** "Der Beginn der Paränese im Galaterbrief." *ZNW* 60 (1969) 83–104. **Mulka, A. L.** "Fides quae per caritatem operatur." *CBQ* 28 (1966) 174–88. **Mussner, F.** *Theologie der Freiheit nach Paulus.* **Nauck, W.** "Das οὖν-paräneticum." *ZNW* 49 (1958) 134–35.

Translation

[1]For freedom Christ set us free! Stand fast, therefore,[a] and do not let yourselves be burdened again by a yoke of slavery.

[2]Mark my words! I, Paul, tell you that if you let yourselves be circumcised, Christ will be of no use to you at all. [3]Again[b] I testify to every man who lets himself be circumcised that[c] he is obligated to obey[d] the whole law. [4]You who are trying to be made righteous by law are alienated from Christ;[e] you are fallen away from grace. [5]For we by the Spirit through faith eagerly await the righteousness for which we hope. [6]For in Christ Jesus[f] neither circumcision nor uncircumcision has any value—only faith expressing itself through love.

[7]You were running well. Who cut in on you to be keeping you from obeying[g] the[h] truth? [8]That contrived persuasiveness does not[i] come from the one who calls you. [9]"A little yeast leavens[j] the whole batch of dough." [10]I am confident in the Lord[k] regarding you that you will take no other view. The one who is throwing you into confusion will suffer the judgment, whoever he may be. [11]Brothers, if I am still[l] preaching circumcision, why am I still being persecuted? In that case the offense of the cross has been abolished. [12]As for those who are troubling you, O that[m] they would go the whole way and emasculate themselves!"

Notes

[a]τῇ ἐλευθερίᾳ ἡμᾶς χριστὸς ἠλευθέρωσεν· στήκετε οὖν ("For freedom Christ set us free. Stand fast, therefore . . . ") is well supported by ℵ* A B P etc. There are, however, a number of variations in the textual evidence, with the data being, as Burton observes, "so complex as to make clear exposition of them difficult" (*Galatians*, 270). The chief variations have to do with (1) the association of an article and/or a relative pronoun with ἐλευθερίᾳ "freedom" (i.e., whether τῇ ἐλευθερίᾳ, or τῇ ἐλευθερίᾳ ᾗ or ᾗ ἐλευθερίᾳ), (2) the position of ἡμᾶς, "us" (i.e., whether ἐλευθερίᾳ ἡμᾶς Χριστός, or ἐλευθερίᾳ Χριστὸς ἡμᾶς, or Χριστὸς ἠλευθέρωσεν ἡμᾶς), and (3) the presence and position of οὖν, "therefore" (i.e., whether after στήκετε, or after ἐλευθερίᾳ, or omitted entirely). All of the variations apparently stem from the syntactical difficulty of τῇ ἐλευθερίᾳ ("for freedom") as a limitation of ἠλευθέρωσεν ("set free") and the absence of a transitional phrase or particle in 5:1a to connect with 4:31.

[b]πάλιν ("again") is omitted by D* G 1739 (10th-century minuscule) vg goth arm.

[c]ὅτι ("that") is omitted by ℵ* 062 (5th-century fragmentary uncial).

[d]ποιῆσαι ("to do," "to obey") is well attested, though πληρῶσαι ("to fulfill") is supported by 440 (12th-century minuscule) syr[h] Mcion (probably to harmonize with Gal 5:14; perhaps also Matt 5:17).

[e]ἀπὸ Χριστοῦ ("from Christ") is well supported by ℵ B C D etc., though some Syriac versions and the Coptic Bohairic reflect ἀπὸ τοῦ Χριστοῦ ("from the Christ").

ᶠ ἐν . . . Χριστῷ Ἰησοῦ is well attested, though Ἰησοῦ is omitted by B Mcion and Clement.

ᵍ The present infinitive construction μὴ πείθεσθαι ("not to obey") is well attested, though the imperative construction. μηδένι πείθεσθε is supported by G it vg⁵. If one accepted this Western reading, v 7b would be taken as two sentences: "Who cut in on you? Obey no one (in such a way as) not to obey the truth."

ʰ The article τῇ with ἀληθείᾳ ("truth") is absent in ℵ* A B etc., but present in p⁴⁶ C D G TR. Perhaps the article was inserted to conform to ἡ ἀλήθεια τοῦ εὐαγγελίου ("the truth of the gospel") of 2:5, 14. Yet the fact that Greek nouns are sufficiently definite of themselves with or without an article means that ἀλήθεια should be read as "the truth" whatever the evidence for or against the article.

ⁱ οὐκ ("not") is omitted by D* it Origen Ephraem, evidently because πεισμονή was understood in a positive sense as "conviction" or "obedience" rather than in a pejorative sense (see *Comment* at v 8).

ʲ The verb ζυμοῖ ("it leavens") is well attested, though δολοῖ ("it falsifies") is supported by D* itᵈ vg goth Mcion Marius Vict Ambst et al., evidently in an attempt to unpack the imagery of the proverb in prosaic fashion (perhaps also influenced by 2 Cor 4:2).

ᵏ ἐν κυρίῳ ("in the Lord") is omitted by B, probably by accident.

ˡ ἔτι ("yet," "still") is omitted by D* G it Ephraem.

ᵐ ἄρα ("so," "then," "therefore") rather than ὄφελον appears in p⁴⁶, thereby making this verse the conclusion of what goes before.

ⁿ The future indicative middle ἀποκόψονται ("they would emasculate themselves") is well attested, though the aorist subjunctive middle ἀποκόψωνται ("they would emasculate themselves") appears in p⁴⁶ D G.

Form/Structure/Setting

Martin Dibelius was the first to identify paraenesis or hortatory material as a distinctive type of material, claiming that the paraeneses of the New Testament and early Christian literature are made up of *topoi* or stock treatments of moral subjects that are frequently strung together without any necessary inner connections and used in a general fashion without any direct application to matters being addressed (cf. *A Fresh Approach*, 217–37; idem, *James*, passim). So he claims that the hortatory sections of Paul's letters differ in style from the argumentative sections, that they lack immediate relevancy to the issues at hand, that they serve only the general requirements of the churches—that, in fact, they have "nothing to do with the theoretic foundation of the ethics of the Apostle, and very little with other ideas peculiar to him" (*From Tradition to Gospel*, 238–39). And many have agreed with Dibelius, so viewing the Pauline paraeneses as being substantially traditional in content (i.e., stock moral aphorisms and cliches), largely stylistic in arrangement, and basically interchangeable without any direct relevance to the issues at hand.

Despite the claims of Dibelius and others, it must be insisted, however, that the exhortations of 5:1–12 are, in fact, directly relevant to all that Paul has said in chaps. 1–4. They give expression to Paul's deepest concerns about his Galatian converts and epitomize his attitude toward the entire Galatian controversy. All that Paul has argued for and exhorted previously in Galatians comes to focus here.

Structurally, the *exordium* of 1:6–10 and the hortatory statements of 5:1–12 form an *inclusio* for Paul's whole treatment of the judaizing threat in the body of his letter, for in both tone and expression they serve as the frame for all that he says regarding that threat. Of particular note are: (1) the sustained severity of 1:6–10 that is paralleled by the sustained severity of 5:2–12; (2) the reference in 1:6 to "deserting the one who called you" that is paralleled by the statement of 5:8 that "that persuasion does not come from the one who calls you," with, of course, "the

one who called/calls you" being a reference to God; (3) the expression "the grace
of Christ" in 1:6 that is paralleled by references in 5:4 to being "alienated from
Christ" and "fallen away from grace"; (4) the use of πάλιν ("again") in both 1:9 and
5:3 to set up corroborating statements; and most dramatically (5) the twice-
repeated anathema of 1:8–9 ("let him be accursed'") that is paralleled by the
threat of divine judgment of 5:10b ("the one who is throwing you into confusion
will suffer the judgment, whoever he may be") and the sarcastic cutting statement
of 5:12 ("I wish they would go the whole way and emasculate themselves"). In
effect, then, though references to the judaizing threat appear again in the
subscription (6:11–18, esp. vv 12–16), the *exordium* (1:6–10) and this last section
of Part 1 of the *exhortatio* (5:1–12) form an *inclusio* for Paul's arguments and exhortations regarding that threat in the body of his Galatian letter.

Looked at on its own, 5:1–12 falls into two parts. The first (vv 1–6) sets out a
ringing declaration of Christian freedom (v 1a) and closes with what appears to
be, in the main, a résumé or précis of what Paul said earlier in the letter regarding the gospel proclamation vis-à-vis the Judaizers' message (vv 5–6). In
between this declaration and this résumé are exhortations and warnings regarding
accepting the Judaizers' message (vv 1b–4). The second part (vv 7–12), as Betz
points out, "is set up in the style of the diatribe" and "is freer [than the first part],
appearing like a rambling collection of pointed remarks, rhetorical questions,
proverbial expressions, threats, irony, and, climaxing it all, a joke of stark sarcasm"
(*Galatians*, 264).

One may, indeed, speak of *topoi* or standardized forms in the Pauline paraeneses, for clearly Paul in exhorting (1) has certain patterns of expression that
repeat themselves in varying contexts, and (2) draws on much that seems to have
become fixed in the ethical tradition of the early church (cf. A. M. Hunter, *Paul
and His Predecessors*). With particular respect to 5:1–12, Wolfgang Nauck has
shown how the particle οὖν ("therefore") of v 1 often has a certain paraenetic
quality, connecting exposition and exhortation, and has identified the verb
στήκω ("stand") that appears also in v 1 as a *topos* in early Christian paraenesis
(*ZNW* 49 [1958] 134–35). Furthermore, the use of athletic imagery in v 7 seems
to have been common for Paul and other early Christians when speaking both of
their own labors in the gospel (cf. Gal 2:2; Phil 2:16; 2 Thess 3:1) and of the ethical life (cf. 1 Cor 9:24, 26; Heb 12:1), as V. C. Pfitzner has shown (*Paul and the Agon
Motif,* esp. 136ff.). As well, the use of proverbs in ethical exhortation (as in v 9),
an expression of confidence (as in v 10a), a threat of judgment (as in v 10b), and
even the "joke" of v 12 can all be related, directly or indirectly, to various *topoi* then
current among the ancients, whether Greek, Jewish, or Christian (cf. Betz,
Galatians, 254, 270).

But to deny the applicability of Paul's exhortations in Galatians (whether from
5:1 onwards or 5:13 onwards) is to draw an inference that is not based on the
evidence. Robert Funk is too polite when he says, "Dibelius may have overstated
his case" (*Language, Hermeneutic, and Word of God,* 270 n. 76). Betz is much more
forthright: "Martin Dibelius's definition ['we call parenesis a series of different
and often unconnected exhortations with a common address'] is clearly too
vague" (*Galatians*, 253–54; Betz's observation regarding Dibelius's work in this
area is also appropriate: "His treatment of the subject is little more than a random
collection of diverse material from a wide range of authors" [ibid., 254 n. 7]).

Comment

1 τῇ ἐλευθερίᾳ ἡμᾶς Χριστὸς ἠλευθέρωσεν, "for freedom Christ set us free!" Chap. 5 begins rather abruptly and rather strangely, for it has no transitional phrase or particle to connect it with what has gone before and it uses the dative τῇ ἐλευθερίᾳ ("for freedom") in a manner that seems peculiar. It was undoubtedly for these reasons that so many textual variations came about in the MSS, versions, lectionaries, and church fathers' quotations (see *Note* a). Yet, as Burton points out, "the weight of external evidence. . . strongly favours τῇ ἐλευθερίᾳ ἡμᾶς Χριστὸς ἠλευθέρωσεν· στήκετε οὖν, and the originality of this reading is confirmed by the fact that it accounts for all the rest" (*Galatians*, 271). It may be that τῇ ἐλευθερίᾳ is "a primitive error" or early scribal corruption for ἐπ' ἐλευθερίᾳ ("for freedom") as Westcott and Hort speculated (cf. 5:1 in their "List of Suspected Readings," *The New Testament in the Original Greek* [London: Macmillan, 1881]) and as many influenced by Westcott and Hort have thought probable (e.g., G. G. Findlay, *Galatians*, 300; Burton, *Galatians*, 271; et al.). But though such a reading would bring v 1 into conformity with v 13, it is unnecessary and unlikely in light of more cogent explanations of the grammar (see below).

In 5:1a Paul states with emphasis the indicative of the Christian gospel: "For freedom Christ has set us free!" His use of ἐλευθερία ("freedom") springs immediately from the statement and vocabulary of 4:31: "Therefore, brothers, we are not children of the slave woman, but of the free woman." In fact, the expression τῆς ἐλευθέρας ("of the free woman") that appears throughout the Hagar-Sarah allegory (vv 22, 23, 30, 31) furnishes the linguistic basis for all that follows in chap. 5 regarding the freedom of believers in Christ. But the idea of freedom is not confined in Galatians to 4:21–31 and what follows in chap 5. In the salutation of the letter (1:1–5) Paul spoke of Christ giving himself "in order that he might rescue us from the present evil age" (v 4); in the *narratio* (1:11–2:14) his emphasis was on freedom for Gentile believers from the restrictions imposed by the Jewish law, with that freedom being termed "the freedom we have in Christ Jesus" (2:4) and equated with "the truth of the gospel" (2:5); and throughout the *probatio* (3:1–4:11) the stress was on no longer being under Jewish prescriptions but having new relationships established "in Christ," with that stress coming to fullest expression in 3:26–28. As Betz aptly says: "ἐλευθερία ("freedom") is the central theological concept which sums up the Christian's situation before God as well as in this world. It is the basic concept underlying Paul's argument throughout the letter" (*Galatians*, 255; cf. my *Paul, Apostle of Liberty*; F. Mussner, *Theologie der Freiheit nach Paulus*).

Because of its linguistic and conceptual ties to the Hagar-Sarah allegory (i.e., an affirmation of "freedom," a call to "stand fast," and a warning about "slavery"), many have considered 5:1 to be the conclusion of 4:21–31 (so, e.g., Souter, UBSGT, Wey, Moffatt, NEB, and such commentators as Lightfoot, Findlay, Ramsay, Duncan, Cole, and Bruce). Others, however, see 5:1 as the heading of a new paragraph, which, though "taking off at a word" from the Hagar-Sarah allegory, introduces a new set of exhortations (so, e.g., Phillips, Knox, JB, NIV [as indicated by the inserted headings], and such commentators as Burton, Mussner, and Betz). Still others prefer to view 5:1 in a more transitional fashion as both a summary of 4:21–31 and a preface to 5:2–12, thus setting it out as a separate paragraph but understanding it to function in a bridging fashion (so WH, Nestle, AmT, ASV, RSV, Berkeley). But the lack of a transitional phrase or particle in the best supported text of 5:1a seems to suggest that this verse was not meant only as the conclusion of the Hagar-Sarah allegory. Furthermore, the parallel expressions τῇ ἐλευθερίᾳ ("for freedom") and ἐπ᾽ἐλευθερίᾳ ("for freedom," "to be free") of 5:1 and 5:13 respectively highlight the fact that each of these verses should be seen as heading up its own section of exhortation. It seems best, therefore, to take the indicative statement of 5:1a as the summary of all that Paul has argued and exhorted regarding the judaizing threat from 1:6 through 4:31, with then 5:1b–12 being his concluding exhortations vis-à-vis that threat in which he urges his converts to hold fast to the freedom they have in Christ.

The major syntactical problem of v 1a is how to understand τῇ ἐλευθερίᾳ as a limitation of the verb ἠλευθέρωσεν ("set free"). Commonly it has been read as a dative of instrumentality or causality ("by" or "through the freedom"), with the relative pronoun ᾗ ("by which") either seen as implied or directly expressed in association (so τῇ ἐλευθερίᾳ ᾗ in corrected copies of D, in E K L and the majority of cursives, in the Peshitta and Harclean versions of the Syriac, and in Marcion, Basil, Chrysostom, Theodore of Mopsuestia [Latin], Theodoret, et al.). Understood in such a fashion, the verse reads: "Through the freedom by which Christ has set us free, stand fast." Lightfoot, in fact, insisted, "The reading τῇ ἐλευθερίᾳ without ᾗ is so difficult as to be almost unintelligible" (*Galatians* [1896], 202).

Yet since Adolf Deissmann's discovery that τῇ ἐλευθερίᾳ was used in the "sacral manumission procedures" of the day to signal destiny or purpose (cf. *Light from the Ancient East*, esp. 326–28), commentators have been more prepared to speak of τῇ ἐλευθερίᾳ here as being a "dative of goal, destiny, or purpose" and so parallel in meaning to ἐπ᾽ ἐλευθερίᾳ of 5:13 (e.g., C. K. Barrett, *Freedom and Obligation*, 55; cf. C. F. D. Moule, who comments: "Gal. v.1 τῇ ἐλευθερίᾳ . . . ἠλευθέρωσεν (if correct reading) seems to be an *emphatic* use, not strictly *instrumental*" [*An Idiom-Book of New Testament Greek*, 44 n. 2, italics his). A similar use of the dative may be found in the phrase τῇ ἐλπίδι ἐσώθημεν ("for hope we were saved") of Rom 8:24, which picks up the expression ἐφ᾽ ἐλπίδι ("unto hope") of Rom 8:20. Understood in this way, Gal 5:1a is a ringing declaration of the indicative of the gospel: "For freedom Christ set us free!"

στήκετε οὖν καὶ μὴ πάλιν ζυγῷ δουλείας ἐνέχεσθε, "stand fast, therefore, and do not let yourselves be burdened again by a yoke of slavery." The second half of v 1 begins with the imperative στήκετε ("stand fast"), which builds on the declaration of the first half of the verse and so contains the inferential particle οὖν ("therefore"). στήκω is a Koine Greek verb in the present tense that is formed from the classical perfect ἕστηκα. It appears as the equivalent of ἵστημι ("stand") in Mark 3:31; 11:25; John 1:26; Rom 14:4; 2 Thess 2:15; and Rev 12:4. It is also used elsewhere in Paul's letters with intensive force in hortatory contexts: 1 Cor 16:13, "stand fast in the faith"; Phil 1:27, "stand fast in one spirit"; Phil 4:1, "stand fast in the Lord" (cf. 1 Thess 3:8). Here in v 1b, of course, "in freedom" is to be supplied.

The passive imperative ἐνέχεσθε ("be held in," "be ensnared") with the dative is well attested in both classical and Koine Greek in the sense of "be subject to" or "be burdened by." The word ζυγός ("yoke") was current in an honorable sense for Torah study and for various kinds of governmental, social, and family responsibilities, as in *m. 'Abot* 3.5: "R. Nehunya b. Ha-Kanah [c. A.D. 70–130] said: 'He who

takes upon himself the yoke of the Law, from him shall be taken away the yoke of
the kingdom and the yoke of worldly care; but he who throws off the yoke of the
Law, upon him shall be laid the yoke of the kingdom and the yoke of worldly care.' "
Also used in an honorable way are such expressions as "the yoke of the kingdom
of heaven" and "the yoke of the commandments" (cf. *m. Ber.* 2.2), "wisdom's yoke"
(cf. Sir 51:26), and, of course, Jesus' invitation to "take my yoke upon you and learn
from me . . . for my yoke is easy and my burden is light" (Matt 11:29–30). But "yoke"
was also used figuratively in antiquity for any disagreeable burden that was
unwillingly tolerated, like slavery (cf. Sophocles, *Ajax* 944; Herodotus 7.8.3;
Plato, *Leg.* 6.770E; Demosthenes 18.289; Gen 27:40 LXX; 1 Tim 6:1). And
paralleling Paul's use here in 5:1b is the statement attributed to Peter in Acts 15:10:
"Now then, why do you try to test God by putting on the necks of the [Gentile]
disciples a yoke that neither we nor our fathers have been able to bear?"

The use of the word πάλιν ("again") does not mean that before becoming
believers in Christ the Galatians had been under the "yoke" of the Jewish law.
Rather, in Paul's words, they had been under τὰ στοιχεῖα τοῦ κόσμου ("the basic
principles of the world"), which for them meant paganism. Yet in Paul's view, from
the perspective of being "in Christ," Judaism and paganism could be lumped
together under the rubric "the basic principles of the world" (see *Comment* on 4:9),
and so a leaving of Christian principles for either one or the other was a
renunciation of freedom and a return "again" to slavery. "The essential point," to
quote Karl Rengstorf, "is that the νόμος is here on the same level as the στοιχεῖα
τοῦ κόσμου. Both rob man of his freedom" ("ζυγός," *TDNT* 2:899).

Summarizing, therefore, all that he has argued and exhorted from 1:6 through
4:31, Paul sets forth in 5:1 the essence of the Christian proclamation and a
believer's response vis-à-vis the Judaizers' message: "For freedom Christ set us
free! Stand fast, therefore, and do not let yourselves be burdened again by a yoke
of slavery." As Betz aptly expresses it: "The whole sentence states in a very concise
form both the 'indicative' and the 'imperative' of Christian salvation in the
Pauline sense" (*Galatians*, 256).

2 Ἴδε ἐγὼ Παῦλος λέγω ὑμῖν ὅτι ἐὰν περιτέμνησθε, Χριστὸς ὑμᾶς οὐδὲν
ὠφελήσει, "mark my words! I, Paul, tell you that if you let yourselves be circumcised, Christ will be of no use to you at all." With this verse Paul's remarks about
the judaizing threat take on a severer tone than has been expressed since the
exordium of 1:6–10, and he sustains that tone up through the cutting comment of v 12.
The first three words of the sentence, while not strictly necessary to the sentence's
thought, serve to emphasize the importance of what follows. ἴδε is properly the
imperative of εἶδον ("see," "look," "perceive") and could easily be considered identical to ἰδού ("behold," "look"), but it came to function in rather stereotyped fashion
as an opening particle meaning something like "you see" or "mark my words" (cf.
the use of ἴδετε in 6:11). Elsewhere in Galatians Paul uses ἐγώ ("I") for emphasis
(cf. 1:12; 2:19–20; 4:12; 5:10–11, 16–17), and elsewhere in his letters he uses ἐγὼ
Παῦλος ("I, Paul") to add the weight of his personal apostolic influence to what he
says (cf. 2 Cor 10:1; Eph 3:1; Col 1:23; 1 Thess 2:18; see also the closing subscriptions
of Col 4:18 and 2 Thess 3:17). So here as he begins v 2 he lays stress on the
importance and seriousness of what he has to say in what follows up through v 12.

The form of the conditional clause ἐὰν περιτέμνησθε ("if you let yourselves be
circumcised"), being a third class conditional construction (ἐάν with the subjunctive

in the protasis and any form of the verb in the apodosis), implies that the Galatians' circumcision was a fact still pending (cf. 1:6; 4:9–10). περιτέμνησθε as a present subjunctive is conative in force, and so suggests that Paul is not thinking of just the future act of being circumcised but of his converts' present decision to become circumcised. The expression Χριστὸς ὑμᾶς οὐδὲν ὠφελήσει ("Christ will be of no use to you at all") may be thought, because of the future tense of ὠφελέω ("help," "aid," "benefit," "be of use to"), to have the future eschaton in mind, meaning thereby that Christ will not come to your aid or help you on the day of judgment. But the absence of any reference to the Parousia or eschatological judgment in this verse and the use of the aorist verbs κατηργήθητε ("alienated") and ἐξεπέσατε ("fallen away") in v 4 make it evident that the future Paul has in mind dates from the time they begin to contemplate seriously becoming circumcised. Paul is not opposed to Jewish Christians continuing to live out their lives as circumcised individuals and in a nomistic fashion (cf. 1 Cor 7:17–24; see also my *Paul, Apostle of Liberty*, 245–67). What he strenuously opposes is the imposition of circumcision and a nomistic lifestyle on Gentile believers as being necessary for living out their Christian faith in a proper fashion, for that takes us right back to the basic issue of righteousness (both forensic and ethical) as being based on either "works of the law" or faith in "the faithfulness of Jesus Christ" (see *Comment* on 2:15–16). For Gentiles to revert to the prescriptions of the Jewish law as a necessary form of Christian lifestyle is, in effect, to make Christianity legalistic rather than Christocentric, and so not to have Christ's guidance in one's life.

3 μαρτύρομαι δὲ πάλιν παντὶ ἀνθρώπῳ περιτεμνομένῳ ὅτι ὀφειλέτης ἐστὶν ὅλον τὸν νόμον ποιῆσαι, "again I testify to every man who lets himself be circumcised that he is obligated to obey the whole law." The postpositive particle δέ is here not adversative but connective, setting up a coordinate reason why the Galatians should not even think of letting themselves become circumcised: because not only would they suffer the loss of Christ's direction and aid in their lives, but they would also bring themselves under a heavy legal burden. The verb μαρτύρομαι ("testify," "bear witness," "affirm") stems from the noun μάρτυς, which was a legal term for testimony or witness and often figuratively used of one who gave witness (so a "martyr" was one who witnessed even to the extent of death). Without an objective accusative, μαρτύρομαι signifies not a call for others to bear witness to something but a solemn declaration on the part of a speaker or writer as to what follows. πάλιν ("again") may refer to a statement previously made to the Galatians when Paul was with them, since the content of v 3 is not identical to that of v 2 nor does v 3 repeat anything previously said in the letter (so Burton, *Galatians*, 274–75). The omission of πάλιν in some MSS (see *Note* b) is probably because some scribe (or scribes) saw that v 3 was not repeating v 2 or any explicit wording of the letter given previously. Still, here πάλιν probably has generally in mind what has just been said in v 2 and so calls attention to v 3 as a reinforcement of what was said there, much as πάλιν of 1:9 sets up a parallel between what is said in 1:8 and what is said in 1:9, with the latter reinforcing the former. For as Bruce points out: "When he was with them there was probably no occasion to mention circumcision. The occasion to mention it had only recently arisen" (*Galatians*, 229; so also Lightfoot, *Galatians* [1890], 203).

The fact that Paul here points out that circumcision obligates one to keep all of the prescriptions of the Mosaic law implies that the Judaizers had not as yet mentioned this. They were urging the Galatians to accept circumcision so as to be more fully related to Abraham, the Abrahamic promise, and the Jewish nation, and they had persuaded them to adopt the Jewish cycle of sabbaths, festivals, and high holy days (cf. 4:10), evidently so as to signal their separation from other Gentiles. In effect, then, Christians in Galatia had accepted the Judaizers' counsel to signal their separation from the Gentile world by keeping the Jewish cultic calendar, and they were seriously contemplating signaling their union with the Jewish world by accepting circumcision. Before they do, however, Paul wants to make it plain that with circumcision comes obligation "to obey the whole law."

Gal 5:3 (cf. also 3:10) has been variously described as "Paul's misrepresentation of Pharisaism" (so A. D. Nock, *St. Paul* [New York: Harper, 1938] 29) or "his overstrained definition of the requirements of the Law" (so G. F. Moore, *Judaism in the First Centuries of the Christian Era*, 3 vols. [Cambridge, MA: Harvard University Press, 1927–30] 3:150 n. 209; cf. W. H. P. Hatch, "The Pauline Idea of Forgiveness," in *Studies in Early Christianity*, ed. S. J. Case [New York: Century 1928] 347; K. Lake, *Paul: His Heritage and Legacy* [London: Christophers, 1934] 70–72). It is possible, of course, to argue that 5:3 reflects more Paul's own Christian understanding of Torah than that of any segment of Second Temple Judaism. Nonetheless, it yet remains true that a doctrine of the necessity of doing all the law was not absent in early or formative Judaism. The Mishnah speaks of being "heedful of a light commandment as of a weighty one" (*m. 'Abot* 2.1), of running "to fulfil the lightest duty even as the weightiest" (*m. 'Abot* 4.2), and it recounts how a reader at the scourging of an apostate or immoral man is to read the ominous words of Deut 28:58–59: "If thou wilt not observe to do all the words of this law" (*m. Mak.* 3.14; cf. *Comment* on Gal 3:10). The Gemaras tell of Rabbi Gamaliel II's turmoil over Ezek 18:1–9, "he that does *all* these things shall live" (*b. Sanh.* 81a, though see Rabbi Akiba's rejoinder countering Ezek 18:1–9 with Lev 18:24), and of Rabbi Jose's teaching that liability is incurred for any infraction (*b. Šabb.* 70b). The Midrashim report that Rabbi Huna taught that adultery is the transgression of all the commandments (*Num. Rab.* 9.12 on Num 5:14). The Tosephta, arguing on the principle that Torah and all of life constitute a single whole stemming from God, insists that the breaking of one commandment reveals a previous denial of the Almighty (*t. Šebu.* 3.6). On the same principle, 4 Maccabees has the aged Eleazar say to his torturer Antiochus: "The transgression of the Law, be it in small things or in great, is equally heinous, for in either case equally the Law is despised" (4 Macc 5:20–21; cf. Sir 7:8: "For in respect of one sin thou art not without guilt"). So also in the DSS the emphasis is on doing all the commandments (e.g., 1QS 1.14; cf. W. D. Davies, "Paul and the Dead Sea Scrolls," 281, n. 80, who reports that he counted seventy-three instances in 1QS alone where the expression "all" is used in connection with doing the law). And in the NT, parallel to Paul's statement of 5:3 is Jas 2:10: "For whoever keeps the whole law, and yet stumbles at one point, is guilty of breaking all of it" (for an excellent treatment of Jas 2:10 along these lines, see J. B. Mayor, *The Epistle of St. James* [London: Macmillan, 1892] 86). It seems, therefore, that David Daube has not overstated the case in saying: "The inter-dependence of all precepts, their fundamental equality, the importance of even the minor ones, or apparently minor ones, because of their association with the weightiest—these were common themes among the Tannaites" (*The New Testament and Rabbinic Judaism*, 251).

4 κατηργήθητε ἀπὸ Χριστοῦ οἵτινες ἐν νόμῳ δικαιοῦσθε, τῆς χάριτος ἐξεπέσατε, "you who are trying to be made righteous by law are alienated from Christ; you are fallen away from grace." Continuing his litany of dire consequences of accepting the Judaizers' message, Paul now adds to "Christ will be of no use to you at all" (v 2) and you are "obligated to obey the whole law" (v 3) the most damning statements of all: "you are alienated from Christ" and "you are fallen away from grace." The Judaizers must have assured the Galatians that in accepting supervision for their lives from the prescriptions of the Mosaic law they were not forsaking Christ or renouncing grace, but rather were completing their commitment to both. Paul, however, tells them just the opposite: commitment to Christ and commitment to legal prescriptions for righteousness, whether that righteousness is understood in forensic terms (i.e., "justification") or ethical terms (i.e., "lifestyle" and expression), are mutually exclusive; experientially, the one destroys the other.

Here in v 4 Paul directly addresses the Galatians using the generic relative plural pronoun οἵτινες ("whoever," "everyone who"), though with the compound οἵτινες being equivalent to the simple relative pronoun οἵ ("you who") as is common in Pauline usage (see *Comment* on Paul's use of compound relative pronouns for simple relative pronouns at 4:24). Such a direct address carries greater force than simply statements of principle as given in vv 2–3. Paul's emphasis in v 4 is on the two aorist verbs and their respective genitive constructions: κατηργήθητε ἀπὸ Χριστοῦ ("you are alienated from Christ") and τῆς χάριτος ἐξεπέσατε ("you are fallen away from grace"), with the positioning of the two verbs at the beginning and end of the sentence signaling where the stress is to be placed, for both the beginning and end positions in a Greek sentence were often reserved for items to be emphasized. The present tense of δικαιοῦσθε indicates that the verb is to be taken as conative in force, signaling their present thought or attempt regarding some future action (thus, "you who are thinking about" or "trying to be made righteous"). The phrase ἐν νόμῳ is either locative ("in the sphere of law") or instrumental ("by law"), with either one being equivalent to ἐξ ἔργων νόμου ("on the basis of the works of the law") of 2:16. The articular τῆς χάριτος ("from the grace") identifies the grace in mind as being the grace of God or of Christ, which, as Paul saw it, was distinctive to his proclamation of the gospel (cf. 1:6). Used together in one sentence, the two aorist verbs denoting a past event viewed as a simple fact coupled with a present conative verb have a certain rhetorical force, as if to say: "Your legal attitude toward righteousness, even though you have not as yet accepted circumcision, has already resulted in your alienation from Christ and fall away from grace." For Paul, it was not circumcision as such that was a problem (cf. 6:15a). Jewish believers in Christ were circumcised and could live out their faith in nomistic fashion without denying the gospel, as he could also (cf. my *Paul, Apostle of Liberty*, esp. 245–67, and Appendix: "Christianity in Jerusalem"). Rather, it was the attempt to combine a legal attitude toward life with faith in Christ that Paul denounces as being incompatible.

5–6a ἡμεῖς γὰρ πνεύματι ἐκ πίστεως ἐλπίδα δικαιοσύνης ἀπεκδεχόμεθα. ἐν γὰρ Χριστῷ Ἰησοῦ οὔτε περιτομή τι ἰσχύει οὔτε ἀκροβυστία, "for we by the Spirit through faith eagerly await the righteousness for which we hope. For in Christ Jesus neither circumcision nor uncircumcision has any value." After speaking negatively in vv 2–4, Paul sets out in vv 5–6 a series of brief positive statements that are, in fact, largely a résumé or précis of what he said before in the *propositio* (2:15–21) and *probatio* (3:1–4:11). That these two verses constitute in the main a précis of what was said before seems to be signaled by the repeated use of γάρ, with the two appearances of the postpositive conjunction expressing neither cause nor inference, continuation nor explanation, but rather, in fashion similar to the conjunction ὅτι, introducing a series of abbreviated statements of significant theological importance (on Paul's use of γάρ to introduce quotations, see *Comment* at 3:27)—statements that may be supposed to be known already to Paul's addressees from their reading the earlier portions of his letter.

Of all the instances of the first person pronoun in Galatians, the use of ἡμεῖς ("we") here could be seen most readily as Paul identifying himself with his Gentile converts. Nonetheless, its appearance here is still somewhat strange, for the pronoun "you" and the second person plural verbal suffix appear consistently in vv 1–4 before vv 5–6 and afterwards consistently in vv 7–10. If, however, Paul is here principally summarizing what he said before, and in those contexts Jewish Christians are in view (cf. *Comment* at 2:15; 3:23–25; 4:5; see also 3:13, which is probably a pre-Pauline Jewish Christian confession), then the use of ἡμεῖς and the first person plural verbal suffix -ομεθα in v 5 is understandable and not to be taken as an exception to his usual usage. Paul's identification with his Gentile converts seems not, in fact, to be signaled in Galatians by his use of the first person plural pronoun or verbal suffix but by his use of the term ἀδελφοί ("brothers"), as appears later in this section at v 11 (cf. 1:11; 3:15; 4:12, 28, 31; 5:13; 6:1, 18).

Understanding vv 5–6a, then, as Paul's own précis of what he said earlier in the *propositio* and *probatio*—or, as Betz characterizes the content of these verses, as "a series of dogmatic abbreviations which had been used before in the letter" (*Galatians*, 262)—we may speak of Paul's emphases and order of thought in Galatians as follows: first, πνεύματι ("by the Spirit"), where he began his argument with his converts in 3:2–5; then ἐκ πίστεως ("through faith"), which is what he discusses in setting out Abraham as the example of faith, in exegeting Scripture, and in developing his theological arguments in 3:6–18; then ἐλπίδα δικαιοσύνης ("the hope of righteousness") that Christians "eagerly await," which undergirds all of Paul's thought; then ἐν Χριστῷ Ἰησοῦ, which comes to most dramatic expression in 2:26–29; and finally οὔτε περιτομὴ . . . οὔτε ἀκροβυστία ("neither circumcision . . . nor uncircumcision"), which linguistically parallels "neither Jew nor Greek" of 3:28 and conceptually summarizes all that Paul proclaimed. Burton has said of v 6: "For the disclosure of the apostle's fundamental idea of the nature of religion, there is no more important sentence in the whole epistle, if, indeed, in any of Paul's epistles. Each term and construction of the sentence is significant" (*Galatians*, 279). And that is true of v 5 as well, particularly when combined with v 6.

6b ἀλλὰ πίστις δι' ἀγάπης ἐνεργουμένη, "only faith expressing itself through love." The clause "but faith expressing itself through love" seems to be Paul's addition to the précis of his teaching given in vv 5–6a, though not less important because of that. Its added character is suggested by the facts that (1) the word ἀγάπη ("love") does not appear earlier in Galatians, and (2) though "faith" and "love" appear often in his other letters, they are nowhere else in his letters brought into immediate association. It seems, therefore, that, having given a précis of his teaching, Paul realizes he needs to emphasize more directly the ethical dynamic inherent in the relationship of being "in Christ Jesus." So as Burton expresses it: "Anticipating the objection that freedom from law leaves the life without moral dynamic, he answers in a brief phrase that faith begets love and through it becomes operative in conduct" (*Galatians*, 280). On the vexing questions (1) whether the participle ἐνεργουμένη is middle or passive, and (2) whether transitive or intransitive, see A. L. Mulka, "Fides quae per caritatem operatur," *CBQ* 28 (1966) 174–88; also Mussner, *Galaterbrief*, 354.

7 ἐτρέχετε καλῶς· τίς ὑμᾶς ἐνέκοψεν [τῇ] ἀληθείᾳ μὴ πείθεσθαι, "you were running well. Who cut in on you to be keeping you from obeying the truth?" While the first half of this section on "Holding Fast to Freedom" is, as Betz notes, a "highly condensed section," the second half beginning with v 7 "is freer, appearing like a rambling collection of pointed remarks, rhetorical questions, proverbial expressions, threats, irony, and, climaxing it all, a joke of stark sarcasm" (*Galatians*, 264). In effect, having argued and exhorted at length, Paul now brings his treatment of the judaizing threat to a close with this loose collection of comments and remarks.

The figurative use of an athlete running in a stadium to represent living one's life is frequent in Paul (cf. 2:2; also 1 Cor 9:24–27; Phil 3:14; 2 Tim 4:7; Acts 20:24). Such athletic imagery for life was common in the ancient world (cf. O. Bauernfeind, "τρέχω, δρόμος, πρόδρομος," *TDNT* 8:226-35; V. C. Pfitzner, *Paul and the Agon Motif*). Here in v 7 the imperfect form of ἐτρέχετε καλῶς ("you were running well") alludes to the Galatians' past responses to the gospel (cf. 4:13–15), with the implication being that at present their response was not that good. The verb ἐγκόπτω ("hinder," "thwart," "block the way") in the context of a race suggests tripping or otherwise interfering with a runner, which inevitably had to do with one runner cutting in on another as they ran and so impeding the other's progress (cf. C. E. DeVries, "Paul's 'Cutting' Remarks about a Race: Galatians 5:1–12," 118–19). In the foot races of the Greek festivals there were rules against tripping or cutting in on an opponent (cf. E. N. Gardiner, *Greek Athletic Sports and Festivals*, 146), just as there are today. Thus Paul asks his Galatian converts: "Who cut in on you to be keeping you from obeying the truth?" The question, of course, is rhetorical and calls for the same answer as the question of 3:1, "Who bewitched you?" In both cases it was the Judaizers.

The verb ἐνέκοψεν ("hindered," "cut in on") is an aorist and functions in a resultant fashion, so signaling what the Judaizers already did in obstructing the progress of the Galatian believers. The infinitive πείθεσθαι ("to obey"), however, is in the present tense and signals a progressing, ongoing activity. Coupled with the negative particle μή ("not") it signifies "to be keeping you from obeying." The lack of the article τῇ in some MSS may signify that ἀληθείᾳ ("truth") should be understood in a qualitative sense (so Burton, *Galatians*, 282), though since Greek nouns are sufficiently definite of themselves, whether with or without an article, ἀληθείᾳ here should probably be read as "the truth" in either case (as some MSS attempt to make explicit, perhaps to conform with 2:5, 14; see *Note* h). Rather than making a noun definite, Greek articles tend to specify. But there is no doubt which truth Paul has here in mind, whether with or without the article.

8 ἡ πεισμονὴ οὐκ ἐκ τοῦ καλοῦντος ὑμᾶς, "that contrived persuasiveness does not come from the one who calls you." The Judaizers had evidently presented their message as God's message encapsulated in Scripture. Paul, however, believed their work and influence to be without divine backing and totally of their own making. The term πεισμονή is a rare word that appears only here in the NT and for the first time in any Greek writing. It can mean "persuasion" as an activity, "conviction" as an accomplished fact, or "obedience." In that Epiphanius later associates it with "empty rhetoric" (*Adv. Haer.* 30.21.2) and Chrysostom with "flattery," contrasting it with God's power (οὐ πεισμονὴ ἀνθρωπίνη, ἀλλὰ θεοῦ δύναμις "not human persuasion, but the power of God"; *Hom.* 1.2 on 1 Thessalonians), it seems best to understand it in a pejorative manner as meaning humanly "contrived persuasiveness" in contrast to God's will and purpose. The article ἡ with πεισμονή identifies that contrived persuasiveness as being what was just spoken of in v 7, its immediate antecedent. By τοῦ καλοῦντος ("the one who calls you") is meant God, as in 1:6. This sentence, then, which is wholly negative, states in sarcastic fashion Paul's opinion of the Judaizers: their work and influence have nothing to do with God's will and purpose.

9 μικρὰ ζύμη ὅλον τὸ φύραμα ζυμοῖ, "'a little yeast leavens the whole batch of dough.'" The occurrence of these exact words in 1 Cor 5:6, introduced by the epistolary formula οὐκ οἴδατε ("do you not know") and the quotation formula ὅτι ("that"), suggests that both there and here Paul is using a proverbial saying having to do with the tendency of small matters to become large concerns and so to dominate a given situation. In 1 Cor 5:6 the proverb has to do with an incestuous man whose conduct had the potential of corrupting the whole Corinthian church. Here it has to do with a false theology that was perverting the Galatian churches. While in one of Jesus' parables the leavening influence of yeast is compared positively to "the kingdom of heaven/God" (Matt 13:33//Luke 13:21//*Gos. Thom.* 96), most often in the NT and antiquity yeast was used figuratively as a negative symbol for the penetrating and corrupting influence of evil (cf. Mark 8:15, par.; 1 *Clem.* 5.6; Ignatius, *Mag.* 10.2; Plutarch, *Quaest. Rom.* 109 [2.289F]; Justin, *Dial.* 14.2.3; *Ps.-Clem. Hom.* 8.17).

10 ἐγὼ πέποιθα εἰς ὑμᾶς ἐν κυρίῳ ὅτι οὐδὲν ἄλλο φρονήσετε, "I am confident in the Lord regarding you that you will take no other view." With an abruptness that characterizes the various comments and remarks of vv 7–12, Paul now turns from the discouraging aspects of the Galatian situation to an expression of confidence regarding his converts. The verb πέποιθα ("I am confident") reflects Paul's past attitude toward his converts, but also the perfect tense signals his present confidence regarding them. The emphatic ἐγώ ("I") emphasizes the personal, subjective character of his confidence, as though saying: However others may evaluate matters, I at least have confidence. εἰς with the accusative plural pronoun ὑμᾶς identifies the persons toward whom this confidence is directed ("regarding you"); ἐν κυρίῳ designates the basis for Paul's confidence ("in the Lord")—with ἐν κυρίῳ here (and forty-six more times in Paul's other letters) being equivalent to ἐν Χριστῷ (cf. Gal 1:22; 2:17, and twenty-four more times in Paul's other letters), ἐν Χριστῷ Ἰησοῦ (cf. Gal 2:4; 3:14, 26, 28; 5:6, and thirty-seven more times in Paul's other letters), and similar expressions found elsewhere in Paul (see *Comment* at 3:26). What Paul is confident about is expressed as ὅτι οὐδὲν ἄλλο φρονήσετε ("that you will take no other view"), which evidently refers back to what was said in vv 8 and 9: (1) the Judaizers' "contrived persuasiveness" is not from God, and (2) there is real danger that their message will pervert the churches.

Just how, amidst their present waverings and undecidedness, Paul can be confident about his converts' final response is a matter that goes beyond any normal reading of the situation. Paul, however, found the basis for his hopes and the ground of his confidence not in the way the situation seemed to be working itself out but "in the Lord" (for similar expressions of confidence "in the Lord" see Rom 14:14; Phil 2:24; 2 Thess 3:4). As Bruce observes: "He knows how the logic of the gospel works, and if they have really received the gospel (as he is convinced they have), they must accept the same logic and think no differently (οὐδὲν ἄλλο φρονήσετε) from himself" (*Galatians*, 235).

ὁ δὲ ταράσσων ὑμᾶς βαστάσει τὸ κρίμα, ὅστις ἐὰν ᾖ, "the one who is throwing you into confusion will suffer the judgment, whoever he may be." Of itself, the present substantival participle ὁ ταράσσων ("the one who is disturbing," "unsettling," "throwing into confusion") may refer to a particular individual, whether known or unknown to Paul, and to any situation of disturbance, whether past, present, or future. But in association with the plural substantival participles οἱ ταράσσοντες ("those confusing") of 1:7 and οἱ ἀναστατοῦντες ("those troubling") of 5:12 that refer to these same opponents, ὁ ταράσσων here must be taken as a generic singular. And in context, what Paul has in mind in referring to "confusion" is certainly the agitation within the Galatian churches caused by the Judaizers. Likewise, of itself the future indicative verb βαστάσει ("he will bear," "endure," "suffer") gives no precise indication as to when in the future the errorists would suffer judgment. But in association with τὸ κρίμα ("the judgment"), which by its articular form suggests God's eschatological judgment, Paul is likely thinking of the Judaizers as coming under God's judicial condemnation at the end of time and not just as experiencing church discipline (cf. *Comment* on ἀνάθεμα ἔστω at 1:8–9).

The conjunction ἐάν in Koine Greek frequently replaces the classical particle ἄν after a relative pronoun (cf. 5:17; 6:7; also Acts 3:23). The vagueness of the generic expression "whoever he may be" implies either that Paul did not know the identities of the agitators in Galatia, for they were certainly not his converts and had entered the churches after he left, or that knowing who they were he preferred to name no names, thereby relegating them to anonymity by a shroud of obscurity.

11 ἐγὼ δέ, ἀδελφοί, εἰ περιτομὴν ἔτι κηρύσσω, τί ἔτι διώκομαι, "brothers, if I am still preaching circumcision, why am I still being persecuted?" Without any preparation of the reader for what follows, Paul here adds another statement to his series of comments and remarks in vv 7–12. It seems that in coming to an end of his treatment of the judaizing threat he feels it necessary to add something further—something evidently occasioned by a false claim made by his opponents—that Paul actually did believe in circumcision and preached it elsewhere in his missionary activity and/or earlier in his ministry, though withheld from the Galatians in order to win their approval (cf. 1:10). Perhaps the Judaizers charged Paul with advocating circumcision because of their garbled version of the Titus episode at Jerusalem (cf. 2:1–5), or, if Galatians be dated later than we have proposed (see *Introduction*, lxxii–lxxxvii), because of Paul's circumcision of Timothy (cf. Acts 16:1–3). Perhaps the charge arose from their knowledge that Paul approved of Jewish believers in Jesus expressing their faith in the traditional forms of Judaism (cf. 1 Cor 7:17–20). Or perhaps they simply knew that Paul himself continued to live a basically Jewish lifestyle (cf. 1 Cor 9:19–23; see also my *Paul, Apostle of Liberty*, 245–63). What they failed to appreciate, however, is that while Paul saw it as perfectly legitimate for Jewish Christians to express their faith in Jesus through the traditional Jewish practices, he strenuously opposed the imposition of those practices on Gentile Christians either for full acceptance by God or as a normative way of life.

κηρύσσειν περιτομήν ("to preach circumcision") is, it seems, Paul's own way of expressing the situation, for it stands in contrast to κηρύσσειν Χριστόν ("to preach Christ"), which is how he usually characterizes his message (cf. Phil 1:15; also 1 Cor 1:23). This has occasioned some to suggest that Paul is not here reacting to an actual charge against him but simply presenting a hypothetical possibility (e.g., Mussner, *Galaterbrief,* 359 nn. 114, 116). Yet though restated in his own words, Paul's question is most likely a response to a charge he knows was being made against him. The presence of the adverb ἔτι ("yet," "still") with κηρύσσω may reflect his opponents' words, but its repetition by Paul implies an acknowledgment on his part that there was a time when he preached circumcision. They may have used the adverb in a logical fashion ("despite what he says, Paul *still* advocates circumcision when it suits his purpose") or in a temporal fashion ("he used to advocate circumcision, either before his conversion to Christ or in an earlier phase of his Christian ministry, and he *still* does when he finds it expedient"). But without any contextual indication that it is to be taken in a logical fashion and with no information in any of his letters that he ever advocated circumcision (particularly for Gentile believers) after he became a Christian, we are left with only the temporal interpretation of ἔτι as having reference to his pre-Christian life and activities. Paul's testimony is: I preached that way once (i.e., before my conversion to Christ), but no more—whatever my opponents say about me. And the practical proof that even his opponents know this, despite what they say about him, is that they treat him not as a friend but as an opponent, and so persecute him and his converts (cf. 4:29).

ἄρα κατήργηται τὸ σκάνδαλον τοῦ σταυροῦ, "in that case the offense of the cross has been abolished." The inferential particle ἄρα ("so," "then," "therefore") may here conclude 5:1–11 (so, e.g., Betz, *Galatians,* 269) or be the reason for what is stated in 5:11a (so, e.g., Mussner, *Galaterbrief,* 360). But in that it is used elsewhere in Galatians to conclude entire sections (cf. 2:21; 3:29; 6:10), it should probably also be seen as signaling Paul's conclusion to his entire discussion of the "judaizing threat" in 1:6–5:11, paralleling ἄρα in 6:10, which concludes his treatment of "libertine tendencies" in 5:13–6:10—with v 12 then thrown in as an additional, sarcastic comment.

The term σκάνδαλον ("stumbling block") with παγίς ("trap," "snare") originally meant something that turns out to be a trap (cf. Josh 23:13 LXX; Pss 69:22 [68:23 LXX]; 141:9 [140:9]; Isa 8:14 Symm. and Theod.; 1 Macc 5:4; Rom 11:9 quoting Ps 69:22), but came to be used on its own for that which gives offense, causes revulsion, or arouses opposition (cf. Sir 7:6; 27:23; Jdt 5:20). The phrase τὸ σκάνδαλον τοῦ σταυροῦ ("the offense of the cross") is probably one that Paul coined himself (cf. 1 Cor 1:23), stemming from his own pre-Christian reactions as a Pharisaic Jew and encapsulating several essential features of his theology of the cross (cf. 3:1; 5:24; 6:12–14). κατήργηται as a perfect, passive verb ("has been abolished") implies that the preaching of circumcision is antithetical to and entirely nullifies the preaching of Christ crucified. It is this point that Paul has been making throughout his discussion of the judaizing threat, and so he closes his treatment of that threat with the repetition of this essential antinomy.

12 ὄφελον καὶ ἀποκόψονται οἱ ἀναστατοῦντες ὑμᾶς, "as for those who are troubling you, O that they would go the whole way and emasculate themselves." Having concluded his treatment of the judaizing threat (cf. ἄρα, "therefore," of v 11), Paul now adds an additional, sarcastic comment meant to caricature and discredit his opponents. The objects of Paul's sarcastic comment are οἱ ἀναστατοῦντες ὑμᾶς ("those troubling you"), which, in line with the plural substantival participle οἱ ταράσσοντες ("those confusing") of 1:7 and the generic singular substantival participle ὁ ταράσσων ("the one throwing into confusion") of 5:10b, identifies the Judaizers within the Galatian churches. The form ὄφελον probably arose as the first person singular second aorist of the verb ὀφείλω ("owe," "be indebted"), but came to be treated as a fixed term for expressing a wish ("O that," "I would that")—an unattainable wish with an imperfect or aorist indicative verb, but a wish viewed as perhaps attainable with a future indicative verb. In Pauline usage the wish is always set in an ironic context (cf. 1 Cor 4:8; 2 Cor 11:1).

The key feature of the sentence is the third person future indicative middle verb ἀποκόψονται. Greek commentators consistently translated it as a term for self-mutilation. John Chrysostom, for example, read v 12, "If they will, let them not only be circumcised, but mutilated," with a long excursus on the phrase ἀποκόπτειν ἑαυτούς ("to mutilate themselves") in which he denounces all who treat the body in such a fashion as though it were a treacherous thing (see his *Commentary on the Epistle to the Galatians* on 5:12). And most modern translations view the verb in this fashion as well: RSV, "I wish those who unsettle you would mutilate themselves!"; NEB, "As for these agitators, they had better go the whole way and make eunuchs of themselves!"; JB, "Tell those who are disturbing you I would like to see the knife slip"; NIV, "As for those agitators, I wish they would go the whole way and emasculate themselves!"; cf. such diverse individual paraphrastic translations as those by James Moffatt, "O that those who are upsetting you would get themselves castrated!", and F. F. Bruce, "If only those who are upsetting you would make a complete job of this 'cutting' business; then we should have no more trouble from them!"

Latin commentators, however, treated the expression more ambiguously, as in the Vulgate's translation *ultinam et abscidantur qui vos conturbant*, which carried over into the KJV, "I would they were even cut off which trouble you." So many have understood "cut off" in terms of a withdrawal from the churches or self-imposed excommunication rather than emasculation (cf., e.g., Phillips: "I wish those who are so eager to cut your bodies would cut themselves off from you altogether!"; Living Bible: "I only wish these teachers who want you to cut yourselves by being circumcised would cut themselves off from you and leave you alone!"). W. M. Ramsay, in fact, mounted a rather vigorous attack against understanding Paul here as using such "foul language" as castration or mutilation, simply because such a "scornful expression would be a pure insult, as irrational as it is disgusting" (*Galatians*, 438; see also 437–40).

Yet as insulting and disgusting as it may seem, Paul's comment should be understood as a sarcastic way of characterizing the Judaizers and his attitude toward them, as most modern commentators recognize (so, e.g., Lightfoot, Burton, Mussner, Betz, Bruce). Indeed, it is the crudest and rudest of all Paul's extant statements, which his amanuensis did not try to tone down (cf. *Introduction* on "Amanuensis" and "Synchronic Rhetorical Analysis"). Underlying the sarcasm and crudity of the comment, however, is Paul's understanding of circumcision as purely a physical act without religious significance (cf. 5:6; 6:15), which when done for societal or physical reasons is acceptable but when done either to gain acceptance before God or to achieve a more acceptable lifestyle becomes simply bodily mutilation (cf. Phil 3:2).

Explanation

Closing off his treatment of the judaizing threat that dominates the Galatian letter, Paul sets out in 5:1–12 (1) a ringing declaration of Christian freedom (v 1a), (2) exhortations and warnings against accepting the Judaizers' message (vv 1b–4), (3) a précis of the gospel proclamation (vv 5–6), (4) a series of somewhat unconnected remarks about the issues at hand (vv 7–11a), (5) a conclusion to the whole discussion that focuses on "the offense of the cross," and (6) an appended sarcastic comment that expresses in a crude, exasperated fashion Paul's view of the Judaizers. Later in the Subscription (6:11–18) Paul will state again the essential points of his argument with the Judaizers (see esp. vv 12–15). For now, however, he has completed his treatment of the judaizing threat, climaxing his arguments and exhortations with the same tone of severity with which he began (cf. 1:6–10 and 5:2–12).

Two dangers threatened Christian freedom in Galatia: the first was the acceptance of Jewish nomism as a lifestyle for Gentile Christians, which in effect brought one right back to the basic question of whether righteousness was to be gained by "works of the law" or by a response of faith to "the faithfulness of Jesus Christ" (cf. 2:16); the second was the corruption of the Christian life by reliance on "the flesh" rather than "the Spirit." The most immediate danger was that of Jewish nomism, which was brought in from outside the church by the Judaizers. So Paul deals with that first and most extensively in 1:6–5:12. The danger of libertinism, however, was also present within the Galatian churches, being there in an indigenous fashion from the very first. And Paul must also deal with that as a threat to the freedom that believers have in Christ, which he does in the remainder of the body of Galatians in 5:13–6:10.

Most often Galatians is viewed as the great document of justification by faith. What Christians all too often fail to realize is that in reality it is a document that sets out a Christ-centered lifestyle—one that stands in opposition to both nomism and libertinism. Sadly, though applauding justification by faith, Christians frequently renounce their freedom in Christ by espousing either nomism or libertinism, and sometimes (like the Galatians) both. So Paul's letter to the Galatians, though directly relevant to the Galatian situation, speaks also to our situation today.

B. Exhortations against Libertine Tendencies (Exhortatio, Part II) (5:13–6:10)

Part II of the *exhortatio* of Galatians (5:13–6:10) contains a number of epistolary conventions that mark it out as a distinguishable unit of material: (1) the reiteration of the declaration of freedom first given in 5:1 that appears as the opening statement of 5:13, ὑμεῖς ἐπ' ἐλευθερίᾳ ἐκλήθητε ("you were called to be free"), with the postpositive γάρ reintroducing that declaration after a brief digression; (2) the "verb of saying" formula λέγω δέ ("so I say") at 5:16 that holds two parts of one unit of material together (cf. 3:17; 4:1); (3) the vocative ἀδελφοί ("brothers") at the beginning of the section at 5:13 and as a minor transition at 6:1

(compare the use of "brothers" elsewhere at the epistolary "seams" of Galatians: 1:11; 3:15; 4:12, 28, 31; 5:11 and 6:18); and (4) the two inferential particles ἄρα ("so," "then") and οὖν ("therefore," "then") that are joined together for emphasis to conclude the section at 6:10. In addition, it should be noted that rhetorically the exhortations of 5:13, "through love serve one another," and 6:10, "do good to all people," function as an *inclusio* for this unit of material.

Whereas previously Paul had argued for Christian freedom against Jewish nomism, here he redirects his thought to argue for Christian freedom against supposedly "Christian" self-centered libertinism. For just as freedom in Christ must never become regulated by law, so it must never become an occasion for "the flesh." Rather than laws or license, the realities that characterize Christian freedom are "love," "serving one another," and "the Spirit." In fact, these three emphases of love, serving one another, and the Spirit appear throughout the exhortations of 5:13–6:10, structuring all that Paul says as the skeleton of a living creature structures all its tissues and form.

The theme of love, for example, informs all of Paul's exhortations vis-à-vis the Galatians' libertine tendencies: serving one another is to be done in love (5:13b); the entire law is fulfilled in the commandment "love your neighbor as yourself" (5:14); the "works of the flesh" are the antithesis of love (5:19–21); the "fruit of the Spirit" is the epitome of love (5:22–23); love restores the erring brother (6:1); love bears the burdens of others (6:2); love is humble (6:3); and love never fails to work for the good of all people, especially those who belong to the family of believers (6:9–10). And as with love, so with service: love is to be expressed in serving one another (5:13b); restoring in a gentle manner someone trapped in sin is an example of service to another (6:1); bearing another's crushing burden is also an example of service (6:2); sharing "all good things" with one's instructor is another form of Christian service (6:6); and doing good to all people, particularly those who belong to the family of believers, is the overriding concern of Christian service (6:9–10).

Yet undergirding all of Paul's admonitions regarding love and service is the reality of life lived "by the Spirit," with references to the Spirit being more frequent in 5:13–6:10 than references to either love or service. Thus Paul sums up his initial exhortation to "serve one another in love" (5:13b) by the admonition to "live by the Spirit" (5:16), which will (1) preserve a person from the influences of "the flesh" (5:16–17), (2) nullify thoughts about nomism and legalism (5:18), (3) produce such "fruit" as "love, joy, peace, patience, kindness, goodness, faithfulness, gentleness, and self-control" (5:22–23), (4) cause one to experience the Spirit's guidance (5:25a), (5) keep one from conceit (5:26), (6) motivate one to restore those who have erred (6:1a), (7) motivate one to bear the oppressive burdens of others, as well as one's own legitimate responsibilities (6:2, 5), and (8) assure one of eternal life (6:7–8).

It may be that 5:13–6:10 should be called Paul's Galatian paraenesis, particularly if one means by "paraenesis" (as influenced by Martin Dibelius' definition) something rather general as "the giving of rules or directions for proper thought and action in daily living in a form which permits a wide applicability of the teachings" (so, e.g., D. G. Bradley, *JBL* 72 [1953] 238, thereby justifying calling 5:13–6:10 the paraenesis of Galatians). But if paraenesis is understood not as a technical term with the definition Dibelius gave it but simply as a synonym for exhortation, then this section should be seen not as a new feature of Galatians but as a continuation of Paul's exhortations in the letter—though, of course, with the thrust of those exhortations now being refocused vis-à-vis another factor to be dealt with in the Galatian churches. For here Paul redirects what he started at 4:12, with the differences of expression and application due to a further matter being addressed: that of libertinism, which was indigenous to the churches, rather than that of nomism, which was brought in from the outside.

1. Life Directed by Love, Service to Others, and the Spirit (5:13–18)

Bibliography

Barclay, J. M. G. *Obeying the Truth,* 106–45, 178–251. **Barrett, C. K.** *Freedom and Obligation.* **Bradley, D. G.** "The TOPOS as a Form in the Pauline Paraenesis." *JBL* 72 (1953) 238–46. **Burton, E. deW.** *Spirit, Soul, and Flesh.* **Davies, W. D.** "Paul and the Dead Sea Scrolls: Flesh and Spirit." In *The Scrolls and the New Testament,* ed. K. Stendahl. New York: Harper, 1957, 157–82. **Deidun, T. J.** *New Covenant Morality in Paul.* **Furnish, V. P.** *Theology and Ethics in Paul.* **Longenecker, R. N.** *Paul, Apostle of Liberty.* **Luther, M.** "The Freedom of a Christian," *Luther's Works.* American Edition, Vol. 31, tr. W. A. Lambert, rev. H. J. Grimm. Philadelphia: Muhlenburg, 1957, 327–77. **Macgregor, W. M.** *Christian Freedom.* **Malherbe, A. J.** *Moral Exhortation.* **Mussner, F.** *Theologie der Freiheit nach Paulus.* **Räisänen, H.** *Paul and the Law.* **Sanders, E. P.** *Paul, the Law, and the Jewish People.* **Westerholm, S.** "Letter and Spirit: The Foundation of Pauline Ethics." *NTS* 30 (1984) 229–48. ———. "On Fulfilling the Whole Law (Gal. 5:14)." *SEÅ* 51–52 (1986–87) 229–37. ———. *Israel's Law and the Church's Faith.*

Translation

[13]*You, brothers, were called to be free! Only do not use your freedom as an opportunity for the flesh, but through love[a] serve one another.* [14]*For all the law is fulfilled[b] in one commandment:[c] "Love your neighbor as yourself."[d]* [15]*If you keep on biting and tearing one another to pieces, watch out that you are not consumed by one another.*

[16]*So I say, live by the Spirit and you will not carry out the desires of the flesh.* [17]*For the flesh desires what is contrary to the Spirit, and the Spirit what is contrary to the flesh. These[e] entities are in opposition to one another, so that you are not able to do what you want.* [18]*And since you are led by the Spirit, you are not under the law.*

Notes

[a] διὰ τῆς ἀγάπης ("through love") is well attested, though τῇ ἀγάπῃ τοῦ πνεύματος ("through love of the Spirit") is supported by D G 104 it vg^cl cop^sa goth Ambst—perhaps by assimilation with 5:22a (cf. Rom 5:5; 15:30).

[b] πεπλήρωται (perfect indicative passive, "is fulfilled") is well attested, though πληροῦται (present indicative passive, "is fulfilled") is supported by D G 0122 Byzantine.

[c] ἐν ἑνὶ λόγῳ ("in one word/commandment") is well attested, though ἐν ὑμῖν ("in/among you") was read by Marcion, ἐν ὑμῖν ἐν ἑνὶ λόγῳ ("in/among you in one word/commandment") by D* G it Ambst, and ἐν ὀλίγῳ ("in brief") by 1611 syr^h Ephr.

[d] ὡς σεαυτόν ("as yourself") is well attested, though ὡς ἑαυτόν ("as oneself") is supported by p^46 G L N* P.

ᵉ ταῦτα γάρ ("for these") is attested by P⁴⁶ ℵ* B D* G etc., though ταῦτα δέ ("but/and these") by ℵ² A C D² Byzantine syrʰ.

Form/Structure/Setting

The exhortations of 5:13–6:10 are to be seen as intimately connected with circumstances in Galatia. They disclose a further problem in the churches of that province. The failure of the Galatians to maintain "the truth of the gospel" (2:5, 14) in their proposed acceptance of Jewish nomism was accompanied by their failure to enter fully into the ethical quality of life consonant with that gospel. Loveless strife was evidently present within the Galatian churches, with such attitudes and actions evidencing the dominance of "the flesh" and certain libertine tendencies within the church—probably not "libertinism" as a conscious, articulated philosophy, but libertine tendencies that took the form of self-promotion, self-vindication, and the disregard of others, with the result that Christian freedom was not being expressed in loving service to others. So Paul in upholding Christian freedom not only speaks of the Spirit as the effective answer to the Judaizers' call for a nomistic lifestyle, but also argues for the Spirit as the effective power for overcoming the flesh and such libertine attitudes as had arisen within the church. For Paul, in fact, the Christian life is wholly determined by the presence and activity of the Spirit.

In 5:13–18 Paul gives two exhortations that serve to govern all that is said in 5:13–6:10 about Christian freedom vis-à-vis so-called "Christian" libertinism: "through love serve one another" (v 13) and "live by the Spirit" (v 16). These two exhortations he connects by the "verb of saying" formula λέγω δέ ("so I say"), as though to highlight the fact that the first is entailed in the second and that both produce comparable results—for while service to others that is motivated and conditioned by love fulfills all the commandments, living by the direction and power of the Spirit counteracts all that springs from "the flesh" and "the law." What follows in 5:19–26 and 6:1–10, then, are basically elaborations and applications of these two exhortations to circumstances within the Galatian churches.

Comment

13 ὑμεῖς γὰρ ἐπ᾽ ἐλευθερίᾳ ἐκλήθητε, ἀδελφοί, "you, brothers, were called to be free!" As at 5:1a, so here Paul begins by emphasizing the indicative of the Christian gospel. In distinction from the statement of v 1a, where the aorist indicative verb ἠλευθέρωσεν ("he set us free") is in the third person singular and active in voice, thereby, particularly with Χριστός as the expressed subject, highlighting the work of Christ. Here the aorist indicative verb ἐκλήθητε ("you were called") is in the second person plural and passive in voice, thereby, in parallel with the use of κληρόω elsewhere in Galatians (cf. 1:6; 5:8), laying stress on the call of God. "The intention of both statements," however, as Betz points out, "is the same: the liberation by Christ and God's call are part of the same process of salvation" (*Galatians*, 271–72).

The postpositive conjunction γάρ (untranslated) may be thought to connect 5:13ff. with what has gone before by providing reasons for the preceding statements. More likely, however, it should be seen in a continuative sense as reintroducing the theme of freedom that was declared in v 1a and is now being refocused after the digressional remarks of vv 7–12, or at least after the sarcastic comment of v 12. ἐπί with the dative is used elsewhere by Paul to express destination or purpose (cf. Eph 2:10, ἐπὶ ἔργοις ἀγαθοῖς, "for good works"; 1 Thess 4:7, οὐ ... ἐπὶ ἀκαθαρσίᾳ, "not ... for uncleanness"; see also Phil 4:10). So ἐπ' ἐλευθερίᾳ has the sense of being called by God "for freedom" or "to be free," with the freedom spoken about being obviously that of freedom from Jewish nomism as argued in the *propositio* (2:15–21) and the *probatio* (3:1–4:11) of Galatians and in Part I of the letter's *exhortatio* (4:12–5:12). The vocative ἀδελφοί ("brothers") is used both affectionately (see *Comment* at 1:11) and as an epistolary convention to identify the beginning of a new section in Paul's letter (cf. the use of "brothers" at both major and the minor "seams" of Galatians: 1:11; 3:15; 4:12, 28, 31; 5:11; 6:18).

μόνον μὴ τὴν ἐλευθερίαν εἰς ἀφορμὴν τῇ σαρκί, "only do not use your freedom as an opportunity for the flesh." The neuter adverb μόνον ("only") functions as a limitation to the action or state designated by the main verb (cf. 1:23; 2:10; 3:2; 4:18; see also Phil 1:27). Here it adds a significant qualification to the ringing declaration of Christian freedom, with the articular τὴν ἐλευθερίαν referring to ἐλευθερία of the preceding clause and having demonstrative force ("your freedom"). The verb of a sentence is sometimes omitted after μόνον (cf. 2:10) or with the negative μή (cf. Mark 14:2), and so here, where both occur, some such imperative as ἔχετε ("do not regard"), ποεῖτε ("do not make") or τρέπετε ("do not turn") is to be understood with τὴν ἐλευθερίαν as its object.

The noun ἀφορμή was originally a military term that meant "the starting point" or "base of operations" for an expedition, but came generally to mean "the resources needed" to carry through any undertaking. In Koine Greek, however, it was also commonly used to mean "occasion," "pretext," or "opportunity" (cf. Rom 7:8; 2 Cor 5:12; 11:12; 1 Tim 5:14). The preposition εἰς with the accusative ἀφορμήν here signals actualization (cf. John 16:20, εἰς χαράν), and so the phrase is to be translated "as an occasion," "as a pretext," or "as an opportunity" for something. The expression τῇ σαρκί ("the flesh") is a dative of advantage limiting the noun ἀφορμήν, with the article being generic (cf. 5:17, 19, 24; 6:8). And since "the Spirit" and "the flesh" are juxtaposed throughout the exhortations of 5:13–6:10, we may assume that just as Paul thought of the one as personal so he meant the other to be taken as at least semi-personified.

Commentators and translators have always had trouble with the term ἡ σάρξ as used in 5:13–6:10. Prior to this section Paul used σάρξ principally to refer to that which is merely human (cf. 1:16; 2:16) or purely physical (2:20; 4:13–14, 23, 29). The only exception might be his use of σαρκί ("by human effort") in 3:3, which verges on being understood in an ethical sense. And later in the subscription of 6:10–18 the term appears again in a purely physical sense (vv 12–13). Here and throughout Part II of the *exhortatio*, however, σάρξ is used in a definitely ethical sense (cf. 5:16, 17, 19, 24; 6:8).

It has often been noted that σάρξ used ethically has to do with humanity's fallen, corrupt, or sinful nature, as distinguished from human nature as originally created by God (cf. esp. E. deW. Burton, *Spirit, Soul, and Flesh*; idem, *Galatians*, 492–95; W. D. Davies, "Paul and the Dead Sea Scrolls," 157–82). Translating σάρξ literally as "flesh" in ethical contexts (as KJV, ASV, RSV) has often encouraged ideas of anthropological dualism, with the physical body taken to be evil per se and the mortification of the body viewed in some manner as necessary for achieving a true Christian experience. In reaction to such ideas, various translators have tried to give to the expression a more interpretive and descriptive rendering. So there have appeared such translations as "physical nature" (AmT), "human nature/natural desires/ physical desires" (GNB), "lower nature" (NEB), "corrupt nature" (Knox), and "sinful nature" (NIV)—or more freely, "self-indulgence" (JB). None of these interpretive options, however, fully captures the ethos of Paul's ethical use of σάρξ. Some, in fact, hardly relieve Paul of the charge of dualism (e.g., AmT, GNB); others imply, conversely, an inherent higher nature that is intrinsically good (e.g., NEB); while still others are so free as to be unable to be carried through for every occurrence of the term in 5:13–6:10 (e.g., JB).

Probably the best of the interpretive translations are those that add the adjective "corrupt" or "sinful" to the noun "nature" (i.e., Knox, NIV), thereby suggesting an essential aspect of mankind's present human condition that is in opposition to "the Spirit" and yet avoiding the idea that the human body is evil per se. As W. Barclay aptly expresses matters:

> The flesh is what man has made himself in contrast with man as God made him. The flesh is man as he has allowed himself to become in contrast with man as God meant him to be. The flesh stands for the total effect upon man of his own sin and of the sin of his fathers and of the sin of all men who have gone before him. The flesh is human nature as it has become through sin. . . . The flesh stands for human nature weakened, vitiated, tainted by sin. The flesh is man as he is apart from Jesus Christ and his Spirit" (*Flesh and Spirit*, 22; though Barclay himself prefers the NEB translation "lower nature" [ibid., 21]).

Nonetheless, it is hard to improve on the nice linguistic balance set up by the translations "the flesh" and "the Spirit" for ἡ σάρξ and τὸ πνεῦμα in 5:13–6:10. So despite the interpretive advantages of such renderings as found in Knox and NIV, a commentary treatment of Paul's ethical use of ἡ σάρξ should probably translate the term literally and comment on it interpretively, as we propose to do in what follows.

In the OT בָּשָׂר (*bāśār*, "flesh") normally means just the physical body, whether of mankind (cf. Gen 2:21; 40:19; Exod 30:32, etc.) or of animals (cf. Gen 41:2–19; Exod 21:28; 22:31, etc.), with such derived meanings as "blood-relations" or "kindred" (cf. Gen 2:23–24; 29:14; Judg 9:2, etc.), the collective use of "flesh" for "all living beings" (cf. Gen 6:17, 19; 7:21; 9:11, 15–17, etc.), and the euphemistic use of "flesh" for the male genitals (cf. Gen 17:11, 14, 23–25; Exod 28:42, etc.) appearing as well. Apart, however, from the occasional use of בָּשָׂר to mean mankind as frail and erring vis-à-vis God (cf. Gen 6:3; 2 Chr 32:8; Job 10:4; Pss 56:5; 78:39; Jer 17:5), there is no use of this term in an ethical sense comparable to what is found in Paul's ethical use of σάρξ. Nevertheless, an ethical use of בָּשָׂר and σάρξ was coming into vogue in Paul's day, as W. D. Davies has pointed out (cf. "Paul and the Dead Sea Scrolls").

Paul speaks of "the flesh" not as itself the culprit, but as a captive of sin. Nevertheless, "flesh" as a captive also acts in behalf of its captor, and so produces "desires and passions" (cf. 5:16–17, 19–21) that are at work against the Spirit. Indeed, the Christian has "crucified the flesh with its passions and desires" (5:24).

Yet the Christian continues to exist, anthropologically speaking, "in the flesh," and so, ethically speaking, "the flesh" continues to be a potential threat. Thus the Christian may choose to use his or her freedom in Christ either as "an opportunity for the flesh" or in response to "the Spirit." Paul calls on his converts to renounce the former, thereby being open to the latter.

ἀλλὰ διὰ τῆς ἀγάπης δουλεύετε ἀλλήλοις, "but through love serve one another." Commitment to Christ carries with it ethical obligation. On that both Paul and the Judaizers agreed. The difference between them, however, was in the manner in which that obligation is to be fulfilled. For the Judaizers, Christian obligation is to be understood in terms of subjection to the Mosaic law as the expressed will of God, with the prescriptions of Torah giving guidance for ethical living. For Paul, the obligation of the Christian is love that expresses itself in service to others, with that obligation being grounded in and guided by the Christian's new existence in "the Spirit." Here in v 13b Paul speaks of love that expresses itself in service to others, evidently picking up the two references to outgoing love that appear earlier in his letter: that of 5:6, where it is said that the only thing having value in the Christian life is "faith expressing itself through love," and, somewhat more contextually distant, that of 2:20, where the confession is made that "Christ loved me and gave himself for me." Later in vv 16ff. Paul will speak of the Christian's new existence in the Spirit, with the "verb of saying" formula λέγω δέ, "so I say," being the epistolary convention that holds these two emphases together.

The strong adversative ἀλλά ("but") often is used to highlight a positive correlative of a preceding negative statement (cf. 1:1; see also Matt 5:17; 7:21; Mark 5:39; Rom 2:13, etc.), as it does here contrasting freedom as "an opportunity for the flesh" and freedom expressing itself "through love" in service to others. The preposition διά ("through") serves to identify τῆς ἀγάπης ("love") as the conditioning cause of Christian service or that which makes possible the action of the verb δουλεύετε (i.e., "through love serve"), and is not to be taken as just instrumental (i.e., "by means of love"). The article τῆς before ἀγάπης is demonstrative, probably having in view "that love" referred to either in 2:20 (Christ's love expressed in action on our behalf) or in 5:6 (Christian love expressed in action on behalf of others), or both. The imperative mood of δουλεύετε ("serve") highlights the ethical obligation in the Christian life; its present tense speaks of such an obligation being continual throughout life. So Christian freedom and love have to do not only with being a "servant of Christ" (1:10) but also with "serving others." The combining of "freedom" and "servant/service" may seem a paradox, as it has to many. Nonetheless, as Betz observes: "Obviously, this juxtaposition of terms is intended. Paul contrasts the slavery under the Law and the 'elements of the world,' which is a one-sided relationship of submission, suppression, scrupulosity, and fear, with the other 'slavery,' which is the free and voluntary act of love" (*Galatians,* 274).

14 ὁ γὰρ πᾶς νόμος ἐν ἑνὶ λόγῳ πεπλήρωται, ἐν τῷ Ἀγαπήσεις τὸν πλησίον σου ὡς σεαυτόν, "for all the law is fulfilled in one commandment: 'Love your neighbor as yourself.'" Somewhat surprisingly, having so definitely denounced legalism (cf. esp. 3:6–14) and set aside the law as a pedagogue in the Christian life (cf. 3:23–4:7), Paul here speaks about Christians fulfilling the law. Is it that having made such a great show of throwing out the law through the front door, Paul now unobtrusively readmits it through the back door? Does v 14 indicate something of

a fundamental inconsistency in Paul's thought? E. P. Sanders has argued that though there is an obvious inconsistency in his statements about the law, there is an underlying coherence to Paul's thought, for "the different things which Paul said about the law depend on the question asked or the problem posed" (*Paul, the Law, and the Jewish People*, 4). So Sanders interprets Paul in the earlier portions of Galatians as arguing against the law for "getting in" to a position of righteousness before God, but what he says here at v 14 reflects his acceptance of "covenantal nomism" as the means for "staying in" such a relationship (ibid., 6, passim)— which understanding of Paul, it must be said, would have delighted the Judaizers of Galatia. Heikki Räisänen, however, dispenses with Sanders' attempt to find an underlying coherence in Paul, insisting, rather, that there are flat contradictions in Paul's view of the law: "Paul states in unambiguous terms that the law has been abolished. . . . The abolition notwithstanding, Paul also makes positive statements which imply that the law is still valid. The claim it justly puts on men is fulfilled by Christians" (*Paul and the Law*, 199).

What, then, is Paul's attitude toward the Christian's relation to the Mosaic law, particularly in light of this verse? Is he inconsistent, not only in his various statements but also in his basic thought? Or did Paul understand the relation of the believer to the law in two ways: one having to do with "getting in" and one with "staying in"? Or is there a consistency here in Paul's commendation of love as "fulfilling" all the commandments vis-à-vis Paul's rejection of "doing" the law for righteousness? And while not allowing the Judaizers to focus all of the law on the one rite of circumcision, is Paul now himself summing up all the law in the one commandment of loving one's neighbor? Is his only argument with the Judaizers that they focused on an external rite while he focused on an internal ethical principle?

Hans Dieter Betz proposed that one must see Paul in v 14 "carefully distinguishing between the 'doing' and the 'fulfilling' of the Torah—the 'doing' of the Jewish Torah is not required for Christians, but the 'fulfilling' is" (*Galatians*, 275). And Stephen Westerholm has taken up Betz's thesis here, developing it more fully (cf. *SEÅ* 51–52 [1986–87] 229–37). As Westerholm points out, (1) in context v 14 cannot be considered a piece of unassimilated theology or an unconscious self-contradiction, but "represents what Paul himself considers a necessary nuance in a presentation of his view" (ibid., 230–31), and (2) solutions that posit irony for Paul's statement here, or a distinction between "getting in" and "staying in," or a distinction between "the whole law" (ὅλον τὸν νόμον) of 5:3 and "all the law" (ὁ πᾶς νόμος) of 5:14 cannot be validated (ibid., 232–33). Rather, as Westerholm cogently argues (following Betz), Paul in his own mind drew a deliberate distinction between "doing" the Mosaic law (as in 3:10, 12; 5:3; cf. Rom 10:5) and "fulfilling" the Mosaic law (as here; cf. Rom 8:4; 13:8, 10), never saying that Christians "do" the law (ibid., 233–35). As Westerholm points out:

For Paul it is important to say that Christians "fulfill" the whole law, and thus to claim that their conduct (and theirs alone) fully satisfies the "real" purport of the law in its entirety while allowing the ambiguity of the term to blunt the force of the objection that certain individual requirements (with which, Paul would maintain, Christian behavior was never meant to conform) have not been "done" (ibid., 235).

Furthermore, as Westerholm continues: "'doing' the law is what is *required* of those 'under the law'; 'fulfilling' the law, is, for Paul, the *result* of Christian living *the norms of which are stated in quite different terms*" (ibid., italics his).

So with respect to Paul's statement here, "Galatians 5:14 is not itself a command to fulfill the law but a statement that, when one loves one's neighbor, the whole law is fully satisfied in the process" (ibid.). And with respect to Paul's statements elsewhere in his letters regarding the Christian and the law, Westerholm aptly concludes:

(i)   Paul never derives appropriate Christian behavior by simply applying relevant precepts from Torah;

(ii)   Paul never claims that Christians "do" (ποιεῖν) the law; they—and they alone—are said to "fulfill" (πληροῦν) it;

(iii) Paul never speaks of the law's fulfillment in prescribing Christian conduct, but only while describing its results (ibid., 237).

The focus of Paul's statement in Gal 5:14, as also in Rom 13:8–10, is not on law but on love. So it is love—love that responds to Christ's love and that expresses a new existence in Christ (cf. 2:20)—that motivates the ethical life of a Christian, with the results of that love ethic fulfilling the real purport of the Mosaic law.

The conjunction γάρ ("for") connects in an explanatory fashion v 14 with the final statement of v 13, thereby giving a reason why Christians are to serve others through love, for such loving service results in all that the law pointed toward in its commandments. The perfect indicative passive πεπλήρωται ("it is fulfilled") signals past completion with a present result, probably having in mind what Jesus did in fulfilling the law (cf. Matt 5:17). So, in effect there remains no more necessity for commandments.

The expression ὁ πᾶς νόμος ("all the law") could have been understood in a Jewish context as referring either to the basic commandments that contain and sum up the whole law (i.e., כללים, *kĕlālîm*, "the principles" or "universals") or to the total number of individual statements of the law (i.e., פרשה, *pārāšâ*, "exact statement" or "detailed rule"). In Jewish lore Moses knew the כללים at Sinai, but learned the פרשה in the tabernacle. Probably the former is here in view (cf. D. Daube, *The New Testament and Rabbinic Judaism*, 65–66). Nowhere in rabbinic writings is Lev 19:18 explicitly said to be the sum of the individual prescriptions and prohibitions of the Torah, though various rabbis are represented as debating how "you shall love your neighbor as yourself" ranks with other specific commandments (cf. *Gen. Rab.* 24.7; *Sipra, Qĕdôšîm* 4.12; *'Abot de R. Nat.* 16.4, 25a). But a negative version of Lev 19:18 is attributed to Rabbi Hillel as the essence of the Torah in *b. Šabb.* 31a:

On another occasion it happened that a certain Gentile came before Shammai and said to him, "Make me a proselyte, on condition that you teach me the whole Torah while I stand on one foot." Thereupon he [Shammai] repulsed him with the builder's cubit which was in his hand. When he went before Hillel he [Hillel] said to him, "What is hateful to you, do not to your neighbor; that is the whole Torah, while the rest is the commentary thereof. Go and learn it."

Although Hillel's "Negative Golden Rule" is not related directly to Lev 19:18 in *b. Šabb.* 31a, it is appended to "You shall love your neighbor as yourself" in *Tg. Ps.-J.*

on Lev 19:18 "and that which you hate, do not do to your neighbor," so suggesting its currency in Hillel's day and Hillel's statement of *b. Šabb.* 31a as having Lev 19:18 in mind.

15 εἰ δὲ ἀλλήλους δάκνετε καὶ κατεσθίετε, βλέπετε μὴ ὑπ' ἀλλήλων ἀναλωθῆτε, "if you keep on biting and tearing one another to pieces, watch out that you are not consumed by one another." Here Paul gives a sarcastic warning. The protasis of the sentence is in the form of a first class condition (εἰ with the indicative), and so assumes the reality of the situation described. The description, of course, is hyperbolic: "you are biting" (δάκνετε, present tense), "you are tearing to pieces" (κατεσθίετε, present tense), and "you are consumed" (ἀναλωθῆτε, resultant aorist). The hyperbole pictures wild beasts fighting so ferociously with one another that they end up annihilating each other. The implication of the portrayal is that this was what was happening—or, at least, what Paul thought was happening—in the churches of Galatia (so Burton, Schlier, Bruce, et al.; contra Oepke, Mussner, and Betz). Perhaps their fighting stemmed from differing attitudes toward the Judaizers' activities among them. More likely, however, it was an expression of their own indigenous and loveless libertine attitudes. So in a comment similar to that of 5:12 Paul here sarcastically denounces the libertine tendencies present among his Galatian converts just as he earlier castigated the Judaizers in their midst.

16 λέγω δέ, πνεύματι περιπατεῖτε καὶ ἐπιθυμίαν σαρκὸς οὐ μὴ τελέσητε, "so I say, live by the Spirit and you will not carry out the desires of the flesh." The truly unique feature of Pauline ethics is the role assigned to the Spirit. Here in v 16 Paul states his thesis regarding how the Christian life is to be lived, viz., "by the Spirit." The "verb of saying" formula λέγω δέ ("so I say"), as noted above, ties together Paul's statements about love in vv 13b–14 with his present statements about the Spirit in vv 16–18. But it also functions as an epistolary convention to direct the emphasis of what is being said to what immediately follows (cf. 3:17; 4:1; also 1 Cor 10:29), that is, to what is being said about life in the Spirit. The statement of v 16 consists of two parts: the first, an exhortation, "live by the Spirit"; the second, a promise, "and you will not gratify the desires of the flesh." This statement is then elaborated on in 5:17–24, exhorted again in 5:25, and applied directly to the Galatian situation in 5:26–6:10.

The verb περιπατέω ("go about," "walk around") appears frequently in Paul's letters and occasionally in the Johannine letters in the figurative sense of "live" or "conduct oneself" (cf. Rom 6:4; 8:4; 13:13; 14:15; 1 Cor 3:3; 7:17; 2 Cor 4:2; 5:7; 10:2, 3; 12:18; Eph 2:2, 10; 4:17; 5:2, 15; Phil 3:17, 18; Col 2:6; 3:7; 4:5; 1 Thess 1:12; 4:1, 12; see also 1 John 2:6; 2 John 4, 6; 3 John 3–4), though its only occurrence in Galatians is here at 5:16. The figurative use of περιπατέω stems from the Hebrew verb הלך (*hālak*), which is the repeatedly used term in the OT for "walk" or "conduct one's life" (the LXX occasionally translates it by περιπατέω, but usually by πορεύομαι) and became the generic designation for all of the rabbinic ethical and social legislation ("Halakah"). Apart from its few uses in the Johannine letters, where it is always more exactly defined than in Paul, the figurative use of περιπατέω in the NT is unique to Paul, being synonymous here in v 16 with πνεύματι ἄγεσθε ("led by the Spirit") of v 18, ζῶμεν πνεύματι ("live by the Spirit") of v 25a, and πνεύματι στοιχῶμεν ("keep in step with the Spirit") of v 25b.

The dative πνεύματι suggests both origin and instrumentality ("by the Spirit"), and therefore a quality of life that differs from both a nomistic and a libertine lifestyle. The present tense of the imperative περιπατεῖτε, which denotes an exhortation to action in progress, implies that the Galatians were to continue doing what they were already doing, that is, experiencing the presence of the Spirit's working in their lives (cf. 3:3–5) and living by faith (cf. 5:5). So the exhortation to believers of Galatia is for them to continue to live their lives in the new reality of "the Spirit," as they had experienced that reality at their conversion and before listening to the Judaizers, and not in the old existence of "the flesh," which has to do with laws and self-indulgent license.

Attached to the exhortation is a promise: "and you will not carry out the desires of the flesh." The verb τελέω ("bring to an end," "finish," "complete"; and so "carry out," "perform," "accomplish") has as its subject the Christian who will not carry out or perform the desires of the flesh. Yet behind the individual believer Paul sees two ethical forces that seek to control a person's thought and activity: the one, the personal Spirit of God; the other, the personified "flesh." What, in such an ethical dilemma, does the Christian do? The promise of the gospel, as Paul proclaims it, is that life in the Spirit negates life controlled by the flesh. In fact, that promise is stated emphatically by the use of the double negative οὐ μή ("no never") with the aorist subjunctive τελέσητε.

17 ἡ γὰρ σὰρξ ἐπιθυμεῖ κατὰ τοῦ πνεύματος, τὸ δὲ πνεῦμα κατὰ τῆς σαρκός· ταῦτα γὰρ ἀλλήλοις ἀντίκειται, ἵνα μὴ ἃ ἐὰν θέλητε ταῦτα ποιῆτε, "for the flesh desires what is contrary to the Spirit, and the Spirit what is contrary to the flesh. These entities are in opposition to one another, so that you are not able to do what you want." Here in v 17 Paul gives a précis of his basic soteriological anthropology, which underlies not only what he has said in v 16 but also his whole understanding of humanity before God since "sin entered the world" (cf. Rom 5:12): "the flesh" and "the Spirit" are diametrically opposed to one another, with the result that one cannot do what he or she knows to be right when in "the flesh" (i.e., when living only humanly according to one's own guidance and the direction of whatever is simply human) but only when in "the Spirit" (i.e., when living in the new reality of being "in Christ" and directed by God's Spirit). The postpositive conjunction γάρ ("for") is used in both a confirmatory and an explanatory fashion, confirming the opposition of flesh and Spirit stated in v 16 and explaining why that opposition exists. It also, however, suggests that such an explanation for the human predicament was commonly held.

What Paul sets forth here in v 17, of course, is an ethical dualism that uses the terms σάρξ and πνεῦμα to express the antitheses of that dualism. Such a dualism, as found not only in Paul's letters but also throughout the Johannine literature (cf. John 3:6 for the terms themselves), has often been treated as the product of Greek thought. But the dualism of Paul and John is an ethical dualism, not cosmological or anthropological in nature, and is best explained in Paul's case as "the complex product of Paul's Old Testament background and his Rabbinic training" (so W. D. Davies, *Paul and Rabbinic Judaism*, 17; see also 17–35), which has parallels with the ethical dualism found at Qumran (cf. W. D. Davies, "Paul and the Dead Sea Scrolls," 157–82).

The neuter plural pronoun ταῦτα ("these things," "these entities") refers back to "the flesh" and "the Spirit," treating them now more as "things" or "entities" than personal forces. The present tense of the verb ἀντίκειται ("they are in opposition to") signals an ongoing opposition of the two entities. The final clause of the statement, cast as a pure purpose clause with ἵνα ("in order that," "so that") and subjunctive verbs and particles throughout, expresses not the divine purpose but the purpose of both the flesh and the Spirit: the flesh opposes the Spirit with the desire that people not do what they want to do when guided by the Spirit, and the Spirit opposes the flesh with the desire that people not do what they want to do when guided by the flesh. So, as Burton encapsulates Paul's thought here, "Does the man choose evil, the Spirit opposes him; does he choose good, the flesh hinders him" (*Galatians*, 302). In effect, Gal 5:17 sets out in rudimentary fashion what is later spoken of more fully in Rom 7:14–25, with both passages expressing the plight of humanity "of itself" (cf. αὐτὸς ἐγώ, "I of myself" or "dependent on my own resources," of Rom 7:25) as being torn between direction by "the flesh" or direction by "the Spirit."

18 εἰ δὲ πνεύματι ἄγεσθε, οὐκ ἐστὲ ὑπὸ νόμον, "and since you are led by the Spirit, you are not under the law." The postpositive δέ ("and") here functions as a simple connective, without any idea of contrast but simply adding a further thought to the thesis statements of this section (vv 13–18). εἰ with the indicative in the protasis is a first class conditional construction that assumes the reality of the statement ("since you are led by the Spirit"), a reality in line with what Paul has recalled about the Galatians' earlier experiences (cf. 3:2–5), with what he has said about their status as "sons of God" (cf. 3:26–4:7), and with what he has declared as to their freedom as Christians (cf. esp. 5:1, 13). πνεύματι is here, as in v 16, God's Holy Spirit, of whom Paul speaks in personal terms. The present passive verb ἄγεσθε ("you are led") is practically synonymous with the present imperative περιπατεῖτε ("live") of v 16, though with an emphasis on the voluntary subjugation of one's will to the Spirit who leads. The phrase ὑπὸ νόμον ("under the law") is undoubtedly to be read, as elsewhere throughout the Galatian letter (e.g., 3:23; 4:4, 5, 21), as referring to the nomistic lifestyle advocated by the Judaizers, against which Paul argued and exhorted from 2:15 through 5:12.

In concluding his thesis statements of 5:13–18, Paul now relates his two exhortations of "through love serve one another" and "live by the Spirit" to the Judaizers' message of a nomistic lifestyle. Here he harks back to what he said in 5:1–6, so causing many to think that throughout Gal 5 there is only one and not two issues in view. Yet though Paul in this chapter exhorts regarding two matters within the Galatian churches, he is addressing the same people among whom both these matters were at issue. So amidst his statements regarding libertine tendencies among his converts, Paul sees it necessary to speak also about how his exhortations on that topic relate to the judaizing threat within the churches. For the Judaizers had undoubtedly argued that only two options existed for Galatian Christians: either (1) a lifestyle governed by Torah, or (2) a lifestyle giving way to license, such as formerly characterized their lives as Gentiles apart from God. The Christian gospel, however, as Paul proclaimed it, has to do with a third way of life that is distinct from both nomism and libertinism—not one that takes a middle course between the two, as many try to do in working out a Christian lifestyle on their own, but that is "a highway above them both" (Burton, *Galatians*, 302). The antidote to license in the Christian life is not laws, as the Judaizers argued, but openness to the Spirit and being guided by the Spirit. For being "in Christ" means neither nomism nor libertinism, but a new quality of life based in and directed by the Spirit.

Explanation

In 5:13–18 Paul sets out his thesis statements regarding the problem of loveless libertinism that was present in the Galatian churches. He begins by reaffirming the indicative of Christian freedom: "You, brothers, were called to be free!" (v 13a). He then speaks about "love," "service to others," and "the Spirit," giving two exhortations: "through love serve one another" (v 13b) and "live by the Spirit" (v 16). So while in 5:1–6 he has spoken negatively with regard to Christian freedom, exhorting that freedom in Christ not be renounced by a retrogression into nomism, here in 5:13–18 Paul speaks positively, exhorting that freedom in Christ be expressed "through love" in "serving one another" and by a life directed by "the Spirit"— certainly not taking Christian freedom as an opportunity for the expression of "the flesh," for "the Spirit" and "the flesh" are diametrically opposed to one another. As a final point in this section of thesis statements, Paul proclaims that life lived by the Spirit's direction is quite another type of existence than life lived nomistically by the precepts of the Torah. He brings this point in at the conclusion of his thesis statements, because though there were two matters that needed to be dealt with in the Galatian churches—the first, that of nomism, which was introduced by the Judaizers; the second, that of libertinism, which was a factor within the churches from the very first—the Galatian Christians were one people who were troubled by both the judaizing threat and certain libertine tendencies.

Contrary to both a legal and a libertine definition of the Christian life, the obligation of the Christian is stated in the two exhortations of this section: (1) "through love serve one another" and (2) "live by the Spirit"—with the former being grounded in and effected by the latter. The Spirit is not an adjunct to the law, assisting in overcoming the desires of the flesh by promoting positive obedience to the law. Nor are the real combatants in the ethical struggle the law and the flesh, with the obedience of the Christian as the prize. Rather, the Spirit opposes the flesh and replaces its works (cf. vv 19–21) with his own harvest of virtues (cf. NEB's translation of v 22: "the harvest of the Spirit"). "Clearly, therefore," as Burton observes, "life by the Spirit constitutes for the apostle a third way of life distinct both on the one hand from legalism and on the other from that which is characterised by a yielding to the impulses of the flesh. It is by no means a middle course between them, but a highway above them both, a life of freedom from statutes, of faith and love" (*Galatians*, 302).

The claim of the Judaizers must have been that the law identified matters contrary to God's will, provided the ethical standard for God's own, and incited the believer to achieve ethical perfection. Undoubtedly the Judaizers also referred to the Spirit, but probably as an auxiliary to the law given by God to aid men and women in their obedience. For Paul, however, the Spirit not only brings the believer into a new realm of spiritual existence but also (1) sensitizes the believer to what is contrary to God's will, (2) gives to the believer an intrinsic standard of values, and (3) enables the believer to do what is good, with expressions of that goodness being for the benefit of others. The Spirit alone is able to overcome the flesh by imparting the new life opened up by the work of Christ. And where the new life in Christ by the Spirit is present, no law is required to command it. It is the Spirit himself who fills the believer's life with rich content. For the one "in Christ," therefore, relationship with God and life lived as a Christian are begun, sustained, directed, and completed entirely by the Spirit.

2. The Works of the Flesh and the Fruit of the Spirit (5:19–26)

Bibliography

Barclay, J. M. G. *Obeying the Truth*, 106–45, 178–251. **Barclay, W.** *Flesh and Spirit*. **Barrett, C. K.** *Freedom and Obligation*. **Deidun, T. J.** *New Covenant Morality in Paul*. **Easton, B. S.** "New Testament Ethical Lists." *JBL* 51 (1932) 1–12. **Kamlah, E.** *Die Form der katalogischen Paränese.* **Malherbe, A. J.** *Moral Exhortation*. **Suggs, M. J.** "The Christian Two Way Tradition: Its Antiquity, Form, and Function." In *Studies in the New Testament and Early Christian Literature*. FS A. P. Wikgren, ed. D. E. Aune. NovTSup 33. Leiden: Brill, 1972. 60–74. **Thomas, J.** "Formgesetze des Begriffskatalogs im Neuen Testament." *TZ* 24 (1968) 15–28. **Vögtle, A.** *Die Tugend- und Lasterkataloge.* **Wibbing, S.** *Die Tugend- und Lasterkataloge.*

Translation

[19] Now the works of the flesh are obvious, which are: sexual immorality,[a] impurity, debauchery, [20] idolatry, witchcraft, hatred, strife,[b] jealousy,[c] fits of rage, selfish ambition, dissensions, factions, [21] envy,[d] drunkenness, orgies, and the like. I warn you, even as I said before: those who do such things shall not inherit the kingdom of God.

[22] But the fruit of the Spirit is love, joy, peace, patience, kindness, goodness, faithfulness, [23] gentleness, and self-control.[e] Against such things there is no law. [24] Those who belong to Christ Jesus[f] have crucified the flesh with its passions and desires. [25] Since we live by the Spirit, let us keep in step with the Spirit. [26] Let us not become conceited, provoking and envying one another.

Notes

[a] πορνεία ("sexual immorality") is well attested as the first in Paul's list of vices, though μοιχεία ("adultery") is added at the head of the list by ℵ² D Byzantine it syr^hel Iren^lat Ambst (the plural μοιχεῖαι, "adulteries," by G)—probably in an attempt to harmonize Paul's list with the catalogue of vices found in Mark 7:21–22 (cf. Matt 15:19).

[b] ἔρις ("discord," "contention") is well attested, though the plural ἔρεις ("discords," "contentions") is supported by C D² G Byzantine it vg syr^hel cop Mcion Cl Epiph Iren^lat.

[c] ζῆλος (in a bad sense: "jealousy," "envy") is well attested, though the plural ζῆλοι ("jealousies," "envies") is supported by ℵ C D² Byzantine it vg syr^hel cop Mcion Cl Epiph Iren^lat Cypr.

[d] φθόνοι ("envies," "jealousies") is attested by P^46 ℵ B cop^sa Mcion Cl Orig Iren^lat Aug, though the assonant couplet φθόνοι φόνοι ("envies and murders") is attested by A C D G Byzantine it vg cop^bo—probably, as at v 19, in an attempt to harmonize Paul's list with the catalogue of vices found in Mark 7:21–22 (cf. Matt 15:19); perhaps also influenced linguistically by Rom 1:29.

[e] ἁγνεία ("purity") is added to the list of virtues by D* G it vg Iren^lat Cypr Ambst.

[f] τοῦ Χριστοῦ ("of Christ") is attested by P^46 D G Byzantine it vg syr, though τοῦ Χριστοῦ Ἰησοῦ ("of Christ Jesus") is somewhat better attested by ℵ A B C P cop.

Form/Structure/Setting

In 5:19–26 Paul elaborates on his thesis statements of 5:13–18, setting out two catalogue lists, the one of vices and the other of virtues, that have to do with "the works of the flesh" and "the fruit of the Spirit" respectively. His purpose in presenting these two lists is to bring his readers to two realizations: (1) that libertinism, which focuses on "freedom as an opportunity for the flesh" (v 13), has dire, negative consequences, and (2) that serving one another "through love" (v 13) and living "by the Spirit" (v 16) have significant, positive results. Paralleling the catalogues of virtues and vices that were developed widely for various purposes in the Hellenistic world of his day, Paul sets out his lists of vices and virtues in order to highlight his two conclusions: (1) that "those who belong to Christ Jesus have crucified the flesh with its passions and desires" (v 24), and so cannot live in a libertine fashion; and (2) that "since we live by the Spirit, let us keep in step with the Spirit" (v 25), thereby expressing "the fruit of the Spirit" in our lives. He then concludes this section with an exhortation, "Let us not become conceited, provoking and envying one another" (v 26), which evidently Paul saw as necessary because of what was going on among his converts in the province of Galatia.

Catalogues of virtues and vices (i.e., systematic lists, often with descriptions of the items listed) were common in Paul's day. In embryonic form they can be traced back to Plato (427–347 B.C.), who, although he did not formulate such catalogues himself, gave an impetus to such endeavors by speaking of four forms of virtue (*Laws* 12.963C), of the ideal society as being "wise, brave, sober, and just" (*Republic* 4.427E), and of "sobriety, and bravery, and loftiness of soul, and all the parts of virtue" as characterizing the ideal citizen of the ideal society (*Republic* 7.536A). Aristotle (384–322 B.C.), however, went further by way of setting out in a systematic fashion the cardinal virtues. So, for example, in *Rhetoric* 1.6.1362b (LCL: 1.6.8) he says:

> To enumerate them one by one, the following things must necessarily be good: Happiness, since it is desirable in itself and self-sufficient, and to obtain it we choose a number of things. Justice, courage, self-control, magnanimity, magnificence, and all other similar states of mind, for they are virtues of the soul. Health, beauty, and the like, for they are virtues of the body.

Then in *Rhetoric* 1.9.1366b (LCL: 1.9.4ff.) Aristotle gives a dual listing of both the cardinal virtues and the cardinal vices:

> The components of virtue are justice, courage, self-control, magnificence, magnanimity, liberality, gentleness, practical and speculative wisdom. . . . Justice is a virtue which assigns to each man his due in conformity with the law; injustice claims what belongs to others, in opposition to the law. Courage makes men perform noble acts in the midst of dangers according to the dictates of the law and in submission to it; the contrary is cowardice. Self-control is a virtue . . . the contrary is licentiousness. Liberality is a virtue . . . the contrary is avarice. Magnanimity is a virtue . . . the contrary is little-mindedness. Magnificence is a virtue . . . the contraries are little-mindedness and meanness. Practical wisdom is a virtue of reason.

The most developed listing of virtues and vices in Aristotle's writings, of course, is to be found in his *Nicomachean Ethics*. In book 2 Aristotle argues that virtue is essentially the observance of a mean or middle way between two extremes, with both such extremes being accounted as vices (2.6.15ff.), though, as he concedes, this is not always true since some vices (e.g., adultery) are wrong of themselves, and so not simply excesses or deficiencies (2.6.18ff.). In 2.7.2–15 he begins an examination of the cardinal virtues, but promises a more detailed treatment to follow (which takes place in books 3, 4, and 5). Then in 3.5.23–5.11.10 appears his full treatment of the virtues, which he prefaces with the statement: "But to resume, let us now discuss the virtues severally, defining the nature of each, the class of objects to which each is related, and the way in which it is related to them. In so doing we shall also make it clear how many virtues there are." In dealing with the virtues "severally," Aristotle takes up such individual virtues as courage (ἀνδρεία), temperance (σωφροσύνη), liberality (ἐλευθεριότης), magnificence (μεγαλοπρέπεια), greatness of soul (μεγαλοψυχία), gentleness (πραότης), and after treating various others concludes with an extensive treatment (all of book 5) on the virtue of justice (δικαιοσύνη).

According to Diogenes Laertius (early 3rd century A.D.) and Stobaeus (5th century A.D.), it was Zeno, the founder of the Stoic school of philosophy at Athens (c. 308 B.C.), who first formulated formal catalogues of virtues and vices, with the virtues having to do with knowledge and the vices with ignorance (cf. Diogenes Laertius, *Zeno* 7.110–16; Stobaeus, *Eklogai Apophthegmata Hypothekai* 2.59.18–62.6). And scholarship has taken their attribution to be credible, as B. S. Easton in 1932 wrote: "It is now generally recognized that the catalogs of virtues and vices in the New Testament are derived ultimately from the ethical teaching of the Stoa" (*JBL* 51 [1932] 1). Lines of dependence, of course, may be debated. There can, however, be no debate that such catalogues were enormously popular in the Greco-Roman world of Paul's day, as witnessed not only in the writings of such Stoics as Seneca (4 B.C.—A.D. 65; cf. his *De brevitate vitae* 10.2–4; 22.11) and Epictetus (A.D. 50–120; cf. his *Discourses* 2.8.23, 14.8, 16.14, 16.41, 16.45, 18.28, 19.19, 19.26, 22.20; 3.2.3, 21.9, 22.13, 24.89–90; 4.3.7, 6.16), but also those of Cicero (106–43 B.C.; cf. his *Tusculan Disputations* 4.7.16–8.22; 11–20, passim), Dio Chrysostom (A.D. 40–120; cf. his *Orations* 2.75; 3.39–41; 8.8; 49.9; 66.1; 69.6, 9), and Plutarch (A.D. 46–120; cf. his *De liberis educandis* 12B; *De tranquillitate animi* 465D, 468B; *Ad principem ineruditum* 782F; *De sera numinis vindicta* 556B), to name only a prominent few.

Catalogue lists of virtues and vices are not to be found in the OT, though, of course, distinctions between formal catalogues and discursive treatments of virtues and vices (e.g., Ps 15:1–5; Prov 6:16–19; 8:13–14; Jer 7:5–9; Ezek 18:5–17; Hos 4:1–2) are not always easy to make. It was only, it seems, when the systematizing tendencies of Greek thought penetrated the Jewish world that Jewish writers in the Second Temple Period began formulating catalogues of the cardinal virtues and vices, with those virtues and vices then subdivided into subordinate virtues and vices almost ad nauseum. Philo of Alexandria (30 B.C.—A.D. 50) is the prime example of such a Jewish writer, with the most obvious instance of such a catalogue of vices (about 150 items!) and virtues appearing in his *Sacrif.* 15–33. But there are also many other such lists in Philo's writings, as witness *Poster. Caini* 52; *Deus* 164; *Opif.* 73; *Leg. Alleg.* 86–87; *Virt.* 182; *Cher.* 71, 92; *Migr.* 60; *Confus.* 47, 117; *Spec.*

1.281; 2.62; 4.84, 87–90; *Mutat.* 197; and *Ios.* 70. Catalogues can be found as well in such overtly hellenistically influenced Jewish writings as Wisdom of Solomon (cf. 14:22–27); 4 Maccabees (cf. 1:18–28, 32a; 2:15); and the *Sibylline Oracles* (cf. 2.254–63 [310–15]; 3.36–41 [43–49], 377–80 [442–46]; 4.31–34 [35–39]). And they appear in somewhat abbreviated form throughout the *Testaments of the Twelve Patriarchs* (cf. *T. Reub.* 3.3–8; *T. Levi* 17.11; *T. Jud.* 16.3; *T. Iss.* 7.2–5; *T. Gad* 5.1; *T. Ash.* 2.58; *T. Benj.* 7.2) and *3 Apocalypse of Baruch* (cf. 4.17; 8.4–5; 13.4)—both writings being extensively redacted by Christians—though hardly at all in the Talmud (only such passages as *m. 'Abot* 3.11; 4.21; *b. Soṭa* 42a; and *b. Sanh.* 74a have anything close in their listings of three or four vices).

Furthermore, it need be noted that lists of virtues and vices appear in the NT not only here at Gal 5:19–23, but also frequently elsewhere: in the Gospels at Mark 7:21–22 (cf. Matt 15:19); elsewhere in the Pauline letters at Rom 1:29–31; 13:13; 1 Cor 5:9–11; 6:9–10; 2 Cor 12:20–21; Eph 4:31–32; 5:3–5; Col 3:5–8; 1 Tim 1:9–10; 2 Tim 3:2–5; Titus 3:3; and in the "hinder parts" of the NT at Jas 3:13–18 (esp. v 17); 1 Peter 2:1; 4:3, 15; and Rev 21:8; 22: 14–15. That such catalogues were considered part and parcel of the way Christians spoke and wrote is evidenced by their continuation during the second and third centuries A.D. in the so-called apostolic fathers (cf. Pol. *Phil.* 2.2; 4.3; *Barn.* 18–20, passim; Herm. *Man.* 5.2.4; 6.2; 8.3–5), the gnostic texts of Nag Hammadi (cf. *Auth. Teach.* [CG VI.3] 23.29–34; 30.26–31.24; *Great Pow.* [CG VI.4] 39.16–33), and the *Ps.-Clem. Hom.* (cf. 11.27). In fact, not only were ethical lists popular among early Christians, as they were within the Greco-Roman world generally, but it appears that they were included within early Christian catechetical teaching, probably in connection with baptism, as Paul's reference to his previous instruction to his Galatian converts in v 21 suggests.

It seems beyond dispute that the catalogue form of virtues and vices had its origin in Greek ethical teaching. Of late, however, while acknowledging the Hellenistic provenance of the catalogue genre, it has been argued that a closer parallel to Gal 5:16–23 is to be found in the "Two Ways" tradition that was taken over by the early Christians from a thoroughly Jewish model (cf. M. J. Suggs, "The Christian Two Way Tradition," 60–74). The "Two Ways" tradition combined with catalogues of virtues and vices is represented at Qumran by 1QS 3.25–4.11, where, in the context of a discussion of "the spirits of truth and of perversity" set by God within every man, there are lists of virtues and vices associated with the activities of these two spirits—though, it need also be noted, there are other lists of virtues and vices in 1QS that are not in a "Two Ways" or "two spirits" context (cf. 2.23–25; 5.3–7; 8.2–4). Likewise, the catalogue of vices in *T. Ash.* 2.5–8 (as noted above) is set within a "Two Ways" context (cf. 1.3–9). And the theme of "Two Ways" was explicitly developed in such second-century Christian writings as *Did.* 1–5, *Barn.* 18–20, and Herm. *Mand.* 6.2.1–7. All of this, it has been proposed, suggests that while catalogues of virtues and vices were common in the Hellenistic world, Gal 5:19–23 is probably more accurately to be seen against the background of a Jewish "Two Ways" ethical tradition that was taken over by the early Christians.

The strongest argument in favor of seeing Gal 5:19–23 as influenced by a Jewish "Two Ways" tradition is the duality of the lists in this passage. Dual lists of virtues and vices, while not altogether absent, appear more infrequently in the Hellenistic catalogues than single lists, while dual lists appear regularly and quite naturally in a Jewish "Two Ways" tradition. With reference to this argument based on duality in Paul's Galatian usage, however, the following considerations must also be taken into account:

1. "Two-ness" is not explicitly referred to in Galatians, whereas in all of the passages cited above where a "Two Ways" tradition can be invoked the word "two" explicitly appears—"two ways," "two spirits," or "two angels." In fact, the appearance of the word "two" seems to be a defining feature of the form; if so, its absence from Gal 5 is telling.
2. While a Jewish "Two Ways" tradition might have left some imprint on the NT lists of virtues and vices, none of the other instances of catalogues in the NT (see above) is associated with "Two Ways" formulations. The fact that every other NT catalogue is devoid of such a context suggests that 5:19–23 should be seen in the same light.
3. That 5:19–23 differs from other NT catalogues in its duality of listing is interesting, but not necessarily conclusive, since duality of listing is not foreign to a Hellenistic catalogue genre. There are significant instances of dual listings in the Hellenistic catalogues (e.g., Aristotle and Philo being most prominent). Moreover, there is an implicit duality in many of the Hellenistic catalogues of vices (i.e., "this is the pattern of behavior you should avoid").
4. Paul's own ethical dualism of "the flesh" versus "the Spirit" provides a sufficient rationale for the dual lists of 5:19–23. Thus the dual nature of his catalogue here does not necessarily imply a Jewish "Two Ways" tradition as formative rather than a Hellenistic catalogue genre being followed.

It seems best, therefore, to view 5:19–23 as modeled after the Hellenistic "catalogue" genre and not a Jewish "Two Ways" tradition. Catalogues of virtues and vices, while originating among the Greeks, had permeated the ancient world before the NT was written and so became a common form in the ethical teaching of Greeks, Romans, Jews (at least those who sought to interact with the Hellenistic world), and Christians alike. While catalogues of virtues and vices appear at times in the "Two Ways" tradition of Second Temple Judaism, that was not their primary context in Jewish writings. The duality of Paul's catalogue in 5:19–23 results, it appears, not from a Jewish "Two Ways" tradition but from the apostle's own ethical dualism of "the flesh" versus "the Spirit."

Comment

19 φανερὰ δέ ἐστιν τὰ ἔργα τῆς σαρκός, "now the works of the flesh are obvious." In the second of his exhortations of 5:13–18 (i.e., "live by the Spirit") Paul pointed to the mutual antipathy of "the flesh" and "the Spirit" (vv 16–18). Now he begins his elaboration on that antipathy, presenting first a catalogue of "the works of the flesh" (vv 19–21). The postpositive δέ ("now") is resumptive in function, not adversative. The noun φανερός ("open to public observation," "evident," "obvious") suggests common knowledge, implying that one does not need the Mosaic law to identify the wrongness of what follows (cf. similar thrusts in Rom 1:24–32; 2:12–15; 1 Cor 5:1). The expression τὰ ἔργα τῆς σαρκός ("the works of the flesh") correlates with, though is not the same as, the phrase ἔργα νόμου ("the works of the law") that Paul used when addressing the judaizing threat (cf. 2:16; 3:2, 5), though admittedly, the conjunction of σάρξ ("flesh") in an embryonically ethical manner with ἔργα νόμου in 3:2–3 may suggest more of a connection than simply a correlation. In speaking against the Judaizers' call for a nomistic lifestyle, Paul began by denouncing what he saw as the basis for their message: that whole legalistic complex of thought having to do with winning God's favor by a merit-amassing observance of Torah (i.e., "the works of the law"). Now in denouncing his converts' libertine tendencies, Paul encapsulates all of their endeavors under the term "the works of the flesh," thereby providing a parallel caption for these further perversions of the gospel. The whole purpose of this list of vices coupled with the list of virtues that follows is, as Burton states, "to enforce the exhortation of V. 13b, not to convert their liberty into an occasion to the flesh, but to rule their lives by love, which is itself to be achieved by the Spirit" (*Galatians*, 304).

19b–21a ἅτινά ἐστιν πορνεία, ἀκαθαρσία, ἀσέλγεια, εἰδωλολατρία, φαρμακεία, ἔχθραι, ἔρις, ζῆλος, θυμοί, ἐριθεῖαι, διχοστασίαι, αἱρέσεις, φθόνοι, μέθαι, κῶμοι, καὶ τὰ ὅμοια τούτοις, "which are: sexual immorality, impurity, debauchery, idolatry, witchcraft, hatred, strife, jealousy, fits of rage, selfish ambition, dissensions, factions, envy, drunkenness, orgies, and the like." In Koine Greek, as different from classical Greek, the compound neuter plural relative pronoun ἅτινα often takes over the function of the simple neuter plural relative pronoun ἅ ("which"), and Paul seems to prefer the longer plural forms of relative pronouns rather than the shorter forms (see *Comment* at 4:24). The third person singular ἐστίν with a neuter plural subject functions to gather all of the items involved into one complex of ideas.

The list of vices that follows is made up of fifteen items, with the expression καὶ τὰ ὅμοια τούτοις ("and the like") indicating that this list is to be taken as only representative of what more might be said. As Betz observes: "Evil occurs in innumerable forms, and only some examples are provided in the list" (*Galatians*, 284). The textual tradition shows that many tried to add to this list by including "adultery/adulteries" at the start and "murders" toward the end (see *Notes* a and d), probably to bring it into line with Jesus' words of Mark 7:21–22 (cf. Matt 15:19). External attestation, however, is not sufficiently strong to warrant such an increase of items, even though obviously Paul viewed both adultery and murder as evil. Interestingly, the various items listed appear sometimes in the singular and sometimes in the plural. Again, the textual tradition shows that many scribes attempted to make the list uniform by recasting the singulars into plurals, but external attestation is not strong enough to warrant our acceptance. Greek abstract nouns are often, though not always, used in the plural to signify manifestations or demonstrations of the quality denoted in the singular, and thus to mean "displays of" or "actions expressing" that quality. So it is possible to translate them into English, as in Greek, by either a singular or a plural form, with the singular often being the more idiomatic.

Of note regarding this catalogue of vices is the fact that the fifteen items seem to be listed without order or system. There have, of course, been many attempts to organize them into categories. Most popular of these is the fourfold classification of Lightfoot (*Galatians*, [1890], 210) and Burton (*Galatians*, 304): (1) three sins of sensuality (i.e., sexual immorality, impurity, debauchery); (2) two associated with heathen religions (i.e., idolatry and witchcraft); (3) eight having to do with conflict among people (i.e., hatred, discord, jealousy, fits of rage, selfish ambition, dissensions, factions, envy); and (4) two that have to do with drunkenness and its natural consequences (i.e., drunkenness and orgies). This fourfold classification has been taken over by NEB and NIV, though a fivefold grouping has also been popularized by JB (dividing the sins that have to do with conflict among people into two sets of five and three). It seems best, however, to take this list of fifteen vices as something of "a random collection of terms, describing the ordinary occurrences of evil among men" (so Betz *Galatians*, 283; cf. J. Thomas, *TZ* 24 [1968] 15–28; Mussner, *Galaterbrief*, 381), as set out by Luther and KJV (though with the two additions of "adultery" and "murders" à la the TR of their day) and as followed by RSV (without the two additions), for the expression καὶ τὰ ὅμοια τούτοις ("and the like") seems to have reference to all the items in the list and not just to drunkenness and orgies. If, in fact, there is any emphasis to be seen in this list of vices, it is probably to be found in the first vice, πορνεία ("sexual immorality"). That is where in a Greek structure one would expect anything being stressed to be placed; furthermore, the parallel list of virtues starts with what appears to be an emphasis on ἀγάπη ("love").

πορνεία has to do with unlawful and immoral sexual relationships, and so is best rendered "sexual immorality." It probably signified originally "prostitution" (πόρνη, the word for "prostitute," is likely related to πέρνημι, "to sell [slaves]," since prostitutes were commonly purchased as slaves), though in the LXX and NT it is used more broadly for sexual immorality generally (cf. Paul's other uses of the word in 1 Cor 5:1; 6:13, 18; 7:2; 2 Cor 12:21; Eph 5:3; Col 3:5; 1 Thess 4:3; also Jesus' catalogue of vices in Mark 7:21//Matt 15:19). This vice was so common in the Greco-Roman world of Paul's day that it was not regarded as particularly reprehensible, except when carried to excess. Thus, as W. Barclay points out: "It is significant that it is with this sin that Paul begins. The sexual life of the Graeco-Roman world in NT times was a lawless chaos. . . . He [Paul] lived in a world in which such sin was rampant, and in that world Christianity brought men an almost miraculous power to live in purity" (*Flesh and Spirit*, 24 and 28; note Barclay's depiction of the state of Greco-Roman morals in Paul's day in the five pages between these two statements).

ἀκαθαρσία has a wide range of meaning: dirt or dirtiness in the physical sense; pus or impurities in a medical sense; unclean or uncleanness in a ritual or ceremonial sense; and lack of purity or looseness in a moral sense. It appears about twenty times in LXX Leviticus in a ritual or ceremonial sense for uncleanness that makes it impossible for a person to enter into the presence of God (e.g., Lev 18:19; 20:25; 22:3). In Josephus it appears twice, once of those afflicted with disease (*Ag. Ap.* 1.307) and once of extreme sexual sins (*J.W.* 4.562). But its normal use in Paul and the rest of the NT has to do with sexual impurity or looseness in a moral sense, with that moral impurity, as with OT ritual impurity, separating a person from God (cf. Paul's other uses of the word to mean sexual impurity or looseness in Rom 1:24; 6:19; 2 Cor 12:21; Eph 4:19; 5:3; Col 3:5; 1 Thess 4:7, though it is used in 1 Thess 2:3 more broadly in the sense of "error").

ἀσέλγεια connotes extreme "licentiousness" or "debauchery"—or, as W. Barclay defines it, "a love of sin so reckless and so audacious that a man has ceased to care what God or man thinks of his actions" (*Flesh and Spirit*, 31). The word does not appear in the canonical books of the LXX, though it does appear in Wis 14:26 linked with various sexual perversions and in 3 Macc 2:26 in describing audacious acts of impiety. Josephus uses the word three times in the *Jewish War*: once in reporting a false accusation against Mariamne that she recklessly "exhibited herself" before another man, so inflaming Herod with murderous jealousy (*J.W.* 1.439);

once describing the Essenes' asceticism in keeping themselves from "women's wantonness" (*J.W.* 2.121); and once in portraying the actions of the Zealot soldiers within Jerusalem in the last days of the city's siege, who in their drunkenness imitated both the dress and the passions of women, "devising in their excess of lasciviousness unlawful pleasures and wallowing as in a brothel in the city, which they polluted from end to end with their foul deeds" (*J.W.* 4.562). And Josephus's seven uses of the word in his *Antiquities* are along these same lines (cf. *Ant.* 4.151; 8.252, 318; 15.98; 16.185; 17.110; 20.112). In the NT the word appears at times without specific restriction to sexual sins (cf. Mark 7:22; 1 Peter 4:3; 2 Peter 2:2, 7, 18), though elsewhere in Paul it has reference always to sensuality (cf. Rom 13:13; 2 Cor 12:21; Eph 4:19), and so should be understood here as well.

εἰδωλολατρία, meaning "idolatry," is not found in the classical writers, the LXX, or Josephus. The cognate term εἴδωλον appears in the LXX and NT either with reference to an image of a god (cf. Acts 7:41; Rev 9:20) or to the god represented by the image (cf. 1 Cor 8:4, 7; 10:19), and εἰδωλολατρία seems to have shared in this ambiguity (cf. 1 Cor 5:10–11; 6:9; 1 Peter 4:3). In Paul's usage, not only is the worship of an image or the god represented by an image idolatry, but also eating food that had idolatrous associations (1 Cor 10:7, 14) and being covetous or greedy (Col 3:5).

φαρμακεία, whence our English word "pharmacy" is derived, while a neutral term meaning to dispense drugs for medicinal purposes, also acquired two negative connotations: the use of drugs to poison people and the use of drugs in sorcery or witchcraft. In the LXX the word is regularly used in a bad sense of the sorcerers of Pharaoh's court (Exod 7:11, 22), of sorcerers in Babylon (Isa 47:9, 12), and of the Canaanites who practiced "detestable works of enchantments" (Wis 12:4). Josephus likewise uses the term and its cognates in a pejorative manner, with φαρμακεία (noun) meaning "murder by poison" (*J.W.* 1.227, 452, 638; *Ant.* 15.47), φαρμακίς (noun) meaning "poisoner/sorceress" and φάρμακον (noun) meaning "poison" (*Ant.* 17.63), φαρμάσσω (verb) meaning "poison" (*J.W.* 1.195), and φαρμακεύς (noun) used in the sense of "sorcerer" or "one who practices witchcraft" (*Life* 145–50). Apart from its occurrence here in Galatians, the only other instances of φαρμακεία in the NT are at Rev 9:21 and 18:23 (though see οἱ φαρμακοί at Rev 21:8 and 22:15), which also have to do with sorcery or witchcraft.

ἔχθραι (plural) is a common word occurring frequently in Greek classical writings, the LXX, and the NT. It denotes "enmity," "hostility," or "hatred" in whatever form expressed. Josephus's uses of the word are representative: Balaam's advice to the envoys from Balak to "renounce that hatred which they bore to the Israelites" (*Ant.* 4.106); Herod's suspicious "hatred" of his former friends at court (*Ant.* 16.239); and the "hatred" of former confederates toward the Jews at the time of Jerusalem's fall (*Ant.* 17.269). In the NT it is used with reference to the hostility between Herod and Pilate (Luke 23:12), but also more significantly of mankind's hostility against God (cf. Rom 8:7; Eph 2:14; Jas 4:4), which undoubtedly is what it connotes here in Gal 5:20. Its opposite among the ancients was φιλία, "friendship." In the NT, however, its opposite is ἀγάπη, "love" (cf. v 22).

ἔρις was commonly used among classical writers to mean "strife," "discord," "quarreling," "wrangling," or "contention." It appears with such a focus of meaning in the LXX (cf. Ps 139:20 [B]; Sir 28:11; 40:5, 9) and Josephus (cf. *J. W.* 1.206; 3.518; 4.109, 131; 5.71, 309, 396, 502; *Ant.*3.96; 7.17, 237; 9.240; 14.470; 16.194; 19.110). And its nine NT instances, all of which are to be found in Paul's letters, continue this same focus on "strife" or "discord" (in addition to here in Galatians, see Rom 1:29; 13:13; 1 Cor 1:11; 3:3; 2 Cor 12:20; Phil 1:15; 1Tim 6:4; Titus 3:9).

ζῆλος occurs commonly in the classical writers as both "a noble passion" (so Plato and Aristotle) and a synonym for φθόνος, "envy" (so Hesiod). In the LXX and NT three meanings for the word appear: (1) "intense devotion" to God, to a person or persons, or to a thing (cf. Num 25:11a; 1 Kgs 19:10, 14; Ps 69:10; 1 Macc 2:24–26, 58; Rom 10:2; 2 Cor 7:7; Phil 3:6); (2) "anger" arising out of devotion to another person or thing (cf. Num 25:11b; Ezek 23:25; Acts 5:17; 13:45; Heb 10:27); and (3) "jealousy," an unfriendly feeling excited by another's welfare, or "envy," a desire to have for oneself what another possesses (cf. Cant 8:6; Eccl 4:4; 9:6; Rom 13:13; 1 Cor 3:3; Jas 3:14, 16). It is often used by Josephus in the sense of "intense devotion" or "anger" arising out of devotion (so, e.g., in many of his references to the Zealots), but in the bad sense of "jealousy" when describing Herod's reactions to stories about Mariamne's supposed moral indiscretions (*Ant.* 15.82). The common feature in all of these meanings has to do with intense feeling, often with an eager desire of some kind. It is only the context, however, that can indicate whether ζῆλος in a particular case is to be understood in a good or bad sense, and here amidst a list of vices it is clearly used in the bad sense of "jealousy" or "envy."

θυμοί (plural), a common word in the classical writings, is like ζῆλος in that it can be used both in a good and a bad sense. It occurs frequently in the LXX (over 300 times) and Josephus (seventeen times) to mean either "disposition" or "courage" in a good sense, or more often "anger" or "fits of rage" in a bad sense. In the NT, the Apocalypse uses it both with reference to God's wrath (Rev 14:10, 19; 15:1, 7; 16:1, 19; 19:15) and Satan's rage (Rev 12:12). Elsewhere in the NT it usually means human expressions of anger or rage (cf. Luke 4:28; Acts 19:28; Heb 11:27), which is how Paul normally uses it as well (in addition to v 20 here, cf. 2 Cor 12:20; Eph 4:31; Col 3:8), though once he uses it of God's anger (cf. Rom 2:8). Often the word is used synonymously with ὀργή ("wrath"), as is evident not only in the phrase ὀργὴ καὶ θυμός ("wrath and anger") of Rom 2:8 but also in the interchangeable expressions ἡ ὀργὴ τοῦ θυμοῦ ("wrath of anger") and ὁ θυμὸς ὀργῆς ("anger of wrath") of the LXX and Rev 16:19 and 19:15. "As compared with ὀργή," as Burton observes, "θυμός denotes an outburst of passion, ὀργή a more settled indignation; in accordance with which distinction θυμός tends to be used of the reprehensible anger of men, ὀργή of the righteous wrath of God. Yet the distinction is not steadfastly maintained" (*Galatians*, 307–8).

ἐριθεῖαι (plural) is a word found only occasionally in the classical writers, once in the LXX, and not at all in Josephus. It first appears in Aristotle where, in a political context, it means "canvassing for office" or "office seeking" (*Pol.* 5.2.9), though in nonpolitical contexts in Hesychius and Suidas it means simply "working for wages." Its cognate is ἔριθος, "a day-laborer" or "wage earner," and it is in this sense of "working for wages" that it is used in Isa 38:12 LXX (cf. the use of the verb ἠριθεύετο in Tob 2:11, where Anna "worked for wages" after Tobit's blindness to maintain her family). It came, however, to acquire the meaning of "self-seeking," "selfish devotion to one's own interests," or "selfish ambition," as is evident in its use in the NT where it appears more often than in all other ancient writings (cf. Rom 2:8; 2 Cor 12:20; Gal 5:20 [here]; Phil 1:17; 2:3; Jas 3:14, 16). For Paul (and James), as Burton points out, the term denotes "the very root-vice of all sin . . . selfishness, the antithesis of the all-inclusive virtue, love" (*Galatians*, 308).

διχοστασίαι (plural) was a common word among classical writers to mean "dissensions" or "seditions," often in a political context. Its one LXX occurrence is at 1 Macc 3:29 where it refers to "dissensions" among the Jews caused by the Seleucid decrees. It does not appear in Josephus. Its only other use in the NT is at Rom 16:17, where Paul urges his readers to watch out for those who cause "divisions" or "dissensions" among them. And this idea of "divisions" or "dissensions" is what is prominent in Paul's use of the term here at v 20.

αἱρέσεις (plural) was used by classical writers to mean either (1) "taking captive," "capture," or "seizure," or (2) "choice," "plan," "purpose," or "preference" (the noun being derived in this latter case from the middle verb αἱρέομαι, "I choose for myself"). So in the LXX the word appears repeatedly in the sense of "free will" or "choice." In later Greek, however, it came to mean as well a "philosophic tendency," "philosophic school," or "philosophic party." Josephus uses it normally to refer to the "three philosophies" within Judaism of his day—the Pharisees, the Sadducees, and the Essenes—though he also uses it in the sense of a "faction" when referring to "the leading men of Antigonus' party" (τοὺς πρώτους ἐκ τῆς αἱρέσεως Ἀντιγόνου) whom Mark Antony killed (*Ant.* 15.6). In Acts the term signifies a body of people who hold a chosen set of opinions—the Sadducees (5:17), the Pharisees (15:5; 26:5), and the Christians (24:5; 2:22)—being a descriptive term without any necessary reproach implied. As a term of reproach, identifying a group or "sect" departing from the main body, it is used of Christians in Acts 24:14, where Paul reports the accusation of his accusers. Its use in 1 Cor 11:19 ("factions" among the Corinthian believers) and 2 Peter 2:1 ("false teachers" who introduce "factions" or "heresies" among the believers), however, has to do more with differences of opinion and action than differing schools of thought, and that is how Paul uses the term here at the close of v 20.

φθόνοι (plural) was regularly used by classical writers in the sense of "ill-will," "malice," or "envy." It appears in the LXX (Wis 2:24; 6:23; 1 Macc 8:16; 3 Macc 6:7) and Josephus (about fifty times, always in the singular) in this negative sense as well. It is this sense of "envy" that dominates its NT uses (cf. Matt 27:18; Mark 15:10; Rom 1:29; Gal 5:21 [here]; Phil 1:15; 1 Tim 6:4; 1 Peter 2:10), except in Jas 4:5 where it is ascribed to the Spirit of God who desires exclusive possession of believers. Here at the start of v 21 φθόνοι ("envies") is closely parallel in meaning to ζῆλος ("jealousy"), which appeared in v 20.

μέθαι (plural) occurs in the classical writings and the canonical books of the LXX in two related senses: (1) "strong drink" and (2) "drunkenness"—though in Hag 1:6 LXX more with the meaning "satiate" ("have your fill") than "drunkenness." In the LXX Apocrypha (Jdt 13:15), Josephus (*J.W.* 5.21,23; *Ant* 1.177, 301; 6.301; 7.134, 175; 10.168, 169; 11.42; 12.188; 13.398; *Ag. Ap.* 2.195, 204) and the NT (Luke 21:34; 1 Cor 5:11; 6:10; Gal 5:21 [here]; Eph 5:18; 1 Thess 5:7), however, it appears only in the sense of "drunkenness."

κῶμοι (plural) occurs in the classical writings in the sense of "revelling," "carousing," or "orgies" such as accompany bouts of drinking and the festivals honoring the gods, particularly the god Dionysus (or Bacchus). In the LXX (Wis 14:23; 2 Macc 6:4), Josephus (*J.W.* 1.570; 2.29; *Ant.* 11.66; 17.65), and the NT (Rom 13:13; Gal 5:21 [here]; 1 Peter 4:3) the term appears with the same meaning as in the classical writers. In the lists of Rom 13:13 and 1 Peter 4:3 it is associated, as here, with drunkenness—in the former, as here, with μέθη; in the latter with οἰνοφλυγία.

21b ἃ προλέγω ὑμῖν καθὼς προεῖπον ὅτι οἱ τὰ τοιαῦτα πράσσοντες βασιλείαν θεοῦ οὐ κληρονομήσουσιν, "I warn you, even as I said before: Those who do such things shall not inherit the kingdom of God." The neuter plural relative pronoun ἃ ("these things") is undoubtedly accusative, not nominative, and so looks forward to the statement introduced by ὅτι ("that"), not back to the fifteen vices just enumerated. Because of the preposition πρό, the verb προλέγω could be understood to mean either "foretell" or "tell forth publicly." But since elsewhere where Paul uses προλέγω its object is a predictive warning (cf. 2 Cor 13:2; 1 Thess 3:4), it probably should be understood here as well to mean "I am predicting" or "I warn." Both the neuter plural relative pronoun ἃ and the verb προλέγω, therefore, refer the reader forward to what will be said as introduced by ὅτι.

But while being pointed forward by the relative pronoun and verb, the phrase καθὼς προεῖπον ("even as I said before") points back to what Paul told his converts before—either in the immediate context of his letter (so, possibly, Gal 1:9; see *Comment* on that verse) or when he was with them earlier (so Gal 5:3; 2 Cor 13:2; 1 Thess 4:6). Here it seems Paul has in mind some portion of his past teaching when he was with them, for there is nothing in the immediate context that matches the content of what he states he is repeating in the last part of the sentence. And while he himself gives no indication as to when in their time together he gave them this instruction, it may be assumed that what we have here is part of Paul's prebaptismal ethical teaching. For as *Did.* 7.1 tells us, new converts to Christ were given ethical teaching just before their baptism: "Concerning baptism, so shall you baptize: Having first repeated all these things [i.e., the ethical instruction of chapters 1–6 on the "Two Ways"], baptize in the name of the Father and of the Son and of the Holy Spirit" (cf. Justin, *Apology* 1.61).

What Paul gave his converts by way of moral teaching when he was with them, and what he now says he is repeating, is evidently a quotation from—or perhaps Paul's own précis of—early Christian catechetical instruction. The language of the statement, "Those who do such things shall not inherit the kingdom of God," seems not quite Pauline at a number of points. First, the term βασιλείαν θεοῦ ("kingdom of God"), while traditional in the early church and common in the Gospels, is somewhat rare in Paul's letters (cf. Rom 14:17; 1 Cor 4:20; 6:9–10; 15:50; see also 1 Cor 15:24; 1 Thess 2:12). Second, the substantival participle οἱ πράσσοντες ("those who do") is not quite what one would expect of Paul in Galatians, for ποιέω is the verb for "doing" in this letter (cf. 3:10, 12; 5:3, 17; 6:9) and the appearance of πράσσω here is the lone exception. Third, the use of the verb κληρονομέω ("inherit") here does not quite match the other instances of the term in Galatians (cf. 3:18, 29; 4:1, 7, 30), but corresponds more closely to the Synoptic sayings that speak of "entering into the kingdom of Heaven/God" (cf. Mark 10:15, par.; Matt 7:21; 18:8–9; 19:17; etc.). So what we probably have here is a ὅτι *recitativum* used to introduce a portion of the catechetical instruction of the early church given by Paul to his converts when he was with them and now repeated by way of warning, the purpose being, of course, that they might again realize the seriousness of allowing their freedom in Christ to degenerate into only "an opportunity for the flesh" (cf. 5:13b).

22—23a ὁ δὲ καρπὸς τοῦ πνεύματός ἐστιν ἀγάπη, χαρά, εἰρήνη, μακροθυμία, χρηστότης, ἀγαθωσύνη, πίστις, πραΰτης, ἐγκράτεια, "but the fruit of the Spirit is love, joy, peace, patience, kindness, goodness, faithfulness, gentleness, and self-control." The catalogue of vices found in vv 19–21a is now contrasted by a catalogue of virtues in vv 22–23a, with the postpositive δέ ("but") functioning in an adversative fashion. The term καρπός ("fruit") appears in a literal sense in 1 Cor 9:7 ("Who plants a vineyard and does not eat of its fruit?") and 2 Tim 2:6 ("The hardworking farmer should be the first to share in its fruits"). Elsewhere in Paul's letters, however, καρπός is used in a figurative sense as a metaphor (1) for converts won to Christ (cf. Rom 1:13; Col 1:6), (2) for the expressions of a godly life (cf. Rom 6:22; 7:4; Eph 5:9; Phil 1:11; 4:17; Col 1:10), (3) for the expressions of an ungodly life (cf. Rom 6:21; 7:5; Eph 5:11), and (4) for the gift of money Paul was taking to Jerusalem from his Gentile churches (Rom 15:28).

The phrase ὁ καρπὸς τοῦ πνεύματος ("the fruit of the Spirit") may be used here in conscious opposition to τὰ ἔργα τῆς σαρκός ("the works of the flesh") that heads the catalogue of vices earlier, and so was meant to suggest (1) the spontaneous quality of a life directed by the Spirit as opposed to human efforts to live according to the directives of the law or the flesh (so, e.g., Burton, *Galatians*, 313; Schlier, *Galater*, 255–56; Oepke, *Galater*, 180; Cole, *Galatians*, 167), (2) the idea of "peaceful growth" in the Spirit-directed life as opposed to "outbursts of undisciplined passion" when guided by fleshly concerns (so Duncan, *Galatians*, 173; cf. also Guthrie, *Galatians*, 148), or (3) that these virtues are given as a gift by God through his Spirit as opposed to being effected through human activity (so, e.g., Schlier, *Galater*, 255–56; Mussner, *Galaterbrief*, 385). C. K. Barrett, for example, aptly elaborates on the first of the above proposals when he says: "If Paul had headed his second list (5.22, 23) 'works of the Spirit' it would not only have led to a clash with 'works of the law,' it would have been positively misleading. Paul's use of 'works' (ἔργα) suggests works that men do, and these [i.e., the items headed by the phrase "the fruit of the Spirit"] are not human products but the result of God's Spirit dwelling within men. . . . All are the consequence of the self-forgetfulness that looks away from itself to God" (*Freedom and Obligation*, 77). And T. J. Deidun well expresses the third proposal when he writes: "The καρπός image evokes the inner dynamics of the Spirit and the 'passivity' of the Christian: the 'fruit' is not the product of the Christian's labouring, but the effect of another's activity. The Christian receives it as a gift" (*New Covenant Morality in Paul*, 81).

It may be, indeed, that Paul had certain features of one or more of the above three proposed ideas in mind where he contrasted "the fruit of the Spirit" with "the works of the flesh." His difference of wording, however, was not because the image of "fruit" and the idea of "fruitfulness" are appropriate only for the activity of the Spirit but inappropriate for discussions of the law and the flesh, for elsewhere Paul uses the metaphors of "sowing," "reaping," and "fruit" for both living according to the flesh and living according to the Spirit (cf. 6:7–8; see also Rom 6:21–22; 7:4–5). Nor was it because "works" and "working" are appropriate only for discussions of the law and the flesh but inappropriate for those having to do with the Spirit, for Paul has no trouble elsewhere speaking about Christians "working out" their faith commitments in terms of good "works" (cf. 5:6; 6:4, 10; see also 2 Cor 9:8; Phil 2:12; 1 Thess 1:3). Likewise, though indeed the virtues listed are given as gifts by God through the Spirit, one must not "unpack" the metaphor of "fruit" in such a manner as to stress only the given quality of the virtues listed, implying an ethical passivity on the Christian's part. For as the exhortations throughout this entire section suggest, combined with the givenness of these virtues by God is the believer's active involvement in expressing them in his or her own lifestyle—or as Paul puts it pointedly a couple verses later: "Since we live by the Spirit, let us keep in step with the Spirit" (v 25).

As with the catalogue of vices of vv 19–21, so here in vv 22–23 the list of virtues is given without any necessary order or system. Some have attempted to classify the nine items in terms of three groups of three each: the first three having to do with dispositions of the mind ("love," "joy," "peace"); the second with qualities affecting human relations ("patience," "kindness," "goodness"); and the third with principles that guide conduct ("faithfulness," "gentleness," "self-control"). Such an ordering was popularized by Lightfoot (*Galatians* [1890], 212), and is carried on in the analysis of Betz (*Galatians*, 287–88) and the punctuation of Nestle (but not that of UBSGT). This threefold classification, however, while possibly of heuristic or homiletic value, is highly artificial and cannot be supported by anything in the text itself. Rather, if there is an emphasis in this list of nine items, it is probably to be seen in the first item, ἀγάπη ("love"), for that is where in a Greek structure one would expect to find anything being stressed. Furthermore, the reference to "love" recalls the opening exhortation of 5:13, "through love serve one another," suggesting, therefore, that all of the other virtues listed result in some manner from love. Perhaps also the last of the items in this list, that is, ἐγκράτεια ("self-control"), should be seen as being emphasized as well, for the final position in a Greek structure is also where one would expect to find anything being stressed. And "self-control," which became by the time of Paul a central virtue in Hellenistic ethics, certainly makes an important, positive contrast to the vices of "drunkenness" and "orgies" that conclude the catalogue of vv 19–21.

ἀγάπη, "love," is a word not found in the Greek classical writings, though the verb ἀγαπάω ("love") appears a number of times. Likewise, in Josephus there are seventy-four instances of ἀγαπάω but none of the noun ἀγάπη. The Greeks used three other nouns for love: φιλία, which refers to warm, intimate friendship of whatever circumstance; ἔρως, which refers primarily to physical love between the sexes; and στοργή, which refers to the love of family members for each other. In the LXX, however, ἀγάπη and ἔρως are often used interchangeably, with no contrast between them suggested. So, for example, the translators used ἀγάπη in relating the story of Amnon's passion for Tamar in 2 Sam 13:15 [LXX 2 Kgdms], and the mutual ardor of the lover and his beloved in Canticles is repeatedly described with ἀγάπη as the noun. Yet in contexts that have to do with God's love, the LXX constantly speaks of that as ἀγάπη.

Likewise in the NT, which is entirely concerned with the redemptive message of God's love expressed to mankind and reflected through his own, the noun ἀγάπη dominates all discussions of personal relationships, whether between God and mankind or between persons in whatever circumstance (ἔρως and στοργή do not appear at all). Particularly among the exhortations of Paul in Gal 5, ἀγάπη is highlighted: the only thing that has any value is "faith expressing itself through love" (v 6); "through love serve one another" (v 13); "all the law is fulfilled in one commandment: 'Love your neighbor as yourself'" (v 14). So as Paul here begins his catalogue of virtues, the first named—and undoubtedly in his mind the most important (cf. 1 Cor 13:13)—is ἀγάπη. In fact, judging by his highlighting of love in Gal 5, as well as later in 1 Cor 13, probably Paul saw all the other virtues of this list as included in and springing from this first-listed virtue.

χαρά, "joy," was a commonly used and highly esteemed noun throughout the Hellenistic world. It was even used as a proper name, so highly was it thought of—just as it is today. In the Greco-Roman world joy was connected with happiness, which in turn resulted from one finding for oneself the mean or middle way in life between all sorts of extremes, with joy in particular being highly dependent on pleasant circumstances. Christians, of course, neither had nor have a monopoly on joy, defined in terms of happiness and pleasant circumstances. Yet for one who is "in Christ" and "in the Spirit," joy becomes transposed into a higher key. For now "in the Holy Spirit" joy is associated with "righteousness," "peace," and "hope" (cf. Rom 14:17; 15:13, 32–33) and not just with pleasant circumstances.

εἰρήνη, "peace," is the universal quest of humanity, though it is defined differently in various philosophies and cultures. Among the Greeks the aim of life was ἀταραξία, "serenity," "tranquillity," or "a quiet mind," which was obtained via αὐτάρκεια or "self-sufficient independence" from all that caused trouble in life. Peace, therefore, was viewed largely in negative terms to mean "absence of pain in the body or trouble in the mind"—particularly among the Stoics, but also throughout Greek thought. Among Jews, however, peace is the term that epitomizes the perfection of relationships in whatever circumstance, and so signifies something quite positive. It means everything that makes for a person's highest good and that promotes the best relationships. So the Jewish greeting *Shalom* means not primarily an absence of opposition, difficulties, or pain, but personal wholeness and beneficial relationships.

Paul and the other NT writers were the inheritors of the Jewish understanding of peace, though they expressed that understanding in Greek words and forms. God is "the God of peace" (cf. Rom 15:33; 16:20; 2 Cor 13:11; Phil 4:9; 1 Thess 5:23; see also Heb 13:20). Relationship with God "in Christ" means that believers receive something of "the peace of God" in their lives, which peace then garrisons their hearts and minds (cf. Phil 4:7) and acts as an arbiter in their communal relationships (cf. Col 3:15). Peace, therefore, in the sense of personal wholeness and beneficial relationships, becomes the hallmark of a believer's life—in the home (cf. 1 Cor 7:15), in the church (cf. 1 Cor 14:33; Eph 4:3), and in the world (cf. Rom 12:18). Thus Paul exhorts believers: "Let us make every effort to do what leads to peace and to mutual edification" (Rom 14:19).

Jesus pronounced a blessing on "the peacemakers," saying that they are the ones who will be called "sons of God" (Matt 5:9). Paul associates "peace" not only with "joy" (as here and Rom 15:32–33) but also with "righteousness" (cf. Rom 14:17) and "hope" (cf. Rom 15:13). The triad "love, joy, and peace" may, in fact, be rooted in early Christian language (cf. Bruce, *Galatians*, 253), stemming from Jesus' words as reported in the Fourth Gospel (cf. the account of the upper room discourse, where Jesus speaks of "my peace," "my love," and "my joy" being given to his own in 14:27; 15:9–10; and 15:11 respectively).

μακροθυμία, "patience," appears rarely in non-Jewish Greek writings (Menander, *Fgm.* 19; Plutarch, *Lucull.* 32.3; 33.1). It occurs, however, four times in the LXX (Prov 25:15; Isa 57:15; Sir 5:11; 1 Macc 8:4), once in Josephus (*J.W.* 6.37), and three times in the *Testaments of the Twelve Patriarchs*, which probably was a Jewish writing heavily redacted by Christians (*T. Dan* 2.1; *T. Jos.* 2.7; 17.2), always with the general meaning of "steadfastness," "patience," or "long-suffering" in the face of persecution or provocation. As an adjective (μακρόθυμος) it appears in the canonical LXX writings as an attribute of God (Exod 34:6; Ps 103:8 [102:8 LXX]); in the NT as a noun it is used of God and Christ in their attitude toward people (Rom 2:4; 9:22; 1 Tim 1:16; 1 Peter 3:20; 2 Peter 3:15). Most commonly, however, it occurs in the NT in the sense of a patient endurance of wrong without anger or taking vengeance (so 2 Cor 6:6; Eph 4:2; Col 1:11; 3:12; 2 Tim 3:10; 4:2; Heb 6:12; Jas 5:10), with Paul urging his readers to live out their faith in terms of μακροθυμία toward one another and toward all people (so Eph 4:2; Col 1:11; 3:12; cf. also the verb μακροθυμέω of 1 Thess 5:14).

χρηστότης, "kindness," is a word used frequently by the classical writers to mean "excellence" when referring to things and "goodness," "honesty," or "kindness" when referring to persons. In the LXX it can mean "goodness" (Ps 14 [13]:1, 3) or "prosperity" (Ps 106 [105]:5), but usually connotes "kindness" (e.g., Pss 21:3 [20:4]; 68:10 [67:11]). In the *Psalms of Solomon* it uniformly means "kindness" (cf. 5.15, 16, 17, 21; 8.34; 9.15; 18.2), as it does also in its twenty-one appearances in Josephus. And "kindness" is its constant meaning in the NT, both when used as an attribute of God (cf. Rom 2:4; 11:22; Titus 3:4) and when used as a virtue expressed by God's people (as here; cf. 2 Cor 6:6 where it is also joined with μακροθυμία, "patience"), except in Rom 3:12, which is a quotation of Ps 14:3 where the word was used in the sense of "goodness."

ἀγαθωσύνη, "goodness," is a word not found in the classical writings, nor in Josephus, nor in such a Jewish sectarian work as the *Psalms of Solomon*. It appears in the LXX as a synonym for χρηστότης, "kindness," with its semantic range of meanings including "goodness" and/or "righteousness" (Ps 51:5), "prosperity" (Eccl 5:10, 17; passim), and "kindness" (Judg 8:35; 9:16; Neh 9:25, 35). In the NT it occurs only in Paul's letters (here at v 22; also Rom 15:14; Eph 5:9; 2 Thess 1:11), being roughly synonymous with χρηστότης but translated with an emphasis on its root idea ἀγαθός to mean "goodness."

πίστις, though used repeatedly elsewhere in Galatians to signify a person's response of trust regarding God's salvation provided in Christ Jesus (cf. 2:20; 3:6ff.; 5:6), here undoubtedly means the ethical virtue of "faithfulness." πίστις as a noun is used by Paul to speak of one of the divine attributes, "God's faithfulness" (Rom 3:3), though more commonly the adjective πιστός is used when referring to that ethical quality of God, "God is faithful" (cf. 1 Cor 1:9; 10:13; 2 Cor 1:18; also 1 Thess 5:24; 2 Thess 3:3). Here, however, the subject is the believer and the context is determinative. For situated, as it is, amidst eight other nouns in a list of human virtues, πίστις must here be understood as well as the human virtue of faithfulness, that is produced in the believer's life by the faithful God through his Spirit. On πίστις as belief and commitment, see *Comment* at 2:20 and 3:6.

πραΰτης, "gentleness," is the Koine spelling of the classical word πραότης, which was used by Plato, Aristotle, and other Greek classical writers to signify "mildness" or "gentleness" in dealing with people. Aristotle, in particular, defined it as the mean between the extremes of an "excessive anger" (ὀργιλότης) and the "inability to be angry" (ἀοργησία) (cf. *Nicomachean Ethics* 2.1108A). Likewise, the LXX uses πραΰτης to mean "mildness" or "meekness" (cf. Pss 45:4 [44:5 LXX]; 132:1 [131:1]), much as it does in the classical writings, though in the apocryphal writings of the LXX it is used both of a "submissive/teachable spirit" toward God (cf. Sir 1:27; 45:4) and of "modesty," "consideration," or "gentleness" toward others (cf. Add Esth 3:13; Sir 3:17; 4:8; 36:28). It does not appear in Josephus. In the NT the term carries on the development of meaning found in the apocryphal writings of Second Temple Judaism, with the idea of "teachableness" or "submission" to God's will found in Jas 1:21 ("in humility [ἐν πραΰτητι] accept the word planted in you, which can save you"), but with the meaning of "considerateness" or "gentleness" toward others found most commonly in 1 Cor 4:21; 2 Cor 10:1; Gal 6:1; Eph 4:2; Col 3:12; 2 Tim 2:25; Titus 3:2; Jas 3:13; 1 Peter 3:15. Here at the start of v 23 Paul undoubtedly means the latter, that of "considerateness" or "gentleness" toward others, which is the opposite of an arrogant and self-assertive spirit.

ἐγκράτεια, "self-control," is a word with a long history among the Greek classical writers. As an ethical term, it was introduced by Socrates (Xen. *Mem.* 1.5.4). Plato set it in opposition to overindulgence in both food and sex (*Republic* 390B, 430E). Aristotle treated it at length in his *Nicomachean Ethics*, discussing the difference between ἐγκράτεια and its opposite ἀκρασία: the ἐγκρατής person has powerful passions but keeps them under control; the ἀκρατής person does not deliberately choose the wrong but has no strength to resist temptation (*Nic. Eth.* 7.4.1145Bff.). In fact, by the time of Paul ἐγκράτεια had become a central concept in Hellenistic ethics.

Neither the noun ἐγκράτεια nor the adjective ἐγκρατής appears in the canonical books of the LXX. They are both, however, repeatedly found in the apocryphal and pseudepigraphical writings of Second Temple Judaism (cf. Tob 6:3; Wis 8:21; Sir 6:27; 15:1; 18:15, 29; 26:15; 27:30; 4 Macc 5:34; *Ep. Arist.* 278; *T. 12 Patr.* [esp. *T. Naph.* 8.8]) and in Josephus (for the noun alone, cf. *J.W.* 2.120, 138; 4.373; *Ant.* 6.63; 8.235; 15.237; 16.218, 246) in the sense of "self-control" in sexual matters, and so "continence" in opposition to allowing the cravings of one's own lusts to dominate. In the NT the noun occurs three times (in addition to here, cf. Acts 24:25; 2 Peter 1:6) and the adjective once (Titus 1:8). As Burton observes: "The position of the word here corresponding to that of μέθη, κῶμοι in the list of the works of the flesh, suggests a special reference in this case to control of the appetite for drink and of the consequent tendency to unrestrained and immodest hilarity. But this parallelism does not warrant the conclusion that the apostle had exclusive reference to this form of self-control" (*Galatians*, 318).

23b κατὰ τῶν τοιούτων οὐκ ἔστιν νόμος, "against such things there is no law." The use of κατά with the genitive to mean "against" is comparable to its use twice in the same manner in v 17. The plural articular substantival τῶν τοιούτων, which is probably to be taken as neuter (not masculine) in gender, is best seen as referring to the items just listed from "love" through "self-control," and so translated "such things." The anarthrous use of νόμος signifies the qualitative sense of "law" or "legal prescription," though certainly with the Mosaic law primarily in view.

In the context of Paul's argument throughout Galatians, the statement "against such things there is no law" is probably best understood as an understatement given for rhetorical effect. As such, it reiterates in a latent manner the assertion made in 5:14 that "such things" fully satisfy the requirements of the law, for they go beyond the law's requirements. Furthermore, the statement makes it clear that the list of enumerated virtues is not given as a set of legal prescriptions—that is, it is not to be taken as some kind of new law for Christians, as though by setting such goals and seeking to put them into practice believers can present themselves as acceptable before God. The statement itself, in fact, may have been proverbial in Paul's day for actions that surpass all legal prescriptions and are therefore beyond any legal accounting. Aristotle in the fourth century B.C. said of people who surpassed their fellows in ἀρετή or "virtue" that κατὰ δὲ τῶν τοιούτων οὐκ ἔστι νόμος, "against such people there is no law" (*Pol.* 3.13.1284A, with τῶν τοιούτων here understood as masculine). Paul, of course, may never have read Aristotle. Yet the statement probably was common coinage in Paul's day as an ethical maxim or proverb to be used by various speakers and writers as best fitted their respective purposes.

24 οἱ δὲ τοῦ Χριστοῦ 'Ιησοῦ τὴν σάρκα ἐσταύρωσαν σὺν τοῖς παθήμασιν καὶ ταῖς ἐπιθυμίαις, "those who belong to Christ Jesus have crucified the flesh with its passions and desires." The catalogues of vices and virtues that Paul gives in vv 19–21 and 22–23, respectively, elaborate on the thesis statements of vv 13–18, in particular showing how libertinism has dire, negative consequences ("the works of the flesh") and how serving others "through love" and living "by the Spirit" have significant, positive results ("the fruit of the Spirit"). But they also set the stage for two conclusions that Paul wants to make in this section: the first here in v 24, that "those who belong to Christ Jesus have crucified the flesh with its passions and desires," and so cannot live in a libertine fashion; the second (cast in hortatory form) in v 25, that "since we live by the Spirit, let us keep in step with the Spirit," so highlighting the Christian life as one lived by the Spirit's direction and enablement.

The substantival use of the plural article οἱ ("those") coupled with the possessive genitive phrase τοῦ Χριστοῦ 'Ιησοῦ ("of Christ Jesus," or "who belong to Christ Jesus") is equivalent to "those in Christ Jesus," as the parallel use of Χριστοῦ ("of Christ") at 3:29 with ἐν Χριστῷ 'Ιησοῦ ("in Christ Jesus") at 3:26 and 28 indicates. The postpositive particle δέ (untranslated) is here used in a connective, continuative fashion, not in a contrasting manner. The expression τὴν σάρκα ("the flesh") has the same meaning as found throughout this section beginning at 5:13, viz., humanity's fallen, corrupt, and sinful nature. The aorist verb ἐσταύρωσαν, since it identifies the crucifixion of the flesh in the Christian's experience as being a past event but assigns that event to no specific time in the past, is best translated as a perfect, "they have crucified"—i.e., a past event with present results or implications. The addition of the phrase σὺν τοῖς παθήμασιν καὶ ταῖς ἐπιθυμίαις ("with its passions and desires") lays stress on the completeness of the crucifixion involved, for not only are the outward manifestations of the flesh destroyed but also its dispositions and cravings put to death.

The self-giving of Christ through death on a cross is the central soteriological theme of Galatians (cf. 1:4; 3:1, 13; 6:12, 14), just as it was the focus of early Christian preaching (cf. the sermons recorded in Acts and the passion narratives of the Gospels). Identification with Christ in his crucifixion means a new type of existence for the believer, for now "Christ lives in me" (2:20). Likewise, just as the proclamation of "Christ crucified" has implications for issues having to do with legalism and nomism (cf. *Comment* on 3:1), so identification with Christ in his crucifixion has implications for issues having to do with libertinism (so here at v 24). For Paul, to claim identification with Christ in his crucifixion means that one cannot espouse a lifestyle that expresses either a legalistic or a libertine orientation. For in being crucified with Christ both the demands of the law and the impulses of the flesh have been crucified as well (cf. Rom 7:1–6; Col 2:13–15).

25 εἰ ζῶμεν πνεύματι, πνεύματι καὶ στοιχῶμεν, "since we live by the Spirit, let us keep in step with the Spirit." Exactly where Paul's elaboration of the antinomy between "the flesh" and "the Spirit" ends and his more specific exhortations begin has always been a problem for translators and commentators. The postpositive δέ of v 24 seems to connect v 24 with what precedes it. Vv 25 and 26, however, have no such connective. Furthermore, v 25 appears to be aphoristic and gnomic in nature, with its balance of indicative and imperative statements comparable to those of 5:1 and 5:13, and so possibly to be seen as the caption for a new hortatory subsection that runs from 5:25 through 6:10. In addition, v 26 appears to be more directly related to some specific situation within the Galatian churches than the catalogues of vv 19–23, and so perhaps to be grouped with what follows in 6:1–10. Some, therefore, have viewed v 24 as closing off the catalogue listings of vices and virtues and v 25 as being the opening affirmation of a new hortatory subsection that runs from 5:25 through 6:10 (e.g., WH; Duncan, *Galatians,* 177; Mussner, *Galaterbrief,* 396; Betz, *Galatians,* 291–93) — or, at least, the beginning of a transitional paragraph that consists of vv 25–26 and so stands between 5:19–24 and 6:1–10 (e.g., JB, RSV).

Yet the contrast that appears between "the flesh" in v 24 and "[the] Spirit" in v 25 seems to continue the contrast of "the works of the flesh" in vv 19–21 and "the fruit of the Spirit" in vv 22–23. So most translators and commentators have been hesitant to break the connection between v 24 and v 25. A few, being convinced of the intimate relation between v 24 and v 25 but believing v 26 to be more related to what follows than what precedes, have posited a minor break in Paul's exhortations between v 25 and v 26, with v 25 concluding Paul's catalogue lists of vices and virtues and v 26 beginning his more directed statements of 5:26–6:10 (e.g., NEB). In our view, however, the use of ἀδελφοί ("brothers") at the start of 6:1 is the epistolary signal that indicates the beginning of a new subsection in Paul's exhortations (cf. the use of ἀδελφοί at 3:15; 4:12, 28, 31; 5:11, 13; 6:18). So we conclude that the final two verses of chapter five should be included within the subsection beginning at v 19 and treated accordingly (so also, e.g., Burton, *Galatians,* 324; UBSGT, NIV; though usually for contextual reasons alone).

Indeed, "since we live by the Spirit, let us keep in step with the Spirit" is a statement that appears to be very much a précis of Paul's message. In form, it is chiastic; in content, aphoristic and gnomic, setting out in balanced form the indicative and the imperative of the gospel. The protasis of the statement is a first class condition (i.e., εἰ with the indicative), which assumes the reality of what is stated (cf. v 18). The expression ζῶμεν πνεύματι ("we live by the Spirit") has not been used by Paul before in Galatians but is synonymous with such expressions already used as πνεύματι περιπατεῖτε ("walk" or "live by the Spirit") of v 16 and πνεύματι ἄγεσθε ("be led by the Spirit") of v 18. And while not verbally synonymous, the thought expressed here is substantially the same as in the expression ζῆ ἐν ἐμοὶ Χριστός ("Christ lives in me") of 2:20, for πνεῦμα and Χριστός are equivalents in Pauline language when speaking of the believer's experience (cf. Rom 8:9–11).

The apodosis of the statement, "let us keep in step with the Spirit," lays emphasis on the obligation of Christian living as being neither to legal prescriptions (nomism) nor to the dictates of the flesh (libertinism) but to the Spirit, who both directs and enables and who is fully sufficient both for bringing to birth a believer's new life "in Christ" and for effecting a truly Christian lifestyle. The verb στοιχέω has as its basic meaning the idea of "stand in a row" (cf. *Comment* on the cognate expression τὰ στοιχεῖα at 4:3; also 4:9), and so came to connote "be in line with" or "agree with." Its use elsewhere by Paul, however, suggests "walking in the footsteps" of another (cf. Rom 4:12) or "living in accordance with a standard" (cf. Gal 6:16; Phil 3:16; also Acts 21:24). So here by exhorting his converts to "be in line" or "keep in step" with the Spirit, Paul is asking those who claim to live by the Spirit to evidence that fact by a lifestyle controlled by the Spirit. That he exhorts believers to do what it is the work of the Spirit to produce (cf. vv 22–23) is typical of Paul's understanding of Christian ethics, for Paul never views the ethical activity of the believer apart from the Spirit's work nor the Spirit's ethical direction and enablement apart from the believer's active expression of his or her faith.

26 μὴ γινώμεθα κενόδοξοι, ἀλλήλους προκαλούμενοι, ἀλλήλοις φθονοῦντες, "let us not become conceited, provoking and envying one another." Paul's own conclusion to his discussion of "the works of the flesh" and "the fruit of the Spirit" is the allusive directive he gives here in v 26: "Let us not become conceited, provoking and envying one another." The directive implies various factions at odds with one another in the Galatian churches. On the basis of this directive alone, we have no idea as to what specifically Paul had in mind here. But evidently he knew what he was talking about, and it must be supposed that they knew as well. For us, however, our only clue is to take v 26 not just as the conclusion to what precedes but also as something of an introduction to what follows, even though the connection of v 26 is closest to what precedes. For in applying the contrasts of a life lived according to "the flesh" and a life lived according to "the Spirit" in an allusive fashion here in v 26, Paul sets the stage for his instructions of 6:1–10 that relate to specific circumstances within the Galatian churches themselves. In effect, what follows in 6:1–10 is Paul's "going off at a word" from the general statement of 5:26, and so spelling out certain specific directives in elaboration of that general statement. It is, therefore, to the directives of 6:1–10 that we must turn to "unpack" what Paul had in mind here in v 26 in speaking of "conceited" or "boastful people" (κενόδοξοι) who "are provoking one another" (ἀλλήλους προκαλούμενοι) and "are envying one another" (ἀλλήλοις φθονοῦντες).

Explanation

The two catalogue lists of vices and virtues that are set out in 5:19–23 are given in support of Paul's thesis statements regarding the antinomy of "the flesh" and "the Spirit" in 5:13–18. Here in vv 19–23 he wants his converts to realize that libertinism, which focuses on "freedom as an opportunity for the flesh" (v 13), has dire, negative consequences, but that serving one another "through love" (v 13) and living "by the Spirit" (v 16) have significant, positive results.

An important observation to make regarding these lists is that they include a number of rather unexpected items. The list of vices, for example, does not focus simply on "carnal" sins and idolatry, but also on such matters as "hatred, strife, jealousy, fits of rage, selfish ambition, dissensions, factions, and envy." These, too, though not always as externally obvious as "sexual immorality, impurity, debauchery, idolatry, witchcraft, . . . drunkenness, and orgies," are called by Paul "the works of the flesh." The common feature in this catalogue of vices seems to reside not in the precise ways in which these fifteen items manifest themselves but in the self-centeredness or egocentricity that underlies all of them. For that which separates us from God is our own idea of autonomy—that is, our attempt to think and live apart from God, believing that what we have stems from ourselves alone—with such an autonomous stance coming to expression in all sorts of egoistic ways that have to do with "hatred, strife, jealousy, fits of rage, selfish ambition, dissensions, factions, and envy," as well as in acts of carnality and idolatry.

It is so, as well, with Paul's catalogue of "the fruit of the Spirit." For while we might have expected such items as alms-giving, evangelism, social service, care of the widows and orphans, etc. to appear in the list, Paul enumerates, rather, such items as "love, joy, peace, patience, kindness," etc. Again, it appears that Paul is not so concerned with precisely how each of these matters works out in practice, but with the underlying orientation of selfless and outgoing concern for others. For in commitment to God through Jesus Christ one discovers a new orientation for life—an orientation that reflects the selfless and outgoing love of God himself. It is not, as in Eastern philosophy, the denial of the ego or the created self. Rather, it is freedom from the contaminating effects of egoism and self-centeredness, with the result that now such virtues as "love, joy, peace, patience, kindness, goodness, faithfulness, gentleness, and self-control" can be expressed in the Christian life in ways that are beneficial to others and that reflect God at work in the Christian's life, apart from one's own sinful egocentricity.

So Paul exhorts his converts to acknowledge that their new relationship "in Christ Jesus" involves being also dead to "the flesh with its passions and desires" (v 24) and to live their lives "in step with the Spirit" (v 25), with such an acknowledgement and lifestyle having direct relevance to how they treat one another (v 26). And Paul's thesis statements (vv 13–18), elaborations (vv 19–23) and exhortations (vv 24–26) are directly relevant to Christians today as we seek to know more fully what it means to "live by the Spirit" and not according to "the flesh."

3. Doing Good to All (6:1–10)

Bibliography

Bammel, E. "Νόμος Χριστοῦ." In *Studia Evangelica* III, ed. F. L. Cross. TU 88. Berlin: Akademie, 1964, 12–28. **Barclay, J. M. G.** *Obeying the Truth,* 146–77. **Barrett, C. K.** *Freedom and Obligation.* **Davies, W. D.** *Paul and Rabbinic Judaism,* 111–46. **Deidun, T. J.** *New Covenant Morality in Paul.* **Dibelius, M.** *A Fresh Approach,* 217–37. **Dodd, C. H.** *Gospel and Law.* New York: Columbia University Press, 1951. 64–83. ————. "ΕΝΝΟΜΟΣ ΧΡΙΣΤΟΥ." In *Studia Paulina.* FS J. de Zwaan, ed. W. C. van Unnik and J. N. Sevenster. Haarlem: Bohn, 1953, 96–110 (repr. idem, *More New Testament Studies* [Manchester: Manchester University Press, 1968] 134–48). **Furnish, V. P.** *Theology and Ethics in Paul,* 51–98. **Longenecker, R. N.** *Paul, Apostle of Liberty,* 181–208. **Malherbe, A. J.** *Moral Exhortation.* **Schrage, W.** *Die konkreten Einzelgebote,* esp. 61–64. ————. *Ethik des Neuen Testaments,* esp. 180–85 (ET *The Ethics of the New Testament*). **Schürmann, H.** "'Das Gesetz des Christus' (Gal 6, 2): Jesu Verhalten und Wort als letztgültige sittliche Norm nach Paulus." In *Neues Testament und Kirche.* FS R. Schnackenburg. Freiburg: Herder, 1974, 282–300.

Translation

¹*Brothers, if someone*ᵃ *is entrapped by some sin, you who are spiritual should restore that one in a spirit of gentleness—though watch yourself, that you be not also tempted.* ²*Bear one another's oppressive burdens, and so you will fulfill*ᵇ *the law of Christ.* ³*For, "If anyone thinks he is something when he is nothing, he deceives himself."* ⁴*Each one*ᶜ *should test his own actions. Then he will have a basis for boasting in himself, and not by comparison with someone else.* ⁵*For, "Each one shall bear his own burden."*

⁶*The one who receives instruction in the word must share all good things with his instructor.*

⁷*Do not*ᵈ *be deceived: God is not mocked. For, "Whatever a man sows, that he also reaps."* ⁸*The one who sows to his own flesh, from the flesh shall reap destruction; the one who sows to the Spirit, from the Spirit shall reap life eternal.* ⁹*Let us, then, not become weary*ᵉ *in doing good, for, "At the proper time we will reap a harvest if we do not give up."*

¹⁰*Therefore, whenever we have*ᶠ *opportunity, let us do*ᵍ *good to all people, especially to those who belong to the household of faith.*

Notes

ᵃ The generic ἄνθρωπος ("man," "anyone," "someone") is well attested, though τὶς ἐξ ὑμῶν ("any one of you") is supported by P syrᵖᵉˢʰ and ἄνθρωπος ἐξ ὑμῶν ("someone of you") by Ψ syrʰᵉˡ copˢᵃ— evidently attempting to make explicit the generic nature of the noun ("anyone," "someone") and/or the concrete situation envisaged ("of you").

ᵇ The future verb ἀναπληρώσετε ("you will fulfill") is attested by B G it vg syrᵖᵉˢʰ Mcion (ἀποπληρώσετε, "you will fulfill," by P⁴⁶), though the aorist imperative ἀναπληρώσατε ("fulfill") is supported almost as well by א A C D Ψ Byzantine Cl. Either tense for the verb is possible, though the future seems to fit Paul's thought better here.

ᶜ The substantival adjective ἕκαστος ("each one," "everyone") is generally well attested, though it is omitted by P⁴⁶ B syrᵖᵉˢʰ copˢᵃ.

ᵈ The negative μή was omitted by Marcion and Tertullian (cf. *Adv. Marc.* 5.4), so reading πλανᾶσθε as a present indicative ("you are deceived") rather than a present imperative ("do not be deceived").

ᵉ ἐγκακῶμεν ("let us [not] become weary") is well attested, though ἐκκακῶμεν ("let us [not] lose heart") is supported by C Byzantine.

ᶠ The present indicative ἔχομεν ("we have") is attested by P⁴⁶ A C D G Byzantine it vg Mcion Cl, though the present subjunctive ἔχωμεν ("we might have") receives equally strong attestation from א B* 33 69 et al.

ᵍ The present subjunctive ἐργαζώμεθα ("let us do") is well attested by א B* C D F G et al., though the present indicative ἐργαζόμεθα ("we do") receives support from A B³ L P etc. Intrinsic probability, however, as well as external attestation, favors the subjunctive.

Form/Structure/Setting

In 6:1–10 Paul gives a series of instructions that spell out in practical terms what it means for his Galatian converts to "live by the Spirit" (5:16, 25a), to "be led by the Spirit" (5:18), and so to "keep in step with the Spirit" (5:25b). The instructions are given in the form of exhortations, with the exhortations generally expressing in somewhat blended fashion two main emphases: (1) personal responsibility and (2) corporate responsibility. Yet the particular situations to which these exhortations speak are not stated, and so commentators are left without any real knowledge of the circumstances within the Galatian churches or how Paul's exhortations fit those circumstances.

"Mirror reading," of course, can be applied not only to the argumentative portions of Galatians but also to the hortatory sections of the letter. But care must be taken in applying mirror reading to a NT letter to distinguish among exposition, polemic, and apology (on "mirror reading" as a method, see pp. lxxxvii–lxxxviii above). Furthermore, the method falls short of its desired goal when an author, for whatever reason, writes in a manner that may be understandable to both himself and his readers but not necessarily to others, as seems to be the case here in 6:1–10.

The most extreme treatment of Galatians in terms of mirror reading is that of B. H. Brinsmead who on the assumption that everything said in the letter is polemical in nature has attempted to read Galatians in terms of this method throughout (cf. *Dialogical Response*), and so treats all that Paul says, whether by way of theological argumentation or ethical exhortation, as being directly opposed in both content and expression to his opponent's message (cf. above, p. lxxxviii). Thus Brinsmead, building on Betz's rhetorical categories, views the ethical statements of Gal 6 as Paul's *refutatio* of his opponent's ethical teachings and traditions. But as J. M. G. Barclay aptly observes regarding Brinsmead's thesis: "This striking proposal is, however, almost entirely arbitrary. Brinsmead provides no evidence for his assertion that these verses are a 'refutatio' and his argument works on the completely unfounded assumption that wherever Paul uses 'traditional' material he must be echoing the *opponents'* traditions" (*Obeying the Truth*, 26 [italics his]; Barclay cites in support "Aune's devastating review of Brinsmead's book in *CBQ* [1984] 145–7"). Indeed, that there were ethical problems within the Galatian churches to which Paul speaks in his exhortations is a thesis that appears prima facie highly probable. But the problems are not just to be equated with the Judaizers' message, but rather have to do with how the Galatian believers themselves understood Christian ethics vis-à-vis how Paul understood life "in the Spirit." Likewise, that there is traditional material incorporated within Paul's exhortations of Gal 6 seems to be a likely hypothesis. But such traditional material is not to be seen as unique to the Judaizers; rather, it probably was drawn by Paul from his own background (whether Jewish, Hellenistic, Christian, or some combination of these factors) and used by him in a manner he believed would be appreciated by his converts with their pagan and Christian backgrounds as well—traditions they would have known, at least to some extent, even before the intrusion of the Judaizers.

The purpose of 6:1–10 has been variously evaluated. Some have taken it as largely unrelated to the body of the Galatian letter, either (1) because it is a gloss or interpolation added by another writer to an original letter by Paul, or (2) because it is traditional material that has no intrinsic relation to what has been argued in the body of the letter. J. C. O'Neill, as noted earlier (see *Introduction*, lviii), views Galatians as a strictly anti-Judaic writing to which over thirty rather disparate glosses from other authors have been added, the longest, continuous gloss being that of 5:13–6:10 (cf. his *The Recovery of Paul's Letter to the Galatians*). So O'Neill concludes regarding this whole section: "I can find nothing specifically Pauline in the collection, and nothing that would have had a specific bearing on the situation facing the Galatians" (ibid., 71). Somewhat similar in conclusion, though entirely different in approach, is Martin Dibelius' argument that the paraeneses of the NT and all early Christian writings are made up of *topoi* or traditional treatments of moral subjects that were frequently strung together without any necessary inner connections and used in a general fashion without any direct relevance to matters being addressed (cf. *A Fresh Approach*, 217–37; see comments on Dibelius's views on 'paraenesis' above, pp. 219 and 234). So Dibelius concludes regarding all the hortatory sections of Paul's letters (e.g., Rom 12–13; Gal 5:13–6:10; Col 3:1–4:6; 1 Thess 4:1–12; 5:1ff.) that, though they are authentically Pauline, they have "nothing to do with the theoretic foundation of the ethics of the Apostle, and very little with other ideas peculiar to him" (*From Tradition to Gospel*, 238–39).

O'Neill's thesis has fallen on deaf ears within the scholarly community, largely because of its implausibility and artificiality. Dibelius' views on Paul's paraenetic materials, however, have gained a rather large following, with many treatments of Gal 6:1–10 reflecting in whole or in part Dibelius' stance (cf. esp. Mussner, *Galaterbrief*, 396–408). Nevertheless, Dibelius is not without his critics. Of late, in fact, there have been significant monographs written advocating the position that "these various maxims are by no means irrelevant to the Galatian churches but are intended to meet their general problems of strife and division" (so J. M. G. Barclay, *Obeying the Truth*, 167; cf. also W. Schrage's two works: *Die konkreten Einzelgebote in der paulinischen Paränese* and *Ethik des Neuen Testaments*). And though the rather general nature of the exhortations themselves prohibits any detailed explication of the "problems of strife and division" within the Galatian churches, we may still believe that in 6:1–10 Paul exhorts regarding personal and corporate responsibility in such a fashion as to be relevant to the circumstances that both he and his converts knew existed within those churches.

As for the structure of these ten verses, that too has been variously evaluated. J. C. O'Neill has declared that "there is no connection between one admonition and the next, except sometimes a similarity of subject or a catch-phrase; the collector is not pursuing a connected argument" (*Recovery*, 67; cf. ibid., 71: "There is no inner idea running through the collection, although each saying shares the family likeness"). Martin Dibelius sees 6:1–10 as being held together only by the use of certain artificial catchwords or *Stichwörter*: βαστάζετε ("bear") and βαστάσει ("shall bear") in 6:2, 5; θερίσει ("shall reap") and θερίσομεν ("will reap") in 6:8, 9; and καιρῷ ("at the proper time") and καιρόν ("opportunity") in 6:9, 10, with one saying attached to another saying only because the same word or a cognate of the same stem appears in both sayings (cf. idem, *James*, 6). Without accepting the views of either O'Neill or Dibelius, most critical texts and commentators view 6:1–10 as a rather loose and diverse series of exhortations that defy any easy grouping or structural ordering. Some refrain entirely from attempting to divide the section into component parts (e.g., Nestle; UBSGT; Schlier, *Galater;* Duncan, *Galatians;* Bruce, *Galatians*); others divide it into two parts, making a break between v 5 and v 6 (e.g., Lightfoot, *Galatians;* Burton, *Galatians*) or between v 6 and v 7 (e.g., Lagrange, *Galates;* Oepke, *Galater*); others into three parts, making a break between v 5 and v 6 and another break between v 6 and v 7, so setting off v 6 as in some way distinctive (e.g., Mussner, *Galaterbrief;* also JB, RSV, GNB, NIV); and still others into four parts, making breaks between v 2 and v 3, between v 5 and v 6, and between v 6 and v 7 (e.g., NEB).

The most atomistic structural analysis of this passage is that done by Betz, who subdivides 5:25–6:10 into eleven subsections because he sees here separate *sententiae* or gnomic sentences composed by the "gnomic poet" Paul, with the practice of composing such sentences having a long history in Hellenistic philosophic writings (cf. *Galatians*, 291–93). J. M. G. Barclay organizes the material on thematic grounds according to whether the exhortations have to do alternately with personal or corporate accountability: v 1a being corporate; v 1b personal; v 2 corporate; vv 3–5 personal; v 6 corporate; vv 7–8 personal; vv 9–10 corporate (*Obeying the Truth*, 149–50).

In our view, after the vocative ἀδελφοί ("brothers") that signals the beginning of a new epistolary subsection and starts this subsection off on an affectionate note (see *Comment* at 1:11; 3:15; and 4:12; also 4:28, 31; 5:11, 13; 6:18), Paul gives a series of exhortations that have to do with both personal and corporate responsibilities within the Galatian churches. The exhortations are expressed in somewhat general terms, without details regarding the specific circumstances they have in mind, though, it must be assumed, Paul thought he knew the circumstances to which he spoke and, furthermore, believed that his converts knew them as well. Most enigmatic in this series is the exhortation of v 6, which speaks of the need to "share all good things" with one's instructor. It is probably best, therefore, to treat this verse separately as containing a distinguishable directive (as JB, RSV, GNB, NIV). Likewise, for paragraphing purposes, v 10 may be set off from what precedes, since it functions not only as the conclusion to 6:1–10 but also as the conclusion to the whole section beginning at 5:13.

The instructions given are, indeed, as Betz proposes, of the nature of *sententiae* or general, aphoristic statements. Probably they incorporate a number of moral maxims that were traditional in Paul's day and so could be used by Paul for his own purposes. His use of catalogue lists of vices and virtues in 5:19–23, which seem to have been common in Paul's day and used by various writers for their own purposes, would lead us to expect something similar in 6:1–10. In fact, it may even be, as seems likely, that Paul signals his use of such maxims at four places in the instructions of 6:1–10 by his use of the explanatory γάρ ("for"), with what follows being a moral maxim of the day that is used generally in support (cf. vv 3, 5, 7, 9).

There is, admittedly, much that must remain uncertain regarding the form and content of the exhortations given in 6:1–10. Despite such uncertainties, however, we must not treat them as only addenda to Paul's previous exhortations of 5:1–26 that were drawn from the ethical wisdom of the day and simply tacked on to what has preceded. For, as Betz points out, "extensive research has not turned up *verbatim* parallels," and "furthermore, the section seems well-integrated into the present context of the letter" (*Galatians*, 291). Rather, as J. M. G. Barclay aptly puts it:

They represent Paul's desire to give concrete instructions, to spell out for the Galatians in practical terms what it means to "walk in the Spirit." Many of these maxims function as practical illustrations of the ingredients of "the fruit of the Spirit"—e.g. πραΰτης (6.2), ἐγκράτεια (5.26; 6.4), μακροθυμία (6.9–10), and ἀγαθωσύνη (6.6, 10)—and thus serve to "earth" these abstract qualities in detailed moral instruction. Throughout Paul endeavours to remind the Galatians of their accountability to God and their responsibilities to one another, and he is especially concerned with the problems of pride and dissension in the Galatian churches which threaten to destroy them altogether. He appeals to them to sow to the Spirit, having shown that only the fruit of the Spirit can counteract and overcome these problems in their midst (*Obeying the Truth*, 167).

Comment

1 ἀδελφοί, ἐὰν καὶ προλημφθῇ ἄνθρωπος ἔν τινι παραπτώματι, ὑμεῖς οἱ πνευματικοὶ καταρτίζετε τὸν τοιοῦτον ἐν πνεύματι πραΰτητος, σκοπῶν σεαυτόν, μὴ καὶ σὺ πειρασθῇς, "brothers, if someone is entrapped by some sin, you who are spiritual should restore that one in a spirit of gentleness—though watch yourself, that you be not also tempted." The first of Paul's exhortations of 6:1–10 contains three parts: (1) a protasis cast in the form of a third class "future more probable" condition (ἐάν with a subjunctive verb in the protasis, with almost any form of the verb appearing in the apodosis) that states the circumstance addressed; (2) an apodosis that gives a directive as to what should be done; and (3) an added concessive statement introduced by the adverbial participle σκοπῶν ("though watch") that gives pointed warning to those who carry out the directive.

The first part of the sentence, the circumstance addressed, is introduced by ἐάν ("if"), which as the initial particle of a future more probable condition connotes some indefiniteness yet also suggests the probability of such a situation in the future. The conjunction καί ("and," "even") is intensive, so putting the emphasis on the immediately following word, the verb προλημφθῇ ("he should be overtaken," or "entrapped"). προλαμβάνω is a frequent word in Greek classical writings that means literally "take beforehand," but came to mean (1) "anticipate," "forestall," or "forecast" in the active voice, and (2) "taken by surprise," "seized unawares," "overtaken," or "entrapped" in the passive. Its only appearances in the LXX are at Wis 17:11 (active voice: "wickedness always forecasts the worst") and Wis 17:17 (passive voice: "mankind was overtaken"). It occurs twenty-nine times in Josephus in these same two ways: in the active voice to mean "anticipate" (e.g., *Ant.* 6.305: David's words to Abigail regarding how she "anticipated" or "forestalled" his action) and in the passive to mean "taken by surprise," "overtaken," or "entrapped" (e.g., *Ant.* 5.79: the Roman Tenth Legion was "taken unawares" or "entrapped" by the Jews). In the NT the word appears in the active voice at Mark 14:8 and 1 Cor 11:21. Here at Gal 6:1, however, it appears in the passive and so suggests being "overtaken" or "entrapped" by something.

The use of ἄνθρωπος ("man") is generic, as a few MSS have attempted to make clear by reading instead the indefinite pronoun τίς ("any one," "someone"; see *Note* a). It is not to be distinguished from ἀδελφοί ("brothers"), as though someone from outside the church is in view, but is to be taken as a generic noun for someone from within the church, as a few MSS have also attempted to make clear by the addition of ἐξ ὑμῶν ("of you"; see *Note* a). The noun παράπτωμα ("transgression," "sin") is a late word in Greek literature that literally means "fall beside" or "false step." It appears a number of times in the LXX and the Greek writings of Second Temple Judaism (though not in Josephus) for various Hebrew words meaning "transgression" or "sin." In the NT it is used repeatedly in the strictly ethical sense of "transgression" or "sin" (cf. elsewhere in Paul's letters at Rom 4:25; 5:15–18, 20; 11:11–12; 2 Cor 5:19; Eph 1:7; 2:5; Col 2:13), with παράπτωμα (rather than such a word as ἁμαρτία) possibly being used here because of its etymological imagery ("fall beside," "false step") that would be in sharp contrast to the imagery of the verb στοιχῶμεν ("walk in a straight line," "conform to a standard," "keep in step") of 5:25. The dative singular indefinite pronoun τινί that functions as an adjective modifying παραπτώματι ("by some sin") continues the indefinite, futuristic tone of the sentence set by the third class conditional structure of ἐάν with a subjunctive verb in the protasis.

Yet while there is something of an indefinite tone to the first part of this sentence, there is also the suggestion in the use of the third class "future more probable" conditional construction that such a circumstance will almost certainly take place. Such a future circumstance probably seemed a near certainty because of past events within the churches of Galatia, with both Paul and his readers knowing of believers in the churches who had been "overtaken" or "entrapped" by moral wrong-doing. In fact, as Betz observes, the previous moral transgressions of some within their churches "would also explain why the Galatians considered introducing the Torah" (*Galatians*, 296).

The second part of the sentence is Paul's directive as to what should be done when sin entraps a fellow believer. He addresses his readers using the designation ὑμεῖς οἱ πνευματικοί ("you who are spiritual"). It has often been thought that οἱ πνευματικοί is used somewhat ironically (so, e.g., Lietzmann, *Galater*, 38; Schlier, *Galater*, 270) or to distinguish one group within the Galatian churches from the rest—either those libertine in their outlook from others who were legalistic (so, e.g., W. Lütgert, *Gesetz und Geist*, 12) or those who were Gnostics from others who may not have been (so, e.g., W. Schmithals, *Paul and the Gnostics*, 46–51). But Paul has repeatedly spoken elsewhere in Galatians of all Christians as being possessed by and in possession of God's Spirit (cf. 3:2–5, 14; 4:6, 29; 5:5, 16–18, 22–23, 25; 6:8). There is, therefore, no reason to doubt and abundant reason to believe that Paul here uses this designation with approval in speaking about *all* his converts in Galatia. They are, despite their legal and libertine enticements, "the true spirituals" simply because by being "in Christ" they have become the recipients of God's Spirit. So by reminding his converts of their status as πνευματικοί Paul calls on them to live up to that status.

The operative expressions in Paul's directive are the present imperative second person plural verb καταρτίζετε ("you restore") and the prepositional phrase ἐν πνεύματι πραΰτητος ("in a spirit of gentleness"). καταρτίζω ("put in order," "repair," "restore," "make complete") is a fairly common word in Greek literature and the LXX. In the NT it appears (1) in material contexts to signify the "repair" of nets to their former usable condition (cf. Matt 4:21; Mark 1:19), (2) in religious contexts to signify the "completion" or "perfection" of one's faith (cf. 2 Cor 13:11; 1 Thess 3:10; Heb 13:21), and (3) in ethical contexts to signify moral "restoration" to a former good state (cf. 1 Cor 1:10). Here in Gal 6:1 it is evidently used in an ethical sense to mean "restore" to a former good state. The accusative singular τὸν τοιοῦτον ("such a one," "that one") parallels the nominative plural τὰ τοιαῦτα ("such ones") that functions as a correlative adjective in 5:21, and so signals that what is in mind here in 6:1 is a person who engages in such "works of the flesh" as those listed in 5:19–21. The πνεῦμα of the prepositional phrase may refer to God's Spirit, as highlighted repeatedly in 5:16–18, 22–23, 25, or the regenerated human spirit, which expresses the virtues enumerated as "the fruit of the Spirit" in 5:22–23. In association with the human virtue of πραΰτητος ("gentleness"), the latter is to be preferred. On the meaning of πραΰτητος in context, see *Comment* at 5:23.

Here in his directive Paul applies the exhortation "keep in step with the Spirit" in 5:25 to the specific problem of how believers are to treat fellow believers who have experienced moral lapses. It is a problem that evidently gave rise to pride and conceit on the part of the Galatian Christians not so entrapped by sin, as 5:26 implies. Paul, however, urges that those guided by the Spirit (οἱ πνευματικοί) be involved in a ministry of restoration with "gentleness," which is one of the expressions of the Spirit's activity in the life (cf. 5:23), characterizing their attitudes and actions.

Significantly, it is more the attitudes and actions of "those who are spiritual" that Paul deals with here than the attitudes and actions of those who have sinned. Libertinism among the Galatian Christians evidently expressed itself in pride, aloofness, and conceit (as sadly it does also among Christians today). And while Paul was always against sin in whatever form, for him pride, aloofness, and conceit were also sinful, being often, in fact, far more damaging to the community of believers and the gospel message than overt moral lapses. So here in a practical manner he brings together his two lists of vices and virtues in 5:19–23, showing how in practice "the fruit of the Spirit" overcomes "the works of the flesh."

The third part of v 1 is a warning to those who attempt to restore an erring fellow believer that they are not to be self-righteous in their attitudes but are to recognize their own vulnerability to those same moral failings that they seek to correct. Suddenly, Paul shifts from the plural address ἀδελφοί ("brothers"), the plural designation ὑμεῖς οἱ πνευματικοί ("you who are spiritual), and the second person plural command καταρτίζετε τὸν τοιοῦτον ("restore that one") to the singular reflexive pronoun σεαυτόν ("yourself"), the second person singular personal pronoun σύ ("you"), and the second person singular aorist subjunctive passive verb πειρασθῇς ("you be [not] tempted"). "The change to the singular after the plural," as Burton points out, "serves to make the exhortation more pointed" (*Galatians*, 328), for it applies the warning to each individual.

The basic meaning of σκοπέω is "look at," "observe," "notice," or "take heed." The verb appears frequently in various Greek writings, with the context determining in each instance whether its purpose has to do with observing in order to avoid, promote, imitate, or honor. Elsewhere in Paul's letters it is used in all these ways (cf. Rom 16:17; 2 Cor 4:18; Phil 2:4; 3:17), and here certainly with the nuance of "watching yourself " in order to avoid the sins in question. As a concessive adverbial participle, σκοπῶν ("though watch") signals the addition of a further statement to the main directive just given. πειράζω ("try," "test") is also a common Greek verb, with the purpose of that "trying" or "testing" being determined by the individual contexts. In the NT it is often used in the sense of "solicit to sin" or "tempt" (cf. esp. Jas 1:13), and that is how it appears here. What Paul, therefore, warns his converts about is their own vulnerability to such moral failings as they seek to correct in others, so that they do not become self-righteous and look down on those they are attempting to restore.

2 ἀλλήλων τὰ βάρη βαστάζετε, καὶ οὕτως ἀναπληρώσετε τὸν νόμον τοῦ Χριστοῦ, "bear one another's oppressive burdens, and so you will fulfill the law of Christ." Central to the believers' new existence "in Christ" is the concept of mutuality. Such a concept is highlighted here in v 2 by the emphatic position of ἀλλήλων ("one another") at the beginning of the sentence. The noun βάρος means literally "weight," but is used in the NT figuratively for an "oppressive burden" (e.g., Matt 20:12, "the burden of the day "; cf. also Acts 15:28; 1 Thess 2:7; Rev 2:24). Here τὰ βάρη has primary reference to "the burdens of temptation" spoken of in v 1, though probably also has in mind more generally oppressive burdens of any kind (cf. Rom 15:1 and 1 Cor 12:26, though without the noun βάρος). It is doubtful, however, that Paul is using βάρος with any idea of "financial support for Jerusalem," as some have posited (so, e.g., J. G. Strelan, "Burden-Bearing and the Law of Christ: A Re-Examination of Galatians 6.2," *JBL* 94 [1975] 266–76; see the rebuttal by E. M. Young, "'Fulfil the Law of Christ': An Examination of Galatians 6.2," *StBibT* 7 [1977] 31–42).

The adverb οὕτως ("in this manner," "thus," "so") with the conjunction καί ("and") correlates what follows with what has immediately preceded, thereby setting out a logical connection between the two. Greek prepositional prefixes often strengthen the verb to which they are attached. Thus the future verb ἀναπληρώσετε ("you will fulfill")—or the aorist imperative verb ἀναπληρώσατε ("fulfill"), if that is the better reading (see *Note* b)—expresses with conviction the fact of a direct correlation between the directive to bear others' oppressive burdens and the assurance that in so doing one is fulfilling "the law of Christ."

The expression ὁ νόμος τοῦ Χριστοῦ ("the law of Christ") has been the focus of extensive discussion. Does it have reference to the principles of the example and teachings of Jesus, as incorporated in the catechetical tradition of the early church, that in some way have external relevance for Christian living, so, in effect, while not being of the same nature as the law of Moses, taking the place of the law of Moses in ethical guidance for the Christian (e.g., Burton, *Galatians*, 329–30; W. D. Davies, *Paul and Rabbinic Judaism*, 111–46; C. H. Dodd, *Gospel and Law*, 64–83; idem, "ΕΝΝΟΜΟΣ ΧΡΙΣΤΟΥ," 96–110; R. N. Longenecker, *Paul, Apostle of Liberty*, 181–208)? Or is it to be interpreted strictly in terms of the command to love given in 5:13b–14, and so understood apart from external principles or propositions (e.g., A. Schweitzer, *The Mysticism of Paul the Apostle*, tr. W. Montgomery [London: Black, 1931] 303; R. Bultmann, *Theology of the New Testament*, tr. K. Grobel, 2 vols. [London: SCM, 1952], 1:262, 268; W. Schrage, *Die konkreten Einzelgebote*, 99–100, 250; V. P. Furnish, *Theology and Ethics in Paul*, 51–98)? Furthermore, is the expression intrinsic to Paul's thought (as seems true of the phrase ἔννομος Χριστοῦ of 1 Cor 9:21), or did Paul use it only polemically in an *ad hominem* fashion either to outclass his opponents in their use of νόμος or to mock his Galatian converts' obsession with Mosaic legislation (e.g., E. Bammel, "Νόμος Χριστοῦ," 12–28; Betz, *Galatians*, 299–301)?

To understand what Paul meant by "the law of Christ" here, much depends on how we understand the purpose and focus of 5:13–6:10. For if we view 5:13–6:10 as a continuation of Paul's arguments and exhortations against the Judaizing threat, then "the law of Christ" must have relevance to what the Judaizers were proposing. One can then, in fact, wonder why this expression does not appear earlier in the Galatian letter. Likewise, if we take 5:13–6:10 to reflect the polemics of Paul's antinomistic stance, then νόμος here may very well be used in contradistinction to the Judaizers' usage. If, however, 5:13–6:10 be seen more in terms of the libertine issues that were also present in the churches of Galatia, then "the law of Christ" may be taken as an expression stemming from Paul's own ethical vocabulary that is used here to check libertine tendencies among his Galatian converts.

Taking this latter approach, and abbreviating a lengthy discussion quite considerably, I propose that ὁ νόμος τοῦ Χριστοῦ here (as does ἔννομος Χριστοῦ of 1 Cor 9:21) stands in Paul's thought for those "prescriptive principles stemming from the heart of the gospel (usually embodied in the example and teachings of

Jesus), which are meant to be applied to specific situations by the direction and enablement of the Holy Spirit, being always motivated and conditioned by love" (so my *New Testament Social Ethics for Today*, 15). Paul is not setting forth Jesus as a new Moses. Nor does he view Jesus' teachings as ethical prescriptions to be carried out in rabbinic fashion. Nonetheless, just as the designation of his readers as οἱ πνευματικοί ("who are spiritual") probably reflects Paul's own understanding of his converts' status "in Christ" and is not used either ironically or polemically (see *Comment* on 6:1), so ὁ νόμος τοῦ Χριστοῦ should probably be seen as expressing an important feature of Paul's own ethical understanding and not taken in an ad hominem or polemical fashion. The expression does not appear earlier in Paul's antinomistic arguments or exhortations, evidently because it did not arise from or have direct relevance to those concerns. Here in countering his converts' libertine tendencies, however, it highlights what Paul sees to be an appropriate check to such tendencies. For when there is mutual concern among believers to "bear one another's oppressive burdens"—which, of course, is the exact opposite of libertine attitudes based on a desire to live solely for one's own self—the whole intent of Jesus' example and teaching comes to fulfillment within the church.

3 εἰ γὰρ δοκεῖ τις εἶναί τι μηδὲν ὤν, φρεναπατᾷ ἑαυτόν, "for, 'If anyone thinks he is something when he is nothing, he deceives himself.'" The verbs δοκεῖ ("he thinks"), and φρεναπατᾷ ("he deceives") of this verse are third person singulars, with their present tenses, active voices, and indicative moods giving them a gnomic quality. The postpositive γάρ ("for") is explanatory. It seems to function not only by way of support for what is said in v 2 but also to set off the statement of v 3 as being a traditional maxim (cf. the use of γάρ at vv 5, 7 and 9; see also its use to introduce traditional material at 3:26, 27–28). Of note also in support of the theory that what we have here is a traditional maxim of the Greco-Roman world that is being quoted by Paul in general support of his previous statement are the following three observations: (1) the verb δοκέω here has a slightly different nuance than it does in 2:2 and 6, for there it meant "to be esteemed (by others) to be important" whereas here it means "to think oneself to be important"; (2) the concessive phrase μηδὲν ὤν ("though" or "when being nothing") is a somewhat harsher statement about the human condition than one usually finds in Paul's letters (cf. Rom 12:3; Phil 2:3–4); and (3) the verb φρεναπατάω ("deceive") is a *hap. leg.* in the NT, which also fails to appear in the LXX or any other Jewish Greek writing.

Understanding, then, the statement of v 3 to be a traditional maxim of the Greco-Roman world, Paul uses it by way of general support for his directive to "bear one another's oppressive burdens" of v 2. His point, it seems, is that conceit—that is, thinking oneself to be something when in actuality we are nothing (as the maxim has it)—results in making one unwilling to bear others' burdens. In effect, the maxim quoted here roughly parallels the exhortation of 5:26, with the warnings against conceit of 5:26 and 6:3 serving as something of an *inclusio* for the exhortations regarding restoring the wayward and bearing one another's oppressive burdens of 6:1–2.

4 τὸ δὲ ἔργον ἑαυτοῦ δοκιμαζέτω ἕκαστος, καὶ τότε εἰς ἑαυτὸν μόνον τὸ καύχημα ἕξει καὶ οὐκ εἰς τὸν ἕτερον, "each one should test his own actions. Then he will have a basis for boasting in himself, and not by comparison with someone else." The first part of v 4 is in the form of a directive or command, like those of vv 1 and 2. The postpositive δέ (untranslated) connects v 4 not with v 3 (οὖν, "therefore," in that case would probably have been a more appropriate connective) but with vv 1 and 2. The adjective ἕκαστος ("each," "every"), serving as a substantive in the nominative case, is the subject of the sentence; it is omitted by some MSS (see *Notec*), evidently inadvertently. The presence of ἕκαστος at the start of v 5 in parallel fashion to v 4 indicates that this substantive was in Paul's mind when he dictated v 4, despite its omission by some worthy textual authorities. δοκιμάζω is a frequent verb in the Greek classical writings, the LXX, other Jewish Greek literature, and the NT. It appears elsewhere in Paul's letter in three different, though roughly complementary, senses: (1) "test" or "examine" (1 Cor 3:13; 11:28; 2 Cor 13:5; 1 Thess 5:21; 1 Tim 3:10); (2) "accept as proven" or "approve" (Rom 2:18; 14:22; 1 Thess 2:4; 2 Cor 8:22); and (3) "think best" or "choose" (1 Cor 16:3); Rom 12:2 could be classified under any or all of these meanings. Here in v 4 the sense is clearly that of "test" or "examine."

The second part of v 4 gives a rationale for the directive just given. The correlative adverbial particle τότε ("then") undoubtedly has temporal force to mean "then, when he has tested his own actions, the following will ensue." The noun καύχημα ("boast") appears frequently in Greek writings and a total of ten times in Paul (elsewhere in Paul's letters at Rom 4:2; 1 Cor 5:6; 9:15, 16; 2 Cor 1:14; 5:12; 9:3; Phil 1:26; 2:16). "It is," as Burton observes, "in itself a less opprobrious term than the English word 'boast,' referring rather to exultation, gratulation, without the implication of the English word that it is excessive or unjustified" (*Galatians*, 333). With the article, τὸ καύχημα carries the idea of "the ground of boasting" or "the basis for boasting." The article also serves to make the noun restrictive (i.e., "his basis for boasting"), with such a nuance emphasized by the neuter particle μόνον ("only," "alone"). The substantival use of the adjective ἕτερος ("other") has in mind "someone else" than those spoken to in the directive. The articular form of the substantival adjective (i.e., τὸν ἕτερον in the accusative) restricts those in view to either (1) a particular wrong-doer with whom someone in the church may compare himself, or (2) a general class of wrong-doers with whom someone in the church may compare himself.

With, therefore, the third person singular future verb ἕξει ("he will have") and the contrast between εἰς ἑαυτόν ("in himself") and εἰς τὸν ἕτερον ("in someone else"), the rationale for testing one's own actions is so that "then" such a one "will have a basis for boasting in himself, and not by comparison with someone else." The warning here is not to live as spiritual people in a state of pride or conceit, always comparing one's own attainments to those of others and so feeling superior, but rather to test one's own actions and so to minimize the possibility of self-deception. Christian feelings of exultation and congratulation should spring from one's own actions as seen in the light of God's approval and not derive from comparing oneself to what others are or are not doing.

5 ἕκαστος γὰρ τὸ ἴδιον φορτίον βαστάσει, "for, 'Each one shall bear his own burden.'" As in v 3, so here the postpositive γάρ ("for") not only connects v 5 to v 4 in an explanatory fashion but also seems to set off the statement of v 5 as being a traditional maxim (cf. also the use of γάρ at vv 7 and 9). The noun φορτίον ("burden") is a common word in Greek literature, including the LXX and other Jewish Greek writings of the Second Temple Period. It is used in Acts 27:10 of a ship's cargo (so also by Josephus, *Ant.* 14.377, and others), in Matt 23:4 and Luke

11:46 of Pharisaically imposed legal burdens, and in Matt 11:30 of Jesus' "burden" imposed on his disciples vis-à-vis the "burden" of the Mosaic law. φορτίον is, of course, synonymous with βάρος. Here in differing contexts it may be used by Paul simply as a parallel to βάρος. Probably, however, the change of nouns has something to do with βάρος in v 2 being Paul's own term and φορτίον here being that of the moral maxim he quotes. The maxim itself, as Betz points out, likely originated within ancient philosophic speculations regarding αὐτάρκεια, or "self-sufficiency" (i.e., the ability to "carry one's own load"), which was the ideal among many ancient philosophers (cf. Betz, *Galatians*, 303–4, and the philosophic literature he cites). Paul, however, uses the maxim in general support of his directive that "each one should test his own actions" in v 4, with ἕκαστος ("each one," "everyone") as the subject of both the directive and the maxim, tying these two statements together and the content of the maxim being generally confirmatory, though admittedly used out of context.

6 κοινωνείτω δὲ ὁ κατηχούμενος τὸν λόγον τῷ κατηχοῦντι ἐν πᾶσιν ἀγαθοῖς, "the one who receives instruction in the word must share all good things with his instructor." The exhortation of v 6 is the most puzzling of all Paul's directives in 6:1–10—or for that matter elsewhere in his Galatian letter. In form it has no supporting ethical maxim attached, as do the directives of vv 2–4 before it and those of vv 7–9 following. In content, it is somewhat different from Paul's other statements regarding financial remuneration for ministers of the gospel. For whereas elsewhere in his letters Paul asserts the right of those who preach and teach to claim support (cf. 1 Cor 9:3–14; 1 Tim 5:18, citing both Scripture and the words of Jesus), here he speaks of the duty of those who are taught to make material provision for their teachers. And whereas in his own practice he personally renounced his rights to such material provision (cf. 1 Cor 9:15–18; 1 Thess 2:9; also Acts 20:33–35) and evidently felt some embarrassment when such was given him (cf. the tone of Phil 4:10–19), here he commands his Galatian converts to "share all good things" with their teachers. Of course, Paul is not here asking for any material provision for himself; rather, he asks on behalf of his converts' teachers in the churches of Galatia—that is, those teachers who teach in accord with Paul's doctrine (cf. 6:16), not the judaizing teachers. Nonetheless, the directive of this verse is still somewhat different from Paul's other statements elsewhere in his letters on the topic of material and/or financial remuneration to Christian ministers and teachers.

Dominating v 6 are two present substantival participles: ὁ κατηχούμενος ("the one who receives instruction") and τῷ κατηχοῦντι ("the one who instructs"). The participles are both singular, thereby signaling a class of persons rather than particular persons themselves. The bringing together of these two classes of people assumes some type of formal association between them. What they have in common is spoken of as τὸν λόγον ("the word"), which must here certainly mean the Christian message (cf. 1 Cor 1:18; 2 Cor 5:19; Eph 1:13; Phil 1:14; Col 1:25; 4:3; 1 Thess 1:6; 2:13; 2 Tim 4:2)—that which was taught by the one and received by the other. The verb κοινωνέω ("share") when used with reference to things connotes "be a partner of" or "share in," though with persons means "give to" or "contribute a share to" someone. Here as a present imperative coupled with a personal object in the dative ("the one who instructs") it is a hortatory command: "Let him share with his instructor." What "the one who receives instruction" is to share is also expressed in the dative, viz. ἐν πᾶσιν ἀγαθοῖς ("in all good things"). The phrase "in all good things" is a rather general expression that may include spiritual benefits as well as material sustenance, but it certainly cannot be understood apart from material sustenance—probably more directly financial support.

Set within the context of exhortations urging mutual helpfulness among Christian believers, as expressed particularly in vv 1–2 and vv 9–10, the directive of v 6 may not be out of place at all. It is just that we today have no knowledge of the circumstance to which this directive was addressed. In fact, no one beyond Paul and his readers has ever been in a position to have any knowledge of the circumstance being addressed, for neither he nor they has ever told us. Nonetheless, certain inferences seem able to be legitimately made: (1) that formal Christian instruction was going on in the churches of Galatia; (2) that the teachers were called as a class ὁ κατηχῶν (from whence comes the title "catechist" for one who instructs in the basics of the Christian faith); (3) that those instructed were called as a class ὁ κατηχούμενος (from whence comes the title "catechumen" for one taking instruction in the basics of the Christian faith); (4) that the content of what was instructed and learned was the Christian message; (5) that Christian teaching was then a full-time—or at least a heavily time-consuming—occupation that deserved material and/or financial compensation; (6) that for some reason Christian teachers were not being adequately compensated materially in some or all of the churches of Galatia; and (7) that Paul thought it incumbent on those who received instruction to take the initiative to rectify this wrong. Paul, of course, had no teachers' union to which to appeal for correcting injustices. His recourse was to lay the onus on those who benefited from Christian instruction to compensate adequately those who gave the instruction, which is still the most appropriate course of action today.

7 μὴ πλανᾶσθε, θεὸς οὐ μυκτηρίζεται· ὃ γὰρ ἐὰν σπείρῃ ἄνθρωπος, τοῦτο καὶ θερίσει, "do not be deceived: God is not mocked. For, 'Whatever a man sows, that he also reaps.'" Verses 7–9 comprise a warning with an explication and an appeal. The unit seems to consist of (1) an introductory formula ("do not be deceived"), (2) the warning itself cast in proverbial form ("God is not mocked"), (3) a traditional maxim given in support of the warning ("whatever a man sows, that he also reaps"), (4) Paul's explication in terms of his own "flesh-Spirit" antinomy ("the one who sows to the flesh, from the flesh shall reap destruction; the one who sows to the Spirit, from the Spirit shall reap life eternal"), (5) Paul's appeal to apply the warning and his explication to circumstances within Galatia ("let us not become weary in doing good"), and (6) another traditional maxim given in support of the appeal and promising a good outcome when such an appeal is heeded ("at the proper time we shall reap a harvest if we do not give up"). Here in v 7 the first three items appear (with the fourth in v 8 and the fifth and sixth in v 9).

By way of introducing the warning, Paul uses the present imperative expression μὴ πλανᾶσθε ("do not be deceived"). Marcion and Tertullian seem both to have known of a text that omitted the negative μή, and so they read πλανᾶσθε as a present indicative ("you are deceived") rather than a present imperative (see *Note* d). But μὴ πλανᾶσθε is used in Stoic writings (cf. H. Braun, "πλανάω κτλ.," *TDNT* 6:244), in 2 Macc 7:18, and elsewhere in the NT (cf. 1 Cor 6:9; 15:33; Jas 1:16; also Luke 21:8) as an interjection before some solemn warning, and so may be assumed to have been a common introductory formula to a statement of warning in Paul's day.

The statement θεὸς οὐ μυκτηρίζεται ("God is not mocked") appears to be a pro-verbial statement of warning, as most commentators since Hans Lietzmann (cf. *Galater*, ad loc.) have assumed. The anarthrous use of θεός ("God") as the subject of the sentence (which is infrequent), the use of the indicative negative οὐ following the negative μή, and the present tense of the verb all tend to support the gnomic quality of this brief statement. Furthermore, while the verb μυκτηρίζω ("turn up the nose at," "treat with contempt," "mock") and its noun μυκτηρισμός ("mockery") both appear frequently in the LXX (cf. 3 Kdms 18:27; 4 Kdms 19:21; 2 Chr 36:16; 1 Esd 1:49; Job 22:19; Pss 44:13 [43:14]; 80:6 [79:7]; Prov 1:30; 11:12; 12:8; 15:5, 20; 23:9; Isa 37:22; Jer 20:7; Ezek 8:17; 1 Macc 7:34) and other Jewish Greek writings of the Second Temple Period (cf. *Pss. Sol.* 4.8; *T. Jos.* 2.3; *Sib. Or.* 1.171), neither appears in the NT except the verb here in this verse, which makes it both a NT and a Pauline *hap. leg.*, and thus presumably not a term rooted in Paul's own vocabulary but attributable to something he quotes.

The purpose of Paul's use of the statement "God is not mocked" is not apparent until one comes to v 8, where Paul gives his own explication. To summarize briefly what he says there, here by way of anticipation, Paul's point in the warning statement of v 7 followed by the explication of v 8 is that one cannot expect to sow to the flesh and then reap eternal life, and so mock the justice of God, for "God is not mocked!"

What follows the warning statement appears to be a traditional maxim given in support. It is introduced by the conjunction γάρ ("for"), which not only functions in an explanatory fashion but also seems to identify what follows as being quoted material (cf. also the use of γάρ at vv 3, 5, and 9). What, then, follows is a well-known agricultural proverb that was used commonly and in various ways in the literature of the Greco-Roman world (cf. Plato, *Phaedr.* 260C; Aristotle, *Rhet.* 3.3.4 [1406B]; Demosthenes, *Cor.* 159; Cicero, *Orat.* 2.65; Plautus, *Mer.* 71), in the LXX (cf. Job 4:8; Ps 126:5; Prov 22:8; Hos 8:7; 10:12–13), in other Jewish Greek writings of the Second Temple Period (cf. Sir 7:3; *T. Levi* 13.6; 4 Ezra 4:28–30; see also Philo, *Confus.* 21; *Mutat.* 268–69; *Somn.* 2.76), and elsewhere in Paul's letters and the rest of the NT (cf. 1 Cor 9:11; 2 Cor 9:6; see also Luke 19:21–22; John 4:35–36). Paul's emphasis in the use of this maxim seems to be twofold: (1) that there is a direct correlation between sowing and reaping, which is how God has established matters; and (2) that the onus rests on the person (ἄνθρωπος) himself as to whether life eventuates in blessing or judgment, for God is not a deity who reverses his laws or can be tricked into believing something to be so when it is not. Thus, generally the maxim supports the proverb: "God is not mocked" by mankind's attempts to ignore the cause-and-effect relationships of justice or to trick God into bestowing blessings instead of judgment.

8 ὅτι ὁ σπείρων εἰς τὴν σάρκα ἑαυτοῦ ἐκ τῆς σαρκὸς θερίσει φθοράν, ὁ δὲ σπείρων εἰς τὸ πνεῦμα ἐκ τοῦ πνεύματος θερίσει ζωὴν αἰώνιον, "the one who sows to his own flesh, from the flesh shall reap destruction; the one who sows to the Spirit, from the Spirit shall reap life eternal." Here in v 8 Paul interprets the proverb of v 7a in the context of his own theology, explicating it in terms of his sharply drawn "flesh-Spirit" antinomy of 5:16–25 and using the metaphors of sowing and reaping that appear in the maxim of v 7b. In effect, the metaphors are now transposed into allegories, for the sower sows either εἰς τὴν σάρκα ("to the flesh") or εἰς τὸ πνεῦμα ("to the Spirit"), as though casting seed into two entirely different fields, and from these two different fields he reaps a harvest that corresponds to the nature of the fields themselves: either φθοράν ("destruction") from "the flesh" or ζωὴν αἰώνιον ("life eternal") from "the Spirit." Whereas ὅτι (untranslated) often is a causal conjunction, here it probably functions in a declarative fashion to set off what follows as being Paul's own explication (cf. Mussner, *Galaterbrief*, ad loc.). The association of "the Spirit" with "life eternal" is in line with Paul's references to living by the Spirit in 5:16, 18, 22–25. That of "the flesh" with "destruction," however, goes somewhat beyond what Paul has said explicitly about the flesh in 5:16–21, though it picks up on and expresses in a graphic manner the warning of 5:21b that "those who do such things [i.e., live in terms of "the works of the flesh"] shall not inherit the kingdom of God."

What Paul seems to have in mind here in speaking about sowing to the flesh are the libertine tendencies of his Galatian converts that he has alluded to earlier in this section: quarrelsomeness (5:15, 26), conceit (5:26), envy (5:26), living aloof from the needs of others (6:1–2; perhaps also 6:6), and pride (6:3–4). Such things not only reflect a misuse of Christian freedom (cf. 5:13) but also have disastrous results both personally and corporately, for "destruction" is their final end.

9 τὸ δὲ καλὸν ποιοῦντες μὴ ἐγκακῶμεν, καιρῷ γὰρ ἰδίῳ θερίσομεν μὴ ἐκλυόμενοι, "let us, then, not become weary in doing good, for, 'At the proper time we will reap a harvest if we do not give up.'" The warning of v 7 and its explication of v 8 are now brought to a practical conclusion by the appeal given here: "Let us not become weary in doing good." The postpositive δέ ("then") connects this verse with what has gone before, and with v 9a being an appeal based on what has gone before should probably here be translated "accordingly" or "then." The expression τὸ καλὸν ποιοῦντες ("doing the good"), as Betz observes, "includes everything the Christian is responsible for doing," and so "is identical with the concepts of the 'fruit of the Spirit' (5:22–23) and of 'following the Spirit' (5:25; cf. 5:16)" (*Galatians*, 309). In particular, it has reference to those matters commanded in 6:1–6: restoring someone entrapped by sin (v 1), bearing the oppressive burdens of others (v 2), and sharing materially with those who teach the gospel message (v 6).

The verb ἐγκακέω ("become weary," "tired") does not appear in classical Greek writings, in the LXX (though it appears later in Theodotion's translation of Prov 3:11, and in Symmachus' translation of Gen 27:46, Num 21:5, and Isa 7:16), or in any extant Jewish Greek writing prior to the NT period. It seems, in fact, to have been first coined sometime in the second century B.C. (cf. Polybius 4.19.10; BGU 1043.3). It does appear, however, in the better attested readings of six NT passages (in addition to here, cf. Luke 18:1; 2 Cor 4:1, 16; Eph 3:13; 2 Thess 3:13), though the TR has ἐκκακέω ("lose heart") at all these places (see *Note* e)—evidently because ἐγκακέω was not that common a word for many scribes. What Paul fears, it seems, is that his converts of Galatia, having begun well (cf. 3:2–5; 5:7a), were losing their enthusiasm about life lived "in step with the Spirit" (cf. 5:25), and so were not only being enticed by a nomistic lifestyle but also were allowing libertine attitudes to take control. In particular, they were beginning to revert from an outgoing type of Christian faith that seeks the welfare of others to a selfish, self-contained religious stance that has little concern for others. So Paul's appeal: "Let us, then, not become weary in doing good."

In support of his appeal, Paul now adds what appears to be another traditional maxim, which is introduced (as are those of vv 3, 5, and 7) by an explanatory γάρ:

"For, 'At the proper time we shall reap a harvest if we do not give up.'" The maxim
here, however, not only adds support to Paul's appeal but also promises a positive
outcome for those who persevere in doing good to others. The expression καιρῷ
ἰδίῳ is probably an idiom for "at the appropriate moment," "in due season," or "at
the proper time," without any specification given as to what moment, season, or
time is in mind (cf. G. Delling, "καιρός," *TDNT* 3:455–62). While both the adjective
ἴδιος and the noun καιρός occur frequently on their own throughout the NT, the
only other instances of their being brought together are at 1 Tim 2:6 and 6:15
(both, however, in the plural). On ἴδιος as meaning "appropriate," "due," or
"proper" in Paul, see 1 Cor 3:8 and 15:23.

The verb θερίζω ("reap," "harvest") corresponds to the agricultural imagery of
vv 7b–8 (cf. also the image of "fruit," καρπός, in the caption "the fruit of the Spirit"
at 5:22). Its appearance here in the future tense (θερίσομεν) is a promise for the
future, but again without any specification as to whether that time is to be a this-
worldly existential future or an other-worldly eschatological future, or both.
Interpreters have easily latched on to one or the other of these understandings
depending on their own theological proclivities. But Paul (as well as the other NT
writers) is not really interested in questions of timing; rather, his attention focuses
on the certainty of God's promises and the inevitability of what will occur when
certain spiritual processes are in place. The verb ἐκλύω ("faint," "become weary,"
"give out," or "give up") is a common word in Greek writings, though it appears only
in the passive in the NT (cf. Matt 15:32; Mark 8:3; Heb 12:3,5). Compared with
ἐγκακέω ("become weary") used in Paul's appeal, ἐκλύω ("give up") of this supporting maxim seems to be the stronger verb, though they are roughly synonymous.
As an adverbial participle, ἐκλυόμενοι has a conditional function, so with the
negative μή the maxim closes with the thought "if we do not give up." For Paul, the
fruit of a spiritual harvest comes through the concurring actions of both God and
the believer, with the believer's perseverance being generally in response to the
Spirit's work in his or her life and specifically an expression of the virtue "patience"
(μακροθυμία, cf. 5:22).

10 ἄρα οὖν ὡς καιρὸν ἔχομεν, ἐργαζώμεθα τὸ ἀγαθὸν πρὸς πάντας, μάλιστα
δὲ πρὸς τοὺς οἰκείους τῆς πίστεως, "therefore, whenever we have opportunity,
let us do good to all people, especially to those who belong to the household of
faith." The inferential particle ἄρα ("then") strengthened by the transitional particle οὖν ("therefore") appears frequently in Paul's letters to signal the conclusion
or main point of a discussion (cf. Rom 5:18; 7:3, 25; 8:12; 9:16, 18; 14:12, 19; Eph
2:19; 1 Thess 5:6; 2 Thess 2:15). Here it sets off the exhortation of this verse as the
conclusion and main point not only of the directives given in 6:1–10 but also of all
that has been said in 5:13–6:10. In effect, the exhortations of 5:13, "through love serve
one another," and 6:10, "do good to all people," function as an *inclusio* for all that
Paul says against libertine tendencies among the believers of Galatia in 5:13–6:10.

The exhortation is prefaced by the phrase ὡς καιρὸν ἔχομεν (present indicative) or ὡς καιρὸν ἔχωμεν (present subjunctive), with both readings of the verb
being almost equally well supported (see *Note* f) and both readings resulting in approximately the same meaning (i.e., "we have" or "we might have"). The adverbial
temporal particle ὡς with an accusative noun means "as long as" or "whenever" and
can be understood either eschatologically ("as long as") or existentially ("whenever"). καιρός, as in v 9b above, suggests "a propitious situation," "a decisive

moment," or "a divinely given opportunity" (cf. G. Delling, "καιρός," *TDNT* 3:455–62). Thus Paul qualifies his exhortation for believers to "do good" in a manner suggesting that such actions be viewed as availing oneself of God-given opportunities and be undertaken as part of a Christian's redemptive mandate. Paul is certainly not relegating ethics to some incidental or optional category of Christian living, as some seem to read his words here. Rather, he is highlighting through his use of the noun καιρός the divinely given and strategic nature of opportunities set before the Christian for doing good.

The exhortation itself is all-embracing: "Let us do good to all people." The better textual authorities read the deponent verb of the exhortation as a present subjunctive, ἐργαζώμεθα ("let us do"), rather than as a present indicative, ἐργαζόμεθα ("we do") (see *Note* g), which is also more internally plausible. The expression τὸ ἀγαθόν ("the good") is fairly general. It corresponds to τοῖς ἀγαθοῖς ("good things") of v 6 and is roughly synonymous with τὸ καλόν ("the good"). In the singular with an article it signifies "that which is advantageous" (cf. Rom 7:13; 15:2). The object of Christian acts of doing good is identified by the prepositional phrase πρὸς πάντας ("to all [people]"). As Betz aptly observes, citing the emphases on "all" in 2:16; 3:8, 22, 26–28 and the new relationships set out in 3:26–28: "The universal character of God's redemption corresponds to the universality of Christian ethical and social responsibility. If God's redemption in Christ is universal, the Christian community is obliged to disregard all ethnic, national, cultural, social, sexual, and even religious distinctions within the human community. Since before God there is no partiality, there cannot be partiality in the Christian's attitude towards his fellow man" (*Galatians*, 311).

Somewhat paradoxically, however, Paul appends to his universalistic exhortation the statement: "especially to those who belong to the household of faith." Is this a lapse from the universalism of concern expressed in 5:13 and immediately previous in 6:10? Or is it rather making the point that amidst our concern for all humanity we as Christians are to have a special concern for the welfare of fellow believers? Undoubtedly it is the latter, in line with Jesus' command to his disciples to "love one another" (John 13:34–35). For Paul, believers "in Christ" make up τοὺς οἰκείους τῆς πίστεως ("the household of faith"), which speaks metaphorically of the corporate unity of Christians, and the members of such a household are to be cared for in particular.

The use of the metaphor οἰκεῖος ("household") for Christians appears elsewhere in Paul's letters explicitly only at Eph 2:19, but the imagery of a building as a communal structure for Christians is fairly common (cf. 1 Cor 3:9–17; 2 Cor 6:14–16; Eph 2:19–22). The expression ἡ πίστις ("the faith") is used here as a locution for the Christian movement (cf. 1:23; see also 3:23, 25).

Explanation

In dealing with the judaizing threat, Paul associated "flesh" with "the works of the law" and circumcision (cf. 3:2–3; see also 6:12–13). Likewise, in dealing with libertine tendencies within the Galatian churches he associates "the flesh" with not being guided by the Spirit or controlled by love, but autonomously expressing one's own sinful nature (cf. 5:13, 16–17, 19–21; 6:8). Whether, therefore, it be "the works of the law" or "the works of the flesh," in either case the result is destruction.

For legalism and libertinism are alike in that they both fail to appreciate or experience the freedom of new existence "in Christ," and so both result in a sorry end.

On the other hand, just as it is "the Spirit" who counteracts legalism and puts an end to nomism (cf. 3:2–5, 14; 4:6–7; 5:5–6), so it is "the Spirit" who counteracts libertinism and enables the believer to do good works that are beneficial to all in need (cf. 5:16–18, 22–23, 25; 6:8). Paul's exhortations really boil down to one point that is expressed in slightly different ways: "live by the Spirit" (5:16), "be led by the Spirit" (5:18), "keep in step with the Spirit" (5:25), and/or "sow to the Spirit" (6:8). Being thus truly "spiritual people" (οἱ πνευματικοί), the result will be that we will serve one another through love (5:13), restore others entrapped by oppressive burdens (6:1–2), adequately compensate those who have provided instruction (6:6), and generally do good to all people, particularly fellow believers (6:10).

In effect, then, whether it be a matter of access to God, a proper Christian lifestyle, or an outgoing, loving expression of the Christian faith, it is the Spirit who both brings such things about and enables the believer to work them out in practice. There is, of course, concurring activity on the part of the Spirit and the believer in these matters. But nothing can be accomplished either by "the works of the law" or "the works of the flesh," but only by reliance on "the Spirit."

IV. Subscription (6:11–18)

Bibliography

Bahr, G. J. "The Subscriptions in the Pauline Letters." *JBL* 87 (1968) 27–41. **Clarke, W. K. L.** "St. Paul's 'Large Letters.'" *ExpTim* 24 (1913) 285. **Clemens, J. S.** "St. Paul's Handwriting." *ExpTim* 24 (1913) 380. **Cuming, G. J.** "Service-endings in the Epistles." *NTS* 22 (1975) 110–13. **Dahl, N. A.** "Der Name Israel: Zur Auslegung von Gal 6, 16." *Judaica* 6 (1950) 161–70. **Davies, W. D.** "Paul and the People of Israel." *NTS* 24 (1977) 4–39, esp. 9–10. **Deissmann, A.** *Bible Studies*, 346–60. ————. *Light from the Ancient East.* 1927 rev. ed. **Dion, P. E.** "The Aramaic 'Family Letter' and Related Epistolary Forms in Other Oriental Languages and in Hellenistic Greek." *Semeia* 22 (1981) 59–76. **Doty, W. G.** *Letters in Primitive Christianity.* **Exler, F.** *The Form of the Ancient Greek Letter,* 73-112. **Fitzmyer, J. A.** "Some Notes on Aramaic Epistolography." *JBL* 93 (1974) 201–25, esp. 201–5, 217. **Gamble, H.** *Textual History,* 57–83. **Jewett, R.** "The Form and Function of the Homiletic Benediction." *ATR* 51 (1969) 13–34. ————. "The Agitators and the Galatian Congregation," *NTS* 17 (1971) 198–212. **Koskenniemi, H.** *Studien zur Idee und Phraseologie des griechischen Briefes bis 400 n. Chr.* **Longenecker, R. N.** "Ancient Amanuenses and the Pauline Epistles." In *New Dimensions in New Testament Study,* ed. R. N. Longenecker and M. C. Tenney. Grand Rapids: Zondervan, 1974, 281–97. **Meecham, H. G.** *Light from Ancient Letters.* **Mullins, T. Y.** "Greeting as a New Testament Form." *JBL* 87 (1968) 418–26. ————. "Benediction as a New Testament Form." *AUSS* 15 (1977) 59–64. **Nijenhuis, J.** "The Greeting in My Own Hand." *BT* 19 (1981) 225–58. **Richardson, P.** *Israel in the Apostolic Church.* SNTSMS 10. Cambridge: Cambridge University Press, 1969, 74–102. **Robinson, D. W. B.** "Distinction between Jewish and Gentile Believers in Galatians." *ABR* 13 (1965) 29–44. **Roller, O.** *Das Formular,* 69–70, 489–93. **Schnider, F.,** and **Stenger, W.** *Studien zum neutestamentlichen Brieff ormular,* 108–67. **Schrenk, G.** "Was bedeutet 'Israel Gottes'?" *Judaica* 5 (1949) 81–94. ————. "Der Segenwunsch nach der Kampfepistel." *Judaica* 6 (1950) 170–90. **Stowers, S. K.** *Letter Writing in Greco-Roman Antiquity.* **White, J. L.** "The Greek Documentary Letter Tradition: Third Century B.C.E. to Third Century C.E." *Semeia* 22 (1981) 89–106, esp. 92–95. ————. *Light from Ancient Letters.* Philadelphia: Fortress, 1986. ————. "Ancient Greek Letters." In *Greco-Roman Literature and the New Testament,* ed. D. E. Aune. SBLSBS 21. Atlanta: Scholars, 1988. 85–106. **Ziemann, F.** *De Epistularum Graecarum Formulis,* 362–65.

Translation

[11] *See what large[a] letters [I use] as I write to you with my own hand!*

[12] *Those who want to make a good showing outwardly are trying to compel you to receive circumcision. [The] only [reason they do this is] to avoid being persecuted[b] for the cross of Christ.[c]* [13] *For those who are circumcised[d] do not themselves keep the law, yet they want you to receive circumcision in order that they might boast about your flesh.* [14] *May I, however, never boast except in the cross of our Lord Jesus Christ, through which the world has been crucified to me and I to the world.* [15] *For, "Neither[e] circumcision nor uncircumcision means anything; all that matters is a new creation."* [16] *Peace and mercy be on all those who will follow[f] this rule, even on the Israel of God.*

[17] *Finally, let no one continue to cause me trouble, for I bear on my body the marks of Jesus![g]*

[18] *The grace of our[h] Lord Jesus Christ[i] be with your spirit, brothers. Amen.*

Notes

a πηλίκοις ("how large") is well attested externally, though ἡλίκοις (the classical form of the word) is supported by P[46] B* and ποικίλοις ("how diversified") by minuscule 642.

b The present subjunctive passive verb διώκωνται ("they might [not] be persecuted") is well attested, though the present indicative passive διώκονται ("they are [not] persecuted") appears in P[46] B K Ψ etc.

c Χριστοῦ ("of Christ") is well attested, though Χριστοῦ Ἰησοῦ ("of Christ Jesus") is the reading of P[46] B and a few minuscules—perhaps influenced by v 14.

d The present passive substantival participle οἱ περιτεμνόμενοι ("those who are circumcised") is attested by ℵ A C D K P et al., though the perfect passive οἱ περιτετμημένοι ("those who have been circumcised") by P[46] B Ψ etc. While the weight of external evidence is almost equally balanced, the present passive substantival participle is more internally convincing and so probably original.

e The shorter reading οὔτε γάρ ("for neither") is attested by P[46] B Ψ 33 1175, though ἐν γὰρ Χριστῷ Ἰησοῦ οὔτε ("for in Christ Jesus neither") is almost equally attested by ℵ A C D TR, as well as most minuscules and many versions. The longer reading, however, is probably influenced by 5:6.

f The future indicative στοιχήσουσιν ("will follow") is well attested, though the aorist subjunctive στοιχήσωσιν ("would follow") appears in P[46].

g The simple name Ἰησοῦ ("of Jesus") is attested by P[46] A B C* 33 et al. Various other readings, however, appear in the textual tradition: Χριστοῦ ("of Christ") is supported by P Ψ 81 cop[bo]; κυρίου Ἰησοῦ ("of the Lord Jesus") by K L Byzantine vg syr[pesh]; κυρίου Ἰησοῦ Χριστοῦ ("of the Lord Jesus Christ") by ℵ it cop[sa]; and κυρίου ἡμῶν Ἰησοῦ Χριστοῦ ("of our Lord Jesus Christ") by D* G Ambst Pel.

h The pronoun ἡμῶν ("our") is omitted by ℵ P 69 1739.

i Χριστοῦ ("of Christ") is omitted by P.

Form/Structure/Setting

The subscriptions of Paul's letters have generally been treated in a rather cursory manner, largely because of (1) the natural tendency of commentators to focus on the weightier matters found in the thanksgivings and bodies of Paul's letters, and (2) the supposition that the salutations and subscriptions that open and close a Pauline letter are primarily conventional in nature and serve only to establish or maintain contact with the readers. The subscription of Galatians, however, has been the object of more scholarly attention than the subscriptions of Paul's other letters. This appears to be so primarily because of its greater length and its more obvious relevance to the body of its letter. J. B. Lightfoot, for example, long ago observed that 6:11–18 functions by way of "summing up the main lessons of the epistle in terse eager disjointed sentences" (*Galatians* [1896], 220); and Adolf Deissmann early insisted regarding Paul's letters in general and Galatians in particular: "More attention ought to be paid the concluding words of the letters generally; they are of the highest importance if we are ever to understand the Apostle. The conclusion to the Galatians is certainly a very remarkable one" (*Bible Studies*, 347–48; cf. also the comments of G. Milligan, *Documents*, 21–28). Since Lightfoot, Deissmann, Milligan, and others drew attention to it, scholars have generally viewed Paul's subscription in Galatians as summing up the contents of the body of the letter—though, it need be noted, their views have usually been based simply on a comparison of topics and without any analysis of epistolary or rhetorical forms.

Of late, Hans Dieter Betz has highlighted the fact that 6:11–18 is not only a summation of Paul's letter but is also "most important for the interpretation of Galatians. It contains the interpretive clues to the understanding of Paul's major concerns in the letter as a whole and should be employed as the hermeneutical key to the intentions of the Apostle" (*Galatians*, 313). Betz, of course, makes this claim from the perspective of rhetorical criticism rather than epistolary analysis. But his assertion that these verses function rhetorically as the *peroratio* of a typical apologetic speech may be doubted. For if Galatians cannot be understood entirely in terms of Greco-Roman forensic rhetoric, but also exhibits, as we have proposed, Jewish ways of arguing (esp. in 3:8–4:7) and Greco-Roman deliberative rhetorical features (esp. in 4:12–6:10), one may legitimately question whether 6:11–18 is properly to be seen in terms of the forensic rhetorical category *peroratio*. Nonetheless, despite his rigid application of forensic rhetorical categories to almost all of Galatians (i.e., apart from the "Epistolary Prescript" of 1:1–5, but including everything else in the letter), Betz's insistence on the importance of 6:11–18 for the interpretation of Galatians is highly laudatory, even though the rationale for such a claim can be better supported on an epistolary rather than a rhetorical basis.

The subscriptions of Paul's letters function like the thanksgivings of his letters, though in reverse: they provide important clues for understanding the issues previously discussed in the bodies of their respective letters. For as the thanksgivings foreshadow and point ahead to the major concerns to be addressed in their respective bodies, the subscriptions serve to highlight and summarize the main points that have been dealt with in those bodies. Galatians, of course, is the primary example of a Pauline letter without a thanksgiving section (probably also 2 Corinthians, though uncertainties regarding how that letter was composed tend to confuse any certain epistolary analysis). But the Galatian θαυμάζω ("I am astonished") subsection of 1:6–10 that begins the long rebuke section of 1:6–4:11 takes its place in setting out the occasion for writing and the issues at stake. And it is to that subsection of 1:6–10 that the subscription of 6:11–18 can be compared when attempting to identify the major concerns of Paul in writing his Galatian letter, and so to seek interpretive keys for understanding what is discussed in the major portion of the body of that letter.

A number of features appear repeatedly in the subscriptions of a Pauline letter. The most frequent of these is the "grace benediction" that occurs in every Pauline letter and usually comes at the close of the subscription (cf. Rom 16:20b [perhaps also v 24, as per D TR et al.]; 1 Cor 16:23; 2 Cor 13:14; Gal 6:18; Eph 6:24; Phil 4:23; Col 4:18b; 1 Thess 5:28; 2 Thess 3:18; 1 Tim 6:21b; 2 Tim 4:22b; Titus 3:15b; Philem 25). Almost as frequent are "greetings" that appear in all of the Pauline letters except Galatians, Ephesians, and 1 Timothy. ἀσπάζομαι ("greet") is the verb always used in the greeting formula—once in the first person singular (cf. Rom 16:22, though here it is Paul's amanuensis Tertius who greets the reader); most often in the second person plural, where the addressees become the agents through whom Paul conveys his greetings (cf. Rom 16:3–16; 1 Cor 16:20b; 2 Cor 13:12a; Phil 4:21a; Col 4:15; 1 Thess 5:26; 2 Tim 4:19; Titus 3:15); often, as well, in the third person singular or plural, where Paul passes on the greetings of others (cf. Rom 16:16b, 21, 23; 1 Cor 16:19–20a; 2 Cor 13:12b; Phil 4:22; Col 4:10–14; 2 Tim 4:21b; Titus 3:15a; Philem 23); and three times using the related substantival phrase ὁ ἀσπασμὸς Παύλου, "the greeting of Paul" (cf. 1 Cor 16:21; Col 4:18; 2 Thess 3:17).

A third feature often found in the Pauline subscriptions is what may be called a "peace benediction" or "peace wish" that appears in many of the letters, except 1 Corinthians, Colossians, the Pastorals, and Philemon (cf. Rom 15:33; 16:20a; 2 Cor 13:11b; Gal 6:16; Eph 6:23; Phil 4:9b; 1 Thess 5:23; 2 Thess 3:16). A fourth is a reference to Paul's own handwriting, or the "autograph," that appears in five letters, always using the phrase τῇ ἐμῇ χειρί, "in my own hand" (cf. 1 Cor 16:21; Gal 6:11; Col 4:18a; 2 Thess 3:17; Philem 19). A fifth is a section of concluding exhortations that either summarizes briefly the central matters discussed within the body of the letter (cf. 1 Cor 16:13–18, 22; 2 Cor 13:11a; Gal 6:12–17) or has to do with further relations within the community addressed (cf. Rom 16:17–19; Phil 4:8–19; Col 4:16–17; 1 Thess 5:27; 1 Tim 6:17–21a; 2 Tim 4:21a; Titus 3:12–14). Within three of these concluding exhortations appears an emphasis on rejoicing, with the verb χαίρω ("rejoice") being used (cf. Rom 16:19a; 1 Cor 16:17–18; Phil 4:10–19). At times, as well, there is a request for prayer (cf. Rom 15:30–32; Eph 6:18–20; Col 4:3–4; 1 Thess 5:25; 2 Thess 3:1–2) and a doxology (cf. Rom 16:25–27; Phil 4:20; 1 Tim 6:16; 2 Tim 4:18), but whether these requests for prayer and doxologies are fixed epistolary formulae in the Pauline subscriptions can be debated. And since such requests for prayer and doxologies do not appear in Galatians, except as part of a confessional portion at 1:5 (see *Comment* there), the issues involved are not of concern to a discussion of the Galatian subscription.

The subscription of Galatians contains no greetings, whether directly from Paul himself, indirectly using the readers as his agents, or simply passing on the greetings of others (the reference to "all the brothers with me" at 1:2 of the salutation is no exception, for there endorsement rather than greeting is to the fore)—probably reflecting something of the strained relations between Paul and his converts that is evident throughout the body of the letter. Likewise, the subscription has no expression of joy, no request for prayer, and no doxology. Each of these items would have assumed a relationship of fellowship and thankfulness between Paul and his readers such as cannot be found elsewhere in the letter.

Other features of a typical Pauline subscription, however, appear in 6:11–18, with each having a nuance appropriate to what Paul has argued and exhorted earlier in the letter. Thus in v 11 there is an "autograph" unit of material such as appears elsewhere in Paul's letters (cf. 1 Cor 16:21; Col 4:18a; 2 Thess 3:17; Philem 19), though here with a particular nuance having to do with "large letters." In vv 12–15 there appears a disproportionately large section of concluding statements that focus on the major issues addressed in the body of the letter and that carry the note not of rejoicing or thanksgiving but of warning. These statements function as implied exhortations. The climax of these statements is the conditional "peace benediction" of v 16, which is followed by the explicit warning and exhortation found in v 17. All of this, then, is concluded by Paul's usual "grace benediction" of v 18.

More directly than in any of his other letters, Paul's subscription in Galatians brings to a head and highlights the central matters discussed within the body of his letter. All of its four features—its autograph (v 11), its implied exhortations (vv 12–15,17), its peace benediction (v 16), and its grace benediction (v 18)—make clear Paul's concerns and message as set out earlier in the body of his letter, particularly those having to do with the judaizing threat dealt with in 1:6–5:12. The subscription of 6:11–18, therefore, is not just a conventional portion tacked on to the weightier material of 1:6–6:10. While it incorporates many of the standard epistolary conventions of a Hellenistic postscript or letter closing, it uses these conventional forms in a manner that reflects the letter's essential concerns and teachings. So 6:11–18 must be seen as something of a prism that reflects the major thrusts of what has been said earlier in the letter, or a paradigm set at the end of the letter that gives guidance in understanding what has been said before. As Betz rightly points out, "It contains the interpretive clues to the understanding of Paul's major concerns in the letter as a whole and should be employed as the hermeneutical key to the intentions of the Apostle" (*Galatians*, 313).

Comment

11 ἴδετε πηλίκοις ὑμῖν γράμμασιν ἔγραψα τῇ ἐμῇ χειρί, "see what large letters [I use] as I write to you with my own hand." Hellenistic letters in Paul's day usually exhibited two styles of handwriting: a more practiced, carefully constructed script of an amanuensis or secretary in most of the letter and the cruder or more casual style of the sender in the subscription (see *Introduction*, pp. lviii–lx). Paul, in fact, seems to have followed the practice of using an amanuensis for the writing of all his letters, though his amanuenses were personal companions or able fellow believers of the various churches rather than professional scribes (see *Introduction*, pp. lx–lxi). And here by the phrase τῇ ἐμῇ χειρί, "in my own hand," Paul's recipients are alerted to the fact that they are not now reading and/or hearing what an amanuensis has written down on his behalf but Paul's own statements that he has inscribed himself.

The second person plural aorist imperative ἴδετε ("notice," "see"), like its derived cognate, the demonstrative particle ἰδού ("notice," "see"), serves to arouse attention and to highlight the importance of what follows. The verb ἔγραψα ("I write") is an epistolary aorist, as used elsewhere in Paul's letters (cf. Rom 15:15 [probably]; 1 Cor 5:11; 9:15; Philem 19, 21; note also ἔπεμψα at Phil 2:28; Col 4:8, and ἀνέπεμψα at Philem 12). The phrase τῇ ἐμῇ χειρί ("in my own hand") not only alerts Paul's converts to a change of handwriting but also signals for them where the body of the Galatian letter ends and its subscription begins. Such a phrase rarely appears in the extant Hellenistic letters of Paul's day, for any difference of script would have been immediately obvious to the recipients of those letters as they read them. Paul's letters, however, were to be read aloud in the churches to which he sent them (so, e.g., 1 Thess 5:27)—even at times to be read aloud to other churches (cf. Col 4:16)—so there was need for him to make such an explicit reference as to where the body of the letter ended and the subscription began, for not everyone would have been in a position to observe the change of script itself.

The correlative pronoun πηλίκοις in the dative ("with what large") and the dative plural noun γράμμασιν ("letters") have in the past been interpreted in a variety of ways. It is true that γράμμα, both in the singular and the plural, was used in early and later Greek for a letter (e.g., Herodotus 5.14; PGrenf 1.30.5; 1 Macc 5:10; *Ep. Arist.* 43; Acts 28:21), a document (e.g., Esth 8:5, 10, passim; Josephus, *Ant.* 7.137; 8.50; passim), the OT generally (e.g., Philo, *Mos.* 2.290, 292; *Praem.* 79; *Leg. Alleg.* 195; Josephus, *Ant.* 1.13; 10.210; *Ag. Ap.* 1.54), and, in fact, for a writing or book of any kind. In Paul's letters, however, ἐπιστολή (whether singular or plural) is the word regularly used for a composition called a "letter" (cf. Rom 16:22; 1 Cor 5:9; 16:3; 2 Cor 3:1; 7:8; 10:9–11; Col 4:16; 1 Thess 5:27; 2 Thess 2:2, 15; 3:14, 17), with γράμμα signaling a letter of the alphabet (cf. 2 Cor 3:7).

Accepting, then, that "large letters" has reference to the style of handwriting that Paul used in writing the subscription of 6:11–18, the question naturally arises as to why Paul wrote with such large letters, and more importantly, what purpose he had in mind in drawing his converts' attention to them. It has been popularly posited that these "large letters" were due to Paul's poor eyesight, appealing to 4:15 in support. But if "you would have torn out your eyes and given them to me" is to be understood more as a popular idiom than as an allusion to a specific physical disability (see *Comment* at 4:15), then such a proposal must be judged as merely a conjecture without foundation. Likewise, Deissmann's view that "writing was not an easy thing to his workman's hand," and so in rather embarrassed, self-conscious fashion, Paul pokes fun at his own clumsy, awkward style of writing as compared with that of his amanuensis (*Light from the Ancient East* [1927], 166), must be declared another conjecture without foundation. Even more unlikely is Nigel Turner's view that Paul "had actually been crucified at Perga in Pamphylia" and so sustained permament damage to his hand (*Grammatical Insights into the New Testament* [Edinburgh: T. & T. Clark, 1965] 94, appealing to 2:19; 6:14, 17 in support).

Much more plausible is the thesis that the "large letters" were intended to emphasize, underscore, or highlight what Paul wanted to say in what follows in his subscription. To quote J. B. Lightfoot: "The boldness of the handwriting answers to the force of the Apostle's convictions. The size of the characters will arrest the attention of his readers in spite of themselves" (*Galatians* [1890], 221). Or as Burton puts it: "The size of the letters would have somewhat the effect of bold-face type in a modern book, or double underlining in a manuscript, and since the apostle himself called attention to it, it would impress not only the one person who might be reading the letter to a congregation, but the listening congregation also" (*Galatians*, 348). And it is with this understanding of Paul's purpose in both closing off his Galatian letter with "large letters" and drawing his audience's attention to them that most modern commentators are content (so, e.g., Schlier, *Galater*, 280; Mussner, *Galaterbrief*, 410; Betz, *Galatians*, 314; Bruce, *Galatians*, 268), thereby calling on us today to read what follows in vv 12–18 with a particular focus of concern and with a realization that here Paul sees himself as coming to the heart of matters, as his original readers and hearers were expected to understand from these final statements of his letter.

12 ὅσοι θέλουσιν εὐπροσωπῆσαι ἐν σαρκί, οὗτοι ἀναγκάζουσιν ὑμᾶς περιτέμνεσθαι, μόνον ἵνα τῷ σταυρῷ τοῦ Χριστοῦ μὴ διώκωνται, "those who want to make a good showing outwardly are trying to compel you to receive circumcision. [The] only [reason they do this is] to avoid being persecuted for the cross of Christ." Vv 12–17 pick up on Paul's arguments and exhortations of 1:6–5:12 against the judaizing threat, without specifically carrying on his arguments and exhortations of 5:13–6:10 against the libertine tendencies. One obvious indicator of this shift back to the major discussion of the letter is his use of σάρξ ("flesh") in vv 12–13, where the term appears in the purely physical sense used earlier in 2:20; 4:13, 14, 23, 29 (probably also 3:3) but not in the ethical sense of 5:16, 17, 19, 24; 6:8. Other rather obvious indicators are his references to the judaizing opponents in vv 12–13, his focus on the centrality of the cross in v 14 (cf. 3:1, 13), his specific repudiation of the relevance of circumcision for the Christian life in v 15, his reference to Gentile belivers as "the Israel of God" in v 16, his warning that others not "trouble" him in v 17a (cf. 1:7; 5:12), and his reference to "the marks of Jesus" in v 17b—each of which, of course, requires comment in what follows.

In vv 12–13 Paul states what he believes motivates his judaizing opponents. While they undoubtedly claimed to be interested only in Gentile believers being fully accepted by God into the chosen people of Israel, and so full recipients of the blessings of the Abrahamic covenant, Paul accuses them of being primarily motivated by a desire to avoid persecution by being able to boast about Gentile Christians being circumcised and so related to the Jewish nation. It is a judgment call on Paul's part that depends on a certain reading of events unfolding within the Jewish world and that is highly subjective in nature. Nonetheless, it is how Paul reads and understands what is really motivating his judaizing opponents within the Galatian churches, and here, after all of his arguments and exhortations against that judaizing activity among Gentile believers of those churches, he highlights his perception of what really lies behind the Judaizers' activities.

As elsewhere in the Galatian letter (cf. 1:7; 5:10, 12), Paul's opponents are not here named; they are identified only by their intent and actions as ὅσοι θέλουσιν εὐπροσωπῆσαι ἐν σαρκί ("those who want to make a good impression in the flesh/ outwardly"). Paul, in fact, may not even have known their names, but he certainly knows of their activities. The verb εὐπροσωπέω ("make a good showing") is a rare word in Greek. Outside of its occurrence here, it appears only in PTebt 19:12 dated about 114 B.C. The expression ἐν σαρκί here is used in the physical sense found earlier in 2:20; 3:3 (probably); 4:13, 14, 23, 29, but not in the ethical sense of 5:16–24; 6:8. Literally, it has reference to circumcision "in the flesh," though more generally it signifies whatever is external as opposed to that which is spiritual and/or internal (cf. Phil 3:3–4). The present tense of the verb ἀναγκάζουσιν ("they are trying to compel") is conative in force (i.e., having to do with mental processes or behavior directed toward action or change, with attendant ideas of impulse, desire, volition, and striving), as also in 2:14 (cf. Acts 26:11). The present infinitive περιτέμνεσθαι ("to be circumcised") is used by Paul elsewhere in Galatians when speaking about the circumcision of adult males (cf. 5:2–3). If he had used an aorist infinitive, Paul would have been speaking about circumcision as a simple fact. In the present tense, however, the infinitive suggests the idea of voluntary action, and so connotes "to let yourselves be circumcised" or "to receive circumcision."

The neuter μόνον ("only," "alone") is used as an adverb (cf. 1:23; 2:10; 3:2; 4:18; 5:13) to qualify the main verb of the sentence, ἀναγκάζουσιν : "they are trying to compel . . . only in order to avoid being persecuted." What the Judaizers wanted, as Paul reads their motives, was to lay the religious compulsion of circumcision on Gentile believers in Galatia—thereby bringing Gentile Christians within the orbit of the Jewish nation on a proselyte basis—and so to relieve themselves and Jewish Christendom generally from persecution at the hands of fellow nonbelieving Jews (cf. 1 Thess 2:14b–16). For, as Robert Jewett observes, in the rising tide of Jewish nationalism in Palestine, with the antagonism of the Zealots being directed against all who had Gentile sympathies and all who associated with Gentiles on a nonproselyte basis, "If they could succeed in circumcising the Gentile Christians, this might effectively thwart any Zealot purification campaign against the Judean church!" (NTS 17 [1971] 206).

The separation of the negative μή ("not") from ἵνα ("in order that") is somewhat unusual, for the normal practice in Greek is to place μή in a negative ἵνα purpose clause immediately after ἵνα. But when Paul wants to highlight something of importance, he at times inserts that item between the conjunction ἵνα and the negative μή in a ἵνα purpose clause (cf. 1 Cor 2:5; 2 Cor 13:10). Here the emphasis is on τῷ σταυρῷ τοῦ Χριστοῦ ("for the cross of Christ"), which he will elaborate on in v 14 as the central focus of the gospel proclamation (cf. 3:1,13).

13 οὐδὲ γὰρ οἱ περιτεμνόμενοι αὐτοὶ νόμον φυλάσσουσιν, ἀλλὰ θέλουσιν ὑμᾶς περιτέμνεσθαι ἵνα ἐν τῇ ὑμετέρᾳ σαρκὶ καυχήσωνται, "for those who are circumcised do not themselves keep the law, yet they want you to receive circumcision in order that they might boast about your flesh." Continuing his emphasis on the motivation of the Judaizers, Paul in this verse adds one further point about his opponents and then reiterates what he sees to be the real reason for their activities. The postpositive connective γάρ ("for") serves to confirm what has just been expressed by the purpose clause headed by the adverb μόνον: that the only reason for the Judaizers' activities was a desire to avoid persecution. And as in the previous verse, so here Paul does not name his opponents but simply refers to them by the substantival participle οἱ περιτεμνόμενοι, that is, "those who belong to the circumcision" or "those who are circumcised."

Johannes Munck, as noted earlier (see *Introduction*, pp. xc–xci), has claimed that the present substantival participle οἱ περιτεμνόμενοι should not be understood as a passive, referring to "those who belong to the circumcision" and so Jewish Christians from Jerusalem, but as a permissive middle, referring to "those who receive circumcision" (i.e., "those who let themselves be circumcised"; cf. 5:3) and so Gentile Christians of Galatia who had become enamored with Jewish practices and taken on the rite of circumcision without any outside pressure (cf. his *Paul and the Salvation of Mankind*, 87–90; idem, *NTS* 6 [1960] 103–16). Munck's view reflects and crystallizes several earlier attempts along these lines to sort out the exact situation at Galatia (e.g., Lietzmann, *Galater*, ad loc.; E. Hirsch, *ZNW* 29 [1930] 192–97; W. Michaelis, *ZNW* 30 [1931] 83–89; H. J. Schoeps, *Paul*, 65, 77). But to have said what Munck and others want him to say, Paul would better have used οἱ ἐν ὑμῖν περιτμηθέντες (the aorist passive substantival participle with the preposition ἐν and the dative ὑμῖν, meaning "those who were circumcised among you") or οἱ περιτετμημένοι (the perfect passive substantival participle, meaning "those who have been circumcised"); this latter reading is found in some MSS, but evidently is not original (see *Note* d). Taken on their own, the subjects of both v 12 and v 13 could be understood as Gentile "Judaizers" who had no connections with Jewish Christians at Jerusalem. In the overall context of the Galatian letter, however, it is very difficult to believe that this is so, particularly in light of the polemic against Jerusalem influence that permeates the *narratio* from 1:17–2:10 and the parallel Antioch episode recounted in 2:11–14. Furthermore, on such an understanding no explanation seems possible for why Gentile "Judaizers" feared persecution (evidently from Jews) when they themselves had no connection with Jerusalem, despite A. E. Harvey's attempt to save Munck's thesis by postulating that the pressure on these Gentile "Judaizers" came from local Jews in their endeavors to recover former proselytes who had become Christians (see his "The Opposition to Paul," in *Studia Evangelica* IV, ed. F. L. Cross, TU 102 [Berlin: Akademie, 1968] 319–32).

Exactly what Paul had in mind when he said that the Judaizers οὐδὲ . . . αὐτοὶ νόμον φυλάσσουσιν ("do not themselves keep the law") is very difficult to say. As noted earlier (see *Introduction*, p. c), this sentence has been used to assert that "these false teachers can hardly have been Judaizers" (so W. Schmithals, *Paul and the Gnostics*, 33–34; F. C. Crownfield, *JBL* 63 [1945] 491–500), or that Paul's Galatian opponents were from non-Pharisaic Jewish backgrounds and so did not hold to a rigid understanding of the law (so J. G. Hawkins, "The Opponents of Paul in Galatia," 344–46). More plausibly, it has been read to mean that Paul thought his opponents were insincere in their own practice of the law (so Lightfoot, *Galatians* [1890], 222), or that he looked on them as not being as scrupulous in their observance as their own teaching demanded (so G. Howard, *Paul: Crisis in Galatia*, 15). Elsewhere in Galatians Paul deals with his opponents in terms of the errors of their teaching and principles, not the shortcomings of their practice. Nonetheless, the fact that in 5:3 he points out to his converts that "every man who lets himself be circumcised . . . is obligated to obey the whole law" suggests that Paul would not have been averse to citing shortcomings of practice as a supplementary argument against any message that advocated "keeping the law" as a means of attainment for the Christian. Probably, therefore, what Paul means here in 6:13 is that despite the loftiness of their assertions and their rigid theology, the Judaizers, at least in Paul's eyes, fell short of keeping all the law scrupulously themselves. For as Paul hints in the *propositio* of Gal 2:15–21 and develops extensively in his letter to the Roman Christians, no one has ever been able to keep the law fully (cf. Rom 1:8–3:20; 3:23; 7:7–25; 8:3; passim).

But while commentators may have difficulty in determining exactly what Paul had in mind in saying that the Judaizers "do not themselves keep the law," there is no difficulty in understanding his meaning in the second part of v 13. For here he repeats his accusation as to the Judaizers' real motives, recasting that accusation to express not just the persecution they wanted to avoid but the boasting they wanted to engage in. The verb καυχάομαι (intransitive: "boast," "glory," "pride oneself"; transitive: "boast about") appears in Paul's letters about thirty-five times to connote both a rightful, healthy exultation and a wrongful, misguided claim, with the context alone determining how it is to be understood. Here, of course, the Judaizers' boast is wrongful and misguided, for they wanted Paul's converts to accede to their call for circumcision only so that they might then use such an act to protect themselves (and probably also Jewish Christians in Judea) from persecution arising from their nonbelieving fellow Jews.

14 ἐμοὶ δὲ μὴ γένοιτο καυχᾶσθαι εἰ μὴ ἐν τῷ σταυρῷ τοῦ κυρίου ἡμῶν Ἰησοῦ Χριστοῦ δι' οὗ ἐμοὶ κόσμος ἐσταύρωται κἀγὼ κόσμῳ, "may I, however, never boast except in the cross of our Lord Jesus Christ, through which the world has been crucified to me and I to the world." What Paul depreciates as wrongful, misguided boasting in v 13 he now dramatically contrasts in v 14 with what he views as rightful, healthy exultation. The contrast is signaled by (1) the adversative use of the postpositive particle δέ ("but," "however") and (2) the optative expression μὴ γένοιτο ("may it never be"), which in all of its fourteen occurrences in Paul's letters expresses an abhorrence to a statement just made or to an inference that could be falsely drawn from the apostle's teaching (cf. 2:17; 3:21; see also Rom 3:4, 6, 31; 6:2, 15; 7:7, 13; 9:14; 11:1, 11; 1 Cor 6:15; apart from Paul, the expression is used in the NT only at Luke 20:16).

Two matters are highlighted in the protasis of v 14. The first has to do with Paul's perspective now as a Christian, which is signaled by the emphatic position of the pronoun ἐμοί ("to me"). In two autobiographical passages elsewhere in his letters, Paul enumerates a number of things in his life that could be the cause for boasting if viewed from a merely human perspective: in 2 Cor 11:21b–29 he attempts to demonstrate the futility of his converts' boasting about their spiritual attainments by setting out a list of his own attainments, evidently to outclass and shame them, but then he concludes with the statement, "If I must boast, I will boast of the things that show my weakness" (11:30); in Phil 3:4–6 he attempts to counter any Judaizer's claimed pedigree by citing his own Jewish pedigree, but concludes with statements regarding his far greater desire to "know Christ" and to experience in his own life all that is his because he is associated with Christ (3:7–14). Becoming one of Christ's people, whether that is expressed as being "of Christ" (Χριστοῦ, cf. *Comment* at 3:29) or "in Christ" (ἐν Χριστῷ Ἰησοῦ, cf. *Comment* at 3:26–28), effects a radical change in one's perspective. As Paul says in 2 Cor 5:16, "So from now on we regard no one from a merely human perspective (κατὰ σάρκα, "according to the flesh"); even if we once regarded Christ from a merely human perspective (κατὰ σάρκα, "according to the flesh"), we regard him now in this manner no longer." Thus with regard to boasting, Paul expresses the fervent wish that he may never exult in matters having to do with "the flesh"—that is, merely human attainments, with particular application here to counting converts and success in ministry—but only in that which has to do with the cross of Christ.

The second matter highlighted in the protasis of v 14 is the cross of Christ. Today, after almost two millennia of the cross as a sacred symbol, it is difficult for Christians to appreciate the repugnance and horror with which the cross was viewed among both Jews and Gentiles in the first century (cf. M. Hengel, *Crucifixion*, passim). The only things comparable in our day would be venerating an electric chair or wearing a hangman's noose around our necks as a symbol of our religious devotion. Indeed, as Paul says in 1 Cor 1:23, the proclamation of "Christ crucified" was "a stumbling block [σκάνδαλον, "scandal"] to Jews and foolishness [μωρία, "senseless"] to Gentiles." Yet for Paul the central feature of the Christian gospel and the focus of the gospel's proclamation is "Christ crucified." By metonymy, such associated terms as "cross" and "death" were used by him to represent the basic Christian κήρυγμα (cf. 1 Cor 1:17–18; 15:3; Phil 2:8; 3:18; Col 1:20; 2:14–15). Thus, as noted at 3:1, the gospel of Christ crucified so completely rules out any other supposed means of being righteous before God that Paul found it utterly incomprehensible for anyone who has once embraced such a gospel to ever think of supplementing it in any way. For to hold before one's eyes "Jesus Christ having been crucified" is to put an end to all forms of legalism. When, in fact, Paul speaks of the work of Christ in Galatians, his focus is entirely on "the cross" and "Christ crucified" (see 1:4; 2:20; 3:1, 13, as well as here at 6:12 and 14; cf. also 1 Cor 1:17–18, 23; 2:2; 5:7b; 8:11; 11:24–26).

The expansive nature of the phrase ὁ σταυρὸς τοῦ κυρίου ἡμῶν Ἰησοῦ Χριστοῦ ("the cross of our Lord Jesus Christ") adds weight and poignancy to the expression, reflecting the emotion with which Paul made the statement. What Paul means by boasting "in the cross of our Lord Jesus Christ" is spelled out in Rom 5:3b–5, 11 (where the deponent verb καυχάομαι appears three times) and 1 Cor 1:18–31 (where καυχάομαι appears twice).

The preposition διά ("through") with the genitive signifies instrumentality, means, or agency. The genitive relative pronoun οὗ ("which") may be either masculine or neuter in gender, and so may refer to either "our Lord Jesus Christ" (masculine) or "the cross" (neuter). Probably Paul means here that it was by means of the cross that his life was radically altered, for it is the cross that receives primary attention in the immediate context (cf. vv 12b, 14a). Yet ultimately, as Betz points out, "Whether δι' οὗ refers to the cross of Christ, or to the person of Christ, is of no consequence, since for Paul 'Christ' is always the crucified redeemer Christ" (*Galatians*, 318).

The result of being identified with "the cross of Christ," and so experiencing the work of Christ in one's life, is depicted by Paul as ἐμοὶ κόσμος ἐσταύρωται κἀγὼ κόσμῳ ("the world has been crucified to me and I to the world"). The perfect indicative passive form of the verb σταυρόω ("crucify") lays stress on a past action with present results. κόσμος ("world") here connotes not the physical world, the world of humanity, or even the world of sinful humanity alienated from God, but rather, as Burton aptly puts it, "the mode of life which is characterised by earthly advantages, viewed as obstacles to righteousness" (*Galatians*, 354, 514; cf. Matt 16:26; Jas 1:27; 4:4; 1 John 2:15). Certainly Paul is not saying that identification with the cross of Christ puts an end to a person's relations with the physical world or humanity generally. The Christian faith, contrary to many Eastern religions that extol disengagement from the physical world and a nonpersonal Nirvana, does not make one less interested in the physical world or less concerned for life as created by God; on the contrary, the gospel proclamation calls on believers to be more related to all that God has created, and so more interested in this physical world, all its created life, and the welfare of people in particular. What identification with the crucified Christ does entail, however, is no longer having "worldly" or "fleshly" advantages dominate one's thinking or living. This might seem, at first glance, somewhat theoretical, but Paul explains what he has in mind in particular in the following verse.

15 οὔτε γὰρ περιτομή τί ἐστιν οὔτε ἀκροβυστία, ἀλλὰ καινὴ κτίσις, "for, 'Neither circumcision nor uncircumcision means anything; all that matters is a new creation.'" The nub of Paul's purpose in writing Galatians and the focal point of his subscription is to be found here in v 15. He has spoken of the Judaizers' motivation in vv 12–13 and the cross of Christ as bringing an end to any "mode of life which is characterised by earthly advantages" in v 14. Now he applies all this to the Galatian situation, stating the essence of his position in a maxim. Following the statement of this maxim, Paul pronounces a "peace benediction" on "all those who follow this rule" in v 16.

Verse 15 has every appearance of being a traditional maxim that Paul here uses for his own purposes, much as he used early Christian confessional material (either directly or by way of summation) at 1:4; 3:1, 13, 26, 27–28; 4:4–5; 5:5–6, and as he used the moral maxims of his day at 6:3, 5, 7, 9 (cf. *Comment* on those verses). The reference to ἀκροβυστία ("uncircumcision") takes one beyond the requirements of Paul's immediate argument against the necessity for circumcision, much as also the confessional portion incorporated at 3:28 ("neither Jew nor Greek, slave nor free, male nor female") and the summation of Christian doctrine at 5:5–6 ("in Christ Jesus neither circumcision nor uncircumcision has any value") state matters more inclusively than Paul's immediate argument requires (see *Comment* on those verses). Likewise, as Betz observes regarding καινὴ κτίσις ("a new creation"): "The brevity of the expression makes it almost a certainty that it was known to the Galatians" (*Galatians*, 319 n. 79).

Furthermore, there is some evidence that this statement of v 15 was considered proverbial in circles other than Paul's. For Georgius Syncellus, the Byzantine historian who about A.D. 806–808 wrote an encyclopedic chronicle (the

Chronographia) that covered events from the creation of the world to the reign of the Roman emperor Diocletian, notes that these same words appear in a writing he calls the *Apocalypse of Moses* (now lost, though perhaps composed of material from the lost ending of the extant *Assumption/Testament of Moses*), which words, he believes, Paul quotes here in v 15. The date and provenance of this so-called *Apocalypse of Moses* may be questioned (Syncellus seems to have derived his information from Euthalius of the fifth century A.D.), but at least Syncellus' noting of the same wording there as here suggests the possibility that "neither circumcision nor uncircumcision means anything; all that matters is a new creation" was something of a proverbial maxim in certain circles of thought, perhaps even stemming from Jewish Christian elaborations of early rabbinic speculations on loving or honoring "mankind" as found in *m. 'Abot* 1.12; 4.1, and 6.1 (cf. B. D. Chilton, *ExpTim* 89 [1977–78] 311–13).

Taking, therefore, the statement of this verse to be a maxim that circulated in certain Christian circles before Paul wrote Galatians, and which Paul believed was also known to his Galatian converts, we may assume that Paul uses it to climax all of his arguments and exhortations in 1:6–5:12 with respect to the judaizing threat. His use of the explanatory γάρ ("for"), which has often been seen to be ambiguous here, would then serve to introduce the statement (cf. the same phenomenon at 3:26, 27–28; 6:3, 5, 7, 9). And the statement itself would reinforce Paul's précis of doctrine given at the conclusion of his exhortations against the Judaizers' message in 5:5–6, especially his summation of early Christian teaching at 5:6: "For in Christ Jesus, neither circumcision nor uncircumcision has any value—only faith expressing itself through love."

What, then, is the epitome of Paul's teaching vis-à-vis the Judaizers' claim that all Christians, whether Jews or Gentiles, must live a nomistic lifestyle in conformity to the Mosaic commandments? It is simply this: that all external expressions of the Christian faith are to be understood as culturally relevant but not spiritually necessitated, for all that really matters is that the Christian be "a new creation" and that he or she express that new work of God in ways reflective of being "in Christ" and directed by "the Spirit." Paul is not against external expressions of one's faith per se, nor against all cultic rituals. One's spiritual life cannot be simply internal; it must also be expressed externally in acts of worship to God and service on behalf of God to people. But Paul is against the Judaizers' attempt to make Gentile believers conform to Jewish laws. For while maintaining continuity with his redemptive activity for his people Israel, God has done a new thing through the work of Christ. For life now "in Christ" is to be lived not in the context of laws but in the context of "the Spirit." It is not just "re-creation" that God effects "in Christ" and by "the Spirit," thereby taking believers back to some primordial state. Rather, what God has done "in Christ" and by "the Spirit" is to effect a "new creation." Therefore, "all that matters" (ἀλλά) for the Christian is the fact of being "a new creation," with that newness of creation reflected externally in culturally relevant lives of worship and service.

16 καὶ ὅσοι τῷ κανόνι τούτῳ στοιχήσουσιν, εἰρήνη ἐπ᾽ αὐτοὺς καὶ ἔλεος, καὶ ἐπὶ τὸν Ἰσραὴλ τοῦ θεοῦ, "peace and mercy be on all those who will follow this rule, even on the Israel of God." That the statement of v 15 was something of a traditional maxim within certain sectors of early Christianity seems confirmed by Paul's reference to it here in v 16 as a κανών ("rule," "standard"). The article ὁ coupled with the adjectival use of the demonstrative pronoun οὗτος ("this") make it clear that the rule or standard Paul has in mind is the statement just cited: "Neither circumcision nor uncircumcision means anything; all that matters is a new creation." The verb στοιχέω ("be in line with," "agree with") undoubtedly is used in the same manner as at 5:25 to connote "live in accordance with" or "keep in step with" (see *Comment* on 5:25). The absolute use of the masculine plural ὅσοι ("all those who") is common in Greek to designate a body of people, with the context or some further descriptive phrase identifying exactly who is in mind (cf. v 12 above; see also Matt 14:36; Mark 3:10; Acts 4:6, 34; 13:48; Rom 2:12 [twice]; 6:3, etc.). Here, of course, it is clear that those on whom Paul pronounces his peace benediction are those who "live in accordance with" or "follow" the Christian teaching that (1) negatively, all external expressions of the Christian faith are to be understood as culturally relevant but not spiritually necessitated, and (2) positively, what matters spiritually is that a person be a "new creation" as he or she is "in Christ" and directed by "the Spirit." The "rule" is expressed in terms of the issues of the day, and so speaks of "neither circumcision nor uncircumcision." Its application, however, has relevance wherever and whenever Christians are confronted with issues having to do with how one's inward spirituality is to be expressed in the contemporary circumstances of the day.

But while the first part of v 16 may seem rather straightforward, not at all clear are (1) the form and extent of the peace benediction that appears in the midst of the verse (assuming the usual punctuation) and (2) how the last clause of the verse relates to what precedes it (assuming that this last clause is something of an appendage). The issues here boil down to two: Does Paul have in mind one group of people on whom he pronounces an expanded peace benediction ("peace and mercy") or is he visualizing two groups of people, the first being the objects of his peace benediction and the second the objects of his mercy benediction? And what does Paul mean by the expression "the Israel of God," for the term "Israel" is never applied elsewhere in the NT to Gentile Christians but always to Jews?

The order εἰρήνη καὶ ἔλεος ("peace and mercy") seems somewhat strange, perhaps even illogical. Elsewhere in NT benedictions when ἔλεος is joined with εἰρήνη it is always "mercy" as the cause that precedes "peace" as the result, not vice versa (cf. 1 Tim 1:2; 2 Tim 1:2; 2 John 3; Jude 2)—so also the oft-repeated benediction χάρις καὶ εἰρήνη, where "grace" as the cause precedes "peace" as the result (cf. Burton, *Galatians*, 357–58; P. Richardson, *Israel in the Apostolic Church*, 76–80). Even more difficult is the interpretation of καὶ ἐπὶ τὸν Ἰσραὴλ τοῦ θεοῦ, "even on the Israel of God"). So it may legitimately be asked: Why does Paul use the double attributes "peace and mercy," and in what appears to be a wrong order? Why two uses of the preposition ἐπί ("on")? Why two uses of the conjunction καί ("and"), if, in fact, he is speaking regarding one group of people? And why, if he is speaking regarding Gentile Christians, does he call them τὸν Ἰσραὴλ τοῦ θεοῦ ("the Israel of God"), when "there is, in fact, no instance of his using Ἰσραήλ except of the Jewish nation or a part thereof" (Burton, *Galatians*, 358; also Richardson, *Israel in the Apostolic Church*, 80–81). Some, therefore, have repunctuated v 16 to read: "Peace on all those who follow this rule, and mercy on the Israel of God," thereby reading the peace benediction as pronounced on Gentile converts of Galatia who follow the rule of v 15, with an additional mercy benediction being pronounced on pious Jews who would yet come to accept the

Christian gospel (cf. Richardson, ibid., 74–84, for a full elaboration of this position, depending heavily on Burton's exegetical insights).

The appearance and order of the double attributes "peace and mercy" is, indeed, highly unusual for a Pauline benediction (contrast Rom 15:33; 16:20; 1 Cor 16:23–24; 2 Cor 13:11, 13; Eph 6:23–24; Phil 4:7, 9, 23; Col 4:18; 1 Thess 5:23, 28; 2 Thess 3:16, 18; 1 Tim 6:13; 2 Tim 4:22; Titus 3:15; Philem 25). It should not, however, be thought of as impossible (cf. the order "peace" and then "mercy" in the added Nineteenth Benediction of the Šěmôněh 'Esrēh [Eighteen Benedictions]; also note that in Rom 5 Paul treats first "peace" and its synonym "reconciliation" as results of justification [vv 1–11] and then "grace" and "the gift of grace" as causes for mankind's new spiritual condition [vv 12–21]). Nor is it impossible that Paul had one group of people in mind throughout this verse, viz., his Gentile converts of Galatia. In fact, in the context of the total argument of Galatians, where the issues focus on the question "Who really are the children of Abraham?" (cf. esp. 3:6–9, 14, 16, 26–29; 4:21–31), to conclude with a declaration that Gentile converts are rightfully "the Israel of God" would be highly significant and telling. In this case the second καί should be seen as being explicative, epexegetically clarifying in a further clause the expression ἐπ' αὐτούς ("on those"): "even on the Israel of God."

Traditionally it has been assumed that Paul's calling Gentile Christians "the Israel of God" means that the Christian church has taken the place of the Jewish nation as "the true, spiritual Israel" (cf. Justin, Dial. 11.5; see also, e.g., John Chrysostom, Commentary on the Epistle to the Galatians, ad loc.; N. A. Dahl, Judaica 6 [1950] 161–70). But as W. D. Davies aptly notes: "If this proposal were correct one would have expected to find support for it in Rom. ix–xi where Paul extensively deals with 'Israel'" (NTS 24 [1977] 10–11 n. 2).

It is sometimes argued that the phrase "the Israel of God" is Paul's way of referring to nonjudaizing Jewish Christians of Galatia (cf., e.g., G. Schrenk, Judaica 5 [1949] 81–94; idem, Judaica 6 [1950] 170–90; D. W. B. Robinson, ABR 13 [1965] 29–44). Others see here an eschatological reference comparable to πᾶς Ἰσραήλ ("all Israel") of Rom 11:26–27, with that expression understood as the totality of Jews who will be saved when "the deliverer will come from Zion" (cf., e.g., Mussner, Galaterbrief, 417; Bruce, Galatians, 275). Yet all of the views that take "the Israel of God" to refer to Jews and not Gentiles, while supportable by reference to Paul's wider usage (or nonusage) of terms and expressions, fail to take seriously enough the context of the Galatian letter itself. For in a letter where Paul is concerned to treat as indifferent the distinctions that separate Jewish and Gentile Christians and to argue for the equality of Gentile believers with Jewish believers, it is difficult to see him at the very end of that letter pronouncing a benediction (or benedictions) that would serve to separate groups within his churches—whether he means by "the Israel of God" a believing Jewish remnant within the broader Church of both Jews and Gentiles, a nonjudaizing group of Jewish Christians in Galatia, or an eschatological Israel that is to be saved at the time of Christ's return. Certain elements within Paul's other letters may be used to support one or the other of these views, but Galatians itself cannot easily be used in such a manner.

Rather, it seems better to argue that here Paul is using a self-designation of his Jewish-Christian opponents in Galatia—one that they used to identify their type of fulfilled Judaism vis-à-vis the official Judaism of their national compatriots (so, tentatively, Betz, Galatians, 323). Furthermore, this was a self-designation that they must have included in their message to Paul's Gentile converts, assuring them that by observing the God-given Jewish laws they would become fully "the Israel of God." The phrase itself is not found in the extant writings of Second Temple Judaism or later rabbinic Judaism, and does not appear elsewhere in Paul's letters. So it may be postulated that it arose amongst the Judaizers and became part of their message to Paul's Galatian converts. If that be the case, then Paul here climaxes his whole response to the judaizing threat in something of an ad hominem manner, implying in quite telling fashion that what the Judaizers were claiming to offer his converts they already have "in Christ" by faith: that they are truly children of Abraham together with all Jews who believe, and so properly can be called "the Israel of God" together with all Jews who believe.

17 τοῦ λοιποῦ κόπους μοι μηδεὶς παρεχέτω, ἐγὼ γὰρ τὰ στίγματα τοῦ Ἰησοῦ ἐν τῷ σώματί μου βαστάζω, "finally, let no one continue to cause me trouble, for I bear on my body the marks of Jesus!" Having given concluding statements against the judaizing threat and then a peace benediction on those who would follow what he said as epitomized in the "rule" of v 15, Paul now adds another remark that seems somewhat strange and cryptic. To some extent, what he does here by way of an additional, personal remark can be paralleled in his exhortations of 5:1–12, where he builds to a theological summation in vv 5–6 and a personal conclusion in v 11 (cf. *Comment* on the use of the inferential particle ἄρα in v 11), and then adds an additional, personal comment at v 12. There his remark was caustic and sarcastic. Here, however, he concludes his treatment of the judaizing threat much as he began it, by highlighting his apostolic authority and warning regarding continued agitation within the Galatian churches.

The adverbial, genitival expression τοῦ λοιποῦ may carry either a temporal nuance (i.e., "from now on," "in the future," "henceforth"; cf. 1 Cor 7:29; 2 Tim 4:8; see also Josephus, *Ant.* 18.272; Matt 26:45; Mark 14:41; Heb 10:13) or a logical nuance (i.e., "beyond that," "in addition," "finally"; cf. 1 Cor 1:16; 4:2; 2 Cor 13:11; Eph 6:10; Phil 3:1; 4:8; 1 Thess 4:1; 2 Thess 3:1; see also Josephus, *Ant.* 6.46; Acts 27:20). It is difficult to decide between the options, and commentators are divided on the question. Probably a logical "in addition" or "finally" is to be preferred simply because a futuristic temporal reading sets up some dissonance when coupled with the hortatory verb παρεχέτω ("let [no one] continue to cause") in the present tense. The noun κόπος is a frequent word for "work," "labor," or "toil" in Greek, even combined by Paul with τῆς ἀγάπης to mean "labor based in love" or "loving service" (cf. 1 Thess 1:3). It was also used, however, to signify "trouble" or "difficulty" (cf. Ps 106 [107]:12; Sir 22:13; 29:4; 1 Macc 10:15; Josephus, *Ant.* 2.257; Matt 26:10; Mark 14:6; Luke 11:7; 18:5, etc.), which is what it undoubtedly means here. The use of the present imperative παρεχέτω suggests an action already in progress; with μηδείς ("no one") the verbal phrase means "let no one continue to cause trouble." The use of the dative of reference μοί ("me") indicates that Paul took the affronts to the gospel caused by the Judaizers quite personally, for he had been commissioned the apostle to the Gentiles (cf. 1:1) and was the one who had evangelized the Galatian churches (cf. 1:8–9; 4:13–15).

Paul's rationale for the warning of the first part of v 17 is to be found in the explanatory clause of the last part of the verse: "For I bear on my body the marks of Jesus!" The term τὰ στίγματα was common in the ancient world for the marks of religious tattooing or slave branding (cf. O. Betz, "στίγμα," *TDNT* 7.657–64), and some have taken from this that early Christians generally and Paul in particular bore tattoo marks or religious brands to signify that they were Christians—perhaps the Greek letter X for "Χριστος." More likely, however, what Paul had in mind by his use of τὰ στίγματα here were the scars and disfigurements left on his body as the effects of his sufferings as an apostle (cf. 2 Cor 6:4–6; 11:23–30; perhaps also Gal 4:13–14). That these were physical scars and disfigurements is made clear by the phrase ἐν τῷ σώματί μου ("on my body"). And that Paul took them to be identifying marks of his Christian apostleship is suggested by the possessive genitive τοῦ Ἰησοῦ ("of Jesus").

There is no self-indulgent pity here in Paul's statement. Rather, it is a statement that highlights Paul's relationship to Jesus and his apostleship established by Jesus. Furthermore, the statement gives a warning regarding any continuing judaizing threat within his Galatian churches. For what takes place in those churches affects him personally as the Galatian Christians' apostle and evangelist. So he warns that he should not be troubled further since he is Christ's "marked man," with those markings suggesting, positively, that he is under Christ's ownership and protection, as well as, negatively, that those who try to harass him will come under Christ's judgment and retribution.

18 ἡ χάρις τοῦ κυρίου ἡμῶν Ἰησοῦ Χριστοῦ μετὰ τοῦ πνεύματος ὑμῶν, ἀδελφοί· ἀμήν, "The grace of our Lord Jesus Christ be with your spirit, brothers. Amen." At the close of every Pauline letter is a grace benediction (cf. also Rom 16:20b [perhaps also v 24 à la D TR etc.]; 1 Cor 16:23; 2 Cor 13:14; Eph 6:24; Phil 4:23; Col 4:18b; 1 Thess 5:28; 2 Thess 3:18; 1 Tim 6:21b; 2 Tim 4:22b; Titus 3:15b; Philem 25). The grace benediction of Gal 6:18 parallels the wording of many of the other Pauline grace benedictions: "the grace of our/the Lord Jesus [Christ]" appearing in all the others except Colossians and the Pastorals; "with your spirit" appearing also in Philippians and Philemon; the simpler forms "with you" or "with all of you" appearing elsewhere (the grace benedictions of 2 Corinthians and Ephesians being slightly expanded). The only difference in the grace benediction of Galatians is the addition of the vocative ἀδελφοί ("brothers"), which highlights Paul's continued affection for his converts even amidst his tones of sternness and severity (on ἀδελφοί in Galatians, see *Comment* on 1:11 and 3:15), and the addition of the final ἀμήν ("Amen"), neither of which appears in the other Pauline grace benedictions. It seems, therefore, that Paul's grace benedictions were rather fixed in their wording, though with some variations in certain cases that serve to highlight the distinctive features of their respective letters.

While the word χάρις ("grace") appears regularly in the Pauline opening salutations and closing benedictions, its appearance in Galatians is particularly meaningful. Thus set between the theological salutation of 1:3 that speaks of grace "from God our Father and the Lord Jesus Christ" and the benediction here at 6:18 that speaks of "the grace of our/the Lord Jesus Christ," Paul refers explicitly to the Galatians being called "by the grace of Christ" (1:6), to his being called "by his [God's] grace" (1:15), to the Jerusalem apostles' recognition that "the grace" had been given him by God (2:9), and, using the verbal form of the word, to the fact that God "graciously gave" the inheritance to Abraham through a promise and not on the basis of the law (3:18). In fact, throughout Galatians grace and law are set out as opposite poles, certainly with regard to being accounted righteous before God (2:15–16, 21; 3:1–18), but also with regard to living a proper Christian lifestyle

(2:17–21; 3:19–4:11). So in closing his Galatian letter, Paul concludes on that note of grace. It may even have been, particularly if Galatians is Paul's earliest extant pastoral letter, that it was this note of grace in Galatians that gave the distinctive character to all of Paul's concluding benedictions.

Explanation

The subscription of Galatians (6:11–18) highlights three matters that are to the fore in all that Paul has written regarding the judaizing threat previously in the letter: (1) the motivation of the Judaizers as Paul saw it (vv 12–13); (2) the centrality of the cross in the Christian gospel (v 14); and (3) the nature of a proper Christian lifestyle as believers attempt to express their faith in the circumstances of their day (v 15). Then there is an expanded peace benediction pronounced on all those who view the Christian life in such a way as set out in v 15 (v 16), which is followed by a further comment of warning and authority (v 17) and a grace benediction (v 18). Thus the subscription provides important clues for understanding the issues discussed throughout Galatians, particularly those having to do with the judaizing threat brought into the churches by certain legalistically oriented Jewish Christians, for it not only summarizes the main points dealt with earlier in the letter but also allows us to cut through all of the verbage and see matters in their essence as Paul saw them.

Historically, Paul's letter to the Galatians has been foundational for many forms of Christian thought, proclamation, and practice. Likewise, today, how one understands the issues and teaching of Galatians determines in large measure what kind of theology one espouses, what kind of message one proclaims, and what kind of lifestyle one lives. May it be, by God's Spirit, that what Paul has written so long ago in this letter finds a new home in our lives, thereby establishing, encouraging, challenging, and transforming us for God's glory.

Index of Ancient Sources

Old Testament Apocrypha and Pseudepigrapha

Rabbinic Literature

Targums

Greek and Roman Writers

Early Christian Authors and Writings

Early Critics of Christianity

Nag Hammadi Texts

Later Greek Versions

Index of Modern Authors

Index of Principal Subjects

Index of Biblical Texts

A. The Old Testament

B. The New Testament